Macroeconomics

Macroeconomics

STEVEN E. LANDSBURG
University of Rochester

LAUREN J. FEINSTONE

The McGraw-Hill Companies, Inc.
NEW YORK ST. LOUIS SAN FRANCISCO AUCKLAND BOGOTÁ CARACAS
LISBON LONDON MADRID MEXICO CITY MILAN MONTREAL NEW DELHI
SAN JUAN SINGAPORE SYDNEY TOKYO TORONTO

McGraw-Hill

A Division of The McGraw-Hill Companies

Macroeconomics

This book was printed on acid-free paper.

1 2 3 4 5 6 7 8 9 0   VNH VNH   9 0 9 8 7

ISBN 0-07-020496-9

This book was set in Times Roman by GTS Graphics, Inc.

The editors were Lucille H. Sutton, Adrienne D'Ambrosio, and Elaine Rosenberg;

the production supervisor was Leroy A. Young.

The design manager was Charles A. Carson.

The designer was Edward A. Butler.

Drawings were done by Fine Line Illustrations.

Von Hoffmann Press, Inc. was printer and binder.

Library of Congress Cataloging-in-Publication Data

Landsburg, Steven E.
Macroeconomics / Steven E. Landsburg, Lauren Feinstone.
    p.   cm.
Includes index.
ISBN 0-07-020496-9
1. Macroeconomics.   I. Feinstone, Lauren J., 1952–   .
II. Title.
HB172.5.L36   1997
339—dc21   96-45453

INTERNATIONAL EDITION

When ordering this title, use ISBN 0-07-020496-9.

http://www.mhcollege.com

About The Authors

Steven E. Landsburg is an associate professor teaching at the University of Rochester. He has also taught at Colorado State University, Cornell University, the University of Iowa, and the University of Chicago. He is the author of two previous books about economics, *Price Theory and Applications* and *The Armchair Economist*. His monthly columns on economic matters have appeared in *Forbes* and the *Washington Post* and are currently appearing in *Slate*.

Lauren J. Feinstone has been a member of the faculty at the University of Rochester and the Economics Institute in Boulder, Colorado. She received a Ph.D. in economics from the University of Chicago. In 1988–1989, she was a Senior Economist on the President's Council of Economic Advisers, with primary responsibility for international macroeconomics. She is the author of the international finance chapter in the *Economic Report of the President* issued in February 1989.

To Cayley Elizabeth

Contents in Brief

Contents

Preface

Macroeconomics today is a different subject than it was just a few decades ago. Old controversies have been resolved, new ones have arisen, and in the process some widespread areas of consensus have emerged. We believe that the paradigm of intertemporal choice is the basis for this emerging consensus in macroeconomics and that the new paradigm is sufficiently developed to serve as the unifying theme of an undergraduate textbook. This is that textbook.

Our strategy is to first develop a basic model whose component pieces are largely noncontroversial and then show how variations in certain key assumptions can lead to alternative conclusions. This enables us to emphasize the existence of an established body of knowledge without denying the controversies that remain.

The fundamental model is one of intertemporal exchange and production. This allows us, right from the start, to address the dynamic issues which are the basis for the modern approach to macroeconomics. As we introduce different sectors of the economy, we repeatedly return to the intertemporal aspects, using these as a unifying theme.

The book's chapters can be roughly classified into "building-block" chapters, "application" chapters, and "institutional" chapters. The building-block chapters introduce the microeconomic foundations of macroeconomics in an environment with flexible prices and perfect information. They include chapters on the dynamic elements of borrowing and lending (Chapter 3), consumption (Chapters 4 and 5), investment (Chapter 7), and labor (Chapter 9). These components are added to the model one at a time, so that the student is able to master equilibrium and comparative statics first in a pure endowment economy and then in successively richer models. Throughout, we emphasize supply, demand, and equilibrium—tools that will be familiar to some students but are developed from scratch with macroeconomic examples.

Early in the development, we incorporate the international economy, highlighting the parallel economics of trade across nations and trade between individuals. We also add another building block—a government sector—and address the traditional concerns of macroeconomics, including government expenditure and taxation (Chapter 6) and the market for money (Chapter 9). Along the way we highlight such issues as the debate surrounding Ricardian equivalence and the causes of inflation.

The application chapters combine these building blocks into more substantial structures—the theory of long-run economic growth (Chapter 8) and the theory of business cycles and short-run income determination (Chapters 11 through 14). Because growth theory requires only some of the building blocks, we have been able to position it even before all of the building blocks are in place. Some instructors will want to cover this chapter in sequence; others will prefer to complete the building-block Chapters 9 and 10 (and possibly some of the subsequent application Chapters 11 through 14) before returning to the topic of growth. We have carefully tailored the presentation so that instructors can follow either sequence without any loss of continuity. Let a thousand flowers bloom.

In the application Chapters 11 through 14, we first discuss some of the evidence and controversies involved in defining, measuring, and predicting business cycles. In Chapter 11, we use this material to call attention to some of the inadequacies of a flexible-price, full-information model. With this as motivation, we integrate the original building blocks into more sophisticated models, incorporating sticky wages (Chapter 12), sticky prices (Chapter 13), and monetary misperceptions (Chapter 14). We emphasize the question of what governments can and cannot do, and how the answer depends critically on what one believes about the existence and nature of distortions in the economy. At the same time, we insist that despite their different policy implications, all of these models are variations on a single theme. We eschew a pedagogy of "dueling models" with nothing in common, which can leave students with the impression that macroeconomists typically have nothing to say to each other. Instead, we provide a common language in which all schools of macroeconomic thought can be communicated and compared.

While we encourage students to think abstractly, we also encourage them to remember that the purpose of abstract thought is ultimately to understand the real world. Real-world institutions and history are referenced repeatedly in every chapter. A few chapters are exclusively devoted to tying the model to reality; these institutional chapters cover, among other topics, the national income accounts (Chapter 2), the money supply process (Chapter 15), and the making of economic policy (Chapter 17). A separate chapter on international finance (Chapter 16) is both an introduction to important real-world institutions and a new sort of building block, which (as we show the student) can be used to embellish the models and analysis elsewhere in the book.

We believe that students learn best by working problems. We have provided a large number of problems, at every level of difficulty. Within the chapters are exercises which should be easy for any student who has understood the preceding few paragraphs; students can use these exercises to slow themselves down and make sure they have grasped one point before rushing on to the next. The end-of-chapter problem sets call for deeper thought and understanding.

There are many other learning aids, including glossary items in the margins and "special warnings" to alert the students to points of particular subtlety. Special warnings are marked with the symbol below.

Supplements

The supplements that accompany Macroeconomics include a Study Guide prepared by William Weber of Eastern Illinois University as well as an Instructor's Manual, a Testbank in printed and computerized versions, Excel spreadsheet software by Tim

Yaeger of Humboldt State, and a set of overhead transparencies. Contact your local McGraw-Hill representative for additional information.

Acknowledgments

The following reviewers made invaluable contributions:

J. Lon Carlson, Illinois State University
A. Edward Day, University of Central Florida
Sharon J. Erenburg, Eastern Michigan University
David W. Findlay, Colby College
Edward N. Gamber, Lafayette College
Fred Graham, The American University
David R. Hakes, University of Missouri, St. Louis
John Huizinga, The University of Chicago
Manfred W. Kell, Claremont McKenna College
Marc Lieberman, Vassar College
Robert G. Murphy, Boston College
Thomas F. Pogue, University of Iowa
Esther-Mirjam Sent, University of Notre Dame
David E. Spencer, Brigham Young University
Christopher J. Waller, Indiana University, Bloomington

We are indebted to the superior editorial and production support we've received at McGraw-Hill. Our development editor Ed Millman was absolutely superb, and Elaine Rosenberg juggled all the production tasks. Lucille Sutton nursed the project to completion. They all did great jobs.

Steven E. Landsburg
Lauren J. Feinstone

Chapter 1

Introduction

Macroeconomics is about *income:* Where does it come from and where does it go? What makes our incomes grow over time, and what makes them fluctuate from year to year? Why do Americans have higher incomes than Koreans, and why are Koreans' incomes growing faster than Americans'? How is income related to employment, wages, interest rates, and prices? Do higher incomes always make us better off? Do inflation, international trade, government budget deficits, and wars affect our incomes, and if so, how? And how can government policies affect our incomes for better or for worse?

More precisely, macroeconomics is about *aggregate* income and *per capita* income: The income of an entire country (or an entire planet) and the income of that

1

country's (or planet's) average citizen. At times, we also are interested in broad questions of how income is distributed: How much, for example, is paid in wages, and how much is collected in rents? But questions about *individual* income—why you earn more or less than your neighbor—are usually reserved for courses in *micro*economics.

Economists study income the same way they study everything else: By examining how people make choices. In macroeconomics, a key observation is that people make choices with an eye to the future. Our decisions about how much to work, how much to consume, how much to invest, and how much to save are all colored by our visions of tomorrow. The choice to consume more or work less today entails a choice to consume less or work more in the future. We cannot separate the two decisions; each action that we take has both present and future consequences. To determine the desirability of the action, we must weigh the two sets of consequences against each other.

This textbook stresses above all the central role of what economists call *intertemporal choices*—choices with consequences in more than one time period. The logic of intertemporal choice is a logic that underlies all of the modern approaches to macroeconomics and unifies what was once a fractured discipline.

Intertemporal choices are made in the context of *markets*. Macroeconomics concerns the interaction among four markets. First is the market for *current goods,* that is, goods that are available for immediate use. We sometimes call it the *goods market* for short. The goods market is an abstraction. In the real world, there are separate markets for pig iron and pig's feet, for matchbooks and comic books, and for shoes and ships and sealing wax. A course in *micro*economics concerns itself with the interactions among these separate markets. In *macro*economics, we aggregate all of them into a single "market for (current) goods," and we pretend that there is a single unit in which all of these goods can be measured. In Chapter 2, you will learn some of the methods by which we maintain that pretense and some of the associated pitfalls to watch out for.

The second market we study is the market for *future goods,* or equivalently the market for *bonds*. As we will see in Chapter 3, a *bond* is a promise to deliver goods at some specified time in the future. Even though the goods to be delivered do not yet exist, the bond market allows them to be traded for current goods. For example, you can trade away one apple in exchange for a bond promising one and a half apples tomorrow. In everyday language, we refer to this as "lending" an apple "at interest," but we shall see that lending and borrowing can always be reinterpreted as buying and selling bonds.

The third market is the market for *labor,* and the fourth is the market for *money.* Our goal in this book is to understand the markets for goods, bonds, labor, and money and the ways in which they influence each other.

To simplify our discussions, we will begin by assuming that markets *clear,* which means that they settle at points of *equilibrium* where the quantities supplied and demanded are equal. If, for example, demanders want to buy more than suppliers want to sell, then demanders bid up the price (that is, they offer to pay more) until an equilibrium is reached. If suppliers want to sell more than demanders want to buy, they bid down the price (by offering to sell for less) to an equilibrium point.

In our first pass through the material on markets (Chapters 3 through 10), we maintain the simplifying assumption that all markets clear at all times. This will enable us to get a feel for how markets behave under ideal conditions.

However, many economists believe that the market-clearing assumption leads to an inadequate description of real-world phenomena such as unemployment, recessions, and the role of government. We discuss the reasons for their discomfort in Chapter 11. In Chapters 12 through 14, we present some alternative hypotheses about how particular markets function, and we explore their consequences both for economic theory and for economic policy. In Chapter 12, we consider the possibility that the labor market fails to clear because wages cannot adjust quickly to changing market conditions. In Chapter 13, we consider the possibility that the goods market fails to clear because prices cannot adjust quickly to changing market conditions. And in Chapter 14, we consider the possibility that markets cannot clear in the traditional sense because people have incomplete information about their economic environment.

The approaches of Chapters 12 through 14 represent variations on a theme, but the underlying model remains the same throughout the book: It is a model of people making intertemporal choices in four interconnected markets. This is the great unifying vision of contemporary macroeconomics, and we will not stray from it. We shall simply tweak it a little in one direction or another.

Models in which markets fail to clear are sometimes called *Keynesian* or *neo-Keynesian* after British economist John Maynard Keynes, who changed the face of macroeconomics in the 1920s and 1930s. In the recent past, economists viewed Keynesian and non-Keynesian approaches as separated by an unbridgeable chasm. Today we agree on enough basics to use a single model to explore and contrast both points of view.

1-2 THE PLAN OF THIS BOOK

Macroeconomists are concerned with two great issues. First, what causes long-run trends in income? This is the topic of *economic growth*. Second, what causes short-run fluctuations in income? This is the topic of *business cycles*.

To address these questions, we need to understand the various markets that make up the economy and how they fit together. Here is a more detailed description of how we will undertake that task.

The Fundamental Variables

In Chapter 2, we define some fundamental macroeconomic variables, such as income, output, and expenditure. We also discuss how these variables are measured in the United States and some of the problems with the official measurements.

The Basic Model

Consumption and the Markets for Goods and Bonds

In Chapters 3 through 5, we discuss the workings of a very simple model economy in which there is no labor, no money, no government, and no productive investment.

You might suspect that such an economy is too simple to be interesting. But in fact the lessons learned from studying this economy will serve as major guideposts as we work our way through increasingly sophisticated models later in the book.

The people who live in this model economy are able to borrow and lend, trading current goods for promises of future goods. Remember that such promises are called bonds. So even our simplest economy contains markets for goods and for bonds and requires that people make intertemporal choices. That is why it provides so many lessons that will serve us well throughout the book.

Chapter 3 lays out the basic language of borrowing, lending, and trading in bonds. Chapter 4 examines the intertemporal-choice problem facing a single individual or household. In Chapter 5, we will see what happens when households can interact in such a way that each one's choices affect all the others. The bottom line will be the determination of the interest rate and an understanding of the circumstances under which the interest rate can change. We will also see what happens to interest rates and borrowing when the citizens of a given country can trade with the rest of the world.

Government

In Chapter 6, we add the government to our economy. We examine the effects of various kinds of government spending and the effects of taxation and borrowing.

Investment

In our first six chapters, we assume that all the goods in the economy must be either consumed or discarded. In Chapter 7, we introduce a third option, allowing the possibility that some goods can be used for productive investment: instead of eating all your grain, you can plant some to create more grain in the future. We address the important issue of how goods are allocated between consumption and investment.

Growth

Chapters 3 through 7 provide sufficient building blocks for us to address the issue of economic growth. Chapter 8 combines those building blocks to provide a complete model of growth in the long run.

Labor

While the building blocks of earlier chapters suffice for studying long-run growth in Chapter 8, we need some additional building blocks before we can go on to study short-run issues in Chapter 11 and beyond. The remaining building blocks are the markets for labor and for money.

In Chapter 9, we add the labor market to the model. Now, for the first time, the quantity of available goods is not fixed: if people work more, they can have more goods, and if they prefer to work less, they must settle for fewer goods. We examine both the labor market itself and the way in which it affects the goods market.

Money

In Chapter 10, we add the money market. Now our basic model of the economy is complete.

Using the Model

Now that the foundations of our model are in place, we can combine them to attack the major questions in macroeconomics: the determination of output and employment, the reasons for recessions, the role of government, and the forces that underlie economic growth.

In Chapter 11, we review the basic model of Chapters 3 through 10, which is often called the *neoclassical* model of the macroeconomy. We compare the predictions of the model with our observations of the real world, and we discuss some of the model's apparent successes and failures. This analysis motivates the variations we discuss in Chapters 12 through 14.

Variations on the Theme

Chapters 12 and 13 present the Keynesian variations. In the former, we assume a sticky wage rate; in the latter, a sticky price level. ("Sticky" means "unable to quickly adjust to an equilibrium level.") Chapter 14 is concerned with a different sort of variation, in which uncertainty about the economic environment plays a major role. In each case we emphasize that the model has been changed only slightly; nevertheless, some of its most important implications can be overturned. In particular, the basic neoclassical model suggests that (aside from providing *public goods* which are inadequately supplied by the marketplace) the government can do very little to improve the workings of the economy. But in the presence of wage stickiness or price stickiness, the model tells us that a far greater range of government policies can be effective.

Domestic and International Monetary Institutions

Chapter 15 fleshes out our basic model by presenting the details of how money is supplied in the United States and surveying the issues faced by the authorities who control the money supply. Chapter 16 extends the analysis to world markets. We discuss the determination of exchange rates (the rates at which one country's currency can be traded for another), the policies that governments can adopt toward controlling those exchange rates, and the reasoning behind those policies.

Economic Policy

In Chapter 17, we bring together the main lessons of the book to study their impact on the issues of macroeconomic policy: How much should governments spend? How much should they tax? How much money should they supply? To answer these questions, we must raise further questions. Some of those are *positive* questions about the probable consequences of alternative policies: Will government spending increase employment? Will a tax cut raise interest rates? Will an increase in the money supply lead to higher prices? Others are *normative* questions about what the government should be attempting to accomplish: Is it more important to combat recessions or to foster long-term growth? Is it more important to improve economic conditions for the average citizen or for the poorest?

Our basic model and its variations offer a range of viewpoints from which to examine these questions, and we survey all of those viewpoints.

1-3   MODELS AND REALITY

We have already discussed, and will continue to discuss for 16 more chapters, the use of economic models. You are already familiar with economic models—such as the model of supply and demand—from your earlier courses. But it is important to recognize that reasoning with models is not unique to economics.

A *model* is nothing but a set of assumptions about the way the world works. A child who falls in the mud and expects his mother to be angry is using a model. His model is "Mom always get angry when I come home with mud on my clothes." In some circumstances the model is inaccurate: perhaps the child will come home and find his mother in an unusually good mood or find an unexpected and sympathetic baby-sitter who is willing to do an extra load of laundry. Nevertheless, if the model is sufficiently close to the truth sufficiently often, the child will find it a useful concept to remember. He might even want to use it as a guide to policy, in this case by steering clear of mud puddles.

In this book we will build models within models within models. We will have a model of labor supply (that is, a set of assumptions about how much people want to work) embedded in a model of the labor market (that is, a set of assumptions about how workers and firms reach agreement on wages and working hours) embedded in a model of the entire economy (that is, a set of assumptions about how the labor market interacts with the markets for goods, bonds, and money). None of these models is "true," in the sense of being infallible. All of them are useful, in the sense of suggesting what we might expect to encounter in the real world.

Because economic models are sometimes more complicated than models of a parent's moods, we frequently—though not always—keep track of them with graphs or equations instead of with words. (In this book, you will encounter many graphs and few equations.) Those graphs or equations are just ways of recording our assumptions and of discovering what those assumptions imply. Throughout the book, we call careful attention to what our assumptions are, how they might differ from a complete description of reality, and the circumstances in which those differences might be important. We repeatedly present evidence from recent economic history to help us decide how well our models—and we—are doing.

Let's get started.

Chapter 2

Income, Output, and Expenditure

E very day newspapers and television newscasts report what is happening to interest rates, unemployment, and income. Sometimes they raise questions: Will the economy suffer another recession soon? Will it improve? Worsen? When? Can the government reduce or eliminate its budget deficit? Prevent inflation? Should taxes be lowered? Raised? What about the trade deficit? Will the rapidly changing European environment improve worldwide economic opportunities? And if so, how?

To discuss such questions, which are all part of macroeconomics, we need to be familiar with the relevant vocabulary. In this chapter, we discuss the meanings of some of the terms commonly used in macroeconomics. We also examine the data—basic quantitative facts about the economy—that give substance to these terms; there is no way to understand what anyone is trying to say about macroeconomics without knowing some of the data.

In most cases, when we define a term, we are really defining a variable—something that can be measured. We therefore face two distinct and equally important problems. The first is choosing an appropriate definition for the purpose at hand. The second is achieving an accurate measurement, consistent with that definition. The *definition* and the *measurement* are usually not the same. It is important to distinguish between the two.

As an example, suppose that we want to study your instructor's height. The first problem is to define what "height" means. We could define her height as the distance from the ground to the top of her head when she is standing up or as the distance from the bottom of her feet to the top of her head when she is lying down. (In general, these distances differ because of the force of gravity.) If your classroom has an unusually low doorway and you want to predict whether your teacher will be able to enter the room without bending, it is more useful to define height as a standing distance. If you want to predict whether your teacher will fit into a tight space capsule when she is weightless, it is more useful to define height as a lying-down distance.

Only after agreeing on a definition can we begin to look for an appropriate method of measurement. For some purposes, it might suffice to count how many 10-inch cinder blocks your teacher's body covers when she stands against the wall; for others, the additional accuracy provided by a ruler might be advisable.

The same sorts of issues arise in macroeconomics. Suppose we want to know how much your city has collected in taxes this month. To compute the answer, we must confront both problems of definition and problems of measurement.

For example, suppose a city ordinance requires that all residents construct birdbaths on their front lawns. The ordinance presents us with a problem of definition: Should the cost of the birdbaths count as a tax? If we are measuring taxes to determine whether government payroll checks will bounce, then the cost of the birdbaths is irrelevant; however, if we are measuring taxes in order to determine the total burden that the government imposes on its citizens, then the cost of the birdbaths is as relevant as any sales or income tax. Once we have decided what our purpose is and chosen an appropriate definition, problems of measurement arise. How can we find out how much all of the birdbaths cost? Surely some errors will be made when we try to collect the figures.

In macroeconomics, as in life generally, there are many ways to go wrong. One is to choose a definition that is inappropriate for the purpose at hand, and another is to make inaccurate measurements. In the remainder of this chapter we discuss several of the most important macroeconomic variables and some potential pitfalls of both types.

2-1   INCOME

Income:
Resources that people acquire through wages, rentals, profits, gifts, etc.

You already have a pretty good idea of what **income** means: Members of your family may work or own a small business from which they earn the resources to help pay for your food, education, and clothes. They might also earn interest or dividends from savings or holdings of stock; these, too, are part of a family's income.

Income arises from many sources: wages, rental income on equipment or apartments, and profits from businesses are all examples of income.

We do not say "making money" when we discuss income. Even though what economists mean by "increasing your income" is the same as what you mean when you say you are "making more money," the economist's vocabulary needs to be much more precise than that of everyday speech. There would be income even if money did not exist. Imagine a simple economy in which some people produce shoes and others produce compact discs; the shoemakers pay their employees with shoes and the recording companies pay their musicians with CDs. There is income in this economy—shoe income and CD income—though not money as we would ordinarily think of it.

Aggregate income:
The sum of all individuals' incomes.

Per capita income:
Aggregate income divided by population.

A country's **aggregate income** is the sum of all the incomes that accrue to all its citizens within a given period of time—a year, a week, or a quarter. (A *quarter* is a specific 3-month period of the year. For example, the second calendar quarter is the months of April, May, and June.) The word "aggregate" means "sum" or "total." Dividing aggregate income by the country's population gives you average income, or **per capita income.** For a given population, a rise in aggregate income means a rise in per capita income.

➡ *Exercise 2-1*
Suppose a country's aggregate income is $500 billion. If its population is 250 million, what is its per capita income? If in the following year aggregate income increases to $600 billion, by what percent does its aggregate income increase? By what percent does its per capita income increase?

Income and Welfare

Welfare:
The well-being of an individual or group.

Economists are interested in knowing about a country's aggregate and per capita income for a variety of reasons. The primary one is that income is a rough measure of its citizens' **welfare**—how well off they are. For the most part, the greater your income, the better off you are: with more income you can afford to buy more goods, live more comfortably, save more so that you can worry less about your future, or give more to the charities of your choice.

Income Approximates Welfare . . .

Layman:
A person who has not studied the subject being discussed; in this book, a person who has never studied economics.

It might surprise you to find out that economists think that it is more important to increase happiness than to increase income. Unfortunately, happiness, which economists call *welfare*, is not easy to measure. Economists know that income is not a perfect measure of welfare, but because they cannot measure happiness at all, they measure income as a rough approximation of welfare.

Economists believe that income is a better approximation of welfare than many **laymen** think. You might argue that money can't buy you love. An economist would agree that it cannot buy you love directly. But it *can* buy you a better education, membership at an athletic club, trips to Mediterranean resorts, and many other things that can increase your chance of finding love. So higher income can at least contribute to greater happiness.

Alternatively, you might say that improving the quality of life—via such things as lower crime rates, happier children, higher literacy and lower teenage pregnancy rates in inner cities, cleaner air, less congestion, better preservation of magnificent parklands—is what matters. A macroeconomist would point out that greater aggregate income can at least help with each of these issues.

The macroeconomist would also use measured aggregate income as a gauge of the country's ability to solve problems that lower the quality of life. Low rates of income growth are sometimes the first and most pronounced symptom of *misdirected* attempts to solve such problems.

. . . But Not Perfectly

Macroeconomists realize that increasing aggregate income is not always an appropriate solution for every social problem. Income and welfare do not always correspond. There are many ways to increase a country's income without making the citizens better off. The following are some examples of ways in which welfare and income might *not* correspond.

More Work   We could increase U.S. income by mandating that everyone work harder and work longer hours. We could force the elderly to work past the normal retirement age. These policies might increase income but certainly would not make people better off.

Inappropriate Goods   Statistics on aggregate income can be deceptive, suggesting greater welfare than is really the case. Consider the former Soviet Union. During the 1970s and 1980s, measured per capita Soviet income averaged about one-third of measured per capita U.S. income. Poor as that is, it does not begin to reflect the miserable quality of life under the communist regime. The Soviet Union's measured income was relatively high because that country produced all kinds of machinery and military equipment that did average citizens no good whatsoever. Of what value was yet another tractor or warplane when people could buy bread only by getting in line at the bakery at five o'clock in the morning? Of what use was greater income when married couples and their children lived with the grandparents in two-room apartments and were not permitted to move elsewhere?

The goods the Soviet Union produced not only were inappropriate for domestic use (within the country) but also could not be sold to the rest of the world either because of poor international relations or because of their poor quality. Many countries in the world with measured per capita incomes far lower than the Soviet Union's had citizens who were much better off.

The Distribution of Income   Neither total nor average income tells us anything about the *distribution* of income. Consider two countries with the same per capita (average) income. In one country everyone has exactly the same income; in the other only a few people have extremely high incomes and everyone else has an extremely low income. Is one country better to live in than the other? Macroeconomists do not attempt to answer this ethical question. There are enough questions to keep us busy without getting involved in ethics. But we contribute to ethical debates by asking questions laymen do not always think of asking: Should we expect income to grow faster in one of those countries than in the other? Do incomes become more disparate within a country over time, or more alike?

These examples show that income and welfare are not identical. Nevertheless, macroeconomists consider aggregate income a good approximation to welfare, and therefore income is well worth studying.

Income and Policy

Policy:
A program of government actions or planned actions that may affect economic outcomes.

As we shall see, many **policies** that are suggested to increase income are difficult to analyze. Some policies effectively increase the incomes of some people, but only at the expense of other people or only far in the future and at the expense of the quality of life in the present. Do welfare programs for the poor increase their income in the long run as well as in the short run? Do lower interest rates increase income? Would a capital gains tax increase income? Whose? Does an increase in your income affect the incomes of others?

Measuring Income

Just like your teacher's height or your city's tax revenue, "national income" can be defined in a variety of ways. The exact value of national income depends on the exact definition that one chooses; by most reasonable definitions national income in the United States is currently in the vicinity of $7 trillion per year.

To make sense of a number like that, we have to compare it with something else. Let's convert it to a per capita basis so that you can compare it with your own income experience. The U.S. population is a little over 250 million, a good round number for you to commit to memory. Then $7 trillion divided by 250 million people comes out to $28,000 per capita—that is, $28,000 for every man, woman, and child in the United States.

Suppose you are the leader of a country and you want to find out your country's income. You can require that everyone fill out and submit a form with the information you think you need, but you will have to do so each time you want to measure aggregate income. Because it is very time-consuming and costly to collect this information from citizens, most countries measure income on an annual basis only. (However, the U.S. government measures income quarterly.) To see how costly collecting data can be for an economy, imagine what would happen if your family had to report its income to the government each week or even each month. Your family would spend so much time doing paperwork that its members would have less time to be together and maybe even less time to work to produce the income.

Problems in Measuring Income Directly

It is not easy to measure aggregate income. At tax time—by April 15 of each year—U.S. citizens must report the income they received during the preceding year. But the resulting aggregate, called **national income,** is *not* what economists use as their measure of the country's income. For many reasons, national income always misses significant sources of a country's income. Discussed below are some omissions.

National income:
The sum of wages, rents, and profits that are reported by citizens.

Underreported Income

Some people have such low incomes that they are not required to report their incomes at all. More importantly, many people who do report their incomes have an incentive to understate their incomes because they have to pay **income tax.** Does a secretary who types evenings on the side and gets paid off the books report all her earnings to the government at tax time and pay income tax on the whole amount? Legally, she must; yet economists know that many people do not report income received in this way. Many people like to get paid in cash so that there are no paper trails the government can follow to track down their true incomes. People who own businesses sometimes understate their reported incomes by overstating their expenses, which are subtracted from their revenues prior to calculating their profits.

Income tax:
A tax paid to the government by the taxpayer, for which the amount paid depends on the income of the taxpayer.

Illegal Activities

Some businesses, like drug dealing and gambling, are illegal. People engaged in these *underground* activities do not usually report their incomes from such activities, not only to avoid taxes but also to hide the nature of their business from the government. The same is true of income from theft; burglars, muggers, and embezzlers surely do not report their misgotten incomes to the government.

Some people argue that because these activities are not good for the economy, it is just as well that the incomes they produce are excluded from aggregate income. However, from the perspective of economists, whose goal is the measurement of welfare, it is clear that some of these sources of income *should* be included. For example, people who gamble illegally do it of their own free will; they get pleasure from it, and thus it contributes to welfare.

Nonmarket Activities; Household Trade

Farm families sometimes produce their own food, which is a form of income that does not show up in official statistics. Moreover, these farmers might not bother to calculate how much income they earn in this form. This is an example of a **nonmarket activity**—the goods are produced and distributed to users but are not traded in any organized markets. Income generated from nonmarket activities accounts for a substantial discrepancy between actual income and measured income.

Nonmarket income is probably a larger percentage of total income for developing countries than for more advanced countries because in developing countries a greater proportion of households do much of their own production. This makes com-

Nonmarket activity:
Any pursuit involving the production and consumption of goods or services that are not traded in organized markets.

parisons of per capita income between countries potentially deceptive. An apparently impoverished country like Mali, with per capita income of about US$100 per year, might not be as bad off as that figure makes it appear; many of Mali's goods are produced in villages and within families without being traded in markets. We're not saying that Mali is well-off. But we are saying that it might not be meaningful to compare the low per capita incomes of many less developed countries like Mali with the high per capita incomes of industrialized nations like the United States.

You might think that in a modern economy like the United States, production within the household is relatively insignificant. But think again. Many of us wash our own dishes, cook our own meals, do our own laundry, and scrub our own floors. The services we provide to ourselves in this way represent income and in principle should enter the official statistics. In practice they do not, because we don't pay ourselves and so we don't report such income.

Imagine instead that we all contracted to do our neighbors' housework for a market wage—person A does neighbor B's housework for a fee, and neighbor B does A's for a fee. We would each do just as much work, and have just as clean a house, as we do now. Measured income would grow enormously. In fact, it has been estimated that, if valued at market rates, the work of Americans in the home would increase aggregate income by one-third! So the undermeasurement of income from nonmarket activities is substantial even in developed countries like the United States.

Indirect Taxes

Pretax income:
The income that is collected before taxes are paid out.

It is important to distinguish between **pretax income** and **posttax income.** Depending on one's purpose, either measurement can be appropriate. But it is also important to be consistent, and many official measurements are not.

Posttax income:
The income that remains after taxes are paid out.

When you buy a candy bar for 55 cents plus 5 cents sales tax, the store owner reports her (pretax) income as only 55 cents—even though she actually collects 60 cents from you at the cash register. But according to the economist's definition, the entire 60 cents is pretax income to the store owner, so what she reports understates her total income.

You might object that the store owner does not get to keep the extra nickel and thus it is actually *correct* not to count it as income. But she doesn't get to keep the whole 55 cents either—some of it gets paid to the government in the form of income tax. Because most measurements of national income count the entire 55 cents as income to the store owner, for consistency these measurements should count the extra nickel as well.

Indirect tax:
A tax that is transferred to the government without ever being reported as someone's income.

Sales tax is an example of an **indirect tax** on business: it passes through the owner's hands to the government without ever being reported as income. Measurements of pretax income that omit indirect taxes are logically flawed.

Dealing with Measurement Problems

Because the government knows the total amount of indirect taxes, it simply adds that amount to the income officially reported by citizens. But the other sources of unreported income are more difficult to correct for. The U.S. government officially estimates and includes some missing nonmarket income. The value of housework, however, is not currently added to U.S. income.

Do these deficiencies seriously distort the picture we get by trying to measure welfare via aggregate income? It depends. If nonmarket activities and underreported income stay at about the same level over time, they present no obstacle to comparing income from year to year or to drawing inferences about welfare changes.

On the other hand, if the level of these activities changes, then the data might have to be handled with caution. For example, tax rates were cut in the early 1980s, and this reduced the incentive to underreport income. Thus, reported income might have increased since then, while actual income remained unchanged.

If more and more women start going to work, as they did in the 1970s and 1980s, and start paying for services like housekeeping and child care, which they used to provide themselves (without pay), then measured income could go up without welfare's rising by very much.

2-2   OUTPUT

Output:
A collective term for the goods and services produced in an economy.

To earn income, a household must produce or help produce something, like shoes, haircuts, cars, insurance services, medical services, education, entertainment, or satellites: some thing or some service. The goods (including services) that are produced are called **output** or *production*.

Measuring Output

Aggregate output or Gross domestic product (GDP):
The total value of goods and services produced in an economy or a specific country.

We measure **aggregate output** for a period by adding the values of all the goods produced in that particular period. Let us suppose that there are two goods in an economy, muffins and magazines. Last year, 10 muffins were produced and sold for $1 each, and 20 magazines were produced, selling for $3 each. The aggregate output was then ($1 × 10) + ($3 × 20) = $70.

Notice that using dollar values allows us to add apparently disparate goods, like apples and oranges or muffins and magazines.

The value of the entire output produced in a country is that country's **gross domestic product,** or **GDP.** Macroeconomists use GDP as their measure of a country's aggregate output.

➡ *Exercise 2-2*
What is a country's GDP if its citizens produce 10 machines, selling for $200 each, and 300 haircuts, selling at $25 each?

Problems in Measuring Output Directly

Several difficulties crop up when output is measured. Two problematic factors are explored below.

Value Added and Intermediate Goods

Suppose a farmer produces $5 worth of wheat, which he sells to a baker. The baker exerts $20 worth of effort to turn the wheat into bread, which she sells for $25. At the end of the day, what has been produced? The answer is just $25 worth of bread. But if we ask the farmer and the baker to report their output for the day, the farmer says, "I produced $5 worth of wheat," and the baker says, "I produced $25 worth of bread."

A statistician who naively adds these numbers might think that there has been $30 of output in the economy. The statistician is led astray by counting the wheat, which is not a **final good** at all but rather an **intermediate good** that disappears after it is used to produce the bread.

Final good:
A good that is not used in the production of another good.

There are two ways to avoid this measurement pitfall:

1. Ask the farmer and the baker to report the value of their sales of *final* goods to consumers. The baker reports $25 and the farmer reports $0, because his wheat is not a final good.

Intermediate good:
A good that is used up in producing another good.

2. Ask the farmer and the baker to report the *contribution* each made to the total. The farmer reports $5 worth of wheat, and the baker reports $20 worth of effort, for a total value of $25 worth of output.

Value added:
The value that a producer adds to intermediate goods by turning them into final goods.

We call the baker's contribution to output her **value added,** which the baker calculates by subtracting her costs, $5, from her revenue, $25. The baker's value added is thus $20. The farmer's value added is $5: in our example, he had no costs. When businesses report their output to the government, they subtract their costs, so they are reporting value added. The government then adds the value added by all businesses to arrive at GDP.

There are many examples of intermediate goods (like wheat) whose value should not be double-counted when output is computed. Three examples are oil, shipping, and advertising.

For businesses to know what to report as their contributions or value added, they have to know how much of their costs they should subtract from their revenues. Thus, the government must define "intermediate goods" quite explicitly. Officially, *an intermediate good or service is one that is used up in the production of other goods or services during the same period in which it was produced.* The key phrases in this definition are "used up" and "same period." Let us see how these concepts clarify which goods are intermediate and which are final.

Inventory:
The quantity of goods that are produced but not used up or sold in a given reporting period.

Inventories What happens if the wheat bought by the baker is not used up by the end of the year? Or if some of the bread remains on the shelves? Goods that are not used up are not intermediate goods. Instead, the unused wheat or unsold bread is called an **inventory** and is classed as a final good. That is, inventories are counted as part of output.

Inventory investment:
Additions to inventory from one reporting period to the next.

The change in the value of a business's inventory from one year to the next is counted as a final good and is called **inventory investment.** Thus, if the baker's inventory is worth $6000 at the end of one year and $7000 at the end of the next year, the baker had $1000 worth of inventory investment during that year. That $1000 is reported as output, in the form of inventory, for the bakery. Inventory investment can be negative: if the baker's inventory had fallen from $6000 to $4000, her inventory investment would have been −$2000.

Capital Goods   What if the baker buys a new oven or some new baking racks? These items are not intermediate goods because they are not used up during the course of the year; nor does the baker sell them to others as final goods. They are examples of **capital goods.**

How does the government account for new capital goods? Capital goods are considered final goods because they are not used up by a business during the period in which they are bought. A business is the final user of any capital good.

From the perspective of GDP accounting—counting up the country's GDP for the year—*a capital good is a long-lived good that is itself produced and is used to produce other goods*. Like an intermediate good, a capital good is used to produce other goods; but unlike an intermediate good, a capital good is not used up right away (although it might deteriorate or be used up eventually).

The total quantity of a country's capital goods is called its **capital stock.** The change in a country's capital stock from the beginning to the end of a year is called the country's **investment** for that year. If the baker starts the year with a **stock** of $2000 in ovens and ends the year with a stock of $5000 in ovens, we say she invested $3000 during the year. By this, we mean that she bought $3000 worth of capital goods—final goods to be reported as output.

The change in a stock is called a **flow.** The flow of capital goods—that is, investment—is counted as part of output for the year.

Depreciation   Just a moment ago we alluded to the fact that capital gets used up—but in the sense that it wears out, or undergoes **depreciation.** Suppose that in a given year, $5000 worth of new capital is created while $3000 worth of old capital wears out—so the total capital stock increases by $2000. Then we say that the country's **gross investment** was $5000 and its **net investment** was $2000. For a given period, gross investment is the amount of new capital created, and net investment is gross investment minus depreciation.

It is difficult to get an accurate measure of the value of depreciation. The U.S. tax law allows businesses to subtract depreciation—called the *capital consumption allowance*—from their revenues before calculating their taxes. Clearly, businesses that overstate the extent to which their equipment has depreciated pay lower taxes. To avoid losing tax revenue, the government publishes a schedule—that is, a table—specifying the percentage depreciation a business can claim, depending on the age of the capital. As a result, economists have little way of knowing if actual depreciation is more or less than the government's allowance.

The business sector's contribution to national output is measured by summing the value added by all businesses to final goods, including the value of capital goods and inventories, and then subtracting the value of depreciation.

Capital good:
A good which is used to make other goods without being used up in the process.

Capital stock:
The value of all the capital in an economy.

Investment:
The addition of capital goods to the capital stock over a period of time.

Stock:
The existing quantity of a good.

Flow:
The change in the stock of a good over a period of time.

Depreciation:
The loss of value of capital goods over time due to wear.

Gross investment:
The amount of new capital created.

Net investment:
Gross investment minus depreciation.

Unfortunately, the process we have just described—summing the value added by each business—is less precise than it sounds. Suppose a car-repair business purchases spreadsheet software to help it keep track of customers, billing, and parts in stock. Is that software an intermediate good or a capital good? If the software becomes obsolete in less than a year, then it is an intermediate good—something that is essentially used up in the process of creating this year's repair services. In that case, the software does not count as output. If the software is still in use a year from today, it is an investment—something that helps create repair services on an ongoing basis. In that case, the software counts as output.

But the government agencies that collect statistics on output must decide today whether to count the software purchase—they do not have the luxury of waiting a year to see if the software is still in use. In practice, they have adopted the following arbitrary rule: Software that is bundled with new computers counts as an investment, while software that is purchased separately for business use counts as an intermediate good. Most software is in the latter category, and hence does *not* count as output. If a different arbitrary rule had been chosen, measured output might be substantially larger than it is today.

Government Output

Some of a country's output is produced by the government, so the country's total output is the sum of government output and business output. But measuring the government's contribution to output is difficult. The government produces but does not sell military and police services. And the tolls the government charges for roads don't come anywhere near the costs it incurs constructing and maintaining them. How then can we calculate the value of government-produced goods and services?

In practice, the government measures its output by its costs: what it pays its employees (including the military), and what it pays for goods and services. Costs are not a perfect measure of the value of the government's output; that output could easily be worth either more or less than what it costs to produce it. Nevertheless, valuing the government's output at cost is probably better than valuing it at nothing at all.

In summary, then:

A nation's output is measured by computing its GDP, which is the sum of business output and government costs.

2-3   RELATING OUTPUT TO INCOME

There is a fundamental relationship between income and output, and it is extremely simple:

$$Output = Income$$

To see this, think of a one-person economy, called a "Robinson Crusoe economy." Imagine Crusoe paying himself at the end of each day for his day's output of fish and home repairs and then using the income to buy, from himself, that very same output. The value of the output he produces is exactly equal to the value of the income he receives.

Now add another person to the economy—Friday—who works for Crusoe in exchange for some of the extra fish he enables Crusoe to catch. Crusoe's income is what he is left with after paying Friday. The sum of their incomes equals the day's catch, so aggregate output and aggregate income are equal.

In the more complicated modern economy, a worker might produce only the windows of an automobile. He is paid a share of the value of the whole automobile. The total value of the automobile—that is, what it sells for in the market—is divided among all the individuals who help build it, design it, conceive of it, ship it, and market it. Everything that is produced adds to the income of those who produce it.

> The total value of income received—composed of wages, rentals, and profits—equals the total value of output produced.

Relating Measured Output to Measured Income

Although output equals income, it does not follow that *measured* output equals *measured* income. This is because the measurement problems we have already discussed introduce ambiguities and discrepancies between the two.

Here is one example of an ambiguity. Suppose you own a business which uses computers to produce graphic artwork. Suppose that in a given year you produce $10,000 worth of artwork but must replace $2000 worth of depreciated computer equipment. What is the value of your output—$10,000 or $8000?

The answer is that your *gross* output was worth $10,000 and your *net* output was worth $8000. Your business contributes $10,000 to the gross domestic product (GDP) but only $8000 to the **net domestic product (NDP),** which is defined by the equation

Net domestic product (NDP):
The amount of income firms have after selling their output; equal to GDP minus depreciation.

$$NDP = GDP - \text{Depreciation}$$

The word "gross" in "gross domestic product" means "before subtracting depreciation."

Net domestic product is the output firms have left after replacing their depreciated capital. That output is sold to produce income, which firms pay out to suppliers, employees, and owners in the form of rents, wages, and profits. However, before that income is paid out, firms may have to pay indirect taxes, which are not counted in the official measurements of national income. Thus we have

$$\text{National income} = NDP - \text{Indirect taxes}$$

Combining the two preceding equations, we see that

$$\text{GDP} = \underbrace{\frac{\text{National}}{\text{income}}}_{} + \underbrace{\frac{\text{Indirect}}{\text{taxes}} + \text{Depreciation}}_{}$$

$$\underbrace{\text{GDP}}_{\text{Output}} = \underbrace{\frac{\text{National}}{\text{income}} + \frac{\text{Indirect}}{\text{taxes}} + \text{Depreciation}}_{\text{Income}}$$

GDP is what macroeconomists use to measure output. The sum of national income and indirect taxes and depreciation is what macroeconomists use to measure income. And the two are equal. As a consequence, GDP is used by macroeconomists as their measure of both income and output.

It is important to remember that national income is *not* the measure economists use when they want a measure of a country's income or output. National income is just one component of a country's aggregate income. Not only is it too low by the size of indirect taxes, but it also excludes depreciation.

We depict the relationship in Figure 2-1. From the figure, you can see that there is more than one way to decompose income or GDP. You can think of it as the sum of business output and government output or as the sum of national income, indirect taxes, and depreciation.

Net Factor Payments Abroad

There is another way to decompose GDP.

Some U.S. citizens earn income by working for businesses owned by foreign companies. At the same time, some of the people who work for U.S.-owned businesses are foreign nationals. This means that if we use the *output* sold by U.S. firms (businesses owned by U.S. citizens) as part of our measure of the total *income* of U.S. citizens, we are making a mistake. If we're interested only in total U.S. income, and we try to measure it by using the output of U.S. firms, we mistakenly include income paid to foreign workers by U.S. firms and mistakenly exclude income earned by U.S. citizens working for foreign-owned firms.

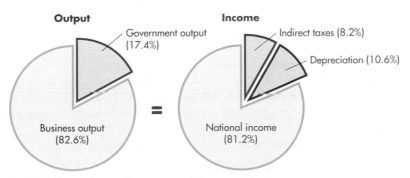

FIGURE 2-1 Measured output equals measured income.
Output and income are commonly subdivided into components, but total output and total income are equal. The percentages are for the United States in 1995.

Net factor payments abroad:

Payments from domestic firms to foreign citizens minus payments from foreign firms to domestic citizens.

The amount that U.S. firms pay foreign workers minus the amount that U.S. citizens earn from foreign-owned companies is called **net factor payments abroad.** Net factor payments abroad have to be subtracted from the total value of U.S. output (GDP) to get U.S. **gross national product,** or **GNP.** That is,

$$GNP = GDP - \text{Net factor payments abroad}$$

Gross national product (GNP):

The output produced by a country's citizens regardless of where they work.

Put simply, GDP is the output produced within a country's borders, whether or not it is produced by the country's citizens. GNP is the output produced by a country's citizens, wherever in the world they work.

For the United States, net factor payments abroad are generally a relatively small percentage of GNP (less than 1 percent in 1990); hence U.S. GNP and GDP are nearly equal. But for some countries, like India and Turkey, many of whose citizens work abroad, the difference between GNP and GDP is substantial. For countries at war or those with domestic difficulties that drive people away, such as Haiti, so many citizens might move abroad that accurate GNP data become impossible to acquire.

Which is a better measure of output for macroeconomists to use, GNP or GDP? It depends on the intended use of the data. If you want to know about the welfare of your citizens, use GNP. If you want to find out about the effects of investment-encouragement programs within your borders, use GDP.

The current accepted measure of output is GDP, and that is the definition we shall use throughout this book. Because output equals income, we shall also use GDP as a measure of income.

2-4 EXPENDITURE

Domestic expenditure:

Spending by a country's citizens.

In this section we discuss **domestic expenditure,** or *expenditure,* which is the total amount that a country's citizens spend on goods and services of all kinds over a period of time. Domestic expenditure includes expenditures by the households, businesses, and government of a country.

Measuring Expenditure

Consumption expenditure:

Spending by households.

It is traditional to subdivide domestic expenditure (that is, spending by the citizens of a country) into three components: **consumption expenditure, investment expenditure,** and **government purchases.** The first two are expenditures by the **private sector;** government purchases are sometimes referred to as purchases by the **public sector.**

Investment expenditure:

Spending (usually by firms) to add to capital and inventory.

Expenditure by the Private Sector

Government purchases:

Spending by the government for goods and services.

Consumption expenditure includes most household purchases, of which some are **durable goods** like furniture and cars, while some are **nondurable goods** like food. Investment expenditure includes the purchase of items like machinery and factory space and additions to inventory.

Private sector:

The segment of the economy consisting of households and firms.

Most investment expenditure is done by firms rather than individuals or households. However, because many households make direct expenditures on investment, *measuring* consumption expenditure and investment expenditure can be a difficult task. For example, expenditure on a child's college education is in principle investment expenditure, although it is counted as consumption expenditure in goverment measures.

Public sector:

The segment of the economy consisting of the government.

Expenditure by the Public Sector

Durable good:

A good that may be used repeatedly for a long time.

Government purchases can theoretically be subdivided into consumption expenditure and investment expenditure by the public sector, although most often they are lumped together. Examples of government investment expenditure are government purchases of military equipment and repaving of highways. Examples of government consumption expenditure are trash collection and wage payments for labor services.

Nondurable good:

A good that is used up in one period.

There are two different kinds of payments which the government makes to private citizens. First, there are payments in exchange for goods and services; these are what we have called "governmental purchases." Second, there are direct payments which citizens receive without having to sell anything to the government. These direct payments are called **transfers.** Examples of transfers include social security (retirement insurance) and welfare payments. Transfers are not part of government purchases, but they are included in a broader category called **government expenditure.** Government expenditure is equal to government purchases plus transfers.

Transfers:

Payments from the government to the private sector (not including payments for goods and services).

Should we count government transfers as part of the country's expenditure? If we did count transfers as expenditure, we would also—to "balance the books"—have to count the welfare and social security payments received by the elderly and the poor as income. If we did that, the country's income would appear larger than it currently does.

Government expenditure:

Government purchases plus transfers.

But that extra income or expenditure does not really represent any additional economic production or activity: the money is simply taxed away from some people and distributed to others. For that reason, economists prefer to exclude transfers from their measure of a country's income and thus (for consistency) to exclude them when measuring expenditure.

Notice that the language we use is potentially confusing: "Government expenditure" is *not* a part of "expenditure." Government expenditure includes both purchases and transfers; only the purchases are included in expenditure.

2-5 THE RELATIONSHIP AMONG INCOME, OUTPUT, AND EXPENDITURE

Closed economy:

An isolated economy whose citizens do not trade with other economies.

Now we want to ask what people do with their income. To simplify the discussion, let us assume (temporarily) the citizens of a certain country do not engage in any trade with foreigners; that is, citizens cannot buy goods from abroad and cannot sell their output overseas. Such an economy is called a **closed economy.** In a closed economy, here are the things you can do with your income:

- You can spend it (for example, to buy a car or an ice cream cone or a college education).
- You can lend it to another individual who plans to spend it. (One way to do this is to make a bank deposit, allowing the bank to lend your income for you.)
- You can lend it to a firm that plans to spend it (for example, to buy a new factory or a new computer).
- You can lend it to the government, which plans to spend it (for example, to buy an aircraft carrier or to pay the president's salary).
- You can pay taxes to the government, which still plans to spend it.

Thus even if you don't spend all of your own income, it is still true that all of your income gets spent. This allows us to write the equation

$$\text{Income} = \text{Expenditure}$$

Income need not equal expenditure for any *individual*—an individual might spend less than his income (if he saves and pays taxes) or more than his income (if he borrows from others). But if we add up over the entire economy, everyone's savings are borrowed by others, who use them to buy things. Hence, from the perspective of an aggregate economy, all income is spent.

Saving

Savings:
The portion of income that is not spent in the present.

What you save—your **savings**—is the part of your income you don't spend. Perhaps you put it in the bank or lend it to a friend. But if you put it in the bank, it doesn't just sit there. The banker lends your savings to someone else: someone who wants those savings precisely in order to *buy* something, like a car, a college course, or the parts needed to build a machine for a factory. Or the government might borrow your savings, spending them on military equipment, schools, or parks. Either way, your savings are spent.

Every dollar saved by one person is a dollar borrowed and spent by someone else.

The fact that income saved by one person is borrowed and spent by someone else is extremely important. This fact is commonly overlooked, and the oversight leads to error and misunderstanding. For example, let's say the economy is in a slump and many people are being laid off from their jobs. Some people think such a problem could be cured if people's confidence returned and they just spent more instead of saving so much. You will see later in this book that for somewhat more complicated reasons, the conclusion that more spending can be desirable is sometimes correct. But the simplistic version of the argument—that spending more will mean more money for businesses, which will add employees and thus put more people back to work—cannot be right: for each additional dollar of my income that I spend, I have to save $1 less; and that means $1 less for someone else to spend.

It is easy to get confused when talking about savings. To an economist, a person's savings are not the total, accumulated amount that the person has in the bank but the amount he adds to that accumulation during the current period. We sometimes call the accumulated amount of savings a person's *stock* of savings to differentiate it from the savings *flow,* which is the change in the amount of savings during the period (for example, a year). The word "flow" emphasizes that we're talking about a *change* in the stock.

Dissaving:

Drawing on stock of savings to spend.

Dissaving is simply negative saving. Borrowing is a form of dissaving. So is withdrawing money from a bank account. When macroeconomists talk about saving, they usually mean the difference between a person's saving and dissaving, that is, the *net saving* for the period. While an individual's net saving can be positive or negative, for the whole economy, net saving must equal zero.

Any saving done by putting the money under a mattress or by the bank's keeping the cash on hand in its vaults is actually a kind of expenditure: the money is spent dollar for dollar buying itself. Hoarding—stockpiling cash under mattresses—makes it difficult for the government to measure total expenditure, but it does not negate the fundamental relationship: income = expenditure.

Taxes

While individuals do not spend the portion of their income used to pay taxes, the government does. Governments spend tax revenue to provide goods and services. Therefore, the portion of your income that goes to pay taxes is also spent—it is spent by the government.

All income is spent somehow: either by the person who earns it, or by someone (either an individual or a firm) who borrows it, or by the government, which acquires it by borrowing or taxation. Therefore, aggregate income equals aggregate expenditure.

The Circular Flow of Economic Activity

The equality among income, output, and expenditure is summarized by the equation

$$\text{Income} = \text{Output} = \text{Expenditure}$$

The relationship is often depicted as a simple circular flow of economic activity between households and businesses, as displayed in Figure 2-2(*a*). Households provide *factor inputs*—that is, they supply labor and rent capital to businesses, which in turn pay wages, rents, and profits as income. That income flows back to the businesses in the form of expenditures by households to buy output. The income that flows from businesses to households, the expenditures that flow from households to businesses, and the value of the output that flows from businesses to households are all equal.

The circular flow is more realistically represented in Figure 2-2(*b*), which includes the government. Now households earn income by selling inputs to both

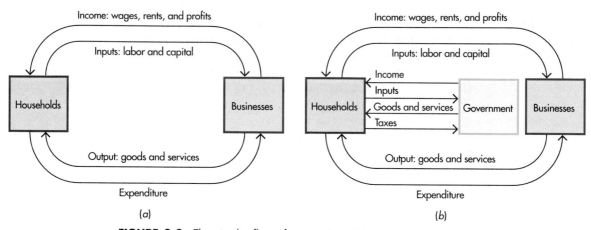

FIGURE 2-2 The circular flow of economic activity.
In (a), households earn income by selling labor and capital to businesses. They use this income to purchase the output of those businesses. The households' income, their expenditures to purchase output, and the value of that output are all equal. In (b), the picture is made more realistic by including a government sector. Now the income that households earn by selling inputs to businesses and government must equal the households' expenditures (including taxes), which in turn must equal the total value of all output produced by businesses and government.

businesses and the government. Their expenditures include both spending to buy output from businesses and paying taxes to the government. The output that households receive from businesses and the government is equal to their expenditures and to their income.

You might object that businesses pay taxes just as households do, and that these business taxes are not represented in Figure 2-2(b). But every business is ultimately owned by households, so business taxes are ultimately paid by households. Hence all taxes are accounted for by the single arrow labeled "Taxes" in Figure 2-2(b).

2-6 INCOME AND EXPENDITURE IN AN OPEN ECONOMY

Open economy:
An economy in which citizens and the government can trade with other economies.

Imports:
Goods from another country that are consumed domestically.

A country whose citizens sell goods to foreigners and buy goods from foreigners is called an **open economy.** In the modern world, most countries have open economies.

Our discussion of the relationship between expenditure and income has to be modified slightly to be applicable to an open economy. Consider what happens when a citizen of the United States buys goods worth $10 from another U.S. citizen. In that case, the value of U.S. income is $10, the same as expenditure.

But suppose the U.S. citizen spends $8 on U.S. goods and $2 on foreign goods, or **imports.** In that case, U.S. income is $8, not $10, but U.S. expenditure remains $10. Total spending by U.S. citizens has to be reduced by the value of imports to maintain the equality between income and expenditure.

Moreover, when an economy is open, some of the goods produced by its businesses are **exports;** they are sold to foreigners, or exported. Suppose a foreigner buys $20 worth of U.S. goods. Then U.S. income is $20, but U.S. domestic expenditure for those goods is $0. Thus, we must add the value of exports to expenditure to maintain the equality between income and expenditure.

For any country, the value of its exports less the value of its imports is called **net exports.** We must add net exports to domestic expenditure to obtain, for an open economy, the equality

$$\text{Income} = \text{Output} = \text{Expenditure} + \underbrace{\text{Exports} - \text{Imports}}_{\text{Net exports}}$$

Because expenditure is the sum of consumption expenditure, investment expenditure, and government purchases (which do not include transfers), we may rewrite this equation as

$$\text{Income} = \text{Consumption} + \text{Investment} + \text{Government purchases} + \text{Net exports}$$

or in symbols as

$$Y = C + I + G + NX$$

where Y represents the country's income, output, or GDP; C represents private consumption expenditure; I represents private investment expenditure; G represents government purchases; and NX represents net exports. The equation is illustrated in Figure 2-3.

Measuring Net Exports

There are various ways to measure net exports, or the **trade balance.** One commonly used measure is the **balance on merchandise trade,** which is the value of exported (physical) goods minus the value of imported goods. This balance does not include services of any kind. A broader measure of the trade balance is the **balance on goods and services,** which includes trade in services such as banking services, travel, and insurance. The broadest measure of the trade balance published by the government is the **balance on the current account.** It includes not only the goods and services included in the balance on goods and services but also trade in debt services—interest payments on loans—plus gifts.

Sidebar definitions:

Exports:
Goods produced domestically and sold abroad.

Net exports or Trade balance:
The value of exports minus the value of imports.

Merchandise trade balance:
A measure of the trade balance that counts physical goods but not services.

Goods and services trade balance:
A measure of the trade balance that counts both goods and services.

Current-account balance:
A broad measure of the trade balance that counts goods, services, debt services, and gifts.

$$
\overbrace{}^{\text{Expenditure}}
$$

Y	=	C	+	I	+	G	+	NX
6932	=	4699	+	1014	+	1315	+	(−96)

FIGURE 2-3 Income (or output) Y equals expenditure plus net exports NX. Expenditure consists of consumption C, investment I, and government purchases G. The numbers are in billions of dollars, for the United States in 1994.

Some major services are still not included in these balances. For example, education, which is exported by the United States whenever foreign students come here to study, is not included. Many exports and imports to travelers, such as meals purchased while traveling in a foreign country, are also not included.

U.S. trade balance data are reported on a country-by-country basis as well as for all foreign countries combined. For example, data are reported on the U.S. trade balance with Japan—the value of U.S. exports to Japanese citizens less the value of U.S. imports from Japanese citizens. Data are also reported on the U.S. trade balance with each of the nation's other trading partners. In macroeconomics, however, such bilateral trade balances are not appropriate measures of net exports; instead, we are concerned with overall U.S. exports to and imports from the entire rest of the world.

The U.S. merchandise trade balance is reported on a monthly basis, while the balance on goods and services and the current-account balance are reported only on a quarterly basis. This difference in reporting sometimes leads people to use the merchandise trade balance as an interim measure of the overall trade balance. Unfortunately, the merchandise trade balance tends to fluctuate from month to month depending on the timing of orders and shipments of various goods. Thus, a delay of a month in the shipment of a large order of airplanes can cause the merchandise trade balance to be reported as a negative number (a **trade deficit**—imports exceed exports) for one month and a positive number (a **trade surplus**—exports exceed imports) the following month, when the airplanes are shipped. The quarterly statistics can sometimes better reflect the overall status of U.S. net exports.

Because of the various limitations of the merchandise trade balance as a measure of the trade balance, in this book we use the current account balance as our measure of the trade balance.

Trade deficit:
An excess of imports over exports for a period of time.

Trade surplus:
An excess of exports over imports for a period of time.

2-7 GROWTH

Economic growth:
The change in output over time.

Growth rate:
Economic growth expressed as a percentage.

Economic growth is the change in a country's output from one year to the next. The **growth rate** is the percent change in the country's output.

Usually, growth is a positive number: a country's output increases from one year to the next. But occasionally output declines. In that case, we say the country has experienced negative growth.

Because output and income are equal, and because income is roughly related to a country's welfare, growth—that is, an *increase* in output—is generally looked upon as desirable.

Problems in Measuring Growth

Gross domestic product, our measure of output, can be used as a rough measure of a country's growth from one year to the next. Let us look at U.S. GDP on a per capita basis—that is, per capita income—to see if it is a good indicator of welfare. For the last four decade-ending years, see Table 2-1. Comparing these income data with what you may know about your own family's income history should suggest that some-

TABLE 2-1

YEAR	PER CAPITA GDP	PERCENT INCREASE PER DECADE
1960	$ 2913	
1970	5050	73
1980	12,226	142
1990	22,979	88

thing is terribly wrong with what we are doing. Did your family's income increase by 88 percent between 1980 and 1990? If average U.S. income rose so much during the 1980s, why doesn't everyone feel that much richer? After all, if the average person's income almost doubled in 10 years, isn't that good news? And just look at the 1970s: during that decade, income increased by 142 percent. Why, then, do people look back on the 1970s as a period of economic troubles?

Real versus Nominal Income

By trying to assess economic well-being as we just did, we make a common mistake: forgetting that the dollars we earn as income are only as useful as the things we can buy with them. If your income rises and the prices of the things you buy also rise, then your income—your **real income**—might not go up as fast as your dollar income, or **nominal income.**

Here is an example that shows the difference between real income and nominal income over time: Imagine that you are an average person in 1970, earning about $5000 per year. That is, your nominal income is $5000. Suppose the only goods in the economy are snacks, selling for $5 apiece. The **price level,** or average price of goods in the economy, is thus $5 per snack. Your *real* income for the year is calculated as

$$\text{Real income} = \frac{\text{Nominal income}}{\text{Price level}}$$

$$= \frac{\$5000/\text{Year}}{\$5/\text{Snack}}$$

$$= 1000 \text{ Snacks/Year}$$

Real income:
Income measured in terms of the goods that it can buy.

Nominal income:
Income measured on the arbitrary scale of dollars.

Price level:
The average price of goods in the economy measured in dollars, thus yielding the quantity of goods a dollar will buy.

You are able to buy 1000 snacks that year. A more general way of saying this is that the value of your annual income, in terms of snacks, is 1000 snacks.

Suppose that in 1980 your nominal income rises to $12,000 per year and the average price of the goods you buy doubles, to $10 per snack. Then your real income in 1980 is

$$\frac{\$12,000/\text{Year}}{\$10/\text{Snack}} = 1200 \text{ Snacks/Year}$$

Your nominal income has risen by

$$\left(\frac{\$12,000 - \$5000}{\$5000}\right) = \frac{7}{5} = 1.40, \text{ or } 140\%$$

but your real income has not. You cannot buy 140 percent more snacks with the increase in your income. Real income rose by the difference in what it could buy each year, or

$$\frac{1200 \text{ Snacks/Year} - 1000 \text{ Snacks/Year}}{1000 \text{ Snacks/Year}} = \frac{200}{1000} = .20, \text{ or } 20\%$$

And real income is the measure that matters, because dollars can hardly be eaten or worn or used for shelter.

Exercise 2-3

Suppose that between 1990 and 2000 your nominal income increases from $12,000 to $24,000. By what percent does your nominal income rise? Suppose that during the same period prices rise from $5 per good to $15 per good. By what percent do prices rise? What is your real income in each year? Does your real income rise or fall? By what percent?

Exercise 2-4

Suppose that between 1995 and 1996 prices rise by 5 percent while nominal income also rises by 5 percent. What happens to real income?

When macroeconomists talk about income, they always mean *real* income. And, since income equals output, when macroeconomists talk about output, they always mean *real* output.

The news media do not always make the important distinction between real income and nominal income in their reports. It is not uncommon for the media to report income, output, and GDP without clarifying whether they are nominal or real.

But it is important for you, as a student of macroeconomics, to be alert to the possibility that the numbers reported by the media are not what they seem; and you must be careful not to draw mistaken inferences by failing to convert nominal data to real terms.

Measuring Real Income: Real GDP

Suppose the price level never changed. Then changes in nominal income would be perfectly good measures of changes in real income. If nominal income rose 10 percent in the 1990s and there were no change in the price level, then we would know that real income also rose by 10 percent.

Unfortunately, the price level *does* change from year to year. But here is a neat trick for measuring real income even when prices change: First, pretend that prices do not change. Calculate the value that output *would* have had if it had been mea-

TABLE 2-2

YEAR	MUFFINS		MAGAZINES		NOMINAL GDP
	QUANTITY	PRICE	QUANTITY	PRICE	
1994	10	$1	20	$2	$ 50
1995	15	2	25	4	130
1996	10	2	30	5	170

Constant prices:
The prices in a given year.

Real GDP:
A measure of GDP that holds prices constant, thus measuring the real value of output for a country.

Base year:
The year whose prices are used to determine real GDP.

sured at **constant prices.** Then, if there was an increase from year to year in the value of output calculated at constant prices, we can conclude that the value of output rose in real terms.

This method is exactly the way the government calculates **real GDP,** which is the macroeconomist's measure of real income. Each year, the real GDP is calculated by valuing that year's output at the prices that prevailed in some earlier year, called the **base year,** which does not change.[1]

Let's try an example. Suppose there are two goods in the economy—muffins and magazines—and they were produced in the quantities and sold at the prices indicated in Table 2-2.

We know that it is meaningless to compare the nominal incomes for the three years because prices changed each year for at least one good. But let us *pretend* that prices in 1995 and 1996 were the same as those in 1994, as shown in Table 2-3.

Since we're assuming constant prices, all changes in the column labeled "Real GDP" are a result of changes in output. That is, all changes in that column are real. Thus, we can say that in 1995 real income rose by

$$\frac{\$65 - \$50}{\$50} = 30\%$$

and in 1996 real income rose by

$$\frac{\$70 - \$65}{\$65} = 7.7\%$$

TABLE 2-3

YEAR	MUFFINS		MAGAZINES		REAL GDP (GDP IN 1994 PRICES)
	QUANTITY	PRICE	QUANTITY	PRICE	
1994	10	$1	20	$2	$50
1995	15	1	25	2	65
1996	10	1	30	2	70

....

[1]This computation of real income fails to account for changes in relative prices over the time period since in the base year. Sometimes the government partially corrects for this problem through a statistical technique called *chain weighting*.

TABLE 2-4

YEAR	REAL PER CAPITA GDP (1992 BASE YEAR)	PERCENT INCREASE PER DECADE
1960	$12,512	
1970	16,520	32
1980	20,252	23
1990	24,559	21

By choosing a base year (1994, in our example) and evaluating each year's output at the base year's prices, we can get a meaningful measure of how real income changes over time. When economists speak of real GDP, they mean GDP as measured in the prices of an agreed-upon base year. We say that it is measured in *base-year dollars*.

Now let us return to the data for the United States. Table 2-4 shows real per capita GDP, measured in 1992 dollars.

Apparently the 1960s were remarkably good economic times, providing the average citizen with a 32 percent rise in real income—an average annual increase of 3.2 percent. The 1970s, however, saw a much lower average annual rise in real income—only 2.3 percent per year, a low rate that became even lower in the 1980s.

 When GDPs are measured in base-year dollars, they are real (not nominal) measures despite being stated in dollars. They are measured in the dollars of only one year, which is equivalent to measuring them in real goods purchased in that year.

Measuring Real Growth

A rise in real output is called economic growth, or just *growth*. The percent change in aggregate real output from one year to the next is called the *annual aggregate growth rate*. The percent change in real output per capita is called the *annual per capita growth rate*. Per capita growth is a rough measure of the rate at which a country's living standards are improving. Although most countries tend to grow each year, how rapidly they grow varies substantially. In some years, real output falls below the output of the previous year. That is, real output decreases, so the country's growth rate is negative.

Exercise 2-5

Suppose real output changes from 1000 goods in year 1 to 900 goods in year 2. What is the annual growth rate?

Recession:

A period in which real output decreases or the growth rate or real output decreases.

Figure 2-4 shows a graph of real U.S. GDP from the 1960s to the present. Although real GDP tends to rise over time, there are occasional declines—such a period is commonly called a **recession**. The figure shows that in 1992 dollars, real GDP rose by just over $1.1 trillion from 1960 to 1970 and by more than that (about

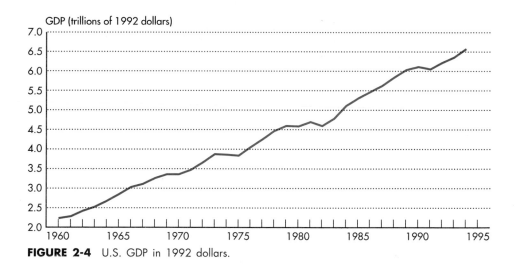

FIGURE 2-4 U.S. GDP in 1992 dollars.

$1.2 trillion) from 1970 to 1980. But $1.1 trillion is 50 percent of 1960's output, while $1.2 trillion is only about 36 percent of 1970's output. Thus the average annual growth rate for the decade 1960–1970 was 5.0 percent, while the average annual growth rate for the decade 1970–1980 was only 3.6 percent. In the decade 1980–1990, the growth rate was even lower, averaging only 3.3 percent.

Earlier we saw that *per capita* real GDP grew by 3.2 percent per year on average from 1960 to 1970; here we have said that *aggregate* real GDP grew by 5.0 percent on average over the same decade. The two figures differ because the population was growing.

Economic event:
Any change that affects the economy.

The data in Figure 2-4 indicate several **economic events** that characterize the period since 1970. In 1974 and 1975, GDP deviated downward from its general upward path, or *trend*. A few years of rapid recovery in the late 1970s were followed by another recession in the period from 1980 to 1982. During the remainder of the 1980s growth was relatively strong, averaging 4.1 percent annually for the 8-year period from 1982 to 1990. In the early 1990s, growth slowed again. Armed with these data, you can begin to understand some of the controversies and debates about the economy that occurred during the presidencies of Nixon, Ford, Carter, Reagan, Bush, and Clinton.

Despite the variability in annual growth rates from one year to the next, worldwide growth rates during the period since World War II tend to fall somewhere between 1.5 and 3.5 percent per year. A growth rate of more than 4 percent per year is extraordinarily large; a year in which income grows 1 percent or less is considered an unusually sluggish year. Toward the end of the 1980s, several Asian countries—

notably Thailand and Korea—experienced growth rates in excess of 10 percent for several years in a row. What factors contribute to such extraordinary success? Can our government do anything to recover the stronger growth rates of the 1950s and 1960s and retain them? We will address these questions in Chapter 8.

Comparing Income over Time

Commentators sometimes decry the fact that U.S. family incomes (after correcting for inflation) have failed to rise as dramatically over the past generation as some had dared to hope. Those commentators overlook the fact that regardless of the measured numbers, U.S. families live far better lives today than their grandparents could ever have imagined.

One reason why life is better today than it was 30 years ago is that there are many more products available. In 1965, your parents used typewriters instead of computers to write their school papers; they watched black-and-white television programs, which could not be taped for later viewing; and they never even imagined the possibility of a video game. While income statistics might make it appear that your college-student income today is lower than your parents' was in 1965, you might still be much wealthier in the sense of having a greater variety of ways to spend that income.

The moral is that over long periods of time, changes in measured income do not accurately reflect changes in economic welfare. The average middle-class American in the twentieth century lives a far more luxurious life than any European monarch did a few hundred years ago, despite having a much smaller measured income. It is not improbable that Henry VIII would have traded half his kingdom for the luxury of hot and cold running water.

2-8   THE PRICE LEVEL AND INFLATION

Inflation:
A rise in the price level over a period of time.

Deflation:
A fall in the price level over a period of time.

In preceding sections, we saw that nominal per capita income rose 142 percent over the entire 10-year period of the 1970s, while real per capita income grew a total of only 23 percent. The large difference between these real and nominal growth rates reflected what had to have been a very large rise in the prices of goods and services during that period.

Recall that the *price level* is the average price of goods and services in an economy. When the price level rises, we say there has been an **inflation;** when it falls, we say there has been a **deflation;** and if it remains the same, we say that prices have been *stable*.

Sometimes a low, constant rate of inflation is loosely called "price stability"; but it is important to understand that if there is an inflation of any magnitude, the price level continues to rise and cannot accurately be called "stable."

Inflation rate:

The percent change in the price level per time period.

The percent change in the price level is called the **inflation rate.** If the price level rises from $20 per good to $22 per good over a period of time, the inflation rate for the period is 10 percent. If the price level falls from $20 per good to $18 per good, the inflation rate is −10 percent; that is, there is a 10 percent deflation.

➡ *Exercise 2-6*

If the price level doubles over a year, what is the annual inflation rate?

Measuring the Price Level and Inflation

The U.S. government measures the price level and inflation in several ways. The measure most frequently cited by the media is the **consumer price index,** or **CPI.** The government starts with a specific bundle of goods and services purchased by households, or *consumers,* and defines this year's CPI to be the cost of that fixed bundle in current dollars. If the dollar cost rises by 10 percent over the course of a year, then the CPI measure of the inflation rate is 10 percent per year.

Consumer price index (CPI):

A measure of the price level that considers the price of a specific basket of consumption goods at current prices.

The government also reports a similar measure for goods purchased primarily by producers (e.g., coal, wooden slats, rolled steel). This measure is called the **producer price index,** or **PPI.**

Producer price index (PPI):

A measure of the price level that considers the price of a specific basket of inputs purchased by producers at current prices.

There are some problems inherent in this measurement process. One problem is that each of the bundles represents only a subset of all the goods and services produced by the entire economy, and thus the price indexes might not accurately reflect all changes in the price level. Consumers make some home improvements themselves, for example, and so buy goods that are classified as producer items. In addition, the quantities and kinds of goods bought by consumers and producers change over time; by fixing the bundle and the quantities once and for all, the government might be measuring the average price of things that are no longer representative.

Because the computation of the CPI entails fixing a bundle of goods, it cannot account for price changes in newly invented goods. The bundle does undergo periodic revision, but that revision tends to lag changes in the actual bundle bought by consumers. Because the prices of new goods, like computers, tend to start high and come down rapidly as output expands, the CPI is believed to overstate inflation rates.

Also, even existing goods change in quality over time; we see this especially in automobiles. When goods improve in quality, CPI price increases tend to overstate the inflation rate, recording as a higher price what is actually the price for the old, unimproved good plus a premium for the higher quality.

Implicit GDP deflator:

A measure of the price level that considers the average price of goods consumed, with each good weighted by the quantity consumed.

The Implicit GDP Deflator

Economists tend to prefer measures of the inflation rate that are broader than the CPI. The broadest such measure is the **implicit GDP deflator** (sometimes called just the *GDP deflator* for short). The GDP deflator is an average of the prices of all goods in the economy, weighted by the quantities of those goods that are actually purchased. The computation of the price deflator is simple. It is equal to nominal GDP (expressed in dollars) as a percentage of real GDP (expressed in the dollars of the base year). That is, for any given year,

$$\text{Implicit GDP price deflator} = 100 \times \frac{\text{Nominal GDP}}{\text{Real GDP}}$$

(To compute the implicit GDP price deflator, we may use either real or per capita GDP in the above equation.)

The inflation rate over any period is then the ratio of the end-of-period deflator to the beginning deflator.

For the example in Table 2-4 (page 30), we have the data in Table 2-5. The total price increase between 1970 and 1980 was nearly 100 percent; that is, prices almost doubled during the 1970s. Our computations also show that inflation in the 1960s averaged only 3.1 percent per year, and inflation in the 1980s, while little more than half that in the 1970s, was still not as low as it had been in the "good old days." These calculations are quite rough, based as they are on only four of the years in the period; nevertheless, they give us an idea of the dramatic shifts that have occurred in the U.S. economy. Figure 2-5 shows the annual implicit GDP deflator in greater detail.

Using the GDP deflator to compute the inflation rate, we find that between 1950 and 1994 the annual inflation rate ranged from a low of 1.2 percent (in 1963) to a high of 9.6 percent (in 1975). By this computation, the 1970s never did reach "double-digit" inflation (that is, an annual inflation rate of 10 percent or more). Computed on the basis of the CPI, however, the annual inflation rate got as high as 13.5 percent between 1979 and 1980.

Based on the implicit GDP price deflator, the average annual inflation rate in the 1950s was only 2.2 percent. From 1960 to 1964 it was only 1.3 percent. Then, in 1965, the inflation rate started to increase rapidly. It went from an average of only 4.1 percent for the remainder of the 1960s to an average of 7.6 percent for the first half of the 1970s and then up to an average of over 9 percent for the next 6 years. Only in 1982 did the inflation rate begin to edge down, averaging just over 4 percent for the remainder of the 1980s.

A student of history can easily match these changes in the inflation rate to political events. The inflation in the late 1960s appears to correspond to the Vietnam War, and perhaps to large U.S. spending programs such as those enacted during President Johnson's administration. The sudden spurt in the mid-1970s matches the much-discussed oil price shock, when the oil cartel OPEC withheld enough oil to drive oil prices up to unheard-of levels. The decline in the 1980s seems to correspond to the much-heralded "tight money policy" of that period.

TABLE 2-5

YEAR	NOMINAL PER CAPITA GDP	PER CAPITA GDP IN 1992 PRICES	IMPLICIT GDP DEFLATOR	INFLATION RATE PER DECADE
1960	$ 2913	$12,512	23.3	
1970	5050	16,520	30.6	31%
1980	12,226	20,252	60.4	97%
1990	22,979	24,559	93.6	55%

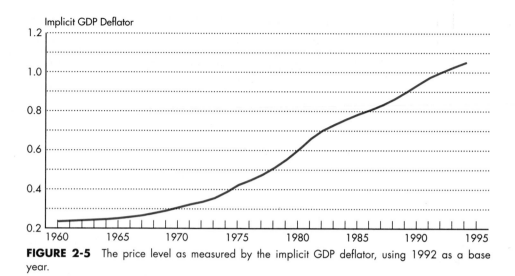

FIGURE 2-5   The price level as measured by the implicit GDP deflator, using 1992 as a base year.

SUMMARY

Aggregate income is the total of all the incomes that all the people in an economy earn. Per capita income is aggregate income divided by the size of the population. Income is generally accepted as an indicator of welfare, but not a perfect one.

Aggregate income can be difficult to measure accurately because some income goes unreported and some is consumed within the household instead of traded in the marketplace (as when people do their own housework).

The total of all goods and services produced is called output. Output includes only final goods, not intermediate goods. One measure of output is gross domestic product (GDP).

Because income is created by the sale of output, aggregate income must equal aggregate output. Therefore, economists use GDP as a measure of income as well as output.

Aggregate expenditure is equal to the total amount that all the people in the economy spend. It includes consumption expenditure, investment expenditure, and government purchases (not including transfers). Since everything a person spends creates income for someone else, aggregate expenditure must equal aggregate income. We express this fact with the equation income = expenditure. Because income is also equal to output, we have

$$\text{Income} = \text{Output} = \text{Expenditure}$$

In an open economy this equation must be modified slightly by adding net exports to expenditure.

Economic growth is the change in a country's output from one year to the next. Equivalently, growth is the change in a country's income from one year to the next. However, it is important to distinguish real growth (changes in real income) from nominal growth (changes in the dollar value of income, caused partly by rising prices). Economists are primarily interested in real growth.

To measure real growth, we measure changes in real GDP (real income), that is, GDP measured in constant prices. To compute real GDP for a period, we multiply the quantity of each item produced in that period by its price as given in the dollars of a chosen base period; then we add the results for all items.

The price level is the average price of goods and services. It is measured by the consumer price index (CPI), which is the price in current dollars of a fixed basket of goods. An alternative measure of the price level is the implicit GDP deflator, which is the ratio of nominal to real GDP for any period. Inflation is the rate of change of the price level and is measured by the percent change in either the CPI or the implicit GDP deflator.

PROBLEM SET

1. *True or false:* If you baby-sit as a favor to your next-door neighbor, output goes up but the official measurement of output does not change.
2. Give some reasons why the real gross domestic product might not accurately measure total real output.
3. Describe some reasons why an increase in total output might not be a good thing.
4. Explain why a major earthquake could cause income to rise and economic welfare to fall at the same time.
5. A mining company mines ore, which it sells to a refiner for $100. The refiner refines the ore into metal, which it sells to a plane factory for $150. The plane factory builds the metal into an airplane, which it sells to a retailer for $200. The retailer sells the airplane to an airline company for $210. In this example, what are the intermediate goods and what is the final output? How much income is earned by the owners of the mining company, the refiner, the plane factory, and the retailer? What is the value of the final output? How do your answers illustrate the equation output = income?[2]
6. "The minute I cook my own dinner or nail four boards together into a chair, I cause the official measures of national income to become less accurate." Discuss.
7. *True or false:* If people's real incomes are too low, they will not be able to afford to buy everything that is produced, and some output will go to waste.
8. Describe the difference between *national income* and *gross domestic product*.
9. Which of the following contribute to GDP? Which contribute to GNP?
   a. An American worker is hired to work in a Detroit car factory.
   b. A Japanese worker is hired to work in a Detroit car factory.
   c. An American worker is hired to work in a Tokyo car factory.
10. In statistics on U.S. expenditure, how does each of the following affect U.S. consumption? How does each affect net exports?
   a. An American buys an American car.

---

[2]This question is based on an example in W. Breit and K. Elzinga, "Ezra Pound and the GNP," *Southern Economic Journal* (1980), 904–912. You can consult this source for an enlightening discussion of the personal and artistic tragedies associated with Pound's misunderstanding of national income accounting.

    b.   A foreigner buys an American car.

    c.   An American buys a foreign car.

11. In the preceding problem, how does each scenario affect U.S. national income? Verify that in each case the equation

Income = Consumption + Investment + Government purchases + Net exports

remains true after the purchase.

12. Show that in a closed economy with no government the total of all saving by households must equal the total of all investment by firms. (*Hints:* Note that households divide their income between consumption and saving. Note that output consists of consumption goods and investment goods. Use the relationship between output and income.)

13. Now consider a closed economy *with* a government. Let S be the total of all saving by households, let I be the total of all investment by firms, let T be the total of all taxes collected, and let G be the value of government purchases.

    a.   Establish the equation

$$S - I = G - T$$

    (*Hints:* Households use their income for consumption, saving, and the payment of taxes. All output goods are used for consumption, used for investment, or purchased by the government.)

    b.   The quantity $G - T$ is called the *government budget deficit*. If the government budget deficit increases, what must happen to saving or investment or both?

14. In the preceding problem, you showed that $S - I = G - T$ in a closed economy with a government.

    a.   In an *open* economy with a government, how must that equation be modified to account for net exports?

    b.   *True or false:* If net exports rise and the government budget deficit $G - T$ remains constant, then either households must increase their spending or firms must decrease their investment.

15. Draw a circular flow diagram like those in Figure 2-2 for an *open* economy, adding a box for the "Rest of the World" and indicating the flows of imports and exports.

16. Suppose that goods X and Y are the only goods produced in the economy, and that they are sold in the quantities and at the prices indicated in the following table:

YEAR	X QUANTITY	X PRICE	Y QUANTITY	Y PRICE
1994	3	$ 5	6	$ 9
1995	4	5	8	12
1996	4	10	8	24

    a.   Compute nominal GDP in each year.

    b.   Compute real GDP in 1994 dollars in each year.

    c.   In which year is there economic growth?

17. Using the table from the preceding problem, suppose that the CPI is computed as the price of a basket containing three X's and six Y's. Compute the CPI inflation rate from 1994 to 1995 and from 1995 to 1996.

18. Using the table from problem 16, compute the implicit GDP deflator for each year, with 1994 as the base year. Based on the implicit GDP deflator, what were the inflation rates for 1994–1995 and 1995–1996?

19. Suppose that in 1990 cups sold for $10 apiece and saucers sold for $5 apiece, while in 1995 cups sold for $5 apiece and saucers sold for $10 apiece. In 1990, two cups and four saucers were sold; in 1995, four cups and two saucers were sold. Using the 1990 basket as a basis, compute the 1995 consumer price index. Using 1990 as a base year, compute the 1995 implicit GDP deflator. According to the consumer price index, has inflation been positive or negative? What has it been according to the implicit GDP deflator?

20. Analyze this statement: The 1980 movie *E.T.* made more money than the 1939 movie *Gone with the Wind*.

Chapter 3

Borrowing and Lending

odern macroeconomic models begin with the observation that time matters. Individuals make decisions based in part on their expectations about the future. In deciding how much of their income to save and how much to spend, they need some idea of what the future might hold. Lending, which is the main way people save, permits people to consume more tomorrow at the cost of consuming less today. Borrowing permits them to do the opposite.

Borrowing and lending account for a large share of economic activity and decision making, and we devote three chapters to them. The goal in this chapter is to be explicit about the nature of the trade-offs involved—what people gain and what they give up when they borrow or lend. The goal in Chapter 4 will be to understand how individuals make choices in light of those trade-offs. The goal in Chapter 5 will be to understand how all those individual choices interact in the context of the market-place.

3-1 BONDS AND LOANS

We begin by introducing the basic terminology of bonds, borrowing, and lending.

Borrowing and Lending

Borrowing:
Trading future goods for current goods.

One way to think of **borrowing** and **lending** is to view them as a form of trade. If you give your aunt an apple and she gives you two oranges, we say that you have traded one apple for two oranges. Likewise, if you lend your aunt an apple today and she pays you back with two apples tomorrow, we can say that you have traded one "current apple" for two "future apples." The apples-for-oranges transaction and the current-apples-for-future-apples transaction are fundamentally similar. The idea is to think of "current apples" and "future apples" as different goods, just as apples and oranges are different goods. From that viewpoint, any lending-and-borrowing transaction is just a form of trading.

Lending:
Trading current goods for future goods.

In ordinary language we would say that you lend your aunt an apple and she repays you with interest. But it is important not to lose sight of the fact that this is just another way to describe a simple trade.

Trading is sometimes described in terms of *buying* and *selling*. When you trade an apple for two oranges, you are simultaneously a seller of apples and a buyer of oranges. When you lend a current apple in exchange for two future apples, you are simultaneously a seller of current apples and a buyer of future apples.

Bonds

Actually, at the moment that you hand over that current apple to your aunt, you receive not the future apples themselves but a *promise* of future apples. Another word for such a promise is "bond." A **bond** is a promise to pay some specified amount at some specified future date.

Bond:
A promise to pay a specified amount at a specified future date.

Bonds are sometimes recorded on paper, computer tape, or fancy certificates. But a fancy certificate is only a *record* of a bond. The bond is the promise itself.

So when you lend to your aunt, you are trading an apple for a bond; you are simultaneously a seller of current apples and a buyer of bonds, while your aunt is a buyer of current apples and a seller of bonds.

It is always the case, as with you and your aunt, that:

The buyer of a bond is a lender, and the seller of a bond is a borrower.

Principal, Face Value, and Interest

Principal:
The purchase price of a bond.

Face value:
The amount that a bond promises to pay.

Interest (debt service):
The amount by which face value exceeds principal.

When you purchase your aunt's bond by giving her one apple, and she promises to repay you two apples in the future, we say that you have lent her one apple as **principal,** that she has issued a bond with a **face value** of two apples, and that the **interest** (or **debt service**) on the loan—the amount by which the repayment exceeds the principal—is one apple.

If your roommate lends you $10 in exchange for your promise to repay $12 tomorrow, then we can say that your roommate has paid $10 to purchase your bond. The principal is the purchase price of the bond, or $10. The face value is the amount to be paid in the future, or $12. The interest is the difference between the two, or $2.

Interest is often expressed as a percentage of the principal. In this case, the $2 interest is 20 percent of the $10 principal, so we say that you are paying 20 percent interest on this loan.

Bonds Sold at Auction

Suppose you want to borrow from your roommate and you need to negotiate the terms of trade. The usual way to do this is to say something like "I would like to borrow $10 till tomorrow; at what interest rate will you lend it to me?" After some dickering you and your roommate might agree on 20 percent interest, or equivalently a $12 payback tomorrow.

Here is a different way to reach the same outcome, although it might seem a bit strange at first: Instead of naming the amount you want to *borrow,* you could name the amount you are willing to *repay* and then dicker over how much your roommate is willing to lend. For example, you could say, "I am expecting $12 from my aunt tomorrow. How much will you lend me today in exchange for that $12?" Your roommate might agree to lend you $10 for it; thus a different negotiation would lead to exactly the same transaction as above. We still say you have borrowed $10 at 20 percent interest.

Although this might strike you as an odd way to negotiate, it is actually quite common. In fact, the U.S. government, which is one of the world's biggest borrowers, initiates *all* of its borrowing in this way. When the government wants to borrow money, it issues a bond promising to pay, say, $10,000 at some specified future date. It then puts the bond up for auction, asking people, "How much are you willing to pay for this bond?" or, equivalently, "How much are you willing to lend today in exchange for a future repayment of $10,000?" Any individual—you, for example, if you have enough cash on hand—can bid for such bonds, and they are sold to the highest bidders. Those high bidders buy the bonds (thereby becoming lenders), which the government sells (thereby becoming a borrower). If the high bidders offer, say,

$9500, then the principal is $9500, the face value is $10,000, and the interest is $500, or 5.3 percent of the principal.

Net Lending and Borrowing

Net lending:
The sum of all lending, counting borrowing as negative lending.

Your **net lending** is the sum of all your current lending, with borrowing counted as negative lending. For example, someone who lends $25 and borrows $20 is a net lender of $5. Alternatively, we can say that *lending is negative borrowing*. Then your **net borrowing** is the sum of all your current borrowing, with lending counted as negative borrowing.

People who lend more than they borrow are called *net lenders*. People who borrow more than they lend are called *net borrowers*.

➡ *Exercise 3-1*
Suppose you lend your uncle five nets and simultaneously borrow seven nets from him. Are you a net borrower or a net lender?

Net borrowing:
The sum of all borrowing, counting lending as negative borrowing.

Aggregate net lending:
The sum of all individuals' net lending in an economy.

Aggregate Net Lending

The **aggregate net lending** in an economy is the sum of all individual net lending. It is positive when the total of all lending exceeds the total of all borrowing, that is, when the average person lends more than he borrows. It is negative when the total of all borrowing exceeds the total of all lending, that is, when the average person borrows more than he lends.

In the economy consisting of the entire world, do you suppose that aggregate net lending is positive or negative? Do you suppose that the absolutely average human being is a net lender or a net borrower?

The answer is to be found not in economics but in arithmetic. Every loan that takes place involves one borrower and one lender. A dollar borrowed is simultaneously a dollar lent, and vice versa. Thus the worldwide sum of all current borrowing and the worldwide sum of all current lending must be exactly equal. Aggregate net lending for the world economy is zero.

The same reasoning applies to any closed economy. (Remember that a closed economy is one that does not trade with outsiders.) However, in an open economy— such as a country that engages in international trade—aggregate net lending can be either positive or negative. Americans can borrow more than they lend, provided the citizens of some other country lend more than they borrow.

The United States as a Net Borrower

Between 1986 and 1994, Americans, on average, lent about 1.8 percent of their income *to* foreigners and borrowed about twice that much *from* foreigners.[1] Thus the average American was a net borrower. We sometimes express this fact (a bit imprecisely) by saying, "The United States is a net borrower."

---

[1]There are a number of measurement problems associated with estimating international borrowing and lending, and hence some uncertainty about their exact values.

After several years of net borrowing, U.S. citizens now collectively owe over $800 billion (somewhat more than $3000 per capita) to foreigners. Although this number is small compared with the average American's income, it does represent a substantial change from the situation prior to the mid-1980s. Following the end of World War II in 1945, the United States served for many years as a net lender to the world, helping Europe and Japan to rebuild from the devastation left by the war.

Creditor:

Someone whose lending exceeds borrowing.

Debtor:

Someone whose borrowing exceeds lending.

During those years, the United States was a **creditor** nation—that is, foreigners owed Americans more than Americans owed foreigners. Now the United States has become a **debtor** nation—Americans owe foreigners more than foreigners owe Americans.

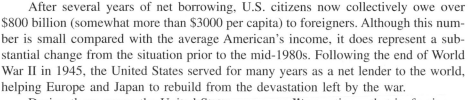

Being a *creditor* is not the same thing as being a *net lender*. You are a net lender if your current lending exceeds your current borrowing. You are a creditor if the total of everything that is owed to you (as a result of all your past lending) exceeds the total of everything you owe (as a result of all your past borrowing).

Similarly, a *debtor* is not the same as a *net borrower*. Being a net borrower depends on current borrowing and lending; being a debtor depends on past borrowing and lending.

The United States has changed from creditor to debtor for a number of reasons. Europe and Japan have completed their postwar rebuilding. Americans may be borrowing more to finance their own investment projects or to finance current consumption—perhaps in anticipation of rising future incomes. In the next several chapters, we will explore all of these factors in detail.

Banks and the Bond Market

Banks are institutions that specialize in borrowing and lending. Adding to your savings account is a form of lending; you lend funds to the bank, which promises to repay them (with interest) in the future. Thus your savings account is a bond: it is nothing more or less than the bank's promise to pay. You are the buyer of the bond, and your bank is the seller.

Market:

Buyers, sellers, and the arrangements that enable them to trade.

Bond market:

Lenders, borrowers, and the arrangements that enable them to carry out loans and repayments.

Banks borrow from their account holders and lend to households, businesses, and governments (including foreign governments). Every time a bank makes a loan, it is buying a bond from the borrower. If you borrow from your bank to finance a car, a house, or a business investment, then you are the seller of a bond and the bank is the buyer.

A **market** consists of buyers and sellers and the arrangements that make it possible for them to trade. In particular, the **bond market** consists of people who want to lend, people who want to borrow, and the institutions (such as banks) that help borrowers and lenders to find each other.

When you hear a phrase like "You can save your money," you should immediately translate it into "You can buy bonds." Thinking of bank deposits and bank loans as bonds makes it clear that buying and selling bonds is an everyday activity for most Americans.

3-2 INTEREST RATES

In this section we distinguish between two kinds of interest rates: *nominal* interest rates and *real* interest rates. We also compare domestic interest rates with foreign interest rates, short-term interest rates with long-term interest rates, and risk-free interest rates with interest rates that incorporate a risk premium.

Nominal Interest Rates

Nominal interest:

A bond's face value minus the principal expressed in dollars.

The **nominal interest** on a bond is the number of dollars that the lender ultimately receives minus the number of dollars that he paid for the bond. For example, when your roommate pays $10 for your promise to deliver $12 tomorrow, the nominal interest is $2.

Nominal interest rate:

Nominal interest as a percent of principal per unit of time.

When the nominal interest is expressed as a percentage of the principal, we call it a **nominal interest rate.** In the example in the preceding paragraph, the nominal interest rate is 20 percent. More precisely, the nominal interest rate is not just a percent but a percent *per unit of time*. A more accurate way to describe the nominal interest rate on this bond is 20 percent *per day* because the length of time between the purchase and the payoff is 1 day. Interest rates are usually reported on an *annual basis,* which means that the unit of time is 1 year.

Real Interest Rates

Suppose you lend $10 to your roommate today and get back $12 tomorrow, so you earn a nominal interest rate of 20 percent per day. Unfortunately, the $12 that you get back tomorrow might not really be worth 20 percent more than the $10 that you lend today. The problem is the possibility of *inflation,* a general rise in the level of prices. If prices increase overnight by 20 percent, then tomorrow's $12 will buy no more than today's $10. In a real sense, you will have earned no interest at all. An economist would say that although you earned a nominal interest rate of 20 percent, you earned a **real interest rate** of 0 percent.

Real interest rate:

A bond's face value minus the principal, expressed in goods or in constant dollars and as a percent of the principal per unit of time.

The inflation rate could, of course, be equal to something other than the 20 percent per day we assumed above. Suppose that the inflation rate is 5 percent. In that case, the first 5 percent of your nominal interest earnings goes to "keeping up with inflation." Only the remaining 15 percent represents a real increase in purchasing power, so we say that you have earned a real interest rate of 15 percent. In general:

> The real interest rate measures that part of your interest earnings which genuinely increases your purchasing power, after accounting for inflation.

To compute the real interest rate, start with the nominal interest rate and subtract the inflation rate. If the nominal interest rate is 10 percent and the rate of inflation is 7 percent, then the real interest rate is only 3 percent. If the nominal interest rate is 10 percent and the inflation rate is 12 percent, then the real interest rate is *minus* 2 percent. If there is no inflation, the nominal and real interest rates are the same.

The real interest rate is equal to the nominal interest rate minus the inflation rate.

Although nominal rates of interest are more familiar to noneconomists, when economists speak of interest rates they are generally more interested in *real* rates of interest. In this book, when we speak of interest rates, we mean real interest rates, unless we specify otherwise.

Real bond:
A bond denominated in terms of goods.

We can even imagine **real bonds**—that is, bonds that promise to pay a certain number of goods instead of a certain number of dollars. Suppose you promise to buy your roommate two hamburgers tomorrow in exchange for one today. Your promise to buy tomorrow's lunch is a bond carrying a real interest rate of 100 percent (two hamburgers is 100 percent more than one). In this case we need not talk about the nominal interest rate. Because no money is involved, inflation cannot change the value of the principal or interest. That value is already expressed in real (purchasing-power) terms in the bond.

Almost all bonds sold in modern economies are stated in nominal terms (that is, they state the dollar amounts rather than the number of goods that must be paid); hence it is simple to compute the nominal rate of interest. However, it is usually fairly difficult to figure out the corresponding real rate. The hard part is predicting what the inflation rate will be.

Despite the difficulty of computing real interest rates, it is real rates that are most interesting to economists. You want $12 back (from your loan) tomorrow only because you expect to use that money to buy something. You do not ultimately want dollars—you want something you can consume. When lenders choose between domestic and foreign bonds, they don't do so by comparing the bonds' nominal interest rates; rather, they compare what they will be able to buy with the particular currency they receive in the end.

We, too, are interested mainly in real rates. Since real and nominal interest rates are the same if there is no inflation, for the remainder of this chapter *we shall assume that the inflation rate is 0 percent.* Then our examples can be stated in nominal units—money—even though we are thinking not of money but of the real goods that the money can buy.

All the lessons that you learn in this chapter will hold even if the inflation rate is something other than 0 percent—provided you remember to apply those lessons to *real,* as opposed to nominal, interest rates.

Foreign Interest Rates

Borrowing and lending take place in *world markets;* lenders can choose among bond offerings from all over the world. (Even when you borrow from your local bank, you have participated in a world market, because your bank can lend to anybody in the world.) However, international bond offerings are usually **denominated** in the currency of the home country, rather than in U.S. dollars. So if a U.S. citizen wants to buy a French bond, that citizen must first acquire French francs; when the bond is repaid, he will receive French francs.

Denominate:
To express the face value of a bond in a particular currency.

The nominal interest on the French loan is the number of French francs that the lender ultimately receives minus the number of French francs he paid for the bond.

The nominal interest rate on this French franc–denominated bond is still the nominal interest expressed as a percentage of the purchase price.

Nominal interest rates vary considerably from one country to another because inflation rates vary considerably from one country to another. If inflation is high (or, more precisely, if inflation is expected to be high between the date on which the bond is sold and the date on which it matures), then borrowers must pay high nominal interest rates to attract lenders.

Figure 3-1 shows the nominal interest rates on bonds issued by four different governments in October 1995. Typically, bonds with distant maturity dates pay somewhat higher interest rates to compensate lenders for the possibility of rising inflation. For example, the Canadian government bond maturing in December 1998 pays an interest rate of 6.95 percent, while the Canadian government bond maturing in June 2025 pays an interest rate of 8.08 percent. You can easily see from the graph that for a given maturity date there is a clear ranking of interest rates: The United Kingdom is the highest, then Canada, followed by Germany and Japan. This ranking reflects the expectations of inflation in the four countries.

The One-Period, Risk-Free Real Interest Rate

T-bill rate:

The interest rate paid on T-bills; equivalently, the rate at which the U.S. government borrows.

Prime rate:

The rate at which corporations in good standing borrow from banks.

Federal funds rate:

The rate at which banks borrow from and lend to each other.

Term (of a loan):

The length of time between a loan and its repayment.

In actuality there are not one but many, many interest rates. Among them are the Treasury bill rate (or **T-bill rate**), at which the U.S. government borrows; the **prime rate,** at which corporations in good standing can borrow from banks; the **federal funds rate,** at which banks borrow money from each other overnight; and hundreds of others.

Interest rates differ depending on whether the **term,** or length, of the loan is long (several years) or short (1 year or less). We will see shortly that they also depend on the default risks presented by different borrowers. When, as economists, we speak of *the* interest rate, which one should we be referring to?

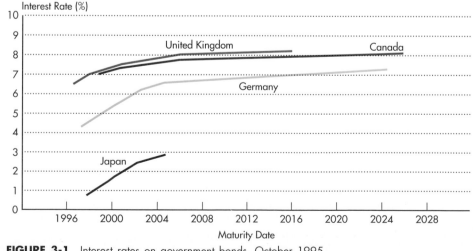

FIGURE 3-1 Interest rates on government bonds, October 1995.

A Multiperiod Bond Is a Series of One-Period Bonds

Any long-term or multiperiod bond can be decomposed into a series of one-period bonds. To see this, suppose you borrow $1000 for 2 years, agreeing to make a $100 interest payment at the end of the first year and to repay the $1000 plus another $100 of interest at the end of the second. But imagine that at the end of the first year, you pay back the entire $1000 plus $100 interest and then instantly borrow the $1000 back again. There is actually no such transaction, but imagining it allows us to pretend that all bonds are repaid after exactly 1 year.

We introduce this useful fiction because it enables us to reduce our discussion of all bonds to a discussion of 1-year bonds (or "one-period" bonds—a *period* might be a year, a day, or a month, depending on the context). Every multiperiod bond can be thought of as a series of one-period bonds, so if we understand one-period bonds, we will understand all bonds.

Here is another example: Suppose you borrow $1000 and agree to make two payments. At the end of the first year, you will repay $200 of the principal plus $100 interest. Then you will owe $800. At the end of the second year, you will repay the remaining $800 plus another $80 of interest. We can imagine instead that you repay the entire $1000 (plus interest) at the end of the first year and instantly reborrow $800 for a year.

Are Short-Term Bonds More Desirable Than Long-Term Bonds?

Historically accountants and the government carefully distinguished between short- and long-term bonds. They argued that short-term bonds (those with terms of 1 year or less) were more desirable because lenders got their cash back sooner. Today economists are wary of distinctions between short-term and long-term bonds, because any long-term bond can be made into a short-term one by prepaying and any short-term bond can be made into a long-term one by reborrowing.[2]

The Risk-Free Rate

Even one-period bonds are offered at a variety of interest rates because they entail varying degrees of risk. Lending a large sum of money to your next-door neighbor is riskier than lending it to the government because there is a bigger chance that your neighbor will repay it late or not repay it at all—that is, a bigger chance of a **default.** (A late payment is legally a default, though not a complete default, on a loan.) Lenders tend to prefer less risk to more, so riskier prospects find that they must offer higher rates of interest if they want to borrow.

If a borrower can truly guarantee repayment, we say the loan is a **risk-free loan** and the interest rate paid is the **risk-free rate**—the lowest interest demanded of any borrower. Few loans meet this criterion. Most economists consider U.S. Treasury bills to be the closest thing to a bond that is free of default risk. However, when Congress

Default:
Any failure to abide by the terms of a loan contract; usually, late or incomplete repayment of a loan.

Risk-free loan:
A loan in which there is no chance of default; thus, timely and complete repayment is certain.

Risk-free rate:
An interest rate that does not include compensation for the risk of default; that is, the interest rate on a risk-free loan.

---

[2]In some cases these changes are prohibited by the loan agreement, but they can usually be accomplished anyway for a fee.

misses the deadline for a final budget agreement, it neglects to tell administrators where to find the tax revenue to make loan payments; in that case, there is a risk that the U.S. government will default on some of its loans. In October 1990, and again in late 1995, the government was forced to shut down temporarily because a budget agreement was not reached in time, although it did continue to service its debt (that is, pay interest) in the interim. Had either crisis continued, the government would have been forced to default.

It is widely believed that the U.S. government has never defaulted on its obligations. This is not correct. For example, it defaulted on Treasury bill GS7-2-179-46-6606-1 in 1984. The federal government delayed payment of the interest (called the *discount*) on that bond for 9 months. During that time the Treasury took the extraordinary position that although the default was entirely the result of its own clerical errors, those errors were irreparable and the interest would never be paid. Only after the intervention of several senators and representatives did the Treasury meet its obligation; and even then it did not pay interest for the extra 9 months in which it unlawfully held the funds.

The authors of this textbook happen to know about this default because they were the lenders in question. The general frequency of such occurrences is not known. However, if incidents such as these became widespread or better publicized, the interest rate on T-bills would have to increase to reflect the higher default risk.

The Risk Premium

Risk premium:
The portion of the interest rate that compensates the lender for the risk of default. This is the difference between the interest paid on a particular loan and the interest rate that would be paid if the loan were risk-free.

Commercial paper:
Collective term for bonds issued by highly trustworthy private corporations.

Many government bonds issued by countries other than the United States are close to risk-free. However, most loans other than government loans command higher interest rates than the risk-free rate to reflect the risk that the borrower will default. The difference between the actual interest rate on the loan and the risk-free rate is called the **risk premium.**

Figure 3-2 shows the behavior of two different interest rates over a period of several years. The lower curve shows the interest rate paid by 6-month Treasury bills (that is, Treasury bills whose maturity date falls 6 months after they are issued). The upper curve shows the interest rate paid by 6-month **commercial paper**—short-term bonds issued by highly creditworthy private corporations.

As you can see, the two kinds of interest rates move up and down together, with the rate on commercial paper always slightly higher than that on Treasury bills. The difference between the two is the risk premium on commercial paper.

When economists speak of *the* interest rate, they mean the *one-period, risk-free real rate of interest* that is available in world markets. We shall conform to that usage throughout this book. In other words, we shall assume that all borrowers repay their debts, so there is no risk of default.

3-3 THE PRICE OF CURRENT AND FUTURE CONSUMPTION

People buy and sell bonds so that they can adjust their consumption levels now and in the future. A lender (that is, the buyer of a bond) agrees to consume less in the

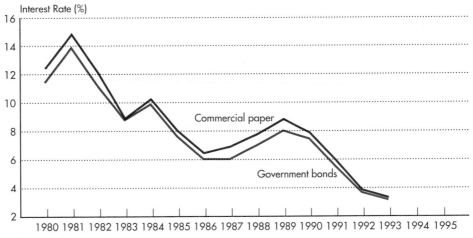

FIGURE 3-2 The risk premium.
The lower curve shows the interest rate on 6-month U.S. Treasury bills, and the upper curve shows the interest rate on 6-month commercial paper. The difference between the two is the risk premium.

present in order to consume more in the future; a borrower (the seller of a bond) agrees to consume less in the future in order to consume more in the present. We have been describing these transactions as trade in bonds, but at a deeper level they come down to trade in current and future consumption goods. In this section, we flesh out that observation and relate the price of consumption to the price of bonds.

The Price of Current Consumption

What does it cost to eat a hamburger today? You might say that it costs a certain number of dollars. But those dollars are valuable only for the spending opportunities that they represent: if you don't spend them today, you can spend them tomorrow. In economics, *costs* always mean forgone opportunities. The cost of today's hamburger is measured in terms of the future hamburgers you must forgo when you decide to eat it.

Suppose the interest rate is 10 percent per day. (We shall continue to assume there is no inflation, so that we need not distinguish between real and nominal interest rates.) Then the cost of 1 current hamburger is 1.1 future hamburgers, to be eaten tomorrow. In other words, you have a choice: you can buy a hamburger now, or you can save money for a day, earn interest, and have enough to buy 1.1 hamburgers tomorrow. When you choose the former, you forgo the latter. In general, the cost of a current unit of consumption (a hamburger, a ticket to a baseball game, or a magazine) is $1 + r$ units of future consumption, where r represents the real interest rate.

When people borrow, they buy current consumption at the expense of future consumption. In other words, we can think of a borrower as *purchasing* current consumption at a price measured in terms of future consumption via the formula

Price of 1 unit of current consumption $= 1 + r$ units of future consumption

> The price of current consumption, expressed in terms of future consumption, is 1 plus the interest rate.

Sometimes people say (incorrectly) that the interest rate is the price of *money*. This is grossly misleading. Even in a world without money, there would still be interest rates: you would still be able to trade a hamburger today for some number of hamburgers tomorrow. The interest rate is *not* the price of money; it measures the price of *current consumption*. More precisely, you can obtain the price of current consumption (in terms of future consumption) by starting with the interest rate and adding 1.

The Price of Future Consumption

The price of current consumption is measured in terms of forgone future consumption. Conversely, the price of future consumption is measured in terms of forgone current consumption.

Suppose that the interest rate is 25 percent and you want to eat five hamburgers tomorrow. How many hamburgers must you forgo today? The answer is four: you give up four hamburgers today, save them at 25 percent interest, and you can have five hamburgers tomorrow.

Because the price of a unit of current consumption is equal to $1 + r$ units of future consumption, it follows that the price of a unit of *future* consumption is equal to $1/(1 + r)$ units of current consumption. That is,

$$\text{Price today of 1 unit of future consumption} = \frac{1}{1 + r} \text{ units of current consumption}$$

At an interest rate of 25 percent, 1 future hamburger costs $1/1.25 = .8$ current hamburgers. This is consistent with the preceding paragraph, since 5 future hamburgers must then cost $5 \times .8 = 4$ current hamburgers.

Discounted Present Value

Discounted present value (DPV):

The price of future goods expressed in terms of current goods.

Present value:

A term used synonymously with "discounted present value."

The price of a future hamburger expressed in terms of current hamburgers is called the **discounted present value,** or **DPV,** of that future hamburger. Sometimes we abbreviate this term and just say **present value,** which means the same thing. Discounted present value is nothing but a fancy term for a price: it is the price of tomorrow's good measured in terms of today's. (In the example above, the discounted present value of 1 future hamburger is .8 current hamburgers.)

The discounted present value of a future meal (or any future good) depends on the interest rate, as is obvious from the formula displayed above; that formula gives $1/(1 + r)$ current hamburgers as the price (that is, the discounted present value) of a future hamburger. If we assume an interest rate of 25 percent per day, the DPV of tomorrow's hamburger is .8 current hamburgers. If we assume an interest rate of 50 percent, the DPV is $1/1.5 \approx .67$ current hamburgers. In general, the higher the interest rate, the lower the discounted present value of future consumption.

Discount rate:

The price of future consumption in terms of current consumption; given by the fraction $1/(1 + r)$, where r is the interest rate.

The fraction $1/(1 + r)$ is called the **discount rate,** or the *rate of discount.* (The phrase "discount rate" is, unfortunately, used to mean several different things in economics; this is only one of them.) If the interest rate is 50 percent, then the discount rate is $1/1.50 = 66.67$ percent.

In general, if we want to know the current cost of any future quantity or value, we divide by $1 + r$, where r is the rate of interest. (Here "future" means "next period"; we shall see shortly how to deal with the more distant future.) If the quantity or value happens to be in nominal terms, we use the nominal rate of interest; if it is in real terms, we use the real rate of interest. (For our purposes here, with the assumption of no inflation, the real and nominal discounted present values are the same.)

➡ *Exercise 3-2*

What is the discounted present value of $400 tomorrow if the interest rate is 25 percent per day?

➡ *Exercise 3-3*

What is the DPV of a promise to deliver 150 bushels of wheat in 1 year if the real interest rate is 10 percent per year?

➡ *Exercise 3-4*

Is the discounted present value usually more or less than the amount to be paid in the future? Why?

The Price of a Bond

Consider now the following two questions:

1. How much would you pay today for a steak dinner tomorrow?
2. How much would you pay today for my (entirely trustworthy) promise to treat you to a steak dinner tomorrow?

It is reasonable to expect that these two questions should have the same answer. The steak dinner tomorrow is a future-consumption good; the promise to treat you to a steak dinner is a risk-free bond. (It is risk-free because of the assumption that the promise is entirely trustworthy.) The good itself should have the same value as the bond.

We will be measuring the prices of future goods and of bonds in terms of current-consumption goods. Thus the questions become these: How many steaks would you give today in exchange for one steak tomorrow? How many steaks would you give today in exchange for my *promise* of one steak tomorrow?

The answer to the first question is precisely what we have already defined as the present value of tomorrow's steak. It is obtained with the expression $1/(1 + r)$, where r is the interest rate. The answer to the second question must be the same. That is:

The price of a bond is equal to the present value of what it promises to deliver.

A bond promising 1 steak tomorrow must sell for a price of $1/(1 + r)$ steaks today.

The price of a bond is inversely related to the interest rate. The higher the bond price, the lower the interest rate, and vice versa. If your uncle pays $10 for your bond, promising $12 tomorrow, the interest rate is 20 percent; if he pays more—say, $11—for the same bond, the interest rate is lower—approximately 9 percent.

When students learn that high bond prices coincide with low interest rates, they sometimes ask which is the cause and which is the effect. Does the high bond price cause the low interest rate, or does the low interest rate cause the high bond price? The answer is that neither causes the other, because a high bond price and a low interest rate are just *two different ways to describe exactly the same thing.* For a bond promising to pay $1 tomorrow, we have

$$\text{Bond price} = \frac{\$1}{1 + r}$$

In view of this formula, it is nothing but the laws of arithmetic that "cause" bond prices and interest rates always to move in opposite directions.

Pricing Bonds with Different Face Values

A bond promising 1 steak tomorrow sells for $1/(1 + r)$ steaks today. A bond promising 2 steaks tomorrow should sell for exactly twice as much, or $2 \times 1/(1 + r)$ steaks today. In general, a bond promising n units of future consumption (that is, a bond with a face value of n) sells for $n \times 1/(1 + r)$ units of current consumption.

Pricing Multiperiod Bonds

Suppose the interest rate is 10 percent per year. Then the present value of $1 delivered 1 year from today is $1 \times 1/(1 + .10) \approx \$0.91$. What is the present value of $1 delivered 2 years from today?

To answer this question, we can use the timelines in Figure 3-3. Part (*a*) shows that $1 to be paid next year has a present value of $0.91 today. Part (*b*) shows that, similarly, $1 to be paid in 2 years has the same value as $0.91 to be paid next year. That $0.91 to be paid next year has, in turn, a present value of $0.83 today. Thus $1 to be paid in 2 years has a present value of $0.83.

To obtain the result in Figure 3-3(*b*), we actually multiplied twice by $1/(1 + r)$, first to convert $1 in 2 years to $0.91 in 1 year and then to convert $0.91 in 1 year to $0.83 today. We could just as easily have multiplied once by $[1/(1 + r)]^2$.

To compute the present value of a payment 2 years from today, multiply that payment by $[1/(1 + r)]^2$.

By extending this reasoning, we arrive at a general formula for the present value of a future payment:

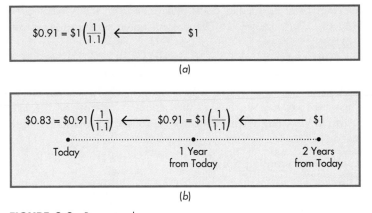

FIGURE 3-3 Present values.
(a) At 10 percent interest, $1 paid next year is worth $0.91 today. (b) Similarly, $1 paid 2 years from today is worth $0.91 a year from today, and $0.91 a year from today is worth $0.83 today.

> To compute the present value of a payment n years from today, multiply that payment by $[1/(1 + r)]^n$.

If you are promised $5 three years in the future, and the interest rate is 25 percent per year, then the present value of the payment is $5 \times [1/(1 + .25)]^3 \approx 2.56.

This calculation has a straightforward interpretation. It means that if the interest rate is 25 percent and you want to have $5 three years from today, you must give up exactly $2.56 today. Suppose you do put exactly $2.56 in a bank account at 25 percent annual interest. At the end of 1 year, your balance will have grown to $3.20 (since you earn 64 cents interest). At the end of 2 years, your balance will be $4. At the end of 3 years, you will have the $5 you wanted.

➡ *Exercise 3-5*
Suppose that the interest rate is 20 percent per year. What is the present value of $50 delivered 4 years from today? Explain how you could trade that number of current dollars for $50 four years hence.

➡ *Exercise 3-6*
Suppose that the interest rate is 10 percent per year. What is the present value of $1 delivered *1 year ago?*

Bonds Promising More Than One Payment

Suppose that your grandfather promises to give you $10 a year from today and another $110 the following year. The interest rate is 10 percent. What is the present value of his promise?

To answer, we break the promise into its two parts and add their present values. In the first part, $10 one year from today has a present value of $10 \times 1/(1 + .10) \approx$

$9.09. And in the second, $110 two years from today has a present value of $110 $\times$ $[1/(1\ +\ .10)]^2\ \approx\ 90.91. The present value of the entire promise is then $9.09 + $90.91 = $100.

This means that it must be possible to purchase a **stream of payments** equal to your grandfather's promise by sacrificing $100 today. And indeed this is true. Put $100 in the bank, let it earn $10 interest in the first year, and withdraw that interest. This gives you $10 at the end of the first year. Now let the $100 sit in the bank for a second year, and then withdraw your entire $110 balance at the end.

Application: Winning the Lottery

Suppose you win a lottery that promises to pay you $1000 now and $1000 per year for 3 years, with the first payment to be made immediately. You would like to use your winnings to start a business or take a vacation. But the lottery board will not give you the entire $3000 up front. Instead, it offers you only $2833.40. Where did the board get that amount? Why isn't it $3000? Angrily, you take your winning ticket to the bank and promise to hand over your two future $1000 payments as they come in if only the bank will give you something for them immediately. How much should the bank be willing to give?

Suppose the interest rate is 6 percent. Then next year's $1000 payment is worth $1000 $\times$ $\frac{1}{1.06}$ = $943.40 right now. The bank is willing to pay $943.40 today for your risk-free promise of $1000 next year.

The final payment 2 years from now is one more step removed. Its present value is $1000 $\times$ $(\frac{1}{1.06})^2$ = $890. The bank will pay only $890 right now for your risk-free promise of $1000 two years hence.

For your two future payments, the bank will give you only $943.40 + $890 = $1833.40. Add to this the $1000 present value of the (immediate) first payment, and we see that your winning lottery ticket is worth exactly $2833.40, just what the lottery board was willing to give you.

Alternatively, if you had not won the lottery but wanted to have a stream of payments identical to what the lottery ticket promises, you could purchase it for $2833.40 by lending that amount to somebody at the market rate of 6 percent interest. Through borrowing and lending, you can either convert the stream of lottery winnings into $2833.40 today or convert $2833.40 today into the stream of lottery winnings. More generally:

Two payment streams with the same present value can always be traded for each other by borrowing and lending.

Exercise 3-7
You win the lottery and are entitled to $1000 per year for 3 years, with the first payment not due to arrive until 1 year from today. Assuming a 6 percent market interest rate, how much have you really won?

Perpetuities

Perpetuity:
A stream of payments that continues forever.

Suppose you win a lottery that promises to pay you $1 per year in **perpetuity**—that is, forever—starting 1 year from today. The present value of the first payment is $1 $\times$ $1/(1 + r)$; the present value of the second payment is $1 $\times$ $[1/(1 + r)]^2$, and so forth. The present value of the entire infinite stream of payments is given by the series

$$\$1 \times \left(\frac{1}{1 + r} + \frac{1}{(1 + r)^2} + \frac{1}{(1 + r)^3} + \cdots \right)$$

This looks formidable, but fortunately it collapses to a much simpler expression. If you have studied infinite series in an advanced calculus class, you should be able to show that the sum of the series in parentheses is just $1/r$. If you are not able to show this, you can take our word for it.

Thus, if the annual interest rate is 10 percent, your winning lottery ticket is worth $1 $\times$ $(\frac{1}{10})$ = $10. If this is correct, there must be a way to convert $10 today into an infinite stream of $1 per year. And there is! Just put $10 in the bank forever at 10 percent annual interest, and withdraw your interest payment of $1 every year. Conversely, you can convert an infinite stream of annual $1 payments to $10 today by borrowing $10, never repaying the principal, but paying the $1 annual interest forever.

Exercise 3-8
If the annual interest rate is 5 percent, what is the present value of a lottery ticket that promises $1 per year forever, starting next year? What if the payments start immediately?

Exercise 3-9
Using the data given in the preceding exercise, describe how you could convert the present value of the stream of lottery winnings into the stream itself, and vice versa.

Comparing Streams of Payments

When you borrow to buy something expensive, say, a house or car, it is a common error to add up all the interest payments and look at the enormous total as if it represents the actual cost of the loan. In fact, the true cost of the loan is the amount you would have to set aside right now to have enough on hand to make those payments exactly—and that amount is not the sum of the interest payments but their discounted present value. This doesn't mean that loans are not costly; it means only that there is no advantage to exaggerating their cost when you are trying to decide whether to borrow.

Exercise 3-10
A worker disabled by an accident will lose the next 3 years' worth of income. The court estimates her income at $45,000 per year. Her lawyer asks for $135,000 to be awarded right now for lost future earnings. What amount should the judge grant,

assuming an interest rate of 10 percent per year? (*Answer:* If we assume that workers collect their earnings at the beginning of each year, then the answer is $123,099.17; if we assume that workers collect their earnings at the end of each year, $111,908.34. The most accurate assumption presumably lies between these two extremes.)

Suppose that you win still another lottery and are given a choice between two prizes. You can have $100 today, or you can have $25 per year for 5 years, starting immediately. Which should you take?

Before we answer this question, let's imagine an even simpler choice. You win a lottery, and as your prize you can claim either a new Mercedes-Benz or a luxury cruise. Which should you take?

Nothing in economic theory can help you decide whether to prefer a fancy car or a fancy vacation. If for some reason you must keep the prize you claim, then your decision can be based only on your personal preferences. If you love driving, take the car. If you love relaxing, take the cruise.

However, if you are able to buy and sell in the marketplace, the economist is ready with some concrete advice: Take whichever prize has the highest market price. If the Mercedes sells for $50,000 and the cruise for $10,000, then you should take the Mercedes *even if you have no use for it*. Then, if you prefer the cruise, you can sell the Mercedes, buy the cruise, and have an extra $40,000 left over.

Likewise with payment streams. If you can collect either $100 today or $25 per year for 5 years starting immediately, no economist can tell you which will make you happier. If you love instant gratification, take the $100. If you love anticipating future pleasures, take the $25 per year.

But if you can borrow and lend in the marketplace, the choice is clear: Take the stream with the higher present value—even if it's not the one you prefer to have. Then borrow or lend until you have the stream you *do* prefer, and you'll come out ahead.

Which stream is better depends on the interest rate. Suppose, for example, that the interest rate is 20 percent. Then a $100 flat payment has a present value of $100, while 5 years of $25 per year has a present value of $89.72. This means that if you place $89.72 in the bank today, you can withdraw $25 per year for 5 years starting 1 year from today. If you want to have that stream of payments, the best way to acquire it is to take the $100, put $89.72 in the bank, and still have $10.28 left over for 2 quarts of high-quality ice cream.

⟶ *Exercise 3-11*
If you put $89.72 in the bank at 20 percent interest and withdraw $25 per year starting immediately, what is your balance at the end of each succeeding year? (*Answer:* $64.72 after your first (immediate) withdrawal; $52.66 after your second; $38.20 after your third; $20.84 after your fourth; zero after your fifth.)

Application: Restructuring Debts in Developing Countries

Beginning in the late 1970s, many developing countries found they were having an increasingly difficult time repaying the large debts previously contracted by their governments. There were many reasons for their difficulties: poor investment projects, declining world prices for the commodities they exported, occasional outright theft of funds by government officials, and, in the early 1980s, soaring real rates of interest on their debts. The **debt restructuring** devised for some of these countries during the 1980s consisted in part of switching payment streams via borrowing and lending. The payment streams to which some of these countries had committed themselves were "traded" for streams with the same present value but with longer terms. Stretching out the terms of the loans allowed the borrowing countries to repay a smaller percentage of their aggregate incomes each year, thereby enabling them to recuperate from bad times.

Debt restructuring:
Renegotiating the terms of a loan by trading one stream of payments for another stream with the same present value.

3-4   ADDITIONAL APPLICATIONS

In this section, we use present values to explain such diverse phenomena as the pricing of corporate stocks, the pricing of durable goods including furniture and artworks, decisions about personal finance, and the effects of government deficits.

Corporate Stocks

Corporate stock:
A share in the ownership of a corporation.

If you own a share of General Motors (GM) stock, then you own a small percentage of the General Motors Corporation. This **corporate stock** entitles you, as a **stockholder,** to a number of things, including a share of GM's profits for as long as you own the stock.

When GM earns $100 in profits, it can do one of two things. It can distribute that $100 to stockholders in proportion to their holdings. If you own 1 percent of all General Motors stock, you receive a check in the mail for $1. Alternatively, GM can purchase $100 worth of assets—say, $100 worth of factory machinery. As a part owner of General Motors, each stockholder owns a portion of the new assets. If you own 1 percent of the company's stock, the value of your shares increases by $1.

Stockholder:
An individual who holds corporate stock, thus owning a portion of the corporation.

Stockbrokers distinguish between these alternatives by referring to the check in the mail as a **dividend** and the increased share price as *growth*. (The stockbroker's definition of "growth" differs from the economist's definition, which we encountered in Chapter 2.) But to the economist, this is a pointless distinction. If you were hoping to see the value of your shares go up but GM chooses to send you a check, you can simply use that check to purchase additional shares; thus the total value of your shares *does* go up, just as you wanted. If you were hoping for a check but GM elects to purchase corporate assets, you can sell stock to achieve your desire.[3]

Dividend:
A gain to the owner of corporate stock that results from dividing the profits of the corporation among the stockholders.

Therefore economists, unlike stockbrokers, use the word "dividend" to describe the stockholder's share of any corporate profit, without regard to whether that dividend is distributed through the mail or realized through an increase in stock prices.

---

[3]This discussion ignores tax consequences and brokerage fees, which can complicate matters in the real world. We are ignoring these complications.

The question on every stockholder's mind—explicitly or implicitly—is this: How much is a share of stock worth? With the economist's definition of dividend, the answer is simple:

> The price of a share is equal to the present value of the stream of dividends that it yields.

If the price were anything else, you could grow infinitely rich. Consider a share of stock whose dividend stream has a present value of $60. Remember that this means the share's owner can convert the dividend stream to $60 today by borrowing $60 and using the dividends to pay off the loan. If the price of the share were less than $60—say, $50—then you could buy a share, convert the dividends to cash by borrowing, and effortlessly earn a clear profit of $10. And you would have no reason to stop there; you could repeat the transaction a limitless number of times. Obviously, such a situation would not be stable; as you and others vied for this golden profit opportunity, the competition would soon bid the share price up to $60.

Likewise, the share price cannot exceed $60; if it did, nobody would buy the stock. (You'd be better off lending the purchase price at market interest rates.) The only possible price at which stocks can be bought and sold is a price exactly equal to the present value of the dividends.

Our discussion so far omits one very important real-world consideration: Usually, when a stock is sold, neither the buyer nor the seller has a very precise idea of what the future stream of dividends will be. Thus the share price cannot literally reflect the actual present value of its dividend stream; it reflects only an estimate of that present value based on the best information available to people at the time of the sale. Sometimes the dividend stream turns out to be unexpectedly high or unexpectedly low, and this is why there are happy and unhappy traders in the stock market.

Durable Goods

Stocks are valuable because they provide a stream of financial dividends. Durable consumer goods—such as houses, cars, furniture, and artwork—yield dividends of a different sort. A house provides living space, a car transportation, furniture a place to rest, and art an uplifting of the spirit. All these benefits may be considered to have monetary values equal to what the goods themselves would command on the rental market. For example, a house that would rent for $10,000 per year yields dividends worth $10,000 per year in the form of living space; a painting that would rent for $100 per month yields a spiritual dividend with that value to whoever enjoys having it on the wall. These dividends are no less real for being intangible, and they determine the price of the durable good just as stock dividends determine the price of the stock.

Consider a painting that yields $1000 worth of pleasure per year for 5 years and can then be resold for $10,000. The market price of that painting is equal to the present value of a stream consisting of five yearly payments of $1000 and a final payment of $10,000. A stock paying the equivalent stream of financial dividends would sell for exactly the same price.

Because the painting can be resold for $10,000 in 5 years, might it be wise to buy the work even if you don't like it? The answer is no. Buying a painting that you don't like is equivalent to buying a stock and throwing away part of the dividend stream. If other people value the painting's appearance on their walls at $1000 per year, that assessment is built into the purchase price. If you buy but won't enjoy the artwork, then you are paying for benefits you won't receive. It is far better to invest in a stock that yields the equivalent stream of dividends in a form you can appreciate.

There is one exception. It might be wise to make the purchase if you think you know more than the rest of the market about future changes in the painting's value. *Expected* changes are fully incorporated into the current price, but unexpected changes cannot be. If you are the one person to accurately foresee an unexpected change, you can get rich—just as you can if you are the one person to accurately guess the outcome of next week's state lottery.

Cash versus Credit

Suppose you decide to buy a new stereo system for $500. Should you pay cash, or should you charge it to your credit card?

To make a first pass at answering this question, let us suppose that the interest rates on your bank account and your credit card arc both 10 percent. You have three ways to pay: Under plan A, you pay $500 immediately. Under plan B, you charge $500 to your credit card, wait a year, and then pay $550 (principal plus interest) to the credit card company. Under plan C, you charge $500 to your credit card, make a $50 interest payment every year, and *never* pay off the $500 principal.

Each of these payment plans has a present value of $500, and therefore all three plans are equally desirable. To verify this, let us examine how each plan affects your savings account balance after 1 year. We begin by assuming that you have, say, $1000 in your account at the outset. Here are the calculations:

- Under plan A, you withdraw $500 to pay for your stereo. This leaves $500 in your account, which grows to $550 after 1 year.
- Under plan B, you withdraw nothing and your balance grows to $1100 in 1 year. You then withdraw $550 to pay your credit card debt and are left with a balance of $550.
- Under plan C, you withdraw nothing and your balance grows to $1100 in 1 year. You withdraw $50 to make your first annual interest payment and are left with $1050 in the account. But of this $1050, there is $500 that you dare not withdraw, since you need it to generate an annual income of $50 to make future credit card payments. This leaves you with a usable balance of $550.

The equality of these results confirms our previous knowledge that payment plans with the same present value are all equally desirable.

In the real world, the situation might be more complicated for a variety of reasons. One is that the interest rate on your savings account might be much lower than the interest rate on your credit card, because lending to you is a riskier prospect than lending to the bank. Another is that paying $500 cash might not be a good option; you might not have access to that much cash without borrowing at a rate even higher than the credit card rate—or dropping out of college to save on tuition. Still another is that the stereo shop might not be willing to lend you $500 "forever," trusting your heirs to continue making payments even after your death. (In some countries, your heirs can be held legally responsible for your debts, but in the United States they cannot be.)

What, then, do we learn from our simplified discussion? We learn that if there *is* any reason to prefer one plan or the other, it must arise from limitations on your ability to borrow at the going market rate. In the absence of such limitations, the plans are equivalent. This lesson is important—and very applicable to the real world—in the discussion of government debt that follows.

Government Debt

Suppose the government decides to build a road. As a citizen, you will be required to pay a portion of the construction costs; let us say that your share comes to $500.

The government has a choice among three ways to pay for the road construction. Plan A is to raise current taxes. Under plan A your tax bill increases by $500 today. Plan B is to leave taxes at their current level and borrow the money for a year at the going 10 percent interest rate. Under plan B, the government must raise taxes next year to pay off its debts, so your tax bill will increase by $550 next year. Plan C is to borrow the money forever, never paying off the debt but continuing to pay $50 interest every year. The interest payments will come from tax revenue. Hence, under plan C, your tax bill will increase by $50 per year forever, starting next year.

Which plan would you prefer to see the government adopt? As in our stereo-purchase example, the payment plans are all equal in present value, so the choice between cash and credit is a matter of indifference. Your usable bank balance next year will be the same regardless of which plan the government adopts.

This suggests that taxpayers should not care whether the government finances its purchases through immediate taxation or through debt. Yet there are two important differences between this example and the stereo-buying example.

In the stereo example we made the unrealistic assumption that the rate at which you borrow on your credit card is the same as the rate at which you lend to your bank. In the government-spending example, the corresponding assumption is far more reasonable. When the government borrows, it borrows at the going rate for U.S. Treasury bills. You *can* earn that rate on your savings, simply by purchasing Treasury bills. So this first difference suggests that the government-spending example is *more* realistic than the stereo example.

The other important difference suggests the opposite: that the government-spending example might be *less* realistic than the stereo example. In the stereo example, your personal decision about whether to use cash or credit has no effect whatsoever on the market interest rate. In the government-spending example, this may not be the case. Our present-value calculations all assume that the market interest rate stays fixed when the government borrows. (That is, we assumed that the interest rate will remain 10 percent whether the government adopts plan A, B, or C.) If government borrowing affects interest rates, then our conclusions may not be valid.

Can government borrowing actually cause a change in the market interest rate? Economists don't agree on the answer. In Chapter 6, we shall examine arguments on both sides of this issue. For now, we can state a qualified conclusion: *If* government borrowing does not affect interest rates, *then* it is a matter of indifference whether the government finances its spending with taxes or with debt.

We can also unambiguously dispose of an argument that is both fallacious and widespread. It is often claimed that when the government borrows and pays interest, taxpayers are saddled with an additional tax burden for which they get nothing in return. This is false. When the government borrows a dollar, it postpones taxing you a dollar. While it is true that next year you must pay taxes equal to the dollar plus interest, it is *not* true that you receive nothing in exchange for that interest payment. What you receive is the opportunity to hold your dollar for an extra year and have it *earn* interest. The 10 cents interest that you earn on your dollar exactly offsets the additional 10 cents that you must pay in taxes to cover the government's interest obligation.

The above discussion suggests that taxpayers should be indifferent between paying for a *given* level of government expenditure through current taxes or paying for it through future taxes as long as interest rates are not affected. It does *not* suggest that taxpayers should be indifferent among different levels of government spending. You might believe that the government's road-building program is too extravagant to justify its cost, or you might believe that the program is insufficient and should be greatly expanded. The extent to which governments build roads is emphatically *not* a matter of indifference. Our argument here suggests only that for a *given* expenditure on road building it does not matter where the money comes from.

Journalists and politicians frequently say that if we don't pay off the national debt, it will be a burden to our grandchildren. But if we *do* pay it off, we pay it out of our grandchildren's inheritances, which is equally a burden.

SUMMARY

A bond is a promise to pay. When you buy a bond, you buy a claim on future consumption. Buying a bond is the same as lending, and selling a bond is the same as borrowing. When you open a bank account, you are buying a bond.

The *nominal* interest rate is the percentage rate paid on a one-period loan denominated in dollars, and the *real* interest rate is the percentage rate paid on a loan denominated in real goods. The real rate can also be thought of as the rate paid on a loan denominated in constant dollars (corrected for inflation). The nominal rate is equal to the real rate plus the rate of inflation.

We can use the interest rate to measure the price of a unit of current consumption in terms of units of future consumption, and vice versa. If the interest rate is r, then a unit of current consumption costs $1 + r$ units of future consumption and a unit of future consumption costs $1/(1 + r)$ units of current consumption.

The discounted present value (sometimes called just the present value) of a future payment is the price of that payment measured in units of current consumption. The present value of 1 unit of consumption delivered one period in the future is $1/(1 + r)$ units of current consumption. The present value of 1 unit of consumption delivered n periods in the future is $[1/(1 + r)]^n$ units of current consumption. The present value of a series of payments is equal to the sum of the present values of the individual payments it comprises.

The current price of a bond is equal to the present value of the stream of payments that it promises. Given a stream of payments, you can always trade it for any other stream with the same present value.

The value of a share of corporate stock or a durable good is equal to the present value of the stream of dividends that it delivers. In the case of the stock, dividends include both cash payments to stockholders and increases in the value of the stock itself. In the case of the durable good, dividends include all of the services, tangible and intangible, that the good provides to its owner.

If you can borrow and lend at the going market interest rate, then it is a matter of indifference whether you pay for your purchases by cash or credit. The same is true for governments.

PROBLEM SET

1. Suppose that your roommate borrows $100 from you and agrees to pay you back $120 in 2 months. Who has sold a bond to whom? What is the monthly interest rate on that bond?

2. Fred agreed to lend Barney $200 for a year at an annual interest rate of 15 percent. Who sold a bond to whom, and what is the face value of the bond?

3. Suppose that you purchase from the government for $850 a bond that pays $1000 a year from today. What is the annual interest rate on that bond? Who is the borrower and who is the lender, and how much has been borrowed or lent?

4. You purchase a bond that pays $1000 in 1 year. The annual interest rate is 20 percent. How much do you have to pay for the bond? Are you a borrower or a lender?

5. In problems 1, 2, 3, and 4, are the interest rates under discussion real interest rates or nominal interest rates? Under what circumstances would there be no need to distinguish these concepts?

6. *True or false:* When interest rates rise, bondholders become wealthier.

7. *True or false:* If you can afford to, it is a good idea to pay off your student loans as quickly as possible, so that the interest charges don't get too high.

8. *True or false:* Chilean banks are paying huge interest rates on loans; therefore, Chile is a good place to put your money.

9. The U.S. government has taken on the responsibility of bailing out failed savings and loan institutions. *True or false:* Although the costs are high, it is best to complete the bailout as quickly as possible to avoid mounting interest charges.

10. You have just bought a car for $10,000 and financed it at 10 percent for 3 years. You are to make three equal payments beginning 1 year from today.

    a. What is your annual payment? (You will probably need a calculator to solve this.)

     b. Now suppose the car dealer offers you a choice: You can get an immediate rebate of $1000 or have your interest rate reduced to 5 percent. Assuming that your savings earn an interest rate of 5 percent, which should you take?

11. Suppose you win a lottery and are entitled to receive payments of $1000 per year for 3 years. What is the present value of your winnings if the interest rate is 10 percent? What if the interest rate is 20 percent? In which case are your winnings worth more? Explain why the value of your winnings changes when the interest rate does and why the direction of change is what it is.

12. Suppose that you plan to live in a house for 3 years. You can rent the house for $10,000 per year (payable in advance at the beginning of each year), or you can purchase it for $100,000. If you do purchase it, you expect to be able to sell it 3 years hence for $100,000. Aside from the financial considerations, you are indifferent between renting and owning.

     a. If the interest rate is 8 percent, should you rent or buy?

     b. If the interest rate is 12 percent, should you rent or buy?

     c. Are your answers to **a** and **b** affected by whether you will pay for the house out of existing savings or will have to borrow to buy the house?

     d. Suppose you change your mind about expecting the house to be worth $100,000 in 3 years; instead, you believe it will lose some of its value. If the interest rate is 15 percent, how much value must you expect the house to lose if you are to be indifferent between renting and buying?

13. A car salesman offers you a choice between two ways to pay for your car. You can pay nothing down, $60 next year, and $55 the following year, or you can pay nothing down, $40 next year, $47 the following year, and $33 the year after that.

     a. At an interest rate of 10 percent, which loan has the lower discounted present value?

     b. What about at an interest rate of 12 percent?

14. Suppose that in Figure 3-2, we were to add a curve showing the market interest rates for home mortgages. What do you think that curve would look like, and why?

15. General Electric makes a light bulb that lasts for 1 year and sells for $3. The company has just figured out how to make a new light bulb that lasts for 5 years instead of 1. *True or false:* If General Electric can get away with it, the company should withhold the new bulb from the market to prevent light bulb sales from plummeting. (*Hint:* How much are consumers willing to pay for the new kind of light bulb?)

16. In the *New Republic* (June 17, 1989), James K. Glassman explains that housing has been a less good investment than stocks: "If you bought a $200,000 house in Foggy Bottom in 1979, it would be worth $316,000 today. But if you bought $200,000 in stock in 1979, it would be worth $556,000 today—and you'd have another $68,000 in dividend income." In words that Glassman might understand, explain what his calculation overlooks.

17. In the *Wall Street Journal* (September 19, 1991), Richard C. Leone (the chairman of the New York Port Authority) explains the impracticality of privatizing New York's airports. The problem, he says, is that the airports are worth well over $2.2 billion but even at that bargain price no investor would be able to earn enough to cover the investment. Comment, in words that Richard C. Leone might understand.

18. The country of Idiovia owes $1 million to the World Bank. The debt is growing at the market rate of 10 percent. The citizens of Idiovia would like to pay off the loan now, but the bank will not allow them to do so until 5 years from now. What strategy can Idiovian citizens and their officials follow that is equivalent to paying off the loan today?

19. Jeeter figures that his personal share of the U.S. national debt is approximately $40,000, and he is distressed that his share is continuing to grow as government interest obligations mount from year to year. He wishes the government would just raise taxes and pay off the debt immediately. If the government refuses to take Jeeter's advice, what strategy can he follow that is equivalent to eliminating his share of the national debt?

20. Columnist George F. Will laments that interest payments on the national debt come from the tax payments of average Americans and are given to "the buyers of government bonds—buyers in Beverly Hills, Lake Forest, Shaker Heights, and Grosse Point, and Tokyo and Riyadh." In words that George F. Will might understand, explain what average Americans get in return for those tax payments.

21. According to the law in many European countries, anybody who resells a work of art must pay a percentage of the resale price to the original artist. Suppose you, a citizen of the United States, are planning to buy a painting that will provide you with $100 worth of pleasure for each of the next 3 years and, you expect, will fetch $500 when you resell it at the end of 3 years.

    a. If the interest rate is 10 percent, what will you pay for the painting?

    b. Suppose that before you buy, the United States adopts the European law, so 20 percent of the resale price goes to the original artist. Now what will you pay for the painting?

    c. If your estimate of a $500 resale price is correct, is this law good or bad for the artist?

    d. If, after you buy the painting, the artist's reputation increases and the resale price grows to $1000, is the law good or bad for the artist?

    e. If, after you buy the painting, the artist's reputation declines and the resale price falls to $200, is the law good or bad for the artist?

    f. *True or false:* Rather than helping all artists as intended, the law helps those artists who do unexpectedly well and hurts those who do unexpectedly poorly.

22. This textbook will be revised after 3 years. Assume that the only reason for the revision is to get copies of the first edition out of the used-book market and force new students to buy new textbooks.

    a. Suppose that a textbook physically lasts for 6 years and is worth $20 to each student who holds it for a year. If there were no revisions, how much would a 5-year-old textbook cost in the used market? How much would a 4-year-old textbook cost? How much would a new textbook cost?

    b. Now suppose that the publisher revises every 3 years, causing the old edition to become obsolete. How much does a new copy (of the new edition) cost?

    c. If it is costly to revise a textbook, is the publisher better off revising or issuing a credible promise never to revise?

    d. Why do you think textbooks get revised?

Chapter 4

Consumption

n 1995, the average American household spent 68 percent of its income on consumption goods. (The remainder went to taxes and savings.) Why 68 percent? To answer such a question, we must go beyond the definitions in the previous chapters and discuss how people make choices about consumption, borrowing, and saving.

A key point is that decisions regarding current consumption are influenced by expectations about the future. Borrowing, for example, allows you to increase your *current* consumption in exchange for a *future* sacrifice; borrowing to finance today's vacation might mean eating bologna sandwiches for lunch next year. Your decision on whether or not to borrow must depend partly on how much income you expect to have in the future.

Similarly, saving (or lending) enables you to increase your *future* consumption in exchange for a *current* sacrifice. And, just as with borrowing, your decision on whether or not to save must depend partly on your vision of the future.

Intertemporal:

Involving more than one period of time; used specifically in relation to decisions regarding behavior in multiple time periods.

The modern economy is a complicated system, intertwining the decisions of households, firms, and governments and offering an array of investment opportunities. Many of these decisions affect people not only in the present, when the decision is made, but also in the future. Such **intertemporal** decision making—that is, decision making with an eye to both the present and the future—is fundamental to understanding macroeconomics. Our goal is to understand intertemporal decision making a step at a time. In this chapter and the next we construct and study a basic model that allows us to focus on the consequences of *borrowing* and *lending*. Lessons learned from this model will continue to apply as we enrich the model in later chapters.

Some Simplifying Assumptions

There are essentially only three things you can do with your income: you can consume it, you can save it, or you can pay taxes with it. Our goal is to understand how consumers allocate their incomes among these three activities. To a first approximation, you have very little choice about how much to pay in taxes; your elected officials make that choice for you. Therefore, the key decisions are how much to consume and how much to save. To focus on those decisions, we will simply pretend in this and the next chapter that taxes and governments do not exist. We shall bring governments into the picture later on, but for now we assume that all of your income is either consumed or saved.

In the real world, there are many ways to save a portion of your income. You can *lend* it to a friend or to a financial institution, with the understanding that you are to be paid back at some future date. Putting money in a savings account is a form of lending: you lend to the bank, and you are repaid (with interest) when you make withdrawals. Another way to save is to purchase a productive asset, such as an apple tree or a Burger King franchise. You sacrifice some current income to purchase the asset, and it yields future income in the form of apples to eat or profits at the cash register.

For our first pass at understanding, we want to keep things as simple as possible. Thus we will imagine an economy in which there are no opportunities to acquire productive assets. In such a simplified economy, *the only way to save is to lend.* In Chapter 7, productive assets will be brought into the model, to make it more like the real economy.

Hence, we now study a world in which households must devote all of their income to either consumption or saving and in which the only way to save is to lend. These two assumptions will be modified in later chapters, but the basic conclusions we obtain here will continue to hold.

Income Streams

Income changes over time. When people are young, their income tends to rise as they gain job experience. When people are older, they retire and their income is likely to fall. Income also goes up and down unexpectedly: people lose jobs, get lucky in the stock market, or suddenly become ill. The sequence of a person's incomes over a lifetime is called his or her *income stream.* To start constructing a model with changing income, consider two consecutive periods of life: the current period and the future period, which you can think of as this year and next year.

The first issue we must address is measurement: In what units do we measure income? We want to discuss real income, in terms of real goods instead of nominal dollars, so the proper unit is a basket containing samples of all the goods and services in the economy.

Hamburgers, pizza, and plumbing services, among many others, should all be represented. Unfortunately, talking about baskets of such diverse goods can get a little clumsy. Therefore, we shall sometimes make a harmless simplifying assumption: We shall imagine that the only good in the economy is apples. Then the natural unit of income becomes "one apple."

If we want to measure consumption in dollars, then we must remember that a "dollar" is just a stand-in for a basket of real goods. We will use apples in some examples and dollars in others. Remember that dollars are valuable only because they represent consumption goods like apples.

Figure 4-1 depicts three separate income streams in our two-period model. Because each stream consists of only a current income and a future income, it can be

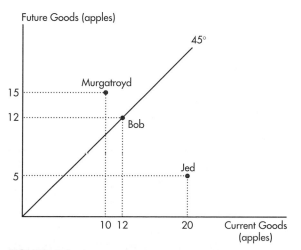

FIGURE 4-1 Income streams.
The horizontal axis measures current goods, while the vertical axis measures future goods. Murgatroyd's income stream is growing over time, while Jed's is declining. Bob's reflects the same income in the future as the one he has today.

graphed as a single point. For example, suppose Murgatroyd's current income is 10 apples and her future income will be 15 apples. Then the point marked Murgatroyd represents her income stream, with current and future incomes measured on the horizontal and vertical axes, respectively. We call that point her **endowment point** or her **income stream point.**

For now we do not ask how Murgatroyd earns her income. We simply envision income materializing *exogenously* each period like manna from heaven to Murgatroyd. By exogenous we mean from outside the model not explainable by the model so far as the model is constituted. We say that income is an **exogenous variable.** In contrast, a variable that is explained or predicted by the model is called an **endogenous variable.**

Murgatroyd's endowment point (10, 15) is above the 45° line. This reflects the fact that her future real income will be greater than today's real income. On the other hand, Bob's endowment point (12, 12) is on the 45° line. Bob's real income is constant over time.

Jed's real endowment point (20, 5) is below the 45° line. His future income of 5 apples will be less than his current income of 20. In a real-world application, this might be because he is planning to retire or because he is planning to quit his job to raise a family for a while.

The important point is this:

If a person's income is rising over time, his or her endowment point is above the 45° line. If income remains constant over time, the endowment point is on the 45° line. If income is declining over time, the endowment point is below the 45° line.

Endowment point *or* Income stream point:
A point representing a person's income for each period.

Exogenous variable:
A variable determined outside the model; its value is taken as a constant in the model.

Endogenous variable:
A variable determined within the model; its value changes when other variables in the model change.

The Intertemporal Budget Line

Credit market:
The market for borrowing and lending, or for exchanging present consumption and future consumption.

With access to a **credit market,** individuals can consume either more or less than their current income, in exchange for consuming either less or more than their future income. The intertemporal budget line is a device for keeping track of the options that are available.

Depicting Borrowing and Lending

Suppose Sandy's income stream consists of 10 apples this year and 10 next year. Figure 4-2 depicts Sandy's endowment point, labeled *Y*.

For our illustration, we assume an interest rate of 10 percent per period, and we assume that Sandy can either borrow or lend at this rate. We don't yet know what Sandy will do, but let us think about some of her options.

One option is to borrow 1 apple now. Then she will be able to consume a total of 11 apples in the present. The cost of this decision is that she must consume fewer apples in the future; in fact, she will have to repay 1.1 apples in the future. Those

1.1 apples will come out of next year's income, leaving her with only 10 − 1.1 = 8.9 apples next year. The outcome of all this is depicted by point *A* in the figure, showing Sandy with a **consumption stream** of 11 apples today and 8.9 tomorrow. Point *A* is Sandy's **consumption stream point** if she chooses to borrow 1 apple.

Consumption stream:

The series of quantities of consumption in each period of time.

Consumption stream point:

A point representing a person's consumption for each period.

Intertemporal budget line:

A line that contains all the possible consumption stream points available to a consumer.

We've worked through one of Sandy's options; now let's work through another. Instead of borrowing 1 apple this year, she might choose to borrow 2. This will allow her to eat a total of 12 apples in the present. She will then have to pay back 2.2 apples next year, leaving her with 10 − 2.2 = 7.8 apples for next year's consumption. This option is depicted by the consumption stream point *B* (12, 7.8) in Figure 4-2.

There are still other options. Instead of borrowing, Sandy might choose to lend. Suppose she lends 1 apple. Then she will be able to consume only 9 apples in the present, but when she collects 1.1 apples next year, she will add them to next year's income and consume a total of 11.1 apples, bringing her to the consumption stream point *C* (9, 11.1).

Yet another option for Sandy is to neither borrow nor lend but to consume exactly her 10-apple income both this year and next year. In this case she remains at point *Y*.

The line in Figure 4-2 that connects all of Sandy's possible consumption stream points is called her **intertemporal budget line.** It includes points *A, B, C,* and *Y,* and all the other points that represent options she can achieve by borrowing or lending. Starting from her endowment point *Y,* she can move rightward to points like *A* or *B* by borrowing or leftward to points like *C* by lending.

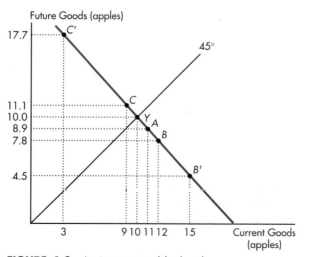

FIGURE 4-2 An intertemporal budget line.
Point *Y* depicts Sandy's endowment. She can achieve point *A* by borrowing 1 apple this year and paying back 1.1 apples (the loan plus 10 percent interest) next year. If she borrows 2 apples instead of 1, she achieves point *B*. She can achieve point *C* by lending. The line connecting these points is Sandy's intertemporal budget line.

→ *Exercise 4-1*

How much must Sandy borrow to reach point B' in Figure 4-2? How much must she lend to reach point C'?

The Relation between Borrowing and Consumption

Suppose that Sandy selects a point to the right of her endowment point, where her current consumption exceeds her current income. She gets there by borrowing, which requires her to consume less in the future. The more she consumes this year, the more she must borrow; the more she borrows, the less she consumes in the future. Saying that "Sandy increases her current consumption," that "Sandy increases her borrowing," and that "Sandy reduces her future consumption" are three different ways of saying that Sandy moves rightward along her budget line. Or to express it in other words:

> An increase in current consumption, an increase in (net) borrowing, and a decrease in future consumption are three different ways to describe the same thing.

Similarly:

> A decrease in current consumption, an increase in (net) lending, and an increase in future consumption are three different ways to describe the same thing.

The Slope of the Intertemporal Budget Line

The intertemporal budget line in Figure 4-2 has slope -1.1. We want now to give an economic interpretation of that slope.

When Sandy borrows an apple, she adds 1 apple to this year's consumption (that is, she moves 1 apple to the right) and subtracts 1.1 apples from next year's consumption (that is, she moves 1.1 apples downward). As she moves 1 unit to the right along the budget line, she moves 1.1 units down; this is exactly what having slope -1.1 means for a given line.

If the interest rate were 15 percent instead of 10 percent, then every time Sandy moved 1 unit to the right by borrowing an apple, she would have to move 1.15 units down. She would have a different intertemporal budget line, and its slope would be -1.15. In general:

> If r is the interest rate, then the slope of the intertemporal budget line is $-(1 + r)$.

In our example, $r = 10$ percent $= .10$; then the intertemporal budget line must have slope $-(1 + .10) = -1.1$, as the line in Figure 4-2 does.

➧ *Exercise 4-2*

Which budget line is steeper: the one with $r = .10$ or the one with $r = .15$?

Drawing the Intertemporal Budget Line

To draw a line, it suffices to have two pieces of information: the slope of the line and the coordinates of one point on that line. We have just seen that the slope of the intertemporal budget line is $-(1 + r)$. We also know that one of the points on the intertemporal budget line is the income stream point *Y*. So you can draw anybody's intertemporal budget line provided you know the interest rate (which gives the slope) and his or her income stream point.

Intertemporal Choice

Intertemporal choice:

The problem of selecting one point on the intertemporal budget line.

When people are faced with making decisions today that take into account the future consequences of those decisions, we say they are faced with a problem of **intertemporal choice.** Sandy's decision about how much to consume today is a problem of intertemporal choice because how much she consumes today affects her consumption tomorrow.

Sandy's budget line is reproduced in Figure 4-3. She must start at her income stream point *Y*, but she can move to any other point on the budget line that she likes better. She can move southeast of *Y* by borrowing or northwest of *Y* by lending. She can choose any point she likes on her budget line.

Optimum:

An individual's favorite among available options. For an individual deciding how much to consume each period, his favorite among the points on the intertemporal budget line.

We assume that of all the points on the budget line, *there is one that Sandy prefers over any other.*[1] We also assume that she can easily identify this point and move to it. If, for example, her favorite point is *A*, then she will move from point *Y* to point *A* by borrowing one apple. If her favorite point is *B*, she will move there by borrowing two apples instead of one. If her favorite point is *C*, she will move there from *Y* by lending an apple. If her favorite point happens to be *Y*, then she will not borrow or lend at all, thereby remaining at point *Y*.

The point that Sandy chooses—her favorite point on the budget line—is called Sandy's *optimum point* or **optimum.**

The Gains from Trade in Bonds

The opportunity to lend and borrow—that is, the opportunity to participate in a credit market—makes Sandy better off. Without a credit market, Sandy would be forced to consume at her endowment point. With a credit market, she can move back and forth along her intertemporal budget line *if she wants to*. If she happens to like her endowment point better than any other point on the line, she can always choose to remain there. Lending and borrowing—or, equivalently, buying and selling bonds—just expand her set of options.

[1]If you have studied indifference curves in a microeconomics course, then you know that this is the point at which Sandy's budget line is tangent to one of her indifference curves.

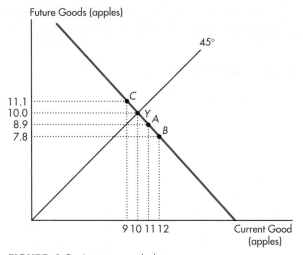

FIGURE 4-3 Intertemporal choice.
Sandy's budget line, reproduced from Figure 4-2. Of the points on the budget line, Sandy will choose her favorite, or *optimum,* point, which could be any point on the line.

When consumers choose to borrow, they calculate that an increase in current consumption is worth the associated future sacrifice. When they choose to lend, they calculate that an increase in future consumption is worth the associated current sacrifice. If they calculated otherwise, they would not behave as they do. Hence trading in bonds leaves both parties better off.

The observation that buying and selling bonds makes both borrowers and lenders better off illustrates the general principle that people gain from trade. Here the trade is in bonds, but more generally people choose to trade what they have for what they do not have when they can be made better off by doing so. Trade does not benefit one person at the expense of another. Everyone benefits.

Prohibiting people from borrowing and lending would force them to consume only at their endowment points. The opportunity to participate in a credit market—to borrow or lend at some interest rate *r*—*expands the* **opportunity sets** of the individuals in the economy to include many more possibilities, namely the entire intertemporal budget line.

Opportunity set:
The set of options available to an individual.

➡ *Exercise 4-3*
Suppose the government considers passing a law that forbids borrowing, in the belief that borrowing causes people to sacrifice their future well-being just for the pleasure of today. Would Dave, a borrower, be likely to vote for such a law? If it were to pass, would he be better off or worse off?

Sometimes people argue that it is better to save up for something you want than to borrow in order to pay for it. If you borrow, it is argued, then you must pay interest in addition to paying the price of the good itself. Is this argument reasonable? Our analysis suggests that it is not. A person who borrows in order to purchase additional current-consumption goods gets the benefit of those consumption goods right away. The cost of that benefit is less future consumption. By borrowing, the borrower is simply revealing his or her assessment that the benefit is worth the cost.

A person always prefers not to pay for something rather than to pay for it. We would all be happier if we could have television sets and tickets to rock concerts for free. But those things do have prices. So does a loan; the only difference is that you pay the price of a loan in a future period rather than at the time you receive the goods.

Do Americans Overborrow?

It is not uncommon to see letters to the editors of newspapers decrying the enormous interest payments that the U.S. government, the nation's firms, or its citizens have racked up in recent years. We cannot yet discuss the question of why they have done so, but we *are* able to make some important clarifying remarks about such worries. In particular, we note that focusing on the size of the interest payments does not address an important issue: that at the time the borrowing was done, the borrowers knew about those future interest payments and nevertheless borrowed because they judged the additional current purchases to be worth the future costs. If a lamentable error was made, it was in how the borrowed resources were used. The fact that interest must be paid is not an additional problem.

Another common complaint is that U.S. citizens consume too much, or that they are on a spending binge. The claim is that they sacrifice their future by borrowing to increase current consumption. It is sometimes pointed out by way of contrast that the Japanese, for example, are saving for their future; and it is suggested that saving is preferable to dissaving—that is, preferable to borrowing to increase current consumption.

Our analysis suggests that it is difficult to decide whether lending is better than borrowing and difficult to decide if a person's current consumption is excessive. A person's tastes concerning the choice between current and future consumption are his or her own private matter. As economists often say, *De gustibus non est disputandum*—"There is no accounting for tastes." Borrowers benefit by borrowing because they get enough extra consumption today to make the future interest payments worthwhile to them.

4-2 EFFECTS OF CHANGES IN THE INTEREST RATE

The intertemporal budget line provides the consumer with a menu of opportunities. Which point on that menu does the consumer select? So far, our answer has been that the consumer selects his favorite, or optimum, point. We have said nothing at all that would enable us to *predict* anything about the location of that optimum point.

And indeed, for an arbitrary consumer with a given intertemporal budget line, we will never be able to say any more than we have already said: The consumer selects the optimum point, and that point could be anywhere on the budget line.[2]

But things get more interesting when there is a *change* in the economic environment. A change in the interest rate or in the consumer's endowment point causes the budget line to shift. The consumer must then pick a new optimum on the new budget line. And although we are unable to say anything about the location of either the old or the new optimum in isolation, we will be able to say quite a bit about the locations of the two optimum points *relative to each other.* Our discoveries in this regard will have substantial economic consequences.

So the goal here is to understand what happens when the budget line shifts. We should begin by asking why the budget line might shift in the first place. The answer is revealed by our earlier observations about what it takes to draw the budget line: The budget line is completely determined by the interest rate (which gives the slope) and the endowment point (which gives a point on the line). Only a change in the interest rate or the endowment point can cause the budget line to shift.

In this chapter we treat both the interest rate and the income stream (endowment) point as *exogenous;* we take them as given, without attempting to explain where they come from. In Chapter 5, when we study the economy as a whole, we will shift focus and treat the interest rate as *endogenous;* its value will be accounted for within an expanded model. In later chapters, we will expand our discussion of the income stream point to make it endogenous as well.

Economic Shocks

A change in an exogenous economic variable is called a *shock.* In contrast to the way we use the word "shock" in ordinary speech, an economic shock need not be either unexpected or undesirable. In this chapter, a shock could be either an increase or a decrease in the interest rate or a shift of the endowment point in any direction.

In this section, we examine the effects of interest-rate shocks on the consumer's optimum. In Section 4-3, we will focus on a geometric means for recording those effects; called the *consumption demand curve,* it will be one of our chief analytic tools throughout the rest of the book. In Section 4-4, we will examine the effects of shocks to the endowment point.

The Case of a Net Borrower

Lisa is a net borrower. She has decided to spend $1000 more than her income this year, and she can do so courtesy of her Visa card.

---

[2]However, we will discover in the next chapter that if our consumer is in some sense "average," then it is possible to say more.

A Rise in the Interest Rate

This morning, Lisa received a notice that the interest rate on her unpaid Visa card balance has been changed from 12 to 15 percent. As a result, she is rethinking her spending plans. In which direction do you think she will revise them?

It is not hard to believe that Lisa's new plan will call for less current consumption than her old plan called for. Let us analyze why.

There are really two reasons why a rise in the interest rate causes Lisa to consume less in the present. First and most obviously, the terms of trade change: a bottle of wine with tonight's dinner now costs 1.15 bottles of wine with a future dinner, rather than just 1.12 bottles. The trade is less attractive at the new interest rate than at the old one, and Lisa is more likely to order ginger ale instead of wine tonight.

Substitution effect:
An individual's response to changes in the terms of trade.

The effect we have just described is called the **substitution effect** of an interest-rate increase; it is so called because it causes the individual—Lisa—to *substitute* future consumption for current consumption. The substitution effect is Lisa's response to a change in the terms of trade between present and future goods. When the interest rate goes up, the substitution effect leads Lisa to consume less today and more in the future.

There is a second reason why Lisa revises her current spending downward after she gets the Visa card notice. As a net borrower, Lisa is made worse off by a rise in interest rates—in a very real sense, she is poorer than she was before. In general, when people become poorer, they consume less of everything, including both current and future goods.[3]

Income effect:
An individual's response to changes in wealth.

Lisa's response to the realization that she is poorer is called the **income effect** of an interest-rate increase. When the interest rate goes up, the income effect leads Lisa to consume less both today *and* in the future.

Now let us combine these conclusions. When Lisa learns that the interest rate is higher than expected, she has two good reasons to cut back on current consumption. One of those is the substitution effect, and the other is the income effect. Therefore, we expect her to cut back on current consumption.

What about her future consumption? Here the result is ambiguous. The substitution effect provides a good reason to *increase* future consumption: Future consumption is cheaper (relative to current consumption) than it used to be; Lisa can now buy 1.15 future bottles of wine for a price of 1 current bottle of wine, whereas before she could buy only 1.12. On the other hand, the income effect also provides a good reason to *decrease* future consumption: Lisa is poorer than before and consequently chooses to cut back on everything. So, does Lisa increase or decrease her future consumption? We cannot say for certain. The answer depends on which is stronger—the substitution effect or the income effect.

The Geometry Figure 4-4 shows Lisa's original budget line (in black) and her new budget line (in blue). Her endowment point is at *Y*. Initially she expects an interest

---

[3]The exceptions to this rule, called *inferior goods,* are unimportant in macroeconomics, and we shall ignore them.

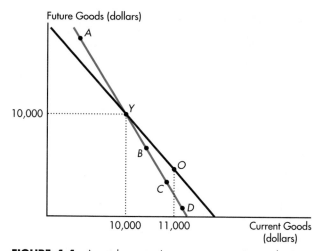

FIGURE 4-4 A net borrower's response to a rise in the interest rate.
Lisa's original budget line (in black) passes through her endowment point *Y*. Her optimum point *O* is southeast of *Y*—that is, Lisa is a net borrower. When the interest rate rises, the budget line pivots clockwise through *Y*, becoming steeper. The new line is shown in blue. Lisa's new optimum point must lie on the blue line. It must be to the left of *O*, because the substitution and income effects combine to make Lisa consume less in the present. Thus Lisa's new optimum point could be *A*, *B*, or *C* but not *D*.

rate of 12 percent and so faces the black budget line, with slope -1.12, through *Y*. After learning that the new interest rate is 15 percent, she faces the blue budget line, with slope -1.15, through *Y*.

Notice that news of an interest-rate change affects only the *slope* of the budget line; the endowment point remains unchanged. (Be sure you understand why.)

> An increase in the interest rate causes the budget line to become steeper by pivoting clockwise about the endowment point.

Lisa's initial optimum is point *O* on the black budget line, which indicates that her current consumption exceeds her current income by $1000. (Remember, she is originally a net borrower.) After the news from Visa, she must find an optimum point on the blue budget line.

We have observed that the income and substitution effects both push Lisa in the direction of reducing her current consumption. Therefore, her new optimum point must involve less current consumption than her old one did, which is to say that *her new optimum point must lie to the left of point O*.

What about the vertical shift of her optimum point? Does Lisa's new optimum point lie *above* or *below* point *O?* This is tantamount to asking whether Lisa increases or decreases her *future* consumption, and we have already noted that we do not know the answer to that question. It depends on whether the substitution effect or the income effect is stronger.

Where, then, is Lisa's new optimum? It could be anywhere on the blue line to the left of point O, at a point like A or B or C. It cannot be anywhere to the right of O, at a point like D.

If Lisa's new optimum is point B or C, she remains a net borrower, though she borrows less than she would have at the old interest rate. If her new optimum is point A, Lisa has decided to become a *lender*, which is another plausible response to a rise in the interest rate.

 *Exercise 4-4*

Suppose that for Lisa the substitution effect is larger than the income effect. Which of points A, B, and C might Lisa move to when the interest rate rises? To which point might she move if the income effect is larger than the substitution effect?

In Figure 4-4, as in many of the other figures in this chapter, the quantity of current consumption is measured in "dollars." Here "dollar" means not a green piece of paper but a (constant) dollar's worth of consumption goods; if apples sell for 50 cents apiece, then "one dollar" is just shorthand for "two apples."

A Drop in the Interest Rate

Suppose now that Lisa gets a second letter, informing her that the first letter was a mistake. The interest rate on her Visa card is not slated to rise from 12 to 15 percent after all; instead, it is slated to *fall* from 12 to 8 percent.

How does Lisa respond? Once again it pays to think separately about the substitution and income effects. A lower interest rate means that current goods have become cheaper relative to future goods and that future goods have become more expensive relative to current goods. The substitution effect therefore leads Lisa to increase her current consumption and reduce her future consumption.

What about the income effect? Because Lisa is a net borrower, a drop in the interest rate makes her better off; in a sense she is richer than before. That leads her to consume more goods in both the present and the future.

Combining the two effects, we find that Lisa's current consumption must increase. She consumes more today both because current consumption has gotten cheaper (the substitution effect) and because she feels richer than she was before (the income effect).

By contrast, the net effect on Lisa's future consumption is ambiguous. She inclines toward reducing her future consumption because future consumption has gotten more expensive relative to current consumption (the substitution effect) but also inclines toward increasing her future consumption because she feels richer (the income effect). On balance, her future consumption could decrease or increase, depending on which effect is stronger.

Figure 4-5 illustrates the situation. When the interest rate falls from 12 to 8 percent, Lisa's budget line changes slope from -1.12 (the black line) to -1.08 (the red line).

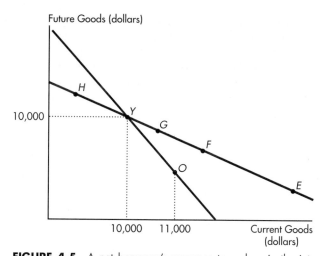

FIGURE 4-5 A net borrower's response to a drop in the interest rate.
Lisa's original budget line (in black) passes through her endowment point Y. Her optimum point O is southeast of Y—that is, Lisa is a net borrower. When the interest rate falls, the budget line pivots counterclockwise through Y, becoming flatter. The new line is shown in red. Lisa's new optimum point must lie on the red line. It must be to the right of O, because the substitution and income effects combine to make Lisa consume more in the present. Thus Lisa's new optimum point could be E or F but not G or H.

> A decrease in the interest rate causes the budget line to become flatter by pivoting counterclockwise through the endowment point.

Lisa starts out at point O on the black budget line. The income and substitution effects combined lead her to increase her current consumption, so her new optimum must lie to the right of O, at a point like E or F on the red line. It can*not* lie to the left of O, at a point like G or H.

➡ *Exercise 4-5*
Suppose that for Lisa the substitution effect is larger than the income effect. Which of points E and F might Lisa move to when the interest rate falls? To which point might she move if the income effect is larger than the substitution effect?

The Case of a Net Lender

The case of a net lender is much like that of a net borrower. Net lenders feel exactly the same substitution effects that net borrowers do. When the interest rate rises, current consumption becomes more expensive and future consumption becomes cheaper. This presents an incentive to consume less in the present and more in the future.

The only difference is that for a net lender, the income effects work in the opposite directions from those for a net borrower. A rising interest rate makes a net lender *richer,* and so leads the net lender to consume *more* of everything. A falling interest rate makes a net lender *poorer,* leading him to consume *less* of everything. (For a net borrower, exactly the opposite is true.)

A Rise in the Interest Rate

Dooney is a net lender. He is living frugally and putting a large part of his income into a savings account so that he can take an exotic vacation next year in Hawaii.

Dooney earns 12 percent interest on his savings. Today the bank announced that it is adjusting that figure upward to 15 percent. How will Dooney respond?

Once again it pays to think in terms of the separate substitution and income effects. First, the substitution effect makes Dooney want to save even more now; that is, he wants to reduce his current consumption even further. It used to be that a $10 steak dinner today meant a $12 reduction in next year's bank balance. Now a $10 steak dinner means a $15 reduction in next year's balance. On this account, Dooney chooses to eat fewer steak dinners now.

But that is only half the current-consumption story. The other half is the income effect. As a net lender, Dooney is made better off by a rise in the interest rate. He feels richer now and on that account is likely to eat *more* steak.

The substitution effect leads Dooney to *reduce* his current consumption, while the income effect leads him to *increase* his current consumption. Depending on which effect is stronger, Dooney's current consumption could go either up or down.

Regarding future consumption, the effects both work in the same direction. The substitution effect leads Dooney to save more (and hence consume more in the future): the dollar he puts in the bank today will allow him to spend $1.15 next year instead of $1.12. The income effect makes Dooney feel richer and hence leads him to consume more both now and in the future. On both accounts, he is likely to revise his future spending plans upward, perhaps deciding to stay 3 weeks in Hawaii instead of 2 or to stay at a plusher hotel.

A Drop in the Interest Rate

Now suppose Dooney has just gotten a letter from his bank announcing a change of plans: The interest rate will *not* rise to 15 percent; it will fall to 8 percent instead. How does Dooney react?

To find out, we examine the substitution and income effects separately, first with regard to current consumption: The substitution effect leads Dooney to consume more in the present, and the income effect leads him to consume less in the present. The net effect is that his current consumption could go either up or down.

➧ *Exercise 4-6*
Explain why the substitution effect leads Dooney to consume more in the present when the interest rate falls. Does a drop in the interest rate make a net lender feel richer or poorer? Explain why the income effect leads Dooney to consume less in the present when the interest rate falls.

Now we do the same for future consumption: The substitution effect leads Dooney to consume less in the future, and the income effect also leads Dooney to consume less in the future. The net effect is that his future consumption decreases.

➥ *Exercise 4-7*

Explain the reasons for the assertions in the preceding paragraph.

In problems 4 through 6 at the end of the chapter, you will be asked to provide geometric representations of Dooney's responses to a change in the interest rate.

The Case of the Representative Agent

In exploring the consequences of an interest-rate change, we have thought separately about net borrowers (like Lisa) and net lenders (like Dooney). Our findings are summarized in Figure 4-6. Which of the two do you think is more typical? Is the average person a borrower or a lender?

Representative agent:

A fictional character who is average in every way. The behavior of this individual may be used as a tool for characterizing aggregate behavior.

By one reasonable interpretation of the word "average," the answer is neither. This follows from the simple observation that every dollar borrowed is a dollar lent, and vice versa. Therefore, in a closed economy the total of all borrowing is exactly equal to the total of all lending. Imagine a **representative agent**—a fictional character who carries on all economic activities at exactly the average levels. That representative agent must borrow exactly as much as he or she lends. The representative agent is thus the citizen who obeys Polonius's advice to Hamlet: "Neither a borrower nor a lender be."

 It is important to recognize that although Polonius would approve of the representative agent's *behavior,* he would surely *dis*approve of the *motives* for that behavior.

When the Interest Rate Rises					
For a Net Borrower			For a Net Lender		
Substitution effect	Income effect	Overall effect	Substitution effect	Income effect	Overall effect
Current consumption goes Down	Down	Down	Down	Up	?
Future consumption goes Up	Down	?	Up	Up	Up

When the Interest Rate Falls					
For a Net Borrower			For a Net Lender		
Substitution effect	Income effect	Overall effect	Substitution effect	Income effect	Overall effect
Current consumption goes Up	Up	Up	Up	Down	?
Future consumption goes Down	Up	?	Down	Down	Down

FIGURE 4-6 How changes in the interest rate affect net borrowers and net lenders.

The representative agent does *not* eschew borrowing and lending because he considers them intrinsically bad; rather, this perfectly average person's endowment point happens to be the agent's favorite among the options presented by his budget line. If some other point were his favorite, he would be quite happy to borrow or lend to get to it.

A Rise in the Interest Rate

When the interest rate rises, what happens to the representative agent's consumption? The substitution effect leads the representative agent to consume less in the present and more in the future, just as it does everyone else. What about the income effect? *For the representative agent, a change in the interest rate has no income effect.* Because the representative agent is neither a borrower nor a lender, he or she feels neither poorer nor richer when the interest rate rises. Therefore, the substitution effect is the entire story. The representative agent's unambiguous response is to consume less today and more in the future.

Suppose Jocko is the representative agent. Figure 4-7 illustrates his response to a rise in the interest rate. Jocko's endowment point is at *Y*, and his budget line is shown in black. His optimum point *O* is the same as his endowment point *Y*, reflecting the fact that Jocko is neither a borrower nor a lender. When the interest rate rises, Jocko's budget line pivots clockwise about point *Y*, perhaps to the position of the blue line. We have just argued that Jocko's new optimum must include less present consumption and more future consumption than his old optimum *O*. Therefore, his new optimum point is northwest of point *O*, at a point like *P* and *not* at a point like *Q*.

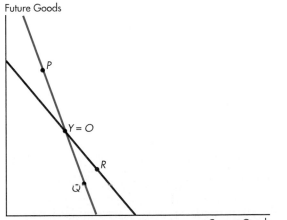

Future Goods

Current Goods

FIGURE 4-7 The representative agent responds to a rise in the interest rate.
Jocko's original budget line (black) passes through his endowment point *Y*. His optimum point *O* coincides with *Y*, indicating that Jocko is neither a net borrower nor a net lender. When the interest rate rises, the budget line pivots clockwise through *Y*, becoming steeper. The new line is shown in blue. Jocko's new optimum point must lie on the blue line. It must be to the left of *O*, because the substitution effect leads him to consume less in the present and more in the future; there is no income effect.

A Drop in the Interest Rate

When the interest rate falls, the representative agent again feels no income effect. He feels only a substitution effect, which leads him to consume more today and less in the future. You should be able to sketch the effects of the interest-rate drop on Jocko's budget line and optimum point.

The Representative Agent, Briefly

We can summarize the above discussion as follows:

> When the interest rate rises, the representative agent always wants to consume less now and more in the future.

> When the interest rate falls, the representative agent always wants to consume more now and less in the future.

Following a change in the interest rate, the representative agent shifts to a new optimum point such as *P* in Figure 4-7. Because *P* is not identical with the income stream point *Y*, this representative agent can no longer be *the* representative agent (unless *Y* has also moved for some reason). But, we will continue to talk about the behavior of *the* representative agent by allowing that the identity of that agent can change.

Are Falling Interest Rates Desirable?

Thinking about representative agents is helpful when it comes to avoiding silly mistakes. In 1992, interest rates fell dramatically. A feature story in the *New York Times* touted the benefits of this turn of events, stressing gains to borrowers who were in the process of buying new cars and houses. A separate and smaller story acknowledged the downside by describing how lenders—such as people saving for retirement—are hurt by lower interest rates, but it characterized these damages as "secondary effects." What the editors failed to notice is that the effects they called "secondary" are of exactly the same magnitude as are the primary effects detailed in the main article. For every borrower there is a lender, and for every winner there is a loser. The representative agent, who neither borrows nor lends, is quite indifferent to changes in the interest rate.

4-3 CONSUMPTION DEMAND CURVES

Consumption demand curve:
A curve showing desired current consumption as a function of the interest rate.

A **consumption demand curve** is a means for keeping track of how an individual changes her or his consumption in response to changes in the interest rate. In this section, we construct and discuss consumption demand curves for current and future consumption.

The Demand Curve for Current Consumption

We can construct a consumption demand curve for any individual. By way of illustration, we will produce one for Lisa, the net borrower of Figure 4-4.

The black line in Figure 4-8(a) is Lisa's budget line. Its slope is -1.12, reflecting the market interest rate of 12 percent. It passes through Lisa's endowment point, consisting of $10,000 this year and $10,000 next year. Her consumption stream point—her favorite point on the black 12 percent budget line—is O, indicating that Lisa spends $11,000 this year (of which $1000 must be borrowed).

To obtain points on Lisa's *current*-consumption demand curve in Figure 4-8(b), we graph interest rate r (on the vertical axis) and *current* consumption (on the horizontal axis). At the going interest rate of 12 percent, Lisa consumes exactly $11,000 this year (meaning "in the current period"). The pair of values (12 percent, $11,000) gives us point O' on the consumption demand curve.

If the interest rate rises to 15 percent, Lisa faces the blue budget line in Figure 4-8(a). She selects her new optimum point on that line, which is necessarily somewhere to the left of O (refer to Figure 4-4 to be reminded of why). Suppose her new optimum is at point A, where she consumes $10,500 today and $9425 tomorrow. We record the current information by plotting in Figure 4-8(b) the pair (15 percent, $10,500) to obtain point A'.

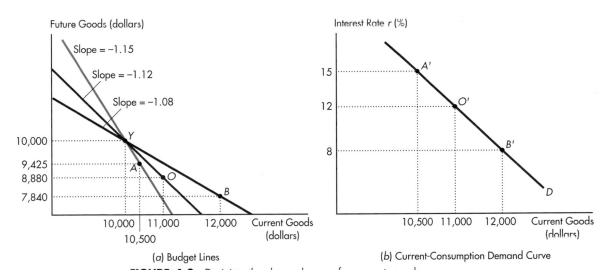

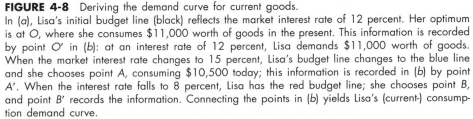

FIGURE 4-8 Deriving the demand curve for current goods.
In (a), Lisa's initial budget line (black) reflects the market interest rate of 12 percent. Her optimum is at O, where she consumes $11,000 worth of goods in the present. This information is recorded by point O' in (b): at an interest rate of 12 percent, Lisa demands $11,000 worth of goods. When the market interest rate changes to 15 percent, Lisa's budget line changes to the blue line and she chooses point A, consuming $10,500 today; this information is recorded in (b) by point A'. When the interest rate falls to 8 percent, Lisa has the red budget line; she chooses point B, and point B' records the information. Connecting the points in (b) yields Lisa's (current-) consumption demand curve.

If the interest rate falls to 8 percent, Lisa faces the red budget line in Figure 4-8(*a*). She selects her new optimum on that line, and it is necessarily somewhere to the right of *O* (refer to Figure 4-5 for the reason why). Suppose her new optimum is at point *B*, with $12,000 in consumption today and $7840 tomorrow. We record the current information in Figure 4-8(*b*) by plotting the pair (8 percent, $12,000) to obtain point *B'* on Lisa's current-consumption demand curve.

The curve labeled *D* that is drawn through points *O'*, *A'*, and *B'* in Figure 4-8(*b*) is Lisa's *demand curve* for current consumption. At each possible interest rate on the vertical axis, the demand curve shows how much current consumption Lisa will choose.

A demand curve usually relates price (on the vertical axis) to quantity (on the horizontal axis). We have seen that the price of current consumption (measured in units of future consumption) is $1 + r$. Thus it would be reasonable to put $1 + r$ on the vertical axis of the demand curve. In Lisa's case, points *O'*, *A'*, and *B'* would then have vertical coordinates 1.12, 1.15, and 1.08.

We have chosen to plot r instead of $1 + r$ on the axis, thereby lowering the vertical coordinates of all points by 1; thus we have points at vertical heights .12, .15, and .08, instead of 1.12, 1.15, and 1.08. The resulting curve, however, is unchanged; it is merely displaced downward a distance of 1. The curve we have plotted still deserves to be called a *demand curve* for current consumption.

To construct a single point on Lisa's demand curve for current consumption, you must follow this five-step procedure: First, imagine an interest rate, such as 15 percent. Second, draw the corresponding budget line, such as the blue line in Figure 4-8(*a*). Third, ask Lisa to identify her optimum point on that line, such as *A*. Fourth, read off the amount of current consumption associated with that optimum point, such as $10,500. Fifth, plot a single point on Lisa's demand curve in Figure 4-8(*b*), such as point *A'*, with the interest rate for its vertical coordinate and the quantity of current consumption for its horizontal coordinate.

To generate another point on the demand curve, repeat the entire five-step process. The demand curve for current consumption connects all the resulting points, one for each rate of interest.

The Slope of the Demand Curve for Current Consumption

Notice that Lisa's demand curve for current consumption slopes downward to the right. This is a consequence of our assumption that Lisa is a net borrower and of our discoveries in Figures 4-4 and 4-5. When the interest rate rises, a net borrower's current consumption must fall; when the interest rate falls, her current consumption must rise.

If Lisa were a net lender, these conclusions might not hold. A net lender might respond to a higher interest rate either by reducing current consumption or by increasing current consumption, depending on whether the substitution and income effects work in the same direction and, if not, on whether the substitution effect or the income effect is the stronger. Therefore, a net lender's demand curve for current consumption might slope either downward or upward to the right.

On the other hand, if Lisa were the representative agent, then her demand curve would necessarily slope downward. The representative agent feels only a substitution effect when the interest rate changes, and this means that she must reduce current consumption when the interest rate rises and increase current consumption when the interest rate falls.

The demand curve for current consumption slopes downward to the right for a net borrower. It may slope downward or upward for a net lender. It slopes downward for the representative agent.

In our examples, we will draw all demand curves for current consumption with negative slopes.

The Demand Curve for Future Consumption

Figure 4-9(*a*) reproduces Figure 4-8(*a*). Part (*b*) of Figure 4-9 shows Lisa's demand curve *D* for *future* consumption.

The first thing to notice about Figure 4-9(*b*) is the unit on the vertical axis. Because the price of a current good is $1 + r$ (in terms of future goods), the price of

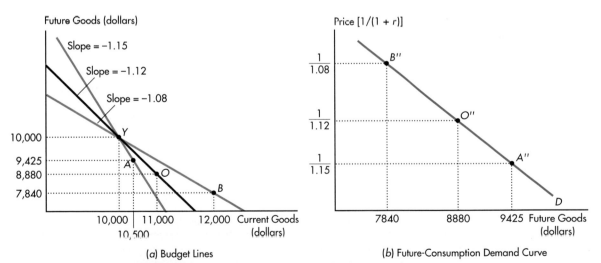

(a) Budget Lines   (b) Future-Consumption Demand Curve

FIGURE 4-9 Deriving the demand curve for future goods.

In (*a*), Lisa's initial budget line (black) reflects the market interest rate of 12 percent. Her optimum is at *O*, where she consumes $8880 worth of goods next year. This information is recorded by point *O*″ in (*b*): when the price of future goods in terms of current goods is $1/1.12$, Lisa demands $8880 worth of future goods. When the market interest rate changes to 15 percent, Lisa's budget line changes to the blue line and she chooses point *A*, consuming $9425 next year; this information is recorded by point *A*″. When the interest rate falls to 8 percent, Lisa has the red budget line, she chooses point *B*, and point *B*″ records the information. Connecting the points in (*b*) yields Lisa's demand curve for future consumption.

a future good (in terms of current goods) is $1/(1 + r)$. That is what we measure on the vertical axis.

Figure 4-9(a) tells us that when the interest rate is 12 percent, Lisa's optimum is O on the black budget line and she consumes $8880 in future goods. This is reflected by point O'' on Lisa's future-consumption demand curve, where $1/(1 + r)$ = $1/1.12$ and the quantity she consumes is $8880. When the interest rate is 15 percent, Lisa's optimum in Figure 4-9(a) is A on the blue budget line and she consumes $9425 in the future; this is reflected by point A'' in Figure 4-9(b). When the interest rate is 8 percent, Lisa's optimum is B on the red budget line and she consumes $7840 in the future; this is reflected by point B''. Points O'', A'', B'', and others derived by the same procedure can be connected to form Lisa's demand curve for future consumption, curve D in Figure 4-9(b).

The Slope of the Demand Curve for Future Consumption

Now let us think about the slope of this demand curve for future consumption. When the interest rate rises, Lisa's future consumption may either rise or fall. Here's why: Recall from Chapter 3 that a *rise* in the interest rate r is the same as a *drop* in the price $1/(1 + r)$ of future consumption. A drop in this price can be associated with either an increase or a decrease in future consumption, depending on the income and substitution effects. The demand curve for future consumption can slope either downward or upward to the right.

Figure 4-9 includes specific assumptions about the locations of Lisa's optimum points A and B and thus shows that they yield a downward-sloping demand curve. But if we had made different assumptions, the demand curve might have sloped upward.

If Lisa were a net lender, however, we could say something less ambiguous. For a net lender, a rise in the interest rate always leads to a rise in future consumption. In other words, a lower value of the price $1/(1 + r)$ (that is, a high value of r) always leads to a higher quantity of future consumption. When lower prices are associated with higher quantities, the demand curve must slope downward. So the net lender's demand curve for future consumption must slope downward.

The same is true of the representative agent, who, like the net lender, always consumes more in the future if the interest rate goes up.

> The demand curve for *future* consumption may slope either downward or upward to the right for a net borrower. It slopes downward for a net lender and for the representative agent.

In our examples, we will draw all demand curves for future consumption with negative slopes.

Aggregate Demand

We have seen how to construct the demand curves for current and future consumption by an individual. Next, we want to construct demand curves showing total con-

Aggregate demand curve:

A curve showing how much all the members of society want to consume in the present as a function of the interest rate.

sumption by all members of the economy. Such curves are called **aggregate demand curves.**

There are two ways to construct the aggregate demand curve for current consumption. One way is to construct the current demand curves for all the individuals in the economy and then add them. If an interest rate of 12 percent corresponds to quantities of 8, 10, and 12 apples on Curly's, Moe's, and Larry's demand curves, then an interest rate of 12 percent corresponds to a quantity of $8 + 10 + 12 = 30$ apples on the aggregate demand curve for an economy consisting of Curly, Moe, and Larry.

The second way is to identify the representative agent and then multiply the quantities on the agent's demand curve by the number of individuals in the economy. If an interest rate of 12 percent corresponds to a quantity of 10 on the representative agent's demand curve, and if there are three individuals in the economy, then an interest rate of 12 percent corresponds to a quantity of 30 on the aggregate demand curve. This works because the representative agent, by definition, consumes the absolute average quantity of everything.

One reason to be a little suspicious of the second method is that in the real world there are *no* representative agents. The absolute "average citizen" is a myth; everyone differs from the norm in one way or another. So, by assuming the existence of a representative agent, we incorporate in our model something that we know is a fiction.

As fictions go, however, the representative agent is a very useful one, at least partly for this reason: Unlike other members of the economy, the representative agent *must* have downward-sloping demand curves for both current and future consumption. Because the aggregate demand curves are just magnified versions of the representative agent's demand curves, we automatically know that the aggregate demand curves are downward-sloping also. This is a very convenient thing to know.

Most of what we can discover by thinking about the representative agent would remain true even if the agent did not exist. However, the representative agent makes such things easier to discover. We will therefore continue to employ him or her wherever doing so is convenient. Here, our knowledge of the representative agent's behavior allows us to draw the following critical conclusion:

Aggregate demand curves for current and future consumption slope downward to the right.

Measuring Aggregate Consumption

The U.S. Department of Commerce measures and reports total spending on consumption goods in the United States. The numbers it reports correspond to points on the U.S. aggregate demand curve for consumption goods. If the (real) interest rate is now 3 percent and aggregate spending is $4 trillion (the approximate figure currently being reported by the Commerce Department), then the point (3 percent, $4 trillion) must be on that aggregate demand curve.

Where does that consumption expenditure go? The largest single category is food, accounting for about 22 percent of household expenditure. The second-largest category is housing, accounting for another 20 percent. That 20 percent includes rental payments, but it does *not* include home purchases. If you buy a new house, the Commerce Department recognizes (quite correctly) that you do not intend to "consume" your entire house this year; instead, you intend to consume the warmth and shelter that it provides, while leaving the house itself intact to continue providing warmth and shelter in the future. Therefore, if you are a homeowner—whether you bought your house recently or long ago—the department pretends that you are renting your own house from yourself at a fair market rental rate and it considers that rental a part of your consumption expenditure.

Another 15 percent of consumption expenditure is for durable goods such as vehicles, furniture, and household equipment. Because cars and furniture last for many years, there is a strong argument for treating them in the same way that the department treats housing—counting not actual purchases but fictional rentals. However, the department does not make this correction in categories other than housing.

Other large categories of consumption include medical services (about 17 percent), household operation including utilities (8.5 percent), clothing (8 percent), transportation services (5 percent), and gasoline (3.5 percent).

The Open Economy

In a closed economy, the representative agent neither borrows nor lends and therefore feels no income effects. This allowed us to conclude that the representative agent's current and future demand curves slope downward and then to infer that the same is true of the aggregate current and future demand curves.

In an open economy, however, it is no longer true that every dollar borrowed is a dollar lent *by someone in that economy.* In an open economy, some borrowing comes *from* foreigners and some lending goes *to* foreigners, so aggregate net lending (and the representative agent's net lending) need not be zero. In this case, the representative agent might be subject to income effects when interest rates change.

Thus, in principle, in an open economy the demand curve for current consumption could slope upward.

At least for the United States, however, aggregate net lending per capita is small enough so that we can safely assume that the income effect is quite small for the representative agent. We can therefore feel quite free to continue assuming that aggregate consumption demand slopes downward, even in the open economy.

4-4   EFFECTS OF CHANGES IN THE ENDOWMENT POINT

Leopold dines nightly at Parnell's House of Liver, where he invariably orders liver casserole with kidney beans. Tonight, however, was different. Although he had planned to order liver casserole as usual, Leopold ended up getting the seafood combination plate instead. Why, do you suppose, did he revise his plan?

There are really only two possible reasons why Leopold deviated from his original intention. One is that he experienced a change in preferences—a sudden realization that he doesn't really *like* liver casserole all that much or that the seafood plate appeals to him more than it used to. The other is that Parnell's changed its menu—maybe casserole is no longer offered or the seafood plate is a new and unexpected option, or maybe the prices have changed.

Any change in consumption behavior must be traceable to either a change in preferences or a change in the menu of opportunities. In macroeconomics, where we study broad categories of goods (with all present consumption lumped together as a single "good" that includes liver casserole, ice cream sundaes, and roller skating), we feel safe in assuming that preferences are fixed. It seems unlikely that people suddenly and frequently revise their feelings about the desirability of liver casserole versus seafood. It seems even *more* unlikely that they suddenly and frequently revise their feelings about the desirability of broad categories like present versus future consumption.

When preferences are fixed, it follows that *all changes in behavior must be traceable to a change in the menu of opportunities.* When we discuss consumption behavior, the relevant menu of opportunities is the intertemporal budget line. So if we want to understand changes in consumption behavior, we only need to understand how people respond to changes in the budget line.

Recall once more that the budget line is specified by two bits of information: the *slope,* which is determined by the interest rate, and the *endowment point,* which is determined by the individual's current and future incomes. In the preceding section, we discussed changes in the interest rate (and hence in the slope of the budget line) and recorded their effects on the consumption demand curve. In this section, we turn to changes in the endowment point. By the end of the section, we will have discussed everything that can affect consumption.

Shocks to Current Income

The endowment point is determined by current income and future income. A change in the endowment point must be caused by a change in current income, a change in future income, or a change in both. Recall that such changes are called *shocks.* We will begin by studying the effects of shocks to current income.

A Rise in Current Income

Consider Horton, who faces the black intertemporal budget line in Figure 4-10. His endowment point Y reflects his income of $1000 a year both this year and next. The slope of −1.25 reflects the current interest rate of 25 percent per year.

Horton happens to be a lender, consuming only $800 this year and lending $200 so that he can consume $1250 next year. His consumption stream point is labeled O.

Suppose that Horton's income suddenly and temporarily increases from $1000 to $1500. By "temporarily" we mean that although *this* year's income has increased, *next* year's income is still expected to be $1000. Maybe he has gotten a $500 bonus or won $500 in a sweepstakes.

Horton's endowment point moves $500 to the right, from Y to Y'. His new budget line must pass through this new endowment point. Because there is no change in

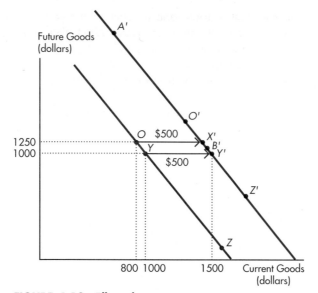

FIGURE 4-10 Effect of a rise in current income.
Horton earns $1000 a year, so his endowment point is at Y. His budget line is shown in black, and his optimum point is at O. Now Horton's current income rises to $1500, while his future income remains fixed at $1000. His new endowment point is Y', and his new budget line is shown in blue. His new optimum must be somewhere on the blue line. We assume that Horton wants to spread out his good fortune, taking some of the benefits now and some in the future. Thus his new optimum contains both more current consumption and more future consumption than his old optimum O; it is at a point northeast of O, like O'. If Horton's original optimum had been at Z, his new optimum would have been at a point northeast of Z, like Z'.

the market interest rate, there is no change in the slope of the budget line. Thus the new budget line must be parallel to the old one, through point Y'. It is shown in blue.

> An increase in current income shifts the endowment point to the right. The budget line shifts rightward parallel to itself until it passes through the new endowment point.

Where is Horton's new optimum point? In principle, it could be anywhere on the blue budget line. However, one plausible assumption suffices to pin down the location a bit more precisely: When people become richer (which is certainly true of Horton) they want more of *everything*—in this case including both current consumption and future consumption. (This is exactly the same assumption we made earlier, when we were discussing the income effect of an interest-rate change.) This rules out a point like A', which contains *less* current consumption than the original optimum point O. It also rules out a point like B', which contains less *future* consumption than O. The only possible new optimum points are points like O', which lie both *to the right* of O and *above* O.

All we are saying here is that when Horton comes by an extra $500, he is unlikely either to spend all of it today or to spend all of it in the future. We expect, instead,

Consumption smoothing:

....

Responding to a change in one period's income by adjusting consumption in all periods, thus avoiding big changes in consumption across periods.

that he will spend *part* of it today and *part* of it next year, spreading his good fortune across his two-period lifetime. Such behavior is called **consumption smoothing.** Rather than taking a bit of good luck all in one lump, Horton smooths it out, taking a little bit now and a little bit later.

Notice that point O' is *less* than $500 to the right of O. You can see this geometrically: A horizontal line from O to point X' (on the new budget line) would have a length equal to $500, and O' is not as far to the right as X' is. You can also see it on simple economic grounds: If Horton uses part of his windfall to increase tomorrow's consumption, then he cannot use all of it to increase today's.

Nothing in this discussion relies on the fact that Horton is a lender. If Horton were a borrower, his original optimum would be at some point below Y on the original budget line (like Z in Figure 4-10). But his new optimum would still lie above and to the right of his old optimum (at a point like Z') on the new budget line.

➡ *Exercise 4-8*

Explain why Horton's new optimum point O' lies less than $500 above point O in Figure 4-10.

A Drop in Current Income

Horton's friend Maisie also starts with an income of $1000 both this year and next year. But Maisie has just gotten bad news. Her current income will not be $1000 after all; it will be only $800. Perhaps this is because an unexpected illness has kept her from work or because she has lost her purse containing $200 (which we count as a loss of income).

Maisie's bad luck, like Horton's good luck, is temporary in the sense that next year's income is unaffected. Maisie's endowment point therefore moves $200 to the left, but its vertical coordinate is unchanged. Figure 4-11 shows Maisie's original endowment point $Y,$ her original budget line in black, her new endowment point Y'', and her new budget line in blue. The new budget line is parallel to the old one because its slope is determined by the interest rate, which has not changed.

A decrease in current income shifts the endowment point to the left. The budget line shifts leftward parallel to itself until it passes through the new endowment point.

Maisie's new optimum point must be somewhere on the blue budget line. To pin down the location, we note that Maisie feels poorer now, so she consumes less of everything in both the present and the future. This means that her new optimum lies both to the left of and below her old optimum $O,$ at a point like $O''.$

Like Horton, Maisie smooths her consumption. Rather than take all of her bad luck in a single lump, she smooths it out, reducing her consumption both this year and next. As a result, her current consumption falls by less than $200.

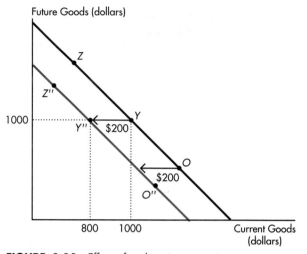

FIGURE 4-11   Effect of a drop in current income.
Maisie earns $1000 per year. Her endowment point is *Y,* her budget line is in black, and her optimum point is *O.* When Maisie's current income falls to $800, her endowment point moves to *Y"* and her budget line is replaced by the blue line. Maisie prefers to swallow her bad fortune in small bites by reducing her consumption both this year and next year. Thus her new optimum is at a point southwest of *O,* like *O".* If her initial optimum had been at *Z,* her new optimum would be at a point southwest of *Z,* like *Z".*

Exercise 4-9
Give a geometric argument to show that *O"* is less than $200 to the left of *O.*

More on Consumption Smoothing

There is strong evidence showing that people prefer to spread out the effects of good and bad luck over their lifetimes. Would you prefer to eat a moderate amount every year or to have some years of feast and some of famine? If you chose the first option, you are a consumption smoother.

The preference for consumption smoothing explains why we tend to think of an event like the Great Depression of the 1930s as a terrible thing. The Depression did decrease most people's total lifetime incomes—but actually, in the context of an entire lifetime, it probably did not decrease them by much. The primary unpleasant aspect of a major depression is not that it lowers people's wealth but that it forces people to have some years of very low consumption relative to that in other years—they cannot smooth their consumption over their lifetimes, as they would prefer to do.

At the time of the Depression, the United States was essentially a closed economy. Its citizens could not borrow from abroad because the Smoot-Hawley tariff (enacted by Congress in March 1930) largely shut down international trade. Hence they could not trade future income for current consumption. If Americans had been able to trade freely with the rest of the world, they might have borrowed to get through the Depression years, thereby spreading the bad effects of the Depression over their lifetimes and thus partly alleviating the pain.

We shall always assume that people smooth their consumption when they are able to. The key consequence of that assumption is this:

> An increase in current income causes an increase in current consumption, but consumption increases by less than income does. A decrease in current income causes a decrease in current consumption, but consumption decreases by less than income does.

Shocks and the Demand Curve

Figure 4-12(*a*) reproduces Horton's old and new budget lines from Figure 4-10. Horton's initial optimum is at *O,* where he consumes $800 this year. Because the interest rate is 25 percent per year, we can plot point *A* in Figure 4-12(*b*), showing that a 25 percent interest rate corresponds to current consumption of $800. By considering budget lines for other interest rates, as we did for Lisa in Figure 4-8, we can find other points of Horton's current demand curve. With several such points, we can draw Horton's initial demand curve *D* in Figure 4-12(*b*).

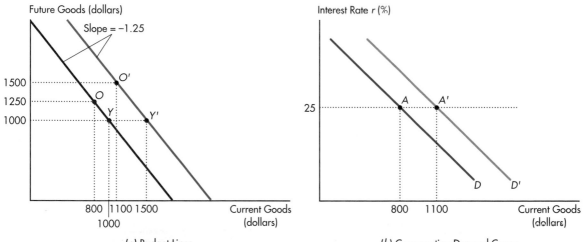

(*a*) Budget Lines

(*b*) Consumption Demand Curve

FIGURE 4-12 An increase in current income.
We assume the interest rate is 25 percent. When Horton's current income and future income are both $1000, he has the income stream *Y* and the black budget line in (*a*). We assume his optimum point is *O,* with $800 in current consumption. This information is recorded in (*b*) by point *A* on his consumption demand curve *D.* When Horton's current income rises to $1500, his new income stream is *Y',* his new budget line is the blue line in (*a*), and his new optimum point is *O'.* Point *A'* on Horton's new demand curve *D'* shows that a 25 percent interest rate corresponds to $1100 in current consumption.

When Horton's current income rises to $1500, his consumption stream point shifts to O' in Figure 4-12(a) and his current consumption rises, say, to $1100. The interest rate is still 25 percent per year. Horton's new current-consumption demand curve must contain a point A' showing that a 25 percent interest rate corresponds to current consumption of $1100. By considering new budget lines for the other two interest rates we chose above, we can find other points on Horton's new demand curve and draw that curve as D' in Figure 4-12(b).

The new current demand curve tells us that, for any fixed interest rate, Horton now consumes more than he would have with his old endowment. Thus every point on his consumption demand curve shifts rightward; in fact, the entire curve shifts rightward. Notice, however, that the rightward shift of the demand curve reflects the increase in Horton's current *consumption,* which is always less than the $500 increase in his current *income* (because of consumption smoothing).

> An increase in current income causes the consumption demand curve to shift rightward. The amount of the shift is less than the increase in income.

➡ *Exercise 4-10*
How does the consumption demand curve shift in response to a *drop* in current income?

Figure 4-12 shows us that *a change in the interest rate or a change in the endowment point can affect consumption behavior.* However, these two types of shocks affect consumption differently:

> A change in the interest rate is reflected by a movement *along* the consumption demand curve (to a new point on the same curve). A change in the endowment point is reflected by a shift *of* the entire consumption demand curve to a new location.

Marginal propensity to consume out of current income (MPC):
The fraction of a dollar increase in current income that an individual chooses to spend in the current period.

Although we have not discussed Horton's demand curve for future consumption, you can infer from Figure 4-12 that it also shifts rightward when Horton's current income increases. Point O' in Figure 4-12(a) lies above point O. Therefore, at any given price for future consumption, the quantity consumed on the new demand curve will exceed that on the initial demand curve.

The Marginal Propensity to Consume out of Current Income

Marginal propensity to save out of current income (MPS):
The fraction of a dollar increase in current income that an individual chooses to save for future consumption.

When current income increases by a dollar, current consumption increases only by some fraction of a dollar because of consumption smoothing. The name for that fraction is the **marginal propensity to consume out of current income** (abbreviated **MPC**). If Jack finds a $10 bill in the street and responds by spending an additional $3 today, then his MPC is 30 percent. Because Jack saves the remaining $7, we say that his **marginal propensity to save out of current income** (**MPS**) is 70 percent.

Because Jack is a consumption smoother, immediately consuming part but not all of any current windfall, his MPC must always lie between zero and 1.

We can also use the MPC to measure the *reduction* in current consumption associated with a decrease in current income. If your MPC is 60 percent and your current income falls by a dollar, then your current spending falls by 60 cents.

⮕ *Exercise 4-11*
If Jill's MPC is .8, how does she respond to finding a $100 bill? How does she respond to losing her wallet, with $50 inside?

Shocks to Future Income

Economics majors and philosophy majors might have equal current incomes, but the economics major who expects to become an investment banker is likely to live more extravagantly than the philosophy major who hopes to find a job washing cars. In other words, consumption smoothing applies to future income as well as to current income. Of two people with the same current income, the one with the higher expected future income will consume more today. That person is already wealthier because future income has a present value. And a wealthier person consumes more of everything—including *current* goods.

Esmerelda earns $1000 a year and has expected that salary to continue in the future. However, today her boss promises her a raise to $1500 next year. As soon as she receives this news, Esmerelda's endowment point moves from *Y* to *Y'* in Figure 4-13(*a*). Her budget line shifts from the black line to the blue line. Because she is now wealthier, she chooses a new optimum point *O'* that is both above and to the right of her old optimum *O;* that is, she increases both her current and her future consumption.

As a result, Esmerelda's demand curve for *current* consumption (as well as her demand curve for future consumption) shifts to the right from *D* to *D'* in Figure 4-13(*b*), just as it would if her *current* income had increased.

If Esmerelda had received bad news instead of good—that she was to be fired next year, for example, and would thus have a future income of $0—then her endowment point would have shifted vertically downward from *Y,* her budget line would have shifted leftward parallel to itself, and her demand curves for both current and future consumption would have shifted to the left.

Marginal propensity to consume out of future income:
The fraction of a dollar increase in future income that an individual chooses to spend in the current period.

We define the **marginal propensity to consume out of future income** as that fraction of additional future income that Esmerelda adds to her current consumption. If a $500 future raise entices Esmerelda to spend an additional $200 immediately, then her marginal propensity to consume out of future income is 200/500 = .4, or 40 percent.

Permanent Income Shocks

Fenster earns $1000 a year every year—or so he thinks. Today, Fenster's boss plans to surprise him with a permanent raise to $1500 a year, starting immediately.

This is much better news than a mere one-time $500 bonus, which would shift Fenster's endowment point $500 to the right. Instead, Fenster's endowment is shifted

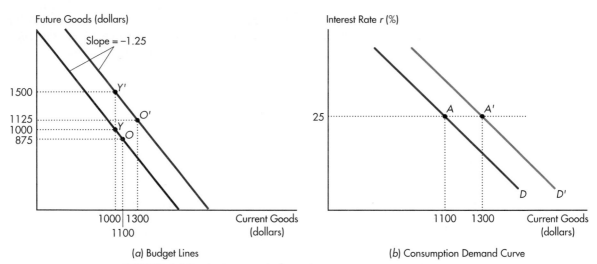

FIGURE 4-13 An increase in future income.
We assume the interest rate is 25 percent. When Esmerelda's current and future incomes are both $1000, she has income stream point Y and the black budget line in (a). We assume her optimum point is O, with $1100 in current consumption. This information is recorded in (b) by point A on Esmerelda's consumption demand curve D. When Esmerelda's future income rises to $1500, her new income stream point is Y', her new budget line is the blue line in (a), and her new optimum point is O'. Point A' on her new demand curve D' shows that a 25 percent interest rate corresponds to $1300 in current consumption.

both $500 to the right *and* $500 upward, because both his current and his future incomes are affected. This is shown in Figure 4-14(a), where Fenster's endowment point shifts from Y to Y' and his budget line shifts from the black line to the blue line. The assumed interest rate is 25 percent per year.

Fenster's initial optimum point is O. Now that he is richer, Fenster wants more consumption both this year and next year, so his consumption point shifts both to the right and upward. How far should we expect it to shift?

Suppose that Fenster wants to spread his good fortune evenly over his lifetime. Because his raise gives him an extra $500 each year, Fenster can afford to spend an additional $500 every year, thereby spreading the benefits perfectly evenly.

To within a reasonable approximation, that is exactly what we expect Fenster to do. A permanent income shock is quite unlike a temporary shock. To spread the benefits of a temporary bonus, you have to spend a portion of it now and a portion of it later. To spread the benefits of a permanent raise, you have to spend the entire raise each year.

Therefore, Fenster's new optimum point O' lies roughly $500 east and $500 north of the old point O. His current consumption and future consumption both rise by about $500.

At any given interest rate, Fenster now wants to consume an additional $500 in the present. This means that his demand curve for current consumption, shown in Figure 4-14(b), shifts rightward by $500, from D to D'.

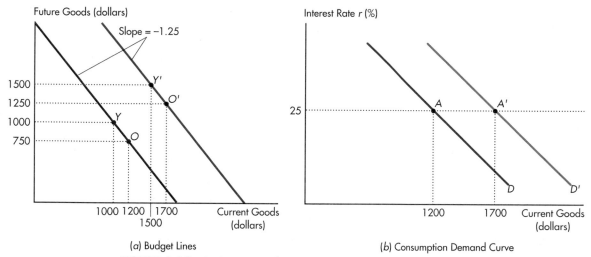

FIGURE 4-14 An increase in future income.
We assume the interest rate is 25 percent. When Fenster's current and future incomes are both $1000, he has income stream point Y and the black budget line in (a). We assume his optimum point is O, with $1200 in current consumption. This information is recorded in (b) by point A on Fenster's consumption demand curve D. When Fenster's current and future incomes both rise to $1500, his new income stream point is Y' and his new budget line is the blue line in (a). In order to spread evenly the benefits of his good fortune, Fenster increases his spending by $1500 a year; therefore, his new optimum point is O'. Point A' on his new demand curve D' shows that a 25 percent interest rate corresponds to $1700 in current consumption.

Fenster's demand curve for future consumption is not shown, but we know that it, too, shifts rightward by $500. At any interest rate, Fenster will consume an additional $500 in the future. For example, at a 25 percent interest rate, Fenster's future consumption will rise a full $500 from $750 to $1250. [You can confirm this in Figure 4-14(a).]

A permanent increase in income causes the demand curves for current and future consumption to shift rightward. They shift by the full amount of the increase in income.

Marginal propensity to consume out of permanent income:
The fraction of a dollar increase in permanent income that an individual chooses to spend in the current period.

A permanent decrease in income causes the demand curves for current and future consumption to shift leftward. They shift by the full amount of the increase in income.

We can define the **marginal propensity to consume out of permanent income** as that fraction of a permanent income increase that is used for consumption. Our expectation about consumption behavior can be restated by saying that *the marginal propensity to consume out of permanent income is approximately 1*.

The Role of Wealth

We have used the term "wealth" several times, more or less as it is used in everyday language. Now we can define a person's **wealth** more specifically as the discounted present value of the person's lifetime income.

Leigh Ann's income is $10 this year and will be $10 next year. She does not expect to live past next year (the future period), and the interest rate is 10 percent. How wealthy is she? Leigh Ann's current income of $10 has a present value of $10. Her future income of $10, discounted at an interest rate of 10 percent, has a present value of $10/1.10. Thus her wealth is

$$\$10 + \frac{\$10}{1.10} \approx \$19.10$$

Notice that to compute Leigh Ann's wealth, you need three pieces of information: her current income y_1, her future income y_2, and the interest rate r. Her wealth W is then given by the formula

$$W = y_1 + \frac{y_2}{1 + r}$$

The people in Figure 4-1 all have two-period endowments consisting of one payment y_1 today and another payment y_2 tomorrow. In Murgatroyd's case, $y_1 = 10$ apples and $y_2 = 15$ apples. If the interest rate is 50 percent, then Murgatroyd's wealth is

$$W = 10 + \frac{15}{1.50} = 20 \text{ apples}$$

➡ *Exercise 4-12*

Using Figure 4-1, at an interest rate of 50 percent, what is Bob's wealth? What is Jed's? What about at an interest rate of 20 percent?

Wealth and the Budget Line

Suppose the market interest rate is 20 percent. Ian's income consists of 3 apples today and 12 apples tomorrow, so his wealth is $3 + \frac{12}{1.2} = 13$ apples. Dave's income consists of 8 apples today and 6 apples tomorrow, so his wealth is $8 + \frac{6}{1.2} = 13$ apples, the same as Ian's. We want to compare Ian's budget line with Dave's.

First, notice that Ian and Dave face the same interest rate, so their budget lines must have the same slope; that slope is -1.20. Ian's budget line must pass through his endowment point I (3, 12), and Dave's budget line must pass through his endowment point D (8, 6). Because Dave and Ian have the same budget line, it turns out that they also have exactly the same wealth, as indicated in Figure 4-15.

There is a good reason for this. Because Ian's income stream has the same present value as Dave's has, either can be traded for the other via borrowing and lending—

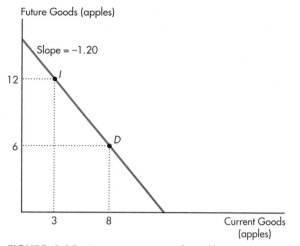

FIGURE 4-15 Income streams and wealth.
Dave's income stream *D* and Ian's income stream *I* both have the same present value. Thus Dave and Ian are equally wealthy. This translates geometrically into the observation that Dave and Ian have the same budget line.

that is exactly what having the same present value *means* for two income streams. And because Dave can trade his income stream *D* for Ian's income stream *I*, it follows that *I* must be one of the points on Dave's budget line. Similarly, *D* must be one of the points on Ian's budget line.

> For a given interest rate, any two individuals with the same wealth face the same budget line, even if their income streams are not identical.

 Suppose that Ian's wealth increases. Is he better off? The answer is not always a rousing yes. *As long as the interest rate is held fixed,* the answer is surely yes. With a fixed interest rate, an increase in wealth must result from a rightward shift of Ian's endowment point and a rightward shift of his budget line. This offers a better set of opportunities, and his new optimum point must be preferable to the old one. However, *when the interest rate is changing, wealth does not measure well being.* For example, a rise in the interest rate can be *good* for net lenders, even when it causes their wealth (measured as the present value of income) to decline. Earlier in this chapter we noted that net lenders "feel richer" (and change their spending habits accordingly) when the interest rate goes up. That is accurate, but a naive calculation of the change in wealth might lead you to the opposite (and wrong) conclusion. (A rise in the interest rate to, say, 50 percent would change Dave's wealth to $8 + 6/1.5 = 12$; if he were a net lender he would feel richer, even though his wealth had

decreased.) The bottom line is that comparisons of wealth are meaningful measures of well-being as long as interest rates are held fixed, but not otherwise.

Only Wealth Matters

Suppose that Karen's endowment consists of 10 apples this year and 10 apples next year and the market interest rate is 50 percent per year. Let us consider three possible scenarios:

1. A 10-apple increase in Karen's current income
2. A 15-apple increase in Karen's future income
3. A 6-apple-per-year increase in both Karen's present income and her future income

Each of the three possible shocks has a present value of 10 apples. (Don't just take our word for this—do the calculation!) That is, each of the three shocks increases Karen's wealth by 10 apples.

Because all three shocks yield the same wealth, all three shocks yield the same new budget line. In Figure 4-16, Karen's initial income stream point Y moves to point X' under the first scenario, to point Z' under the second, and to point Y' under the third. In any case, her new budget line is the blue line in the figure.

Karen's new optimum is her favorite point on the blue line; it is labeled O' in Figure 4-16. This is so *regardless* of which of the three scenarios caused her budget line to shift in the first place. (Actually, point O' could be any point on the blue line; we have arbitrarily drawn it between Y' and Z'.)

However, the following observation is critical: *The location of point* O' *is entirely independent of which scenario caused the budget line to move.* Consequently, Karen's

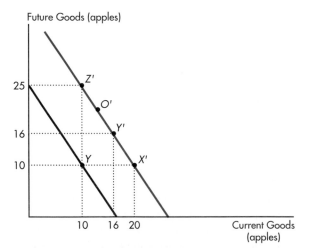

FIGURE 4-16 Shocks and wealth.
Karen could experience different shocks bringing her income stream from point Y to point X', Y', or Z'. All three shocks leave Karen equally wealthy, so they all yield the same budget line and hence all lead Karen to the same optimum point O'.

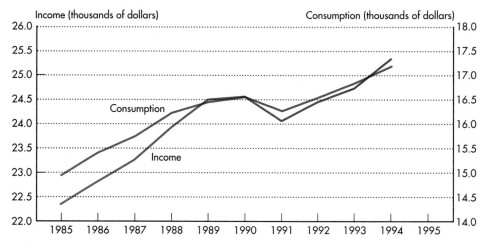

FIGURE 4-17 Income versus consumption.
The graph shows per capita income (measured in constant 1992 dollars on the left-hand axis) and per capita consumption (measured in constant 1992 dollars on the right-hand axis).

current and future consumption levels would be the same under all three scenarios. In slightly different language:

> The effect of an income shock on current consumption depends only on the present value of that shock.

It is irrelevant whether the shock itself occurs entirely in the present, entirely in the future, or partly in each.

Some Evidence on Consumption Smoothing

Figure 4-17 illustrates, in constant 1992 dollars, the income and the consumption expenditure of the average American from 1985 to 1994. Both income and consumption generally rose during the period.

The first thing to notice is that the consumption curve is considerably flatter than the income curve. In most cases, when income rises, consumption also rises—but by less than the rise in income. And when income falls, consumption also falls—but by less than the drop in income.

This is exactly what we would expect from a nation of consumption smoothers. Over the course of a year, the typical individual receives quite a few income shocks, some of them temporary (like an auto accident that causes $500 worth of damage) and some of them permanent (like an unexpected wage cut that reduces expected income for the next several years). According to the theory of consumption smoothing, permanent shocks to income should reduce or increase consumption approximately dollar for dollar, but temporary shocks to income should have a smaller effect on consumption.

From 1990 to 1991, annual per capita income (measured in constant 1992 dollars) fell by $501, from $24,559 to $24,058. Of this $501, part was due to temporary conditions (the economy was in a deep recession, from which it was expected to recover), while the remainder was caused by permanent conditions. Only the permanent component should have had a large impact on consumption; that is why consumption fell by only $283 (from $16,532 to $16,249), and not by the full $501.

There is another way in which Figure 4-17 confirms the theory of consumption smoothing. To see it, first compare the years 1989 and 1992. In 1992, income was lower (by about $50) but consumption was higher (by about $90).

Now note that a 1989 consumer faced a bleaker immediate future than did a 1992 consumer. There was very little income growth from 1989 to 1990, and income actually fell dramatically in 1991. By contrast, a 1992 consumer could look forward to a healthy rise in income by 1993. Insofar as these changes were foreseeable, they would have influenced contemporary consumption choices—leading the 1989 consumer to be frugal in the face of hard times to come and the 1992 consumer to spend a bit more liberally in anticipation of a brighter future.

SUMMARY

In order to focus on consumption decisions, we imagine a world with no taxes and no productive assets. In such a world, the only way to save is to lend.

We consider a simple economic model in which people must choose between consumption today and consumption in the future. Consumption is measured in units of some real good, like apples. Sometimes we measure consumption in "dollars," but it is important to remember that these dollars are only stand-ins for apples or other consumption goods.

To illustrate consumption opportunities, we use a diagram with current consumption on the horizontal axis and future consumption on the vertical. An individual's two-period income stream can be represented by a point in that diagram called the income stream point or endowment point. In this chapter, we do not inquire into the source of that income stream. An income stream point lies on, below, or above the 45° line, depending on whether the individual's income is constant, falling, or rising over time.

The intertemporal budget line illustrates the set of consumption points that the individual can achieve by borrowing or lending. Its slope is $-(1 + r)$, where r is the interest rate. It passes through the individual's endowment point.

The individual chooses his favorite, or optimum, point on the budget line. This determines how much the individual will consume both now and in the future. Any change in consumption plans must result from either a change in preferences or a change in the menu of opportunities (the budget line). We rule out changes in preferences, so any change in consumption plans must come from a change in the budget line. The budget line can change only if either the interest rate or the endowment point changes.

A change in the interest rate causes the budget line to pivot through the endowment point, becoming steeper if the interest rate rises or flatter if the interest rate falls. The individual chooses an optimum point on the new budget line. The location of that new optimum point is governed by the income and substitution effects.

When the interest rate rises, the substitution effect leads everyone to consume less in the present (because current consumption is now more expensive than it was before, with the price measured in terms of forgone future consumption). The income effect leads borrowers to consume less in the present (because they feel poorer) and lenders to consume more in the present (because they feel richer). The representative agent, who is neither a borrower nor a lender, feels no income effect and therefore certainly consumes less in the present.

All of the above effects work in reverse when the interest rate falls.

An individual's current (or future) consumption demand curve shows how much current (or future) consumption he demands at each possible interest rate r. The representative agent's consumption demand curve must slope downward to the right. The aggregate consumption demand curve can be derived by multiplying the size of the population by the consumption quantities on the representative agent's consumption demand curve. It follows that the aggregate demand curve for current consumption slopes downward. The same is true of the aggregate demand curve for future consumption, which has $1/(1 + r)$, rather than r, on the vertical axis.

When an individual's income changes, the endowment point shifts and the budget line shifts parallel to itself. The individual picks a new optimum point on the new budget line. If the budget line shifts rightward, the individual feels richer and consumes more in both the present and the future.

We assume that people engage in consumption smoothing, trying to spread good and bad luck evenly over their lifetimes. This means that a temporary change in income leads to smaller changes in current and future consumption. However, a permanent change in income leads to changes in current and future consumption that are about as large as the income change.

A change in the interest rate causes a movement *along* the consumption demand curve, while a change in the endowment point causes a shift *of* the consumption demand curve.

An individual's wealth is the present value of his income stream. For a fixed interest rate, two income shocks leading to the same wealth both lead to the same budget line, hence to the same optimum point, and hence to the same levels of current and future consumption.

PROBLEM SET

1. *True or false:* A person can never consume more than his income.
2. *True or false:* A person whose consumption stream is increasing over time must have an income stream that is increasing over time.
3. Humbert's income is $10 this year and will be $0 next year. Lolita's income is $0 this year and will be $15 next year.
    a. Draw Humbert's and Lolita's budget lines for an interest rate of 10 percent per year.
    b. Repeat part **a** for an interest rate of 75 percent per year.
4. Dooney is a net lender. His savings account has been paying 12 percent per year, but the bank has just announced that the interest rate is being increased to 15 percent.
    a. Draw Dooney's original budget line, his income stream point, and his optimum point.
    b. Draw Dooney's new budget line, after the bank's announcement.
    c. Indicate the portion of the new budget line on which Dooney's new optimum might

lie. Does it include portions to the left of the old optimum? To the right? Above? Below? Explain your reasoning in terms of the income and substitution effects.

    d. Suppose you know that, for Dooney, the substitution effect of an interest-rate change is bigger than the income effect. Can you further limit the portion of the new budget line on which Dooney's new optimum point could lie? Do so.

5. Repeat problem 4, assuming that Dooney's bank announces not an increase in the interest rate from 12 to 15 percent but a decrease from 12 to 8 percent.

6. In problem 5, when the interest rate falls to 8 percent, might Dooney decide to become a net borrower if, for him:

    a. The substitution effect is greater than the income effect?

    b. The income effect is greater than the substitution effect?

7. Jocko is the representative agent in an economy in which the going interest rate is 12 percent. One day the interest rate falls to 8 percent.

    a. Draw Jocko's original budget line, his endowment point, and his optimum point.

    b. Draw Jocko's new budget line, after the change in the interest rate.

    c. Indicate the portion of the new budget line on which Jocko's new optimum might lie. Does it include portions to the left of the old optimum? To the right? Above? Below? Explain your reasoning in terms of the income and substitution effects.

    d. Give an alternative argument for your conclusion in part **c,** using geometric reasoning rather than the income and substitution effects.

    e. Following the change in the interest rate, does Jocko become a net borrower or a net lender? Is he still the representative agent?

8. Suppose that you have an income of $10 in your youth and $0 in your old age. The market interest rate is 10 percent per stage of life; that is, $1 saved in youth returns $1.10 in old age.

    a. Draw your intertemporal budget line.

    b. Suppose that the government imposes a 100 percent "consumption tax"; at each stage of life you must pay the government an amount equal to the amount you consume. Draw your new intertemporal budget line.

    c. Now suppose that, instead, the government imposes an income tax of 50 percent on all income earned in your youth. Draw your new intertemporal budget line.

    d. Now suppose that, instead, the government imposes an income tax of 50 percent on all income earned in your youth *and* on all interest income earned in your old age. Draw your new intertemporal budget line.

    e. If the government is trying to decide between a consumption tax and an income tax that does *not* include interest income, explain why you don't care which is selected.

    f. Suppose that in your youth the government imposes an income tax and in your old age it decides to switch to a consumption tax. Does it follow from part **e** that you are indifferent to this switch?

9. *True or false:* Lenders gain at the expense of borrowers because they get the interest payments.

10. *True or false:* A rise in the interest rate is a bad thing because it makes borrowing more expensive.

11. *True or false:* A net lender always benefits from a rise in the interest rate.

12. *True or false:* When the interest rate rises, net lenders are sure to remain net lenders but net borrowers might not remain net borrowers.

13. *True or false:* If the interest rate rises, savers can afford to save less and still increase their future consumption. Therefore, economywide saving might go down.

14. When the interest rate rises from 10 to 25 percent, Beany switches from net borrowing to net lending. *True or false:* Beany is certainly better off as a result of the interest-rate change.

15. *True or false:* A person who neither lends nor borrows cannot be made worse off by a change in the interest rate.

16. Suppose the going market interest rate is 10 percent. This is the rate at which you can lend. However, because of your bad credit history, you are able to borrow only if you pay 20 percent. Your income stream consists of $1000 each year.

    a. Carefully draw your intertemporal budget line. (*Hint:* It is *not* a straight line.)

    b. Suppose you choose to consume $1100 this year. Assume that the market interest rate at which you can lend rises from 10 to 15 percent, though you can still borrow only at 20 percent. Draw your new intertemporal budget line. What points on the new budget line might you prefer?

    c. Suppose now that the market interest rate remains 10 percent and that you acquire a cosigner to guarantee your loans, so lenders are willing to lend to you at 10 percent as well. Draw your new budget line. What points on the new budget line might you prefer?

17. Your employer offers you a choice between a salary increase of $1 per month, beginning at the end of this month, and an annual bonus of $12, beginning 1 year from today. *True or false:* If you expect to spend a lot of money at the end of the year, then you should take the bonus; but if you want to smooth your consumption, then you should take the raise.

18. Describe how and why your demand curve for current consumption shifts in each of the following circumstances:

    a. You find a $10 bill in the street.

    b. You lose your wallet containing $100.

    c. You learn that your grandfather is planning to leave you a large inheritance.

    d. Your college announces a large tuition hike that will take effect next year.

    e. Your roommate agrees to pay a larger share of the rent if you clean the refrigerator every month.

    f. Your roommate agrees to pay you $20 to clean the refrigerator one time.

    g. Your parents disown you and stop paying your weekly $100 allowance.

19. Your boss announces she is going to give you a $1000 bonus 1 year from today. Immediately after you get the good news, a gorilla throws an exploding banana through your window and does $800 worth of damage.

    a. Suppose the interest rate is 5 percent per year. What happens to your demand for current consumption?

    b. Suppose the interest rate is 50 percent. What happens to your demand for current consumption?

    c. Suppose the interest rate is 25 percent. What happens to your demand for current consumption?

20. Suppose Dino's marginal propensity to consume out of current income is 80 percent and his income is $10,000.

    a. *True or false:* We can conclude that Dino consumes $8000 and lends the rest.

    b. *True or false:* We can conclude that if Dino loses $1, his consumption falls by 80 cents.

21. Suppose Beanstalk's marginal propensity to consume out of current income is 30 percent and he faces an interest rate of 10 percent.

    a. Describe in detail what happens to Beanstalk's demand curve for current consumption when his current income increases by $1.

    b. Describe in detail what happens to Beanstalk's demand curve for *future* consumption when his current income increases by $1.

22. At an annual interest rate of 10 percent per year, what is the wealth of someone who will make $20,000 per year for 3 years?

23. Calculate your wealth, assuming that the interest rate is 10 percent and that you will make $30,000 per year for 40 years. (You might want to write a computer program to do this.) What salary would you have to expect for 40 years to be worth $1 million today?

24. Fredonia is an open economy in which the aggregate demand curve for current consumption slopes upward to the right. On average, are the residents of Fredonia net lenders or net borrowers?

25. *True or false:* In an open economy, it is possible that the demand curves for current and future consumption *both* slope upward.

Chapter 5

Interest Rates

and Equilibrium

The modern world is a complicated place. To completely model the U.S. economy, we would need to account for the productivity of agriculture and industry, medicine and banking, entertainment and education, and many other activities. We would need to think about what determines how resources are allocated among all these activities and what determines which resources are simply consumed immediately. We would need to discuss how individuals allocate their time between labor and leisure and how that allocation is affected by wage rates, working conditions, and investment opportunities. We would need to completely understand the market for money, the role of government, and the workings of international finance.

It would be absurdly difficult to learn about every aspect of the U.S. economy at once. Instead, we shall continue as in Chapter 4, studying a much simpler economy—a fictional world in which there is no productive activity, no government, no money, and no uncertainty about the future.

The world we describe in this chapter is so simple that it can be understood completely. In later chapters, we shall add complications one by one. Soon, our fictional world—our model—will become similar enough to the world we inhabit that we can use it to illustrate and understand the issues and controversies of real-world macroeconomics.

This learning strategy would be very frustrating if each new complication forced us to unlearn everything that had gone before. Fortunately, that is not the case. While the simple model of this chapter can address only a few issues, the things you learn about those issues will remain valid and useful in understanding *any* model; and, more importantly, they will remain valid and useful in understanding the real world.

The simple model of this chapter allows us to address a single fundamental question: What determines interest rates? In previous chapters, we discussed at length how people respond to a *given* interest rate, but we did not ask why the interest rate should have one value rather than another.

In Sections 5-1 through 5-3, we discuss interest rates in a closed economy—an economy whose citizens trade only with each other. The most obvious example of a closed economy is the economy of the entire world. Until we discover extraterrestrial life, we earthlings can trade only with others of our species.

The closed-economy model can be used to approximate the economy of a large country like the United States, which sells over 90 percent of its output domestically. In Section 5-4, we examine some recent U.S. history in light of the model's predictions.

Nevertheless, there are two reasons for expanding our model to include open economies—economies whose citizens trade with outsiders. First, many smaller countries trade so extensively with other countries that their economies cannot be approximated by closed-economy models. Second, we sometimes want to ask and answer questions that specifically involve foreign trade—and we can't ask these questions unless our model admits that foreign trade exists. Therefore, in Section 5-5 we extend the model so that it applies to open economies. This allows us to use the model to make predictions about trade deficits and trade surpluses.

5-1 THE ENDOWMENT ECONOMY

Our model begins with the simplest fictional world in which it is possible to discuss interest rates. It is a world in which there is no productive activity. People's income is derived entirely from endowments, as it was in Chapter 4; that is, consumption goods simply arrive on people's doorsteps, free of charge and without any effort on their part.

To fix ideas, it is useful to continue imagining a world in which the only good is apples. People own apple trees, and apples fall from the trees. The apples that fall from your apple trees constitute your income. The total of all the apples that fall from everyone's trees constitutes both the total *income* and the total *output* of the entire economy.

In the real world, there are many ways to increase the apple crop. One is to plant more trees. Another is to acquire a ladder and devote some effort to apple picking. For the time being, we shall assume that no such activities are possible. Neither productive investments nor labor input can increase the apple yield.

Another opportunity that the real world offers is *storage*. When Joseph told the Egyptian pharaoh that his dreams predicted 7 years of good harvests followed by 7 years of famine, the pharaoh was able to store grain from the good years to carry Egypt through the hard times to come. This option is also excluded from our model world. We assume that apples must be eaten as they arrive; unless they are eaten, they rot.

In short, we assume a world with *no production, no labor, and no storage.* Such a world is called an **endowment economy.**

> **Endowment economy:**
>
> An economy in which there is no production, no labor, and no storage and in which individuals are endowed with a given quantity of income each period.

Supply

> **Supply:**
>
> The quantity of goods an individual provides to himself and others in a given period of time, expressed as a function of the interest rate.

Each resident of our endowment economy has a current income, consisting of apples that fall from his trees this year (or, more generally, this period), and a future income, consisting of apples that fall from his trees next year (or, more generally, next period). We assume that these incomes are perfectly foreseeable. As we saw in Chapter 4, they can be represented by a single endowment point. Consider, for example, Eve, who receives five apples today and will receive seven tomorrow. Eve's endowment point is labeled Y in Figure 5-1(*a*).

What can Eve do with her five current apples (her **supply**)? In the simple economy we've described, she has only two choices: One is to eat them, and the other is

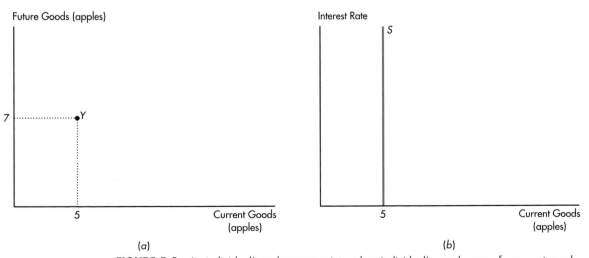

FIGURE 5-1 An individual's endowment point and an individual's supply curve for current goods. (a) Eve's endowment consists of 5 apples this year and 7 next year, as illustrated by point Y. (b) She supplies 5 current apples to the economy, so her supply curve for current consumption is vertical at 5 apples.

to lend them to somebody else who wants to eat them. If she eats them, we think of Eve as a supplier of apples to herself; if she lends them, we think of her as a supplier of apples to others. Of course, Eve might supply some apples to herself and some to others, say, by eating three and lending two. But no matter what she does, she always supplies a total of exactly five apples to the entire economy (which includes herself).

Supply curve:
A curve illustrating the quantity supplied at every interest rate.

Aggregate supply:
The quantity of goods that all individuals in an economy provide in a given period of time, expressed as a function of the interest rate.

Figure 5-1(*b*) depicts Eve's **supply curve** *for current apples.* Regardless of the interest rate r, she supplies five current apples. Therefore, her supply curve is a vertical line at the quantity 5.

If Eve's neighbor Adam has nine current apples in his endowment, then Adam's supply curve is a vertical line at the quantity 9. The **aggregate supply** of current apples is the sum of all the apples that everyone supplies. If Eve supplies five apples and Adam supplies nine, and if Adam and Eve are the only people in the economy, then the aggregate supply curve is a vertical line at the quantity 14, as shown in Figure 5-2.

The Market Demand for Current Consumption

What if Eve wants to eat more than five apples today? She has no way to produce additional apples, but she still has a way to acquire them: she can borrow apples at the going interest rate. Alternatively, suppose that Eve wants to increase her *future* consumption above seven apples. Although she cannot produce additional apples or store apples for the future, she can still raise her future consumption by lending apples now. As we saw in Chapter 4, borrowing and lending enable Eve to reach any point along her budget line.

We know from our analysis in Chapter 4 that Eve chooses to consume at the optimum point on her budget line. We also know that when the interest rate changes,

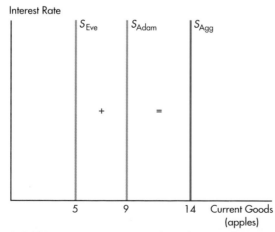

FIGURE 5-2 Aggregate supply is the sum of individual supplies. Eve supplies 5 current apples, and Adam supplies 9. If Eve and Adam are the only members of the economy, then the aggregate supply of apples is 14.

Eve's budget line rotates and she then chooses a new optimum point. In Chapter 4, we saw how we can use this observation to construct Eve's demand curve for current consumption.

Eve's neighbor Adam might differ from Eve in either or both of two ways. First, he might have a different endowment point; and second, he might have different preferences for current and future consumption. (Conceivably he differs in other ways as well, but unless they affect the demand for apples, those differences do not concern us here.) Consequently, Adam's demand curve for current apples might be quite different from Eve's. Figure 5-3 displays both Adam's and Eve's demand curves for current consumption.

Suppose again that Eve and Adam are the only people in the economy. Then the **aggregate demand curve** for current goods in that economy is the sum of their individual demand curves. To determine a point on the aggregate demand curve, we first choose an interest rate, say, 10 percent. At that interest rate, Figure 5-3 reveals that Eve demands 4 current apples and Adam demands 10. The total is 14. Thus a 10 percent interest rate corresponds to 14 apples demanded on the aggregate demand curve D_{Agg}, as shown by point A in Figure 5-3.

Additional points are determined similarly: At a 5 percent interest rate, Eve demands 11 apples and Adam demands 12. The total quantity demanded is 23, and this yields point B in Figure 5-3. At a 15 percent interest rate, Eve demands 3 apples and Adam demands 6, for a total of 9 apples demanded; this yields point C. A curve drawn through these points yields the aggregate demand curve D_{Agg}.

In similar fashion, we can construct an aggregate demand curve that combines the demand curves of any number of consumers. If Adam and Eve acquire a new neighbor, Mr. Sibilant, there will be three individual demand curves that sum to the aggregate curve.

Aggregate demand curve:

A curve that illustrates the quantity of goods that all members of an economy want to consume as a function of the interest rate.

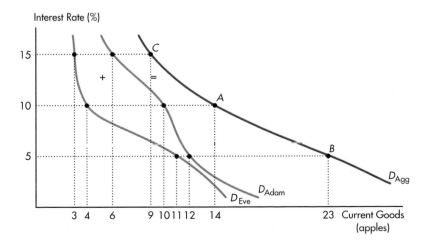

FIGURE 5-3 Aggregate demand.
Eve's demand curve D_{Eve} is derived from her preferences, as in Chapter 4. Adam's demand curve D_{Adam} is derived similarly. To get the aggregate demand curve D_{Agg}, we add Eve's and Adam's quantities of current consumption at each interest rate.

We will often be interested in the marketwide demand curve for current consumption, sometimes called simply the *aggregate demand curve*. We can construct it by adding the demand curves of everybody in the economy, just as we did for a two-person economy in Figure 5-3.

5-2   EQUILIBRIUM IN THE ENDOWMENT ECONOMY

Equilibrium point:

The point where the aggregate demand and supply curves intersect.

Figure 5-4 shows the aggregate supply and aggregate demand curves for the endowment economy. Recall that the aggregate supply curve displays the quantity of apples actually available, that this quantity does not vary with the interest rate, and consequently that the aggregate supply curve is vertical. The aggregate demand curve displays the total number of apples that individuals want to consume this year at each interest rate. In general, people want more current consumption when the interest rate is low and less when it is high. Hence the aggregate demand curve slopes downward.

Equilibrium interest rate:

The interest rate at which the quantities supplied and demanded are equal.

The point at which the two curves intersect is called the **equilibrium point** and is labeled *E* in Figure 5-4. The corresponding interest rate, in this case 10 percent, is called the **equilibrium interest rate,** and the corresponding quantity (in this case, 14) is called the **equilibrium quantity.**

There are good reasons to believe that the equilibrium interest rate is the one that actually prevails in the economy. We shall now explore those reasons.

Getting to Equilibrium: Market Forces

Equilibrium quantity:

The quantity of goods supplied (and demanded) at the equilibrium interest rate.

Suppose for the moment that the interest rate is 15 percent. Each individual in the economy, taking account of that interest rate, decides how many apples to consume

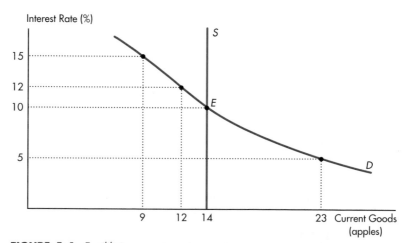

FIGURE 5-4 Equilibrium.
When aggregate demand *D* and aggregate supply *S* are plotted on the same graph, their intersection point *E* indicates the equilibrium interest rate and consumption quantity.

this year. The demand curve in Figure 5-4 reveals that the sum of those quantities is 9 apples. But the supply curve shows that a total of 14 apples is actually available. Hence, people are holding 5 more apples than they want to eat this year. What becomes of that **excess supply** of apples?

Excess supply:
The amount by which the quantity of goods supplied exceeds the quantity demanded, at a given interest rate; occurs when the interest rate is above the equilibrium interest rate.

The answer is that the people holding them attempt to *lend* those excess apples. They don't want to eat them this year (at least, not if they can be lent out at 15 percent), and they certainly don't want to leave them on the ground to rot. Instead, they turn to their neighbors and say, "Would you like to borrow an apple?"

Unfortunately, the neighbors are also likely to be holding excess apples and probably reply "What a coincidence! I was just hoping that *you* might want to borrow an apple." With everybody simultaneously trying to lend, and nobody willing to borrow, it will not be long before some lender hits on the strategy of offering a lower interest rate in an attempt to attract a borrower. Consequently:

When the interest rate starts out above equilibrium, it has a tendency to fall until the equilibrium point is reached.

Suppose that it falls to 12 percent. Now people collectively are willing to consume 12 apples, which is still fewer than the 14 that are available. There are still frustrated would-be lenders who are prepared to bid the interest rate down even further to induce the neighbors to borrow.

Market clearing:
The condition under which borrowers can find lenders for all the goods they wish to borrow and lenders can find borrowers for all the goods they wish to lend. The market clears when the quantity demanded is equal to the quantity supplied—that is, when the market is in equilibrium.

This process continues until the interest rate falls to 10 percent. At that rate, the equilibrium interest rate, the number of apples that people want to consume immediately, is exactly equal to the number that are immediately available. Every lender finds a borrower, and there is no reason for the interest rate to fall any further.

We say that the equilibrium interest rate of 10 percent *clears the market;* that is, it enables every lender to find a borrower and every borrower to find a lender. Under **market clearing,** people want to eat exactly the number of apples that are available; there is neither a shortage nor a surplus of consumption goods. We sometimes express this condition by saying that the market is *in equilibrium.*

What happens when the interest rate starts out *below* equilibrium? Suppose, for example, that the interest rate is 5 percent. At that rate, the total quantity of apples demanded is 23. Unfortunately, 23 apples is 9 more than the 14 that are available. There is an **excess demand** for apples.

Excess demand:
The amount by which the quantity of goods demanded exceeds the quantity supplied, at a given interest rate; occurs when the interest rate is below the equilibrium interest rate.

Now there are unsatisfied demanders, who are unable to obtain as many apples as they would like. These demanders attempt to borrow from their neighbors, and in the process they bid up the current interest rate. The process continues until the equilibrium interest rate is achieved.

When the interest rate starts out below equilibrium, it has a tendency to rise until the equilibrium point is reached.

In this section, we have described what *would* happen if the market interest rate were different from the market-clearing equilibrium rate. We concluded that market forces would quickly push the interest rate in the direction of equilibrium. Because our conclusion indicates that the market cannot remain out of equilibrium for any appreciable length of time, we will assume (at least for the next several chapters) that *the market is always in equilibrium.* Hence only the equilibrium interest rate need concern us.

The Market for Future Consumption

We have seen that the interest rate is determined by equilibrium in the market for current consumption. In this subsection, you will see that the interest rate is simultaneously determined in the market for *future* consumption and that the rates determined in both markets must agree.

Consider again Eve, whose endowment point is shown in Figure 5-1(*a*). Eve is endowed with five apples this year, from which we inferred that her *current-apple supply curve* is vertical at the quantity 5. Because Eve is endowed with seven apples next year, we can similarly infer that her *future-apple supply curve* is vertical at the quantity 7. Eve will have seven apples next year, and she must supply them all to the economy. She supplies exactly seven apples regardless of the interest rate, which is why her supply curve must be vertical.

Before we actually draw Eve's supply curve for future apples, we must give a moment's thought to what belongs on the vertical axis. Recall from Chapter 3 that the price of a future apple is $1/(1 + r)$ current apples, where r is the interest rate. A supply curve must display the price on the vertical axis, so the appropriate vertical axis measures $1/(1 + r)$.

Figure 5-5 shows Eve's supply curve for future apples, as well as Adam's and the aggregate supply curve. Because Eve is endowed with 7 future apples, her sup-

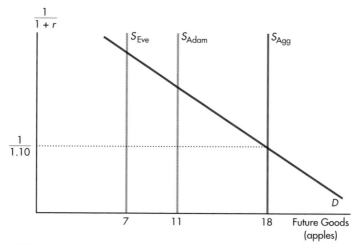

FIGURE 5-5   The market for future goods.
The aggregate supply S_{Agg} of future goods is derived by adding Adam's supply curve S_{Adam} to Eve's supply curve S_{Eve}. D is the aggregate demand curve.

ply curve is vertical at the quantity 7. We assume that Adam is endowed with 11 future apples, so his supply curve is vertical at the quantity 11. Because Eve and Adam are the only two people in their economy, the aggregate supply curve is vertical at the quantity 18.

The same graph shows the aggregate demand curve D for future apples, constructed by adding together everyone's (meaning Eve's and Adam's) individual demand curves. The demand and supply curves intersect at a price of $1/1.10$. That is the price that clears the market for future apples; because that price corresponds to an interest rate of 10 percent, the equilibrium interest rate for the economy is 10 percent.

We now have two ways to determine the equilibrium interest rate: We can obtain it from either the market for current goods, as in Figure 5-4, or the market for future goods, as in Figure 5-5. Both methods are correct and therefore must lead to the same outcome.

Figure 5-6 shows the supply and demand curves for another endowment economy, where the equilibrium interest rate is 7 percent per year. The market for current goods [illustrated in part (*a*)] clears at an interest rate of 7 percent, and the market for future goods [illustrated in part (*b*)] clears at the price of $1/1.07$ current goods per future good (which corresponds to an interest rate of 7 percent).

The point to be drawn from Figure 5-6 is that as soon as we observe the equilibrium rate of 7 percent in part (*a*), we know that the market-clearing price must be $1/1.07$ in part (*b*); alternatively, as soon as we observe the market-clearing price in part (*b*), we know what the equilibrium rate in part (*a*) must be.

Recall that the market for future goods is the same thing as the market for bonds. Therefore:

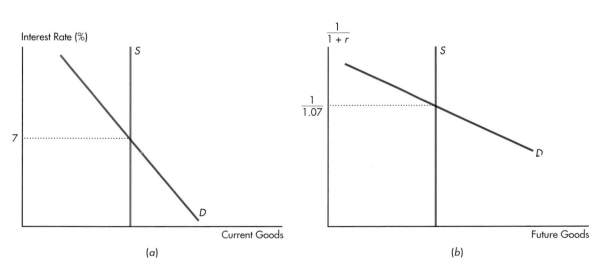

FIGURE 5-6 The relation between the markets for current and future goods. (*a*) The market for current goods in a certain economy. (*b*) The market for future goods in the same economy. Equilibria in the two markets lead to the same 7 percent interest rate.

The same interest rate that clears the current-goods market simultaneously clears the bond market.

Here is another way to think about this result: If there is an excess supply of current goods, the situation exists because people are trying to trade goods for bonds to a greater extent than is physically possible. Such a situation can equally well be described as an excess supply of current goods or an excess demand for bonds. Thus disequilibrium in one market implies disequilibrium in the other. By the same token, equilibrium in one market implies equilibrium in the other; that is why a single relative price is able to clear both markets.

Exercise 5-1

Suppose the interest rate is too low to clear the current-goods market. Explain why there must necessarily be an excess supply of future goods (or of bonds).

Walras's Law

The story above has a moral that applies to all economies (not just the simple endowment economy of this chapter): Any excess supply (or excess demand) in one market must be matched by an equivalent excess demand (or excess supply) in another. It is not possible for all markets but one to clear. This remarkable relationship among markets is called *Walras's Law* after economist Léon Walras.[1] According to Walras's Law, *whenever all markets but one have cleared, the remaining market must clear also.* A corollary is that in an economy with n markets, only $n - 1$ relative prices are necessary to clear them all. Our endowment economy has two markets (current goods and future goods) and therefore needs only one relative price (the interest rate). An economy with three markets would need two relative prices, an economy with four markets would need three, and so on.

5-3 COMPARATIVE STATICS

The economic environment changes continuously. Current output moves up or down for random reasons like changes in the weather. Expected future output increases or decreases because of new information about the state of technology or population growth. Wars are fought; epidemics break out; and government policies change. In this section, we will analyze how such changes affect the market equilibrium. Economists refer to such problems as exercises in **comparative statics.**

Remember always that the market equilibrium is determined by the intersection of the supply and demand curves for current goods (or equivalently by the intersection of the supply and demand curves for future goods). In the endowment economy we are studying, an event can change the equilibrium only by causing one or both of these curves to shift. Therefore, when you are confronted with a question like "How

Comparative statics:

The analysis of how exogenous changes in the environment affect the equilibrium point and thus the endogenous variables.

[1] Pronounced "val·rah′." He developed this law around 1874.

does a temporary improvement in the weather affect the interest rate?" you should always begin your analysis by asking separately "How does the demand curve respond?" and "How does the supply curve respond?" Only after you've answered these preliminary questions can you put the answers together in a graph to see what happens to the interest rate.

In every case, if you think carefully about supply and demand, your graph will reveal how the interest rate changes. It can also be instructive to think about the underlying story, imagining the adjustment process that causes the changes. The examples that follow illustrate both the graphical technique and the underlying stories.

An Increase in Future Income

Suppose we learn now that next year's weather is going to improve, perhaps because of changes in cloud formations or because of better technology controlling auto emissions or smog. Or suppose we discover something that will enable us to improve our future lives: a new type of air bag that will contribute to a longer average life span, or an idea for a new machine that will make it possible to produce more with the same amount of effort. Or suppose the populace elects a new president or a new Congress whose policies are expected to make us more productive. Each of these advances results in an increase in our expected *future* output—in the form of more agricultural products, longer productive lives, or greater per capita production—and thus in our expected future incomes.

The scenarios in the preceding paragraph concern the real world, but they have an analogy in the model world we have developed: Something happens to convince us that tomorrow's apple crop will be larger than what we had been expecting.

We begin by asking what happens to the *supply* of current apples. The answer is that nothing happens. News about the future has no effect on the number of apples that are physically available for consumption today.

Next we ask what happens to the *demand* for current apples. To answer, recall the concept of consumption smoothing from Chapter 4: Individuals respond to an expected increase in future income by increasing their demand for *current* consumption. That strategy allows them to spread the effects of the future windfall throughout their lives instead of taking it in one lump when the future arrives. Another way to say the same thing is that future income is part of wealth, and when people become wealthier, they want to consume more immediately.

Now we record these effects in a graph—Figure 5-7(*a*). There is no change in the supply curve. But the demand curve shifts to the right, from *D* to *D′*, reflecting the increase in the economy's aggregate demand for current consumption. The graph reveals that the equilibrium interest rate increases from *r* to *r′*.

Taking Stock

Let us be very clear about what went into this analysis. When we think about the *supply* of current goods, we think about the physical goods that are *actually available*. When we think about the *demand* for current goods, we think about the quantity of goods that people actually *want* to consume. The supply curve can shift only

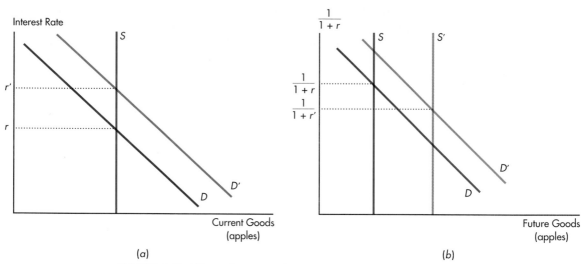

FIGURE 5-7 Effects of a rise in future income.
(a) The current-goods market: There is no change in the *supply* of current goods, but the demand for current goods increases because people are now wealthier; they want to consume more now in order to smooth their consumption. The result is a higher equilibrium interest rate r'. (b) The future-goods market: The supply of future goods increases; the demand for future goods increases but by less than the increase in supply, again because of consumption smoothing. The result is a decrease in price, to $1/(1 + r')$, and thus an increase in the equilibrium interest rate to r'.

in response to changes in what is available for immediate consumption; in this particular example, there is no supply change. The demand curve shifts in response to changes in how much people want to consume, which can result from changes in *wealth*. In this example, people have become wealthier, so the demand curve shifts.

Another Way to Do It

Figure 5-7(*b*) shows an alternative path to the same conclusion. Instead of thinking about the market for *current* apples, we can examine the market for *future* apples. Once again, we think separately about supply and about demand.

What happens to the supply of future apples? The answer is that it increases, by the amount of the future windfall. Thus, in Figure 5-7(*b*), the supply curve shifts to the right, from S to S'.

What happens to the demand for future apples? The future windfall makes people wealthier, so they want to increase their consumption of apples both in the present and in the future. Since people want to increase their future consumption, the demand curve shifts to the right, from D to D'.

What happens to the equilibrium point? When the supply and demand curves both shift to the right, the equilibrium price can either rise or fall. To determine which direction it moves in this case, we need one additional piece of information.

Once again, the key is to think about consumption smoothing. People want to spread the benefits of the future windfall over their lives, taking some of their gain now and some tomorrow. This means that their demand for future apples must increase by *less* than the amount of the windfall. If you know that you will receive a $100 gift tomorrow, and you respond by spending part of that $100 today, then you must increase your spending by *less* than $100 tomorrow.

The upshot is that in Figure 5-7(*b*), *the demand curve shifts rightward less than the supply curve does.* So we can conclude unambiguously that the equilibrium price moves down.

To reach a conclusion about the interest rate, we must recall that the price of future apples is measured by $1/(1 + r)$. Since $1/(1 + r)$ falls, it follows as a matter of arithmetic that r must rise. Indeed, the graph shows that the interest rate increases from r to r', just as in Figure 5-7(*a*).

The two parts of Figure 5-7 must both lead to exactly the same conclusion— that is, they must both lead us to exactly the same value of r'—because each represents a correct method of attacking the problem. In the examples that follow, we shall usually work the problem in just one way. But you can always check your work by analyzing the same problem in both ways, once via the current-goods market and once via the future-goods market, and then making sure that your results agree.

The Adjustment Process

We began with the question "What happens when there is an increase in future income?" Figure 5-7 reveals the answer: the interest rate goes up. In one sense our job is now complete. But it is also instructive to give some thought to the mechanism that drives the interest rate up.

Imagine life in the model economy. Initially, the market is in equilibrium, with everyone having chosen an optimum point and satisfied with his consumption plans. One day, we learn that our future incomes have increased. We all respond to this news by thinking, "Now that I am richer, I think I will start eating more apples immediately." But we *have* no more apples; the windfall does not take place until next year. Where can we go to get more apples this year? The only possibility is to borrow them. So we all simultaneously turn to our neighbors and ask to borrow an apple. As it happens, the neighbor to whom you turn is in no mood to accommodate you; she's trying to borrow apples herself. As everyone tries to borrow more, and nobody finds a willing lender, the interest rate must be bid up.

Ultimately, the number of apples eaten this year cannot increase—because the number of apples in the world does not increase. When everybody gets the idea to eat more apples, the interest rate must rise by enough to talk them out of it.

It might be tempting to use the reasoning in the above paragraph as a shortcut to the answer without relying on the graphs in Figure 5-7. As soon as we noticed that people wanted to smooth their consumption by borrowing against their future incomes, we could have predicted that at the old rate of interest there would be excess demand to borrow. Since we know already that excess demand to borrow results in a rise in the interest rate, we can immediately predict that the market rate of interest rises when expected future income increases. That is certainly right.

But drawing a graph allows us to do two additional things. First, it organizes our approach to the problem, something that will matter a great deal when we want to analyze more complicated situations. Verbal stories tend to become convoluted and can easily lead us astray unless we keep track of everything. And graphs do just that: they keep track of everything—not just the things our story happens to bring out. Second, if we know the shapes of the supply and demand curves, a graph allows us to work out the *size* of the change: it tells us just how *far* the interest rate must rise.

In summary, the graph reveals the answer to the comparative-statics question. After you know the answer, it can be instructive to think about the underlying story— the process that leads to the new equilibrium. But it is always a good idea to draw a graph.

An Increase in Current Income

Imagine a year with an unusually good harvest, a year in which very few people become ill with the flu, or a year with no snowstorms, earthquakes, or tropical storms. In such years, current output increases, and thus so does current income. How does the interest rate respond?

We begin by translating the problem into terms that our model can deal with. In the model world, an increase in current output corresponds to an increase in this year's apple harvest, or a shift of the endowment point to the right.

First, we ask what happens to the supply of current goods. The supply shifts to the right *by exactly the amount of the windfall,* from S to S″ in Figure 5-8. Recall that the current supply curve reflects the quantity of goods that are physically available now. Because the trees bear more apples, the supply of goods increases.

What about demand? The increase in current output makes people wealthier. Thus, demand for current goods increases: the demand curve shifts to the right.

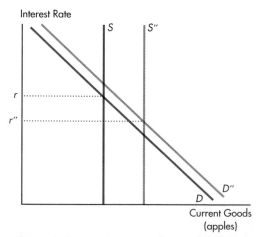

FIGURE 5-8   An increase in the supply of current goods.
The supply curve shifts to the right from *S* to *S″,* a distance that represents the amount of the current windfall. The demand curve shifts to the right from *D* to *D″,* which is a smaller distance because of consumption smoothing. The equilibrium interest rate falls from *r* to *r″.*

But the demand curve does not shift as far to the right as the supply curve does. Because the increase in income is temporary, people smooth their consumption streams by attempting to spend only part of the windfall now and to save some of it for the future.

Following a temporary increase in income, the demand for current goods shifts to the right, but not as far as the supply shifts.

What happens to the interest rate? As you can see in Figure 5-8, it falls from r to r''. The inference that r'' is below r follows from our observation that demand shifts less than supply does.

➡ *Exercise 5-2*
Analyze the effect of an increase in current output by examining the market for *future* goods. Do you get the same result as that suggested by Figure 5-8?

The Adjustment Process

Figure 5-8 reveals that an increase in current income causes the market interest rate to fall. Let us think about the underlying reasons for this result.

Prior to the news about the windfall, the market is in equilibrium and everyone is satisfied with his consumption pattern. When the windfall occurs, everyone simultaneously decides to consume some of it now and save some for the future. The way to save is to lend. As we all turn to our neighbors and ask "Would you like to borrow an apple?" and as we all receive the reply, "No. Would *you* like to borrow an apple?" we recognize that in order to attract borrowers, we must offer lower interest rates. The market interest rate is thus bid down to a new equilibrium level, r'' in Figure 5-8.

At the moment of the windfall, people have more apples than they want to eat. The interest rate must fall by enough to convince them to eat the apples that are available.

A War

In 1991, the United States went to war with Iraq on behalf of Kuwait. It was estimated (incorrectly, as it turned out) that $40 billion worth of U.S. goods would be destroyed in the war. Those goods were primarily tanks and weapons; had the war taken place on U.S. soil, the destruction might have taken other forms.

Let us analyze how such a war—if it had turned out as predicted—might have affected the interest rate. If physical goods worth $40 billion are destroyed, the supply of current goods shifts to the left by $40 billion, from S to S' in Figure 5-9.

There is a complication here, because our current-apples/future-apples model encompasses only goods that are used for consumption, whereas tanks and weapons are not generally thought of as nutritious. However, the lost weapons must be replaced, and the act of replacing them uses $40 billion worth of resources, which are then unavailable for the production of consumption goods. So the bottom line is that $40

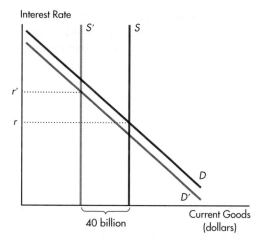

FIGURE 5-9   The effects of a war.
The war destroys $40 billion worth of current goods, causing the supply curve to shift leftward from *S* to *S'*. The demand curve shifts leftward from *D* to *D'* because of the reduction in wealth, but demand shifts less than supply does because of consumption smoothing. The interest rate rises from *r* to *r'*.

billion worth of consumption goods is eventually removed from the economy. The analysis can become more subtle if we believe that the replacement process takes an appreciable length of time; for purposes of illustration we assume here that it takes place immediately. That is, we assume that the destruction of a $100,000 tank causes an instantaneous $100,000 reduction in goods that people have available to consume.

Americans are made poorer by this war and therefore reduce their demand for current consumption. However, the drop in demand (from *D* to *D'*) is small relative to the drop in supply because people want to smooth out the unpleasant effects of war over their entire lifetimes. Rather than cut consumption by the full amount of the loss in a single year, people attempt to cut consumption by a little bit in each of several years. Therefore, as you can see in Figure 5-9, the interest rate must rise (from *r* to *r'*).

Why must the interest rate rise? Because $40 billion worth of goods has disappeared from the economy, something must happen to convince people to cut their consumption by $40 billion. What is that something? Everyone's initial inclination is to cut consumption by much less than $40 billion. People want to go on eating about as much as they ate before, or only slightly less, even though there is much less food available. To maintain their old living standards, people attempt to increase their borrowing or reduce their lending; the interest rate is therefore driven up until people are willing to cut their consumption by amounts totaling the full $40 billion.

We can go a little further and give some thought to the question of exactly how *far* the interest rate must rise. Divided among the U.S. population of about 250 million, $40 billion comes to $160 per person. In the new equilibrium, the average American must reduce his consumption by this amount. There is less to go around now, and as a matter of physical necessity people must consume on average that much less.

The drop of $160 per person comes to $640 per family of four. How much of a change in the interest rate would be necessary to convince your own family to cut its consumption this year by that amount? (If your family is of a different size, make the corresponding adjustment in the dollar amount.) That is, how much would the interest rate have to increase before your family either reduced its borrowing or increased its lending by $640? (Remember that keeping a bank account is a form of lending.) If your family is reasonably typical, then the answer to that question tells us how far the interest rate would have to rise if the United States became involved in a war that really did destroy $40 billion worth of U.S. property.

Actually, $160 per person may be an overestimate. If Americans can borrow from foreigners, then it is not necessary for them to reduce their current consumption by the full $160 per person. The question is whether the economy consists of the United States alone, in which case we divide $40 billion by a population of 250 million, or of the United States plus some trading partners, in which case we divide $40 billion by the total population of all the relevant countries. But the United States constitutes a large fraction of its trading bloc, and therefore the two sets of numbers might not be very different.

→ *Exercise 5-3*
Verify the result of Figure 5-9 by examining the market for future goods.

A Permanent Increase in Income

Suppose income increases permanently. That is, suppose income rises today and, instead of returning to its old level next year, is expected to remain at its new, higher level. For example, suppose a vaccine against AIDS becomes instantly available (allowing resources now used in hospitals to be applied to alternative productive uses) or a favorable change in the climate appears to be permanent (promising higher crop yields now and in the future).

The effects of a permanent increase in income are depicted in Figure 5-10. Current output increases, so the supply curve shifts to the right, from S to S', by the amount of the increase.

Demand also increases (from D to D'); and in this case the demand curve shifts to the right *by exactly the same amount as the supply curve*. The reason for this is simple. If income increases permanently, consumption is automatically smoothed without any need to shift part of it from one time period to another. If your income increases by a permanent $100 per year, then the way to keep your consumption smooth is to increase it by the same $100 per year.

> Following a permanent increase in income, the demand for current goods shifts rightward as far as the supply does.

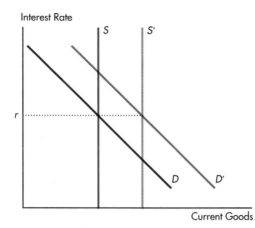

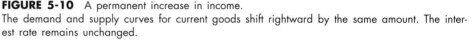

FIGURE 5-10 A permanent increase in income.
The demand and supply curves for current goods shift rightward by the same amount. The interest rate remains unchanged.

Since demand and supply increase by the same amount, the interest rate stays the same. Since the increase in income is expected to persist into the future, there is no increase in the desire to lend or to borrow. There is no reason for the interest rate to change.

General Changes in Income

In the real world, news about the economy can affect current and future incomes in different ways. We have discussed the economy's response to a change in current income, a change in future income, and equal changes in both current and future incomes. The interest-rate response depends on the change in current income *relative* to the expected change in future income.

To see this, let us review our results so far. Recall that if income increases this period but people do not expect the windfall to repeat itself in the future, the interest rate will fall as people attempt to smooth their consumption streams by lending (see Figure 5-8). But if future income increases by the same amount as current income, people's consumption streams are already smooth, so people do not change their lending patterns and interest rates do not change (see Figure 5-10).

Suppose that current income increases by one apple and that, simultaneously, expected future income increases by two apples. Then in order to smooth their consumption streams, people attempt to increase their current consumption by *more* than one apple, which requires borrowing. The supply of current consumption shifts rightward by one apple, while the demand for current consumption shifts rightward by more than one apple, as in Figure 5-11. Thus, the equilibrium interest rate must rise.

➧ *Exercise 5-4*
Suppose the economy enters a downturn and current income falls by one apple. At the same time, people expect that the downturn will become worse in the future and that future income will fall by two apples. Show what happens to the supply and the demand for current consumption. What happens to the equilibrium interest rate?

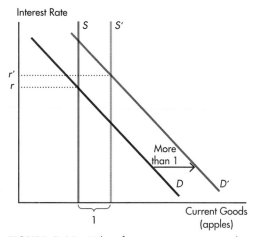

FIGURE 5-11 When future income increases by more than current income, the demand for current goods moves farther to the right than the supply. The interest rate rises.

5-4 INTEREST RATES: RECENT HISTORY

Figure 5-12(a) shows the nominal interest rate paid by 3-month U.S. Treasury bills from 1950 to 1994. Notice that it is very volatile—that is, the plot is not as smooth as, for example, the plots of real GDP and the price level in Figures 2-3 and 2-4. Nominal interest rates fluctuate a great deal and do not exhibit the upward trend of those other economic variables.

Interest-rate fluctuations get a lot of attention in the financial press. If you pick up the business section of your favorite newspaper, you will always find a report on the latest changes in nominal interest rates and will often find one or more articles attempting to analyze and explain those changes.

In any such analysis, the most important thing to remember is that the nominal interest rate is the sum of the real interest rate and the inflation rate. So a change in the nominal interest rate might be attributable to a change in the real interest rate, to a change in the inflation rate, or to a combination of the two.

Which component—the real interest rate or the inflation rate—is more important as a determinant of changes in the nominal interest rate? To explore this question, we have superimposed graphs of the inflation rate and the real interest rate on the graph of the nominal interest rate. The inflation rate and the nominal interest rate [Figure 5-12(b)] seem to move together, at least approximately. This is not the case, however, for the real interest rate and the nominal interest rate [Figure 5-12(c)]. These observations suggest that most of the volatility of nominal interest rates can be attributed to changes in the inflation rate.

However, you can see in Figure 5-12(c) that the real interest rate is quite volatile in its own right. Most of the time, it falls within the range of 1.5 to 3.5 percent. But in 1951, in 1955, and again in 1975, the real interest rate plunged far below that range, even becoming negative. In 1984, it soared to almost 6 percent.

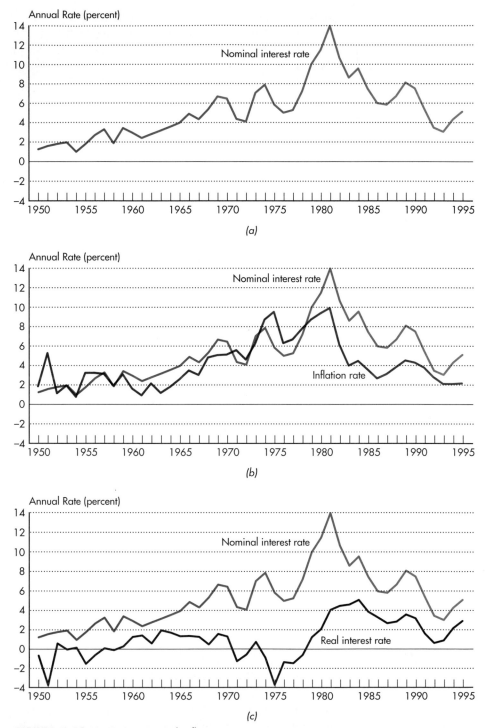

FIGURE 5-12 Interest rates and inflation.
The nominal interest rate for 3-month Treasury bills: (a) alone; (b) with the inflation rate; (c) with the real interest rate.

Ex ante real interest rate:

The real interest rate that borrowers and lenders believe they are agreeing to when a loan is contracted.

Ex post real interest rate:

The real interest rate that borrowers and lenders actually face when the loan is paid off.

To interpret these fluctuations, we must distinguish between the *ex ante* real interest rate and the *ex post* real interest rate. The **ex ante real interest rate** is the real interest rate that borrowers *think* they will be paying (and that lenders think they will be receiving) when a loan is negotiated. The **ex post real interest rate** is the real interest rate that borrowers *actually* pay (and that lenders actually receive) when the loan is paid off. These two measures of the real interest rate differ when the inflation rate is misperceived. Suppose that the nominal interest rate is 8 percent, the inflation rate is widely expected to be 5 percent, but the true inflation rate turns out to be 7 percent. Then the ex ante real rate is $8\% - 5\% = 3\%$ and the ex post real rate is $8\% - 7\% = 1\%$.

In 1975, inflation (as measured by the implicit GDP deflator) hit a record high of 9.4 percent. It seems likely that few people at the time realized how high the inflation rate had gotten. Thus, when they sold bonds at a nominal interest rate of about 6 percent, lenders might have expected to earn a positive real rate even though the ex post real rate turned out negative—as low as -3.6 percent.

What other factors have contributed to large dramatic changes in the real interest rate? The three downward plunges (1951, 1955, and 1975) all occurred in periods of recession—times when income had declined for several calendar quarters in a row and unemployment was increasing. That is, they occurred when current income was down. Our model tells us that in order to explain the behavior of the interest rate, we need to know not only what happens to income in a given year but also what people expect to happen the following year. One explanation of the decline in the interest rate during a recession is that people are familiar enough with recessions to know the recession will persist; they know that conditions—mainly, the decline in their current incomes—are likely to get worse in the near future. Consequently, they expect their future incomes to be even lower than their current incomes. To smooth their consumption streams, they reduce their borrowing or increase their lending. The interest rate falls.

⇒ *Exercise 5-5*

Use Exercise 5-3 to justify the final sentence of the preceding paragraph.

What about the rising real interest rate of 1980–1984? Our model suggests that it should have been tied to a general expectation of rising incomes. The technological revolution that brought us VCRs, personal computers, and compact discs was just getting under way in the early 1980s. If people believed that computers would increase productivity and therefore income throughout the 1980s, that belief could explain the rising real interest rate.

5-5 | THE OPEN ECONOMY

The model in Sections 5-1 through 5-3 shows how the interest rate is determined in a closed economy—an economy whose citizens trade only with each other. Now we extend the model to open economies, which trade with each other inside the closed *world* economy.

To study trade between countries, we use exactly the same techniques we used to study trade between individuals. Just as we added Adam's and Eve's supply curves to get an economywide supply curve, we add all the different countries' supply curves to get a worldwide supply curve. Then we add all the different countries' demand curves to get a worldwide demand curve. And finally we use the worldwide supply and demand curves to find an equilibrium interest rate for the world.

World Supply and Demand Curves

We divide the world into two parts: the *domestic* country (meaning whatever country we are currently interested in studying) and the rest of the world, which we sometimes call the *foreign* country, even though the rest of the world is not really a single country.

In Figure 5-13(a) we add the domestic and foreign supply curves for current goods to get the world supply curve: S_d is the domestic country's supply curve, S_f is the foreign country's supply curve, and their sum, S_w, is the world's supply curve. In Figure 5-13(b) we add the domestic and foreign demand curves to obtain the world demand curve.

World Markets: Reinterpreting Our Assumptions

The horizontal axes in our graphs now represent goods currently demanded and supplied in *world markets*. An individual endowed with an apple can now sell it to the highest bidder anywhere in the world; likewise, anyone who wants to buy an apple can search the entire world for the best—that is, the lowest—price. This situation requires that we make two simplifying assumptions. First, we assume that apples can be costlessly transported from one country to another. Second, we assume that there

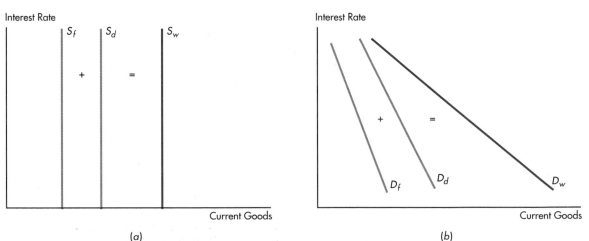

FIGURE 5-13 World supply and demand curves.
(a) The world supply curve S_w is the sum of the domestic and foreign supply curves S_d and S_f.
(b) The world demand curve D_w is the sum of the domestic and foreign demand curves D_d and D_f.

are no *barriers to trade;* that is, there are no import taxes or export taxes and no quotas or subsidies for imports or exports.

These two assumptions are not new. In Sections 5-1 and 5-2 we implicitly assumed that Adam and Eve could trade apples without incurring transportation costs and without running into government-imposed barriers to trade. Those assumptions are probably better approximations to reality within a single country than they are in the world economy, but we make them here as well. However, you need to be aware that our conclusions about the world economy depend on those assumptions and that when the assumptions fail, the conclusions may need to be modified.

Given our assumptions, the aggregate world demand and supply curves look and behave just like the aggregate demand and supply curves for any closed economy. For example, the aggregate world demand curve slopes downward, and the aggregate world supply curve is vertical.

Equilibrium in the World Economy

In Figure 5-14 we have superimposed the demand and supply curves from Figure 5-13. Examining the aggregate world demand and supply curves, we see that they intersect at an interest rate which, we assume for illustration purposes, is 10 percent. That is the interest rate that clears the world market for current goods.

Trade Deficits and Trade Surpluses

We can use Figure 5-14 to determine the effects of international trade in each component country. At the equilibrium interest rate of 10 percent, we see that the

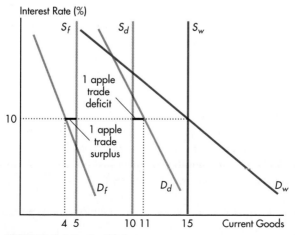

FIGURE 5-14 Equilibrium.
The world interest rate is 10 percent, because that is where the world supply and demand curves cross. At that interest rate, domestic citizens supply 10 apples and consume 11. The extra apple is borrowed from abroad and constitutes the domestic country's trade deficit. At the same time, foreign citizens supply 5 apples and consume only 4; the extra apple is the one that domestic citizens borrow.

domestic country demands 11 apples and supplies 10 apples, while the foreign country demands 4 apples and supplies 5 apples.

How can domestic citizens choose to consume 11 apples when they have only 10 available? The answer is that they borrow 1 apple from abroad. Foreigners have 5 apples available and choose to consume only 4; the extra apple is the one that is lent to somebody in the domestic country.

Alternatively, we can say that the domestic country imports (on net) 1 apple from abroad, while the foreign country exports (on net) 1 apple.

Figure 5-14 tells us that the foreign country must export one more apple than it imports. (That is why we use the phrase "on net" above.) There are many ways this could come about. The foreign country could export one apple and import zero, or it could export three and import two, or it could export five and import four.

A country that imports more than it exports is borrowing. A country that exports more than it imports is lending.

Trade balance (balance of trade, net exports):
The value of an economy's exports minus the value of its imports during a given period of time.

The difference between a country's exports and imports is called its **trade balance,** its **balance of trade,** or its **net exports.** Letting *EX* stand for exports, *IM* for imports, and *NX* for the balance of trade, we can write this as

$$NX = EX - IM$$

In Figure 5-14, the trade balance of the domestic country is −1 apple, and the trade balance of the foreign country is 1 apple.

In this book, we use the term "net exports" to mean the same thing as "trade balance." Recall from Chapter 2 that there are several different official *measures* of the trade balance. "Net exports" as reported by the government excludes trade in services, as does the merchandise trade balance. In this book, we use the more inclusive current account balance to measure net exports.

Net imports:
The value of an economy's imports minus the value of its exports during a given period of time.

We use the phrase **net imports** to mean the opposite of net exports; that is, net imports equal *IM* − *EX*.

Whenever an apple is imported, it must be paid for either now (with an export of equal value) or in the future (in which case the citizens of the importing country are incurring debt). The amount the country must borrow is always equal to the excess of imports over exports—that is, net imports.

Net imports equal net borrowing. Equivalently, net exports equal net lending.

Trade deficit:
The size of an economy's trade balance if that trade balance is negative.

Trade surplus:
The size of an economy's trade balance if that trade balance is positive.

If a country's trade balance is negative, we say the country is running a **trade deficit.** If a country's trade balance is positive, we say the country is running a **trade surplus.** In Figure 5-14 the domestic country runs a trade deficit of one apple, while the rest of the world runs a trade surplus of one apple.

A country that runs a trade deficit is borrowing. A country that runs a trade surplus is lending.

Because borrowing is the same as dissaving and lending is the same as saving, we can also say:

A country that runs a trade deficit is dissaving. A country that runs a trade surplus is saving.

The laws of arithmetic dictate that if the domestic country runs a trade deficit, the foreign country must run a trade surplus of equal size. This is just an application of the general law that every dollar borrowed by someone is a dollar lent by someone else. Thus:

The sum of all countries' trade balances must be zero; they cannot all be positive or all be negative at the same time.

In particular, not all countries can run trade surpluses (or trade deficits) at the same time.

Exercise 5-6
Draw a graph like the one in Figure 5-14 assuming the domestic country runs a trade surplus.

Bilateral Trade Deficits

Bilateral trade deficit:
The difference between the value of an economy's exports to one other economy and the value of its imports from that one other economy during a given period of time.

The U.S. trade deficit is equal to all U.S. imports minus all U.S. exports. The U.S. **bilateral trade deficit** with, say, Japan, is equal to all U.S. imports *from Japan* minus all U.S. exports *to Japan*.

While the overall U.S. trade deficit measures the borrowing of U.S. citizens, bilateral trade deficits do not directly measure anything of economic significance. To see why, think of the trade deficits run by your family. Your family "imports" food from grocers, clothing from department stores, and education from a college. At the same time, your family supplies goods or services, some to itself and some for "export" to the marketplace. Your family's income measures the value of the goods and services that the family supplies.

If your family spends more than its income (that is, if your family runs a "trade deficit"), then we can conclude that your family is accumulating debt. If your family spends less than its income (that is, if your family runs a "trade surplus"), we can conclude that your family is accumulating savings. But if we observe only that your family spends more *at the grocery store* than it earns from selling goods and services *to the grocery store* (that is, your family runs a "bilateral trade deficit" with the grocer), then we can conclude nothing at all about whether your family is choosing to borrow or to save.

Similarly, if we observe only that the U.S. runs a bilateral trade deficit with Japan, we can conclude nothing except that U.S. citizens happen to like Japanese goods and that the products sold by Americans are being sold in countries other than Japan. This is no more a problem for the United States, or for U.S.-Japanese relations, than is the fact for you that you buy food from your grocer, or education from your college, and finance it with income earned from, say, a computer manufacturer.

Are Trade Deficits Bad?

Once a month, the U.S. government (and other governments as well) releases its latest measure of the nation's trade balance, and newspapers publish analyses of what the most recent statistics portend. If the trade deficit has grown, journalists frequently report a "worsening of the trade balance"; if it has shrunk, they report an "improvement." But such value judgments are typically misguided. A large trade deficit is neither inherently better nor worse than a large trade surplus.

Indeed, a country with a trade deficit is just a country whose citizens are borrowing, on net, from abroad—or, equivalently, selling bonds to foreigners. At the end of Section 4-1 we discussed the gains from trade in bonds and pointed out that everyone—borrowers and lenders—gains from the opportunity to participate in credit markets. In particular, borrowers gain because they are able to consume more in the present at a price (in terms of future consumption) that they deem acceptable. And when we discuss investment in Chapter 7, you will discover another way in which borrowers can gain: by using borrowed resources to create new capital, which in turn leads to greater future income.

Because there is nothing inherently bad about borrowing, it follows that there is nothing inherently bad about a trade deficit. It is true that in the real world people sometimes miscalculate and borrow more than is wise—that is, less than they would have with perfect hindsight. But it is equally true that in the real world people sometimes miscalculate and borrow *less* than is wise. So, in principle, a country's citizens can run a trade deficit that is too large, or they can run a trade deficit that is too small. But in the absence of widespread miscalculations, either a trade deficit or a trade surplus is just a sign that people are benefiting from the opportunity to participate in international capital markets.

Can a Country Run a Permanent Trade Deficit?

We saw in Chapter 2 that the U.S. government reports various measures of the trade deficit. According to some of these measures, the United States has been running a trade deficit since 1982, and this fact has led some commentators to wonder whether the trade deficit has become a permanent feature of the U.S. economy.

But it would be exceedingly difficult for a country to run a permanent trade deficit—just as it would be exceedingly difficult for an individual to borrow in every year of his life. Lenders lend because they expect to be repaid at some time in the future. Foreign countries allow Americans to import their goods because they expect to be repaid—via American exports—at some future date. It is unlikely that they would be willing to wait forever.

A country that could run a permanent trade deficit would be a fortunate country indeed. Citizens of that country could consume more than their incomes on a permanent basis. Some economists like to drive this point home by observing that in any year in which the United States runs a trade deficit, American citizens receive cars, appliances, and other goods from abroad in exchange for green pieces of paper which the government can print at essentially no cost.

This almost makes the trade deficit sound like the source of an extravagant free lunch. But no lunch is truly free, and foreigners will surely use those green pieces of paper to buy American goods—at the expense of U.S. consumption—at some future time.

A trade deficit is borrowing. A permanent trade deficit is borrowing without ever repaying the debt. The former can be a good opportunity. The latter is an opportunity that is too good to be true.

5-6 COMPARATIVE STATICS IN THE OPEN ECONOMY

When we studied the closed economy, our comparative-statics experiments focused on changes in the interest rate. Now we will try some similar comparative-statics experiments for the open economy, focusing on changes in both the interest rate and the trade balance.

An Increase in Domestic Future Income

What happens to a nation's interest rate and trade balance if its citizens come to expect higher incomes in the future?

Figure 5-15 shows the current domestic (subscript d) and foreign (subscript f) demand and supply curves, as well as the aggregate demand and supply curves for the entire world (subscript w). Initially, the world supply and demand curves determine the interest rate r. We have assumed in the figure that the domestic economy runs a trade deficit, which is necessarily matched in size by a trade surplus in the rest of the world. These trade balances are represented by the black bars along the horizontal line at the interest rate r.

Now suppose that a new invention or the outcome of an election causes people to expect that next year's income in the domestic economy will increase. Because the change in income does not take place until next year, there is no change in any of the current supply curves. However, U.S. citizens, attempting to smooth their consumption, increase their *demand* for current goods, so the domestic demand curve shifts rightward from D_d to D_d'. Because foreign citizens foresee no change in their incomes, the foreign demand curve D_f does not shift. The world demand curve D_w shifts rightward (to D_w') by the same distance that the domestic demand curve shifts.

The equilibrium interest rate, now determined by S_w and D_w', rises to r'. It is easy to understand the reason for this increase: Domestic citizens, who want to start spending their future windfall immediately, attempt to borrow more in world markets. Because the number of goods available to the entire world is unchanged, those attempts bid up the interest rate.

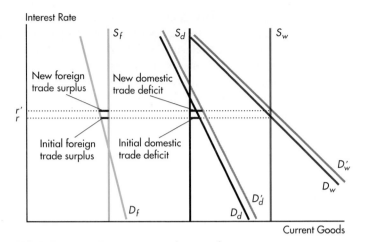

FIGURE 5-15 An increase in domestic future income.
Initially, the interest rate is r, and the black bars at level r represent the trade deficit for the domestic economy and a trade surplus of the same size for the foreign economy. When expected future income rises in the domestic country, the domestic demand for current goods shifts rightward from D_d to D_d'; the world demand for current goods shifts rightward by the same amount, from D_w to D_w'. The interest rate rises to r', and the black bars at that level represent the new trade balances.

When the interest rate changes, the trade balances change as well. The new trade balances are represented in the figure by the black bars at level r'.

The new foreign trade surplus is obviously larger than the inital surplus: the black bar at level r' extends farther to the left of S_f than the black bar at level r does. When the interest rate increases, the foreign trade surplus must increase.

Now what about the domestic trade deficit? The black bar at level r' has been drawn to extend farther to the right of S_d than has the black bar at level r, indicating an increase in that trade deficit. Why must the graph be drawn this way? From the figure, it seems possible that if the interest rate increases by enough, the domestic trade deficit could decrease. But that is wrong, and here's why: *The domestic trade deficit must always be equal to the foreign trade surplus.* Because the foreign trade surplus unambiguously increases, we know that the domestic trade deficit must increase by the same amount.

Exercise 5-7
Analyze the effects of a drop in the future income of the foreign country. (As in Figure 5-15, begin by assuming that the domestic country is running a trade deficit.)

An Increase in Domestic Current Income

Figure 5-16 shows what happens when domestic citizens experience a temporary increase in current, as opposed to future, income.

In the initial equilibrium determined by S_w and D_w, the interest rate is r, the domestic country runs a trade deficit, and the rest of the world runs a trade surplus of the same size. Those trade balances are represented by the dark bars at level r.

Now suppose that the domestic economy is blessed with a temporary rise in cur-

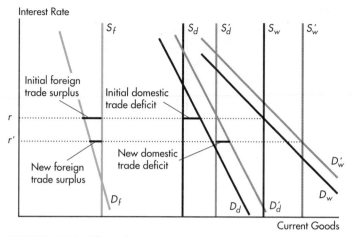

FIGURE 5-16 Effect of an increase in domestic current income.
Initially, the interest rate is r; the black bars at level r represent a trade deficit for the domestic economy and a trade surplus of the same size for the foreign economy. When current income rises temporarily in the domestic economy, the domestic supply of current goods shifts rightward from S_d to S_d'; the world supply of current goods shifts rightward by the same amount from S_w to S_w'. The domestic and world demand curves also shift rightward, but not as far as the supply curves. The interest rate falls to r', and the black bars at that level represent the new trade balances.

rent income. The domestic supply curve shifts rightward by the amount of the windfall (from S_d to S_d'), and consumption smoothing dictates that the domestic demand curve shift rightward but not as far (from D_d to D_d'). Because there is no change in the fortunes of foreign citizens, the foreign supply and demand curves do not shift.

The world supply and demand curves S_w and D_w shift rightward by the same distances as the domestic supply and demand curves. Thus the world demand curve shifts less far than the world supply curve. The equilibrium interest rate falls from r to r'.

Again the trade balances change; the new ones are represented by the black bars at level r'. The foreign trade surplus has clearly shrunk. The domestic trade deficit has therefore shrunk as well, because the domestic trade deficit is always equal in size to the foreign trade surplus.

Figure 5-16 could have been drawn differently. Then, if the current windfall were sufficiently large, the interest rate could fall so far that the foreign country switches to running a trade deficit and the domestic country switches to running a trade surplus.

Opening an Economy to Trade

Not all economies are open to trade in goods and bonds. Let us analyze what happens when a closed economy decides to open its borders to trade.

Figure 5-17 shows the domestic and foreign equilibria both before and after the borders are opened. When there is no international trade, the demand for goods in the domestic economy can be filled only by suppliers in the domestic economy. Thus the

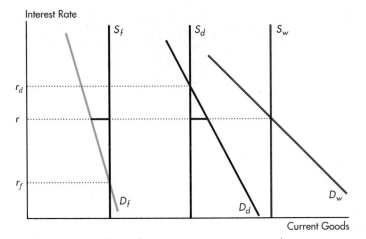

FIGURE 5-17 Effects of opening an economy to trade.
If the domestic and foreign countries are closed economies, the initial domestic interest rate is r_d and the initial foreign interest rate is r_f. After the economies are opened to trade, the world interest rate is r; the black horizontal bars represent the trade balances.

domestic equilibrium interest rate r_d is determined by the intersection of the domestic demand and supply curves D_d and S_d.

Similarly, the foreign interest rate r_f is determined by the intersection of the foreign demand and supply curves D_f and S_f.

In Figure 5-17, the domestic interest rate happens to be higher than the foreign interest rate. We could equally well draw the figure to make the foreign interest rate higher than the domestic interest rate. Either way, the following holds:

> The equilibrium interest rate in a closed economy can be different from the interest rate in the rest of the world.

Now suppose these economies agree to open their borders to trade. Then equilibrium is determined by the world supply and demand curves S_w and D_w. They determine the equilibrium interest rate r, and that is the interest rate that prevails worldwide. The domestic and foreign economies run trade balances represented by the black bars at level r.

> Trade equalizes interest rates across countries.

 In Figure 5-17, opening the domestic economy to trade leads to a trade deficit. This is a consequence of our earlier assumption that the domestic interest rate is higher than the foreign interest rate with no international trade. If we had made the opposite assumption, we would have found that opening the domestic economy to trade leads to a trade surplus.

Also, recall that "interest rate" always means *real* interest rate. Even when economies are entirely open, nominal interest rates will differ in countries with different inflation rates.

As it happens, the interest rate r that clears the *world* market for goods is *between* the two interest rates r_d and r_f. Is that a coincidence? The answer is no. In our example, r_d is higher than r_f. But once the domestic economy is opened to trade, citizens who want to borrow no longer have to pay the high rate r_d; they can turn instead to foreign lenders. This bids down the domestic interest rate. At the same time, foreign citizens who want to lend no longer have to settle for the lower rate r_f; they can turn to domestic borrowers. This bids up the foreign interest rate. The domestic interest rate falls and the foreign interest rate rises until they meet at the new equilibrium rate r. Thus r must lie between r_d and r_f.

➡ *Exercise 5-8*
Suppose that initially the domestic interest rate were below the foreign interest rate. After the economies are opened to trade, what forces would cause the new world interest rate to lie between the two initial interest rates?

The Gains from Opening an Economy to Trade

Who gains and who loses when an economy is opened to trade? To answer, first recall that opening an economy to trade can cause its interest rate to change. A drop in the domestic interest rate is good for lenders and bad for borrowers.

Because the representative agent is neither a lender nor a borrower, you might be tempted to conclude that opening an economy to trade is neither a good thing nor a bad thing for its average citizen. But such a conclusion would be incorrect, because trade brings new, and potentially beneficial, opportunities to borrow and lend. In an open economy, the domestic representative agent has the option to become a borrower or a lender.

Recall that in a closed endowment economy, aggregate consumption must equal aggregate income; the only way for Adam to consume either more or less than his endowment is for Eve to consume either less or more than *her* endowment. But when their economy opens its borders, Adam and Eve can *simultaneously* consume either more or less than their endowments—by borrowing from foreigners or by lending to them. Another way to say this is that a closed economy must operate on its (domestic) supply curve, whereas an open economy is freed from that constraint. New opportunities to borrow and lend become available, and those opportunities represent a net gain to the average citizen.

Thus, although opening to trade may hurt some individuals and help others, the gains to the winners generally exceed the losses to the losers. The average citizen benefits from having a wider range of options.

Government Policies

Although opening an economy to trade improves economic welfare, those groups that are hurt by trade—such as domestic lenders in Figure 5-17—frequently lobby their government to close the country's borders, or at least to reduce the size of the trade balance. In 1995, President Clinton responded to such concerns by pressuring Japanese citizens to buy more auto parts from the United States. By threatening to impose a crippling tariff on Japanese cars, the president was able to force an agreement that, he hoped, would increase U.S. exports and thereby lower the U.S. trade deficit.

But while that action may have increased the export of U.S. auto parts, it was unlikely to have much effect on U.S. exports in general. Japanese citizens in 1995 wanted to save; that is, they wanted to spend less than their incomes. If they were forced to buy more auto parts from the United States, they were liable to compensate by buying less of some other good.

Likewise, Americans in 1995 were eager to spend *more* than their incomes. They bought a lot of different goods, including auto parts. When more of those auto parts were exported to Japan (making them unavailable domestically), Americans had to find other goods to buy instead—and those goods had to be imported from abroad. Thus there was no reason for U.S. *net* exports (the U.S. trade deficit) to change as a result of the president's action.

The trade balance—as we saw in Figure 5-14—is determined entirely by the domestic and foreign demand and supply for current goods. When the president intervenes in the market for a *particular* good (in this case, auto parts), he is unlikely to affect the market for goods *in general*—and hence unlikely to affect the trade balance.

The U.S. Trade Balance: Recent History

Figure 5-18 shows the recent history of the U.S. current-account balance. (Recall that the current-account balance is one measure of the trade balance.) The horizontal line at 0 separates years of trade surplus from years of trade deficit. Until the late 1970s, the U.S. trade balance tended to be a surplus. After the early 1980s, though, the United States not only ran continual trade deficits but ran remarkably large ones: in 1987 the trade deficit was close to 4 percent of GDP.

What accounts for the shift from the trade surpluses of the 1950s through the

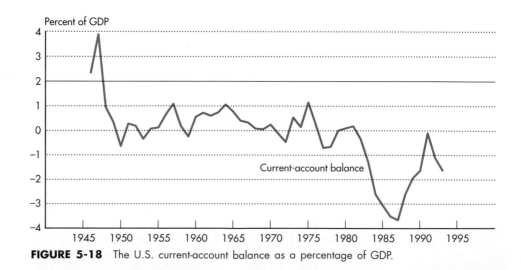

FIGURE 5-18 The U.S. current-account balance as a percentage of GDP.

1970s to the trade deficits of the 1980s? Recall that a country's trade surplus is equal to its net lending. Beginning immediately after World War II, the United States lent heavily to countries in Europe and Asia that were rebuilding war-damaged factories and industries. Recall also that a country's trade surplus is equal to its net exports. From this point of view, we can point to the fact that foreigners used loans from the United States to buy American goods, particularly the physical capital—as well as the managerial know-how—of American entrepreneurs.

But by the 1970s, Europe and Japan were largely rebuilt. The postwar loans were repaid. Instead of continuing to lend abroad, U.S. citizens increased their consumption spending. So one explanation for rising U.S. imports is that Americans had begun to claim their rewards for more than two decades of saving.

At least two other factors contributed to U.S. trade deficits in the 1970s. First, in the early part of the 1970s the cost of the Vietnam War caused U.S. spending to exceed U.S. output. Second, in later years favorable foreign exchange rates made foreign goods relatively cheap and encouraged Americans to spend more. (We will discuss the subject of exchange rates more deeply in Chapter 16.)

In the 1980s, U.S. trade deficits got much larger, growing to almost 4 percent of GDP by the middle of the decade. While 4 percent is large in comparison with deficits of the 1960s and 1970s, it is not exorbitant in a broader historical context, at least for a country as productive and secure as the United States. Indeed, a large trade deficit is often a sign of optimism concerning the future. We should not be at all surprised by substantial borrowing in a country where people expect the future to be much brighter than the present.

SUMMARY

An endowment economy is an economy with no production, no labor, and no storage. People have current and future incomes, which we can think of as apples that fall from trees. The total quantity of apples that fall in a given year is called that year's aggregate supply.

In a graph with the interest rate on the vertical axis and the quantity of current consumption on the horizontal, supply is represented by a vertical line at the existing quantity supplied. On the same graph, we can overlay the market (aggregate) demand for current consumption, which is the sum of the individual demand curves of all the members of the economy.

The equilibrium point is the point where the demand curve intersects the supply curve. We assume that the endowment economy is always at the point of equilibrium.

We can also examine the market for *future* consumption, using a graph with $1/(1 + r)$ (the relative price of future goods) on the vertical axis and the quantity of future consumption on the horizontal. The equilibrium interest rate as determined in the future-goods market must coincide with the equilibrium interest rate as determined in the current-goods market.

Because aggregate demand is the sum of individual demands, the aggregate demand curve responds to shocks in the same way that individual demand curves do. The key to keeping track of demand is consumption smoothing. Aggregate supply is determined by the physical availability of consumption goods. Together, aggregate demand and aggregate supply determine how the economy responds to shocks.

An increase in future income increases current demand because of consumption smoothing but has no effect on current supply; therefore, the market interest rate goes up. An increase in current income increases current demand by *less* than the amount of the windfall because of consumption smoothing but increases current supply by the full amount of the windfall; therefore, the interest rate goes down. A permanent increase in income increases current demand and current supply by the amount of the windfall; therefore, the interest rate remains unchanged.

In general, interest rates rise when demand increases by more than supply, and they fall when supply increases by more than demand.

If the domestic economy is open to trade with foreigners, the equilibrium interest rate is determined by the intersection of the aggregate world supply and demand curves. Aggregate world supply is the sum of domestic and foreign supplies, and aggregate world demand is the sum of domestic and foreign demands.

At the world equilibrium interest rate, a country's citizens might demand either more or fewer goods than they supply. If the quantity demanded exceeds the quantity supplied, then the excess is borrowed from abroad. If the quantity supplied exceeds the quantity demanded, then the excess is lent to foreigners.

A country's net exports (that is, its exports minus its imports) are equal to its net lending. Equivalently, net imports are equal to net borrowing. A country with positive net exports is said to run a trade surplus and a country with negative net exports (or, equivalently, positive net imports) is said to run a trade deficit.

When a country's future income rises, both that country's demand curve and the world demand curve shift rightward. This raises the world interest rate. At the new, higher interest rate, the foreign economy (the rest of the world) runs a larger trade surplus and the domestic economy runs a larger trade deficit.

When current income rises in the domestic economy, the domestic and world supply curves shift rightward; the domestic and world demand curves also shift rightward, but not as far. The world interest rate falls. At the new, lower interest rate, the foreign economy runs a smaller trade surplus and the domestic economy runs a smaller trade deficit.

Opening borders to trade has the effect of equalizing interest rates across countries. This allows citizens of the domestic economy to operate at a point off the domestic supply curve. This new opportunity improves economic welfare on average, though not for every individual.

PROBLEM SET

Answer problems 1 through 16 using the closed-economy model presented in Sections 5-1 to 5-3.

1. Suppose that the current apple harvest increases by five apples. Which of the following shift to the right by five apples? Which shift to the right by fewer than five apples? Which do not shift?
    a. The supply curve for current goods
    b. The supply curve for future goods
    c. The demand curve for current goods
    d. The demand curve for future goods
2. Suppose the expected future apple harvest increases by five apples. Which of the following shift to the right by five apples? Which of the following shift to the right by fewer than five apples? Which do not shift?
    a. The supply curve for current goods
    b. The supply curve for future goods

    c. The demand curve for current goods

    d. The demand curve for future goods

3. *True or false:* The supply of current goods depends only on current income, but the demand for current goods depends on both current income and future income.

4. Suppose the interest rate that clears the bond market is 10 percent. *True or false:* If the government passes a law requiring that all borrowing and lending take place at a 15 percent interest rate, there will be an excess demand for current goods (that is, the quantity demanded will exceed the quantity supplied).

5. When the interest rate rises, the quantity of goods demanded falls. But when the demand for goods falls, the interest rate falls. Does this mean that a rise in the interest rate is always followed by a fall in the interest rate?

6. *True or false:* The interest rate determined in the bond market is usually higher than the interest rate determined in the market for future goods because bonds are riskier than goods.

7. Suppose a major new oil field is discovered in the United States. What happens to the supply of current goods in the United States? What happens to the demand for current goods? What happens to the interest rate?

8. Suppose a decrease in world tensions reduces the probability that there will be a devastating nuclear war in the near future. What happens to the supply of current goods? What happens to the demand for current goods? What happens to the interest rate?

9. A ravaging disease permanently renders the population of a country less able to work. What happens to the supply of current goods? What happens to the demand? What happens to the interest rate?

10. Contrast the effects on the interest rate of:

    a. A year of bad weather that lowers agricultural productivity

    b. A global climate change that lowers agricultural productivity permanently

11. The government of Fredonia has decided to raise taxes immediately in order to collect resources with which to build an aircraft carrier immediately. Unfortunately, the aircraft carrier is entirely worthless. What happens to the interest rate?

12. The government of Fredonia has announced that next year it will raise taxes and use the resources to build an aircraft carrier, which Fredonian citizens expect will be entirely worthless. What happens to the interest rate?

13. The government of Fredonia has announced that beginning immediately, it will set higher tax rates and use the revenue to build one new, entirely worthless aircraft carrier every year. What happens to the interest rate?

14. The leaders of a country embezzle funds from the country's tax revenues, spend the money on the sly, and take the resources out of the country. What happens to the supply curve for consumption goods in that country? Suppose that the citizens do not know about the embezzlement. What happens to the demand curve, and why? What happens to interest rates in the country? Do the interest rates change by more or by less than they would if people were aware of the theft?

15. Suppose that environmental predictions of global warming are widely believed to be accurate. That is, suppose everyone believes now that in the future the world is going to warm enough to devastate crops. What happens to current supply? Current demand? Interest rates? Now suppose that next year new evidence arises suggesting that global warming in the future will not have effects anywhere near as severe as those initially announced. What happens to interest rates?

16. *True or false:* If the inflation rate turns out to be lower than expected, then the ex post real interest rate will exceed the ex ante real interest rate.

Answer problems 17 through 25 using the open-economy model presented in Sections 5-5 and 5-6.

17. Suppose the domestic economy experiences a permanent increase in income. Use a graph to show that there is no effect on the world interest rate and on either the domestic or foreign trade balance.

18. Assume that the domestic economy runs a trade deficit and the foreign economy runs a trade surplus, as in Figure 5-14.
    a. Discuss the effects of an expected increase in foreign future income.
    b. Discuss the effects of an increase in foreign current income.

19. Assume that the domestic economy runs a trade deficit and the foreign economy runs a trade surplus, as in Figure 5-14.
    a. Discuss the effects of an expected increase in future income throughout the world (that is, in both the domestic and foreign economies).
    b. Discuss the effects of an increase in current income throughout the world (that is, in both the domestic and foreign economies).

20. Suppose the citizens of a certain country come to expect a drop in their future incomes. What happens to the world interest rate, and what happens to that country's trade balance?

21. Suppose a war is expected to reduce future income throughout the world. What happens to the world interest rate, and what happens to trade balances?

22. Suppose the United States, which is running a trade deficit, makes a one-time gift of 1 million tractors to the countries of eastern Europe. What happens to the supply and demand curves for current goods, both in the United States and abroad? What happens to the world interest rate, and what happens to the size of the U.S. trade deficit?

23. *True or false:* If a country opens its borders to trade and immediately begins to run a trade deficit, then we know that the interest rate in that country must have fallen.

24. If a country running a trade deficit decides to close its borders to trade, what happens to the interest rate its citizens face?

25. *True or false:* A large trade surplus is as likely to be an economic problem as is a large trade deficit.

An open economy is said to be *small* if changes in its demand or supply do not cause the world interest rate to change. Answer questions 26 through 29 for a small open economy.

26. A small country faces a world demand curve for its output that is flat at the world interest rate. Sketch the demand and supply curves for a small open economy and the world demand curve. Assume the domestic (small open) economy experiences a trade deficit.

27. Suppose the citizens of a small open economy experience a drop in their current income. What happens to that country's trade balance?

28. Suppose the citizens of a small open economy experience a drop in their expected future income. What happens to that country's trade balance?

29. Suppose the world rate of interest rises. What happens to the trade balance of a small open economy? Does the answer depend on whether the country is running a trade surplus or a trade deficit at the time of the interest-rate rise? Discuss the income and substitution effects.

Chapter 6

The Government

Our work in Chapters 4 and 5 has produced a simple model that explains how interest rates are determined in an endowment economy. Our goal in the next several chapters is to bring the model closer to reality by incorporating other factors that can affect interest rates and output.

In the model so far, no individual's actions can significantly affect economywide variables. In reality, there is one institution that is certainly large enough to make its presence felt. That institution is the government. In recent years, the federal, state, and local governments in the United States have purchased nearly 20 percent of the nation's output.

In Section 6-1 we examine the figures to see how much the government spends in the United States, and in Section 6-2 we discuss some of the reasons for all of that spending. Those sections are meant to convince you that it is important to add the government to our model. Beginning in Section 6-3, we do just that.

6-1 GOVERNMENT SPENDING

The word "government" most frequently suggests the *federal* government—the U.S. president, Congress, and the Judiciary. However, to economists, "government" always includes all levels of government: the federal government along with state and local (town, county, and city) governments. We consolidate these governments to get aggregate government statistics. Thus, when we say that in 1990 the government purchased 20 percent of output, we mean government at all levels. About 63 percent of that government spending was done by the federal government; the remainder, by state and local governments. In Figure 6-1 we compare the spending of several countries' governments.

The distinctions between federal, state, and local governments do not exist in many foreign countries, most of which have only one consolidated government that is not subdivided into smaller units. This sometimes causes people to make misleading comparisons. The press often quotes statistics about the U.S. federal government, excluding state and local governments. You should not compare such statistics to statistics on consolidated foreign governments.

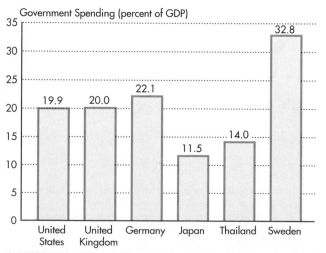

FIGURE 6-1 Government spending in the 1980s as a percentage of GDP.
[*Source: International Financial Statistics* (Washington, D.C.: International Monetary Fund, 1995).]

The government can spend money only if it first acquires the necessary resources—which it can obtain in several ways. For instance, the government can run a business, selling the output just as the owner of a private business would. In the United States, this method of raising revenue is best exemplified by the Postal Service, which charges to deliver letters. User fees, like tolls for using highways and admission charges at government-owned parks, are a small source of government revenue and are also examples of selling the output of government-owned "firms." In some countries, the government owns industries that represent a major proportion of the country's production. For example, in Mexico and Saudi Arabia the governments own and run the oil industry, selling oil to earn revenue. In some countries, a government can raise revenue through **nationalization:** it takes over, or *nationalizes,* an industry that has been set up by private owners. However, in the United States, most businesses are privately owned and legally protected against nationalization, so the sale of government output constitutes only a tiny portion of U.S. government revenue.

Nationalization:
The taking of private property by the government.

Another method of acquiring the resources for government spending is to print money. Although you might think that this method would provide a potentially infinite supply of revenue, printing money actually generates a relatively small and unreliable percentage of the real resources a government can use to finance its expenditures. You will be able to understand why this is so later in this book.

By far the most common method of raising government revenue is *taxation.* Taxes take many forms. Income taxes, property taxes, and sales taxes are probably the most familiar. Most of every dollar the government spends is acquired by taxing someone.

Of course, there's yet a fourth method of acquiring resources—borrowing. Borrowing resources does allow the government to acquire expendable revenue today. But every dollar borrowed must be repaid at some future time. Whenever the government borrows, its citizens know they will have to pay enough taxes in the future to cover the debt. Borrowing is thus only a temporary way for the government to acquire resources; eventually someone must be taxed.

Government Budgets

Usually, the government begins to develop a spending plan—called a *budget*—a year in advance of the actual spending. The budget describes how much money will be spent, what it will be spent on, and how it will be raised. (Actually, in the United States, the different levels of government—federal, state, and local—all produce their own budgets, but we can combine them all into "a budget.") The legislative unit—Congress, in the federal case, and state legislatures or city councils or even the voters in small local communities—discuss the consequences and benefits of the completed budget and vote on whether to pass it or revise it. Eventually, a budget must be agreed upon or the government will have to shut down.

Budget surplus:
The amount by which a government's revenue exceeds its expenditures.

If the government's revenue exceeds its expenditures, the government is said to run a **budget surplus.** In that case, the government lends the excess.

Budget deficit:
The amount by which a government's expenditures exceed its revenue.

If the government's revenue falls short of its expenditures, the government runs a **budget deficit.** The government must borrow the shortfall, and it must anticipate future taxes sufficient to cover the loan repayments.

Balanced budget:

The condition that results when a government's revenue exactly equals its expenditures.

A budget in which the government's revenue exactly covers its expenditures is called a **balanced budget.**

Governments spend, tax, and borrow so routinely that you might be surprised to hear an economist ask: "But is there any economic *rationale* for allowing our governments to spend our money?" In the next section, we turn to this question.

6-2 MARKETS VERSUS GOVERNMENTS

In this section, we discuss some of the costs and benefits of government spending.

Failures of the Marketplace

Private good:

A good that can be supplied efficiently by private competitive markets.

Public good:

A good that tends to be undersupplied in private competitive markets.

Nonexcludable good:

A good that people cannot be excluded from using.

Economists distinguish between **private goods,** which can be efficiently supplied by competitive firms under appropriate market conditions, and **public goods,** which competitive firms tend to supply in inefficiently small quantities. What distinguishes public goods is that they are either *nonexcludable, nonrivalrous,* or both. Let's see what these terms mean.

Nonexcludable Goods

Something is a **nonexcludable good** if there is no way to exclude people from using it. The most common example is national defense. A radar system that monitors the coastline for foreign invaders confers benefits on everyone. There is no practical way for the system to protect some people but not others.

Local police protection is another example. If the police patrol your neighborhood, their very presence reduces your chance of being robbed. Even if the police wanted to protect your neighbors without also protecting you, they would not be able to do so. In the course of protecting your neighbors, they would scare away criminals and you would automatically reap some of the benefits.

City parks may be nonexcludable if there is no practical way to prevent people from entering—say, because the boundaries can't be effectively patrolled. An outdoor concert is nonexcludable if there is no way to prevent nonpaying customers from hearing the music.

When a good is nonexcludable, consumers are reluctant to pay for it, since they know they can consume it for free. Suppose the United States Army or your local police department threatened to withdraw its protection unless you made a voluntary donation. You might very well refuse, secure in the knowledge that the army or the police department is quite incapable of withdrawing its protection from you alone. As long as soldiers or police continue to protect your neighbors, you are also protected and without charge. Likewise, if your city park is nonexcludable and tries to charge admission fees, many people may simply choose to walk in without paying. If a downtown concert charges admission and if the concert can be heard equally well from a block away without paying, not many tickets will be sold.

Because consumers are reluctant to pay for nonexcludable goods, private producers are reluctant to provide them. Who will organize the downtown concert if nobody is willing to pay for tickets? Who will construct and maintain the park if nobody is willing to pay the entrance fee? Who will set up a police force or an army if nobody will pay for protection? In such cases, people can make themselves better off by allowing the government to tax them and provide the services that no private producer will provide.

Nonrivalrous Goods

Nonrivalrous good:
A good that unlimited numbers of people can use without interfering with each other's enjoyment.

Something is a **nonrivalrous good** if an unlimited number of people can use it at once without interfering with each other's enjoyment. Ordinary goods like oranges and medical care don't qualify as nonrivalrous. Once you eat an orange, nobody else can eat it, and once you take an hour of your doctor's time, nobody else can have that hour.

But *The Simpsons* is a nonrivalrous good. No matter how many people watch *The Simpsons*, it is still there for other people to watch. If 10 million individuals tune their television sets to the proper channel at the proper time, then all 10 million can watch Homer giving bad advice to Bart. If 20 million individuals tune their sets to the program, then 20 million can watch. An unlimited number of people can watch *The Simpsons*, and they don't interfere with each other at all.

National defense is largely nonrivalrous. Many of the military programs that currently protect 250 million Americans could protect 300 million just as well at no additional expense.

An uncrowded park is nonrivalrous. New people can enter without affecting the ones who are already there. But a crowded park is rivalrous. In a crowded park, each new entrant uses up some of the other people's elbow room.

Computer disks are rivalrous. If you are using a computer disk, then I can't use it at the same time. But computer *software* is nonrivalrous. If you are using Word-Perfect, I can use WordPerfect at the same time without affecting your copy's performance one bit.

When a good is nonrivalrous, it seems churlish not to let everybody use that good. After all, no user is hurting any other user or keeping any other person from becoming a user, so what is the harm in making the good available to everyone? You might have heard people make exactly this argument to defend illegal cable television hookups and the use of pirated software.

The firms that produce nonrivalrous goods don't see it that way, though. They are in business to make a profit, and if their goods were available for free, then nobody would pay for them. Network television *does* make its services available for free, financing its operations through commercials. But cable stations and software manufacturers insist that people pay for their products.

If cable television costs $100 a year and you are only willing to pay $50, then— if you play by the rules—you don't get cable. An economist looks at that situation and sees a wasted resource. It just seems a shame not to let you have a cable hookup for the $50 that you are willing to pay; the deal would make you happy, and it wouldn't hurt anybody. The only reason it doesn't happen is that the cable company knows that if word of your special discount got around, everybody else would want one too.

In a sense, then, nonrivalrous goods like cable TV and computer software really "ought" to have unlimited distribution. But because no private firm is willing to provide unlimited distribution, there is an argument for the government to finance the production of those goods and then distribute them to everyone without charge.

Private versus Public Goods

Nonexcludable goods include police protection, outdoor concerts, and national defense. Nonrivalrous goods include cable hookups, computer software, and national defense again. Goods that fit into one or both of these categories are public goods. Goods that fit into neither category (like pumpkin pie, legal assistance, and bungee jumps) are private goods.

Most of the goods and services we purchase are private goods. An automobile is both an **excludable good** (if you don't pay, you don't get a car) and a **rivalrous good** (if you have the car, then somebody else doesn't have it). Therefore, an automobile is a private good.

Excludable good:
A good that is not nonexcludable.

Rivalrous good:
A good that is not nonrivalrous.

Competitive markets can provide private goods efficiently to the marketplace. In microeconomics classes, one spends a lot of time first being precise about what is meant by "efficiently" and then explaining *why* competitive markets are so efficient when it comes to private goods. But even without taking a lot of time, you can see why such a statement might be plausible. Because cars are excludable, manufacturers are able to charge for them and make a profit. Because cars are rivalrous, the fact that manufacturers don't give them out willy-nilly is a good thing; if they did, they would have to make so many cars that they would drain important resources from other industries.

However, as we saw, competitive markets tend to undersupply nonexcludable and nonrivalrous goods. When a good is nonexcludable, producers can't stop people from helping themselves, so they don't produce in the first place. When a good is nonrivalrous, producers really ought to let everybody use it, but they can't do that and make a profit, so they don't.

It is therefore at least possible that everybody can benefit when public goods are supplied not by private firms but by the government. The fact that this is *possible* doesn't make it true; governments have their own unique sources of inefficiency, which we shall discuss before the end of this section. Nevertheless, it is at least sometimes true that by providing public goods, governments can improve the lives of their citizens.

Equity

Equity:
Justice or fairness in the distribution of resources.

We have just discussed why the government should sometimes spend tax money for public goods. There is also a justification for government spending on *private* goods. It comes under the heading **"equity"** or "distribution." In an economy left to evolve on its own, some people will be poor and others will be rich. Some will be handicapped and others will be endowed with better-than-average skills. Should the government help those who have fewer resources at the expense of those who have more?

Most people have a natural desire to help those less fortunate than themselves. Religions and secular society encourage charity and compassion in all forms. The interesting question is not "Should we be charitable?" but "Should the *government* of a country tax those who have more to confer benefits on those who have less?"

Here is one argument that answers yes: We know that people voluntarily insure themselves against disasters. A typical middle-class American is likely to be insured against illness, injury, premature death, fire, burglary, and, perhaps, earthquakes. From this it is reasonable to infer that if we could purchase insurance before being born— and before knowing the circumstances we were to be born into—we would choose to insure ourselves against being born poor or otherwise disadvantaged. It can be argued that although such insurance is impossible, we are morally bound to act *as if* we had signed insurance contracts before birth, on the grounds that we all know that we *would* have signed them if we could have. From this viewpoint, government intervention to even out the distribution of income has the same moral status as government intervention to make sure your fire insurance company honors a legitimate claim.

Cash Transfers versus Goods and Services

There are two different ways governments can act to even out the distribution of wealth. One is by making cash transfers, such as welfare payments. The other is by directly providing those goods and services that are perceived to be most valuable to the poor or disadvantaged. There lurks a problem, however: Government officials might guess wrong about *which* goods and services are really most valuable to recipients.

Medical care is primarily a private good because its benefits are both excludable and rivalrous.[1] It can therefore be provided efficiently by the marketplace. Unfortunately, it might be provided by the marketplace at a price that makes it inaccessible to those at the lower end of the income scale. For this reason many people prefer to see the government provide medical care to the poor at below-market rates.

Similar arguments can be made to justify government provision of transportation services for the handicapped, or at least government subsidies to bring about private provision of those services. Yet in each case it can also be argued that the poor or the handicapped would be better off receiving simple cash transfers that they could spend as they please—on medical care, transportation, or whatever else they perceive to be in their best interests.

Whatever you think about such arguments, it is important to remember that whenever the government spends, it must raise revenue either by increasing taxes or by reducing its expenditure on some other item in its budget.

---

[1]An exception is the prevention and cure of contagious diseases. When you avoid contracting a contagious disease like smallpox, all your neighbors benefit automatically; this benefit might well be nonexcludable or nonrivalrous or both. Thus smallpox vaccinations could reasonably be classified as public goods.

Failures of the Government

We have argued that private markets can fail to provide adequate supplies of public goods and that therefore, in principle, it can be better for these goods to be supplied by the government. In this section, we examine the opposite argument, pointing out that governments, too, can fail to provide optimal outcomes.

Inefficiency in Production

WordPerfect is a popular software package used for word processing. To use Word-Perfect legally, you must pay a license fee of several hundred dollars to the Word-Perfect Corporation. This fee excludes many potential users. But the exclusion serves no economic purpose, since software is a nonrivalrous commodity: your use of Word-Perfect does not in any way limit your neighbor's ability to use it. This provides an argument for having the government develop and distribute the software free of charge.

Notice first that this argument has nothing at all to do with the costs of developing WordPerfect. If the government supplied software, it would have all of the same development costs that the WordPerfect Corporation has. Taxpayers would foot the bill for those costs, just as WordPerfect's customers do under the private market system. The one advantage of government provision would be wider distribution of the software.

However, the argument is conclusive only if the government can produce software as efficiently as the WordPerfect Corporation can. In practice this is unlikely to be the case. Faced with a profit motive and dozens of competitors, WordPerfect is under intense pressure to provide a high-quality product at the lowest possible cost. A government agency might not feel the same urgency about responding to market forces. While government-supplied software could be made available to everyone, it probably would not provide the array of features that have made WordPerfect so popular.

Lack of Information

Even when government bureaucrats are sincerely motivated to provide high-quality services at low cost, they face an overwhelming disadvantage compared with competitive suppliers. When the WordPerfect Corporation incorporates a new feature into its latest release, it wants to implement that feature in ways that will be especially valuable to users. It is hard to predict what users want, so WordPerfect's task is difficult. But the corporation can observe customer response to similar features in the variety of competing products that the marketplace provides. If all software came free from the government, this valuable information would be unavailable.

Thus governments fail to provide goods efficiently for at least two reasons. First, bureaucrats insulated from competitive pressure can be insufficiently motivated to provide quality products and to minimize costs. Second, even when they *are* fully motivated, bureaucrats may not have access to the vast flows of information that a market system automatically provides.

6-3 GOVERNMENT SPENDING IN THE ENDOWMENT ECONOMY

Now that you have an idea of what government spending entails, we are ready to add the government to the model presented in Chapter 5. We are going to explain how different kinds of government spending affect the equilibrium interest rate.

Categories of Government Spending

Productive government spending:
Government spending with benefits that exceed its cost.

Wasteful government spending:
Government spending with benefits that are less than its cost.

Pure transfers (transfer payments):
Government spending with benefits that are exactly equal to its cost; usually in the form of cash payments from one person to another.

Productive government spending provides benefits that exceed its cost, as can happen when the government supplies a public good that would be inefficiently supplied by the private sector. In **wasteful government spending** the cost exceeds the benefits. There is also government spending in which the cost is exactly equal to the benefits. This kind of spending consists of **pure transfers** (also called **transfer payments**), in which the government takes resources from one person and gives them to another. The transfer benefits (to the recipient) and the cost (to the person whose resources are taken) are exactly equal.

Let us consider a few examples and some of their economic effects.

Productive Spending

Sometimes the government is able to spend resources more effectively than the private sector can, as in the case of public goods. In exchange for a $1 million expenditure for police officers, parks, or pothole repair, the government may be able to provide services that people value at far more than $1 million. In this case the net value of all goods and services produced and consumed in the economy increases because of the spending, and people as a whole become wealthier.

In graphical terms, productive spending shifts the aggregate supply curve in Figure 6-2 to the right by an amount that is equal to the net benefit from the govern-

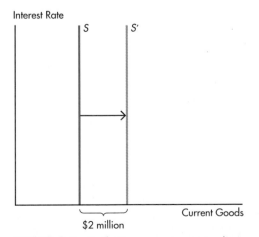

FIGURE 6-2 Productive government spending.
Suppose that by spending $1 million, the government can produce goods and services that citizens collectively value at $3 million. As a result, the total value of all resources in the economy increases by $2 million, and the supply curve moves to the right by that amount, from S to S'.

ment's undertaking. Remember that the aggregate supply curve reflects the total value of all of the goods that are actually available for consumption. Productive government spending increases that total value. In the figure, we assume that the government provides $3 million worth of benefits, using up $1 million worth of resources in the process. The total value of all available goods increases by $3 million minus $1 million, or $2 million. Therefore, the aggregate supply curve shifts to the right by $2 million.

Wasteful Spending

We use the term "wasteful spending" to characterize government expenditures that produce benefits less valuable than their costs. If the government spends $10 million to provide a public school that could have been provided privately for $6 million, then the economy is $4 million poorer than before. The additional $4 million in resources consumed by the government is now unavailable for consumption. Figure 6-3 shows that this spending causes the aggregate supply curve to shift to the left by $4 million.

 The adjective "wasteful" carries no moral connotations. If the government spends $15 million to provide $5 million worth of health care to the poor, then society is $10 million poorer, and the aggregate supply curve shifts $10 million to the left. Many people—perhaps even everyone—might support this program if its distributional effects (such as transferring income from one group of people to another) are perceived as desirable. Nevertheless, we will continue to characterize such spending as wasteful, meaning *only* that it reduces society's resources. We do *not* mean to imply that the reduction is necessarily a bad thing.

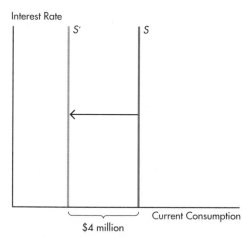

FIGURE 6-3 Wasteful government spending.
If the government spends $10 million (uses up $10 million worth of resources) to produce $6 million worth of educational services, the total value of all resources in the economy falls by $4 million. Therefore, the aggregate supply curve shifts left by $4 million, from S to S'.

Transfer Payments

Productive spending produces benefits in excess of its cost; wasteful spending produces benefits that are less valuable than its cost. One remaining possibility is that the benefits of a government spending program just happen to offset the cost exactly. In general, this would require a remarkable coincidence. But there is one case in which this outcome is to be expected, and that is the case of a transfer payment. If the government taxes Peter $100 in order to make a $100 cash payment to Paul, then the cost (to Peter) is $100 and the benefit (to Paul) is also exactly $100. Resources are transferred from Peter to Paul, but *no resources are either created or destroyed*. In this case, the government's spending is neither productive nor wasteful. In contrast to the situation in Figures 6-2 and 6-3, now the aggregate supply curve does not move, because there is no change in the total quantity of goods and services available to the entire economy.

Sometimes the government spends on projects that yield no immediate benefits but are expected to be highly productive in the future. A highway is useless while it is under construction but might be very valuable after it is completed. Anticipating the language of Chapter 7, we shall call such construction an example of *productive investment* by the government: the spending occurs now, but the benefits of the spending accrue later.

How do the government's productive investments affect the aggregate supply curve? Remember that the aggregate supply curve illustrates the quantity of goods available *in the present*. If the current costs of a government project exceed the *current* benefits, then the aggregate supply curve shifts to the left, as in Figure 6-3—just as if the spending were wasteful.

Temporary government spending:

Government spending that lasts only a single period of time.

Does this mean that a government program to build useful highways and a government program to build useless ditches have exactly the same effects? No; it means only that they have the same effect on the aggregate supply curve in the market for current goods. They have quite *different* effects on the aggregate supply curve in the market for *future* goods, and therefore quite different effects on citizens' well-being in the long run.

Temporary Spending versus Permanent Spending

Permanent government spending:

Government spending that is repeated in each period of time.

Some government expenditures are of a "one-shot" nature, while others continue over time. The purchase of a single nuclear submarine or the construction of a new highway is an isolated event (**temporary government spending**), whereas a permanent expansion of the army or an annual highway maintenance program entails a series of expenditures over many years (**permanent government spending**). Temporary and permanent spending programs have very different costs and benefits, and hence very different effects on the way citizens organize their lives. Whenever we analyze the effects of a government program, we need to know both whether it is productive, wasteful, or neither *and* whether it is temporary or permanent.

Comparative Statics

Let us now analyze the effects of various government spending programs. To get the analyses correct, it is critical to remember that all spending must ultimately be financed by taxation. In order to spend more, the government must tax more.

In some cases, taxes are raised immediately; in other cases, the government borrows resources temporarily and does not raise taxes until some future date. *In this section, we will always assume that taxes are raised simultaneously with spending.* Later in the chapter, we will ask how our conclusions would change if the tax increase is deferred to the future.

A Temporary Increase in Wasteful Spending

Suppose that the government undertakes a one-time-only project representing wasteful spending. Real-world examples might include the purchase of an unnecessary aircraft carrier, the installation of handicapped-access ramps at an office building rarely visited by the handicapped, or a temporary agricultural program that subsidizes farmers to cut back on their production. The common thread in these examples is a reduction in the resources available for other uses, including consumption. The parts that go into making the aircraft carrier could have been used for automobiles; the effort that goes into the access ramps could have been used to construct new office buildings; the grain that farmers choose not to grow could have fed the hungry.

In the endowment economy represented by the simple model in Chapter 5, a temporary wasteful spending program would be that the government confiscates apples and throws them away. As we have seen in Figure 6-3, such a program means that the aggregate supply curve shifts to the left by the amount of the waste. Figure 6-4

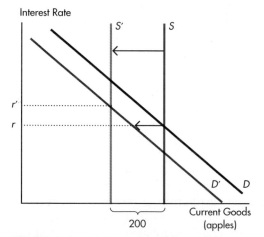

FIGURE 6-4 Temporary wasteful spending.
When the government spends wastefully, aggregate supply shifts leftward by the amount of the waste (from S to S'). Aggregate demand shifts also, but by less than the shift in supply (from D to D') because the spending program is not permanent. The equilibrium interest rate rises from r to r'.

illustrates the effect of a program in which the government destroys a total of 200 apples. The aggregate supply curve shifts 200 apples to the left, as shown.

What happens to the aggregate demand for current goods? Having lost a total of 200 apples, people are poorer and will therefore choose to consume less. The result is that the demand curve shifts to the left. But how *far* to the left? Here the key observation is that the wasteful spending program is temporary. Current incomes are effectively reduced, but future incomes are unchanged. Consumption smoothing dictates that people will attempt to spread their bad fortune over several years. That is, rather than reduce their current consumption by a full 200 apples, people will want to reduce current consumption by something *less* than 200 apples and to reduce future consumption a bit as well.

Thus the demand for current consumption shifts leftward but by less than 200 apples, from D to D' in Figure 6-4. When supply and demand both shift leftward but demand shifts less than supply, then the equilibrium interest rate must rise. In this case it rises from r to r'.

Note that the diagram looks qualitatively exactly like Figure 5-9 (page 122) ("The effects of a war"). If we were to illustrate the effects of a tornado or of Hurricane Andrew, the diagram would look the same again. *Any* one-time destruction of consumption goods causes the supply of current consumption to shift leftward by the amount that is destroyed and the demand for current consumption to shift leftward by less (because of consumption smoothing).

From a macroeconomic viewpoint, all that matters is that current resources are destroyed. It does not matter whether the destruction is caused by the weather, a hostile foreign power, or our own government.

 Many economists model wasteful spending by the government *not* as a reduction in the *supply* of current goods but as an addition to the *demand* for current goods. Either method is legitimate, but it is important to adopt one method and use it consistently. In this book, we shall always treat wasteful government spending as a reduction in supply.

Exercise 6-1
Suppose that the 200-apple wasteful spending program causes the demand curve to shift leftward by only 150 apples. If the interest rate did not adjust immediately to r', would there be a momentary excess supply or excess demand for apples? How would individuals' response to this situation cause the interest rate to rise?

A Temporary Increase in Productive Spending

Figure 6-5 illustrates the effect of a temporary government program whose benefits exceed its cost. Typically, such a situation arises when the government seizes an opportunity to provide a valuable public good that cannot be supplied efficiently by the marketplace.

In terms of the model, productive spending means the government has found a

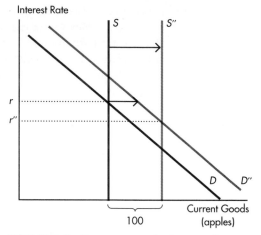

FIGURE 6-5 Temporary productive spending.
When the government effectively creates 100 new apples, the supply of current goods shifts right by 100 apples, from S to S''. Consumption smoothing dictates that the demand for current goods shifts right by *less* than 100 apples, from D to D''. The net effect is a drop in the interest rate from r to r''.

way to increase the number of apples. To visualize this idea, imagine a machine that converts five apples into six. The government collects 500 apples through taxation, puts them through its machine, and returns 600 apples to a grateful populace.

The first effect of such a program is an increase in the supply of current goods. The supply curve shifts rightward by the full amount of the windfall—in this case 100 apples—from S to S'' in the figure. The second effect is an increase in the *demand* for current goods: people are wealthier and therefore want to eat more apples. Once again we must face the question: How far does the demand curve shift? And once again, the key is consumption smoothing. If you are given one extra apple today with no promise of extra apples in the future, you will want to consume only *part* of the apple today, spreading your good luck over several years. Therefore, the consumption demand curve shifts rightward by *less* than the amount of the windfall, from D to D''. As a result of the supply and demand shifts, the interest rate falls from r to r'' in Figure 6-5.

Notice that Figure 6-5 is qualitatively identical to Figure 5-8 on page 120 ("An increase in the supply of current goods"). All that matters in either figure is that the quantity of current-consumption goods has increased and that people choose to smooth their consumption streams. Whether the good fortune comes from nature (as in Figure 5-8) or from the halls of Congress (as in Figure 6-5) is unimportant.

Many economists count government-distributed goods separately from private consumption demand. In this textbook, we will not make that distinction: all the apples that Eve chooses to consume are counted as apples demanded by Eve, whether she owns them originally, buys them from Adam, or receives them as gifts from the government.

Our method is not consistent with the way that official statistics (called *national income accounts*) are kept in the United States, where "consumption spending" (by individuals) is placed in a separate category from government spending. There is, however, a good argument for the alternative method that we are using here. It makes little difference whether you buy corn flakes from a store or have them delivered to you by a government agent, but the U.S. national income accounts treat these transactions differently—the corn flakes you buy are counted as consumption, while the corn flakes you get from the government are counted as government spending. Many European governments have adopted accounting systems that eliminate such false distinctions, and we have done the same thing in this book.

Throughout this book, then, we will usually lump government spending into other categories. Thus, if the government purchases consumption goods for people, we will count these purchases as consumption; if the government purchases investment goods, we will count these purchases as investment; if the government spends wastefully, we will usually think of the spending as reducing the supply of goods. This approach is neither more nor less legitimate than the accounting methods discussed in Chapter 2, but it sometimes makes it easier to see what is going on.

To avoid confusion, though, you should recognize that the accounting system in Chapter 2, which describes how official statistics are compiled in the United States, is not identical with the accounting systems in this and later chapters.

A Temporary Increase in Transfer Payments

Suppose the government decides, on a one-shot basis, to take one apple from Peter and give it to Paul.

We first observe that there is no change in the aggregate supply of current apples. Peter has one less and Paul has one more, but there is no change in the total number of apples.

Our second observation concerns current-consumption demand. Peter, being poorer, will reduce his demand (by *less* than one apple, because of consumption smoothing). Paul, being richer, will increase his demand (also by less than one apple). The aggregate demand for apples can change in either direction, depending on whether Peter's demand reduction is more or less than Paul's demand increase.

In Chapter 4, we gave a name to the quantity by which Paul increases his current-apple consumption: It is his *marginal propensity to consume out of current income,* or *MPC.* Paul's demand increases by his MPC. Peter's demand falls by his own MPC. The direction of the shift in aggregate demand depends on which MPC is greater.

In the problem as stated, we have no information about whose MPC is greater, and in such circumstances we will assume that the two MPCs are equal or at least close enough so that we can pretend they are equal. Thus we expect in this example that there is no shift in aggregate consumption demand.

Because neither supply nor demand shifts, there is no change in the interest rate.

The quantity of goods and the aggregate demand for those goods are both unchanged, so the market maintains its equilibrium without any change in the interest rate.

> *Exercise 6-2*
> Suppose that Peter's MPC exceeds Paul's. Which way does the interest rate move? What if Paul's MPC exceeds Peter's?

A Permanent Increase in Wasteful Spending

Suppose the government institutes a wasteful program whereby 200 apples are destroyed every year and announces that this program will continue forever. The first 200 apples have just been destroyed.

In this case, the supply of current consumption shifts leftward by 200 apples as shown in Figure 6-6. *Future* reductions in the apple harvest do not affect the supply of *current* goods; only the immediate 200-apple loss is reflected in the supply curve.

The demand for current consumption, however, reflects all the current *and future* effects of the program. Citizens are told that their incomes will be effectively reduced by 200 apples per year forever. To smooth their consumption of apples, they must reduce their consumption demand by 200 apples per year this year and forever. The demand curve shifts leftward by 200 apples—the full amount of the current wasteful spending.

Since supply and demand shift leftward by the same amount, the interest rate remains unchanged. Although a certain number of apples have disappeared from the world, people voluntarily reduce their consumption by exactly that number of apples. The market remains in equilibrium without change in the interest rate.

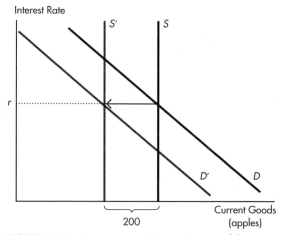

FIGURE 6-6   A permanent increase in wasteful government spending. When the government announces a plan to destroy 200 apples each year, starting immediately, the supply curve shifts left by 200 apples, from S to S' (because 200 apples are instantly destroyed). Consumption smoothing dictates that the demand curve shifts leftward by a full 200 apples, from D to D'. The interest rate r remains unchanged.

Government Spending in the United States

Figure 6-7 illustrates the recent history of federal, state, and local government spending as a percentage of GDP in the United States. The lower curve (labeled "Purchases") includes all government purchases of goods and services, while the upper curve (labeled "Expenditures") adds direct cash transfers from the government to individuals. If your state government constructs a new highway, the costs of labor and raw materials are included in both purchases and expenditures. If your state government makes welfare payments to families with dependent children, the payments are included in expenditures but not purchases.

Many economists argue that government purchases are the best measure of the burden that governments impose on their citizens. Goods and services purchased by the government are no longer available to be purchased by anyone else. The real resources that you and I have available to us are diminished by what the government purchases. By contrast, cash transfers do not consume any resources at all: they shift wealth from some citizens to others without using up any of that wealth in the process.

When we speak of the "burden" of government on citizens, we must not forget that citizens receive a stream of government services in exchange for bearing that burden. The graph of government purchases measures the cost of government; such a graph does not show the offsetting benefits—which are far harder to measure and which may be either much greater or much less than the cost.

While government purchases may be the best measure of the burden that government places on its citizens taken as a whole, government expenditures may be the best measure of the burden that government places on those of its citizens who pay

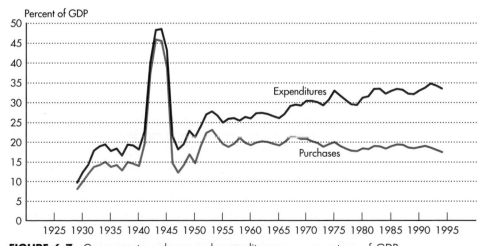

FIGURE 6-7 Government purchases and expenditures as a percentage of GDP. Purchases include all goods and services that the government buys; expenditures also include cash transfer payments.

taxes. A $10 million highway and a $10 million welfare program are equally costly to those who foot the bill.

The most striking thing about Figure 6-7 is the enormous peak in the early 1940s, when the United States was fighting World War II. If you examine the purchases curve, you will find a much smaller blip upward in the early 1950s and an even smaller one in the late 1960s, corresponding to the wars in Korea and Vietnam.

Another striking feature of the graph is that government spending (relative to GDP) is much larger now than it was in 1929, before the Great Depression. In the 1930s, the scope of government grew considerably, and it has not returned to its former level. Economists do not have a good and widely accepted model of what causes such dramatic and long-lasting changes in the level of government spending.

In more recent years, as the graph illustrates, there has been a remarkable divergence between purchases and expenditures. While purchases have leveled off or even exhibited a slight downward trend, expenditures have grown rapidly, reflecting a great expansion of the government's role as a dispenser of transfer payments. In the early 1990s, there was a slight downturn in the level of expenditures—but it is too soon to know whether it will be a blip in the graph or the beginning of a long-term trend.

6-4 TAXATION

To spend, the government must tax. Once the decision to spend has been made, the only remaining decisions are *when* to tax and *what* to tax.

Regarding *when* to tax, the choice is between *now* and *later.* One option is to spend and tax simultaneously. Another is to spend borrowed revenue and then raise taxes later to pay the debt. Much of Section 6-5 is concerned with the choice between these options.

Regarding *what* to tax, you are probably aware that there are many candidates. Governments can and do tax income, consumption, labor, investment, and savings. These are all examples of **variable taxes,** whereby your tax bill varies according to the dollar value of some item. An income tax varies with the dollar value of your income, a consumption tax varies with the dollar value of your consumption, and so forth. You can probably think of several variable taxes that you or people you know pay regularly. When you buy a pad of paper, you might pay a *sales tax* proportional to the price, with the percentage depending on the city and state where you make your purchase. Homeowners pay *property taxes* that vary with the value of their property (the value is decided by assessors, who periodically evaluate the market prices of houses in each community); businesses that bring foreign goods into the country pay *import duties* that vary with the value of the imported goods; and most citizens pay *income taxes,* to both federal and state governments, that vary with their earnings.

Some variable taxes are invisible in the sense that government statistics fail to record them. For example, when you buy an automobile, part of the purchase price pays for mandatory pollution control equipment. There is no difference between pay-

Variable tax:
A tax in which the amount paid is dependent on the value of some quantity that is within an individual's control.

ing $1000 for a catalytic converter and paying a $1000 "pollution tax" that the government uses to provide you with a catalytic converter. Whenever a firm or an individual is required to purchase a good, the resulting expenditures should be considered a form of taxation.

In the example of the catalytic converter, all car buyers pay the same amount. Nevertheless, this (hidden) tax is still an example of a *variable* tax because people who don't buy cars pay nothing. One way to think of this is that your tax is zero if you have zero dollars' worth of car (that is, no car) and $1000 if you have *more* than zero dollars' worth of car—so the tax does vary with the dollar value of your car.

Lump-sum tax:
A tax in which the amount paid is not dependent on any variables that are within an individual's control.

Head tax (poll tax):
A type of lump-sum tax in which each person pays the same amount.

Disincentive effect:
The substitution effect that results from taxing consumption or production of a specific good, thereby discouraging the activity by raising the price of doing it.

An alternative to variable taxes is a **lump-sum tax** requiring that everybody pay a constant amount that is independent of the value or quantity of any item or activity. For example, a lump-sum tax might require that each household pay a $100 annual fee to the government regardless of a family's income, property holdings, or spending behavior. A lump-sum tax such as this, which treats everybody equally, is also called a **head tax** or a **poll tax.** Poll taxes of this sort were a significant source of government revenue in the United Kingdom in the 1980s. Requiring that each family send a member to perform some government service, such as serving in the military, is another form of lump-sum tax.

It is a fundamental observation that *taxing an activity discourages that activity.* This law is called the **disincentive effect** of taxation. In general, the more heavily an activity is taxed, the more that activity is discouraged. If you tax gasoline, people buy less gasoline. If you tax imported cars, people buy fewer imported cars. If you tax developed land (land that has a structure on it or that has been prepared for cultivation) more heavily than undeveloped land, less land gets developed. If you tax income, people choose to have less income (by working less); since income equals output, this means that output must fall.

In these examples of the disincentive effect the taxes are variable. Lump-sum taxes, because they are not taxes on any activity, do not generally have significant disincentive effects. This means that lump-sum taxes are a bit easier to work into our models. When we study lump-sum taxes, we need to think only about the effects of the tax itself. When we study variable taxes, we need to think both about those effects and about disincentive effects. Therefore, we will concentrate our attention, especially at the beginning, on lump-sum taxes. What we conclude will still be applicable when we return to the study of variable taxes; we will only have to incorporate the disincentive effects of variable taxes to obtain the complete picture.

Actually, even lump-sum taxes can have some disincentive effects. For example, if a law imposes an annual head tax of $20,000 per person, couples might choose to have fewer children. But these effects are generally less significant than the disincentive effects of variable taxes, and we will generally ignore them.

By concentrating on lump-sum taxes, we can defer the question of *what* to tax. We now return to the question of *when* to tax.

6-5   DEBT AND DEFICITS

Deficit:

The amount that a government borrows in a given period of time.

When the government borrows to finance current spending, it is said to run a **deficit.** A deficit should be distinguished from outstanding **government debt,** which includes debt from past years that has not yet been repaid. If the government already owes $100 billion and borrows an additional $10 billion, then the debt—total outstanding debt—increases to $110 billion, while the (current) deficit is just the additional $10 billion borrowed.

The History of Government Debt in the United States

Government debt:

The cumulative amount that a government owes as a result of all past borrowing.

The U.S. government was born in debt, and it has been in debt ever since. To help finance the Revolution, the Continental Congress issued about $6 million in bonds. Early American patriot Thomas Paine encouraged such borrowing, arguing that the citizens of a new nation would feel more loyalty toward a government that owed them money. Alexander Hamilton, who would become the first secretary of the Treasury, agreed.

By the time the Constitution was ratified, the federal debt had grown to about $50 million. In Figure 6-8 you can see that this debt was slowly paid off over a period of about 50 years, with a bit of backsliding to finance the War of 1812. By 1835, the total outstanding debt of the federal government had been reduced to just $38,000. (Coincidentally, $38,000 is very close to the federal debt *per capita* today.) This virtual elimination of the debt was the work of President Andrew Jackson, who never wavered in his near-fanatical devotion to the principle that governments should be free of debt. Once Jackson left office, the debt proceeded to grow, and except for a

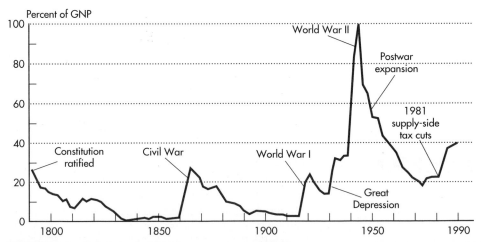

FIGURE 6-8   U.S. federal debt as a percentage of GNP.
[*Source:* D. Stabile and J. Cantor, *The Public Debt of the United States* (New York: Praeger, 1991).]

brief time just prior to the U.S. entry into World War I, it has never again threatened to approach zero.

If you look again at Figure 6-8, you will see that the public debt has tended to increase in times of war. This is not surprising; in wartime governments need funds in a hurry. The enormous debts that were incurred to finance World War II were largely paid off at an extremely rapid rate: the debt (as a percentage of national income) had fallen to prewar values by about 1970.

Since then the national debt—again, expressed as a percentage of national income—has been on the rise. However, it is still far lower than it was in 1950, a time of economic growth and prosperity. This hardly proves that the national debt is not a matter for concern—but it does show that the nation has lived quite comfortably with levels of government debt far in excess of those we face today.

Recent History of the U.S. Federal Deficit

Figure 6-9 illustrates the outlays and receipts of the U.S. government in recent years. They are measured in constant 1992 dollars and on a per capita basis. In the first year of the second Reagan administration (1985), the federal government spent $5059 per American while collecting $3924 per American in taxes. The difference of $1135 was added to the average American's share of outstanding federal debt—in other words, the federal deficit in 1985 was $1135 per capita.

By the last year of that same administration (1988), outlays had been reduced by $15 to $5044 per American (after having fallen all the way to $4971 in 1987), while receipts had grown by $385 to $4309 per American. In that year, the average American's share of the federal debt grew by only $735. Clearly this reduction in the per capita deficit, from $1135 to $735, was almost entirely the result of rising tax revenues, not cuts in government spending.

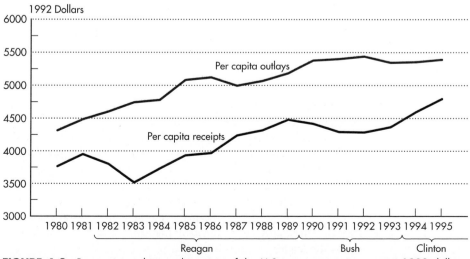

FIGURE 6-9 Per capita outlays and receipts of the U.S. government, in constant 1992 dollars.

Over the course of the Bush administration, there was a substantial increase in government spending, with outlays growing to $5415 per American per year by 1992, the last year of that administration. Compared with the spending of $5044 four years earlier, annual outlays grew by $371 per American while President Bush was in office. At the same time, annual receipts fell by $33 per American, to $4276. The average American's share of the annual deficit rose by $371 + $33 = $404, to $1139.

In President Clinton's first year in office—1993—outlays fell to $5321, while receipts rose to $4357. In that year, the federal debt grew by $964 per American. The fact that it was $964 rather than the previous year's $1139 can be attributed to $94 in spending cuts and $81 in tax increases. Over the next two years under Clinton, annual outlays rose again (by $45), while annual receipts rose much more dramatically (by $428), reducing the per capita annual deficit by $383, to $581.

Taxation versus Deficits

Suppose once again that the government has decided to undertake a spending program. The program might be wasteful or productive, temporary or permanent. In Figures 6-4, 6-5, and 6-6 we analyzed the effects of various spending programs under the assumption that these programs were financed by current tax revenues. But suppose now that instead of taxing citizens currently, the government borrows the resources it is going to spend. How do our conclusions change?

Consider this concrete example: Suppose the government has decided to spend 200 apples wastefully—say, by throwing them into the ocean. It is considering two different plans for acquiring the apples. Senator Tarcomed proposes to increase current taxes by a total of 200 apples. Senator Nacilbuper suggests borrowing the apples at the going annual interest rate of 10 percent, in which case the loan will have to be repaid next year. Under Senator Nacilbuper's plan, next year's taxes will be increased by 220 apples to repay the loan with interest.

Figure 6-10 reproduces Figure 6-4 to illustrate the effect of Senator Tarcomed's plan to raise current taxes. Let us review the analysis of that figure in the context of this example. Because 200 apples are destroyed, the supply curve shifts leftward by 200 apples, from S to S'. Because people are made poorer by being taxed 200 apples, the demand curve shifts leftward as well, from D to D'. However, demand does not shift leftward as far as supply shifts; because people attempt to spread their bad fortune over a lifetime, they cut their current consumption by something less than 200 apples. The interest rate rises from r to r'.

Let us now consider Senator Nacilbuper's alternative plan to borrow the apples. Here 200 apples are still destroyed, but citizens are not taxed to cover the expenditure until a year in the future. Once again the current supply curve in Figure 6-10 shifts to the left by 200 apples, because 200 current apples are destroyed. The supply curve reflects the number of apples that are physically available today, and that number is reduced by 200 at the moment that the government throws 200 of them away. The supply curve shifts by that same amount regardless of how the government gets the apples.

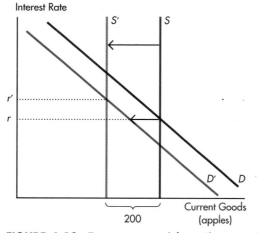

FIGURE 6-10 Taxation versus deficits: The case of temporary wasteful spending.
If the government institutes a temporary wasteful spending program that destroys 200 apples, then the supply of current apples shifts leftward by 200. In addition, the demand for current apples falls, because people are poorer. It falls by the same amount, from D to D', whether the government finances the spending by taxation or by borrowing. In both cases, the interest rate rises from r to r'.

> When the government spends wastefully, the leftward shift of the aggregate supply curve is independent of where the government gets the resources to pay for the wasteful spending.

Next let us determine what happens to the demand curve. By running a deficit, the government manages to avoid raising taxes in the present. However, the deficit today commits the government to raising taxes in the future. Anticipating the future tax increase, people already feel poorer; indeed, they already *are* poorer. Rather than feel all the pain in the future, people prefer to smooth consumption, cutting back a bit today and a bit tomorrow. Thus consumption demand moves leftward as in Figure 6-10.

Now comes the critical comparison: Under which plan does the demand curve shift farther left, Senator Tarcomed's taxation plan or Senator Nacilbuper's deficit plan? The key to answering that question is the observation that *current-consumption demand is determined by wealth.* The taxation plan reduces people's wealth by 200 apples today. The deficit (borrowing) plan reduces people's wealth by 220 apples tomorrow, which have a present value of $220/1.10 = 200$ apples today. Both plans result in the same present value, so *both plans reduce people's wealth by exactly the same amount.* Therefore, both plans reduce current-consumption demand by exactly the same amount. The current demand curve in Figure 6-10 moves to the same location, D', under either plan.

Both plans cause S to shift to S'; both plans cause D to shift to D'. Figure 6-10 applies equally to both plans. Under either plan, the interest rate rises from r to r'.

In a simple endowment economy, when the government spends wastefully on a temporary program, the interest rate rises by the same amount whether the spending is financed by current taxation or by borrowing.

A similar argument based on Figure 6-5 shows that:

In a simple endowment economy, when the government spends *productively* on a temporary program, the interest rate *drops* by the same amount whether the spending is financed by current taxation or by borrowing.

Ricardian Equivalence

The great economist David Ricardo, writing in the early 1800s, thought that these conclusions were so obvious as to need no elaboration. Ricardo saw that the choice between current taxation and government borrowing is a choice between two tax collections of equal present value. It was clear to Ricardo that two payment schemes of equal present value must have identical effects.

In Ricardo's honor, the principle that taxation and borrowing have identical effects is known as the principle of **Ricardian equivalence.** There is no question that Ricardian equivalence holds in a simple endowment economy such as we have described. But even Ricardo himself had doubts about applying the principle to the real world. In fact, the applicability of Ricardian equivalence to real economies remains controversial among modern economists, for reasons we shall soon explore.

While economists today debate the importance of Ricardian equivalence, politicians and journalists seem to overlook it entirely. In ancient times (1984), a politician named Walter Mondale gave eloquent voice to a common misconception when he asserted during a televised presidential debate that "everybody, every economist, every businessman" agrees that deficits are an important factor affecting interest rates. Perhaps someday economists will be unanimous on the subject of deficits, but Mondale certainly spoke too soon.

> **Ricardian equivalence:**
> The proposition that taxation and government borrowing have identical effects on an economy.

The principle of Ricardian equivalence can be summarized by the slogan "Deficits don't matter." Do not confuse this slogan with the *wrong* slogan, "Spending doesn't matter." Temporary government spending programs definitely affect interest rates, current consumption, and people's happiness, as you can see in Figures 6-4 and 6-5. The only assertion of Ricardian equivalence is that once the spending has been undertaken, the decision to finance it by borrowing has no *additional* effect on anything of economic consequence.

The Geometry of Ricardian Equivalence

The idea behind Ricardian equivalence can be summarized in a paragraph: When the government spends a dollar, the present value of all current and future taxes must rise by exactly one dollar. It is a matter of indifference to taxpayers whether the government collects one dollar today or $1 + r$ dollars tomorrow. Since the choice of tax policies is a matter of complete indifference to everyone, it can have no effect on anyone's behavior.

A verbal argument can make an idea seem reasonable—sometimes misleadingly. To see whether Ricardian equivalence really makes sense, let's translate its argument into geometry.

Figure 6-11 is a graphical analysis of the case for Ricardian equivalence. The graph displays the budget line L of Terry Taxpayer, who accounts for 1 percent of the economy. Terry's income this year is five apples and her income next year will be seven apples, so point Y depicts her income stream. We assume Terry consumes at optimum point O on L. (Note that point O is drawn to the left of point Y; this is for convenience only. If point O were drawn to the right of point Y, the argument to follow would remain the same.)

If the government raises taxes by 200 apples today, then, because Terry accounts for 1 percent of the economy, her tax bill must rise by 2 apples today. Her income stream point (showing her current and future after-tax income) must then shift 2 apples to the left, to point T (for "taxation"). Terry's new intertemporal budget line L' must pass through point T. If the interest rate is 10 percent, then the slope of both L and L' is -1.10. We assume that Terry consumes at optimum point O' on her new budget line. (Point O' is drawn between points T and D, again, for convenience only. Point O' could occur anywhere along line L', and the argument to follow would remain the same.)

Suppose, on the other hand, that the government borrows 200 apples at 10 percent interest and raises taxes by 220 apples next year to pay off the debt. Then Terry's

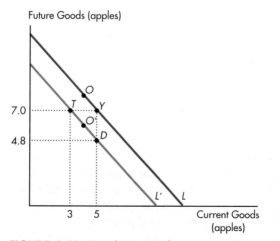

FIGURE 6-11 Ricardian equivalence.
Terry Taxpayer starts with budget line L and endowment point Y. The government decides to spend 200 apples, of which Terry's share is 2 apples. If the government taxes Terry 2 apples today, her endowment point moves to T and her new budget line is L'. Alternatively, if the government borrows 2 apples and taxes her 2.2 apples next year to repay the debt, Terry's endowment point moves to D and her new budget line is again L'. Either way, she chooses the same optimum point O'. Therefore, Terry's demand for current consumption is the same under either program.

current taxes do not rise at all, and so her current income remains unchanged. Her future taxes, however, rise by 2.2 apples, which is her 1 percent share of the total future tax bill; her expected future income falls to 4.8 apples. Instead of moving from Y to T, her income stream point moves from Y to D (for "deficit spending").

Terry's intertemporal budget line is now a line of slope -1.10 through point D. The key observation is that *this is exactly the same budget line* L' *we obtained when Terry's income stream point moved to* T. This is the geometric equivalent of the statement that both financing plans leave Terry with exactly the same level of wealth.

Since Terry's budget line is L' regardless of how the government spending is financed, her consumption point is O' regardless of which financing plan is chosen. Her present- and future-consumption demands are the same under either plan.

 Notice that Terry's optimum point (representing desired present- and future-consumption demands) is *not* the same whether the government spends or not. In the absence of any spending program, Terry's optimum would be at point O on line L.

Once we know that Terry has the same current-consumption demand under either plan, Ricardian equivalence follows. The two plans certainly have identical effects on the supply of current goods. If they also have the same effects on the demand for current goods, then *all* of their effects are identical.

6-6 RICARDIAN EQUIVALENCE AND REALITY

The argument for Ricardian equivalence is simple and appears definitive. Nevertheless, many economists believe that the argument omits some important features of the real world, and they are therefore skeptical of its conclusion. In this section, we examine both sides of the issue.

A Bad Argument against Ricardian Equivalence

When newspapers and politicians express concern about government deficits, they often rely on one simple argument that almost all economists agree is incorrect. We begin our examination by disposing of that argument. (If you can learn to avoid making this argument, you will know more about deficits than most of the people who earn a living discussing them.) Then, in the next subsection, we shall concentrate on arguments that many economists *do* find plausible.

The Government as Competitor

Noneconomists frequently argue that when the government borrows, it must compete for lendable resources with existing private borrowers. They say that when this happens, the added demand for those resources drives the interest rate up.

What the argument overlooks is that governments borrow *on behalf of* private citizens. Suppose that today Oscar's government plans to tax him $10 to finance its operations, and suppose also that today Oscar plans to borrow $1 with which to buy a banana peel. But the government suddenly announces a change in policy: instead of taxing Oscar $10, it will tax him only $9 today, borrow the additional dollar now, and raise Oscar's taxes in the future. At this point, Oscar has an extra dollar in his pocket as a result of the tax cut, and he can use that dollar to buy his banana peel. There is no longer any reason for him to borrow.

It would surely be incorrect to argue here that the government competes with Oscar to borrow a dollar. The correct analysis of this situation is that when the government decides to borrow a dollar instead of raising Oscar's taxes, Oscar no longer needs to borrow a dollar. The total demand for borrowing is unchanged.

Argument by Geometry

Figure 6-12 illustrates the geometry of another example. In (*a*), Terry Taxpayer's initial income stream point is *Y*. A new, wasteful government-spending program is instituted, and Terry's share is $200. If she is taxed in the present, her income stream point

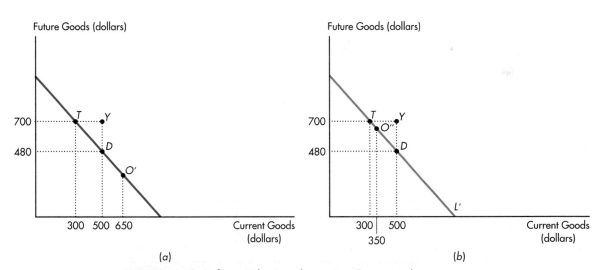

FIGURE 6-12 Deficits and private borrowing: Two examples.
Terry's income stream point is initially at *Y*. The government institutes a wasteful spending program that it can finance by taxation (moving Terry to *T*) or borrowing (moving Terry to *D*); either way, her new budget line is the blue line. (*a*) Suppose that Terry's optimum point happens to be *O'*. Under the taxation scheme, Terry borrows $350 to get from *T* to *O'*. Under the deficit scheme, the government borrows $200 and then Terry borrows $150 to get from *D* to *O'*. Either way, the total amount of borrowing is $350; either way, there is the same amount of upward pressure on the interest rate. (*b*) Suppose that Terry's optimum point happens to be *O"*. Either Terry borrows $50 to get from *T* to *O"*, or the government borrows $200 and Terry lends $150 to get from *D* to *O"*. Either way, net borrowing is $50; either way, there is the same upward pressure on the interest rate.

falls from Y to T; if she is taxed in the future, her income stream point falls from Y to D. In either case she chooses to consume at O'.

If Terry is taxed, she moves from T to O' by borrowing $350 to consume what she wants. If, instead, the government runs a $200 deficit on Terry's behalf, then Terry moves from D to O' by borrowing $150. Thus, when the government borrows $200 more, Terry borrows $200 less. There is no change in the total demand for borrowing, and hence no additional upward pressure on the interest rate.

Figure 6-12(b) illustrates what might happen if Terry's optimum were not at point O' but elsewhere along her budget line. (Recall that her optimum can lie anywhere along that line.) In this case, if Terry is taxed $200, placing her at point T, she can move from T to the optimum point O'' by borrowing $50. If the government runs a $200 deficit on Terry's behalf, placing her at point D, she can move from D to O'' by lending $150.

We can think of lending as negative borrowing. When the government borrows $200 more, Terry borrows $200 less (reducing her borrowing from +$50 to −$150). Once again there is no change in the total demand for borrowing—and so once again there is no additional upward pressure on the interest rate.

Borrowing at Gunpoint

If a masked gunman enters your room and demands that you borrow $200 against your will, what do you do? The prudent thing is to borrow $200. What do you do with the money? Clearly you don't want to spend it immediately; if that were your preference, you would have borrowed it before the gunman showed up. The rational thing is to *lend* the $200, which effectively undoes the damage. By simultaneously borrowing and lending, you can satisfy the gunman without changing your consumption stream.

When the government borrows $200 on Terry's behalf (instead of taxing her), it acts as a gunman forcing her to borrow $200. That is, she finds herself with $200 extra in her pocket (as a result of lower taxes) and a debt to pay in the future. But if Terry is rational, the gunman can do her no real harm. She simply reduces her other borrowing by $200, or increases her lending by $200, or does some combination of the two. The net effect is that her optimum consumption stream is maintained.

In either part of Figure 6-12, taxation "forces" Terry to point T, while deficit spending "forces" her to point D. But Terry always wants to consume at her optimum (either O' in the first example or O'' in the second) and always finds a way to get there by adjusting her other borrowing or by lending. She technically obeys the gunman, but she can easily undo his orders all the same. The gunman has no effect on the total quantity of borrowing.

When borrowing is counterbalanced by equivalent lending, it has no effect on the market interest rate. If you doubt this, try the following experiment: Find a friend and lend each other $1 trillion for 1 year. Make sure that you borrow your $1 trillion and lend your $1 trillion at exactly the same instant. Now go buy a *Wall Street Journal* and see what effect you've had on the market interest rate.

Good Arguments against Ricardian Equivalence

Having disposed of a bad argument, we turn now to the good arguments against Ricardian equivalence. Each good argument begins by observing that the simple model we have been using ignores some aspect of the real world. If that aspect is significant, then the conclusion of Ricardian equivalence may not hold true.

Misestimating Future Taxes

The model assumes that when the government borrows a dollar at 10 percent interest, all taxpayers immediately become aware that their future taxes must rise by $1.10, and they adjust their current behavior accordingly. If, instead, taxpayers fail to notice the future tax burden until it comes due, then the government's current deficit spending leads them to overestimate their wealth. They want more current consumption and therefore bid up the interest rate.

In Figure 6-13, Terry Taxpayer starts at point Y on the dark blue budget line L. If she is taxed $200, she moves to point T, acquires the light blue budget line L', and consumes at her optimum point O'. That is, she consumes $550 worth of goods today.

If, instead, the government borrows $200, Terry moves from point Y to point D but *thinks* that she is still at Y because *Terry fails to realize that her future taxes must rise.* Therefore, she attempts to consume at her optimum on the dark blue line, point O. She does this by consuming $600 worth of goods today.

Because the demand for current goods (by Terry and others like her) is now

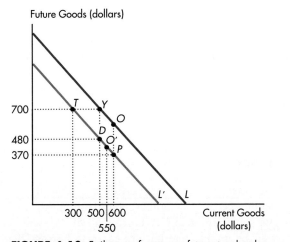

FIGURE 6-13 Failure to foresee a future tax burden.
Ricardian equivalence suggests that taxation and deficit spending both leave Terry with the light blue budget line L' and that in either case she chooses the same optimum O'. But if the government borrows and Terry fails to foresee the future tax burden, she might believe that she has the dark blue budget line L and then might attempt to consume at point O. Her demand for current consumption is thus higher when the government borrows than it is when the government taxes. Under these circumstances, the argument for Ricardian equivalence breaks down.

higher, the equilibrium interest rate rises: the interest rate is higher under the borrowing plan than under the taxing plan. That is, if Terry fails to foresee her future tax burden, deficit spending raises the interest rate.

Although Terry attempts to consume at point O in Figure 6-13, she is not really able to do so because it is outside her true budget line L'. What actually happens is that she spends $600 today and so—to her surprise—has only $370 left next year. Her actual consumption point is P.

In their response to this argument, pro-Ricardians contend that it is unreasonable to think that people are unaware that their future taxes must rise when the government borrows. Not only are the government's budget and tax plans well publicized, but citizens have years of experience with the consequences of government borrowing and would have to be terribly naive not to have noticed that they eventually pay for whatever the government buys.

In their response to this response, anti-Ricardians point out that in everyday experience we never hear people say that their consumption decisions are affected by the government budget deficit and the realization that taxes must rise at some future time. Pro-Ricardians counter this by observing that we *do* hear people say they are trying to be frugal because they expect the government to be unable to continue funding Medicare or Social Security for many more decades. Expecting the government to close down Medicare or Social Security and expecting it to raise taxes are essentially equivalent; there is no difference between canceling Social Security payments and taxing them at 100 percent.

Some economists even believe that government borrowing causes undue fear about the size of future interest payments, leading citizens to *over*estimate their future tax burden. In this case, people would respond to government borrowing by overadjusting—reducing their consumption demand *below* where it would otherwise be and driving interest rates *down*! So until we know more about people's psychological reactions to government borrowing, it seems that we cannot say for sure whether this argument provides a reason for interest rates to move up or to move down when the government borrows.

Borrowing Constraints

Our model assumes that everyone can borrow and lend at a single market interest rate. But many people, because of limited creditworthiness, must pay premium rates when they borrow; some are unable to borrow at all. We will see that if many people can't borrow at the market rate but are eager to borrow, then Ricardian equivalence can fail.

Figure 6-14 illustrates the problem. Terry Taxpayer has missed a few mortgage payments and is now considered a bad candidate for credit. She is effectively unable to borrow.

When the government taxes Terry, her income stream moves from point Y to point T. She prefers to consume at point O'', which she could ordinarily reach by bor-

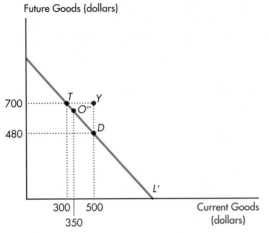

FIGURE 6-14 Borrowing constraints.
Taxation moves Terry to *T* on budget line *L'*; deficit spending moves her to *D*. Either way, her optimum is *O"*. But if Terry is a bad credit risk, she might not be able to borrow the $50 she needs to get from *T* to *O"*. Thus under taxation she is stuck at *T*, whereas under deficit spending she can reach *O"* by lending $150. Her consumption demand is different in the two cases, and the argument for Ricardian equivalence breaks down.

rowing $50. Under the circumstances, though, *O"* is unavailable to her. Terry is stuck at point *T*.

When the government borrows instead of taxing, Terry's income stream moves from point *Y* to point *D*. She still prefers point *O"*, which she can now reach by lending $150. There are no limits on Terry's ability to lend, so she is able to move to *O"*.

Under taxation, then, Terry consumes at *T*; but under deficit financing, she consumes at *O"*. Her current-consumption demand is therefore higher under deficit financing. If there are many taxpayers like Terry, then economywide consumption demand is significantly higher under deficit financing (that is, government borrowing), and hence so is the equilibrium interest rate.

The point here is that Terry, at point *T*, wants to borrow to increase her current consumption. Although Terry is unable to borrow in her own name, the government, with a somewhat better repayment record, is able to borrow on her behalf. By raising future taxes instead of current taxes, the government effectively provides Terry with a loan that she could not get elsewhere and thus enables her to increase her current consumption.

Therefore, constraints on borrowing can create a significant barrier to Ricardian equivalence in the real world.

Death and Taxes

Another potential breakdown of Ricardian equivalence is predicated on the sad but inescapable fact that people do not live forever. We ordinarily argue that it makes no difference whether you are taxed now or in the future. But what if you expect to depart this mortal vale before the future tax bill comes due? In that case you certainly prefer a future tax to a present tax. Present taxes reduce your disposable income and induce you to cut back your consumption; future taxes, if you don't think you are going to have to pay them, do you no harm and have no effect on your behavior. You consume more in the case of future taxes (that is, government borrowing) than you do in the case of present taxes. If there are many like you, economywide consumption demand (and therefore the interest rate) is significantly higher when the government borrows.

Pro-Ricardians make the counterargument that even people with short life expectancies usually *do* care about future taxes because they care about their children, who *will* be there to answer the door when the tax collector finally arrives. If this counterargument is correct, then Ricardian equivalence might continue to hold.

As always, a little geometry will help us keep track of the issues. The trade-off here is not between your own present consumption and your own future consumption; instead, it is between your own consumption (in the present) and your children's consumption (in the future). You can increase your children's consumption at the expense of your own by spending less and thereby increasing their inheritance.

Figure 6-15 shows two possible configurations. In each part, you begin at endowment point *Y*, which here means that your own (current) income is $500 and your children's (future) income is $700. In each part, we assume that the government spends $200 wastefully. And in each part, the government can either tax you $200, which moves you to point *T*, or borrow and then tax your children $220, which moves

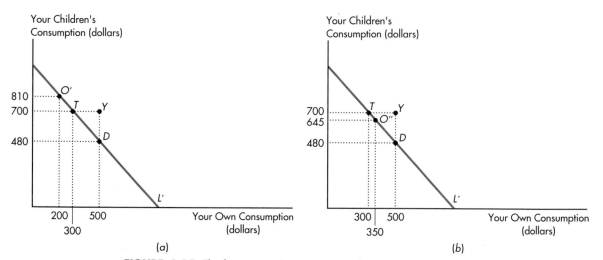

FIGURE 6-15 The bequest motive.
Government spending moves you from your original endowment point *Y* to *T*; government borrowing moves you from *Y* to *D*. In either case you have the same budget line *L'*. (*a*) If your optimum is at *O'*, then you will lend enough to get there regardless of whether you start from *T* or *D*. (*b*) But if your optimum is at *O''*, then you cannot get there from *T*, as that move would require that your children pay back what you borrow today, which you cannot force them to do. So you are stuck at *T* under taxation, whereas you can lend to get to *O''* under deficit spending. In this case, the argument for Ricardian equivalence breaks down.

you to point D. In part (a) we assume that your preferred consumption point is O'; in part (b) we assume it is O''.

In Figure 6-15(a) your optimum choice is to consume \$200 of your income and leave the remainder to your children. In the case where the government borrows \$200 (so you are at point D), you have \$500 in your pocket, so you spend \$200 and put aside \$300 to leave as an inheritance. With interest—and after your children are taxed \$220 to pay off the debt—this inheritance raises their income to \$810.

In the case where you are taxed (so you are at point T), your after-tax income is \$300, of which you spend \$200 and put aside \$100 to leave as an inheritance. With interest, this inheritance raises your children's income to \$810.

In either case, you achieve point O', where you consume \$200 worth of goods today and your children consume \$810 worth of goods tomorrow. Both deficit financing and taxation lead to the same demand for current consumption and hence to the same interest rate. Ricardian equivalence holds.

In Figure 6-15(b) your optimum choice is to consume \$350 of your wealth and leave the remainder to your children. In the case where the government borrows \$200 (so you are at point D), you have \$500 in your pocket, so you spend \$350 and put aside \$150 to leave as an inheritance. With interest—and after your children are taxed \$220 to pay off the debt—this inheritance raises their income to \$645.

In the case where you are taxed (so you are at point T), your after-tax income is \$300. To reach your optimum point O'', you want to *borrow* \$50 and let your children pay the debt after you are gone. But the legal system renders this ploy impossible, because your children cannot be held responsible for your debts. Potential lenders, realizing this, will not lend you the \$50 in the first place. You are stuck at T, unable to move to your optimum point O''.

With deficit spending you consume \$350 worth of goods today, while with taxation you consume only \$300 worth. Consumption demand differs under the two policies, and so does the interest rate. Ricardian equivalence breaks down.

The upshot of all this analysis is that if most people have optimum points like O' in Figure 6-15(a), then Ricardian equivalence holds; but if a substantial number have optimum points like O'' in Figure 6-15(b), then Ricardian equivalence fails. Therefore, it is worth investigating which configuration is most common in reality.

Bequest motive:
The desire to leave an inheritance.

The consumer with an optimum like O' in Figure 6-15(a) is eager to leave behind a positive inheritance; we say that she has a positive **bequest motive.** The consumer with an optimum like O'' in Figure 6-15(b) would prefer, when taxed, to take resources *from* her children; the bequest motive here is lacking. So the question becomes: Do most people have positive bequest motives?

Casual observation suggests that positive bequest motives are the norm. One bit of evidence is that most people do leave positive bequests. A counterargument to that evidence is that someone who leaves a positive bequest might have preferred to spend all the money before dying; the only reason something is left over is that he failed to perfectly anticipate the hour of his death.

Other evidence for a strong positive bequest motive is that during their lifetimes parents routinely give gifts to their children. If parents choose to feed, clothe, and buy sports cars for their children in life, is it not reasonable to assume that they would also want to do the same after death?

Possibly not. In an article titled "The Strategic Bequest Motive," economists B. D. Bernheim, Andrei Shleifer, and Lawrence Summers argue that gifts from parents to children, including bequests, are motivated not so much by pure altruism as by a desire to influence the children's behavior toward the parents.[2] For example, they present evidence that adult children expecting large bequests visit their parents more often than do those expecting smaller bequests. If the primary purpose of a bequest is to keep one's children in line, then the analysis of Figure 6-15 is incomplete. Older consumers care not just about achieving their optimum points but about how they get there. In (*a*), they would prefer a deficit finance scheme that enables them to leave a large bequest over a taxation scheme that forces them to leave a smaller one.

Under this analysis, taxing and deficits are not equivalent and Ricardian equivalence fails.

Variable Taxes

Our analysis implicitly assumes that taxes are of the lump-sum type and are unavoidable. But in the real world most taxes are variable, and there are ways to escape them. The most important example is the income tax, which can be partly avoided by choosing to earn less income.

Our endowment economy model does not yet incorporate labor (we shall remedy this in Chapter 9), so we cannot discuss this issue here with precision. But the basic point is easy to describe. If people are taxed in the present, they work less and produce less in the present. If they are taxed in the future, they work less and produce less in the future. Therefore, the timing of taxation can affect the *supply* of consumption goods. Even if consumption demand is the same under both taxation and deficit financing, the interest rate can differ as a result of differences in supply.

Do Government Budget Deficits Matter?

We don't know.

If Ricardian equivalence holds, then it really doesn't matter whether the government taxes people today or tomorrow in order to accomplish its spending plans. Private wealth is reduced by the same amount with either approach. The interest rate and people's welfare are unchanged by a switch from taxation to deficit spending.

On the other hand, if people do not foresee future taxes, if they face major borrowing constraints, if they have only imperfect bequest motives, or if taxes can be avoided, then government budget deficits do affect the interest rate.

But even in those cases, it is likely that the effects of government borrowing are small compared with the effects of government spending. Here is a parable to help you see why: If your father comes home tonight and announces that he has just bought a yacht, your mother's first question is *not* likely to be "Did you pay cash, or did you put it on the credit card?" She is far more likely to ask something like "What makes you think that a yacht is something we ought to be spending our income on right now?" To your mother, who is concerned for the economic health of the family, what

[2]*Journal of Political Economy* 93 (1985), 1045–1076.

your father is buying and how much it costs are primary; the question of cash versus credit is relatively minor. Similarly, when your government spends your money to buy you an interstate highway, a school lunch program, or a military aircraft, the wisdom of the spending itself is almost always a more critical issue than the question of how that spending is financed.

This parable suggests that government spending has much greater consequences than government borrowing. But on the basis of historical evidence, it is difficult to be sure of this conclusion. When governments increase their spending, they often increase their borrowing simultaneously. Thus, it may be difficult to disentangle the effects of new spending from the effects of new borrowing.

Measuring the Deficit

It is difficult to measure the government's budget deficit in a meaningful way. And if we cannot measure the deficit, then we cannot be sure when it is low and when it is high. If we cannot be sure when it is low and when it is high, then we cannot tell whether years of high deficits correspond to years of high interest rates.

Perhaps you find it surprising that nobody really knows how to measure the deficit. After all, government agencies routinely announce deficit numbers, and news sources routinely report them. But economists are quite skeptical about whether the reported numbers bear any close resemblance to the underlying economic reality.

In principle, a deficit is *an increase* in outstanding government debt. If the government owes $3000 billion at the beginning of 1997 and owes $3300 billion at the end of 1997, then the 1997 deficit is reported to be $300 billion. But in a world with inflation, this figure can be highly misleading.

Suppose, for example, that the inflation rate is 10 percent. Then the $3300 billion that the government owes at the end of the year is worth no more in real terms than the $3000 billion that it owed at the beginning. In this example, the *real* value of the debt is unchanged over the course of the year, so the *real* deficit is actually zero!

Because official deficit numbers are reported in nominal terms, the presence of inflation always makes the deficit look bigger than it is. In 1980, President Jimmy Carter was running for reelection. His challenger, Ronald Reagan, was highly critical of the $49 billion budget deficit that had been reported for 1979. But that criticism was unjustified. With the appropriate correction for inflation, the government had not really run a deficit at all that year—but rather a $3 billion *surplus*.

Reagan defeated Carter and quickly became a victim of the same statistical fallacy that he had exploited in his campaign. During Reagan's first year in office (1981), the budget deficit was measured as being at a historic high of $86 billion, an event for which the new president was subjected to heavy criticism. But a correction for inflation would have shown that the year's deficit was a relatively modest $18 billion— far lower than the deficit during Carter's own first year in office, and lower yet than the true historic highs that were achieved under Carter's predecessor, Gerald Ford.

➡ *Exercise 6-3*
Suppose that over the course of a year, Fredonia's outstanding debt rises from $100 to $150 and that Fredonian inflation is 100 percent per year. What deficit is reported by Fredonian newspapers? What is the actual deficit?

The right way to measure the deficit is to calculate what the government owes in *real* terms at the beginning and end of the year and to take the difference as the year's deficit. But a stumbling block is figuring out what the government owes! It is in the nature of governments to make promises. Is a promise a debt? If I promise to build you a $10,000 swimming pool, there is a very real sense in which I owe you $10,000, and I ought to account for that when I am totaling up all of my debts. But if your congressman promises to build you a $10,000 swimming pool with government funds, the government fails to account for that debt in its official figures.

In many cases, it is hard to decide whether a promise has really been issued. Suppose that your congressman promises to build you a swimming pool, but you don't believe him. Is the cost of the swimming pool part of the government's debt? What if you think he might be telling the truth, but you aren't sure?

By far the largest outstanding promise of the U.S. government is its promise to pay Social Security benefits to everyone now living. In exchange for that promise, most of us make annual payments to the Social Security system, which are typically deducted directly from our paychecks.

The federal government's official figures count Social Security payroll deductions as *taxes* and Social Security payments to beneficiaries as *transfer payments*. However, it is very easy to make a case for counting Social Security payroll deductions as *loans* to the government and Social Security payments to beneficiaries as *repayments of these loans*. That simple change of viewpoint would more than double the outstanding government debt, from approximately $5 trillion to approximately $12 trillion. If the measurement of the debt can vary by $7 trillion depending on a completely arbitrary choice of terminology regarding Social Security, then how can that measurement be meaningful?[3]

Another problem with the official deficit figures is that they fail to account for changes in the value of government-owned property. If the value of your home grew from $100,000 to $200,000 over the past year, then you have had a good year even if your net income from other sources was negative. If the value of a national park increases, the deficit figures fail to credit the government with that gain. In principle, this correction should be made; in practice, it is very difficult to assess changes in the market value of Yellowstone National Park.

One of the government's greatest assets is its ability to tax its citizens. It can be argued that anything that enriches the general populace adds to the value of this asset and should be counted on the plus side of the government's balance sheet, just as an increase in the value of a national park should be. In particular, productive government spending adds to the tax base, and assessments of the government's financial status ought somehow to reflect this benefit. In practice, productive spending and wasteful spending are treated identically in the government's accounts.

If we carry this criticism through to its logical conclusion, then any borrowing used to finance a tax cut should not be counted as part of the deficit. The tax cut puts more resources into the pockets of citizens, who are then equipped to pay higher taxes

---

[3]This question, along with others of a similar nature, is raised forcefully by L. Kotlikoff in his book *Generational Accounting* (New York: Free Press, 1992).

in the future. The government's situation is analogous to that of a farmer who borrows $1000 to buy feed that enables him to fatten his hogs so that they will be more valuable next year at the butcher shop. He is in quite a different situation from the farmer who borrows $1000 to finance a wild night in Las Vegas. The accountant who does these farmers' books would consider their financial situations to be quite different. But the accountants who do the government's books make no distinction between frivolous spending projects and spending to fatten the hogs.

It is hard to decide what "the deficit" should mean and hard to measure it once you have decided. Even if we could overcome these difficulties, we would still be hard-pressed to decide what economic effects deficits have. It is unfortunate that detailed economic statistics have been kept for only the last 50 years or so: not enough evidence has yet accumulated to enable us to settle the most interesting problems regarding deficits.

SUMMARY

Public goods can be provided more efficiently by the government than by the private sector, because they are either nonexcludable or nonrivalrous or both. When the government provides public goods, it can increase the total amount of goods available for consumption.

Government spending falls into three categories. Some government spending is wasteful—meaning its benefits are less than its cost. Wasteful spending is not necessarily undesirable; for example, we may be willing to accept some waste in exchange for the ability to redistribute income.

Some government spending is productive—meaning it provides an excess of benefits over cost. Productive spending can occur when the government supplies public goods.

Some government spending consists of pure transfers, in which case the benefits are exactly equal to the cost.

In analyzing the effects of a government spending program, it is important to know whether the spending is wasteful or productive or is a pure transfer and whether the program representing the expenditure is temporary or permanent.

Wasteful government spending causes the supply of current goods to shift leftward, productive government spending causes the supply of current goods to shift rightward, and pure transfers have no effect on supply.

Wasteful government spending makes people poorer and therefore causes the demand for current goods to shift leftward. Productive government spending makes people richer and therefore causes the demand for current goods to shift rightward. Pure transfers have no effect on demand.

In each case, the demand shift is smaller than the supply shift for a temporary spending program and as large as the supply shift for a permanent program.

Deficit spending only delays taxation; it has no effect on the present value of all taxes. Therefore, in our simple model, government spending financed by a deficit affects people's wealth, their demand for current consumption, and the interest rate in exactly the same way as does government spending financed by current taxation. This conclusion is known as Ricardian equivalence and can be summarized as "deficits don't matter."

In the real world, Ricardian equivalence might fail as a result of misestimates of future taxes, constraints on borrowing by individuals, imperfect bequest motives, or the disincentive effects of variable taxation. Unfortunately, it is very difficult to find a meaningful measure of the current deficit and of its effects. Therefore, the effects of deficits remain controversial among economists.

PROBLEM SET

1. Which of the following goods are nonrivalrous? Which are nonexcludable? Which are both? Which are neither?
   a. Seats in an uncrowded movie theater
   b. Seats in a full movie theater
   c. Broadcast television
   d. Cable television
   e. Coca-Cola
   f. The formula for producing Coca-Cola
   g. Patentable ideas
   h. The idea of a department store

2. Upper and Lower Slobbovia are identical endowment economies. The governments of both countries have decided to raise taxes and spend the proceeds wastefully. The only difference is that in Upper Slobbovia, the tax-and-spend plan is in effect for this year only whereas in Lower Slobbovia the plan is permanent and will be repeated every year. In both countries, this year's taxes have just been collected and wasted. Compare the two countries' interest rates and their levels of current consumption.

3. Paul is having an unusually bad year; his income is only $20,000 as opposed to the $100,000 that he expects to earn next year. Peter is having an unusually good year; his income is $100,000 as opposed to the $20,000 that he expects to earn next year. The government has decided to tax Peter in order to make a transfer payment to Paul.
   a. Who do you expect has the greater marginal propensity to consume out of current income, Paul or Peter?
   b. Now suppose that Paul and Peter have poor credit ratings that prevent them from borrowing. How does this affect your answer to **a**? In this case, how does the transfer payment affect the current interest rate?
   c. Now suppose that the policy of transferring from high-income to low-income individuals is permanent, so everyone knows that next year, when Paul is prosperous, he will be taxed to make a payment to Peter. How does this affect your answer to part **b**?

4. Use a graph to illustrate the effects of a permanent increase in productive government spending.

5. Suppose that the government constructs a new highway. The construction will be very costly and yield no immediate benefits, but the stream of *future* benefits is expected to more than justify the highway's cost.
   a. What happens to the aggregate supply curve in the period in which the highway is being built?
   b. What happens to the aggregate demand curve in the period in which the highway is being built?
   c. How much can you say about what happens to the equilibrium interest rate?

6. Because of a reduction in world tensions, the United States will be able to reduce its military expenditures by $100 million this year. Senator Smith says that the government should take this opportunity to cut taxes by $100 million. Senator Jones says that instead of cutting taxes, the government should use the $100 million to reduce the deficit. Use a simple model to compare and contrast the effects of the Smith and Jones plans. Your answer should include a careful discussion of how people's current consumption decisions are affected under each plan.

7. A presidential candidate says that the government needs to raise taxes and use all of the revenue to reduce the deficit.
   a. Show how a typical taxpayer's endowment point would move under this plan.
   b. What happens to that taxpayer's demand for current consumption? Why?
   c. What happens to the supply of current consumption? Why?
   d. What happens to the interest rate?

8. Figure 6-11 illustrates that when the government spends wastefully, the choice between taxation and borrowing has no effect on Terry Taxpayer's demand for current consumption. This problem is intended to illustrate that the same is true when the government spends productively.

   Suppose that the government has discovered a way to turn a $100 investment into $150 worth of immediate benefits. Terry Taxpayer is to receive all of the program's benefits. Terry's initial income stream consists of $500 today and $700 tomorrow.
   a. Suppose that the program is financed by a $100 increase in Terry's current taxes. Draw Terry's initial income stream, her new endowment point, and her new budget line. (Don't forget to account for the $150 gift she is receiving from the government.)
   b. Suppose instead that the program is financed by borrowing at 10 percent interest and taxing Terry next year to pay the debt. Draw Terry's new endowment point and her new budget line.
   c. Explain how your solutions to **a** and **b** illustrate the principle of Ricardian equivalence when government spending is productive.

9. Suppose that in Figure 6-12 Terry's optimum is not at O' or O'' but at a point O''' with a horizontal coordinate of $100. How much does Terry borrow or lend if the government chooses to finance its spending through taxation? How much does she borrow or lend if the government chooses to finance its spending by borrowing? In each case, what is the total demand for borrowing and/or lending by Terry and the government?

10. Suppose that the government undertakes a productive spending program to provide public goods whose value exceeds their costs. In particular, the government spends $200 on Terry's behalf and returns $300 worth of benefits to her.

    The government can pay for this program either by taxing Terry $200 in the present or by borrowing $200. Suppose that in the latter case, Terry fails to foresee the associated future tax burden. Draw a figure similar to Figure 6-13 that shows Terry's consumption points under taxation and under deficit spending. Be sure that your figure accounts for the $300 in benefits that Terry receives today.

    How does your diagram illustrate the failure of Ricardian equivalence when future tax burdens are misperceived?

11. How would Figure 6-13 look if Terry made the mistake of *over*estimating her future tax burden as the result of government deficits?

12. Suppose the government needs to raise lump-sum taxes to finance the purchase of a new aircraft carrier. *True or false:* People would prefer to have their taxes raised a small

amount in each of several years than to have them raised a much larger amount for 1 year only.

13. The government has decided to raise taxes by $10 billion this year to finance some entirely worthless projects. Although the taxes are collected today, the government has not yet decided whether to spend the revenue immediately or to save it for a year at 10 percent and spend $11 billion next year.

   a. Compare the effects that the two alternatives have on the *demand* for current consumption.

   b. Compare the effects that the two alternatives have on the *supply* of current consumption.

   c. *True or false:* If Ricardian equivalence holds, then it doesn't make any difference to the interest rate whether the government does its spending now or in the future.

14. In Figure 6-14, Ricardian equivalence fails because of borrowing constraints. Would Ricardian equivalence still fail if point O'' were above and to the left of point T? What if point O'' were below and to the right of point D?

15. "If the government borrows money instead of raising my taxes, I will be able to buy a fancy car. My grandchildren, who are not yet born, will get no benefit from that car but *will* have to pay a higher tax bill. Therefore, deficit spending benefits me at the expense of my grandchildren."

   a. Under what circumstances is this statement true?

   b. *True or false:* If the statement is meant to explain why the speaker opposes deficit spending, then the statement is wrong. If it is meant to explain why the speaker favors deficit spending, then it is right.

16. *True or false:* If government deficits cause significantly higher interest rates, then it is likely that there are many people who cannot borrow as much as they want to at the going market rates.

17. *True or false:* If it becomes much easier for people to emigrate from the United States to other countries, then a given level of U.S. government debt will have a bigger effect on interest rates. (*Hint:* How does the prospect of low-cost emigration affect people's assessment of their probable future tax burdens?)

18. Refer to Figure 6-15. Suppose that Mark, a typical consumer, has an optimum point in this figure not at O' or O'' but at a point with a horizontal coordinate of $600.

   a. If the government taxes Mark $200 to finance current spending, how much will Mark want to borrow or lend today? Given that he cannot require that his children pay his debts, how much will Mark actually be able to borrow or lend?

   b. If the government borrows $200 to finance current spending and raises future taxes to pay the debt, how much will Mark want to borrow or lend today? Given that he cannot require that his children pay his debts, how much will Mark actually be able to borrow or lend?

   c. If most consumers have preferences like Mark, does Ricardian equivalence hold? Why or why not?

19. Suppose the government owes $10,000 at the beginning of this year and $11,000 at the end of the year. Over the course of the year there is a 20 percent deflation. What is the size of the "deficit" as reported in the newspapers? What is the size of the real deficit?

Chapter 7

Investment

Until now, we have assumed that all consumption goods simply fall on the economy like manna from heaven; that is, we have assumed that people are born with apple trees, and we have not asked where the trees come from or why output changes over time.

Capital:
Goods that are used to produce consumption goods.

In this chapter we enrich our model by admitting the importance of **capital,** by which we mean goods (like trees) that are used to produce consumption goods (like apples). A person with $100 worth of trees can produce more apples than a person with $20 worth of trees. We continue, however, to simplify matters in potentially important ways. In the model, we do not actually distinguish different *forms* of capital, like apple trees and heavy machinery; instead, we treat all kinds of capital as identical.

Investment:

An addition to capital.

Capital is acquired through **investment,** which is just a fancy name for producing new capital. Growing trees or building machines is a form of investment. So is building a house, because a house provides consumption goods (like warmth and closet space) that can be used in the future. Accumulating an inventory of goods to be used in the future is yet another kind of investment.

In the United States, investment by the private sector typically accounts for something on the order of 15 percent of the gross domestic product, though that percentage tends to change quite a bit from year to year—investment is far more volatile than consumption. Fluctuations in investment are therefore a major source of fluctuations in GDP.

In an economy with capital, many of the same resources can be employed either for investment or for immediate consumption. You can use your trees either to build a house that will keep you warm tomorrow or to build a fire that will keep you warm today. In our model, we will approximate this truth by assuming that there is only one kind of good and that it can be used either for consumption or for investment.

This necessitates enriching our model of aggregate demand. The model of consumption demand that we developed in Chapter 4 remains unchanged. But now the same goods that are being demanded for consumption are simultaneously being demanded for investment. (I want to eat the same corn that my neighbor wants to plant.) So an important innovation in this chapter is that investment demand must be added to consumption demand.

With our new, enriched model of demand, we shall revisit all the issues we considered in Chapter 5. In general, the answers to the questions raised there will not change. But new questions will arise, and our old techniques can be adapted to answer them.

7-1   CAPITAL, INVESTMENT, AND PRODUCTION

Capital and Investment

Capital goods (or *capital* for short) are goods that are used to produce other goods.

Physical capital:

Physical goods that are used to produce consumption goods.

Human capital:

Individual skills or knowledge that is used to produce consumption goods.

There are two kinds of capital: physical and human. Examples of **physical capital** include machinery and factories. **Human capital** consists of knowledge, talents, and skills that people are born with or acquire over their lifetimes. An entrepreneur's human capital—her knowledge of how to run her business—gives that business value beyond that of the physical capital it owns.

Investment, or *investing,* is any activity that adds to the stock of capital. Building a new machine is an investment in physical capital. So is accumulating an inventory of goods. An entrepreneur at a business lunch, learning new ideas from clients, suppliers, and competitors, is investing in human capital. By reading this book and attending college, you are making one of the most substantial investments you will ever make—increasing your own human capital. Research and the development of new products are important investments in human capital.

When General Motors builds a new assembly line, both GM and the economy as a whole are investing. When General Motors purchases an assembly line from another automaker, GM is investing, even though the economy as a whole is not. The transfer of ownership adds to GM's capital but not to the total of all capital in the economy.

Financial "Capital" and Financial "Investment"

Money, shares of stock, and bonds are sometimes called "financial capital" in everyday speech. But from the perspective of economics such *financial capital is not capital*. Capital consists solely of goods that are directly useful in the production process, like machinery, factories, and the special skills of corporate managers. Stock certificates symbolize the *ownership* of capital, but they themselves are not capital.

Buying shares of stock is sometimes called "investing" or "investment" in everyday speech. But from the perspective of economics, *buying stocks is not investment.* Investment is the creation of *new* capital. When you buy stocks, you acquire ownership of capital that already exists. Nothing new is created.

"Suppose a company sells stock to finance the purchase of new capital, say, a new factory?" you might ask. "Isn't that investment? After all, some new capital is created." The answer is that the new factory *is* indeed investment, but the purchase of the new stock is *not* investment. The company might sell stock equal in value to its investment, or to one-fifth of that value, or half, or none at all. The fact that the stock is sold to *finance* an investment does not make the stock purchase *itself* an investment.

Buying bonds or money market funds is not investment either. Investment occurs only when new capital—real productive assets—either physical or human, is created.

The Volatility of Investment

In the United States today, about two-thirds of all output is purchased by households for consumption, and another one-seventh is purchased by firms for investment. (The remainder is purchased by the government.) Thus, compared with consumption, investment appears to be a relatively small fraction of output. But investment is far more *volatile* than consumption—it is subject to much larger swings in both directions.

You can see this in Figure 7-1, which shows the annual percent changes in U.S. output, consumption, and investment over several recent years. Notice that the percent change in consumption tracks the percent change in output fairly closely. Do not misinterpret this to mean that changes in consumption are of the same general *magnitude* as changes in output. Because only two-thirds of output is used for consumption, a 1 percent change in consumption is only about two-thirds as large as a 1 percent change in output.

Changes in investment swing much farther in both directions than changes in consumption. In periods of relatively low output growth, such as 1990–1991, investment often declines (showing negative growth). The decline from 1990 to 1991 was 9.7 percent. When output growth rebounded the following year, investment rose by

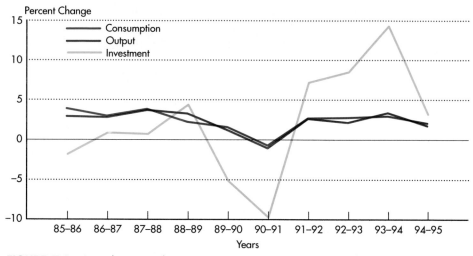

FIGURE 7-1 Annual percent changes in U.S. output, consumption, and investment.

7.1 percent. Two years later, from 1993 to 1994, the annual quantity of investment grew by an astonishing 14.3 percent, more than canceling the drop in 1991 and returning investment to its former level.

Production

So far in our model, we have imagined that the supply of goods simply appears in the economy each period. Now we shall enrich the model by assuming that goods can be *produced* via the use of capital. The goods that are produced can be used in either of two ways: for consumption in the present or for investment to create new capital, which in turn will produce more goods in the future.

The apple trees of our model economy are its capital. Each additional tree planted this year will produce a stream of additional apples in future years.

In the real world, in order to harvest those apples, some *labor* might be required. But we shall defer questions about labor until the next chapter. Here, we hold the quantity of labor constant and consider only variations in the quantity of available capital.

The Marginal Product of Capital

Marginal product of capital (MPK):

The additional output that results when capital is increased by 1 unit and all other productive factors are held constant.

Suppose Anne Jones owns an apple orchard, and her 10 trees produce 1500 apples per year. She knows that if she planted an eleventh tree, she would be able to produce 1600 apples per year. Hence, the eleventh tree would increase her output by 100 apples per year.

This quantity—100 apples per year per tree—is called the **marginal product of capital,** or **MPK,** in Anne's 10-tree orchard. The marginal product of capital is the *additional output* that results when *1 new unit of capital* is brought into service.

Diminishing Marginal Product

The marginal product of capital need not be constant. In fact, at a given firm, the marginal product of capital is *usually* not constant. An eleventh tree would allow Anne to produce an additional 100 apples per year, but a twelfth tree might allow her to produce only an additional 80 apples, for a total of 1680 apples per year. For the 11-tree orchard, the marginal product of capital has fallen to 80 apples per year per tree.

Why would the eleventh tree add 100 apples and the twelfth tree only 80? Anne has only a limited amount of time to spend harvesting; adding trees does not add hours to her day. The more trees she must attend to, the less attention she can give to each additional tree.

Economists call this phenomenon the **diminishing marginal product of capital.** Each additional tree at the orchard, or each additional machine at a factory, means that other resources—in particular, the employees—have to be spread more thinly. As a result, the marginal product of capital falls as the quantity of capital increases.

Diminishing marginal product of capital:

The concept that each additional unit of capital adds less to output than the previous unit added.

In discussions about the diminishing marginal product of capital, it is important to isolate the particular capital item that is being discussed. Other inputs to the production process, like labor and other forms of capital, must be held constant.

You might think that you can concoct an example of increasing marginal product by imagining that Anne's first few trees are learning experiences for her. Only after she has five trees under way has she learned how to recognize insect pests, choose the right fertilizers, and so forth. Thus each of these first few trees adds more to the apple crop than any of its predecessors.

But in that example, one of the inputs—Anne's knowledge, or human capital—is allowed to increase. You are not describing the marginal product of trees, because you are not holding Anne's knowledge fixed.

Even though we assume that the marginal product of capital is diminishing, we still assume that it is never zero. Each additional tree will always add *something* to Anne's annual output, though if there are already many trees in the orchard, it may not add much.

The Production Function

Figure 7-2 depicts a typical relationship between capital and output. The quantity of capital in the economy is measured along the horizontal axis; the quantity of goods that get produced (that is, the output) is measured along the vertical axis. The graph in Figure 7-2 is called a *production function.*

Implicit in the production function is a unit of *time.* Figure 7-2 tells us, for example, that K_0 units of capital can produce Y_0 units of output *per year* or *per month* or per whatever period of time is fixed at the outset of the discussion. We shall sometimes draw production functions without being explicit about the time periods

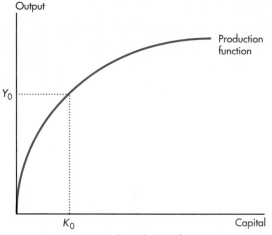

FIGURE 7-2 A typical production function.
Capital is measured on the horizontal axis and output on the vertical. The curve slopes upward to indicate that more capital can produce more output.

to which they apply, but it is important to remember that *some* time period is always implicitly specified.

The Slope of the Production Function

Figure 7-3 illustrates the relationship between the production function and the marginal product of capital.

The curve in the figure is the production function for Anne Jones's orchard, showing (among other things) that 10 apple trees can produce 1500 apples and 11 apple trees can produce 1600. Using the points A (10, 1500) and B (11, 1600), we obtain the slope

$$\frac{1600 \text{ apples} - 1500 \text{ apples}}{11 \text{ trees} - 10 \text{ trees}} = \frac{100 \text{ apples}}{1 \text{ tree}} = 100 \text{ apples/tree}$$

which is exactly the marginal product of capital when there are 10 trees in the orchard.

Likewise, using the points B (11, 1600) and C (12, 1680), we compute a slope of 80 apples per tree, which is the marginal product of capital when there are 11 trees in the orchard.

The slope of the production function at any point is equal to the marginal product of capital at that point.

The same time period that is implicit in the production function is also part of the MPK. In most of our examples, that time period will be 1 year. Thus, more precise descriptions of the MPKs at the apple orchard are 100 apples per tree *per year* and 80 apples per tree *per year*, in keeping with the units discussed earlier. We shall,

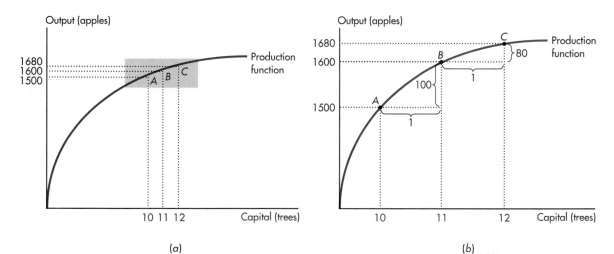

FIGURE 7-3 The slope of the production function is equal to the marginal product of capital. You can see this most clearly in (b), which is a blowup of the shaded region in (a). The slope of the curve at point A is rise/run = 100 apples/1 tree. The slope at point B is rise/run = 80 apples/1 tree. These are exactly the MPK values at points A and B, respectively.

however, often omit explicit mention of the time period, relegating it to the back of our minds just as we frequently do with interest rates.

Exercise 7-1
Suppose that the point (13, 1720) is also on the production function in Figure 7-3. What is the MPK at point *C* (12, 1680)?

Firms

It is sometimes useful to think of the producers in our model economy as *firms,* or businesses. We can think of each individual in the model as setting up a firm to purchase capital and produce output on his behalf. We then must divide each individual into a "consumer" part and a "firm" part. The firm part of the person produces output with whatever capital—physical and human—that person owns, and the consumer part either consumes that output, lends it, or borrows additional output to consume.

This division is a good way to describe the behavior of professionals like doctors and lawyers and of small-business owners like grocers and day-care providers. It might also describe the behavior of people who own shares of stock as one of their income sources. In our model we can even imagine a person who cooks at McDonald's as owning a business that sells labor services—which are really services produced by his human capital—to McDonald's. The model is not yet rich enough to distinguish between people who set up their own businesses and those who work for businesses owned by others; that will come in Chapter 9.

Although our division of all people into firms and consumers is merely a useful abstraction, what is not an abstraction is that *all firms are owned by people.* In the real world, businesses do not exist on their own; they do not earn profits, pay taxes, or purchase capital. Only the people who own them do these things.

7-2 THE DEMAND FOR CAPITAL AND INVESTMENT

Demand for capital:

The quantity of capital firms wish to hold, expressed as a function of the interest rate.

The **demand for capital** tells us how much capital a firm (or a collection of firms) wants to *own*, at each interest rate. The **demand for investment** tells us how much capital a firm (or a collection of firms) wants to *add* to its existing capital, at each interest rate. The two demands are closely related; we shall discuss the demand for capital first.

The Demand for Capital

Demand for investment:

The quantity of investment (per period) firms wish to undertake, expressed as a function of the interest rate.

How much capital does a firm demand? If a firm owns 10 units of capital, should it invest—that is, should it acquire more capital—or not? And if its owners choose to invest, how much should they invest? To make this decision, the owners must compare the cost of increasing the firm's capital with the benefits of doing so—namely, the output the new capital can produce.

To keep track of costs and benefits, and for ease of comparison, it is important to measure everything in the same units. The most obvious unit that can be applied to both machinery and output is probably monetary value—the "dollar's worth." Thus we shall measure everything in dollars, but we must remember that these dollars are measures of real goods and not simply pieces of green paper.

Suppose Davo owns a firm with $100 worth of machinery. If he adds another $1 worth of machinery, then he can produce an additional 20 cents' worth of output per year. Therefore, his marginal product of capital (MPK) is equal to 20 cents per dollar per year, or .20 dollars per dollar per year.

When capital and output are both measured in the same units, it is convenient to express the MPK as a percentage, in this case 20 percent. (More precisely, we should say 20 percent *per year*.)

Should Davo invest another dollar in machinery? The answer can be found by comparing costs and benefits. First, let us find the cost of the investment. To buy the additional $1 worth of machinery, Davo must acquire a dollar. He can get the dollar by *borrowing* at the market rate of, say, 10 percent, or he can get the dollar by *removing* it from his savings account, forgoing interest earnings of 10 percent. Either way, the machinery costs him a dime a year for as long as he owns it.

The annual cost of an additional $1 worth of capital is equal to the annual interest on a $1 loan.

What about the dollar itself? Why haven't we counted it as a cost of the new machinery? The answer is that the dollar is fully recoverable, since (as far as we know) Davo can always resell his machinery for $1. This is true, however, only if the machine doesn't wear out. If machines *do* wear out, or *depreciate,* then we need one additional wrinkle in the analysis, and we shall add it at the end of this section. Even with depreciation, though, the main cost of capital is usually the annual interest charge.

Now that we have measured the cost of Davo's investment, let us turn to the benefits. We have already said that a $1 machine would increase output by 20 cents per year; this 20 cents per year is the benefit of adding that machine. Notice that the 20 cents, or .20, is also Davo's marginal product of capital.

The annual benefit of an additional unit of capital is equal to the MPK.

Finally, we return to the question: Should Davo invest another dollar in machinery? The answer is clearly yes, as the cost is 10 cents a year and the benefit is 20 cents a year. As long as the benefit exceeds the cost, Davo should add to his capital stock.

Now we must ask whether Davo should invest still *another* dollar. The annual cost, determined by the market rate of interest, remains 10 cents a year. But the annual benefit is now only, say, 18 cents a year because of the diminishing marginal product of capital: as Davo's business expands, the MPK decreases.

Still, 18 cents exceeds 10 cents, so Davo should expand further. He should continue to expand until the MPK falls all the way to 10 cents, at which point the benefit of further expansion no longer exceeds the cost.

Perhaps the MPK hits 10 cents when Davo has expanded to $104 worth of machines. In that case, Davo wants to have exactly $104 worth of capital. Thus, when the interest rate is 10 percent, the quantity of capital that Davo demands is "$104 worth."

To summarize, the firm adjusts its capital stock until the equation

$$MPK = r$$

is satisfied. In this equation, the market interest rate r is taken as given (that is, a constant that the firm cannot change), and the MPK depends on the firm's choice of capital stock.

Graphing the Demand for Capital

MPK curve:

A curve expressing the marginal product of capital as a function of the quantity of capital held.

Demand curve for capital:

A curve illustrating the demand for capital.

The **MPK curve** in Figure 7-4(*a*) depicts the MPK at Davo's firm as a function of the amount of capital he owns. Among other things, it shows (at point *A*) that when Davo has $104 worth of capital, the MPK is 10 percent per year.

Figure 7-4(*b*) shows Davo's **demand curve for capital,** which expresses demand for capital as a function of the interest rate r. This demand curve can be derived directly from the MPK curve.

We start by asking this question: When the interest rate is 10 percent, how much capital does Davo want to own? We have just figured out that he wants $104 worth. We record this as point *A'* in Figure 7-4(*b*).

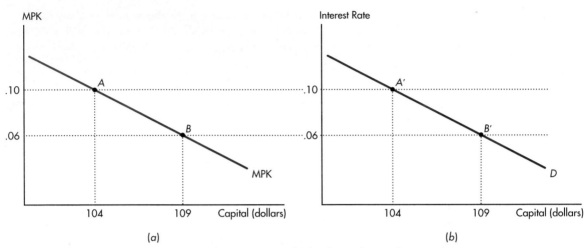

(a)   (b)

FIGURE 7-4   (a) The MPK curve; (b) the demand curve for capital.
To get a point on the firm's demand curve for capital, proceed as follows: Start with an interest
rate (say, 10 percent). At that interest rate, the firm wants to expand until the MPK is equal to 10
percent, or .10; we see on the MPK curve in (a) that this happens when the capital stock is $104.
Thus we record in (b) that an interest rate of .10 corresponds to a capital stock of $104. Con-
tinuing in this way, we generate the entire demand curve for capital. When we are done, we
have constructed an exact replica of the MPK curve in the first panel.

Now we suppose that the interest rate falls to 6 percent. How much capital will
Davo then want? He will want to keep investing until the annual benefit from an additional dollar's worth of capital (the MPK) is equal to the annual cost (6 cents per
year) of an additional dollar's worth of capital. We see from point B in the MPK plot
that this occurs at $109 worth of capital. Therefore, we record in the capital demand
plot that when the interest rate is 6 percent, Davo wants to own $109 worth of cap-
ital. This gives us point B'.

Continuing in this way, we can generate all the points on Davo's demand curve
for capital. Like points A' and B', each of these points will correspond exactly with
a point on the MPK curve. The moral is:

The firm's demand curve for capital is identical with its MPK curve.

The Demand for Investment

Remember that an investment is an addition to capital and that the demand for investment tells us how much capital a firm wants to add to its existing capital.

Figure 7-5(a) reproduces Davo's demand curve for capital from Figure 7-4. We
see there that when the interest rate is 10 percent, Davo wants to have $104 worth of
capital. But this does not mean he wants to *acquire* $104 worth of capital; he may
have some capital already. If he already has $100 worth of capital (as we have
assumed), then he wants to acquire only an additional $4 worth; that $4 is the quan-

tity of *investment*—the addition to capital—that Davo demands at the 10 percent interest rate.

So point A' on the capital demand curve yields point A'' on the investment demand curve in Figure 7-5(*b*). Likewise point B' yields point B'': at an interest rate of 6 percent, Davo wants $109 worth of capital, so he demands to invest $9.

Continuing in this way, we obtain the entire demand curve for investment. We note the following:

> The firm's investment demand curve is identical to its capital demand curve, but it is shifted to the left by the quantity of existing capital.

➡ *Exercise 7-2*
Suppose Davo starts with $50 worth of capital, and suppose his demand curve for capital is still that in Figure 7-5(*a*). Give the coordinates of two points on his investment demand curve.

The Slope of the Investment Demand Curve

Why does the investment demand curve slope downward? One way to answer is to say that it does so because it has the same shape as the capital demand curve; that the capital demand curve slopes downward because it has the same shape as the MPK curve; and that the MPK curve slopes downward because of the diminishing marginal product of capital.

Another way to say the same thing is to say that the interest rate is the cost of investment. That is, firms that invest must forgo the opportunity to save and earn interest. When the interest rate is high, firms can do better by lending another dollar (or

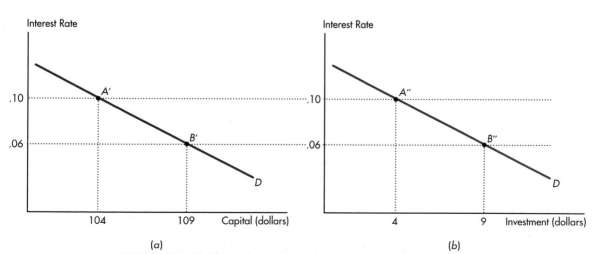

FIGURE 7-5 The firm's demand curve for investment, in (*b*), looks just like its demand curve for capital, in (*a*), except that the horizontal scale is shifted to the left by the quantity of existing capital, in this case $100 worth.

by borrowing one less dollar) than by investing it. When the interest rate is low, they can do better by investing (even if they have to borrow to do so) than by lending. Hence, investing increases as the interest rate falls, causing the investment demand curve in Figure 7-5(*b*) to slope downward.

Aggregate Investment Demand

Figure 7-6(*a*) gives the investment demand curves of two firms: Good Grades with Less Work (GG), Inc., and Better Grades with More Work (BG), each of which buys desks for students. The curves show that GG demands 10 desks when the interest rate is 10 percent, while BG demands 14 desks at that interest rate. Figure 7-6(*b*) gives the **aggregate investment demand curve,** derived by adding all the firms' curves (in this example, only two) horizontally. For example, at an interest rate of 10 percent, aggregate investment demand is equal to 24 desks.

It is possible that an individual firm would want to invest a negative amount. To see this, imagine a firm that starts the year with $100 worth of machinery but prefers to downsize to $75 worth; this firm demands *minus* $25 worth of investment. However, when we add all firms' demands to obtain aggregate investment demand, we rarely find it to be negative. Thus, whenever we look at aggregate demand for investment, we will assume that it is positive.

Aggregate investment demand curve:

A curve illustrating the total demand for investment by all firms as a function of the interest rate.

Depreciation

No bow or brooch or braid or brace, lace, latch, or catch or key, can keep capital from wearing out over time. Unpoetic economists use the ugly word "depreciation" to

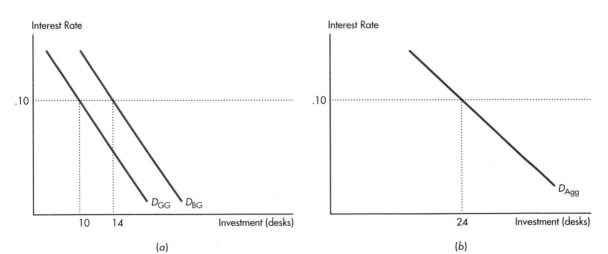

FIGURE 7-6 Aggregate investment demand.
To get the aggregate investment demand curve in (*b*), horizontally add the curves of the individual firms in (*a*).

describe this process of vanishing away. Our analysis until now has ignored depreci-ation; this section incorporates it.

By ignoring depreciation, our model so far has suggested that if a firm under-takes no investment at all, its capital stock stays constant forever. But in reality, the older capital gets, the less productive it gets. Often the very act of using capital causes it to deteriorate, as with a light bulb or unfertilized soil. Capital that has become less productive produces less output, exactly as if the quantity of capital had diminished. Therefore, we can think of next period's capital stock as being smaller by the amount that this period's capital stock wears out, or *depreciates*.

It is not difficult to modify the model to account for depreciation. When we first discussed the demand for capital, we noted that firms continue adding capital until the annual *benefit* of adding 1 more unit (the MPK) is equal to the annual *cost* of adding 1 more unit (the interest rate r). The same principle holds in the presence of depreciation, but there is one more cost to account for: the depreciation of capital, which is itself a cost.

Suppose that capital depreciates at the percentage rate δ (for example, if $\delta = .05$, capital loses 5 percent of its value every year). Then the annual cost of employ-ing 1 additional unit of capital is no longer just r but rather $r + \delta$. (The machinery's annual loss of value—δ—is a cost that must be added to the interest cost r.) Instead of adding capital until MPK $= r$, firms now add capital until MPK $= r + \delta$, or equiv-alently until

$$\text{MPK} - \delta = r$$

This equation tells us that the demand curve for capital is no longer identical to the MPK curve but to the MPK curve shifted downward by the depreciation rate, as shown in Figure 7-7. Then at an interest rate of 10 percent, firms would demand $100.25 worth of capital rather than $104 worth. In other words, depreciation decreases the desired stock of capital.

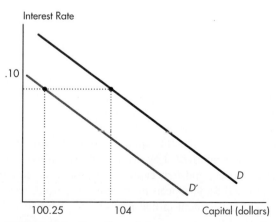

FIGURE 7-7   The effect of depreciation.
A depreciation rate of 3 percent depresses the demand curve for capital by 3 percent, from *D* to *D'*.

What about the demand for investment? It is true that in the presence of depreciation, firms want to maintain a smaller capital stock. But it is also true that in the presence of depreciation, firms need to keep investing just to keep that capital stock constant. If a firm demands 100 machines in a world without depreciation and if it already has 100 machines, then its demand for investment is zero. If a firm demands 100 machines in a world where 5 percent of all machines wear out every year, then its demand for investment is 5 machines per year, just to maintain its desired capital stock. So depreciation can *increase* the demand for investment.

It remains true that the demand for investment and the demand for capital are essentially determined by the marginal product of capital.

> Given a fixed depreciation rate, the only thing that can cause the demand for capital to change is a change in the MPK. The only things that can cause the demand for investment to change are a change in the demand for capital or a change in the existing quantity of capital.

7-3 EQUILIBRIUM AND THE MARKET INTEREST RATE

The investment demand curve shows how much firms would want to invest at each *given* rate of interest. But what determines the rate of interest? In Chapter 5—in the model without investment—the equilibrium interest rate was that rate at which the quantity of *consumption* goods demanded was equal to the quantity supplied. Now that we have added investment to the model, it will still be the case that the equilibrium interest rate is determined by the intersection of supply and demand. But we need to rethink what we mean by supply and demand.

Aggregate Supply

What determines supply in a world with investment and capital? To keep our model simple and focus on the important points, let us assume that investment cannot be used for immediate production. If a firm buys a new machine in one period, we imagine that the machine is not ready for use until the next period. Alternatively, if capital consists of trees, we imagine that trees planted today do not bear fruit until tomorrow, or until next year. (Later, in Chapter 8, we will consider what happens in subsequent periods.)

The assumption that investment cannot be used for current production means that the supply curve remains unaffected by investment activities. A certain amount of capital is already in existence, and that capital can produce a certain amount of output. That output is what will be produced in the current period, regardless of the interest rate and regardless of investment in that period. This is indicated by the vertical supply curve *S* in Figure 7-8.

The supply of goods, then, is the same as it was in the simpler model in Chapter 5. It measures the goods that are physically available for immediate use.

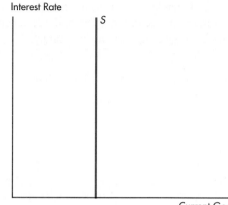

FIGURE 7-8 Aggregate supply.
The aggregate supply curve for *current* goods is perfectly vertical because current investment neither adds to nor subtracts from the quantity of goods that are currently available.

Aggregate Demand

Next, consider demand. Figure 7-9 shows the consumption demand curve D_C and the investment demand (curve D_I). Note that investment represents a smaller percentage of output than consumption; that is, the investment demand curve is to the left of the consumption demand curve. This reflects the usual relation between measured consumption and investment in most countries, but our analysis does not require that assumption.

The aggregate demand curve D is the horizontal sum of the consumption and investment demand curves. Suppose that the goods in this economy are sunflower

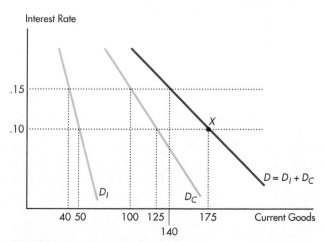

FIGURE 7-9 Aggregate demand.
The aggregate demand curve D is the horizontal sum of the consumption and investment demand curves, D_C and D_I.

seeds, which investors plant and consumers eat. At an interest rate of 10 percent, firms demand 50 seeds for investment and consumers demand 125 seeds for consumption. In the aggregate, 175 seeds are demanded, giving us point X.

➡ *Exercise 7-3*
In Figure 7-9, what quantity should correspond to an interest rate of 15 percent on the aggregate demand curve? Why?

Equilibrium Explored

In Figure 7-10 we have overlaid the aggregate demand and supply curves. They intersect at the equilibrium point X. Thus the equilibrium interest rate is 10 percent. Of the 175 seeds supplied to the market, 125 are eaten and 50 are planted to create next year's crop.

To convince ourselves that the economy will settle at this equilibrium rate, let us ask what would happen if the interest rate were something else, say, 15 percent. At that interest rate, Figure 7-9 shows that consumers would demand 100 seeds and investors would demand 40. The total quantity demanded, 140, is less than the supply of 175 seeds. Someone, somewhere—or some combination of firms and consumers—is holding 35 more seeds than he or she wants to hold.

Consumers with more seeds than they want act exactly as the people did in Chapter 5: they try to lend the excess. But nobody wants to increase personal borrowing at the current interest rate, so the interest rate is bid down. Investors with more seeds than they want do exactly the same thing that consumers do. They try to lend the excess, and they put additional downward pressure on the interest rate. This process continues until the equilibrium interest rate of 10 percent is reached.

➡ *Exercise 7-4*
If the interest rate is below the equilibrium level of 10 percent, how does the quantity of seeds demanded compare with the quantity supplied? What pressures force the interest rate back to the equilibrium level?

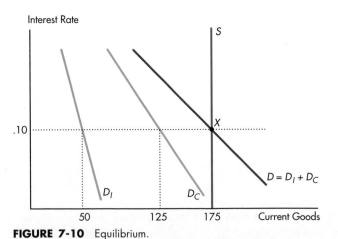

FIGURE 7-10 Equilibrium.
The equilibrium interest rate is determined by the point where supply equals demand.

Saving versus Investment

In the simple models discussed in earlier chapters, there was no net saving in the economy as a whole. Whatever one individual saved (by lending) another individual had to dissave (by borrowing resources and consuming them). Counting dissaving as negative saving, this means that in a closed economy

Economywide net saving $= 0$

Now that our model includes investment, this conclusion no longer holds. When an individual saves by lending goods that are used for investment (as opposed to consumption), those goods are *not* dissaved. Every dollar's worth of goods invested means a dollar's worth of net saving for the economy. In that case, again in a closed economy, we have

Economywide net saving $=$ Economywide investment

This observation is frequently summarized in a (somewhat sloppily worded) slogan: "Saving equals investment."

 Although saving must equal investment for the economy *as a whole*, no *individual* needs to save and invest equal amounts.

Suppose, for example, that you decide to save $100 by depositing it in your bank account. Suppose that the bank lends $30 of that $100 to a consumer who uses it to finance a night of partying and $70 to a firm that uses it to finance the purchase of a new fax machine. Then you have saved $100 and the party animal has saved *minus* $30, for a total of $70 worth of saving. The firm has invested $70, for a total of $70 worth of investment.

In this example, no one individual saved and invested equal amounts; in fact, the savers did no investing at all. Nevertheless, the laws of arithmetic force the total of all saving to equal the total of all investment.

In Figure 7-11 we use the aggregate supply and demand curves to show the relationship between saving and investment. The intersection of the curves determines the equilibrium interest rate r_0. Let's begin by thinking about what would happen if the interest rate were above equilibrium, say, at r_1. At this interest rate, consumers demand C_1 goods in the present, which is less than their income of Y_0. The difference, $Y_0 - C_1$, is the amount they want to save. This desired quantity of saving is represented by the horizontal distance from the consumption demand curve to the aggregate supply curve.

Desired investment at the interest rate r_1 can be read off the investment demand curve; it is I_1. This quantity is also the horizontal distance between the consumption demand curve and the aggregate demand curve, as marked in the figure. The reason for this equality is the definition of the aggregate demand curve as the sum of consumption demand and investment demand; if we subtract consumption demand from this sum, we are left with investment demand.

Note also in Figure 7-11 that at the equilibrium interest rate, desired saving and desired investment are equal.

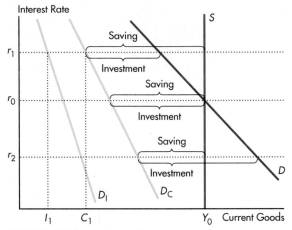

FIGURE 7-11 Saving = Investment.
Desired saving is represented by the horizontal distance between the consumption demand curve and the aggregate supply curve; desired investment is represented by the horizontal distance between the consumption demand curve and the aggregate demand curve. At the equilibrium interest rate, desired saving and desired investment are equal.

You can see in Figure 7-11 that at the interest rate r_1 (above equilibrium), desired saving exceeds desired investment; people want to save more than investors want to borrow. As a result, the interest rate is bid down toward the equilibrium rate.

At an interest rate below equilibrium, such as r_2, desired saving falls short of desired investment. Investors cannot borrow enough to acquire capital for their projects, and the interest rate is bid up toward equilibrium.

We noted earlier that the equilibrium interest rate is the rate at which the aggregate demand for goods is equal to the aggregate supply of goods. You can see now that it is also the rate at which desired saving equals desired investment.

The Government

When we say that saving equals investment in a closed economy, it is important to remember that borrowing counts as negative saving. Borrowing includes both direct borrowing by individuals and borrowing by the government (which must ultimately be repaid by those same individuals).

Thus suppose that individuals add $100 billion to their private savings in a year in which the government runs a deficit of $70 billion. Net saving for that year equals $30 billion, and investment must therefore equal $30 billion as well.

What happens if the government decides to increase its deficit from $70 billion to $80 billion? The answer depends on how individuals react. If they continue to save just $100 billion, then net saving (and hence investment) falls to $20 billion. In this case, an increase in the government budget deficit causes investment to fall.

However, if Ricardian equivalence holds, then individual saving does not stay fixed at $70 billion. Foreseeing a future tax burden with a present value that has increased by $10 billion, individuals increase their private saving by exactly $10 billion, to $110 billion. Net saving (and hence investment) remains fixed at $30 billion ($110 billion in private savings minus an $80 billion government budget deficit).

> If Ricardian equivalence fails to hold, an increase in the government budget deficit causes investment to fall. If Ricardian equivalence holds, an increase in the government budget deficit has no effect on investment.

The Open Economy

In an open economy, it need no longer be true that saving equals investment. To see why, refer to Figure 7-11. If the economy is closed, the equilibrium interest rate is r_0, at which saving and investment are equal. But if the economy is open, then the interest rate is determined in world markets and can have a value other than r_0.

Suppose, for example, that the world interest rate is r_2. In that case, you can see from Figure 7-11 that domestic saving is less than domestic investment. The difference between domestic investment and domestic saving is represented by the horizontal distance from the supply curve S to the demand curve D at level r_2. We know from Figure 5-14 that this distance is also equal to the trade deficit. Thus:

> In an open economy, domestic saving *plus the trade deficit* equals domestic investment.

7-4 COMPARATIVE STATICS

In this section we explore again how changes in the economic environment affect equilibrium.

An Increase in Future Income

We considered the effect of an increase in expected future income in Chapter 5. There, we saw that the consumption demand curve shifts to the right, as it does (from D_C to D_C') in Figure 7-12. Why? Because an increase in future income is an increase in wealth, and consumers respond by increasing current as well as future consumption.

Does the investment demand curve D_I shift? The answer is no, because the marginal product of capital has not changed. Hence there is no reason for firms to increase or decrease investment. *Only a change in the marginal product of capital affects the investment demand curve.*

Thus, the aggregate demand curve D shifts to the right by the same amount as the consumption demand curve, from D to D'.

The current supply of goods, S, is unaffected by an increase in future income. Current supply is affected only by a change in what is physically available now. Our

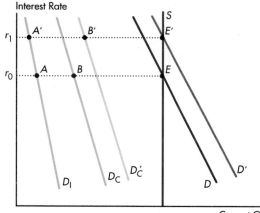

FIGURE 7-12 An increase in expected future income.
Consumption demand shifts to the right, from D_C to D_C', and therefore aggregate demand shifts from D to D'. There is a rise in the equilibrium interest rate from r_0 to r_1, a drop in investment (a leftward move from A to A'), and a rise in consumption (a rightward move from B to B').

model assumes that new investment goods do not produce additional output until at least the next period.

Thus, the equilibrium point moves from E to E' in Figure 7-12. The market interest rate, determined at the intersection of supply and demand, rises from r_0 to r_1.

What happens to investment? We can read the effect off the (fixed) investment demand curve. As the interest rate rises from r_0 to r_1, firms move along the investment demand curve D_I from point A to point A', where they invest less than before. When future income increases, current investment falls.

What happens to consumption? Consumers move from point B on the old consumption demand curve D_C to point B' on the new consumption demand curve D_C'. But is consumption up or down? That is, does point B' lie to the right or to the left of point B? Here is how to figure that out: All goods are used either for consumption or for investment. The quantity of goods is unchanged, and we have seen that the quantity being invested has fallen. Thus the quantity being consumed must rise. So point B' must lie to the *right* of point B.

In Figure 5-7, we saw that an increase in future income encourages consumers to borrow against their future prospects, thereby driving the interest rate up in the current period. The same thing occurs in our enriched model with investment. Current consumption demand increases, causing the total demand for current goods to increase. The interest rate is driven up in the process. At the higher interest rate, both consumers *and* investors are dissuaded from borrowing. Investment declines. For consumers, the initial impulse to increase their borrowing dominates the damping effect of the higher interest rate, so consumption increases.

➡ *Exercise 7-5*
Draw a graph that shows what happens when expected future income *falls*.

An Increase in the Marginal Product of Capital

Suppose that a remarkable innovation increases the marginal product of capital, so people can produce more in the future with the existing capital stock. Clearly people are better off: they are wealthier because future income will increase. But to predict the effects on consumption and investment, we must look deeper.

As in the preceding discussion (an increase in future income), current supply is unaffected. Also as before, consumption *demand* shifts to the right as consumers look to borrow against their future gain. So far, an increase in the marginal product of capital looks just like any other change that causes an increase in future income.

But when the marginal product of capital changes, there is one additional effect: The investment demand curve moves. The marginal product of capital is now higher for any given quantity of capital. This makes capital more desirable. Firms seeking more capital increase their current demand for investment. The investment demand curve shifts rightward, from D_I to D_I' in Figure 7-13.

Also shown in Figure 7-13 is the rightward shift in consumption demand from D_C to D_C'. Total demand—the sum of consumption demand and investment demand—shifts rightward by the sum of the consumption demand shift and the investment demand shift. As a result, the equilibrium point moves from E to E'; the interest rate rises from r_0 to r_1.

Investment moves from point A to point A'. Is that an increase or a decrease? In other words, does point A' lie to the right or to the left of point A? Either outcome is possible. The immediate impact of the increased MPK is that investors want to invest more. On the other hand, the rise in the interest rate (brought about partly by the rise in *consumption* demand) tends to discourage investment. The net effect

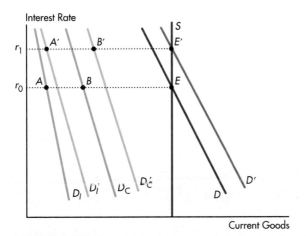

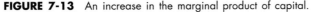

FIGURE 7-13 An increase in the marginal product of capital.
Consumption demand shifts rightward because future income increases. Investment demand shifts rightward because each unit of capital is now more productive. Aggregate demand shifts rightward because it is the sum of consumption and investment demand. The interest rate rises, and the quantities of consumption and investment can either rise or fall.

depends on how far the investment demand curve moves, how far the consumption demand curve moves, and how steep the investment demand curve is.

What is the effect on consumption? It moves from B to B', but does point B' lie to the right or to the left of point B? We can't say; we can only note that if current investment increases, then current consumption must decrease (because total output is fixed), and vice versa.

Finally, although it is not visible in the graph, we can consider the effect on future output. By itself, the increased marginal product of capital will lead to higher future output. If there is increased investment (that is, if A' is to the right of A), future output will increase even more. But if investment falls, might it fall far enough to cause a drop in future output? The answer is no. In fact, future consumption must rise. We know this because we can analyze the substitution and income effects of a rise in the marginal product of capital. When the marginal product of capital rises, future consumption becomes less expensive relative to current consumption; thus the substitution effect leads to more future consumption. At the same time, the rise in the marginal product of capital has made people wealthier, leading them to demand more of everything, including future consumption. (This is the income effect.) The two effects reinforce each other, ensuring that future income rises.

➡ *Exercise 7-6*
Draw a graph that shows what happens when the marginal product of capital falls.

An Increase in Supply

Let us suppose that the economy experiences a one-time increase in current output. A remarkably good harvest or an unusually mild winter might give that result.

Figure 7-14 shows the picture. The supply of goods shifts to the right by the amount of the windfall, from S to S'. Consumption demand shifts to the right because people are wealthier, but it shifts by less than supply shifts because of consumption smoothing. Investment demand stays fixed because there is no change in the marginal product of capital. Hence aggregate demand shifts to the right by the same amount as consumption demand. The equilibrium point moves from E to E', yielding a lower interest rate and, consequently, an increase in investment, from I_0 to I_1.

➡ *Exercise 7-7*
Draw a graph that shows what happens when the supply of current output falls.

7-5 MEASURING INVESTMENT

Productivity:
The quantity of output per worker; aggregate output divided by the number of workers.

Economists are concerned with how to increase **productivity**—that is, the quantity of output per worker. Productivity is closely related to per capita output, but it is not the same thing. To get per capita output, we divide aggregate output by the total population, including those who are unemployed. To get productivity, we divide aggregate output by the number of people who work.

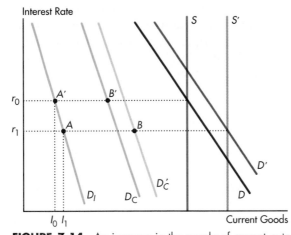

FIGURE 7-14 An increase in the supply of current output.
Supply shifts to the right from *S* to *S'*. Consumption demand shifts right by less than supply shifts. Total demand shifts right from *D* to *D'*, exactly as far as consumption demand shifts. The interest rate falls from r_0 to r_1, and investment increases from I_0 to I_1.

In general, the more capital a country has, the more productive its economy. All kinds of capital—physical and human alike—contribute to a country's productivity. A faster machine and a better-quality education can both make a worker more productive.

Economists want to understand the real-world relationship between investment and productivity. To do this, we measure investment and changes in productivity, and we see how they compare. But we face the obstacle that many kinds of investment are hard to measure. Learning to use existing capital more efficiently is a form of investment—it is investment in human capital—but such learning is difficult to observe and measure. Managers invest in human capital when they figure out how to relocate assembly lines so that the output of one line feeds directly into the next or when they encourage preventive medicine, frequent exercise, and friendly relations among their workers. It is relatively easy to measure the resulting increase in output per worker—that is, the change in productivity—but much harder to measure the investment that led to the increase.

Government regulations and the openness of a country's borders can also affect investment and productivity by influencing the efficient transfer and creation of ideas and knowledge. When a country's government opens its borders to trade with other countries or when computer links such as the Internet create new channels for worldwide communication, there are new opportunities for citizens to learn from the mistakes and inspirations of their counterparts abroad. Immigration of educated workers, or of workers whose ideas are different and thought-provoking, increases human capital and is thus a form of investment. Better highways and railroads can yield similar benefits by facilitating communication, the relocation of workers, and the formation of whole new towns and cities. Such investments are, again, difficult to measure.

A government like the former Soviet Union that suddenly permits its citizens to choose where they wish to live and which job skills they want to acquire might experience a long-run boom in output as citizens relocate and learn new skills. But there is no clear way to determine how much of the boom was associated with that single change in regulations and how much with other simultaneous policy changes. This inability to attribute results to specific causes leads to further problems in measuring the contribution of investment to productivity increases.

By understanding the nature of measurement problems, economists have come to understand what the data do and do not tell us. In this section we discuss measurement difficulties associated with real net investment, using the United States as an example. In the next section we turn to measurement problems that arise in open economies, again focusing on the United States as our example.

Measured Real Net Investment

Real net investment:

Investment consisting of additions to capital minus depreciation; expressed in constant dollars.

Figure 7-15 shows the government's measure of **real net investment** in the United States as a percentage of GDP. The most obvious feature of the graph is that investment fluctuates greatly. As an example, in 1979 real net investment represented 7.5 percent of GDP, but only 3 years later it fell to under 3 percent of GDP. And then only 2 years after that, it was back up to over 7 percent of GDP.

Notice that the average level of investment appears to be declining over time. The peak investment levels of the fluctuations seem to get lower and lower, as do the troughs. During the 1960s, net investment fluctuated around an average level of just over 7 percent of GDP, a pattern that also characterized the preceding decade. How-

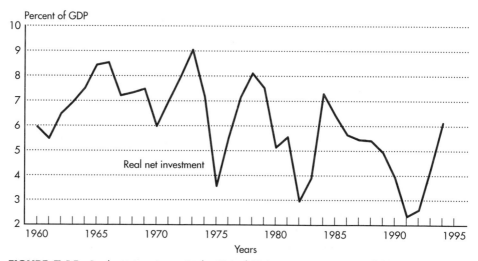

FIGURE 7-15 Real net investment in the United States as a percentage of GDP. Investment in the United States slowed, on average, during the 1980s. Net investment is gross investment minus depreciation.

ever, starting in the early 1970s, net investment dropped to an average of less than 7 percent of GDP, followed by an average level of just over 5 percent of GDP in the 1980s. The pattern of decline appears to be continuing into the 1990s.

Why Has Measured Real Net Investment Decreased since the 1970s?

Is the decline in net investment since the early 1970s a troubling phenomenon for the United States? Some studies imply that the decline in investment is more likely a measurement problem than an actual slowdown in net investment. Discussed below are some particular ideas suggested by researchers as possible explanations. As you will see, each of these ideas tends to be only a partial explanation: none of them alone accounts for the entire period or the entire magnitude of the decline.

Computers

Measurements of investment activity since the 1970s probably have not fully accounted for the technology boom that has accompanied the introduction of computers.

If a company purchases new desktop computers for its staff, the value of that hardware is counted as investment. However, according to U.S. government classification rules, most computer software purchases are deemed intermediate goods rather than investment goods. Thus, if a firm that already owns a computer decides to purchase an accounting software package to improve its billing procedures, that software is considered to be an intermediate input, which is used up fully in that particular year's production.

Some software products depreciate in value quickly enough to make the assumption that they are used up within a year quite reasonable. Other software products maintain their value over longer periods. The decision to classify software as an intermediate good is obviously an arbitrary one. But because some software is clearly an investment good, and because software purchases have boomed since the 1970s, completely omitting them from measured investment tends to undervalue investment as a percentage of GDP.

Education

Traditionally, education is not counted as investment when governments measure investment. Neither is on-the-job training. But both are very much investments in human capital.

Since the 1970s, especially in the United States, higher degrees such as M.B.A.s have become much more common. The large influx of women joining the workforce in the last three decades might have reduced the average experience level of the workforce, and therefore the average investment in human capital, but continued participation by women has likely been accompanied by increased learning on the job. (Estimates suggest that the average experience level of the workforce did decline slightly between 1963 and 1992 but that the decline was more than offset by an increase in education levels.) Because the overall increase to investment represented by extra education and learning on the job is not included in investment measures, the measures have probably understated investment since the 1970s.

Depreciation

Because repairing and replacing older capital is costly, producers of capital equipment frequently invest in methods to increase the longevity of their products in order to appeal to buyers. Many capital items, such as tires, television sets, and heavy machinery, now last longer and require fewer repairs than they did 20 years ago. Thus, it is likely that actual depreciation has decreased over time.

However, when firms report to the U.S. government the amount their capital has depreciated, they do not report the actual extent of depreciation. Instead, they use a table the government publishes that specifies how much depreciation they may report on the basis of the age and basic type of the capital. The table does not account for quality improvements and more efficient uses of capital that affect the longevity of capital, and the table is rarely adjusted. Thus, over time, actual depreciation tends to be less and less than reported depreciation.

Recall that net investment is gross investment minus depreciation. If we could measure actual depreciation and subtract it from gross investment instead of subtracting reported depreciation, average net investment since the 1970s would likely be higher than the graph shows. It may be that real net investment has not in fact declined since the 1970s or that, if it has declined, the magnitude of the decline has been very small.

7-6   INTERNATIONAL INVESTMENT

When overseas investment opportunities become more promising than opportunities at home, U.S. citizens invest abroad. Similarly, foreign firms take advantage of investment opportunities in the United States. How have these international capital flows changed over time?

In comparison with many other nations, U.S. laws permit relatively free sales and purchases of capital across national borders (except for transactions that might affect national security). Thus U.S. citizens can invest abroad in any country that permits such investment, and foreigners can invest in the United States as long as their countries' laws allow them to do so. Foreign firms investing in the United States, say, by building and equipping factories, are subject to U.S. tax, employment, and environmental laws (as well as the laws imposed by their own countries concerning their investments in the United States); similarly, U.S. citizens investing abroad are usually subject to foreign laws as well as U.S. tax laws that are specific to foreign investments.

Measuring International Investment

Net international investment:

The difference between U.S. investment abroad and foreign investment in the United States.

U.S. direct investment position abroad (U.S. DIPA):

A measure of the capital owned by U.S. citizens but located abroad.

Foreign direct investment position in the U.S. (foreign DIPU):

A measure of the capital owned by foreign citizens but located in the United States.

Net U.S. direct investment position abroad (net U.S. DIPA):

U.S. DIPA minus foreign DIPU.

Measuring **net international investment**—the difference between U.S. investment abroad and foreign investment in the United States—is even more difficult than measuring domestic investment because it includes all the problems discussed in Section 7-5 as well as additional problems. In this section we discuss some of these additional measurement problems.

To measure net international investment, the U.S. government reports several figures. First is the **U.S. direct investment position abroad (U.S. DIPA),** which is a measure of the capital owned by U.S. citizens but located abroad. Next is the **foreign direct investment position in the U.S. (foreign DIPU),** which is a measure of the capital owned by foreign citizens but located in the United States. Subtracting the foreign DIPU from the U.S. DIPA gives the **net U.S. direct investment position abroad (net U.S. DIPA).**

Although the word "investment" appears in the names of these measures, they do not measure investment at all. Instead, they measure existing capital. To measure this year's investment (which is an *addition* to capital), we must subtract last year's capital from this year's capital. Thus, if you want to know, for example, how much U.S. citizens invested in foreign countries in 1995, you would subtract the U.S. DIPA for 1994 from the U.S. DIPA for 1995.

Unfortunately, the number you would come up with in this way might still be very misleading. The problem is this: When a U.S. citizen purchases shares of stock in a foreign firm, the government sometimes counts that purchase as an addition to the U.S. DIPA (the purchase is counted if it amounts to more than 50 percent of the value of the foreign firm). Similarly, when a foreign citizen purchases stock in a U.S. firm, the government sometimes counts that purchase as an addition to the foreign DIPU. But economists do not count stock purchases as investment; to an economist, only the creation of new capital counts as investment. It is difficult to evaluate how much this measurement problem distorts conclusions about international investment.

Figure 7-16 compares the U.S. DIPA to the foreign DIPU and also shows their difference, the net U.S. DIPA, all as percentages of U.S. GDP. While both the U.S. DIPA and the foreign DIPU tended to rise between 1985 and 1993, the *net* U.S. DIPA declined during the late 1980s and early 1990s. In other words, throughout that time period, American ownership of foreign assets and foreign ownership of American assets both increased, but the latter increased more than the former did.

Note, however, that the net U.S. DIPA never became negative. That is, during the 1980s and 1990s, the value of foreign capital held by Americans—accumulated holdings of foreign land and factories—continued to exceed the value of American capital held by foreigners. And although the net U.S. DIPA did decline slightly in the late 1980s, in 1993 it reached nearly the same level—approximately 4 percent of GDP—that it had held in 1985.

Market Value versus Historical Value

Most U.S.-owned assets abroad were purchased long ago, shortly after or even long before World War II. Because many of these assets have increased in value and

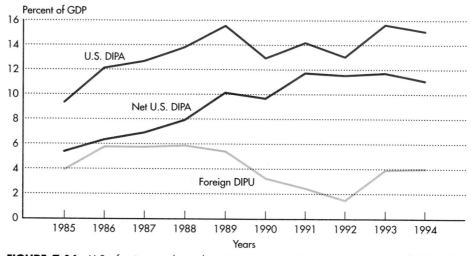

FIGURE 7-16 U.S., foreign, and net direct investment positions as percentages of U.S. GDP. The U.S. and foreign investment positions include asset holdings valued at market prices wherever those data are available.

because of decades of inflation, the original purchase prices of those assets greatly understate their current market values. On the other hand, most U.S. assets owned by foreigners were purchased fairly recently, since the late 1970s. The original purchase prices of those assets reflect their current market values far more accurately.

Until recently, asset positions abroad were computed using original purchase prices rather than current market values. This procedure undervalued U.S. holdings of foreign assets more than it undervalued foreign holdings of U.S. assets. To eliminate this discrepancy, asset positions are now computed using current market values. Unfortunately, current market values can be difficult to estimate, so the new procedure has introduced new inaccuracies. Most economists believe that assets are still systematically undervalued in official statistics and that U.S. holdings abroad are undervalued to a greater extent than foreign holdings in the United States.

Exchange-Rate Changes

In order to do the subtraction necessary to compute the net U.S. DIPA, statisticians must first convert the U.S. DIPA to U.S. dollars. If a U.S. citizen owns a French factory worth 40,000 French francs and a foreign citizen owns a U.S. factory worth $10,000, we must figure out how many U.S. dollars the piece of foreign capital is worth before we can perform the subtraction.

However, **exchange rates**—the value of one currency in terms of other currencies—often change rapidly from day to day. Should a factory worth 40,000 French francs on December 31 be converted to U.S. dollars at the price of francs at the middle of the year, at the end of the year, or perhaps at an average of the year's exchange rates? The choice of which exchange rate to use affects the measured net U.S. DIPA and causes it to fluctuate partly because exchange rates fluctuate.

Exchange rate:
The price of one nation's currency in terms of another's.

In periods of relatively rapid U.S. inflation, the U.S. dollar tends to lose some of its value relative to other currencies. Thus, the measured value of the U.S. DIPA, and hence of the net U.S. DIPA, tends to decline. So depending on inflation rates, measured year-end investment positions might or might not accurately reflect the actual value of investment.

Do International Investment Positions Matter?

Are Americans adversely affected when foreigners own a lot of capital in the United States? Does it matter if a golf course or an automobile factory in the United States is owned by someone in Japan? The answer is: probably not. Most golfers don't care—or don't even know—whether the course they are playing is owned by a Japanese stranger or an American stranger. In neither case can they control the owner's decision about how often to water the greens or whether to convert the course to a parking lot.

Indeed, foreign ownership of U.S. assets offers at least one strategic advantage to the United States: In the event of war, those assets can be seized. Perhaps the prospect of such seizures encourages nations to seek alternatives to war.

On the other hand, that same prospect can be a source of inefficiency and international friction. Suppose that a U.S. firm owns an oil well in Saudi Arabia. The firm must always be wary of an unexpected deterioration in U.S.-Saudi relations that could lead the Saudi government to seize the well. Consequently, the firm might be eager to deplete the well as quickly as possible and thus might remove oil at a much faster rate than a Saudi-owned firm would.

But the primary thing to remember about international investment is that it is a form of trade. If you can sell your land to a foreigner for a better price than you can get from your neighbors, you will be better off if you do so—for you will end up with more resources to use as you desire. International trade, like domestic trade, occurs when it will benefit both parties.

People who express concern about foreign ownership of land and capital frequently forget that the land and capital were paid for and that the seller—that is, the original owner—presumably considered the exchange a good deal. If that seller applied the proceeds to a productive investment, the net effect could well have been an *increase* in the total value of assets held by domestic citizens. And even if the seller consumed all the proceeds—say, in a single riotous weekend—we should remember that a sufficiently riotous weekend can be well worth the expense.

SUMMARY

Capital goods are used not for current consumption but to produce goods for future consumption. An investment is an addition to capital.

In our model economy, the level of output is determined by the stock of capital. The relationship between the two is given by the production function. The production function is characterized by a diminishing marginal product of capital (MPK), which means that each additional unit of capital adds less to output than any previous unit. The MPK for any quantity of capital is equal to the slope of the production function at the point which represents that quantity of capital.

The demand curve for capital is identical with the MPK curve, which represents the MPK versus capital on hand, and is therefore downward-sloping. The demand curve for investment is the difference between the demand curve for capital and the amount of capital already in existence; it has the same shape as the demand curve for capital.

Even in a model with capital and investment, the aggregate supply of current goods is represented by a vertical line. Because current investment has no effect on the production of current goods, the quantity of current goods is fixed.

The aggregate demand for current goods is the sum of consumption demand and investment demand.

The equilibrium interest rate is determined by the intersection of the aggregate supply curve and the aggregate demand curve for current goods. The equilibrium interest rate can also be characterized as the interest rate at which desired saving is equal to desired investment.

In comparative-statics exercises, consumption demand and aggregate supply are still subject to all of the same rules as applied in earlier chapters: Supply is affected by current physical availability of goods, and demand is governed by the principle of consumption smoothing. Investment demand is determined by the marginal product of capital, and so it changes only if something happens to change the MPK.

Measured real net investment appears to have declined over time. However, this drop in investment might be the result of the difficulty of measuring investment, including problems in accounting for the values of computer software, education, and depreciation. Measurements of the U.S. net asset position abroad may understate the relative value of foreign assets purchased many years ago and are subject to rapid fluctuations when exchange rates change.

PROBLEM SET

1. Suppose that Anne Jones has an orchard with 10 trees, producing 1500 apples per year, and that with 11 trees she could produce 1600 apples. Trees sell for $100 apiece, and apples sell for $0.10 apiece. Express the MPK at Anne's orchard in percentage terms.

2. Suppose a violent storm destroys a significant quantity of existing capital. What happens to the demand for capital? What happens to the demand for investment?

3. Suppose the depreciation rate increases from 3 percent per year to 5 percent per year.

    a.   In which direction does the demand for capital shift? How far does it shift in the vertical direction?

    b.   Give a reason why the investment demand curve might shift to the left. Give a reason why the investment demand curve might shift to the right.

    c.   If the demand curve for capital is nearly vertical, which of the two effects in part **b** is larger? Which way does the demand for investment shift?

4. A certain shoemaker can buy a new hammer for $10, and by doing so he can increase his profits by $2 per year forever. A certain rental property returns a net flow of income equal to $10,000 per year forever. What is the market price of the rental property. (*Hint:* What must the market interest rate be, and why?)

5. In 1981, the personal computer was introduced, creating a whole range of new opportunities for productive investment. Shortly thereafter, interest rates rose dramatically. Give a full explanation of how the new computers might have contributed to the rise in interest rates. If you draw a graph and shift curves, be sure to explain why the curves shift as they do.

6. Certain government regulations tend to reduce the productivity of capital. Consider two plans to make capital more productive:

    Plan A: An *immediate, temporary* easing of such regulations. This easing would end in 3 months, whereas it takes 6 months to complete any new investment project. Thus there would be no effect on the demand for investment.

    Plan B: A *temporary* easing of regulations, announced today but scheduled to take place *next year*, to give firms time to adjust their investment plans.

    a. Under plan A, what happens to the interest rate and to the level of current consumption?

    b. Under plan B, what happens to the interest rate and to the level of current consumption?

    c. *True or false:* Because plan A ends before any investment projects can be completed, it would not lead to any new investments being undertaken.

7. Suppose the government levies a tax of 10 percent on investment. Draw the investment demand curves before and after the tax is levied.

8. What would happen to the interest rate and to the quantities of consumption and investment if a war in eastern Europe reduced expected future income throughout the world? Explain.

9. Suppose there is a temporary drop in the marginal product of capital, say, because bad weather makes it difficult to operate machinery effectively. What happens to the equilibrium interest rate and to the quantities of goods used for consumption and investment?

10. Suppose an epidemic wipes out half the population. What happens to the equilibrium interest rate and to the quantities of goods used for consumption and investment? (*Hint:* Keep in mind that capital is less productive when there are fewer people around to operate it.)

11. The government has decided to increase taxes temporarily and use the revenue to reduce the deficit.

    a. Suppose the tax takes the form of a new sales tax on consumption goods. How does this policy affect the interest rate, the quantity of current investment, and the quantity of current consumption?

    b. Suppose, instead, that the tax increase takes the form of a new tax on investment. How does this policy affect the interest rate, the quantity of current investment, and the quantity of current consumption?

    c. Suppose, instead, that the tax increase takes the form of a flat $100-per-person head tax (that is, a tax that everyone must pay regardless of what he or she consumes or invests). How does this policy affect the interest rate, the quantity of current investment, and the quantity of current consumption?

12. Suppose an open economy with a trade deficit decides to stop all trade with the rest of the world.

   a. What happens to the amount of saving in that economy?

   b. What happens to the amount of investment?

   c. Which changes by more—the amount of saving or the amount of investment?

Chapter 8

Economic Growth

Y ou are living in the most prosperous era in history. A generation ago, your parents could choose among only three television channels, broadcasting mainly in black and white and showing programs that could not be taped for later viewing—because there were no VCRs. They used electric typewriters, of which the latest models provided a wonderful innovation: a "delete" key that enabled you to automatically erase the last character you had typed. If you wanted to erase the character *before* that one, you were out of luck. There were no automatic ice dispensers, no car stereos, and no telephone answering machines. Only a few generations earlier, there were no refrigerators, no cars, and no telephones.

Just as your standard of living will exceed that of your parents, your children's standard of living will almost surely exceed your own. We can be reasonably confident of that prediction, because nearly every generation in history has lived better than its predecessors. That march of progress—the increase in per capita income from one year to the next—is what we call **economic growth.**

The rate of economic growth varies considerably from decade to decade and from country to country. In the United States, from the late 1940s to the early 1970s, per capita output grew at an average rate of over 2.5 percent per year. Since the 1970s, the growth rate has slowed to an average of less than 1.5 percent per year. That 1.5 percent looks low compared with the rate immediately after World War II, but it is not far different from the nation's average rate of 1.6 percent over the past 120 years. Over that long horizon, Japanese per capita output grew much faster, averaging 2.5 percent per year. Other countries, such as Australia and the United Kingdom, did worse, averaging 1.1 percent and 1.3 percent, respectively.

The difference between annual growth rates of 1.1 percent and 2.5 percent is enormous. Consider a middle-class American earning $50,000 per year who expects his children, 25 years from now, to occupy the same middling rung on the economic ladder as he occupies today. With a 1.1 percent growth rate, those children will earn the equivalent of about $65,000 a year; with a 1.5 percent growth rate, the equivalent of about $73,000; and with a 2.5 percent growth rate, the equivalent of about $93,000.

And the benefits of growth multiply from generation to generation. With a 1.1 percent growth rate, the grandchildren of that $50,000-a-year middle American will earn the equivalent of about $86,650 a year; with a 1.5 percent growth rate, the equivalent of about $106,000; and with a 2.5 percent growth rate, the equivalent of about $174,500.

Clearly growth is the engine of economic prosperity. In this chapter we examine the workings of that engine. The *neoclassical model* we have been constructing in Chapters 3 through 7 is now sufficiently rich so that we can use it to predict how economies develop over time. We do so in Section 8-1, where the model leads us to some important distinctions between short-run and long-run (or "steady-state") growth patterns.

However, the model in Section 8-1 is too simple to perform certain important tasks. First, it cannot easily be used to describe an economy with a growing population. Second, it is a clumsy model to use for comparative statics. To repair these and other shortcomings, we develop a more general model in Section 8-2: the *Solow model,* which is the model that economists most often use to organize their thinking about growth.

Then, in the remainder of the chapter, we tie the theory together with facts about real-world growth, and we examine the question of how much and how fast an economy "ought" to grow.

8-1 GROWTH IN THE NEOCLASSICAL MODEL

Our incomes depend on how much we produce, and the amount we can produce depends on how much capital we have. So the story of economic growth—that is,

Capital stock:

The amount of capital available to an economy at a point in time. Remember that capital refers to goods that are used to produce consumption goods.

the story of how our incomes increase over time—must begin by describing the growth of the **capital stock.**

Remember that an increase in the capital stock is called investment and that in Chapter 7 we were able to determine the equilibrium quantity of investment for a given period. In this section, we extend that story by investigating how today's investment affects the capital stock in the more distant future.

Roughly, our extended story will go like this: Today's investment adds to tomorrow's capital stock. That change in the capital stock affects tomorrow's demand for investment and hence tomorrow's equilibrium quantity of investment. That in turn affects the capital stock on the day *after* tomorrow, and so on. We will trace this scenario through several days (or years, or "periods") to determine the long-run behavior of the capital stock and its implications for economic growth.

How the Capital Stock Grows from One Period to the Next

Figure 8-1(a) provides a quick review of the goods market with investment—the material of Chapter 7—for the current period. The demand curve D is the sum of the consumption demand curve D_C and the investment demand curve D_I. The demand curve D intersects the supply curve S to determine the market interest rate r_0. At that interest rate, the quantity of investment, read off the curve D_I, is I_0.

How the Curves Shift from One Period to the Next

Figure 8-1(b) shows the supply and demand curves from Figure 8-1(a). Now let us see how those curves will shift in response to this period's I_0 units of investment.

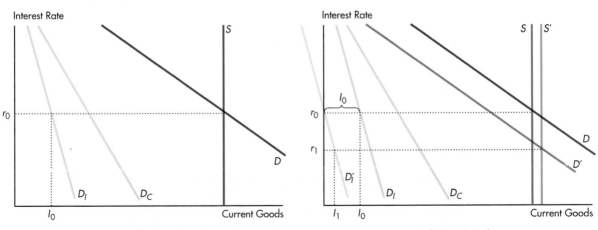

(a) This Period   (b) Next Period

FIGURE 8-1 Goods market equilibrium during (a) this period and (b) next period.
Because this period's investment adds I_0 units to the capital stock, output increases in the next period, so the aggregate supply curve shifts rightward from S to S'. But this period's investment also causes investment demand D_I to shift leftward by I_0 units to D_I', so total demand also shifts leftward from D to D'. The interest rate falls from r_0 to r_1 and a smaller quantity, I_1, is invested in the second period.

First, consider the supply of goods S. This period's investment adds to the capital stock, so more output can be produced next period. Thus next period's supply of goods is greater than this period's. In other words, the supply curve shifts to the right, from S to S'.

Next, consider the demand for consumption D_C. Recall that D_C changes primarily in response to changes in wealth. But wealth has not changed, so the consumption demand curve D_C does not shift.

We have argued repeatedly in this book that an increase in output makes people wealthier and so leads to an increase in consumption demand. But we have made that argument only when output has increased *unexpectedly*. Foreseeable increases are already included in current wealth and therefore do not cause the demand curve to shift.

What about the demand for investment D_I? At any given interest rate, investors have a target stock of capital—namely, that capital stock at which MPK $= r$. (We discovered this in the discussion accompanying Figures 7-3, 7-4, and 7-5.) Investment demand—that is, the demand for *additions* to capital—is the difference between the target stock and the existing stock.

But following this year's investment of I_0 units, the capital stock is I_0 units closer to its target value. Therefore, next period's investment demand is *reduced* by the quantity I_0. In other words, the investment demand curve shifts I_0 units to the left, from D_I to D_I' in Figure 8-1(b).

Finally, consider the aggregate demand curve D. The aggregate demand curve is the sum of the consumption demand curve D_C, which does not shift, and the investment demand curve D_I, which shifts I_0 units to the left. Therefore, the aggregate demand curve D shifts I_0 units to the left, to D'.

When we say that investment I_0 increases the capital stock by I_0 units, we ignore the effects of depreciation, which reduces the capital stock and so contributes to a net increase of fewer than I_0 units. We shall continue to ignore the effects of depreciation in this first pass at exploring the long-run effects of capital accumulation. Later on, we will see that including depreciation leaves the spirit of the model intact.

How the Equilibrium Changes from One Period to the Next

Because the demand curve shifts leftward from D to D' and because the supply curve shifts rightward from S to S', the equilibrium interest rate falls from r_0 to r_1.

The new equilibrium quantity of investment can be read off the new investment demand curve D_I' at the new equilibrium interest rate r_1. That new equilibrium quantity is I_1. Under reasonable assumptions about the slopes of the curves, it is possible to demonstrate that I_1 must be less than I_0, and that is how the figure has been drawn.

Remembering that I_0 is the amount invested in the first period and I_1 is the amount invested in the second period, we conclude:

According to the model, investment decreases from one period to the next.

Incorporating Depreciation

Our discussion has ignored depreciation, but that is not hard to remedy. In Figure 8-1(a), we see that I_0 units are added to the capital stock (that is, invested) in the current period. Suppose that at the same time, some quantity δ units are subtracted from the capital stock via depreciation. Then investors begin next period not I_0 units closer to their target capital stock but only $I_0 - \delta$ units closer. Thus in Figure 8-1(b), the investment demand curve D_I must shift leftward not by I_0 units but by $I_0 - \delta$ units. The remainder of the analysis is unchanged.

How the Capital Stock Grows in the Long Run

Now let us ask what happens in the even more distant future. We have seen that from this period to next period the curves D_I, D, and S of Figure 8-1(a) are replaced by the curves D'_I, D', and S' of Figure 8-1(b). The equilibrium quantity of investment drops to I_1. We can now repeat the entire process shown in Figure 8-1, using the new (primed) curves and the new equilibrium as a starting point. In the period after next, then, all the curves shift again in the same directions as before, and investment falls to an even lower level.

In each period, investment is lower than it was before. Eventually, one period's investment becomes indistinguishable from zero, and the growth of the capital stock comes to a virtual halt.

According to the model, the capital stock grows ever more slowly over time and eventually stops growing.

Incorporating Depreciation

This description of the long run also ignores the effects of depreciation, but again they are not hard to include. If a portion of the capital stock depreciates each period, then investment must exceed depreciation in order to add to the capital stock. When it does, investment decreases from period to period, as in Figure 8-1. However, instead of approaching zero, investment approaches that quantity which is just necessary to replenish the capital stock. At that point, the capital stock essentially stops growing.

Economic Growth

Figure 8-2 shows the economywide production function that was first introduced in Figure 7-2. The capital stock in each of several successive periods is plotted along

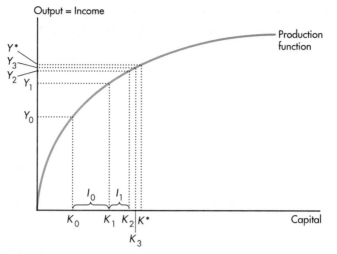

FIGURE 8-2 Convergence to the steady state.
The capital stock grows from K_0 to K_1 to K_2 and so forth, converging to the steady-state value K^*.
The production function determines the output Y_i that corresponds to each capital stock K_i. Thus
output grows from Y_0 to Y_1 to Y_2 and so forth, converging to the steady-state value Y^*.

the horizontal axis: K_0 is the capital stock now, K_1 is the capital stock next period, K_2 is the capital stock in the period after that, and so on.

Our model does not attempt to explain how the current capital stock got to be exactly K_0. However, it *does* explain why next period's stock is K_1: K_1 is equal to the current capital stock K_0 plus this period's investment I_0. (More realistically, we should say that K_1 is equal to K_0 plus I_0 *minus depreciation,* but we shall ignore the effects of depreciation for simplicity.) Recall that I_0, the equilibrium quantity of current investment, was determined in Figure 8-1(*a*).

Similarly, K_2 is equal to K_1 plus I_1, where I_1 is next period's investment, as determined in Figure 8-1(*b*). And K_3 is the following period's investment, which we could determine similarly.

The values of K_0, K_1, and so forth, plotted in Figure 8-2 illustrate our conclusion that while the capital stock grows from period to period, it grows by ever-smaller increments and eventually comes to a virtual halt. After several periods, the capital stock gets very close to a level that we have labeled K^*, and further increases are so small as to be imperceptible. For all practical purposes, the capital stock reaches K^* and then stops growing.

Although the capital stock never becomes exactly equal to K^*, we will speak loosely and say that it "reaches" K^* once it has gotten so close that the difference is of no practical importance.

The vertical axis of Figure 8-2 illustrates the growth in aggregate output (or, equivalently, aggregate income) over time. Initially, the capital stock K_0 produces the output Y_0. Then, as the capital stock increases, output rises to Y_1 next period, then rises again (but by less) to Y_2 the following period, and eventually gets very close to a level Y^*, after which there is no further growth of any appreciable magnitude. Essentially, aggregate annual income reaches Y^* and then remains there (because the capital stock remains at K^*).

The Steady State

According to Figure 8-2, the economy eventually reaches a *steady state*—a situation in which all economic variables retain the same values from one period to the next. Once the capital stock reaches K^*, it remains K^* for all time. Income remains Y^* for all time. Other variables, such as the equilibrium interest rate, are determined by graphs like Figure 8-1(*a*) in which no curve ever moves, so the values of those variables do not change either. We say that each variable has achieved its **steady-state level.** There is no further economic growth.

> **Steady-state level:**
> The level of an economic variable when the economy reaches a steady state.

With some simple reasoning, we can figure out something about the steady-state level of investment. Because the capital stock is fixed from one period to the next in the steady state, it follows that each period's investment must be just enough to replenish depreciation losses. In an economy with no depreciation, this means that in the steady state investment must equal zero.

Comparative Statics

In all previous chapters, we have used our model to predict the values of economic variables at a single time. By contrast, Figure 8-2 illustrates the behavior of the capital stock and of income at a series of different times. It shows both where the economy is headed [to (K^*, Y^*)] *and* the path it is following to get there [from (K_0, Y_0) to (K_1, Y_1) to (K_2, Y_2) and so forth].

When you are on a journey, your plans can change in either of two different ways: you can change your route, or you can change your destination. Similarly, an economic shock can affect the path to the steady state, or it can affect the steady state itself.

Suppose, for example, that the economy has reached the point (K_3, Y_3) in Figure 8-2 when a tornado destroys enough capital to set it back to the point (K_1, Y_1). What happens? The same thing happens that happened the first time the economy was at that point: Equilibrium investment is I_1, and the economy proceeds in the following period to the point (K_2, Y_2). It then continues on as before, always two steps behind where it would have been but converging to the same steady state (K^*, Y^*) toward which it had always been headed.

What if the tornado sets the capital stock back to some value not on the original path, say, between K_1 and K_2? Does the economy follow a new path to the original steady state K^*, or does it travel toward some new steady state? The answer is that it follows a new path to K^*. The reasons for this will be much easier to understand after we cover the material in Section 8-2.

....

Suppose alternatively that the production function itself rotates upward because of some permanent technological improvement like the invention of the personal computer, a better system of transportation, or a reform of the legal system that reduces the cost of organizing commerce. In that case, the point (K^*, Y^*) is no longer on the production function and hence cannot possibly represent a steady-state outcome! In fact, more is true: The new production function makes people richer and raises the marginal product of capital, affecting the consumption and investment demand curves in Figure 8-1; it also means that more goods are produced, affecting the supply curve. For both reasons, equilibrium investment in each period is affected, so the entire sequence $K_0, K_1, \ldots, K^*$ is replaced by a new sequence, converging to a new steady-state capital stock.

A change in the path also changes the destination. Where on the graph should we locate that destination—the new steady state? At the moment we do not have the tools to answer that question. In Section 8-2 we shall develop such tools.

Economic Growth and Population Growth

....

The sequence $Y_0, Y_1, \ldots, Y^*$ in Figure 8-2 shows how aggregate income increases over time. But this is not quite an illustration of economic growth; economic growth is an increase in *per capita* income, not aggregate income.

This problem is easy to remedy, at least when the size of the population is constant. Simply divide all of the quantities Y_i by the population to get a sequence of per capita incomes $y_0, y_1, \ldots, y^*$. This sequence behaves exactly like the aggregate income sequence in the sense that it increases ever more slowly, eventually approaching a steady-state value y^* at which it remains.

But what if the population is *not* fixed in size? What if the population, like that of most countries in the world today, is rapidly growing? Then how can we compute the rate of per capita income growth? Here is a simple idea: Divide each quantity Y_i by the population in period i; that is, divide Y_0 by the current population, divide Y_1 by next period's population, and so forth.

Unfortunately, this idea is *too* simple, and here is why: Changes in the population affect the quantity of output that can be produced with any given quantity of capital—a larger workforce can produce more output with the same capital stock. Thus a world with a growing population is one in which the production function itself keeps moving. This movement in turn causes continuous motion of all the curves in Figure 8-1. And all of this motion has been left out of our model.

Therefore, although Figure 8-2 is an adequate picture of economic growth in an economy with a fixed population, it is quite *in*adequate for describing an economy whose population grows every year. For that, we must replace the *aggregate* production function of Figure 8-2 with an *individual worker's production function,* which does not shift when the population changes. This will be the starting point for the more sophisticated model in Section 8-2.

8-2   THE SOLOW MODEL OF ECONOMIC GROWTH

We have now gone as far as we can with the tools from earlier chapters. Those tools have been useful; they have allowed us to discover the important concept of a steady state. But our ability to study growth is still deficient. First, our graphs are not well suited to illustrate the outcomes of comparative-statics experiments. Second, and more important, our model is limited to the highly artificial circumstance in which there is no population growth.

In the 1950s, economist Robert Solow, a professor at MIT, figured out how to reinterpret the neoclassical growth model in a way that overcomes both of these limitations.[1] In this section, we discuss the ideas for which Solow was eventually awarded the Nobel Prize.

Returns to Scale

The first thing we need to think about is how one worker's productivity is affected by the presence of other workers.

Constant returns to scale:

The condition under which the doubling of (or any percent increase in) all factors of production results in the doubling of (or the same percent increase in) output.

Let's start with a thought experiment. Suppose that you could simultaneously double the world's population and its capital stock. What would happen to each individual worker's productivity? Would it decrease, increase, or remain the same? There are good arguments in favor of each possibility.

One argument goes like this: Because the capital stock increases in the same proportion as the population, each worker still has just as much capital to work with as ever. Therefore, each worker can carry on exactly as before, with no change in productivity. In cases such as this, we say that the economy exhibits **constant returns to scale.**

Decreasing returns to scale:

The condition under which the doubling of (or any percent increase in) all factors of production results in less than doubling (or less than the same percent increase in) output.

An alternative argument is that overcrowding would reduce individual productivity. A carpenter can saw fewer boards per hour when he has a neighbor whose shoulder keeps bumping into his elbow. In this case we say that the economy exhibits **decreasing returns to scale.**

Many economists would counter this argument by pointing out that elbow room is a form of capital and our thought experiment specified that all capital was doubled. Therefore, we ought to have imagined a world with twice as much room to work. But a counter-counterargument is that even in a thought experiment, we should refrain from doubling things that cannot be doubled even in principle. The counter-counter-

_____

[1]R. Solow, "A Contribution to the Theory of Economic Growth," *Quarterly Journal of Economics* (February 1956), 65–94.

Increasing returns to scale:

The condition under which the doubling of (or any percent increase in) all factors of production results in more than doubling (or more than the same percent increase in) output.

argument goes on to suggest that the *right* thought experiment involves doubling only the more traditional forms of capital.

Finally, it can be argued that in a larger population each worker becomes *more* productive than before, because there are more opportunities to collaborate with other workers and more opportunities to specialize. In this case we say that the economy exhibits **increasing returns to scale.**

The Solow model—the model used in this section—takes as an assumption that the economy exhibits constant returns to scale. In Section 8-3, we shall discuss some of the consequences of relaxing this assumption.

The Per-Worker Production Function

In Figure 7-1 we developed the production function for an entire economy. That curve shows aggregate (economywide) output as a function of the aggregate capital stock. Figure 8-3 shows the production function for an *individual worker.* It shows the output produced by a single worker as a function of the capital used by that worker. If the worker in question is the average citizen of the economy—the representative agent—then we can label the horizontal axis "*Per Capita* Capital" and the vertical axis "*Per Capita* Output" (or income).

Capital-labor ratio:

Commonly used term for "per capita capital"; that is, the average quantity of capital per worker.

The phrase "per capita capital" is so ugly that economists have given the concept a different name. It is usually called the **capital-labor ratio** because it is the economywide capital stock divided by the number of workers. The capital-labor ratio is denoted by a lowercase k to distinguish it from the economywide capital stock K.

We assume throughout Section 8-2 that the economy exhibits constant returns to

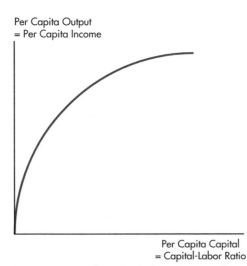

FIGURE 8-3 The individual worker's production function.

scale. This means that *the per-worker production function of Figure 8-3 is unaffected by changes in the population.* The arrival of new neighbors does not change the amount that a worker can produce with a given amount of capital.

Why the Capital-Labor Ratio Evolves

Now let us think about what causes the capital-labor ratio (or, equivalently, the per-worker stock of capital) to change from period to period.

Suppose that your parents jointly own an apple orchard, which they plan to give to their children 10 years from today. Do you expect that you and your siblings will eventually receive more or fewer trees per capita than your parents own?

There are two reasons to answer "fewer" and one reason to answer "more." On one hand, your share may indeed *shrink*. First, you may inherit fewer trees because of *depreciation:* over the next 10 years, some trees will die. Second, your inheritance may be affected by *population growth:* if you have three sisters, then the orchard that is now shared by two parents must eventually be shared by four siblings; this situation cuts the per capita shares in half. But on the other hand, your share may *grow* because of *investment:* over the next 10 years, your parents may do some planting.

In summary:

- Depreciation reduces the aggregate capital stock (that is, the total number of trees) and consequently also reduces the capital-labor ratio (that is, the number of trees that each child inherits).
- Population growth does not change the aggregate capital stock, but it does reduce the capital-labor ratio.
- Investment *increases* the aggregate capital stock and consequently also *increases* the capital-labor ratio.

Our next goal is to depict these effects in graphs.

Depreciation and Population Growth

Our goal here is to construct a graph that shows how depreciation and population growth affect the capital-labor ratio. For the time being, we ignore the effects of investment.

Let us begin with a concrete example. Suppose that the depreciation rate is 10 percent per period; that is, in an orchard of 100 trees, 10 trees can be expected to die from one period to the next. Suppose also that the population doubles each period, so this period's family of two workers has four working descendants next period.

To make this even more concrete, suppose that in the first period—call it period *t*—the capital-labor ratio is 100 trees per worker. Thus each married couple owns 200 trees. By period *t* + 1, 10 percent of these trees will die, leaving 90 per worker. But because of population growth—the 180 remaining trees belonging to two parents must be divided among four descendants—each worker in the next period inherits 45 trees.

This calculation is recorded by plotting the point (100, 45) in Figure 8-4. In that figure, the horizontal axis records period t's capital-labor ratio, and the vertical axis records period ($t + 1$)'s capital-labor ratio. The point (100, 45) tells us that when this period's workers own 100 trees per capita, next period's workers inherit 45 trees per capita.

Survival line:

A line mapping the capital-labor ratio from one period to the capital-labor ratio in the next period. Its slope is dependent on population growth and depreciation.

Similarly, if two parents begin this period with 200 trees apiece, then each of their four descendants begins next period with 90. This is recorded by the point (200, 90) on the graph in Figure 8-4.

The **survival line** for this economy is obtained by drawing a line through the plotted points.

Exercise 8-1
Explain how the number 90 in (200, 90) is calculated.

Changes in the Depreciation Rate

Suppose the spread of a new disease causes apple trees to die at a rate of 20 percent per year instead of 10 percent. What happens to the survival line?

We can quickly calculate some points on the new line. If a couple owns 100 trees per capita (200 altogether), then 80 percent of the trees (160 altogether) survive to next period; after the inheritance is divided four ways, each heir receives 40 trees. Thus (100, 40) is a point on the new survival line.

Exercise 8-2
On the new survival line, what is the vertical coordinate of the point that has horizontal coordinate 200?

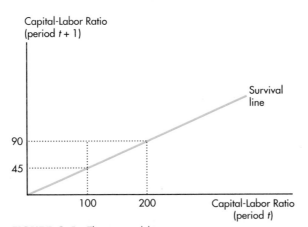

FIGURE 8-4 The survival line.
Of 100 trees per capita alive today, 45 per capita will survive to next period. The reduction is due partly to depreciation (in this case the death of trees) and partly to population growth, which means that trees must be shared by more people.

Figure 8-5 exhibits both the original survival line from Figure 8-4 (representing a 10 percent depreciation rate) and the new survival line (representing a 20 percent depreciation rate).

A rise in the depreciation rate causes the survival line to become flatter. Similarly, a drop in the depreciation rate causes the survival line to become steeper.

➡ *Exercise 8-3*
Suppose that the depreciation rate falls to zero. Give the coordinates of two points on the new survival line.

Changes in the Population Growth Rate

Suppose the depreciation rate remains fixed at 10 percent but the population growth rate increases: instead of doubling each period, the population now triples each period.

We can calculate a point on the new survival line by noting that if two parents own 100 trees per capita, then again 90 per capita (or 180 altogether) remain next period after depreciation. These 180 trees must be divided now among not four children but six. So each child receives 30 trees. Thus, the point (100, 30) is on the new survival line, shown in Figure 8-6. When the depreciation rate rises, the survival line becomes flatter.

A rise in the population growth rate causes the survival line to become flatter. Similarly, a drop in the population growth rate causes the survival line to become steeper.

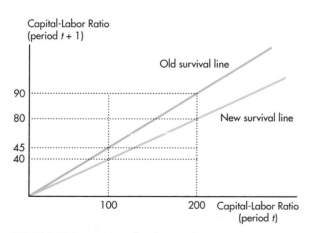

FIGURE 8-5 A rise in the depreciation rate.
When the depreciation rate increases, the survival line becomes flatter.

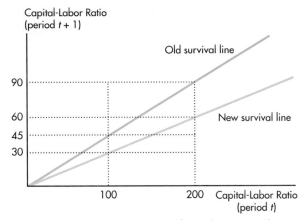

Capital-Labor Ratio
(period *t* + 1)

Old survival line

90

60

45

30

New survival line

100   200   Capital-Labor Ratio
(period *t*)

FIGURE 8-6 A rise in the rate of population growth.
When the population growth rate increases, the survival line becomes flatter.

⇒ *Exercise 8-4*
Suppose that the population growth rate falls to 1.5; in other words, two parents in
this period produce three children who become workers in the next period. Give the
coordinates of two points on the new survival line.

Saving and Investment

The survival line depicts the two forces—depreciation and population growth—that
tend to shrink the capital-labor ratio from period to period. Now we turn to the
forces—saving and investment—that work in the opposite direction. To account for
their effects, we need to make the following assumption:

Each year, people save an amount that is an increasing function of their current income.

In other words, the more you earn this year, the more you'll want to save. Plausible as this may sound, it is really quite an inadequate description of saving behavior; we have stressed throughout this book that saving decisions are as much a function of expected future income as they are of current income. Nevertheless, we will
accept this somewhat troubling—though still quite plausible—assumption for the
sake of simplification.

We already know that income is an increasing function of capital stock (as shown
in Figure 8-2). More capital means more income, and by our new assumption, more
income means more saving. So individual saving is an increasing function of the capital-labor ratio, as shown in the **saving curve** of Figure 8-7. (The shape of the curve
in Figure 8-7 is derived from the shape of the curve in Figure 8-3.)

We know from Figure 7-9 that at equilibrium economywide saving must equal
economywide investment. This means that for the average citizen—the representative

Saving curve:

A curve representing
saving per worker
as an increasing
function of the capi-
tal-labor ratio.

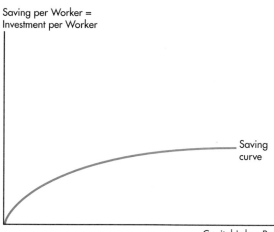

FIGURE 8-7 The saving curve.
The capital-labor ratio determines individual income, and individual income determines individual saving. Therefore, we can depict individual saving as a function of the capital-labor ratio. It is an increasing function because income is an increasing function of the capital stock and saving is an increasing function of income.

agent—individual saving must equal individual investment. So although Figure 8-7 is drawn to show individual saving as a function of the capital-labor ratio, it also shows individual investment as a function of the capital-labor ratio. (The vertical axis is labeled to indicate this.)

Changes in the Saving Rate

Saving rate:
The portion of an economy's income that individuals choose to save.

The **saving rate** is the fraction of an economy's income that people choose to save. If the saving rate increases, then the saving curve in Figure 8-7 rotates upward.

What factors could cause a change in the saving rate? One important factor is the tax treatment of interest earnings and of *capital gains* (that is, increases in the value of financial assets such as stocks and bonds). Currently in the United States, such earnings are taxed at roughly the same rate as other forms of income. In the 1980s and 1990s, there have been recurring political controversies about whether to lower the tax rate on interest and capital gains to encourage saving. The most dramatic proposal has been to scrap the income tax entirely and replace it with a *consumption tax*— essentially, a national sales tax—which would allow interest earnings to accumulate tax-free until they are spent.

Another factor that might influence the saving rate is the government budget deficit. An increase in the deficit amounts to a decrease in national saving because citizens incur the obligation to pay higher taxes in the future. (An obligation to make future payments is a form of negative saving.) If Ricardian equivalence holds, any increase in the deficit is matched by a dollar-for-dollar increase in personal saving, so the country's saving rate is unchanged. But if Ricardian equivalence fails, then a higher budget deficit means a lower saving rate—and a downward rotation of the saving curve in Figure 8-7.

The Transformation Curve

**Transformation
curve:**

A curve illustrating
next period's capi-
tal-labor ratio as a
function of the sum
of the survival line
and the saving
curve.

How much capital will be available to the individual worker of tomorrow? The answer is the sum of two components: the capital that survives from today and the capital that is created by today's investment.

Capital that survives from today is represented by the survival line in Figure 8-4, and capital that is created by today's investment is represented by the saving curve in Figure 8-7. Figure 8-8 combines both curves and adds them to create the **transformation curve.**

The transformation curve shows next period's capital-labor ratio as a function of the current period's capital-labor ratio.

The vertical axis in Figure 8-7 is labeled "Saving per Worker" and "Investment per Worker." Saving and investment are measured in units of *goods* (like apples). The capital-labor ratio is measured in the same units. Because the vertical units are identical, we can superimpose the saving curve on the survival-line graph in Figure 8-8.

For example, suppose that the capital-labor ratio in the current period is 100 trees per worker. Of these, 65 trees per worker survive the processes of depreciation and population growth, as indicated by the point (100, 65) on the survival line. Another 55 trees per worker are created by investment, as indicated by the point (100, 55) on

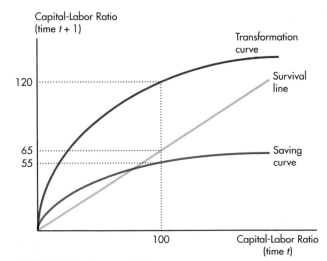

FIGURE 8-8   The transformation curve.
The transformation curve is the vertical sum of the survival line and the saving curve. It illustrates next period's capital-labor ratio as a function of this period's capital-labor ratio.

the saving curve. Thus next period's capital stock consists of $65 + 55 = 120$ trees per worker, as indicated by the point $(100, 120)$ on the transformation curve.

Changes in the Transformation Curve

The transformation curve shifts whenever the survival line or the saving curve shifts. In particular:

A rise in the depreciation rate flattens the survival line (see Figure 8-5) and hence the transformation curve.

A rise in the rate of population growth flattens the survival line (see Figure 8-6) and hence the transformation curve.

A rise in the saving rate (that is, the percentage of their incomes that people want to save) rotates the saving curve upward and hence raises the transformation curve.

Of course, a drop in the depreciation rate, the population growth rate, or the saving rate has the opposite effect to that of a rise.

How the Capital-Labor Ratio Evolves

Figure 8-9 shows the transformation curve of Figure 8-8 together with a 45° line.
To see how the capital-labor ratio evolves over time, let us suppose the repre-

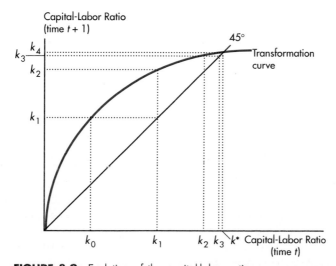

FIGURE 8-9 Evolution of the capital-labor ratio.
From a value of k_0 in the current period the capital-labor ratio evolves to k_1 next period, from k_1 it evolves to k_2 the following period, and so on, eventually converging to its steady-state value k^*.

sentative agent—Anne Jones—owns k_0 units of capital in year 0 (represented by the point k_0 on the horizontal axis). According to the transformation curve, she will own k_1 units in year 1 (represented by the point k_1 on the vertical axis).

Having found the value k_1 on the vertical axis, we can reflect it in the 45° line to find the same value on the horizontal axis. Now the transformation tells us that because Anne owns k_1 units of capital in year 1, she will own k_2 units in year 2 (represented by the point k_2 on the vertical axis).

We can continue in this way, finding that Anne will own k_3 units of capital in year 3, k_4 units in year 4, and so on. The capital-labor ratio increases each year, but the increments get successively smaller. Eventually, the capital-labor ratio comes very close to some value k^*, and further changes are small enough to be insignificant. In essence, the capital-labor ratio settles down at k^* and grows no further. In other words, k^* is a steady-state capital-labor ratio.

When the capital-labor ratio reaches its steady state, this period's and next period's capital-labor ratios are identical; thus the point (k^*, k^*) must be on the transformation curve. The point (k^*, k^*) is also on the 45° line. Thus:

> The steady-state capital-labor ratio can be found at the point where the transformation curve crosses the 45° line.

It is worth comparing the prediction of the Solow model with the prediction of the very simple neoclassical model in Section 8-1. The Solow model predicts that the capital-labor ratio—that is, the *per capita* capital stock—approaches a steady state and stops growing. This means that after the economy has reached its steady state, the *aggregate* capital stock and the population must grow at exactly the same rate. (For example, if the population doubles every 20 years, then the aggregate capital stock must double every 20 years to keep the capital-labor ratio unchanged.)

In the particular case of an economy with no population growth, then, the Solow model predicts that after the economy reaches its steady state, there is no growth in the aggregate capital stock. This was precisely the conclusion of the simple neoclassical model in Section 8-1.

Exercise 8-5
Suppose that Anne Jones starts with k_2 units of capital (as opposed to k_0 units, as we assumed above) in year 0. How much does she own in year 1? In year 2? How much sooner does she reach the steady state?

Economic Growth

We have studied the evolution of the capital-labor ratio, but that topic is only a stepping-stone on the way to our real interest: the evolution of per capita income, which is what we mean by "economic growth." We need to take one more step.

Figure 8-10(*a*) reproduces Figure 8-9 and Figure 8-10(*b*) reproduces Figure 8-3 ("The individual worker's production function"). The annual capital-labor ratios k_0, $k_1, \ldots, k^*$ of Figure 8-10(*a*) have been marked off in part (*b*), as have the corresponding output values $y_0, y_1, \ldots, y^*$ on the vertical scale. As you can see, growth of the capital-labor ratio in (*a*) translates directly into growth of per capita output in

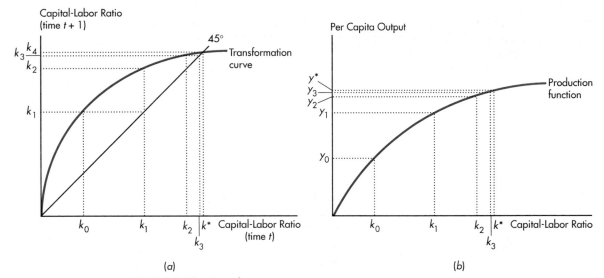

FIGURE 8-10 Growth.
As the capital-labor ratio evolves from k_0 to k_1 and so on in (a), per capita output evolves from y_0 to y_1 and so on in (b). That is, the economy grows. But economic growth slows down over time and comes to a virtual halt when per capita output reaches the steady-state value y^*.

Steady-state per capita output:

The level of per capita output when the economy is in a steady state.

(b). Like the growth of the capital-labor ratio, the growth of per capita output is initially rapid but slows down and eventually approaches y^*, the level of **steady-state per capita output.** At that point, the economic growth rate is essentially zero.

> According to the Solow model, economic growth is initially rapid but slows down from period to period. Eventually, per capita output reaches its steady state and the economy stops growing.

Comparative Statics

The Solow model is sufficiently rich for us to perform a variety of experiments in comparative statics. As in Section 8-1, we must be alert to the difference between a change in the steady state (the economy's long-run destination) and a change in the path that the economy follows to reach that state.

An Increase in the Saving Rate

Suppose that people decide they want to save more—perhaps because of a spontaneous burst of thriftiness or perhaps because of a change in tax policies that rewards saving relative to consumption. Then in Figure 8-8, the saving curve rotates upward. Consequently, the transformation curve, which is the sum of the saving curve and the survival line, rotates upward also—as shown in Figure 8-11(a).

The steady-state capital-labor ratio, which is at the intersection of the transformation curve and the 45° line, shifts rightward from k_0^* to k_1^*. In the long run, the

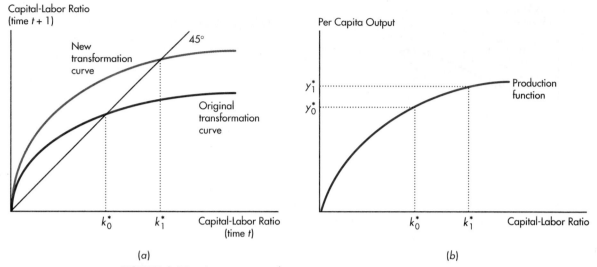

FIGURE 8-11 An increase in the saving rate.
If people decide to save more, the transformation curve in (a) rotates upward. The steady-state capital-labor ratio shifts from k_0^* to k_1^*, and in (b), steady state per capita output rises from y_0^* to y_1^*.

capital-labor ratio approaches k_1^*, and, as the production function in Figure 8-11(b) shows, output approaches y_1^* instead of y_0^*.

➡ *Exercise 8-6*
Illustrate the effect of a *decrease* in the saving rate.

A One-Shot Improvement in Technology

A technological improvement, such as the invention of the computer, has two effects. First, the production function rotates upward from the old production function in Figure 8-12(b) to the new—indicating that we can now obtain more output per unit of capital. Second, this improvement in the production function leads to an increase in people's incomes and hence in their saving. (Recall our assumption that saving is an increasing function of income.) The saving curve rotates upward, and so does the transformation curve, as shown in Figure 8-12(a).

The combined effects of a new steady-state capital-labor ratio k_1^* [from Figure 8-12(a)] and a shifted production function produce a higher output y_1^*, as shown in Figure 8-12(b). Thus:

A one-shot improvement in technology leads to a higher steady-state level of per capita income.

➡ *Exercise 8-7*
Suppose that in Figure 8-12(b) the economy has not yet reached its steady-state capital-labor ratio k_0^*; instead, the current capital-labor ratio is k_0. Now a technological

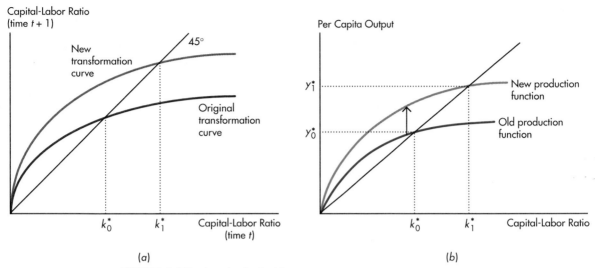

FIGURE 8-12 A technological improvement.
In (a), higher wealth leads to higher saving, which rotates the transformation curve upward and increases the steady-state capital-labor ratio from k_0^* to k_1^*. In (b), steady-state output increases from y_0^* to y_1^*.

improvement occurs, causing the production function to rotate upward, as in the figure. What happens to *current* per capita income? Is it true that the technological improvement increases per capita income in both the short run and the long run?

A *one-shot* increase is not the same thing as a *temporary* increase. Figure 8-12 shows the effect of a single technological improvement, such as the invention of the computer, which happens all at once but *improves productivity permanently.*

Technological progress is not limited to marvels of engineering. The design of a new insurance contract, a better legal system, or an improved pattern of crop rotation can contribute as much to our prosperity as the design of a new kind of plastic can. Any such event causes the production function to rotate upward.

An Ongoing Improvement in Technology

In the first century A.D., Julius Frontinus said, "Inventions reached their limit long ago, and I see no hope for further development." He was wrong. The U.S. Patent Office now issues nearly 100,000 new patents every year.

At least in the modern world, technology appears to improve continuously. This might not always have been the case. Perhaps in the ancient world, there were long periods with no significant innovation at all, punctuated by world-shaking one-shot improvements such as the development of agriculture or of written language. More recently, in the Middle Ages, the pace of technological growth may have been insubstantial for centuries at a time. But since the Industrial Revolution of the nineteenth century, continuous inventiveness seems to have become a fixture of the economic environment.

If technology improves continuously, then we must modify Figure 8-12(*b*) so that next period's new production function is replaced two periods hence by a higher, newer production function, which in turn is replaced by an even higher production function in the period after that, and so on. As a result, the steady-state capital-labor ratio moves continuously to the right, and steady-state per capita income moves continuously upward.

The steady state, then, becomes a moving target that the capital-labor ratio might never reach. Each time the capital-labor ratio takes a step rightward toward the steady state, the steady state itself can take an even larger step in the same direction. This allows the possibility of unlimited growth.

An alternative story—and probably a more realistic one—is that the capital-labor ratio eventually does reach (or, more precisely, does come arbitrarily close to) its steady-state value but then continues growing to keep pace with that value's upward march. The economy is always in the steady state, but the steady state—and hence the economy—never stops growing.

We have just discovered a major result:

Continuous improvements in technology can yield unlimited economic growth.

This is the first time in this chapter that we have encountered *any* mechanism that can account for the apparently unlimited economic growth that much of the modern world seems to have experienced over the past two centuries. Indeed, according to the Solow model, continuous technological improvements constitute the *only* plausible mechanism that can account for such growth.

A One-Shot Increase in Population

A one-shot increase in population has no effect on the survival line or the saving curve in Figure 8-8 and hence no effect on the transformation curve. It does, however, cause a one-shot jump downward in the capital-labor ratio, because a fixed amount of capital is now divided among more people. Thus, for example, an economy that had already reached a capital-labor ratio of k_2 in Figure 8-10(*a*) might be set back to a capital-labor ratio of k_0. The setback would reduce per capita output to y_0 in Figure 8-10(*b*). However, two periods later, per capita income would be restored to its level at the time of the shock, and it would then continue on its original growth path. In the long run, the economy would achieve the same steady state it had been headed for in the first place—but would do so somewhat later in time.

➧ *Exercise 8-8*
Suppose that the capital-labor ratio is well below the steady state and that there is a one-shot decrease in the population. What happens to the current capital-labor ratio and to the length of time until the steady state is reached?

An Increase in the Rate of Population Growth

Suppose that the population growth rate increases. As we saw earlier (in Figure 8-6), the survival line becomes flatter and therefore the transformation curve becomes flatter as well. We see the result in Figure 8-13(a). When the transformation curve becomes flatter, the steady-state capital-labor ratio (which must be on the 45° line) shifts downward from k_0^* to k_1^* percent. In the long run, then, a higher population growth rate means a lower steady-state capital-labor ratio. Now the production function in Figure 8-13(b) tells us that this results in a lower steady-state per capita output (y_1^* instead of y_0^*).

We conclude as follows:

An increase in the rate of population growth reduces the steady-state capital-labor ratio.

In Section 8-4 you will see that this conclusion can be overturned when the assumptions of the Solow model are relaxed.

The Solow Model So Far

The Solow model demonstrates that under the assumption of constant returns to scale, capital accumulation alone cannot account for sustained economic growth. Unless there is a continuous stream of technological improvements, investment shrinks from one period to the next until the economy reaches a steady state. In that steady state, the capital-labor ratio and per capita income stop growing; in other words, the aggre-

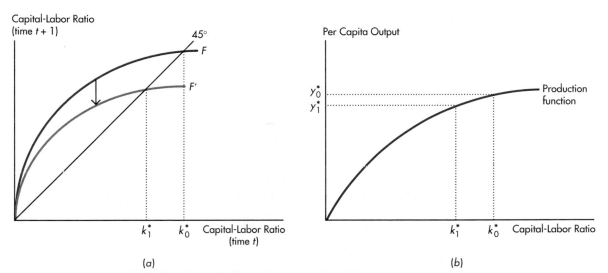

(a)   (b)

FIGURE 8-13 An increase in population growth.
In (a), the transformation curve shifts downward. In (b), the steady-state capital-labor ratio falls from k_0^* to k_1^*, and the steady-state per capita output level falls from y_0^* to y_1^*.

gate capital stock and aggregate income grow at exactly the same rate that the population grows.

Thus the main moral of the Solow model is that a continuous stream of technological improvements is necessary to sustain growth. The good news is that in the modern world, a continuous stream of technological improvements appears to be the norm.

8-3 INTERNATIONAL EVIDENCE

Before we confront the Solow model with evidence, let us review its major implications. According to the model, an economy goes through two stages: first it progresses toward the steady state, and then it remains there. However, technological progress can cause the steady state itself to move. Thus there are really two kinds of economic growth: growth in **developing economies,** which have not yet reached their steady states, and growth in **mature economies,** which have reached their steady states but continue to grow as the steady state advances.

In a developing economy, the rate of growth depends critically on the slope of the transformation curve in Figure 8-8: the steeper the transformation curve, the faster the progression toward the steady state. The slope of the transformation curve depends in turn on the slopes of the survival line and the saving curve. Of these, the saving curve is often the critical factor in the sense that its slope differs dramatically from one country to another. Japanese citizens typically save over 30 percent of their incomes, making the Japanese saving curve (and hence the Japanese transformation curve) very steep. Mexican citizens typically save less than 20 percent of their incomes, making the Mexican transformation curve far flatter than the Japanese curve.

We say that the Japanese *saving rate* is over 30 percent and the Mexican saving rate is under 20 percent. One lesson of the Solow model is this:

> In a developing economy, the saving rate is the major factor in determining the rate of economic growth.

By contrast, a mature economy is not striving toward a steady state but is moving from one steady state to another. The advance of the steady state is driven by technological progress, which therefore takes on a central role as the engine of growth. Thus the next lesson of the Solow model is this:

> In a mature economy (as opposed to a developing economy) growth can depend more on technological progress than on the saving rate.

To test these implications, we need to measure saving rates and rates of economic growth in several countries. The saving rate is the fraction of a country's income that is saved. But we know that income equals output, and we know from Chapter 7 that aggregate saving equals aggregate investment. Therefore, the saving rate is equal to the fraction of a country's output that is invested. In practice, then, we can measure saving by measuring investment.

Developing economy:

An economy that has not yet reached its steady state and experiences growth as it approaches the steady state.

Mature economy:

An economy that has reached its steady state and experiences growth resulting from changes in the steady-state level.

 A more complete analysis would account for the fact that an open economy can have a non-zero trade balance, so that domestic saving and domestic investment need not be equal.

Pacific Rim:

Term used in reference to the Asian nations along the coast of the Pacific Ocean that have experienced high growth rates in recent years—primarily, Japan, Korea, Hong Kong, and Singapore.

Figure 8-14 is a plot of saving (measured by investment) against growth rates for 14 countries.[2] Both the saving rates and the growth rates are 12-year averages for the period 1980–1991. Figure 8-14(b) is a blowup of the boxed area in Figure 8-14(a).

The figure demonstrates the remarkable rewards that the **Pacific Rim** countries of Japan, Korea, Hong Kong, and Singapore have earned for their extraordinarily high saving rates. In Korea, economic growth averaged a remarkable 7.7 percent per year over the period in question.[3] By 1991, the income of the average Korean was 2.3 times its 1980 value. If that same growth rate continues, Koreans in the year 2005 will have 7 times the income of their 1980 counterparts: a shopkeeper who earned $20,000 in 1980 will have children with incomes of $140,000 in 2005!

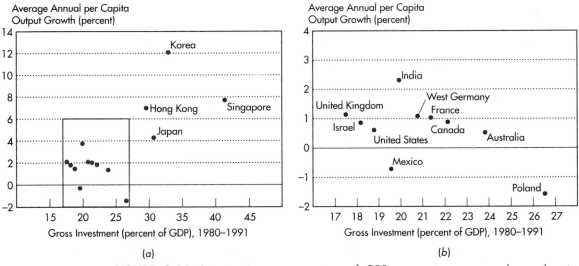

FIGURE 8-14 Investment as a percentage of GDP versus average annual growth rate, 1980–1991.
Panel (b) is a blowup of the boxed area in (a).

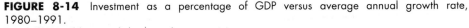

[2]The graphs measure *gross* investment, which includes both the component of investment that creates new capital and the component that replaces depreciated capital. Economists speak of *net* investment when they mean only the first of these components.

[3]The figure of 7.7 percent, like the other numbers recorded in the graph, is based on reports by the OECD. The World Bank, using somewhat different methods, measured Korea's annual growth over the same period as an even more remarkable 8.7 percent. And over the slightly longer period 1980–1993, as reported by the World Bank, the Korean annual growth rate was 9.1 percent!

By contrast, countries like Mexico, with much lower saving rates, tend to cluster at the lower left of Figure 8-14(*a*), indicating that they experienced very little growth over the period in question. This gives broad support to the Solow model's prediction that high saving rates are crucial for growth in developing economies.

However, Figure 8-14(*b*) appears at first to cast doubt on that prediction. For the countries in this group, there seems to be little relation between saving rates and growth rates. But this too is consistent with the Solow model, because most of the countries in Figure 8-14(*b*) are mature economies: the United States, the United Kingdom, France, and Germany have been heavily industrialized for two centuries now. These are economies that can be presumed to have reached their steady states and to be relying for further growth on technological advancements.

One striking data point is Poland, where a very high saving rate in the 1980s was associated with a *negative* rate of economic growth. To understand this, we need to recall why it is that high saving rates cause growth in the Solow model: the key is that saving equals investment, so saving in one period leads to more capital and more production in the next period. This model, however, presumes that investment will be directed toward *useful* forms of capital. Poland in the 1980s was a command economy, directed by bureaucrats with little sense of market reality. Much of their investment ended up being wasted. The lesson of Poland is that even if you must invest to get rich, you can't get rich by investing unwisely.

Because growth is the engine of prosperity, and because saving is—for developing economies—the engine of growth, it follows that economies which encourage saving will become prosperous while those that discourage it will linger for decades on a tortuously slow path toward the steady state. Why have the Pacific Rim countries gone to one extreme while Mexico has gone to the other? Economists can point to factors like favorable tax treatment of saving and investment in the Pacific Rim and a relatively small number of restrictive regulations on the way capital can be invested there. (Such an environment can also allow a given amount of capital to produce more output, thus raising the production function—which also speeds the pace of growth.) Other factors, such as cultural attitudes and preferences for current versus future consumption, may also play significant roles.

Yet another possibility is that the Pacific Rim countries, which started in the 1960s and 1970s with substandard technology, have been playing technological catch-up for the past 20 years. Thus, technological progress would have been unusually rapid in the Pacific Rim during this period of modernization. If this model is right, then the extraordinarily high levels of investment and growth that we have seen in the Pacific Rim cannot be sustained forever: Once the Pacific Rim has caught up with western technology, the entire world can be expected to progress technologically at a single rate. If Japanese citizens continue to save more than Americans do, they will enjoy a higher steady-state income—but not necessarily a faster growth rate.

The model in the preceding paragraph, while treated with respect by many economists, is *not* consistent with standard economic theory, which posits that all countries have access to identical technology—though the countries with more capital can use that technology more effectively.

8-4   ENRICHING THE MODEL

Figures 8-12 and 8-13 show how changes in technology and population affect economic growth. But what factors *cause* changes in technology and population? One factor is economic growth! Our model so far accounts for influences in one direction, but not in the other.

Moreover, changes in technology can affect population growth and changes in population growth can affect the rate of technological advancement. A fully satisfactory growth model should account for all of the complex relationships among these variables. Economists do not yet have a fully satisfactory model, though much recent progress has been made in this area. In this section, we discuss some of the ideas behind that progress.

Increasing Returns to Scale

The Solow model introduced in Section 8-2 assumes that production exhibits constant returns to scale. In other words, it assumes that per-worker output depends only on the capital available to each individual worker (the capital-labor ratio).

But many economists believe that there are circumstances in which *increasing* returns to scale are a more realistic assumption. In other words, these economists believe that if both the population and the aggregate capital stock were doubled (thereby leaving the capital-labor ratio unchanged), aggregate output would *more* than double (thereby raising per capita output or, equivalently, per capita income).

In the presence of increasing returns to scale, then, every increase in population causes the per-worker production function to rotate upward—just as the technological improvement does in Figure 8-12. And in the presence of increasing returns, an *ongoing* increase in population causes the per-worker production function to rotate continuously upward—just as an ongoing sequence of technological improvements does. In this case, the steady state becomes a moving target that may never be hit. Even if it *is* hit, it continues to move and the economy continues to grow to keep up with it. In other words:

> When there are increasing returns to scale, then economic growth can continue forever without reaching a steady state—even if there are no technological improvements.

In view of this happy conclusion, it is worth asking what reasons we have to expect increasing returns to scale.

Why Increasing Returns?

Why might we expect increasing returns to scale? There are a number of reasons. One is that a larger economy allows workers to specialize. No one worker can produce an automobile (at least not in a reasonable amount of time), because no one worker can be simultaneously a mechanic, an electrician, a metalworker, and an engineer. But 1000 workers, each specializing in a particular task, can produce perhaps 5000 automobiles per year, which is more than 1000 times zero. When the population increases from 1 to 1000, productivity per worker increases from zero cars per worker per year to five cars per worker per year.

The advantages of specialization come in two different forms. First, specialization allows people to emphasize their natural talents. If you are a natural gardener and a clumsy tailor, you will benefit from living in a world where you can grow vegetables and trade them to your neighbor for clothing. The more neighbors you have, the more such opportunities you will find.

Second, even when natural talents are not at issue, it is often useful to concentrate on a single task rather than divide your attention among several. Baking two dozen cupcakes is less than twice as much work as baking one dozen; if you bake all the cupcakes while your neighbor makes all the frosting, both of you are likely to end up with more frosted cupcakes than will be the case if each of you tries to do everything without the other's help. Once again, it pays to have a lot of neighbors.

Another reason for increasing returns to scale—and one that modern growth theorists find particularly intriguing—is the *external benefit of human capital accumulation*. Human capital accumulation is the acquisition of knowledge and skills. The **external benefit** of a person's human capital accumulation is the benefit it confers on that person's neighbors. If you want to repair your car's engine, it pays to have a neighbor who knows something about automobiles. If you want to install a new operating system on your computer, it pays to have a neighbor with some knowledge of computer architecture.

People engaged in similar professions frequently meet at conventions, where they exchange ideas. Presumably they do this because it makes them more productive. Indeed, people in similar professions often go to great lengths to work and live near each other for exactly the same reason. Investment bankers live in New York City and filmmakers live in Los Angeles because they want to be near other investment bankers and filmmakers. Apparently, they believe that there is prosperity in numbers—evidence of increasing returns to scale.

In short, it is easier to be productive when you have a lot of neighbors. If you are a printer, you will welcome the arrival of an inkmaker. If you are a physician with a tough case to diagnose, you may benefit from brainstorming with other physicians. Having more neighbors means having more people to trade with, more opportunities to participate in specialized markets, and more colleagues willing to share ideas. Many growth theorists believe that these advantages may far outweigh the costs of living in a crowd.

External benefit:
The benefit that individuals realize from another person's resources, such as that person's human capital stock.

Increasing Returns and International Trade

We have several times run the thought experiment of suddenly "increasing the size of the population" and then asking what happens to productivity. That might strike you as a purely theoretical exercise. But there is at least one sense in which the experiment has a real-world counterpart, and that is in the liberalization of trade between countries. When two countries of about equal populations open their borders to trade, they are, in a sense, combining two economic units into a new unit of twice the size.

The benefits of increasing returns—more neighbors to trade with—are then available to citizens in both countries.

When a large country and a small country agree to trade, the citizens of the large country gain, in relative terms, only a few new neighbors. But the citizens of the small country can see their economic world multiply to many times its size. This is one reason why economists believe that trade between a large and a small country is disproportionately beneficial to the small one. Both countries benefit, although the small country benefits more.

Population Growth and Technological Progress

The comparative-statics exercises in Figures 8-12 and 8-13 suggest that from an economic growth perspective, technological progress is good and population growth is bad. But Nobel Prize–winning economist Simon Kuznets pointed out that technological progress requires ideas and ideas come from people.[4] Thus it may be that technological progress is *caused* by population growth, so you can't have one without the other. Professor Kuznets argued that the indirect benefits of population growth (via its positive effect on technology) outweigh its direct costs (via its negative effect on the capital-labor ratio).

In making that argument, Kuznets assumed that a world of 10 billion people will have twice as many geniuses as a world of 5 billion people. But it may be possible to make an even stronger argument. If the world population doubles, inventors will be able to sell their products to twice as big a market and earn twice as much income. The prospect of such increased rewards might tempt a greater fraction of the population to become inventors. Indeed, two economists at the Federal Reserve Bank of Richmond have recently argued that the Industrial Revolution of the nineteenth century—and the massive ongoing growth spurt that it triggered—had to wait until the world's population grew large enough to make inventiveness profitable.[5] As a result, a double-size world could produce *more* than twice the number of inventions, and even Kuznets's optimistic perspective on population growth is not optimistic enough.

One Million Years of Growth

A recent paper by Professor Michael Kremer of MIT has the provocative title "Population Growth and Technological Change: One Million B.C. to 1900."[6] Building on the ideas of Kuznets, Kremer argues that economic growth leads to increases in population, increases in population lead to improvements in technology, and—to complete the "virtuous circle"—improvements in technology fuel economic growth.

In more detail: Economic growth causes population growth because families can afford to support more children when they are wealthier. Population growth causes

---

[4]S. Kuznets, "Population Change and Aggregate Output," in *Demographic and Economic Change in Developed Countries* (Princeton, N.J.: Princeton University Press, 1960).

[5]M. Goodfriend and J. McDermott, "Early Development," *American Economic Review* 85 (1995), 116–133.

[6]*Quarterly Journal of Economics* 108 (1993), 681–716.

technological progress in the way that Kuznets envisioned—larger populations have more geniuses, whose creativity can be exploited by everyone.[7] Technological progress fuels economic growth, just as we saw in the discussion accompanying Figure 8-12.

Kremer's argument predicts not only that technology and population will grow forever but that they will grow forever at an increasing rate. He notes that his prediction has been borne out by long-term trends for the past million years.

8-5 EVALUATING GROWTH

Is rapid growth always desirable? The answer is clearly no. Suppose a government takes the country's entire output during a certain period and uses it for investment. Then next period's output will increase dramatically; but before people can enjoy the benefits of this growth, they will starve. Future growth comes at the expense of current consumption.

Alternatively, a country can grow too slowly, eating into its future by consuming all its current output and devoting none to investment. In the extreme, we can imagine a country choosing to consume not only all its output but its entire capital stock, so the country's future output is destroyed by current consumption.

It is important to distinguish the destruction of a country's capital stock from a mere change in the kind of capital a country owns. Suppose a nation's citizens willfully cut down and sell every tree in their country because the world price of trees is unusually high. Have they destroyed their capital stock? Perhaps. That depends on what they do with the proceeds of their tree sales. If they go on a spending spree and purchase TV sets and fancy motorcycles, they will be left with no capital stock. If, on the other hand, they use the proceeds to send their children to school or to invest in new factories or more seeds to plant, then the value of their capital stock might actually increase.

Consumption versus Investment

What, then, is the right balance between investment and consumption? The consumption and investment demand curves in Figure 8-1 represent the choices made by individuals in their dual roles as consumers and producers. Those choices reflect individual preferences. The people in our model have every reason to save for the future, either by buying bonds or by purchasing investment goods for their firms, because they want to ensure their future consumption. They know that current investment means higher future income, and higher future income means they can choose higher future consumption. They balance current and future consumption, and they make

---

[7]Kremer quotes with approval "newscaster" Ted Baxter on the old *Mary Tyler Moore Show*, who wanted to have six children because he was hoping that one of them would grow up to solve the overpopulation problem.

their choices. Let us examine some recent history for evidence as to whether those choices have been reasonable ones.

The 1980s

Figure 8-15 shows U.S. investment and consumption as percentages of GDP since 1959. In the 1980s, investment was unusually low and consumption was unusually high. Moreover, compared with that of other countries during the same period, U.S. consumption was extremely high. Does this mean that U.S. citizens were sacrificing their future by refusing to replenish their capital stock? Were they on a spending spree that the government should have discouraged for the good of the country? The answers are not obvious.

First, it is possible that the increased consumption of the 1980s was not a spending spree at all. To a large extent, consumers were purchasing durable goods, such as cars and furniture, which provide services not just in the present but also in the future. Although official statistics count such purchases as pure consumption, they should really be considered partly as investment.

Purchases of education are also counted as consumption in official statistics, even though from the perspective of economics they are clearly investment. Education purchases in the United States increased substantially in the 1980s. That increase adds to the statistical image of a "spending spree," producing an inaccurate picture. For most students, the college years are not just an orgy of consumption.

On the other hand, even if you correct for the effects of education purchases, you will still find that U.S. consumption exceeded foreign consumption (as percentages of income), though not by as much as is widely believed.

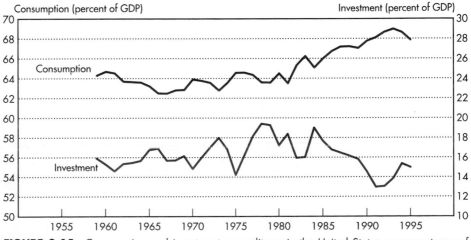

FIGURE 8-15 Consumption and investment expenditures in the United States as percentages of GDP.

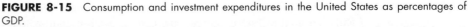

Consumption is measured on the left vertical axis, and investment is measured on the right vertical axis.

Second, our economic model suggests that if people *do* choose to go on a spend-ing spree, they are doing so for a reason. People chose to increase consumption more than investment in full knowledge of the long-term consequences. They perceived the benefits of spending as outweighing the costs, and who is to say that they were mis-taken?

On the other hand, it is possible that high consumption was not entirely a result of weighing costs and benefits accurately but was partly the artificial by-product of government policies that encouraged consumption at the expense of investment. If so, the right response for the government would have been to identify those policies and eliminate them. But to date, nobody has been able to say with confidence what those policies might have been.

Future Generations

Economists always want to judge the desirability of market outcomes and ask whether the outcomes can be improved by government policies. Often the hardest part of the evaluation is deciding what to count as an improvement. By encouraging investment, today's government can make your grandchildren richer at your expense: Current investment increases future output, but it leaves fewer goods available for current con-sumption. Is that an improvement? If your grandchildren could be here today, they might have a different opinion than you do.

Insofar as your own present investments affect your own future consumption, you might argue that you are perfectly capable of weighing costs and benefits with-out prodding from the government. But when your present investments affect the con-sumption of people who have not yet been born, that argument becomes more diffi-cult to defend.

Nevertheless, at least two arguments can be made for believing that the market equilibrium investment rate is in some sense a "good" outcome. The first argument is that people care very much about their children and their children's children, and so have every incentive to make reasonable trade-offs between their own consump-tion and their children's consumption. The other argument, which is of a very differ-ent flavor, is that the world's present inhabitants have no moral obligation to future generations and therefore have every right to squander resources if they choose to. Many economists reject the first argument on the grounds that people care less about their descendants than about themselves, and most reject the second for reasons that go beyond economics.

In thinking about these difficult issues, economists have found inspiration in sources of wisdom that predate even Adam Smith. Next we shall see how the most ancient ethical principle plays a role in modern economic thought.

The Golden Rule

The Bible tells us to do unto others as we would have them do unto us. That Golden Rule, applied to future generations, can be used to analyze the desirability of differ-ent rates of economic growth.

How do we know when an investment project is socially desirable? The answer depends on what we mean by "socially desirable." One reasonable criterion—and a plausible interpretation of the biblical Golden Rule—is that a project is desirable when its benefits (as measured by people's willingness to pay for them) exceed its costs, without regard to who pays the costs and who receives the benefits.

Within a single time period, it is relatively easy to interpret this criterion. If a certain project costs me $1 and confers benefits on you worth $2, then it is a good project. If it costs me $1 and confers benefits on you worth 50 cents, it is a bad one.

(To relate this criterion to the Golden Rule, notice that you would certainly be willing to incur $1 in costs to gain benefits of $2 for yourself and that you would certainly be *un*willing to incur $1 in costs to gain benefits of 50 cents for yourself. The suggestion here is that you should evaluate benefits to others exactly the way you evaluate benefits to yourself.)

However, when we think about investments, such calculations become trickier, because we are usually thinking about at least two separate time periods. Costs (building factories, educating workers, accumulating inventory) can occur in the present, while benefits (increased output) occur in the future. Now the question arises: When we compare this year's costs with next year's benefits, how should we measure next year's benefits—by their *face* values or by their *present* values?

Suppose, for example, that by spending $1 today you can produce $1.05 worth of output next year and that the market interest rate is 10 percent per year. Is this project a good one because $1.05 (the face value of the benefits) exceeds $1? Or is it a bad one because the present value of that $1.05 is *less* than $1?

From the individual investor's point of view, the answer is easy: Only present values matter. In terms of the example, an investor can earn more by lending $1 at interest than by investing it, so the project will be rejected.

But from a broader social viewpoint, it is less clear which criterion is the right one. If we imagine that next year's population consists of the same individuals who are alive today, then it is surely still correct to use present values. After all, each individual makes choices with an eye to the future and chooses an optimal mix of consumption and investment. The individuals—quite rationally—make present-value calculations, and any alternative would lead to inferior decisions (that is, decisions which would leave people less happy).

But suppose we imagine next year's population to be quite different from this year's, because children are born and their grandparents die. Those who will not be born until next year do not get to participate in the advantages of consuming earlier rather than later—indeed, today's consumption is of no benefit to them whatsoever. That makes a present-value calculation much harder to justify. If people can invest $1 today to create $1.05 worth of benefits for their descendants, and if we treat all generations as equally worthy, then the $1.05 benefit exceeds the $1 cost and the project is desirable. In other words:

If all generations are treated equally, then the Golden Rule tells us to undertake a project if its future benefits exceed its current costs when those future benefits are assessed at their *face* values.

On the other hand:

> Individual investors will undertake a project if its future benefits exceed its current costs when those future benefits are assessed at their *present* values.

That is, individual investors do *not* follow the Golden Rule. Instead, they reject some projects that the Golden Rule would recommend.

 However, if individual investors value their descendants' happiness as much as their own, then they might choose to follow the Golden Rule.

 The Golden Rule is an ethical principle, not an economic one; nothing in economic theory can tell us whether it is the "right" guide to policy. Many economists reject the notion that people living today have as strong an obligation to future generations as the Golden Rule requires.

Here is one argument *against* asking the present generation to make sacrifices according to the Golden Rule: Because of the forward march of technology, future generations will almost surely be much wealthier than we are. Should the relatively poor (that is, us) eat less so that the relatively rich (our descendants) can eat more?

Applying the Golden Rule

If you believe that the Golden Rule is the right social criterion for evaluating invest-ment, you will want to encourage investors to undertake more projects than they are naturally inclined to. This is the motivation behind many government programs that give favorable tax treatment to investors, and it has been used to justify government-sponsored research and development.

Evaluating the Steady State

When we evaluate economic growth, we have to distinguish two questions. First, do we approve of the steady state (that is, the values of the steady-state income and cap-ital-labor ratio) toward which the economy is heading? Second, do we approve of the path the economy is following en route to that steady state?

So far, our discussion in this section has dealt with the general issue of trade-offs between current consumption and future consumption. This discussion is applic-able both to evaluating steady states and to evaluating paths. Now we shall focus more specifically on evaluating steady states. What is the most desirable steady state for an economy to achieve?

We can reword this question as follows: Suppose the per-worker production func-tion is the curve shown in Figure 8-16(*a*). Suppose the economy is destined to settle permanently at some point on this curve, representing the capital-labor ratio and per capita income that all future generations will enjoy. (In making this supposition, we

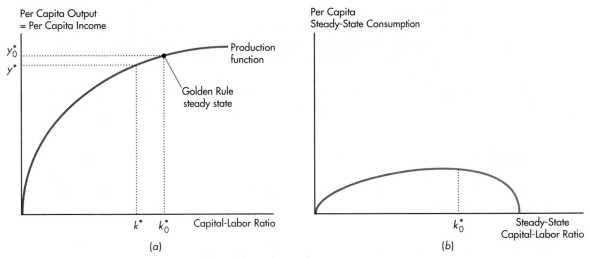

FIGURE 8-16 The Golden Rule steady state.
The economy can achieve its steady state at any point on the production function in (a). In this case we assume it is (k^*, y^*). The Golden Rule steady state is the steady state that maximizes per capita consumption. To find it, we locate the highest point on the curve in (b), find the corresponding capital stock k_0^*, and then plot (k_0^*, y_0^*) in (a).

temporarily ignore future changes in the steady state due to technological progress.) What point on the curve will make those generations happiest?

At first glance, the answer seems obvious. Points farther out on the curve correspond to higher per capita incomes. It would seem that workers want to be as far out along the curve as possible.

But that is wrong, and here is why: Workers care about their consumption, not about their incomes. A high income is of little value if you spend most of it replenishing depreciated capital. An economy that is far out on the production function is an economy with an enormous capital stock, which can be so expensive to maintain that little income remains for citizens to consume.

Figure 8-16(b) is a graph of per capita steady-state consumption as a function of the steady-state capital-labor ratio. An economy with no capital produces no output, and, consequently, its citizens consume nothing; thus the curve in Figure 8-16(b) passes through the point (0, 0). As the capital-labor ratio grows, per capita income increases [as shown in Figure 8-16(a)], but an increasingly large share of that income is spent on maintaining the capital stock. If the capital stock is very large, the amount of income that is available for consumption can be quite small. That is why the curve in Figure 8-16(b) eventually turns downward, passing through points with high capital-labor ratios and low per capita consumption.

The ideal steady-state capital-labor ratio is the one for which per capita consumption is at a maximum: k_0^* in Figure 8-16(b). It is possible to demonstrate (see problems 24 through 26 at the end of this chapter) that k_0^* is also the steady-state cap-

Golden Rule steady state:

The steady state that would result if investors undertook all projects whose future benefits exceed their current costs.

ital-labor ratio that is achieved when investors follow the Golden Rule criterion. Therefore, k_0^* is called the *Golden Rule steady-state capital-labor ratio,* and the point (k_0^*, y_0^*) in Figure 8-16(a) is called the **Golden Rule steady state.**

As we have already seen, investors typically underinvest relative to what the Golden Rule criterion recommends. Consequently, the actual steady state is typically below and to the left of its Golden Rule value, at a point like (k^*, y^*) in Figure 8-16(a). Thus the consumption of future generations fails to achieve its maximum potential.

When technology changes, so does the Golden Rule capital-labor ratio. The capital-labor ratio that will maximize steady-state consumption in the twenty-first century would have been ridiculously expensive to maintain with the technology available in, say, 1890.

Income versus Welfare

We have had much to say in this chapter about the relations between population growth and income growth. Income is important, and economists often use it as an approximation of economic welfare, although the approximation is imperfect. It is important to recognize, however, that in the context of a changing population, income is a worse approximation of welfare than it is when the population is fixed.

To see this, note that if income measured welfare, then the birth of a child (which immediately reduces the family's per capita income) could never be considered a "blessed event." Economist Peter Bauer has pointed out that if income measures welfare, then the birth of a farm animal is a blessing but the birth of a child is a curse.

The fact that people do *not* view the world in that way—the fact that people actually *celebrate* childbirth—means that even as population growth reduces our per capita incomes, it increases our welfare in other forms. And it is not only our own children who make us happy. A world with many people offers more potential friends who share our interests, more small acts of kindness between strangers, and a better chance of finding love.

People frequently *like* to have other people around, even if their own incomes are smaller as a consequence. That is why so many people choose to live in Manhattan instead of Montana, or in Calcutta instead of the countryside. New Yorkers complain about crowds, but they reveal by staying in the city that they value the benefits of being in a large population center as more than enough to compensate.[8]

But modern growth theory holds out the hope that we might not even have to consider such trade-offs. In Section 8-4, we saw that a growing population can contribute to economic growth, both through increasing returns to scale and by accelerating the pace of technological progress. When you are stuck on a freeway, it is easy to imagine that if the population were smaller, the driver in front of you might never

---

[8]In a recent survey, 39 percent of New Yorkers said that they would live someplace else "if they could." Because anyone who wants to leave New York is free to do so, economists interpret this result as evidence that 39 percent of New Yorkers lie to pollsters.

have been born. But it is important to remember also that if the population were smaller, the engineer who figured out how to widen the road from four lanes to its present six might not have been born either. Perhaps we should think of our neighbors not as competitors for the world's resources but as important resources in their own right.

Our neighbors might be the *source* of our prosperity, rather than competitors for shares of it.

SUMMARY

According to the neoclassical model explored in Chapters 3 through 7, any positive quantity of investment brings investors closer to their target capital stock. This lowers the demand for investment next period. As a result, investment declines from one period to the next. Eventually, there is only enough investment each period to replace depreciated capital. At that point the economy has reached its steady state, where the capital stock and income stop growing.

This model is deficient in a number of ways. First, it accounts for *aggregate* output, not *per capita* output (or income), which is an accurate measure of economic welfare. Second, it is not well suited for doing comparative-statics experiments, such as determining the effect of an improvement in technology. The more general Solow model of economic growth does not suffer from these shortcomings.

The first assumption of the Solow model is that the economy exhibits constant returns to scale. This means that each worker's output depends only on the amount of capital he has available (the capital-labor ratio), not on the size of the population. Therefore, it makes sense to draw a per-worker production function giving per capita output as a function of the capital-labor ratio.

In the Solow model, economic growth is driven by the evolution of the capital-labor ratio. The capital-labor ratio shrinks over time because of depreciation, shrinks over time because of population growth, and grows over time because of investment. The survival line represents the first two effects, the saving curve represents the third, and the transformation curve—which is the sum of the survival line and the saving curve—represents all three.

The capital-labor ratio grows from one period to the next, but grows by less in each succeeding period. When it reaches its steady-state value, which is the value at which the transformation curve crosses the 45° line, it stops growing.

Per capita output grows along with the capital-labor ratio, in a way that can be read off the per-worker production function. As the capital-labor ratio approaches its steady-state value, per capita output approaches a corresponding value and essentially stops growing.

A one-shot change in the saving rate or in technology can change the steady state and cause the economy to grow until the new steady state is reached. Ongoing improvements in technology can cause the steady state to move continuously, allowing unlimited economic growth. In the Solow model, the only plausible source of continued growth is a stream of improvements in technology.

A one-shot increase in the population affects current growth but not the steady state. An increase in the population growth rate reduces the steady-state capital-labor ratio.

The Solow model leads us to distinguish between developing economies, which have not yet reached their steady states, and mature economies, which have reached their steady states. In developing economies, investment should be the primary engine of growth, while in mature economies, growth hinges on technological progress. International evidence is broadly consistent with these predictions.

Many economists believe that, contrary to the Solow model, economies frequently benefit from population growth. There are several reasons why population growth can be desirable. First, there may be increasing returns to scale: workers become more productive by living in large communities where there are opportunities to specialize and to benefit from the expertise of their neighbors. Second, in a larger population, there may be a greater stream of technological advancements, both because a larger population breeds more inventors and because a larger population offers greater rewards for inventiveness.

In evaluating the desirability of growth, economists note that individuals weigh the costs and benefits of consumption and investment and invest accordingly. However, some economists argue that from an ethical standpoint, future benefits ought to be measured at their face values, not at their present values, and that this discrepancy leads to underinvestment relative to what the Golden Rule would recommend. Other economists reject the stringent ethical demands of the Golden Rule, partly on the grounds that, in any event, future generations will be much wealthier than we are.

In growth theory as in macroeconomics in general, economists use income as a rough measure of welfare. But it is important to recognize that in the context of a growing population, the correspondence between income and welfare may be weaker than usual.

PROBLEM SET

Answer problems 1 through 4 using the model in Section 8-1.

1. As the economy grows from one period to the next, in what direction does the real interest rate move?
2. Suppose the consumption demand curve is nearly horizontal. How does this affect the speed at which the economy approaches its steady state?
3. Suppose the depreciation rate is 100 percent per period: the current period's investment is available for use next period but becomes worthless in all future periods. How must Figure 8-1 be modified? Does the economy still approach a steady state?
4. *True or false:* If the production function in Figure 8-2 were flat, then the capital-labor ratio would grow over time but output would remain fixed. (*Hint:* Under the assumptions of the problem, what is the marginal product of capital? What does it imply about the investment demand curve and about the equilibrium quantity of investment?)
5. In Lower Slobbovia, capital takes the form of personal computers. Workers sit in isolated booths, each with a computer, and produce manuscripts that are sold to foreigners. In Upper Slobbovia, capital takes the form of ideas, which are available for all workers to use. Workers use ideas to create services that are sold to foreigners. Which economy is more likely to exhibit constant returns to scale? Which is more likely to exhibit increasing returns to scale? (*Hint:* In Upper Slobbovia, what do you think would happen if you

doubled the number of workers while holding the number of ideas fixed? What if you doubled both the number of workers *and* the number of ideas?)

6. *True or false:* If there are constant returns to scale, then population growth causes the aggregate production function, but not the individual worker's production function, to shift.

7. *True or false:* If there are decreasing returns to scale, then population growth can cause the aggregate production function and the individual worker's production function to shift in opposite directions.

8. *True or false:* If there are increasing returns to scale, then population growth causes the aggregate production function and the individual worker's production function to shift in the same direction.

9. If capital never depreciates and the population never changes, what does the survival line look like?

10. Suppose that δ is the fraction of capital that depreciates from one period to the next and that n is the fraction by which the population increases from one period to the next. (Thus, if the population doubles from one period to the next, $n = 100$ percent $= 1$.) Derive a formula for the slope of the survival line.

11. Suppose that capital depreciates more rapidly when there is more of it: in a small orchard, 10 percent of the trees die each year, but in a large orchard 15 percent die. What does this imply about the shape of the survival line?

12. Suppose that workers with more capital reproduce more quickly (say, because they are able to afford better health services). What does this imply about the shape of the survival line?

13. Suppose that the government institutes a permanent program of wasteful spending: every year it purchases $1 billion worth of output to discard. The program is financed by lump-sum taxes.
    a. What happens to the saving curve? (*Hint:* People divide their after-tax income between current consumption and saving for future consumption. When their after-tax income falls, the principle of consumption smoothing tells us that they will choose less of both activities.)
    b. What happens to the transformation curve?
    c. What happens to the steady-state capital-labor ratio?
    d. In the long run, does annual consumption go down by more than $1 billion, less than $1 billion, or exactly $1 billion?

14. If the capital-labor ratio starts out above its steady-state value k^*, how does it behave over time? Illustrate your answer with a graph similar to Figure 8-9.

15. In the fourteenth century, the Black Death killed one-third of the population of Europe. If the capital-labor ratio was at its steady state before the Black Death, what path did it follow afterward? Where did it end up?

16. Suppose half the nation's capital stock is destroyed by a war. What is the immediate effect on per capita output? Illustrate the behavior of the capital-labor ratio over time. Does the economy ever return to its original steady state?

17. Suppose a new rustproofing process slows the depreciation rate of physical capital. What happens to the capital-labor ratio and to per capita income, both in the short run and in the long run?

18. Suppose there is a one-shot *temporary* increase in technology. What happens to the growth rate in the current period? What happens to the growth rate in the next period? What happens to the steady state?

19. In Middle Slobbovia, only women work. If a major upheaval in social norms convinces all the men to join the workforce, what happens to per capita output? To the growth rate? To long-run per capita output? In the long run, do married couples have more or less income to consume between them than they had before? How much more or less? Can you tell whether they are better or worse off than before?

20. How might your answers to the preceding question change if only those people who are actively engaged in the workforce are capable of discovering innovative ideas to improve productivity?

21. In an economy with increasing returns to scale, suppose there is an increase in the rate of population growth. How does the transformation curve shift in the near future? How does it shift in the more distant future?

22. According to Figure 8-15, do consumption and investment tend to move in the same direction or in opposite directions? What is the reason for this pattern?

23. Using Figure 8-15, can you identify those years when the economy seems to have been growing more slowly than usual? Which variable seems to respond more dramatically to changes in the growth rate: consumption or investment?

24. The Golden Rule may be restated as: "Invest whenever the face value of future benefits exceeds current costs." In this problem, we will find a more quantitative formulation of the Golden Rule.

    a. Suppose the current generation invests $1 worth of resources. Explain why the benefit to the next generation is $(1 - \delta + \text{MPK})$, where MPK is the marginal product of capital and δ is the depreciation rate.

    b. Using part **a,** explain why the Golden Rule can be translated as follows: Keep investing as long as $\text{MPK} > \delta$, and stop when the two become equal.

25. In Figure 8-16, we defined the Golden Rule steady-state capital-labor ratio k_0^* to be the ratio that maximizes steady-state per capita consumption. In this problem, we will find another characterization of the Golden Rule steady-state capital-labor ratio.

    a. Explain why the following statement is true: Once the economy has reached its steady state, consumption equals output minus depreciation. (*Hint:* First recall that in *any* period, output equals consumption plus investment. Then explain why, once the steady state has been reached, investment equals depreciation.)

    b. Suppose the economy is in its steady state and something happens to cause the steady-state capital-labor ratio to increase by 1 unit. Explain why steady-state consumption increases by $\text{MPK} - \delta$, where MPK is the marginal product of capital and δ is the depreciation rate.

    c. Explain why, at the Golden Rule capital-labor ratio k_0^*, we have $\text{MPK} = \delta$.

26. Using the preceding two problems, explain why an economy that follows the Golden Rule will eventually reach the Golden Rule steady state.

Chapter 9

Labor

I n Chapters 5 and 6 we analyzed an endowment economy in which all goods simply appear each period. In Chapter 7 we enhanced our model by allowing the possibility that goods could be *produced* with capital. In this chapter, we bring our model economy still closer to the real world by incorporating *labor* into the production process. The quantity of goods produced will thus depend on both the amount of capital available *and* how much people work.

Our first step is to examine the simplest kind of economy in which labor is important. Our prototype is the Fern Hill Apple Orchard, whose proprietor, Anne Jones, has no contact with the outside world and no opportunities for investment. She picks her own apples and consumes whatever she picks.

In Section 9-1, we examine Anne's decisions regarding how many hours to work each day. In Section 9-2, we allow Anne some contact with the outside world to see how her labor decisions interact with her choices about borrowing and lending. While Anne and her apple orchard constitute a very simple economy, the lessons we draw from them will carry over to Section 9-3, where we examine the **labor market,** in which people buy and sell labor. Finally, in Section 9-4, we incorporate the labor market into the basic model used in earlier chapters.

> **Labor market:**
>
> A market consisting of the individuals who buy and sell labor and the arrangements that make it possible for them to buy and sell.

Incorporating the labor market will enrich our model in two different ways. The first is this: Until now we have dealt only with the markets for current and future goods. Only one price (the interest rate) is required to clear both these markets. Now that we are introducing an additional market—the market for labor—we must introduce an additional price to clear it. That price is the *wage rate.* It will appear in Section 9-3.

The second way our model becomes richer is that labor supply decisions affect the *supply of current goods.* (This contrasts with investment decisions, which affect only the demand for current goods and the supply of future goods.) As a result, the supply curve will now slope upward instead of being vertical, and there will be new forces that can cause that curve to shift.

9-1 A VERY SIMPLE MODEL

Our main simplifying assumption is that there are only two ingredients in the recipe for human happiness: leisure and consumption.

> **Leisure:**
>
> Time spent in activities other than work.

Leisure, as the word is used in economics, means time devoted to any activity other than work. Thus leisure includes time spent surfing, watching television, and sleeping.

All of our time must be divided between leisure and working. Leisure contributes directly to our happiness. Working contributes indirectly to our happiness by allowing us to earn income, which we can use to purchase consumption goods. Consumption goods include food, theater tickets, works of art, and Nintendo games.

All of our income must be divided between consumption and saving, with the latter including productive investment. Consumption contributes directly to our happiness. Saving contributes indirectly to our happiness by allowing us to consume more in the future. Certain kinds of saving also contribute indirectly to our happiness by increasing our leisure: purchasing a microwave oven is a form of investment (saving) that allows us to spend less time working in the kitchen.

As in earlier chapters, we shall often pretend—only for simplicity's sake—that there is a single consumption good, such as apples. To this pretense, we shall often add another: that there is a single leisure activity, such as sleep. In translating between the model and the real world, "apples" will stand for everything we consume, and "sleep" for everything we do when we are not working.

The key new idea in this chapter is the recognition that if you sleep less, you can work more and therefore eat more. Rather than falling from trees as in earlier chapters, apples must now be picked. There are a fixed number of hours in the day;

you can use some of them for picking apples (or more generally for working), and you have the remainder free for sleep (or more generally for leisure). The more time you spend working in the orchard, the more you can eat at the end of the day.

The Production Function

Production function:

Output as a function of labor, assuming that all other inputs are held fixed.

The relation between labor and consumption is depicted by a **production function** like that in Figure 9-1. Point *A* shows that if Anne Jones, the proprietor and sole employee of Fern Hill Apple Orchard, spends 40 hours per week picking apples, she will collect 800 apples per week. Point *B* shows that if she spends 60 hours per week picking apples, she will collect 1000 per week.

Figure 9-1 incorporates the assumption that the number of *trees* at Fern Hill (that is, the amount of available *capital*) is held fixed. At the end of this section we will examine the consequences of planting additional trees. For now, we assume that the number of trees cannot change.

The production function shown in Figure 9-1 is *not* the same as the production function we discussed in Chapter 7, which relates the quantity of *capital* to the quantity of output produced. Instead, the production function in Figure 9-1 relates the quantity of *labor* to the quantity of output (in this case, apples at the Fern Hill Apple Orchard).

Notice the symmetry between our treatment of labor here and our treatment of capital in Chapter 7. When we draw a production function relating capital to output, we hold the quantity of *labor* fixed; when we draw a production function relating labor to output, we hold the quantity of *capital* fixed.

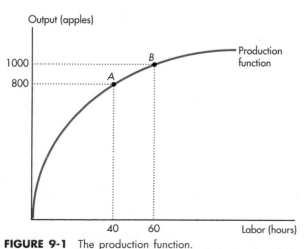

FIGURE 9-1   The production function.
The production function shows how many apples of output Anne can produce for each possible quantity of labor input. The production function is drawn assuming that the quantity of capital (in this case apple trees) is held fixed.

The Marginal Product of Labor

The **marginal product of labor (MPL)** is the additional output that Anne generates when she works an additional hour. Suppose that in a given week, 40 hours' work can produce 800 apples while 41 hours' work can produce 814 apples. Then when Anne is working a 40-hour week, the marginal product of labor is 14 apples per week per labor hour. We usually shorten this to "14 apples per hour."

We will assume that the marginal product of labor declines as additional labor is applied. If the forty-first hour of labor produces 14 additional apples, the forty-second might produce only 13, and the sixty-first only 6. However, an additional hour of labor always produces some additional output.

The primary justification for this assumption is our earlier assumption that the quantity of capital—that is, the number of apple trees—is fixed. The more you work, the harder it is to coax additional apples from a given population of trees (or to coax additional autos from a given assembly line). In the early stages, you can pick from the lowest branches; later on, you spend a lot more time climbing ladders (or maintaining heavily used machinery).

Geometrically, the marginal product of labor is represented by the *slope* of the production function. More specifically, the MPL for any quantity of labor is given by the slope of the production function at the point which represents that quantity. Anne's production function is reproduced in Figure 9-2(*a*), and the MPL values derived from it are graphed in Figure 9-2(*b*).

The production function slopes upward to reflect our assumption that additional labor always produces additional output. However, the production function becomes flatter as more labor is applied, reflecting our assumption that the marginal product

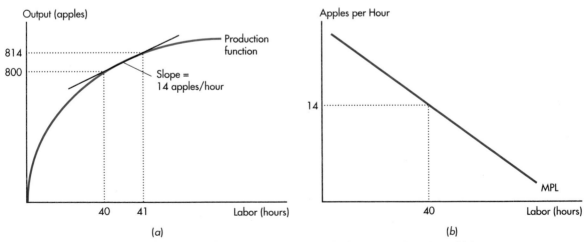

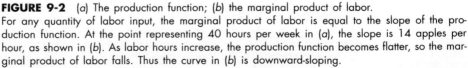

FIGURE 9-2 (*a*) The production function; (*b*) the marginal product of labor.
For any quantity of labor input, the marginal product of labor is equal to the slope of the production function. At the point representing 40 hours per week in (*a*), the slope is 14 apples per hour, as shown in (*b*). As labor hours increase, the production function becomes flatter, so the marginal product of labor falls. Thus the curve in (*b*) is downward-sloping.

of labor declines. The downward slope of the MPL curve in Figure 9-2(*b*) and the flattening of the production function in Figure 9-2(*a*) are two ways of illustrating the same effect.

The Labor Model

At this point, our model of the Fern Hill Apple Orchard includes the following explicit assumptions:

- Apples are the only consumption good.
- The quantity of capital—that is, the quantity of apple trees—is fixed. Anne Jones has no opportunities for productive investment.
- The level of output—that is, the number of apples picked—depends on the quantity of labor—that is, the number of hours that Anne works each week—as illustrated by the production function in Figure 9-1.
- The orchard is isolated, so Anne has no opportunities to borrow or lend. She must immediately consume all the apples she produces. (We will relax this assumption in Section 9-2.)
- Because the orchard is isolated, Anne has no opportunity to hire labor or to sell her own labor. All labor at the orchard is done by Anne, and all of Anne's labor is done at the orchard. (We will relax this assumption in Section 9-3.)

Anne's Optimum

Each week, Anne decides how many hours to work by balancing her desire to relax against her desire to eat. She can choose any point on the graph of the production function in Figure 9-1. Points farther to the left represent decisions to work very little and eat very little; points farther to the right represent decisions to work a lot and eat a lot. Among these points, Anne chooses the one that makes her the happiest. We

Optimum point:
The point on the graph of the production function which a given individual prefers to all other points on that graph.

call that point her **optimum point.**

  Anne's problem is analogous to that of a consumer picking an optimum point along an intertemporal budget line, as discussed in Chapter 4. The production function, like the budget line, presents a menu of opportunities. As long as that menu remains fixed, there is no reason for Anne's optimum point to move. We will, however, want to know what happens to her optimum point in situations that cause the production function to shift to new locations.

Changes in the Environment

In this subsection we consider how Anne responds to changes in her economic environment.

An Increase in Nonlabor Income

Suppose Anne finds a source of free apples that come to her without any work. Maybe one of her apple trees begins to drop 40 apples a week that she can eat without having to pick them. Maybe a mysterious stranger leaves 40 apples on her doorstep each week.

Because Anne's newfound income is independent of her work, she has an extra 40 apples each week regardless of whether she works zero hours or a hundred. Consequently, her output quantity increases by 40 apples at every quantity of labor. Thus, *Anne's production function shifts vertically upward parallel to itself,* as in Figure 9-3.

When Anne's nonlabor income increases, her optimum point moves from *O* on the old production function to *O'* on the new one. We take the location of *O* as given and want to determine where *O'* might lie in relation to *O*.

Anne is now richer, and this means that she is subject to an **income effect** and wants more of everything. To Anne, "everything" means apples and leisure hours. Because she chooses to have more apples, her optimum point moves upward. Because she chooses to have more leisure (that is, to work less), her optimum point moves leftward. *The income effect pushes Anne's optimum point up and to the left of its original location.*

Notice that while Anne's apple consumption increases, it increases by *fewer* than 40 apples. (Point *P* is 40 apples above point *O*; the new optimum point *O'* is not as high as *P*.) Anne works less but can still consume more apples. She smooths out her good fortune by taking some of it in the form of leisure and some in the form of apples.

> An increase in nonlabor income causes the production function to shift vertically upward, parallel to itself. The new optimum shows an increase in consumption and a decrease in work hours. The increase in consumption is smaller than the increase in nonlabor income.

Income effect:

The effect of a change in income. When income increases, people choose to increase both their consumption and their leisure.

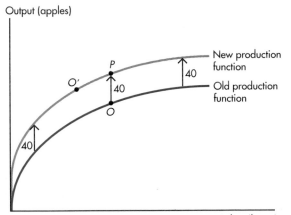

FIGURE 9-3   An increase in nonlabor income.
When Anne's nonlabor income increases, her production function shifts upward parallel to itself, in this case by 40 apples. Because Anne is richer, she now wants more of everything, so her new optimum is at a point like *O'*, with more consumption *and* more leisure (that is, less work) than her original optimum point *O*. While *O'* is above *O*, it is above *O* by fewer than 40 apples.

An Increase in the Productivity of Labor

Suppose that Anne's labor becomes more productive than it used to be. This might happen if she discovered a more efficient way to organize her day or if an improvement in her health made her a stronger apple picker. Or perhaps better weather has improved the crop and made apple picking easier.

In any of these circumstances, Anne's MPL—the number of apples she can pick in an additional hour of work—increases. This means that her production function shifts upward and *becomes steeper,* as in Figure 9-4. It shifts upward because any given amount of work produces more apples than it used to. It becomes steeper because each *additional* hour of work adds more to the total than it used to.

Anne's new optimum point is O'' in Figure 9-4. To investigate the location of O'' relative to the old optimum point O, we must consider two effects separately.

First, the **substitution effect** leads Anne to work more hours because each additional hour is rewarded more heavily than it was before. If Anne used to work 45 hours a week, her reason was that working a forty-sixth hour for, say, an extra 13 apples didn't seem quite worth the effort. If she can now work a forty-sixth hour for an extra 16 apples, she is likely to do so.

As the substitution effect leads Anne to work more hours, it also leads her to consume more apples. So it pushes her optimum point up and to the right.

Second, there is an income effect: Anne's extra productivity makes her richer. Just as she did when her nonlabor income increased, Anne wants to use her new wealth in two ways. One way is to eat more apples; the other is to work less. This pushes her optimum point up and to the left.

Both the substitution effect and the income effect lead Anne to consume more apples, pushing her optimum point up. In Figure 9-4, this means that point O'' is above point O, as shown.

Substitution effect:
The effect of a change in the reward for an additional hour of work. When the marginal product of their labor increases, people choose to increase their consumption and reduce their leisure.

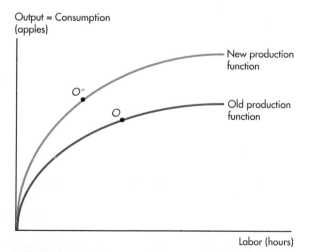

FIGURE 9-4 An increase in the marginal product of labor.
Anne's production function is now higher and steeper; you can think of it as having rotated upward. Her new optimum point is O''.

Regarding work hours, the substitution and income effects move Anne in opposite directions. Anne wants to work *more* because her efforts are more substantially rewarded (the substitution effect), but at the same time she wants to work *less* because she has become wealthier (the income effect). Because either effect could dominate, Anne could decide to work either more or less than she did before. Thus, in Figure 9-4, point *O″* could be either to the left or to the right of point *O*. Figure 9-5 illustrates both possibilities.

An increase in the productivity of labor leads to an increase in consumption. It can lead to either an increase or a decrease in the number of work hours.

An Increase in Capital

Our model holds the number of apple trees fixed, in the sense that Anne can do nothing to change it. However, we can imagine the quantity of capital changing *exogenously*. (Recall that this means *for reasons outside the model*.) If a blight destroys some apple trees, Anne's capital stock falls. If nature takes its course and new trees take root, grow, and bear fruit, her capital stock increases.

A change in the capital stock affects Anne's productivity. For example, when she has more trees, Anne can pick more apples from low branches before she has to get out the ladder. Or she can pick more apples in one corner of the orchard without having to spend time traveling from one part of the orchard to another. An increase in capital yields an increase in productivity, as discussed in the preceding subsection.

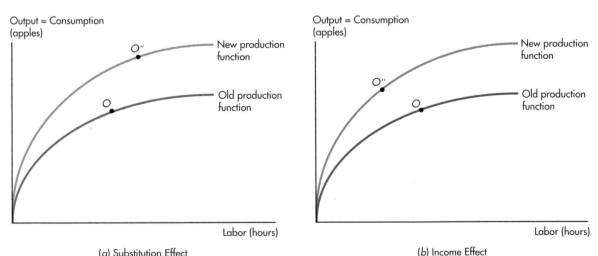

(a) Substitution Effect   *(b)* Income Effect

FIGURE 9-5 Substitution and income effects due to an increase in productivity.
Both effects lead Anne to consume more, so her new optimum point *O″* is above the old point *O*. The substitution effect leads Anne to work more, while the income effect leads her to work less. Either could dominate, so *O″* could lie either to the right of *O* as in *(a)* or to the left of *O* as in *(b)*.

And, as shown in Figure 9-5, Anne eats more apples and might decide to work either more or fewer hours.

The Model versus Reality

When you think about workers in the modern economy, you probably do not think about people like Anne Jones, who is self-employed. If you have not studied macroeconomics before, your image of the economy might include a rigorous distinction between employers, who hire labor, and employees, who provide it.

But Anne Jones is closer to the typical worker than that image suggests. We are all, in reality, employers. Each time you buy a candy bar, you are, by proxy, employing every confectionery worker, sales representative, and truck driver who participated in the manufacture, marketing, or distribution of that candy bar.

Does the *average* person—the representative agent whom we met in Chapter 5—buy more or less labor than he sells? The answer is neither. Every hour of labor bought is an hour of labor sold. So the "average" person hires exactly the same number of labor hours that he or she provides.

Anne Jones is that average person. Because she employs only herself and works only for herself, she hires (from herself) exactly the same number of labor hours that she provides. Insofar as we can analyze the economy by thinking about the behavior of a typical individual, we ought to think about the behavior of Anne Jones.

In coming sections, we will expand this basic labor model by allowing some workers to borrow and others to lend and allowing some to hire help and others to be hired. Nonetheless, the economywide response to a change in nonlabor income, productivity, or capital stock will always be the same as Anne Jones's response here. Anne Jones in her isolated orchard is the representative agent; she is perfectly average and her behavior reflects the behavior of the economy as a whole.

9-2 THE MODEL WITH BORROWING AND LENDING

Our goal for this chapter, which we will achieve in Section 9-4, is to incorporate the effects of labor into the macroeconomic model of earlier chapters. That will mean redrawing the supply and demand curves for current consumption to account for the labor market and reexamining how we use those curves.

The lessons we have learned about Anne and her apple orchard will guide us in that task. To get some further guidance, we can relax some of the assumptions of our labor model and imagine how Anne reacts.

To that end, we now consider what happens if we relax one of our earlier limitations and assume the following instead:

• Anne can borrow and lend apples at a market interest rate.

One lends today in order to consume tomorrow. Hence, to fully analyze a labor model with borrowing, we would need at least a four-dimensional diagram relating apples today, apples tomorrow, work today, and work tomorrow. (Here, as usual, "today" and "tomorrow" stand for "this period" and "next period.") Rather than attempt to draw four dimensions on a two-dimensional page, we will talk through the model's implications. In general, when Anne trades apples today for apples tomorrow, she is governed by the considerations in Chapter 5, and when she trades labor for apples, she is governed by the considerations in Section 9-1.

Changes in Current and Future Nonlabor Income

Current Changes versus Future Changes

We have just seen that when Anne's nonlabor income goes up, she works less and consumes more. In earlier chapters, we saw that an increase in future income is interchangeable with an increase in current income if they have the same present value.

Thus, if there is a 10 percent daily interest rate, Anne responds to a 44-apple increase in tomorrow's nonlabor income exactly as she would respond to a 40-apple increase in today's nonlabor income. In either case, she responds by working less and consuming more *both today and tomorrow.*

Just as the citizens of the endowment economy smooth their good fortune over current and future consumption, Anne smooths her good fortune over *four* categories: current consumption, future consumption, current leisure, and future leisure.

Any increase in current or future nonlabor income leads to more consumption and less work beginning immediately. The size of the effect depends only on the present value of the windfall.

Permanent Changes versus Temporary Changes

Let us compare the effect of a permanent increase in nonlabor income with the effect of a temporary increase.

Suppose Anne discovers that she is to receive 40 free apples every day from now on. Then her (daily) production function rises vertically by 40 apples. We have seen the consequences in Figure 9-3: Anne takes her benefits partly in the form of increased consumption and partly in the form of increased leisure (less work). That is, her consumption rises by less than the full 40 apples and her work hours decrease.

Now suppose, instead, that Anne receives 40 free apples *today only.* Her wealth increases by 40 apples, and she spreads the benefits over a lifetime. She saves (by lending) most of the 40 apples, which then do not contribute to her current consumption. Thus it is as if Anne's *current* production function has shifted vertically, but by much less than 40 apples.

As in Figure 9-3, there is an increase in Anne's current consumption and a decrease in her current work hours. But these effects are smaller than those shown in the figure, because the production function has effectively shifted by only a fraction of the total windfall.

A permanent increase in nonlabor income shifts the current production function upward by the full amount of each period's windfall. Consumption rises by less than that full amount, and work hours decrease.

A temporary increase in nonlabor income shifts the current production function upward by a fraction of the windfall. Consumption increases and work hours decrease, but by relatively little.

Changes in Current and Future Productivity

Current Changes versus Future Changes

We have seen that Anne's reaction to an increase in her *current* productivity is governed by the *substitution* effect and the *income* effect. When Anne's current productivity increases (so work is rewarded more heavily), the substitution effect leads her to work more hours and consume more apples. The income effect (because Anne is wealthier) leads her to work fewer hours and consume more apples. Overall, she will eat more but may work more or fewer hours.

A change in *future* productivity makes Anne feel wealthier starting immediately. Thus she feels an income effect and wants to work less starting immediately. However, *there is no immediate substitution effect,* as *current* work is no more productive than it ever was. For the current period, then, *an increase in future productivity is just like an increase in future nonlabor income.* Anne consumes more and works less.

An increase in current productivity leads to a rise in current consumption and either an increase or a decrease in current work hours. An increase in future productivity leads to a rise in current consumption and a decrease in current work hours.

Temporary Changes versus Permanent Changes

Suppose that you work 20 hours a week at McDonald's making $5 per hour and that one day your boss amazes you by giving you a raise to $20 per hour. What happens to your work hours? From your point of view, your work has become more productive. You might decide to work less because you are richer (the income effect) or more because your wage is higher (the substitution effect).

In this example, it is not clear that you are actually more productive in the sense that you now flip more burgers per hour or wait on customers more efficiently. You might be more productive only in the limited sense that each hour of work now produces more income *for you* than it did before the raise. But for purposes of deciding on your work schedule, it is only this limited sense of "productivity" that you care about.

However, in a market economy people usually don't get raises unless they have begun producing more output per hour. So when we describe you as "more productive" now, that phrase is probably accurate from both your personal viewpoint and the viewpoint of the McDonald's manager.

Now suppose your boss tells you that the raise is in effect for *this week only.* You are not so much richer any more, and the income effect largely disappears. The substitution effect remains at full strength, so you increase your working hours this week.

But there is a third effect, which we have not yet discussed. Suppose you had been planning to take this Wednesday off to go rock climbing. There is now an excellent chance that you will reschedule your rock-climbing trip to the following week. When productivity fluctuates over time, people try to schedule their vacations and other leisure activities accordingly so as to concentrate their work at times when they are most productive.

Consequently, when productivity rises *temporarily,* people often respond by increasing their work hours by far more than we would expect on the basis of the substitution effect alone. This *additional* impetus to work a lot in the present is called the **intertemporal substitution effect** of a temporary productivity change.

Anne Jones might well exhibit intertemporal substitution at her apple orchard. If Anne faced the production function of Figure 9-1 year-round, she might choose to work 45 hours per week throughout the year. But a real-life Anne would more likely face that production function only in October, when the number of ripe apples on the trees is at a maximum. She would likely work far *more* than 45 hours per week in October, recognizing that nature will sharply reduce her apple-picking prospects as autumn gives way to winter. And if, instead, she faced the same production function in September, she might work far *less* than 45 hours a week in September, gathering her strength for a burst of activity the following month, when she becomes even more productive.

Because people rearrange their affairs to take advantage of short windows of productive opportunity, a *temporary* increase in productivity (as occurs, for example, in a month when all the apples ripen) can lead to a very great increase in the number of work hours, and hence to a very great increase in output.

If people are reasonably indifferent about the timing of their vacations,[1] then intertemporal substitution effects can be quite large. Even a small increase in productivity, if it is expected to be short-lived, can convince people to increase their work hours this week and compensate by taking part of next week off.

Small increases in productivity, if they are perceived to be temporary, can lead to very large increases in work hours and in output.

Intertemporal substitution effect:

The effect of a temporary change in productivity. When people are temporarily more productive, they concentrate more of their working hours into the current period.

---

[1]The word "vacations" should be interpreted broadly to include 2-week trips to the Bahamas, year-long sabbaticals to find one's inner soul, and 2-hour absences from work to visit the dentist's office.

Conversely, if productivity falls slightly but temporarily this month, many people might decide that this is a good month to take off from work and visit the beach. Work hours and output can decline substantially.

In recessions, employment and output fall far more than wages do. Intertemporal substitution might be an important reason for that phenomenon. If wages fall slightly, the ordinary substitution effect leads people to work slightly less. But if the drop is expected to be temporary, intertemporal substitution can lead people to reschedule planned future vacations and work far less in the present.

Changes in the Interest Rate

It is better to earn a dollar that can be saved at 15 percent interest than a dollar that can be saved at 10 percent interest. This means that if the interest rate goes up, current earnings become more desirable and therefore a net lender works more.

The effect is the same for a net borrower. Borrowing at 15 percent interest is less pleasant than borrowing at 10 percent interest. If the interest rate goes up, the borrower prefers to borrow less and therefore works more hours to increase her current income.

Another way to see this is to recall that a higher interest rate means that the relative price of current goods (in terms of future goods) is higher. Therefore, a high interest rate makes it more desirable to acquire current (as opposed to future) income and provides an incentive to work more in the present. This is called the **interest-rate effect.**

Interest-rate effect:
The effect of a change in the interest rate. When the interest rate rises, people work more.

A rise in the interest rate leads to an increase in work hours.

A Summary of Four Effects

The various changes we have discussed in this section can be grouped into four effects:

1. *Income effect: When people become wealthier, they work less and consume more.* The increased wealth can result from current or future increases in nonlabor income or in productivity. In general, permanent changes have bigger income effects than temporary changes have.

2. *Substitution effect: When people become more productive, they work more and consume more.* The effect is the same whether the productivity change is temporary or permanent. Only current changes can have substitution effects.

3. *Intertemporal substitution effect: When current productivity and expected future productivity differ, people work more in the more productive period.* Anything that affects the *difference* between current productivity and future productivity can have an intertemporal substitution effect.

4. *Interest-rate effect: When the interest rate increases, workers work more hours in the present.*

Historical Evidence

The four effects listed above will guide our investigation of the model world in which Anne Jones lives. But first we shall pause to demonstrate that these same effects are important not just in Anne Jones's world but also in our own.

Income Effect

Real U.S. per capita income has increased over the last century by a factor of more than 6. According to Figure 9-3, an increase in wealth should lead to a decrease in the number of hours worked. And so it has: a hundred years ago, the average workweek in American manufacturing industries was about 60 hours; today it is just under 40 hours. Figure 9-6 shows how times have changed.

When you first look at Figure 9-6, you might be tempted to focus on the dramatic but temporary downward plunge in working hours during the Great Depression of the 1930s. But in terms of long-run effects, the most important thing about the graph is not that plunge but the steady long-term downward trend in the average workweek.

We work less than our grandparents did because we are wealthier than they were. We have already mentioned the sixfold increase in real per capita income between 1890 and 1990. But even that figure understates how much richer we are than our ancestors. Like Anne Jones in Figure 9-3, we have chosen to take only part of our good fortune in the form of higher income (or "apples"); we have taken the remainder in the form of additional leisure time. If you want to measure economic welfare, a proper accounting should include the value of that leisure.

Within the home, the length of the workweek has fallen even more dramatically.

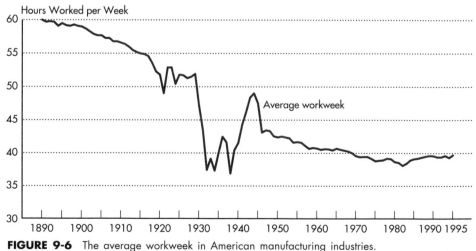

FIGURE 9-6   The average workweek in American manufacturing industries.
(*Note:* The post–World War II data in this graph are based on workweeks reported by households. Workweeks reported by employers are considerably shorter, by about 5 hours per week.)

In 1900, the average housekeeper spent 12 hours a day on laundry, cooking, sewing, and cleaning. By 1966 that figure had fallen to 5 hours, and today it is lower still.

Not only do we work fewer hours per week than our ancestors did; we also work fewer weeks per year. In 1901, only 6 percent of manufacturing workers took vacations. The figure has steadily grown to about 90 percent today. This too is surely a direct consequence of the growth in workers' incomes.

And there is more: We work fewer hours per week, we work fewer weeks per year, *and* we work fewer years per lifetime. In 1890, 18 percent of all males had entered the full-time labor force by age 13; today, the corresponding percentage is essentially zero. In 1890, only 26 percent of male workers had retired by age 65; today, well over 80 percent of 65-year-old males are retired.

Together, these changes are evidence of a strong income effect on work efforts.

Substitution Effect

In 1981, newly elected President Ronald Reagan fulfilled a campaign promise by signing into law a massive cut in income tax rates. Reagan and the supply economists who advised him were particularly eager to cut **marginal tax rates**—rates specifying the percentage of each additional dollar earned that is claimed by the government. Cutting marginal income tax rates is tantamount to raising after-tax wages. The president argued that workers who can earn more per hour will choose to work more. In other words, he expected a substantial substitution effect.

Marginal tax rate:

The amount by which your tax bill grows when your income grows by one dollar.

(According to the previous subsection, the substitution effect kicks in when a worker becomes more productive. Wage earners measure their own productivity by their after-tax wages.)

The Reagan tax cuts were indeed followed (though not immediately) by a great increase in the amount of labor supplied—an event that has been accurately described as the "greatest peacetime expansion (of the economy) in history." Over the course of Reagan's two terms in office, the employed fraction of the population rose from 59 to 63 percent. As we will see shortly, there is room for considerable controversy about what role the tax cuts played in triggering that expansion. But Reagan and many others were sufficiently encouraged to propose another round of marginal tax cuts that took effect in 1988.

In 1980, a married couple who had two children and earned $40,000 a year were permitted to keep 68 cents of every additional dollar they earned. (That is, the income tax took 32 cents of each additional dollar.) After the tax cuts of 1981, that 68 cents rose to 72 cents.

For couples with higher incomes, the tax cuts had more dramatic effects. If that same married couple had earned $100,000 a year instead of $40,000, they would have been allowed to keep only 46 cents of each additional dollar earned in 1980—but that amount rose to 55 cents after the first round of Reagan tax cuts and to 67 cents after the second round.

Figure 9-7 shows how the two rounds of Reagan tax cuts affected families in four different income brackets. But were these tax cuts actually responsible for the ensuing increase in employment and in hours worked? To assess their impact, we need

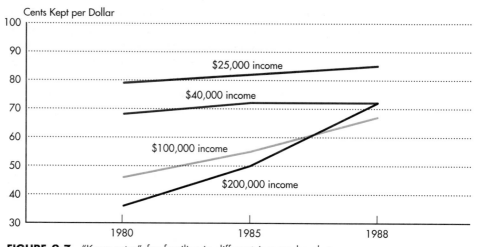

FIGURE 9-7 "Keep rates" for families in different income brackets.
The figure shows how many cents out of each additional dollar earned a family of four was permitted to keep before and after the Reagan tax cuts. The curves track the keep-rate increases for families at four different income levels. [*Source:* J. Hausman and J. Poterba, "Household Behavior and the Tax Reform Act of 1986," *Journal of Economic Perspectives* 1 (1987), 101–119.]

to sort out several effects. First, if the tax cuts made people feel wealthier, there would have been an income effect—leading to a *reduction* in the amount of labor supplied. Second, offsetting the income effect, there would have been the substitution effect that the president was counting on, leading to an increase in labor supplied. As in Figure 9-5, the net effect could have been either an increase or a decrease in the amount that people worked.

However, one can argue that in the case of a tax cut there is really no income effect—because a tax cut now means an increase in government debt and a tax increase in the future, with no change in the present value of after-tax income. Thus we will concentrate on the substitution effect. (There might have *also* been an intertemporal substitution effect if people perceived the tax cuts as temporary. We shall return to this later.)

The question now becomes this: How big, typically, is the substitution effect? Many studies have concluded that the answer is very different for male workers than it is for female workers. If the after-tax wage rate rises from, say, $10 an hour to $11 an hour, the average male worker might add about 1.5 hours to his 40-hour week, whereas the average female worker might add anywhere from 4 to 8 hours. (If there is an offsetting income effect—as in the case of a worker's getting a raise as opposed to a tax cut—then the average male actually *reduces* his work hours while the average female increases hers.)[2]

These numbers are at least broadly consistent with the experience of the eight-

[2]These estimates are based on J. Pencavel, *Labor Supply of Men: A Survey,* and M. Killingsworth and J. Heckman, "Female Labor Supply: A Survey," in the *Handbook of Labor Economics,* O. Ashenfelter and R. Layard, eds. (North Holland, 1986).

ies. Among males, employment actually fell through much of the eighties, and it returned to its pre-Reagan level only around the time the president was leaving office. But among females, employment increased substantially, from 47.7 percent of the population when Reagan took office to 54.3 percent when he left. (Similarly impressive gains were evident for nonwhite workers of both genders. Black employment rose from 52.3 percent of the population to 56.9 percent.)

Still, no economist is sure how much of the experience of the 1980s can be attributed to the Reagan tax cuts and how much to other factors. We are not even certain how many different effects the tax cuts themselves might have had. Did people feel wealthier, or did they foresee their responsibility for the growing federal deficits that followed? Did people view the tax cuts as permanent, or did they view them as temporary? We would need to know the answers to these questions in order to know whether the income effect and the intertemporal substitution effect—as well as the substitution effect—played a significant role in people's labor supply decisions.

Intertemporal Substitution Effect

We have already noted, in discussing Figure 9-6, that workers supplied far less than the usual amount of labor during the low-wage years of the Great Depression. Some economists have argued that this great drop in average work hours can be explained at least partly by intertemporal substitution—essentially, workers were waiting to put forth more effort in the more rewarding years to come.[3] (In later chapters, you will see that there are other competing theories as to what happened to employment during the 1930s.)

There has been a lot of disagreement among economists about the importance of intertemporal substitution, especially in regard to explaining why employment falls during recessions. In 1987, economist George Alogoskoufis reviewed the evidence on both sides of the debate and concluded that it is important to distinguish between two issues.[4] Workers have to decide, first, whether to hold a job at all and, second, how many hours a week to devote to that job. Alogoskoufis found that intertemporal substitution plays a much bigger role in the first decision than in the second. He found that people do enter and exit the labor force in significant numbers in response to temporary changes in the wage rate and that these entries and exits are large enough to explain big observed fluctuations in aggregate employment and *average* workweek length.

While Alogoskoufis focused on economywide data, we can also measure intertemporal substitution effects in particular industries. For example, taxicab drivers can often foresee the difference between a good day (when fares will be easy to find because of a special event or a rainstorm) and a bad day (when fares will be difficult to find). The intertemporal substitution effect should lead drivers to work substantially

---

[3]This hypothesis was first proposed and defended by R. Lucas and L. Rapping in "Real Wages, Employment and Inflation," *Journal of Political Economy* 77 (1969), 721–754.

[4]G. Alogoskoufis, "On Intertemporal Substitution and Aggregate Labor Supply," *Journal of Political Economy* 95 (1987), 938–960.

more hours on the good days than on the bad ones, and, in fact, one study shows that, at least for experienced drivers, this is the case.[5]

In March 1989, the *Exxon Valdez* oil tanker ran aground in Alaska, creating an oil spill of historic proportions. The urgent cleanup created a (foreseeably) temporary rise in the wage rate for Alaskan workers. Figure 9-8 shows the result: average work-weeks shot up from 35 to 49 hours as workers rushed to take advantage of the temporary peak in wage rates. A few months later, wages returned to where they had been before the spill, and hours fell below the norm—presumably because workers were now taking some of their deferred leisure.

University of Chicago economist Casey Mulligan has reviewed the evidence for large intertemporal substitution effects (including Alogoskoufis's work, the study of cab drivers, and the facts from Alaska) and concluded that overall the evidence is quite strong.[6]

Interest-Rate Effect

Alogoskoufis combined his study of intertemporal substitution with an investigation of the interest-rate effect. His results for the two effects were very similar. Specifically, he found that the interest-rate effect is small for individual employed workers

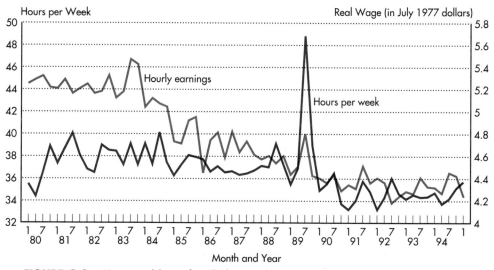

FIGURE 9-8 Wages and hours for Alaskan workers.
The *Exxon Valdez* oil spill occurred in March 1989. (*Source:* Professor Casey Mulligan, based on data from the Bureau of Labor Statistics.)

[5]C. Camerer, L. Babcock, G. Loewenstein, and R. Thaler, "A Target Income Theory of Labor Supply: Evidence from Cab Drivers," working paper, California Institute of Technology, March 1995.

[6]C. Mulligan, "The Intertemporal Substitution of Work—What Does the Evidence Say?" working paper, University of Chicago, June 1995.

but large for the economy as a whole, because many workers enter or exit the labor force in response to changes in the interest rate.

It should not be surprising that the intertemporal substitution effect and the interest-rate effect are so similar. Both rely on the willingness of workers to increase their current work hours in response to unusually large rewards—a temporarily high wage rate in the first case, and the chance to earn and save at a high interest rate in the second.

9-3　THE LABOR MARKET

In this section we investigate the workings of a market where labor is bought and sold at a going market price, or wage. Our earlier discussions of the income, substitution, intertemporal substitution, and interest-rate effects continue to apply. Our objective is to see how the market wage is determined.

Real and Nominal Wage Rates

The first and most important step is to understand the units in which the market wage is measured. Remember that in our model economy apples are the only good. Hence we must pay workers in *current apples*.

In the real world, of course, people are paid in *dollars*. But those dollars are only useful for the apples (or other goods) that they can buy. If you receive a salary of $20 per hour and apples cost 50 cents apiece, then we can equally well say that you receive a salary of 40 apples per hour. In the model, we will *always* quote wages as an hourly rate, in units of (current) apples per hour.

Because there are no dollars in our model, we can study it without worrying about changes in the value of a dollar. However, if we want to relate the model to reality, then changes in the value of the dollar can be very important.

Nominal wage rate:

The number of dollars paid for an hour of work.

Real wage rate:

The quantity of goods paid for an hour of work.

Suppose that apples sell for 50 cents apiece and your salary is $20 per hour, which translates to 40 apples per hour. Now suppose that one day the price of apples rises to $1 apiece and your wage rate rises to $40 per hour. This *still* translates to 40 apples per hour. Your **nominal wage rate**—your wage rate quoted in dollars—has risen, yet your **real wage rate**—your wage rate quoted in apples (or other goods)—is unchanged.

For us, the term "wage rate" (or "wage") will always refer to the *real* wage rate.

The Demand for Labor

Now let's leave the apple orchard and enter a world in which people hire other people to work for them.

We assume there is an economywide production function with the general shape of the one in Figure 9-1. The production function flattens as the quantity of labor increases; thus the economywide marginal product of labor is a decreasing function of labor input, as indicated in Figure 9-2(*b*).

Employers hire additional labor as long as its marginal product exceeds the going wage rate *W;* they stop hiring when the two become equal. That is, employers choose that quantity of labor at which $W = \text{MPL}$. This means that the demand curve for labor coincides with the MPL curve, as illustrated in Figure 9-9. (In Figure 7-4, we saw that the demand curve for capital coincides with the MPK curve; the same basic principle governs both cases.)

The Supply of Labor

Fred Flintstone is a net supplier of labor; that is, Fred supplies more labor than he hires. When Fred's wage rate goes up, he feels both a substitution effect, which makes him want to work more, and an income effect, which makes him want to work less. As usual, either effect could dominate. Thus, when the wage rate goes up, Fred's quantity of labor supplied could either increase or decrease. Another way to say this is that Fred's labor supply curve could slope either upward, as in Figure 9-10(*a*), or downward, as in Figure 9-10(*b*).

Fred's neighbor Mr. Slate is a net demander of labor; he hires more labor than he supplies. When the wage rate goes up, Mr. Slate, who *pays* wages, becomes *poorer.* Thus the income effect leads Mr. Slate to work *more,* unlike Fred, who is led by the income effect to work *less.* At the same time, Mr. Slate responds to the substitution effect just as Fred does: the rewards for additional work hours have gone up, so Mr. Slate works more hours. For Mr. Slate there is no ambiguity. The income and substitution effects work in the same direction, so when the wage rate goes up, he certainly works more. Mr. Slate's labor supply curve must slope upward.

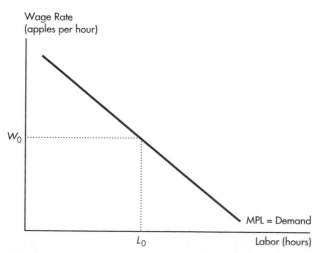

FIGURE 9-9 The market demand curve for labor.
The demand curve coincides with the marginal product of labor curve.

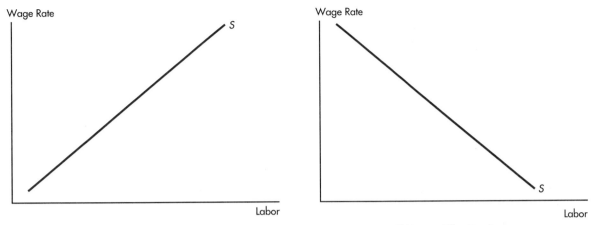

(a) Substitution Effect Dominant   (b) Income Effect Dominant

FIGURE 9-10   The individual labor supply curve.
If the substitution effect dominates the income effect, then higher wages lead the individual worker to supply more labor, so the labor supply curve slopes upward, as in (a). If the income effect dominates the substitution effect, then higher wages lead the individual worker to supply less labor, so the labor supply curve slopes downward, as in (b).

The *average* person (our old friend the representative agent) is neither a net supplier of labor nor a net demander. The average person demands and supplies labor in equal quantities; this is a simple consequence of the observation that every time one person sells an hour of labor, somebody buys that same hour.

When the wage rate goes up, then, the average person is made richer and poorer in equal amounts; the wages he collects and the wages he pays rise equally. Thus the average worker feels no income effect when the wage rate goes up. He feels only a substitution effect, which leads him to work more. Like Mr. Slate's, the average worker's labor supply curve must slope upward.

The economywide labor supply curve must behave like that of the average worker and therefore must slope upward as well.

Individual labor supply curves can slope either upward or downward. The economywide labor supply curve must slope upward.

Equilibrium

To find the equilibrium wage rate and the equilibrium quantity of labor, we superimpose the labor demand and labor supply curves D and S, as in Figure 9-11(a). The equilibrium point is the point E, at which they intersect; there, L_0 hours of labor are hired at a wage rate of W_0.

To discover how much output is produced, we can use the production function in Figure 9-11(b). It tells us that the equilibrium quantity of labor L_0 produces the quantity Y_0 of goods. Thus Y_0 is the economywide output at equilibrium.

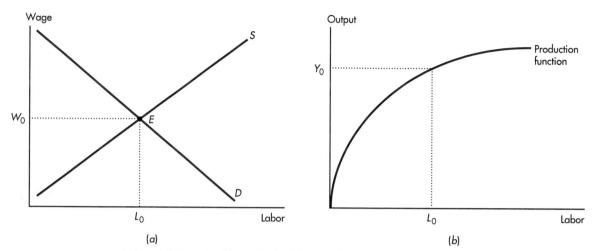

FIGURE 9-11 Equilibrium in the labor market.
(a) The equilibrium wage W_0 and quantity of labor L_0 are determined in the labor market. (b) The production function shows that, because L_0 units of labor are employed, the quantity of output must be Y_0.

Comparative Statics

We will now examine how the labor market's equilibrium changes in response to changes in the economic environment.

As always in studying changes in equilibrium, it pays to think about the behavior of the demand and supply curves separately. Regarding demand, the key observation comes from Figure 9-9: the demand curve coincides with the MPL curve. Therefore:

> The labor demand curve shifts if, and only if, there is a change in the marginal productivity of labor.

Regarding supply, it is critical to distinguish movements along a given supply curve from shifts of the curve itself. Changes in the wage rate are adequately modeled by moving along the curve. Changes in anything else require shifting the curve.

In Section 9-2, we listed four reasons why a worker might work more or fewer hours. One of these—the substitution effect—is the result of increased productivity, which the worker feels through an increase in the wage rate. Therefore, the substitution effect *cannot* cause the supply curve to shift.

The other three effects do cause shifts in the supply curve. So in deciding whether to shift the supply curve, they are the three effects to look out for.

> The labor supply curve shifts in response to income, intertemporal substitution, and interest-rate effects. The curve shifts leftward when people become

wealthier, leftward if wages are expected to be higher in the future, and rightward if the interest rate rises.

Later in this section we will see that a tax on labor income can also shift the labor supply curve.

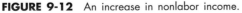 You might object that, like the substitution effect, the intertemporal substitution effect works through changes in the wage rate: workers provide more labor in times when their wages are unusually high and less in times when wages are unusually low. But these are not responses to the wage rate itself; instead, they are responses to *differences* between current and future wage rates. Thus we model them not by movements *along* the supply curve but by shifts *of* the supply curve.

An Increase in Nonlabor Income

Suppose there is a general increase in wealth, of such a nature that its size does not depend on how much people work. This can come about, for example, if a country is suddenly able to reduce its defense expenditures or a vast new oil field is discovered where only a negligible amount of labor is necessary to extract the oil.

There is no change in the marginal productivity of labor and hence no change in the demand for labor.

Labor *supply,* however, moves leftward because of the income effect. The average citizen is wealthier than before and therefore chooses to work fewer hours at any given wage.

Figure 9-12 shows the old equilibrium at quantity L_0 and wage rate W_0 and the

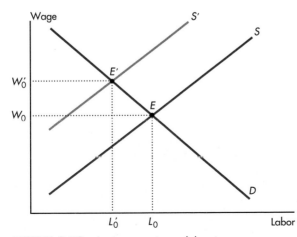

FIGURE 9-12 An increase in nonlabor income.
People work less (because they are richer), so the supply of labor shifts leftward. There is no effect on the marginal product of labor, and hence no effect on the demand curve. The equilibrium point moves from E to E'.

new equilibrium at L_0' and W_0'. Employment (that is, the number of hours worked) goes down, and the wage rate goes up.

Whether the windfall is in the present or the future, the size of the income effect is determined solely by its present value. If the annual interest rate is, say, 10 percent, then a $1 billion cut in this year's defense spending has exactly the same consequence as a $1.1 billion cut in next year's defense spending.

A *permanent* defense cut of $1 billion per year forever has a much larger present value than a temporary defense cut and thus has a much larger income effect. In terms of Figure 9-12, the supply curve would shift much farther to the left if the defense cut is permanent than it would if the cut is temporary. Therefore:

> An increase in nonlabor income causes employment to fall and the wage rate to rise. The size of the effects depends only on the present value of the windfall. A permanent change has a much larger effect than a temporary change of the same magnitude.

Exercise 9-1

Draw a graph that illustrates the effect of a decrease in nonlabor income.

A Permanent Increase in the Marginal Product of Labor

Suppose something happens to make each hour of labor permanently more productive. Examples include technological progress, an increase in the capital stock, or a favorable long-term climate change in an agricultural economy. Because the marginal product of labor increases, the demand for labor increases also. In other words, the demand curve shifts rightward.

Because the average citizen is now wealthier, the income effect causes the supply curve to shift leftward.

When the MPL curve rises, people are wealthier for *two* reasons. They are wealthier in their capacity as workers, because wages go up when the MPL curve goes up. (This is because the labor demand curve coincides with the MPL curve, and when the labor demand curve rises, so does the equilibrium wage.) They are also wealthier in their capacity as employers, because the people they employ are more productive. The first of these income effects, because it is felt through a change in wages, does *not* shift the supply curve. The supply curve shifts because of the second income effect. The average person is wealthier because his capital, coupled with more productive workers, is now worth more. Therefore, the average person chooses to take more leisure (at any given wage).

The shifted curves are shown in Figure 9-13. The wage rate obviously rises, from W_0 to W_0'. But it is impossible to tell what happens to employment. Depending on

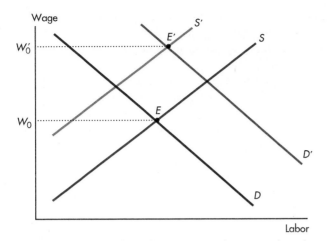

FIGURE 9-13 A permanent increase in the marginal productivity of labor.
The labor demand curve shifts rightward from D to D' (because the demand curve *is* the MPL curve), and the labor supply curve shifts leftward from S to S' (because of the income effect). The equilibrium point moves from E to E'. The wage rate rises from W_0 to W_0', but it is impossible to tell what happens to employment.

the magnitudes of the shifts, employment could move in either direction. This is consistent with the lesson of Figure 9-4: When Anne Jones becomes more productive, she may end up working either more or less than before.

A permanent increase in the marginal product of labor causes the wage rate to rise. Employment may increase or decrease.

Exercise 9-2
Draw a graph that illustrates the effect of a permanent decrease in the marginal product of labor.

A Temporary Increase in the Marginal Product of Labor

Marginal productivity (represented by the MPL curve) could increase temporarily if, for example, a year of unusually good weather allows each worker to accomplish more per hour in an agricultural economy.

The demand for labor then shifts rightward exactly as in Figure 9-13. The magnitude of the shift is independent of whether the increase in productivity is temporary or permanent; for shifts in the demand curve, only current productivity matters.

The supply curve, however, does not behave as in Figure 9-13, for two reasons.

First, because the good fortune is temporary, people are only slightly wealthier. Therefore, the income effect is small and causes the supply curve to shift only slightly to the left.

Second, there is now an intertemporal substitution effect. Recognizing that their opportunity to earn high wages is of limited duration, workers cancel vacations and work overtime. This leads to an increase in labor supply—a rightward shift in the supply curve.

Because the income effect and the intertemporal substitution effect push the supply curve in opposite directions, the curve's final position could be either to the left or to the right of its original position. But the income effect is small, so we shall assume that the intertemporal substitution effect dominates. The result, as shown in Figure 9-14, is a rightward shift in the supply curve.

Notice that the new equilibrium point E' is to the right of the old equilibrium point E; that is, employment increases. Notice also that E' could be either above or below E, depending on which curve, S or D, shifts farther.

However, if we step beyond the geometry to the underlying economics, we can say more. We have noted that the supply curve shifts right because of the intertemporal substitution effect—workers trying to grab high wages in the short interval when they are available. This story makes no sense unless the new wages are unusually high. It follows that point E' must be above point E.

Wages therefore rise, but not by as much as they did in Figure 9-13, where the supply curve shifted to the left.

A temporary increase in the marginal productivity of labor causes employment to rise and also causes the wage rate to rise, but not by as much as when the increase in productivity is permanent.

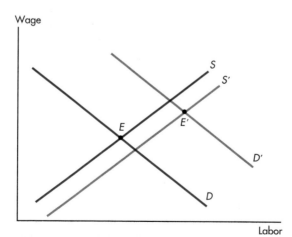

FIGURE 9-14 A temporary increase in the marginal product of labor.
The demand curve shifts rightward to reflect the increased marginal product. Supply is shifted slightly left by the (small) income effect, but it is also shifted right by the intertemporal substitution effect. We assume that the intertemporal substitution effect dominates, so the net shift in supply is to the right. The equilibrium shifts from E to E'.

→ *Exercise 9-3*
Draw a graph that illustrates the effect of a temporary decrease in the marginal productivity of labor.

An Increase in the Interest Rate

When the interest rate rises, working is more desirable. Figure 9-15 shows the consequences. The demand for labor D is unaffected (because nothing has happened to the MPL), but the supply of labor shifts rightward from S to S*. The equilibrium shifts from E to E*. Consequently, employment rises and the wage rate falls.

> An increase in the interest rate causes employment to increase and the wage rate to decrease.

→ *Exercise 9-4*
Draw a graph that illustrates the effect of a fall in the interest rate.

The Government

The government can affect the labor market by spending and by taxing.

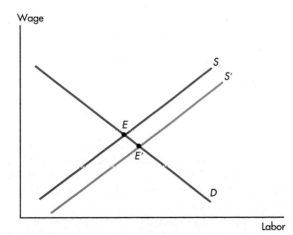

FIGURE 9-15 A rise in the interest rate.
Working is more desirable, so the labor supply curve shifts rightward from *S* to *S'*. The labor demand curve is unaffected. The equilibrium moves from *E* to *E'*.

Spending

Government spending, as we saw in Chapter 6, can be wasteful, productive, or a pure transfer. If it is wasteful, the average citizen is made poorer and the labor supply curve shifts rightward. If it is productive, the average citizen is made richer and the labor supply curve shifts leftward. If it is a pure transfer, the labor supply curve is unaffected.

Conceivably, productive government spending can increase the marginal product of labor. As an example, if the government constructs an efficient interstate highway system that for some reason could not have been provided by the private sector, then productivity is likely to rise: workers who drive trucks can now travel longer distances in a given amount of time. In that case, the demand curve for labor shifts rightward.

Taxing

Lump-sum taxes (head taxes) do not affect the demand for or supply of labor because they do not change the MPL or wealth. By contrast, a tax on labor income causes the labor supply curve to shift leftward via the substitution effect because working is less desirable when you don't get to keep all your wages.

We have just met an exception to a rule. The rule is that the substitution effect does not shift the labor supply curve. The exception is a tax on labor income—which reduces the hourly reward for labor and thereby discourages work through the substitution effect. This is the one case in which the substitution effect *does* cause the labor supply curve to shift.

The reason for this exception is that the direct impact of a tax on labor is not a reduction in your wage rate but a reduction in the fraction of your wage that you get to keep. Changes in the wage rate are already built into the supply curve and therefore do not cause that curve to shift. But changes in the fraction you get to keep are *not* built in and therefore *do* require shifts.

When a tax on labor income is perceived to be temporary, people also engage in intertemporal substitution. They reschedule their vacations to take place in the high-tax year, and they either delay their productive activities until the year is over or rush to complete them before the year begins.

Thus, any tax on labor income has a substitution effect. A temporary tax on labor income has an intertemporal substitution effect as well. Therefore, any tax on labor income shifts the labor supply curve to the left, but a temporary tax shifts it farther to the left than a permanent tax does.

Intertemporal Substitution in the Early Nineties

In December 1992, monthly income in the United States shot up by over 10 percent as people rushed to complete work projects and productive activities before the new year began. Figure 9-16 illustrates just how dramatic that spike in income was.

To understand this pattern, recall that shortly after taking office, President Clinton proposed a substantial rise in income tax rates. Although Clinton did not clarify his precise intentions until well after taking office in January 1993, by December 1992 the average American could quite reasonably have expected that the new administration would propose some sort of tax hike.

Since the (lower) tax rates of 1992 were now perceived as only temporary, conditions were ripe for intertemporal substitution. Projects that had been planned for 1993 were rushed to completion in 1992 so that the income they generated could be taxed at the old rates. Vacations scheduled for the week before Christmas were rescheduled for the week after New Year's Day.

It would be a mistake to attribute the December spike in income entirely to genuine intertemporal substitution. Part of it must have been due not to changes in the actual timing of labor efforts but to the creative efforts of accountants, who are sometimes able to shift profits from one month to another via transactions that take place only on paper. (The accountants themselves must have been among the great intertemporal substituters of the decade, as they rushed to complete those creative efforts before the end of the year.) The first lady herself was reported to have sold stock in late 1992 in order to avoid taking profits in 1993. But the December jump in income was large enough to suggest that income was being shifted not just on paper but in actuality, in a broad range of activities across the economy.

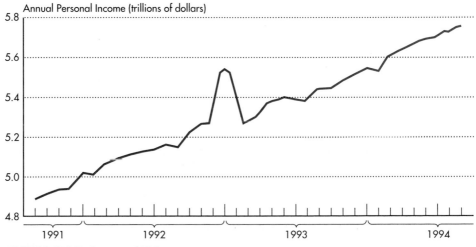

FIGURE 9-16 Income of U.S. citizens.
(*Source: Wall Street Journal*, October 3, 1994.)

9-4   THE GOODS MARKET WITH LABOR

Our final task in this chapter is to integrate our model of the labor market into the goods market model that has occupied the previous several chapters.

We will see that the existence of the labor market affects the supply of goods in two ways. First, it causes the supply curve for goods (which is vertical in a model without labor) to slope upward. Second, it creates new forces that can cause the supply curve to shift.

By contrast, the theory of the *demand* for goods remains just as it was in previous chapters.

The Supply of Goods

We begin by deriving the new supply curve for goods. The process is illustrated in Figure 9-17. Recall that the supply of labor shifts rightward when the interest rate rises; Figure 9-17(*a*) shows three labor supply curves, corresponding to interest rates of 10, 15, and 20 percent. With the labor demand curve, they yield equilibrium levels of employment L_0, L_1, and L_2. Using the production function in Figure 9-17(*b*), we find that these employment levels produce outputs of Y_0, Y_1, and Y_2.

The supply curve for goods is a graph of interest rates versus outputs. To obtain it, we plot points (10 percent, Y_0), (15 percent, Y_1), and (20 percent, Y_2) and then draw the supply curve S through them, as shown in Figure 9-17(*c*).

It is important to recognize that the supply curve in Figure 9-17(*c*) contains no new information. It is simply a different way to record information that is already contained in Figures 9-17(*a*) and 9-17(*b*).

Each supply curve in Figure 9-17(a) depicts the supply of *labor* as a function of the *wage* rate. The supply curve in Figure 9-17(c) depicts the supply of *goods* as a function of the *interest* rate. These are entirely different curves; take care not to confuse them.

Equilibrium in the Goods Market

We have thus replaced the vertical supply curve of previous chapters with the upward-sloping supply curve S derived in Figure 9-17. The new curve tells us that when there is a labor market, higher interest rates call forth more goods for consumption and investment. The reason is simple: When the interest rate rises, workers supply more working hours, so that more goods are produced.

In Chapter 7, we derived the demand for current goods as the sum of a consumption demand curve and an investment demand curve. There is no need to modify that derivation or its result. The demand curves in the goods market are exactly the same as those in Chapter 7.

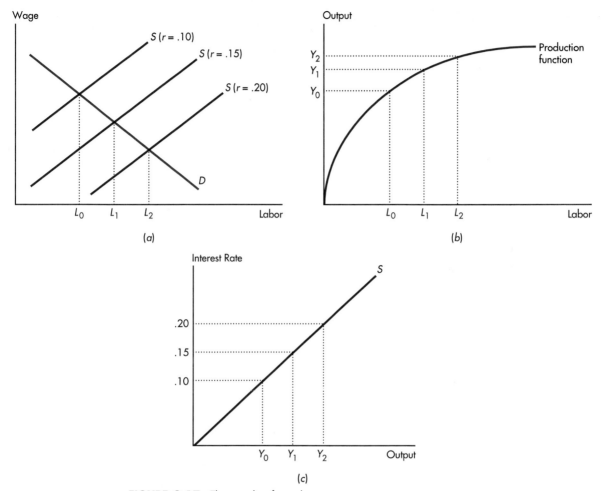

FIGURE 9-17 The supply of goods.
The supply of and demand for labor in (a), together with the production function in (b), contain
the information needed to construct the supply curve for goods. To get a point on the goods supply curve, fix an interest rate (say, 10 percent), draw the corresponding supply curve for labor
[from panel (a)], read off the equilibrium quantity of labor (say, L_0), and read off the equilibrium
quantity of output (say, Y_0). Plot the point (10 percent, Y_0) in panel (c). This is one point of the
goods supply curve. Repeat for other interest rates, and construct the goods supply curve S.

Figure 9-18 shows the curves that now make up the goods market and indicates
the equilibrium point E.

Comparative Statics

In Section 9-3, we considered how various changes in the environment affect the *labor*
market equilibrium. Now we will consider how some of the same changes affect equilibrium in the *goods* market.

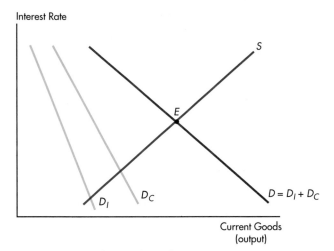

FIGURE 9-18 The goods market.
The demand curves for investment D_I and for consumption D_C are the same as those in Chapter 7, as is the aggregate demand curve D. The supply curve S is derived in Figure 9-17. Equilibrium is at point E, the intersection of S and D.

A Permanent Increase in Nonlabor Income

Let us suppose that the government is able to cut its defense expenditures by $1 billion per year forever. This is equivalent to a permanent increase in nonlabor income, because the resources previously devoted to constructing weapons are now available to be spent in other ways. We shall think separately about how this affects the supply of and demand for current goods.

First, supply: Initially, new goods worth $1 billion are available for current consumption and investment. (This is because $1 billion worth of resources that were formerly destined for conversion to tanks and missiles can now be converted to automobiles and satellite dishes.) Thus you might expect the supply of goods to shift rightward by a full $1 billion. In Chapter 7, this would have been exactly the right expectation.

With labor in the model, though, there is an additional factor to consider. People are wealthier now, and therefore work less (this is the income effect). Thus fewer goods are produced, and the total supply of goods rises by *less* than $1 billion, say, from S to S' in Figure 9-19(*a*).

How do we know that the income effect is not strong enough to take S' to the *left* of the original supply curve S? For the answer, think back to Anne Jones and Figure 9-3: When nonlabor income increases, Anne unambiguously chooses to have more apples. Anne is typical, so we can conclude that the average worker does produce less than before but still produces enough so that the total number of goods available is greater after the windfall.

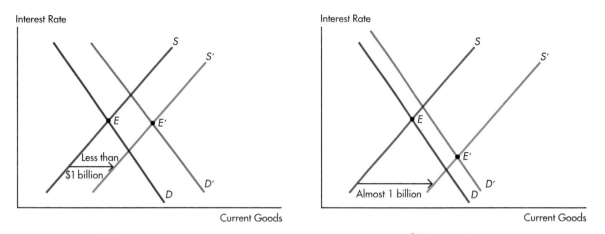

FIGURE 9-19 Increases in nonlabor income.
(a) A permanent $1 billion increase in nonlabor income initially shifts supply to the right by $1 billion. But this is partially offset by the income effect—wealthier people work less—and that reduces output. The result is that supply shifts right by less than $1 billion. Demand shifts right (because people are wealthier) about as much as supply. (b) When the increase in income is temporary, the income effect is small, so supply shifts almost the full $1 billion. Demand shifts right much less than supply.

Next, demand: An increase in nonlabor income makes people wealthier, and wealthier people demand more goods, so the demand curve shifts rightward from D to D' in Figure 9-19(a). Because of consumption smoothing, demand moves rightward about as far as supply does. The two rightward shifts cause the equilibrium point to move rightward from E to E'. Output obviously rises, but there is no reason to expect the interest rate to move in one direction rather than the other.

A Temporary Increase in Nonlabor Income

Now imagine a one-time-only defense cut of $1 billion (as opposed to the permanent cut of $1 billion per year that we have just finished analyzing). People feel wealthier, but much less so; hence the income effect is now much smaller, so people work only slightly less than they were working before. Therefore, after a temporary defense cut, the supply curve shifts from S to S' in Figure 9-19(b)—almost, but not quite, the full $1 billion to the right of the original curve.

Because people feel only slightly wealthier, the demand curve shifts only slightly to the right, as shown in Figure 9-19(b). Together, the two effects cause the equilibrium point to move from E to E'. Output rises and the interest rate falls.

A Permanent Increase in the Marginal Product of Labor

A permanent increase in marginal productivity leads to increased output, as we know from Anne Jones, who picked more apples when her productivity increased (see

Figure 9-4). The increased output makes people wealthier and increases the demand for current consumption. Hence both the demand for current goods and the supply of current goods move rightward, and the picture looks just like Figure 9-19(*a*).

A Temporary Increase in the Marginal Product of Labor

We know from Figure 9-14 that a temporary increase in the MPL causes employment to increase (the key to that analysis was the intertemporal substitution effect). Hence output increases for two reasons: because labor is more productive, and because more of it is being applied. Therefore, the supply of current goods shifts quite far to the right, from *S* to *S'* in Figure 9-20(*a*).

When the MPL increases temporarily, consumption demand increases slightly because people are slightly wealthier. The demand curve moves rightward, but only slightly. The result, as Figure 9-20(a) shows, is greater output and a lower interest rate.

Figure 9-20(*b*) reproduces Figure 9-19(*b*) for comparison. In both cases, demand shifts slightly rightward and supply shifts farther rightward. But when there is a temporary increase in the MPL, the supply curve moves *farther* than when there is a temporary increase in nonlabor income. In both cases people tend to work less because of the income effect, but when the MPL increases, there is an offsetting intertemporal substitution effect, leading people to work more. Obviously, when people work more, the supply of goods rises more.

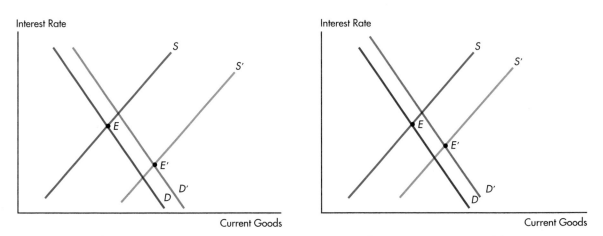

(*a*) Temporary Increase in MPL

(*b*) Temporary Increase in Nonlabor Income

FIGURE 9-20 A temporary increase in the marginal product of labor.
In (*a*), a temporary increase in the MPL causes the supply of goods to shift far to the right (from *S* to *S'*) and the demand for goods to shift slightly to the right (from *D* to *D'*). The effect of a temporary increase in the MPL is similar to the effect of a temporary increase in nonlabor income, shown in (*b*). The only difference is that in (*a*), the supply curve shifts farther because of the intertemporal substitution effect.

Taxes
....

We saw in Section 9-3 that an income tax shifts the labor supply curve leftward and thus leads to less employment. We also saw that this effect is greater when the income tax is temporary than when it is permanent.

Because an income tax reduces employment, it causes the supply of goods to shift leftward. Therefore, it causes the interest rate to rise and output to fall, and these effects are greater when the income tax is temporary than when it is permanent.

Additional effects come about if the tax revenue is spent either wastefully or productively. If the government spends wastefully, people are poorer, so the demand for goods falls and the supply of labor (and hence of goods) increases. If the government spends productively, the opposite is true. These effects are large for permanent spending programs and relatively small for temporary programs.

9-5 TRENDS IN REAL WAGES

Real Wages and Real Compensation

Until about 25 years ago, real wage rates in the United States generally rose over time. In the early 1970s, this trend was dramatically reversed, as you can see in Figure 9-21(*a*), which shows the average hourly real wage rate (measured in 1982 dollars) of civilian workers in the United States.

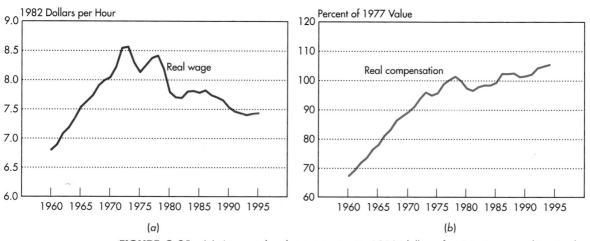

FIGURE 9-21 (*a*) Average hourly wage rate, in 1982 dollars, for Americans working in the private sector; (*b*) real compensation (wages plus fringe benefits) as a percentage of its 1977 value.

Politicians and journalists have viewed the decreasing trend in real wages with alarm, suggesting that it means that today's college students will be the first generation in American history to be worse off than their parents. Are they right?

There are several reasons to be skeptical of the alarmist conclusion. First, workers today can spend their wages on higher-quality goods than were available 20 years ago. You might have to work more hours to earn a car than your parents did at your age, but the car you buy will be a lot more reliable than anything that was on the market in 1970. In other words, a fully accurate measure of the real wage rate should account for changes in quality over time, but official statistics often do a poor job of making that adjustment.

For example, suppose that your grandmother had to work 1 hour to buy a light bulb that lasted a month and you have to work 2 hours to buy a light bulb that lasts a year. Official statistics might show that your real wage rate is lower than your grandmother's: she earned one light bulb per hour, and you earn only half a light bulb per hour. But a more reasonable assessment is that despite this official measurement, your real wage rate is actually *higher* than your grandmother's: she earned 1 month of light per hour, and you earn 6 months of light per hour.

A second reason why Figure 9-21(*a*) is misleading is that when we measure real wages alone, we fail to count the value of fringe benefits such as health insurance, on-the-job training, longer coffee breaks, and opportunities to play Tetris on corporate computers. The value of these benefits has increased substantially in recent years, partly compensating for the drop in actual wages.

Real compensation:
The real value of wages plus fringe benefits.

Figure 9-21(*b*) corrects for this problem by showing **real compensation**—that is, wages plus measurable fringe benefits like health insurance. You can see that unlike real wages, real compensation has risen steadily throughout the 1980s and 1990s. If Figure 9-21(*a*) presents a riddle—"Why have real wages fallen?"—then Figure 9-21(*b*) presents a partial answer—"Because workers have been taking their compensation in other forms."

This partial answer raises new questions. *Why* have workers started taking so much of their compensation in other forms? One answer is tax avoidance: by accepting $500 worth of health insurance instead of $500 in additional wages, workers avoid having to pay tax on that $500. But why has this kind of tax avoidance increased since 1977, and why has it expanded every year since? (We infer that it has expanded because the gap between real wages and real compensation has expanded.) Why didn't workers determine their optimal level of tax avoidance long ago, achieve that level, and remain there?

A possible response to that question is this: Tax avoidance requires ingenuity, and it has taken time to devise new and more extensive employee benefit plans. Many large employers now routinely pay for their workers' child care, an idea that had to be invented before it could become widespread. Company "insurance" plans now cover regular dental checkups, eyeglasses, and other foreseeable expenses that are far outside the traditional scope of insurance as a hedge against unforeseen catastrophes. Over time, personnel offices have thought of more and more new ways to exploit such opportunities—and hence to increase compensation without increasing wages.

And why did this stream of ingenuity begin in the 1970s? Again we can only guess, but it is worth noting that the high inflation rates which began in the early 1970s caused big increases in nominal income—and higher nominal incomes are taxed at higher rates. When people pay higher tax rates, they search harder for ways to avoid taxes.

So from the average worker's point of view, the good news is that Figure 9-21(*a*) paints a misleadingly bleak picture by omitting the rapid growth in fringe benefits. But the bad news is that even with fringe benefits included, real compensation has grown much more slowly since the mid-1970s than in the decades before. This is evident from Figure 9-21(*b*): since 1980, the upward trend has been a very mild one.

Real Compensation and Productivity

Productivity:

Output per worker-hour.

How surprising is it that real compensation has been growing so slowly? For comparison purposes, in Figure 9-22(*a*) we have superimposed the graph of real compensation from Figure 9-21(*b*) on a graph of **productivity**—that is, output per worker-hour. There are two things about Figure 9-22(*a*) that economists find extremely puzzling.

The first—and the one that probably jumps out at you when you look at the graph—is that until about 1977, productivity and real compensation moved almost in lockstep. In 1977, real compensation was about 70 percent of output per hour—that is, a worker who produced $10 of output in an hour could expect to earn an hourly wage of about $7 (the remaining $3 went to the owners of the capital that the worker employed). This 70 percent ratio had been remarkably constant for many years, as

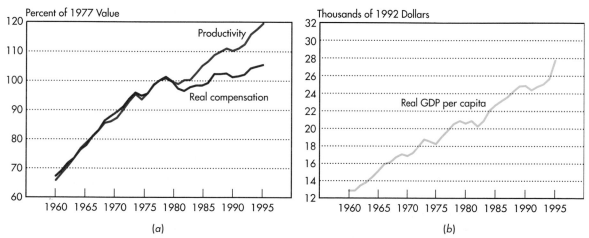

FIGURE 9-22 (*a*) Real compensation superimposed on a graph of productivity (output per hour of work), as a percentage of its 1977 value; (*b*) real per capita GDP.

indicated by the close coincidence of the curves in Figure 9-22(*a*). Since about 1977, the curves have diverged, and no economist is sure why.

Many economists suspect that the curves have diverged partly because real compensation is being measured inaccurately and changes in the nature of the workforce since the late 1970s have magnified the inaccuracies. In the past 15 to 20 years, there have been a number of striking new trends in the labor market: One is a great increase in participation by women; another is a great widening of the gap between rewards to skilled and unskilled workers. Perhaps in some ways that we do not fully understand, these new trends have undermined the accuracy of the way we measure fringe benefits.

(Here is one purely speculative example: Suppose that women, more than men, value flexibility in their hours and that employers have become more accommodating of this preference as the fraction of women in the workforce has increased. Flexible work hours are a form of fringe benefit that does not get counted in government statistics.)

The second thing that economists find extremely puzzling about Figure 9-22(*a*) is this: Productivity is not growing as fast as it used to grow. This *productivity slowdown* may not be obvious from a casual inspection of the graph, but it becomes strikingly apparent if you compare numbers on the graph by computing their ratios. In the 15 years from 1960 to 1975, the measure of productivity (as a percentage of its 1977 value) grew from 65.7 to 95.6—a 46 percent rise, or almost 3 percent per year. In the next 15 years, from 1975 to 1990, the measure of productivity grew from 95.6 to 110.8—a 16 percent rise, or just over 1 percent per year.

To explain the productivity slowdown, some macroeconomists have again resorted to the hypothesis that the problem is not real and the findings are the result of measurement error. As in our earlier discussion of real wages, the quality of goods becomes a major issue: if goods are increasing in quality, then the true value of output is increasing in ways that the official measurements—and hence the graph in Figure 9-22(*a*)—may ignore.

But economists do not know whether measurement errors can explain the graphs entirely. Productivity appears to have slowed dramatically, and real compensation has failed to keep up even with the slow pace of productivity. These are puzzles that economists are still working to solve.

Comparison with Economic Growth

In evaluating our economic welfare, it is important to remember that not all of our income arises from wages or even from wages plus fringe benefits. Figure 9-22(*b*) reminds us that real per capita income—from all sources—has grown at a healthier pace than productivity and at a *much* healthier pace than real compensation.

 Per capita income is income per person, which is the same as output per person. Productivity is output per hour of work. Per capita income has grown faster than

productivity because, since the expansion during the 1980s, hours of work have grown more rapidly than the population.

The rate of per capita income growth *has* slowed a bit (as we noted in the introduction to Chapter 8), but per capita income is unquestionably growing, just as it has since long before your parents' time. Much of that income is derived from the ownership of capital, which is all to the good: for most people, it is a lot more fun to earn income *without* working than it is to earn income in the labor market.

To see how life has really changed since the 1970s, find a Sears catalog from that decade. Look carefully at the quality of the goods for sale and at their real prices, and ask yourself whether you would prefer to shop from that catalog (at inflation-adjusted prices, of course)[7] or at Sears today. (Be guided by the fact that prices have roughly tripled in the past 20 years.) We predict you will have no hesitation about choosing the latter. Such comparative "shopping" is an excellent way to confirm that in ways that really matter, the current generation is a lot richer than the last one.

For the average citizen, then, economic growth continues to yield ever-greater prosperity. But taken together, the graphs in Figures 9-21 and 9-22 do tell a story that might be a source of some concern: Those Americans whose income is primarily or entirely from wages may no longer be sharing in the benefits of economic growth to the extent that they did in the past.

SUMMARY

Workers balance consumption against leisure. When they become wealthier, they tend to choose more of both, so they consume more and spend less time at work; this is called the income effect. When they become more productive, the substitution effect leads them to consume more and work more. An increase in productivity is typically accompanied by an increase in wealth, so the substitution and income effects work in the same direction regarding consumption but in opposite directions regarding work.

People work much more during temporary periods of high productivity. This is the intertemporal substitution effect. People also work more when the interest rate is higher; this is the interest-rate effect.

In the market for labor, the demand curve coincides with the MPL curve. It therefore slopes downward. It shifts only when the MPL shifts.

The labor supply curve slopes upward. It shifts to the left when people become wealthier (due to the income effect), to the right when there is a temporary opportunity to be more productive than usual (due to the intertemporal substitution effect), and to the right when the interest rate rises. It does *not* shift in response to substitution effects that are felt through

---

[7]If you prefer, you can imagine shopping from, say, the 1975 catalog at the published prices—but then, of course, you must also imagine that you are earning a 1975 wage rate.

changes in the wage rate. However, it *does* shift in response to substitution effects that are felt through a tax on labor income.

The labor market affects the goods market. First, the labor market causes the supply curve for goods to slope upward: higher interest rates call forth more labor, which means that more output is supplied. Second, changes in the labor market can cause the supply curve for goods to shift.

PROBLEM SET

1. Moe and Curly are farmers with identical skills, but Moe enjoys his work more than Curly does. If both farmers are forced to work one additional hour this week, which of them will produce more output in that hour? Why?

2. Suppose a permanent change in technology causes the production function to both rise and become flatter, as in Figure 9-23. Can you determine whether people work more or less after the change than they did before? Explain your answer in terms of the income and substitution effects.

3. Suppose it is discovered that technological improvements will increase the productivity of labor beginning *next year*. What is the effect on the number of hours people work *this year*? Describe the directions (if any) of the income, substitution, and intertemporal substitution effects. Does the interest rate change, and if so, how does that change affect the number of hours worked?

    After accounting for all effects, can you determine whether the number of hours worked increases or decreases? (*Hint:* What happens to current consumption?)

4. In each of the following circumstances, determine what happens to the supply of labor, the market interest rate, and the level of current consumption.

    a.   A temporary increase in the pleasantness of working conditions

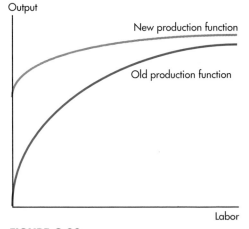

FIGURE 9-23

b. A permanent increase in the pleasantness of working conditions

c. A flu epidemic from which everyone eventually recovers

d. A polio epidemic that leaves many people permanently handicapped

e. A decision by the U.S. government to give away several billion dollars' worth of food to the countries of eastern Europe

f. A decision by the U.S. government to guarantee a yearly shipment of food to the countries of the former Soviet Union for several years to come

g. A cut in the income tax, in effect for this year only

h. A permanent cut in the income tax

i. A cut in the income tax, to be followed by further cuts in future years (all of which is announced in advance)

5. Suppose the government has an opportunity to undertake a spending program that produces consumption goods far more efficiently than people can produce them for themselves. The spending will be financed with a tax on income.

a. Explain why the supply of labor might shift farther if the tax-and-spend program is permanent than if it is temporary.

b. On the other hand, explain why the supply of labor might shift farther if the tax-and-spend program is temporary than if it is permanent.

6. Compare the effects of each of the following on wages and hours worked:

a. A flood that lowers agricultural productivity for 1 year

b. A prediction of a flood that will lower next year's agricultural productivity

c. A climate change that permanently lowers productivity

7. The government has undertaken a large building project that will create enormous benefits far beyond anything that the private sector can produce at similar expense. *Assume that the only kind of tax that can ever be raised is the income tax.*

a. Assume the project is financed by a temporary tax increase. Describe the income, substitution, and intertemporal substitution effects on hours worked.

b. Assume the project is financed by running a deficit. Describe the income, substitution, and intertemporal substitution effects on hours worked. How do they compare in both magnitude and direction to the effects you described in part **a**?

8. In Upper Slobbovia, all output is produced by robots; in Lower Slobbovia, people have to work for a living. Both countries have just been hit by tornadoes. In which country do you expect a bigger increase in the interest rate?

9. In Upper Slobbovia, the labor supply curve is very nearly vertical; in Lower Slobbovia, the labor supply curve is very nearly horizontal. Both countries have just been hit by tornadoes. In which country do you expect a bigger increase in the interest rate?

10. Compare the effects of each situation below on current consumption, current investment, and the interest rate:

a. A flood that destroys much of the grain that is stored in silos and ready for consumption

b. A flood before the harvest season that makes it much more difficult to plant and grow new grain

11. What happens to current consumption and current investment when there is an increase in nonlabor income? Are the changes larger or smaller if the increase is temporary rather than permanent?

12. What happens to current consumption and current investment when there is an increase in the marginal productivity of labor? Are the changes larger or smaller if the increase is temporary rather than permanent?

13. Suppose that the government raises income taxes to finance a new spending program. What are the effects on the supply and demand for goods and on the market interest rate?

   a. Answer assuming that the spending program is wasteful.

   b. Answer assuming that the spending program is exceptionally productive.

   c. Answer assuming that the spending consists of pure transfers.

Chapter 10

Money

ee Tapioca, the pudding tycoon, earns $25 million per year in salary and twice as much in bonuses. He owns a 20-room mansion in Beverly Hills, another in Palm Springs, and a magnificent 30-acre estate on Long Island. He travels around the world in his private Learjet, staying at the world's finest hotels and dining in the most exclusive restaurants. His investment empire includes substantial shares in some of America's largest corporations. The annual income from his bond portfolio alone is 10 times what the average American earns in a lifetime.

Would you say that Lee has a lot of money? In everyday parlance, nobody could object to such a statement. But if we speak the precise language of economics, we must observe that we haven't been told anything at all about how much money Lee has. He certainly has a lot of houses, a jet plane, and a lot of stocks and bonds. But none of those things is money. In economics, we reserve the word "money" for assets that are actually used to purchase things. In the United States, such assets are pieces of green paper bearing pictures of presidents and the words "This note is legal tender for all debts, public and private."[1]

To determine whether Lee Tapioca has a lot of money, we would have to look in his wallet and his desk drawers and count the currency there. It might be a lot or a little, depending on Lee's habits and on whether he has been to the bank lately. The key point is that *money is not the same thing as wealth.* Stocks, bonds, and houses are forms of wealth, but they are not money.

Credit cards are also on the list of things that are not money. Lee Tapioca has a credit card with a $100,000 credit limit; but if you have a $20 bill in your pocket, you might have more money than Lee has.

In this chapter, we examine the demand for money and the supply of money, and we investigate what it means for the **money market** to be in equilibrium. The notion of a "demand for money" would seem strange if you used the word "money" loosely, in reference to wealth. After all, everyone wants to be as wealthy as possible, so it seems there is little more to say. But if you remember that "money" refers only to pieces of green paper, then you can see that people do demand limited quantities and that those quantities vary with circumstances. A man like Lee Tapioca, whose credit is good everywhere, might demand no money at all; that is, he might decide not to keep *any* pieces of green paper in his pocket or his nightstand. A relatively poor college student heading out to purchase his back-to-school wardrobe might temporarily demand a lot of money, withdrawing, say, $200 in cash from his bank account. Elsie Corner, who owns the Corner Grocery Store, might also demand a lot of money, to keep in her cash register so that she can always make change. Toward the end of the day, she might choose to hold even more money, since she collects a lot of cash from her customers but doesn't take it to the bank until the store closes. At closing time, she might carry several thousand dollars to the bank to deposit; then, the moment she hands over the cash, her demand for money goes down by several thousand dollars.

Money market:
A market consisting of the individuals and institutions that supply and demand money and the arrangements that allow them to do so.

10-1	THE PRICE LEVEL AND THE PRICE OF MONEY

Before we can discuss the *demand* for money, we must determine what is meant by the *price* of money. And before we can discuss the price of money, we must define the *price level*.

....

[1]In economics, the word "money" usually includes not just currency but other assets that are used for purchases, such as checking account balances. In this chapter, however, we shall simplify matters by using the word "money" to mean just currency. In Chapter 15, we will adopt a more inclusive definition of money, but the lessons learned in the present chapter will continue to be applicable.

The Price Level

The **price level** is the average price of all goods in the economy, measured in dollars. On average, goods cost about three times as much in 1991 as they did in 1971. We say that the price level roughly tripled between 1971 and 1991.

Notice that the price level is *not* the price of any *particular* good. The price of videotape recorders actually *fell* dramatically between 1971 and 1991. The price of housing in many parts of the country increased *more* than threefold. But *on average,* the price of goods was multiplied by about 3 over that 20-year period.[2] Thus the price level in 1991 was three times as great as the price level in 1971.

To fix ideas, it is useful to imagine a fictional "average good." We will adopt the fiction that the average good is apples. That is, we will pretend that the price of apples always behaves exactly like the average of all prices in the economy. This will enable us to think about the price level very concretely: *If apples are the average good, then the price level can be measured by the price of apples.* But remember that if the price of apples behaves atypically (for example, if a frost causes the price of apples to increase relative to the prices of all other goods in the economy), then apples are no longer the average good and we can no longer use their price as a measure of the price level.

Within an economic model, we can simplify even further by pretending that apples are the *only* good, in which case the price level *is* the dollar price of apples.

We will use the letter P to denote the price level. Perhaps the price level was \$1 per apple in 1971 and \$3 per apple in 1991. (Of course, these estimates are not intended to be realistic; they are intended to illustrate the idea with simple numbers.) These amounts are consistent with our earlier assertion that the price level tripled over this time period.

> If apples are the average good and the price of apples is P dollars per apple, then the price level is P dollars per apple.

The Price of Money

What does it cost to hold a dollar? In other words, what opportunities do you forgo when you choose to hold a dollar? The answer is that you forgo the opportunity to hold some goods—such as apples—instead. If apples sell for \$1 apiece, then a decision to hold a dollar in cash is a decision to forgo owning one apple. Consider Johnny Dollarseed, who owns ten dollar bills and three apples. If he were willing to own only nine dollar bills, he could own four apples. His decision to hold an extra dollar costs him one apple.

Of course, if apples sell for \$3 apiece, then Johnny's decision to hold an extra

---

[2]In computing the price level as an average, it is important to take an appropriate *weighted* average. We don't want to count the price of bread and the price of ruby slippers as equally important, because bread consumes a much larger fraction of aggregate income than ruby slippers do. The problem of choosing appropriate weights can be surprisingly subtle, but it does not concern us here. It was discussed briefly in Chapter 2.

**Price of money
(in terms of goods):**

The number of
goods that must be
sacrificed to gain 1
unit of money equal
to the reciprocal of
the price level.

dollar costs him only one-third of an apple. So, in general, if the price of apples is P dollars per apple, then the price of dollars (that is, the **price of money**) is $1/P$ apples per dollar. We will continue (for a while) to pretend that apples are the average good, so that the price of apples can stand for the general price level. This result is worth emphasizing:

....

If apples are the average good and the price of apples is P dollars per apple, then the price of money is 1/P apples per dollar.

....

The Quantity of Money

There are two natural ways to describe the quantity of money in your pocket. One way is to count the number of dollars: "I have six dollars in my pocket." The other way is to describe the purchasing power of those dollars: "I have enough in my pocket to buy lunch," or "I have enough in my pocket to buy two apples."

Nominal measure:

A measure expressed in terms of dollars.

The number of dollars in your pocket is called the **nominal measure** of your money holdings, and the purchasing power of those dollars is called the **real measure** of your money holdings. Suppose that all prices double and that you simultaneously double the number of dollars in your pocket. Then your *nominal* money holdings have doubled (say, from $6 to $12), but your *real* money holdings have remained constant (you started with enough to buy one lunch and continue to have enough to buy one lunch).

Real measure:

A measure expressed in terms of purchasing power.

We denote **nominal money holdings** by the letter M. If you choose to hold $10, then we say that you are demanding the quantity $M = \$10$.

Nominal money holdings:

The number of dollars that a person holds.

If your money holdings are M and the price level is P, then your **real money holdings** can be described as the ratio M/P. For example, if you have $10 and the price level is $2 per apple, then $M = \$10$, $P = \$2$ per apple, and you are holding

Real money holdings:

The purchasing power of the dollars that a person holds.

$$\frac{M}{P} = \frac{\$10}{\$2/\text{apple}} = 5 \text{ apples}$$

worth of money. Notice that if M and P are multiplied by the same number, then M/P is unchanged; this is the case in our example above, where M and P are both doubled but your *real* money holdings remain constant.

10-2 THE DEMAND FOR MONEY

Why do people hold money at all, when they could hold apples or race cars instead? One reason for holding, or *demanding,* money is that doing so makes buying things easier. If the only thing you have to trade is apples and you want to buy a haircut, then you have to find a hairstylist who likes apples. But if you hold some of your wealth in the form of money, then pretty much any hairstylist will be willing to deal with you.

So people hold money in order to carry out **transactions.** Some transactions are foreseeable and others are not. You might carry $5 in your pocket because you know that you are going to use it to buy lunch and another $10 because you know that you might want to buy something else unexpectedly before the day is out.

Money is a good. Carrying more of it makes your life easier. The more you carry, the less likely it is that you will have to make an unanticipated trip to the bank or pass up an unexpected bargain. As with any good, you choose to have more of it when its price is low and less when its price is high. Since the price of money is $1/P$, when $1/P$ is high (that is, when P is low), you will carry relatively little money, and when $1/P$ is low (that is, when P is high), you will carry more. This relationship is illustrated in Figure 10-1, which is a graph of your demand for money, or **money demand.** As with any demand curve, we plot the price (in this case, $1/P$) on the vertical axis and the quantity (which we denote by M) on the horizontal axis. The point labeled A shows that when $1/P = 6$ (that is, when $P = \frac{1}{6}$), you carry 20 dollar bills; the point labeled B shows that when $1/P = 4$ (that is, when $P = \frac{1}{4}$), you carry 30 dollar bills.

There are a lot of ways to think about the underlying story that causes the money demand curve to slope downward to the right. Perhaps the easiest is this: When $1/P$ is high, the price level is low, so people don't need very much money to carry out their transactions. Likewise, when $1/P$ is low, prices are high, so people choose to carry lots of money.

Real Money Holdings

The money demand curve in Figure 10-1 measures *nominal* money holdings—actual dollar bills. Let us give some thought to the demand for money in *real* terms.

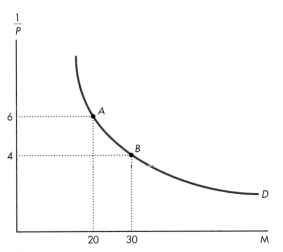

FIGURE 10-1 The demand for money.
The quantity demanded depends on the price, which is $1/P$, where P is the price level. When the price level is higher, the price of money is lower and people demand more of it. (The shape of the curve is explained in the text.)

When you decide how much money to carry with you, all you really care about is its purchasing power. You might think, "I'm going to carry just enough to buy lunch," or "I'm going to carry enough to buy lunch and get a cab ride home," or "I'm going to carry twice as much as I expect to spend today, just in case I see something interesting in a store window." If the price level changes, there is no reason for these real considerations to change. That is, if all prices double, you will continue to think "I'm going to carry enough to buy lunch," or "I'm going to carry enough for lunch and a cab ride." To accomplish this, however, you must now double your nominal money holdings.

More generally, recall that the purchasing power of your money is given by the fraction M/P. When P changes, you must adjust M proportionately to keep M/P constant.

> When the price level P changes, there is no change in how much *real* money people want to hold. Therefore, people adjust their *nominal* money holdings M so that the fraction M/P remains constant.

We can summarize this observation by saying that real money demand is governed by the equation

$$\frac{M}{P} = \text{constant}$$

The Money Demand Equation

Figure 10-1 illustrates a downward-sloping demand for money. Now we can say more about the exact shape of that demand curve.

In the preceding subsection we discovered the equation $M/P =$ constant, which we can also write as

$$M \times \frac{1}{P} = \text{constant}$$

Money demand equation:

The equation that describes the graph of the money demand curve; written as $M \times (1/P) =$ constant.

This equation, known as the **money demand equation,** describes the money demand curve. Because the demand curve is plotted with nominal money holdings (M) on the x axis and the inverse of the price level ($1/P$) on the y axis, we can think of the demand curve as the graph of an equation in the familiar form

$$xy = \text{constant}$$

The graph of this type of equation is a hyperbola. So:

> The money demand curve is a hyperbola whose equation is $M \times (1/P) =$ constant.

Notice that the constant in your money demand equation simply measures the purchasing power you choose to carry. The value of the constant might be "five apples," meaning that you carry enough to buy five apples. Or, if we measure the price level in terms of lunches and you carry enough to buy lunch, then the constant is "one lunch."

➠ *Exercise 10-1*

Use point *A* in Figure 10-1 to find the value of the constant in the money demand curve. Use point *B* to verify your solution.

Demand versus Quantity Demanded

With any demand curve, we must distinguish between a change in quantity demanded and a change in demand. A change in *quantity demanded* is caused by a change in price and is represented by a movement *along* the demand curve. A change in *demand* is caused by a change in anything *other* than price and is represented by a shift *of* the demand curve.

We apply this general principle to the money demand curve of Figure 10-1, where the relevant price is $1/P$. A change in $1/P$ (which is the same thing as a change in P) causes a change in *quantity demanded*, represented by a movement along the demand curve. When P changes from ⅙ to ¼, for example, you move along the money demand curve from point A to point B, demanding 30 dollar bills instead of 20. There is no shift of the demand curve. Another way to say this is that the constant in the money demand equation M/P = constant does not change.

A change in anything *other* than the price level *can* cause a shift in demand. Suppose you decide to start riding in taxicabs instead of on buses. (In that case, you will probably want to carry more money with you.) This is a change in something other than the price level P. Hence it causes a change in your *demand* for money, represented by a shift of the money demand curve as indicated in Figure 10-2. Another

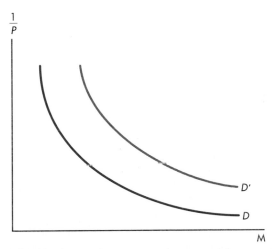

FIGURE 10-2 An increase in the demand for money.
The money demand curve shifts rightward from *D* to *D'* if money becomes more desirable for some reason other than a change in the price level *P*. The rightward shift of the demand curve means that the constant in the money demand equation is replaced by a new and larger constant.

way to say this is that in the equation M/P = constant, the constant changes, so the entire curve shifts.

There is another, equivalent way to distinguish between changes in quantity demanded (movements *along* the money demand curve) and changes in demand (movements *of* that curve). Each money demand curve represents a certain fixed *real money demand*. When the price level increases, people demand more nominal money to keep their *real* money holdings *constant*. Hence they move along the original money demand curve. By contrast, when people switch from buses to taxis, they demand more nominal money to make their real money holdings *increase* (from "enough to pay the bus fare" to "enough to pay the cab fare"). Hence they shift to a different money demand curve (as in Figure 10-2).

A movement along the money demand curve never represents a change in the amount of real money people want to carry. A shift of the money demand curve always represents a change in the amount of real money people want to carry.

Determinants of the Demand for Money

The demand curve for money has the equation M/P = constant. The size of the constant controls the exact location of the curve. A shift of the curve is the same thing as a change in the value of the constant.

What sorts of things might cause the money demand curve to shift? The answer is anything (other than the price level) that affects the desirability of holding real money. We will now discuss a few examples.

A Change in Income

Generally speaking, people with higher real incomes make more purchases and therefore demand more (real) money. This need not be universally true. For example, people with high real incomes might have easy access to credit and therefore demand relatively *little* money. But as a general rule, we believe that money demand increases with real income. Thus, if there is an increase in real income—due, for example, to an increase in productivity—we expect money demand to increase. That is, a rise in real income causes the money demand curve to shift rightward, say, from D to D' in Figure 10-2. Similarly, a drop in real income causes the money demand curve to shift leftward.

Remember that income equals output and that one component of output is government spending. It is unclear whether changes in that component should affect money demand. Certainly, when there is an increase in consumption—with people buying more clothing, better haircuts, and new VCRs—we expect an increase in the demand for money. It is a little harder to describe a link between the number of aircraft carriers and the amount of cash that people want to carry in their pockets.

A Change in the Interest Rate

One cost of holding money is the forgone opportunity to hold an interest-bearing asset, such as a savings account or a Treasury bond. A dollar in your pocket earns no interest. If you are willing to sacrifice that dollar, you can increase your bank balance and earn additional interest.

If the interest rate rises, this cost becomes more significant, so the demand for money falls. The money demand curve of Figure 10-1 shifts to the left. By the same token, a drop in the (nominal) interest rate makes money more attractive relative to bonds and causes the money demand curve to shift rightward to D' in Figure 10-2.

These interest-rate effects are particularly important to firms that must keep a lot of cash on hand. At a supermarket that must keep $2000 cash in the registers to make change, the owner sacrifices $140 per year in interest when the interest rate is 7 percent. If the interest rate rises to 14 percent, the sacrifice rises to $280 per year and the owner becomes more diligent about finding ways to reduce the store's cash reserves.

Other Changes

We have already seen that if people start taking cabs instead of buses, the demand for money rises. More generally, any change in people's purchasing habits can affect the demand for money. The invention of credit cards caused a significant drop in the demand for money, since many people began using cards instead of money to make purchases.

Suppose that, for some reason, you decide to visit your bank less often. Maybe you have a new job, with hours that conflict with banking hours; maybe you have sold your car and getting to the bank is less convenient. In any case, you are now visiting the bank to make withdrawals once a month instead of once a week. Consequently, you will probably increase the size of your withdrawals, and this change means that your demand for money has increased.

Let us elaborate on that last point. Originally you went to the bank once a week, withdrew $50, and spent it at a uniform rate so that it lasted until your next trip to the bank. At the beginning of the week you demanded $50, at the end of the week (just before your next trip) you demanded $0, and on the average day you demanded $25. Now you decide for some reason to visit the bank only once a month, withdraw $200, and spend it at a uniform rate for a month. At the beginning of the month you demand $200, at the end you demand $0, and on the average day you demand $100. Your average money demand has increased fourfold, from $25 to $100.

10-3 THE SUPPLY OF MONEY AND EQUILIBRIUM

Money supply:
The quantity of money supplied by the authorities.

Money supply curve:
A curve showing the money supply as a function of the interest rate. It is vertical at the quantity chosen by the authorities.

United States currency is supplied by the U.S. monetary authorities. The details of money creation are discussed in Chapter 15 and need not concern us here. The bottom line is that the **money supply** is whatever the authorities want it to be.[3]

Because the authorities set the money supply at whatever quantity they choose, the quantity supplied is unaffected by changes in the price level. This means that the **money supply curve** S is vertical, as in Figure 10-3, at the chosen quantity M_0.

By superimposing the supply and demand curves for money, we can find the equilibrium point (E in Figure 10-3) for the money market. We expect the money market to be at the equilibrium point for all of the same reasons that we expect any market to be in equilibrium. In Figure 10-3, the equilibrium price of money (that is, $1/P$) is $\frac{1}{2}$; therefore, the equilibrium price level (that is, P) is 2.

Once we have found the equilibrium point, it is natural to ask what could cause that equilibrium to shift. The answer, of course, is a shift in supply or a shift in demand. We begin by considering the former.

Changes in Supply

Suppose that for some reason the monetary authorities decide to double the supply of money, from M_0 to $2M_0$ in Figure 10-4. As you can see from the figure, the equilib-

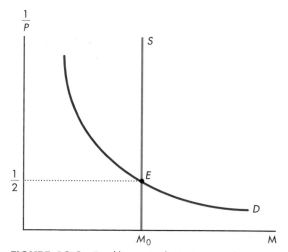

FIGURE 10-3 Equilibrium in the money market.
The demand curve D is that of Figure 10-1. The supply curve S is vertical at whatever quantity of money M_0 the authorities choose to supply. The equilibrium point determines the price level.

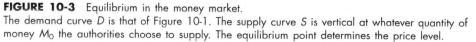

[3] If checking account balances are counted as money, then the authorities no longer have full control of the money supply. We will continue to use the word "money" to mean only actual currency.

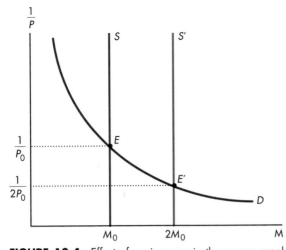

FIGURE 10-4 Effect of an increase in the money supply.
An increase from M_0 to $2M_0$ causes the equilibrium price level to rise. (The illustrated *decrease* in the price of money from $1/P_0$ to $1/2P_0$ is equivalent to an *increase* in P.) From the equation of the demand curve we can infer that P exactly doubles.

rium point moves from E to E' and the price of money $1/P$ falls. This means that the equilibrium price level, P, has to rise.

An increase in the money supply causes the equilibrium price level to rise.

We can determine exactly how far the equilibrium price level must rise by using the equation of the money demand curve:

$$\frac{M}{P} = \text{constant}$$

In Figure 10-4, the equilibrium point moves along a fixed money demand curve, so the constant remains unchanged. Therefore, if M doubles, P must also exactly double.

More generally, if the money supply M increases (or decreases) by any proportion, the price level P must increase (or decrease) by exactly the same proportion so that the fraction M/P remains constant.

Why Does the Price Level Change?

What happens when the money supply doubles? We see in Figure 10-4 that the price level must increase, and we learned from the money demand equation that in fact the price level must exactly double. In some sense, this completely answers the question. But it is still instructive to think more carefully about the process by which the price level rises to its new equilibrium value.

To fix ideas, we need to examine what happens when new money is introduced into the economy. Suppose that your college community is a closed society, having no contact with the outside world. Everybody in this community likes to carry just enough money to buy lunch. One day, while you and all your friends are milling about on the quad, a dozen helicopters appear and start dropping money. In fact, they drop enough money to double the money supply at your college. What do you think happens?

First, of course, people rush to pick up the money, because money is a form of wealth and everyone welcomes the opportunity to be wealthier. Once the money has been pocketed, everybody is carrying more money than he really wants. That is to say, each person has more than just enough to buy lunch, or more than the person had decided to carry upon leaving home that morning. Anybody who wanted to carry extra cash that day could have easily acquired it by making a trip to the bank. The extra money from the helicopters is more than anybody ever wanted.

What then will people do? They will certainly not throw the money away, because that would be discarding wealth. Instead, they will attempt to trade their money for goods. That is, they will attempt to *buy things*.

Unfortunately, when everybody tries to buy things at once, people run into a problem: There are no sellers. When you turn to your neighbor and offer to buy his watch, your neighbor says, "What a coincidence. I was just going to offer to buy *yours*." As everyone attempts to purchase goods from everyone else, the prices of all goods—and thus the general price level—are bid up.

As the price level starts to rise, a remarkable thing happens: The *real* value of the money in people's pockets begins to fall. Even if you are completely unsuccessful in finding goods to purchase, your real money holdings decrease. No dollar bills leave your pocket, but their real value falls.

If prices rise only a little, people still have more than enough to buy lunch. They still have more money than they want, and therefore they bid up prices further. Eventually, prices rise to twice their original level. People have twice as much (nominal) money as they had before, prices are twice as high as they were before, and once again everybody has just enough to buy lunch. At this point, people are satisfied with their money holdings, and the economy has reached its new equilibrium.

Notice that the people in this model accomplish their goal, though not in the way they would have preferred to accomplish it. When the helicopters come by and real money holdings (M/P) increase, everyone tries to reduce his real money holdings back to their original level by reducing M (that is, by buying things). Although nobody succeeds in buying anything, everybody *does* end up reducing M/P—but through an increase in P. This is the less enjoyable way to reduce one's real money balances: successfully purchasing goods at low prices is more fun than just watching prices rise. The better outcome, unfortunately, is not in the cards. But at least the people in this economy *do* achieve the limited goal of holding exactly the amount of real money that they want to hold.

What are the relations among this story, Figure 10-4, and the money demand equation? Essentially, Figure 10-4 and the money demand equation tell us how the story must end. Together, they reveal the new equilibrium price level to be twice the old equilibrium level. The story fleshes out the process that leads from one equilibrium to the other.

How long does the bidding-up process take? Much depends on the details, including how far people must travel to attempt to purchase goods. But there is no reason why the process should not happen very quickly, and so we shall abstract from reality and assume that it happens instantly. Therefore:

> When new money is introduced into the economy, the price level is immediately bid up to its new level.

Students sometimes ask, "If people want to dispose of the new money and are unable to purchase goods with it, why don't they just buy bonds or put the money in the bank?" The answer is that then the *banker* is stuck with more money than he wants and so tries to spend it. There is no way to make the new money disappear other than destroying it. While some individuals may succeed in disposing of it, the money must always be in *somebody's* hands. Until the price level doubles, that somebody will continue attempting to hand it on to somebody else.

Welfare

How does a helicopter money drop affect economic welfare? That is, are people made better off or worse off when the helicopters fly by and double the money supply?

A moment's reflection will convince you that the helicopters do no good and no harm. When money holdings M and prices P move exactly in proportion, nobody's real wealth is changed; nobody's real money holdings M/P are changed; nobody's stock of capital or stream of consumption is changed; nothing real is changed.

In fact, this conclusion would be clear even if we had not thought through the process by which the price level is bid up. The new money supplied by the government cannot be eaten; it does not transport people where they want to go; it does not add to knowledge or to beauty. Scraps of green paper cannot make the world a better place.

Changes in Real Income

We turn now to changes in the money market equilibrium that result from a shift in demand. One thing that can cause a shift in the demand for money is a change in real incomes, so let us work through an example of that.

When people's real incomes increase, people engage in more transactions, so they want to carry more money. Notice that they want to carry more money in real terms; they want more **purchasing power.**

Purchasing power:
The ability to acquire goods.

Because people have increased their demand for real money, the money demand curve shifts to the right, from D to D' in Figure 10-5. The equilibrium value of $1/P$ rises, and therefore the equilibrium value of the price level falls from P_0 to P_1.

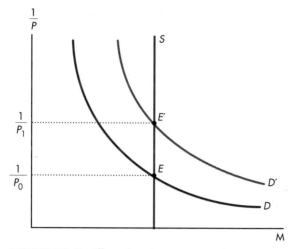

FIGURE 10-5 Effect of an increase in real income.
When real income rises, the demand for money shifts rightward from *D* to *D'* and the price level
P falls (that is, $1/P$ rises).

An increase in real income causes the equilibrium price level to fall.

As it was for a change in supply, it is instructive to think about the process that
brings about the new equilibrium. We start with a rise in real incomes: instead of
earning enough to buy 5 apples per week, people now earn enough to buy 10 apples
per week. To spend their additional incomes, all the people simultaneously decide to
carry more money than before. But there *is* no more money than before; an increase
in real incomes does not affect the number of dollar bills in circulation. Everybody
simultaneously attempts to acquire more money, but it is impossible for everyone to
succeed. In order to increase their money stocks, people must attempt to sell goods.
As everyone attempts to sell, prices are bid down.

Why must people sell goods to obtain more money? Can't they demand it from their
employers or from their banks? The answer is no, for the simple reason that there is
no more money available than there was before. When everybody demands more
simultaneously, something has got to give. Exactly what gives depends on the details
of institutional arrangements. Perhaps the bank does guarantee its customers the right
to make cash withdrawals; in that case, the *banker* must sell something to obtain
more dollar bills. Perhaps employers do guarantee that they will pay their employees
in cash; in that case, the *employers* must sell something. The overall effect is that
people try to sell goods to obtain dollars and thus the price level drops.

The general decrease in prices has the effect of increasing everyone's real money
holdings, even though people's *nominal* money holdings remain unchanged. The

increase in real money holdings happens to be just what everybody is aiming for. Eventually, the price level falls just enough so that people are able to achieve their desired new level of real money holdings. At that point, the market has reached its new equilibrium.

Once again, we shall assume that this bidding-down process takes no appreciable time and that the market jumps to the new equilibrium immediately. And once again, we note a remarkable irony: People end up accomplishing exactly what they set out to do but not in the way they set out to do it. The goal is to increase real money holdings M/P. Initially, people seek to do this by increasing M (that is, by selling goods for money). Because everyone is trying to sell, everyone fails; but in the process, P falls and therefore M/P does rise after all.

Welfare

What happens to economic welfare when the price level falls as a result of an increase in real income? Do people gain or lose when prices change?

We first observe that people certainly gain from the increase in real income, which is presumably the result of an increase in productivity. The question is whether the events that ensue in the money market add anything *more* to people's welfare.

This time, the answer is yes. When the price level adjusts downward, people who are holding money are beneficiaries. The real value of the money in their pockets increases, and they are genuinely wealthier. Since the quantity of (nominal) money M does not change and since each dollar bill is worth more now than it was before (because P has decreased), there has been a net increase in wealth. This increase in wealth is separate from the earlier increase that came when real incomes rose. It is an *extra* increase.

But that extra increase poses a riddle: Where is the additional wealth coming from? How can money holders get richer when nobody else becomes poorer? The events that occur in the money market seem to have no effect on anything real. Prices fall, but there is no corresponding increase in the availability of any real goods. An increase in money demand creates no more food, no more cars, no more of anything we value.

But there is one exception to that last statement, and it solves the riddle: A rise in money demand, by causing a decrease in the price level, leaves people with more *real* money in their pockets than they had before. The person who put enough money in his pocket this morning to buy lunch now finds himself carrying enough to buy a large dinner. This change has real effects. It means that if you see a sweater you like in a store window, you can buy it without first running to the bank to make a withdrawal. It means, more generally, that you can visit the bank less often, saving on time and transportation costs. In other words, **transactions costs** are reduced, and that is a genuine benefit that adds to society's wealth.

Transactions costs:

The costs of carrying out transactions, including time spent acquiring money.

This benefit of a rise in money demand is made possible by the accompanying increase in the real quantity of money. Everyone who holds money at the moment that prices fall shares in this real social gain.

 Students sometimes think that a drop in prices is a good thing because it means that people can buy things more cheaply. This is *incorrect*, because the drop in prices applies both to the things you buy *and* to the things you sell. For example, if you sell labor, your wages fall. Since everything that is bought is simultaneously sold, any gains to buyers are exactly canceled out by losses to sellers. The only sense in which a drop in prices is a good thing *on net* is that it increases the value of people's money. If you happen not to be holding any money at the moment that the price level adjusts, then you do not benefit from the adjustment.

Other Factors That Change Money Demand

Anything that shifts the demand for money can change the price level. We saw earlier that when the interest rate rises, the demand for money shifts to the left. Thus $1/P$ falls and the price level P rises.

→ *Exercise 10-2*
What happens to the price level as credit cards become more generally available?

Following any shift in the demand for money, there is a change in the equilibrium price level, a change in real money holdings, and a consequent net gain or loss in economic welfare. When money demand increases, prices fall, real money holdings increase, and there is a net welfare gain. When money demand decreases, prices rise, real money holdings decrease, and there is a net welfare loss.

These results contrast with the effects of a shift in the money supply. Following a shift in the money supply, there is a change in the equilibrium price level but no change in real money holdings; in fact, the equilibrium price level changes by just enough so that real money holdings stay fixed. Because there is no change in real money holdings, there is no change in economic welfare.

The Demand for Money and Foreign Trade

An increase in the demand for money creates positive net benefits. Suppose, for example, that Americans purchase automobiles from Japanese firms and that the firms choose to hold onto the American dollars they receive in payment. Is this a good thing or a bad thing for Americans?

Editorial writers often bemoan the dangers of letting dollars pile up in foreign hands. But what really happens when Japanese firms decide to hoard American dollars? The answer is that the demand for dollars rises and the price level falls. Every American who holds money is a winner, because the purchasing power of his money increases.

If the Japanese firms eventually elect to spend their dollars, then the demand for money drops to its original level, the price level rises to its original value, and the stream of benefits to Americans comes to a halt. But in the interim, Americans get to hold more real money and experience a real increase in wealth. The longer that interim period lasts, the better off American citizens are.

Here is another way of looking at the same situation: It costs Americans, as a society, practically nothing at all to print pieces of green paper with George Washington's picture on them. If somebody is willing to trade us valuable goods for those pieces of green paper, there must be a net gain to Americans. The only question is this one: Exactly what form does that gain take? The answer is a rise in real money balances, accomplished through a drop in the price level. But even if we couldn't figure that out, we should have known that there had to be a net gain *somewhere,* because Americans as a group were essentially getting something for nothing.

Testing the Theory

Figure 10-6 shows the behavior of the price level and the money supply in the United States over an 11-year period. The price level is normalized to equal 100 in 1987. The money supply is measured in units of $7.5 billion each and is thereby also normalized to 100 in 1987 (when the money supply was equal to $750 billion).

The theory in this chapter suggests that *if* the demand for money was constant over this 11-year period, then the price level and the money supply should move together; in particular the two curves should always exhibit the same slope. You can see from the graph that there are important deviations from this prediction. The rapid money supply growth in 1985–1986 was not matched by comparable growth in the price level; neither was the even more rapid money supply growth in 1991–1993. The fall in the money supply in 1994–1995 is not accompanied by a fall in the price level.

There are several possible explanations for these deviations. One explanation is

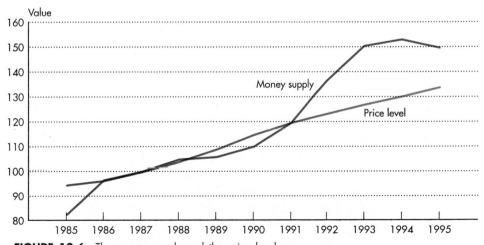

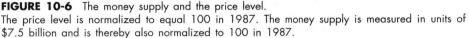

FIGURE 10-6 The money supply and the price level.
The price level is normalized to equal 100 in 1987. The money supply is measured in units of $7.5 billion and is thereby also normalized to 100 in 1987.

that we might be measuring money incorrectly. The "money" that is measured in Figure 10-6 consists of cash and checking account deposits. This measure of the money supply is called M1, and it is discussed further in Chapter 15.[4] But there are alternative measures of the money supply. Perhaps we should have been *more* restrictive and excluded checking account balances. Perhaps we should have been *less* restrictive and included savings account balances as well.

A more promising explanation is that the *demand* for money must have been changing over the course of the sample period. This should come as no surprise, because real income rose every year in that period, and we know that real income affects money demand.

To test whether this explanation is sufficient, we need a more quantitative model of the relationship between income and money demand. Let us experiment by assuming a particularly simple relation: Changes in income affect money demand *proportionately,* so a 10 percent increase in income yields a 10 percent increase in money demand.

This means that the money demand equation can be written in the form

$$\frac{M}{P} = kY$$

where Y represents real income and k is a constant of proportionality. (This is perfectly consistent with our money demand equation M/P = constant; we always knew that the constant depends on Y, and now we have specified *how* that constant depends on Y.) This equation can be rewritten as $M = kPY$.

But PY is the product of the price level times real income; in other words, it is nominal income. Thus we have discovered that when money demand is accounted for—at least if it is accounted for in a particular (possibly oversimplistic) way—we should expect the money supply to move proportionately not with the price level but with nominal income.

Figure 10-7 serves as a test of that prediction. The price level is measured just as it was in Figure 10-6, but here it is compared with nominal GDP (a measure of nominal income), which is measured in units that force its value in 1987 to be 100.

If you compare Figures 10-6 and 10-7, you will see that changes in nominal GDP track changes in the money supply better than changes in the price level do. This suggests that we have gained some ground by adding money demand considerations to our model. However, important discrepancies remain to be explained. The rapid money supply changes at the beginning and end of the sample period are fully reflected in the behavior of nominal GDP.

We cannot really expect a perfect fit, because our money demand model remains quite primitive. It assumes a proportional relation between income and money demand, and it completely ignores the influence of other variables, most notably the interest rate. Yet we have been able to narrow the gap.

....

[4]Thus, in this section only, we are departing from the convention adopted elsewhere in this chapter, where we count only currency as money.

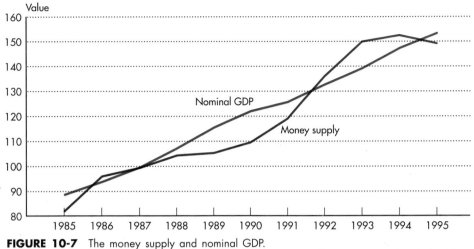

FIGURE 10-7 The money supply and nominal GDP.
The money supply is normalized to equal 100 in 1987. Nominal GDP is normalized to 100 in 1987.

10-4 INFLATION

Inflation:

A continuous increase in the price level, sustained over a period of time.

Inflation is a continuous increase in the price level, sustained over a period of time. The price-level jumps that we have examined in previous sections are *not* examples of inflation, because they are one-time jumps that occur in an instant. Figure 10-8 illustrates two different ways in which the price level might change over time. In part

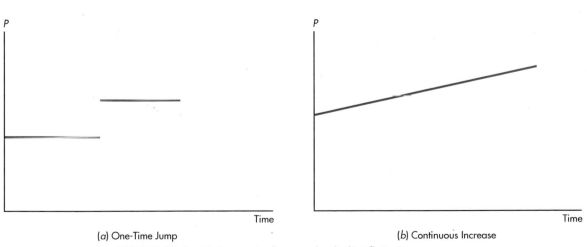

(*a*) One-Time Jump

(*b*) Continuous Increase

FIGURE 10-8 (*a*) A jump in the price level; (*b*) inflation.

(*a*), we see a one-time jump in the price level, which is not inflation. In part (*b*) we see inflation.

Suppose that the price level rises by 10 percent from January 1, 1998, to January 1, 1999. Then official statistics will report a 10 percent inflation rate for 1998, regardless of whether prices rose continuously (in a genuine inflation) or whether they jumped all at once on June 1 (which is not inflation at all). Thus, although it is important to distinguish in principle between inflation and a price-level jump, a naive reading of reported statistics is inadequate to make that distinction.

What can cause inflation? The only possible answers are a continuous increase in the supply of money, a continuous decrease in the demand for money, or some combination of the two. Of these, the first is by far the more common. Governments might very well—and often do—increase the money supply continuously, for reasons that will occupy us later in this chapter. By contrast, it is hard to think of very many things that could cause a continuous fall—as opposed to a one-shot drop—in the demand for money.

Figure 10-9 is an attempt to illustrate a continuous increase in the money supply, though a moving picture would be needed to illustrate it with complete accuracy. As the supply of money shifts continuously to the right at a steady pace, the point of equilibrium moves continuously downward along the demand curve and the price level rises continuously. Because the money demand curve does not shift, the price level rises just enough to keep the real quantity of money M/P constant. If, for example, the money supply increases at a rate of 10 percent per year, then the price level increases at the same rate.

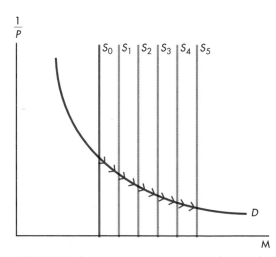

FIGURE 10-9 A continuous increase in the supply of money.
The supply curve S is seen in "snapshots" at various times during an inflationary period. Higher subscripts denote later times. As the supply of money shifts rightward, the equilibrium point moves down and the price level P increases.

Inflation around the World

If the demand for money were fixed, then the price level would grow at the same rate as the money supply. In practice, rising real incomes usually cause the demand for money to rise over time. This tempers the inflationary effect of money supply growth, and so the price level typically grows more slowly than the money supply. But we should still expect higher rates of money supply growth to cause higher rates of inflation.

Figure 10-10 confirms this expectation. The graph shows, for the decade of the 1980s, the average annual rates of money supply growth and inflation in 18 countries. As expected, inflation rates are lower than the growth rates of the money supply. But you can see that for the most part, countries with relatively high money supply growth (like Italy, Australia, and Finland) also experienced relatively high inflation rates. Those with relatively low money supply growth (like Germany) experienced relatively low inflation rates.

There are a few striking exceptions, most notably Singapore, where inflation averaged only 1.9 percent per year despite money supply growth of 13.5 percent per year. But this is easily explained. Singapore experienced extraordinary economic growth in the 1980s. Thus the demand for money in that country rose quite rapidly, offsetting most of the effects of the rapid increase in the money supply.

The Onset of Inflation

We assumed above in our discussion of inflation (Figure 10-9) that the demand curve for money never shifts. That is, the inflation results from the continuously increasing money supply, which in turn causes a continuous increase in the price level; but this

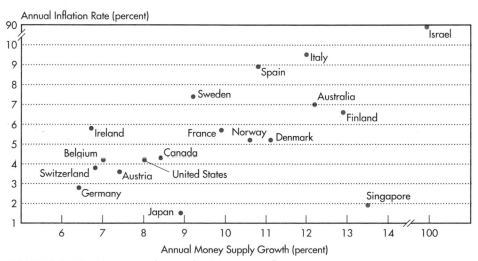

FIGURE 10-10 Money supply growth rates versus inflation rates. These are average annual rates for the decade of the 1980s. [*Source: World Development Report of the OECD* (Paris: 1993).]

is due to continuous movement *along* the demand curve. The quantity of money demanded increases, but demand itself remains fixed.

Now let us start all over, with a slightly different scenario. Suppose that the money supply and the price level are constant, with no inflation. Then one day the authorities announce that beginning immediately, they will increase the money supply at the rate of 10 percent per year. What happens?

Figure 10-9 shows what the picture looks like once the continuous money supply increase is under way. There is inflation of 10 percent per year. However, we want now to think specifically about what happens at the instant the new policy goes into effect.

First, notice that in a world of inflation, money loses value as it sits in your pocket. You can begin the week carrying enough money to buy lunch, but a day or two later, without having spent anything, you are carrying only enough to buy a snack. Inflation reduces the desirability of holding money, which causes people to want less of it.

Hence the prospect of inflation makes people want to hold less money in *real* terms. Recall that a change in the demand for real money holdings causes a shift in the money demand curve (as opposed to a movement along that curve). Therefore, *the demand for money jumps downward at the moment the new policy is initiated.* This decrease in demand causes the price level to jump upward.

These events are graphed in Figure 10-11(*a*). Initially the supply of money is

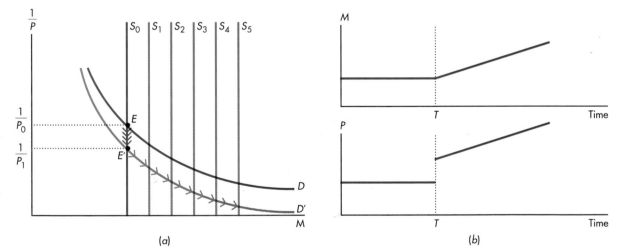

FIGURE 10-11   The onset of inflation.
(*a*) The economy starts in equilibrium at *E*, the intersection of money demand curve *D* and money supply curve S_0. The price level is P_0. At some time *T*, the government begins a policy of increasing the money supply at a steady rate. Once the policy is under way, the price level increases at the same rate as the money supply. However, just at time *T*, there is a drop in the *demand* for money, shifting the demand curve down to *D'* and the equilibrium point from *E* to *E'* and creating a sudden jump upward (to P_1) in the price level. From that time on, the inflation proceeds smoothly along the new demand curve *D'*. (*b*) *Top*, the behavior of the money supply *M* over time; *bottom*, the behavior of the price level over time. Although the money supply does not jump at time *T*, the price level does.

represented by the supply curve S_0, and the economy is in equilibrium at point E with a price level of P_0. Now people are informed that the government will immediately begin pushing the supply of money rightward at a rate of 10 percent per year. Recognizing that this means they will be living in an inflationary world, people immediately demand less money, so the demand curve jumps down to D'. The equilibrium point is now E', indicating that the price level has jumped *upward* to P_1. Then, as the supply curve undertakes its rightward march, equilibrium follows along the new demand curve D', as shown by the arrows, with the price level rising continuously at 10 percent per year.

Figure 10-11(b) shows the behavior of the money supply and the price level over time. At time T, when the new policy is announced and takes effect, the price level jumps even though the money supply does not. Thereafter, the price level and the money supply move upward at exactly the same rate.

A change in price can cause only a change in quantity demanded, not a change in demand. In Figure 10-11(a), we observe an immediate shift in demand *not* because the price level is changing but because people know that the price level is *going* to change. Demand shifts from what is appropriate in a noninflationary world (curve D) to what is appropriate in an inflationary world (curve D'). This is a one-shot change, and the new demand curve remains in effect for as long as the inflation does. The inflation itself—as opposed to the *anticipation* of future inflation—causes only changes in quantity demanded, as the equilibrium point moves along the new demand curve D'.

Overshooting:

An effect that occurs at the onset of an inflation, when money demand drops and therefore the equilibrium price level jumps upward.

The additional jump in the price level that occurs at the beginning of an inflation is sometimes called the **overshooting** of the price level because the price level rises by more than the money supply does. The word "overshooting" can be misleading, since it seems to connote that people have made some sort of miscalculation and have gone beyond their goals. Do not be misled by this. In fact, overshooting occurs precisely because people accomplish just what they set out to do. In a time of inflation, people want to hold less real money. If the price level and the money supply rose at exactly the same rate, then real money holdings would remain fixed. It is only through overshooting that people are able to reduce their real money holdings.

Welfare

Suppose the government initiates a policy of increasing the money supply at a rate of 10 percent per year. In the long run, the price level and the money supply both increase by 10 percent. Nothing real changes, and society as a whole is neither enriched nor impoverished.

However, we must also consider what happens at the very beginning of the inflation. At that moment the demand for money jumps downward and the price level overshoots to a new, higher level. Instantly, people who are holding money all lose because their real money holdings decline. Their loss is not offset by any gain to anyone.

When real money holdings decline, life becomes less convenient. You have to visit the bank more often, as you run out of money more frequently. You sometimes must pass up a bargain because you have insufficient cash. If you own a grocery store, you are keeping less in the cash register and will run out of change more often.

In Germany in 1922, prices multiplied by a factor of 600 million in a single year. Economist John Maynard Keynes reported that because prices were rising so rapidly, tavern goers routinely ordered several beers at the beginning of their evening out. Waiting an hour before ordering a second round meant ordering the second round at a substantially higher price. As a result, tavern goers drank a lot of warm beer that was poured at eight o'clock but not consumed until midnight. One cost of the German hyperinflation was the forgone opportunity to drink cold beer.

The Hungarian Hyperinflation

For about a year after World War II, Hungary experienced a hyperinflation that made the early German experience look tame. Between August 1945 and July 1946, Hungarian prices multiplied (on average) by a factor of more than 100 every month.

At that rate, a cup of coffee that cost 10 cents on June 1 would have cost $10 on July 1, $1000 on August 1, $100,000 on September 1, $10 million on October 1, and $1 billion by November 1. By New Year's Day, that same cup of coffee would have sold for $10 trillion, which exceeds the total (nominal) annual income of all present-day Americans.

The consequences for Hungarians were devastating. Workers were paid as often as three times a day, as nominal wage rates changed continuously. Once they received their wages, it was imperative to spend the money—either on goods or on bonds—immediately: even an hour's delay meant a significant loss in the money's value. In many households, one family member took on the full-time job of shuttling back and forth between the workplace and the marketplace.

The time and effort that were expended on dodging the effects of inflation could otherwise have been devoted to productive pursuits, and Hungarian real output fell dramatically as a consequence.

Expected versus Unexpected Inflation

We have so far discussed the effects of an expected inflation. When inflation comes unexpectedly, we get exactly the same effects (the overshoot occurs as soon as people recognize that an inflation is under way and therefore adjust their money demand). But when inflation is unexpected, there are additional effects.

An unexpected inflation is a boon to net borrowers and a burden to net lenders. When loans are denominated in dollars, as they usually are in this country, an unexpected inflation offers borrowers the opportunity to repay their loans in inflated dollars. The loans are repaid in nominal dollars; the real value of those dollars is less than what either the borrower or the lender originally intended.

The same thing is *not* true of an expected inflation. If it is known in advance what the amount of inflation will be, then the nominal interest rate reflects this knowledge and compensates lenders for the effects of the inflation. Suppose that the equilibrium real interest rate is 5 percent. Then in a period of zero inflation, the nominal rate will also be 5 percent. But if a 10 percent inflation is expected, the nominal rate will be 15 percent, so the real value of loan payments is not affected.

If you receive a pension of $100 per month, fixed in nominal terms, then you are a lender (since most of your wealth is currently on loan to the pension fund, which pays it back to you in monthly installments). An unexpected inflation is bad for you and good for the owners of the pension fund. An expected inflation, by contrast, would have been factored into the calculation of the nominal payment at the time your pension contract was first negotiated.

Thus an unexpected inflation creates additional winners and losers. However, *for every additional loser there is an additional winner, and for every additional winner there is an additional loser*. Every dollar borrowed is a dollar lent. There are two parties to each transaction, one of whom loses and one of whom wins.

From a viewpoint that encompasses all of society, then, an unexpected inflation is neither better nor worse than an expected one. Both an expected and an unexpected inflation cause people to demand less money (once they become aware of the new economic environment), and that reduces their real money holdings, creating real net social costs. An unexpected inflation has the additional effect of shuffling wealth around, but it does not destroy any additional wealth in the process.[5]

It is important to distinguish between two related questions: First, "Did people foresee the inflation *before* it began?" Second, "Did people perceive the inflation *after* it began?" In this chapter, we've called inflation "expected" or "unexpected" according to whether or not it was foreseen, but we have always assumed that everyone is aware of the inflation from the moment it begins.

In Chapter 14 we will relax that assumption, so that even once the inflation is under way, people might not be aware of it. Therefore, we will call inflation "expected" or "unexpected" according to whether people perceive it while it is happening.

Thus the phrase "expected inflation" (like its opposite "unexpected inflation") has two different meanings depending upon the context.

10-5 THE ROLE OF GOVERNMENT

It will not surprise you to learn that in real life money does not come from helicopters. The helicopter story illustrates many valuable lessons, but the time has come to replace it with a more realistic picture of how money is supplied.

The details of the money supply process do not concern us here; you can read something about them in Chapter 15. For now, we simply note that governments create money and put it into circulation by using it to buy things. Conversely, when

---

[5]In Chapter 14, we will discuss some additional ways in which an unexpected inflation can cause social disruption by making it difficult for people to determine the real prices of the goods they buy and sell. But that phenomenon does not concern us here.

governments want to decrease the supply of money, they can do so by selling things, collecting money, and destroying the money after it is collected.

Suppose the government decides to increase the money supply from M_0 to M_1. It does so by printing $M_1 - M_0$ new dollar bills and using them to purchase goods. This increase in the money supply causes the price level to rise just as it did after the helicopter drop of Figure 10-4: those who sell goods to the government end up with more money than they would prefer to hold, and in their efforts to trade it away they bid up prices.

As in the case of the helicopter drop, there is no change in real money holdings and no change in the quantity of goods available. There is, however, one additional effect worth noting. Although the quantity of goods in the economy does not change, some of those goods do change hands. For example, if the government buys turkeys for postal workers, then postal workers end up with more turkeys. (We shall assume that the goods purchased by the government are given to somebody. If the government spends wastefully, there are additional effects, but those effects are due to the waste, not to the printing and spending of money.) So some people gain from the government's actions.

Because printing and spending money does not increase society's net wealth and because some people gain from it, there must be others who lose. We don't have to look far to discover who those others are. They are the people who are holding money at the moment the price level increases. These people see the value of their money decrease because of the rise in prices, and they are made poorer by the process. The wealth lost by money holders exactly equals the amount gained by the beneficiaries of the government's largesse.

Therefore, *an increase in the money supply is exactly like a tax on money holdings*. It takes wealth from the pockets of money holders and transfers that wealth to the government (which then passes it on). A direct tax on money held would have precisely the same effects. The two alternatives are equivalent in every meaningful way, and there is no reason to distinguish between them. Hence we say that an increase in the money supply *is* a tax on money held.

Seigniorage:
The right to create money.

The right to print and spend money is called **seigniorage** and is jealously guarded by most national governments. There is no reason, in principle, why individuals or firms could not print and circulate their own money; indeed, that was standard practice in the United States during the nineteenth century. But governments today generally prefer to maintain a monopoly on seigniorage.

The Algebra of Seigniorage

We have noted that when the government prints and spends money, the gains of the winners (those who receive the proceeds) precisely equal the losses of the losers (those who are holding money at the moment the price level jumps). We know that the gains must exactly equal the losses because there is no change in the quantity of goods. However, it can be instructive to reach this same conclusion in a different way, by actually calculating the gains, calculating the losses, and seeing that they are equal.

Suppose that the money supply is initially M_0 and the price level is initially P_0. The government decides to increase the money supply to M_1, thereby causing the price level to rise to P_1. Because the price level rises in exactly the same proportion as the money supply, we can write

$$\frac{M_0}{P_0} = \frac{M_1}{P_1}$$

To calculate the gains and losses, we must make an assumption about the exact timing of the jump in the price level: Does it occur before or after the government actually spends the new money? Different assumptions lead to different calculations, although both choices ultimately lead to the conclusion that gains equal losses. For illustrative purposes, we arbitrarily assume that prices do not jump until just *after* the moment that the government spends the money.

In that case, the government is able to spend $M_1 - M_0$ new dollars to purchase goods at the old price level of P_0. The quantity of goods that the government buys is equal to

$$\frac{M_1 - M_0}{P_0}$$

This measures the gains of the winners—those who get the goods that the government buys.

Next we shall calculate the losses of the losers. After the government spending, people hold M_1 dollars, which at the old price level are worth M_1/P_0 in real terms. However, at this point the price level jumps to P_1 and the real value of money holdings drops to M_1/P_1. The loss to money holders is

$$\frac{M_1}{P_0} - \frac{M_1}{P_1}$$

Using our earlier equation $M_0/P_0 = M_1/P_1$, we can rewrite this expression as

$$\frac{M_1}{P_0} - \frac{M_1}{P_1} = \frac{M_1}{P_0} - \frac{M_0}{P_0} = \frac{M_1 - M_0}{P_0}$$

which is exactly the same expression that we found for the gains to the winners. The algebra confirms our expectation that when the government prints money, the gains of the winners just equal the losses of the losers.

The Inflation Tax

When the government increases the supply of money in a single burst, it taxes money holdings at a particular moment. When it raises the supply of money over time, creating inflation, it taxes money holdings on an ongoing basis. We are about to contrast the effects of one-shot changes in the money supply with the effects of ongoing changes. However, the conclusions we will draw apply equally well to *all* taxes. Therefore, we should first digress to discuss some general phenomena common to any tax on any good. Then we will apply what we learn to the case of inflation.

A Digression on Taxation

Suppose the government imposes a one-time-only, unannounced, and unexpected tax on coffee. Everyone holding a coffee cup at the moment the tax is announced must pay $1. If 15,000 people are drinking coffee at that moment, then the government collects $15,000 and coffee drinkers lose $15,000. The gains exactly match the losses. Wealth is transferred, but society as a whole (which includes the people to whom the government gives the $15,000) is neither richer nor poorer.

Suppose, on the other hand, that the government institutes an *ongoing* tax on coffee. Now the consequences are quite different. The new policy creates an incentive to learn to drink tea or to eat one's donuts dry. Many people will choose to drink less coffee. Some may give it up altogether.

The revenue that the government collects is still equal to the taxes that the coffee drinkers pay. But coffee drinkers now suffer an additional loss: they now drink less coffee than before. This additional loss to coffee drinkers is not offset by a gain to anyone. A loss with no offsetting gain is called a **deadweight loss.**[6]

Now the losses of the losers actually exceed the gains of the winners. Coffee drinkers pay (say) $10,000 in taxes per year and reduce their coffee consumption by (say) 1000 cups with a monetary value to them of $2000 per year. Their net loss is $12,000. But the gain to the winners is only the $10,000 that is collected in taxes. The remaining $2000 per year is a deadweight loss.

An ongoing tax has another unsettling aspect, separate from the issue of deadweight loss. It is this: If the tax rate is set too high, the tax might yield very little revenue to the government. A coffee tax of $1 per cup might bring in $10,000 per year, but a coffee tax of $100 per cup would certainly not bring in $1 million per year. In fact, a coffee tax of $100 per cup would likely bring in almost no revenue at all, because almost nobody would drink coffee that is taxed so heavily.

Figure 10-12, a graph of tax revenue as a function of tax rate, illustrates the tax collector's dilemma. When the tax rate is set at 0, there is no tax revenue. When the tax rate is set very high, at T_H, there is also no tax revenue. Some intermediate tax rate—T_M in the graph—yields the maximum possible revenue. Once the tax rate is set at T_M, there is simply no way to earn additional revenue by adjusting the coffee tax. The curve shown in the figure is sometimes called the **Laffer curve** after economist Arthur Laffer, who argued that U.S. income tax rates were above T_M in the early 1980s.

What is the optimal tax rate? You might say that the obvious answer is T_M. However, this is correct only if you believe that it is desirable to maximize government revenue. A skeptic who dislikes government might argue that the optimal tax rate is *zero*. Certainly if your only goal is to minimize deadweight losses, then the optimal tax rate is zero. In many situations, there is a trade-off between the need to raise government revenues (say, to purchase public goods that people cannot easily purchase for themselves) and the desire to minimize deadweight losses. If your primary inter-

Deadweight loss:
A loss to one party that is not offset by a gain to any other party.

Laffer curve:
A curve showing tax revenue as a function of the tax rate.

---

[6]If you have studied microeconomics, you may recognize the deadweight loss as a reduction in consumers' surplus. If the supply of coffee is upward-sloping, there is a reduction in producers' surplus that contributes to the deadweight loss as well.

Tax Revenue

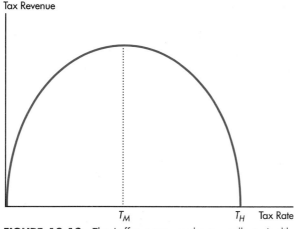

T_M T_H Tax Rate

FIGURE 10-12 The Laffer curve, or the tax collector's dilemma. Tax revenues fall when tax rates are increased beyond a certain point T_M.

est is maximizing government revenue, you will prefer a tax rate near T_M; if your primary interest is maximizing the welfare of coffee drinkers, you will prefer a tax rate near zero.

But the crucial point is that *nobody* prefers a tax rate higher than T_M. At such rates, coffee drinking is heavily discouraged, there is a lot of deadweight loss, *and* government revenue is less than it could be. Only somebody whose goal is to discourage coffee drinking might support such a high tax rate.

The concept of the Laffer curve has been summarized this way: Any tax at all creates a deadweight loss, which is unfortunate. A very high tax also leads to low government revenue, which is insane.

Morals for Inflation

Now back to the effects of money supply changes. A one-shot jump in the money supply is a one-shot tax on money holdings. Like a one-shot tax on coffee, it creates winners and losers but no deadweight loss. What the losers (money holders) lose, the winners (recipients of government purchases) win.

An ongoing increase in the money supply is an ongoing tax on money holdings. Just as an ongoing tax on coffee reduces the demand for coffee, reduces the quantity of coffee consumed, and thereby leaves coffee drinkers worse off, so an ongoing increase in the money supply reduces the demand for money, reduces the amount of real money held, and thereby leaves money holders worse off. The government collects revenues, which are exactly equal to what money holders lose on a day-to-day basis. But there is an additional loss to money holders that is not offset by gains to anyone.

That additional loss manifests itself through overshooting. Refer again to Figure 10-11(*b*). It shows that after time *T*, the price level and money supply rise at the same rate. The rising price level costs money holders exactly the amount by which the rising money supply increases the government's spending power. But the overshoot at time T represents a jump in the price level that does not correspond to any new money created by the government. The overshoot hurts money holders without benefiting anyone. It creates a deadweight loss perfectly analogous to the deadweight loss associated with an ongoing tax on coffee.

Now let us consider another problem, separate from the problem of deadweight loss. We just saw that when tax rates are set too high, tax revenues can be very low. In the case of the inflation tax, here is what that means: When the government sets too high an inflation rate, there is a very large decrease in the demand for money and so a very large overshoot. The overshoot reduces the value of newly printed money even before the government has a chance to spend it. Dollar bills come off the printing presses rapidly, but each bill is worth so little that the government's real purchasing power is less than it would be if the presses were slowed down.

10-6 MONEY AND INTEREST RATES

Financial journalists frequently report that the government wants to raise or lower interest rates by changing the money supply, and government officials speak in similar terms. Are they correct in assuming that the size of the money supply can affect the rate of interest?

First, let us dispose of a widely used but incorrect argument that goes like this: "The interest rate is the price of money. When the supply of a good increases, its price must fall. Therefore, an increase in the money supply must lead to a decrease in the interest rate."

This argument goes wrong in its first sentence. The real interest rate, as we know from earlier chapters, is not the price of money at all. Instead, it is a measure of the price of *current consumption* relative to future consumption. Even in a world without money people would borrow and lend, and so there would be a prevailing interest rate. But in a world without money there would be no "price of money." Because an interest rate can exist without a price of money, they must be two different things.

Indeed, we already know that the price of money is $1/P$, where P is the price level. The term $1/P$ is unrelated to the interest rate.

Disposing of an incorrect argument does not settle the question. Can the money supply affect the interest rate, or can it not? Actually, we should ask two separate questions: First, can the money supply affect the *real* interest rate? Second, can the money supply affect the *nominal* interest rate?

We have already seen that the real rate of interest is determined by the demand and supply curves for current consumption. A change in the money supply has no effect on either of these curves and so cannot affect the point of equilibrium. *The money supply has no impact on the equilibrium real interest rate.*

Some economists, however, believe that a change in the money supply can cause a temporary disequilibrium in the market for current consumption and consequently can have a temporary effect on the real interest rate—but only until equilibrium is restored. In Chapters 12 and 13, we will see how this possibility can occur.

To see whether the money supply affects the *nominal* interest rate, recall that the nominal interest rate is the sum of the real interest rate and the inflation rate. Although the supply of money does not affect the equilibrium real interest rate, it can affect the nominal interest rate by changing the inflation rate. Now we can apply what you have learned in this chapter: A one-shot increase in the money supply does not cause inflation (it causes only a one-shot increase in the price level) and therefore does not affect the nominal interest rate. A continuous increase in the money supply does cause inflation, and so it does increase the nominal interest rate.

Notice that the direction of this effect is the opposite of what you would expect if you had bought into the widely used but incorrect price-of-money argument. A continuous increase in the money supply causes nominal interest rates to *rise,* not fall.

SUMMARY

Individuals demand money in order to engage in transactions—buying and selling goods and services. Because the price level P is the average price of goods in terms of money, the inverse of the price level $1/P$ is the price of money in terms of goods.

The money demand curve has the price of money ($1/P$) on the vertical axis and the quantity of money (M) on the horizontal axis. The shape of the curve reflects the fact that people have a target value for their real money holdings M/P; thus the equation of the curve is given by M/P = constant, where the constant is equal to that target value.

When people decide to hold more money in real terms (that is, more purchasing power), the value of the constant increases and the money demand curve shifts rightward. Such a shift could be caused by a rise in income or a fall in the interest rate. Similarly, a fall in income or a rise in the interest rate reduces the demand for money and causes the money demand curve to shift leftward.

Money is supplied by the government's monetary authority. In equilibrium, the quantity of money supplied equals the quantity of money demanded. The price level adjusts until the money market is in equilibrium.

If the government increases the money supply, the price level rises by the same proportion, so the fraction M/P remains constant. The rise in the price level occurs because each individual tries to spend the extra dollars he receives from the government; with no new goods available, prices of goods are bid up. There is no net change in economic welfare.

An increase in money demand (due to, say, an increase in income or a fall in the interest rate) causes a drop in the equilibrium price level. The drop occurs because people attempt to sell goods to acquire more money. There is a net increase in economic welfare due to the fact that people hold more real money, making transactions more convenient.

Inflation is a continuous rise in the price level. Only a continuous rise in the money supply or a continuous decline in the money demand can cause inflation. The former is much more common.

When the money supply is growing continuously, the price level grows at the same rate as the money supply. When the growth rate of the money supply increases, the demand for money falls. Thus the price level must jump upward to maintain equilibrium in the money market. This jump is called overshooting.

Unexpected inflations benefit borrowers at the expense of lenders because most loans are denominated in nominal terms. Expected inflations do not redistribute wealth.

When a government issues money, it earns the benefits of seigniorage—the government can use newly printed money to buy goods. The resulting rise in the price level costs money holders an amount equal to what the government earns through seigniorage. Thus the issuance of new money is equivalent to a tax on the holders of existing money.

When a government continuously issues new money, it continuously earns the benefits of seigniorage. However, the ongoing inflation that results causes individuals to hold less real money. This reduces the real value of the government's seigniorage and also creates a deadweight loss: a reduction in economic welfare due to the fact that people now hold less real money.

The equilibrium real interest rate is unaffected by changes in the money supply. The nominal interest rate is the sum of the real interest rate plus the inflation rate and hence is affected by changes in the inflation rate, which in turn is affected by changes in the growth rate of the money supply.

PROBLEM SET

1. Suppose the government confiscates and burns half of everybody's money.
   a. What happens to the price level?
   b. Explain the process by which the new price level is achieved.
2. Suppose that a new law is passed declaring that every dollar bill is now worth only 50 cents, every $5 bill is now worth only $2.50, and so forth.
   a. What happens to the price level?
   b. Explain the process by which the new price level is achieved.
3. Suppose that a fall in productivity leads to a decline in real incomes.
   a. What happens to the price level?
   b. Explain the process by which the new price level is achieved.
   c. What can you say about economic welfare in this situation?
4. *True or false:* In hard economic times, people don't have enough money to buy all the goods that are produced. The government could help to solve this problem by printing and distributing enough money so that people can afford to buy the existing goods.
5. *True or false:* The invention of credit cards probably caused the price level to rise.
6. *True or false:* If automatic teller machines were installed on every street corner, the price level would rise.
7. *True or false:* A rise in the interest rate would cause the price level to rise.
8. *True or false:* If crime in the streets were eliminated, the price level would rise.
9. *True or false:* The *nominal* quantity of money is determined by what the authorities choose to supply, but the *real* quantity of money is determined by what individuals choose to demand.
10. Scrooge McDuck is a fabulously wealthy businessman who keeps a vault full of cash so that he can bathe in money every night. *True or false:* When Scrooge hoards cash, he

benefits nobody but himself. It would be better for the rest of us if he would spend some of that money.

11. The government has decided to raise taxes by $10 billion this year only, but it has not yet decided whether to spend the proceeds on an entirely worthless aircraft carrier or to convert the proceeds to dollar bills and burn them.

    a. How does each plan affect the demand for and supply of current goods, and how does each affect the interest rate?

    b. How does each plan affect the demand for and supply of money, and how does each affect the price level?

12. In Lower Slobbovia, the price level and the money supply have both been constant for a long time. However, the productivity of Lower Slobbovian workers has just begun to fall and is expected to continue falling steadily over time.

    a. How does the Lower Slobbovian price level behave over time?

    b. How does the Lower Slobbovian price level behave immediately?

13. Until 1980, Upper and Lower Slobbovia had equal money supplies and equal price levels. In 1980, Upper Slobbovia's money supply began to increase slowly, and it is still doing so. Lower Slobbovia's money supply remained fixed until 1990; then it began to increase rapidly, and it is still doing so. The Lower Slobbovian money supply has just caught up with the Upper Slobbovian money supply; at this moment, the money supplies in the two countries are equal. In which country is the price level higher, and why?

14. In Llareggub, all money is stamped with an expiration date. Once a year, citizens bring their money to government offices to have it restamped; without a current stamp the money is worthless. The government charges a fee of $1 to stamp $10 worth of currency.

    a. What happened to the price level in Llareggub when this plan was first put into effect?

    b. Who gains and who loses from this plan? Do the losses exceed the gains?

15. Suppose that the government of France institutes a policy of trading French francs for U.S. dollars and stockpiling the dollars. What are the consequences in the United States?

16. Suppose that the price level and the money supply are initially constant. Then the government announces that henceforth it will *decrease* the money supply at 10 percent per year. What is the immediate effect on the price level? What are the welfare consequences?

17. Suppose that the price level and the money supply have been steadily growing at 10 percent per year when the government announces that henceforth the money supply will grow at only 5 percent per year. What is the immediate effect on the price level?

18. Suppose that the supply of and demand for money are initially constant but that one day people's real incomes begin to rise at a steady rate of 2 percent per year. The growth in real incomes is expected to continue at this rate forever.

    a. In the long run, how does the price level behave?

    b. At the moment that incomes begin to rise, what happens to the price level?

    c. *True or false:* In the situation described, the government can increase the money supply on a continuous basis without causing inflation.

19. Suppose that the government prints money and that the price level jumps just *before* the government actually spends the new money. Write algebraic expressions for the seigniorage gains and the losses to money holders. Are the two expressions equivalent?

20. *True or false:* If all prices, wages, and other payments were indexed so that they automatically adjusted to changes in the price level, then inflation would have no bad effects.

21. Suppose that all dollar bills are stamped with their date of issue and that their value grows over time at the nominal rate of interest. For example, if the nominal interest rate is 10 percent, then a 1-year-old dollar bill is worth $1.10.

    a. How does inflation affect the demand for money?

    b. At the beginning of an inflation, is there more or less overshooting than there would be in the absence of this plan?

    c. Is the deadweight loss from the inflation tax greater or less than would be the case in the absence of this plan?

Chapter 11

The Neoclassical Model

We have reached a milestone. Our basic model is now complete. We began by modeling a simple endowment economy in which people trade goods today for goods tomorrow. We then embellished the model to account for the role of government, investment, labor, and money. The resulting *neoclassical model* of the economy, as developed in Chapters 3 through 10, is a powerful engine for understanding how the economy responds to shocks and to policy changes.

The neoclassical model describes the entire economy using only tools (like supply and demand analysis) that are well understood and well accepted in microeconomics. Better yet, there is general agreement among economists that at least in the long run, the model provides a good basis for making accurate predictions about consumption, investment, labor markets, inflation, trade balances, and economic growth.

However, many economists believe that the model as it stands is inadequate for describing certain aspects of the macroeconomy, especially in the short run. In this chapter we put all the parts of the neoclassical model together. Then we examine the model with a critical eye, paying special attention to its potential inadequacies. Chief among these are the following:

- According to the model, changes in the money market should have no effect on real output. But this seems to be contradicted by evidence.
- According to the model, all unemployment is "voluntary" in a sense that we shall discuss in Section 11-2. Many economists have questioned the reasonableness of this implication.
- The model as it stands may be inadequate for describing business cycles—the tendency of the economy to oscillate back and forth between recessions and prosperity.
- The model suggests that the only way in which governments can improve their citizens' welfare is through the provision of public goods. By contrast, many economists believe, on empirical grounds, that carefully chosen government policies can alleviate unemployment and smooth out business cycles. The model fails to offer any support for this belief.

Because of their concern about these shortcomings, many economists have suggested modifications to the basic neoclassical model. These modifications take the model in several different—and mutually contradictory—directions. We will discuss three of these directions in Chapters 12 to 14, after elaborating on the motivation for them in this chapter.

11-1 THE NEOCLASSICAL MODEL: AN OVERVIEW

The neoclassical model of the macroeconomy is the model we have presented in Chapters 3 through 10. It is a description of the economy at a particular time and can be summarized by the graphs in Figure 11-1. In those graphs, S means supply and D means demand, as usual.

Figure 11-1(a) shows the market for current goods. Equilibrium in this market determines the level of output Y_0 and the interest rate r_0.

Figure 11-1(b) shows the market for labor. The supply curve is labeled $S(r_0)$ to remind us that its location depends on the interest rate, which is currently r_0. If the interest rate were higher, the supply curve would be shifted to the right; if the interest rate were lower, it would be shifted to the left. Equilibrium in this market determines the quantity of labor utilized L_0 and the real wage rate w_0.

[Recall that the *real* wage rate is measured in units like apples per hour, or, more generally, output goods per hour, as opposed to the *nominal* wage rate, which is measured in dollars per hour. It is the *real* wage rate that is determined in panel (b) of Figure 11-1.]

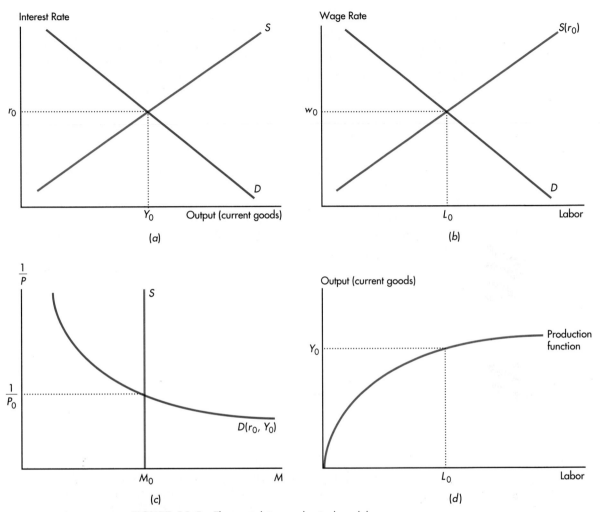

FIGURE 11-1 The complete neoclassical model.
(a) The market for current goods; (b) the market for labor; (c) the market for money. The production function (d) connects the markets for goods and labor.

These first two graphs are related by the production function in Figure 11-1(d). The equilibrium quantity of labor L_0 must be just sufficient to produce the equilibrium quantity of output Y_0.

Figure 11-1(c) shows the market for money. The demand curve has been labeled $D(r_0, Y_0)$ to remind us that its location depends on both the interest rate, which is currently r_0, and the level of income, which equals output and is currently Y_0. If the interest rate were higher, the demand for money would be lower; if the interest rate were lower, the demand for money would be higher. If income were higher, the demand for money would be higher; if income were lower, the demand for money would be lower. Equilibrium in this market determines the price level P_0.

The Locations of the Curves

The curves in Figure 11-1 depend on a variety of factors that are not explicit in the diagram. However, *all these factors can ultimately be traced back to just two things: tastes and technology.*

Consider the market for current goods. Here the demand curve is the sum of the demand curves for consumption and investment. The demand curve for consumption arises from individual **tastes**—people's preferences among various options. The demand curve for investment arises from the marginal product of capital, which depends on the state of **technology**—the relationship that transforms inputs into outputs—and the quantity of labor available (and that depends, in turn, on the tastes of workers). The demand curve for consumption shifts in response to changes in wealth (that is, current or future income), and the demand curve for investment shifts in response to changes in technology or the availability of labor.

The supply curve in the goods market is derived from equilibrium in the labor market, with the production function serving as an intermediary. To get each point on this supply curve, we proceed as follows: Fix an interest rate r; draw the corresponding labor supply curve, as in Figure 11-1(b); read off the equilibrium quantity of labor L; use the production function to find the corresponding quantity of output Y; plot the point (r, Y), which is on the goods market supply curve. This procedure is based on both technology (as embodied in the production function) and workers' tastes (as embodied in the labor supply curve).

Next consider the market for labor. The labor demand curve is derived from the marginal product of labor, which depends on the state of technology and on how much capital is available for workers to employ. (That quantity of capital in turn depends on past investment decisions, which were themselves guided by tastes and technology.) It shifts when there is a change in technology or a change in the quantity of existing capital.

The labor supply curve reflects the tastes of individual workers. It can shift in response to anything (other than the wage rate) that leads workers to supply more or less labor. (Changes in the wage rate are reflected by movements along the supply curve, not shifts of the curve.) Chief among the factors that can shift the supply curve are:

- *Changes in wealth* (that is, current or future income). When workers are wealthier, they work less and the curve shifts left.
- *Intertemporal substitution.* If workers learn that they are unusually productive in the present, they work more; if they learn that they are unusually unproductive, they work less.
- *Interest-rate effects.* If the interest rate rises, workers work more and the supply curve shifts right.

The label $S(r_0)$ in the labor market diagram emphasizes only the interest-rate effect.

Finally, Figure 11-1(c) shows the market for money. The money supply curve depends on what the authorities choose to supply. This is the only curve in the model that does not depend directly on tastes and technology for its location. On the other

Tastes:

Individuals' preference orderings among various options; reflected in the demand curve for goods and the supply curve for labor.

Technology:

The functional relationship that transforms inputs such as labor and capital into outputs; represented by production functions that help give rise to the supply curve for goods and the demand curve for labor.

hand, an adequate model of how the authorities make decisions (which we have not provided) would presumably have tastes and technology as its foundation.

The money demand curve depends on technology (like the technology of banking services, credit cards, ATMs, etc.) and tastes (how much people are willing to sacrifice in exchange for the convenience of carrying an extra dollar). It depends also on the interest rate and income, as determined in panel (*a*). The label on the demand curve in Figure 11-1(*c*) emphasizes these latter dependencies.

Market Clearing in the Neoclassical Model

The chief distinguishing characteristic of the neoclassical model is that *all markets are always in equilibrium*. Each market is cleared by a freely adjusting price that responds to the forces of supply and demand. That is:

In the neoclassical model, all markets clear.

You can see in Figure 11-1 that *the interest rate* r *clears the goods market, the wage rate* w *clears the labor market, and the price level* P *clears the money market.*

We saw in Chapter 5 that it is possible to find the equilibrium interest rate by looking at the market for future goods (or bonds) instead of the market for current goods. The price (discounted present value) of a bond is $1/(1 + r)$. Because the bond market yields the same interest rate as the goods market does, it is unnecessary to include both markets in the model.

11-2 INADEQUACIES OF THE NEOCLASSICAL MODEL

The neoclassical model is the microeconomic foundation of all modern macroeconomics. Each of the pieces—labor supply and demand, production, consumption, investment, government borrowing and lending, and money—is treated as it would be treated by a microeconomist specializing in that field. None of the pieces is controversial by itself.

Yet, when we put the pieces together, the composite picture does not seem to confront many of the most important economic phenomena we observe around us. The model fails to acknowledge that changes in the money market can affect output and employment. It does not deal adequately with unemployment—the inability of people to find jobs. Neither does it seem to account for the occasional declines in output known as **recessions.**

Recession:

A temporary economywide decline in output.

If we are interested only in the long run, we can largely ignore these concerns. Recessions, for example, are by definition temporary. Thus most economists are reasonably comfortable with the neoclassical model as a description of the economic long run (though different economists might give very different answers if you ask them to tell you how long the long run is). On the other hand, many economists believe that to describe the short run adequately, the model must be either expanded or modified. In this section, we elaborate on the reasons for that belief.

The Real–Nominal Dichotomy

Real–nominal dichotomy:

The conclusion that changes in the real market affect the money market but changes in the money market have no effect on the markets for goods and labor.

Neutrality of money:

A phrase used synonymously with "real–nominal dichotomy."

In Figure 11-1, panels (*a*) and (*b*), augmented by the production function, represent the "real" side of the neoclassical economy, while panel (*c*) represents the "monetary" side. The goods and labor markets in panels (*a*) and (*b*) interact in complicated ways. For example, the supply of goods, in (*a*), and the demand for labor, in (*b*), are both derived from the production function in panel (*d*); anything that affects the production function will affect the goods market and the labor market simultaneously. For another example, any change in the equilibrium interest rate, from (*a*), causes a shift in the labor supply curve, in (*b*). For yet another example, if a change in working conditions causes a shift in the labor supply curve, in (*b*), then the supply of goods, in (*a*), will shift also.

In short, the goods market affects the labor market, and the labor market affects the goods market. By contrast, the money market interacts with the goods and labor markets in one direction only. Changes in the goods market can affect the equilibrium interest rate and output level, and hence the location of the money demand curve. But in the neoclassical model, *changes in the money market have no effect at all on the goods and labor markets*. Economists summarize this observation by saying that in the neoclassical model, *money is neutral*. That is, the model exhibits a **real–nominal dichotomy,** which is sometimes referred to simply as the **neutrality of money.**

➡ *Exercise 11-1*

When the money supply increases, does the *nominal* wage rate change?

Changes in the price level are sometimes called *nominal* changes because they affect only the *names* of things that people care about, rather than the things themselves. When the price level is $1 per apple, three apples are called "$3 worth of apples." If the price level doubles, those same three apples are called "$6 worth of apples." But three apples are three apples, whatever they are called. In the neoclassical model, if your real income is three apples per year when the price level is low, it remains three apples per year when the price level is high. In the model, changes in the price level cannot affect anyone's real income. In summary:

> In the neoclassical model, changes in the money supply have no effect on real variables: quantities and relative prices. Changes in the money supply affect only nominal values.

Yet a majority of economists believe that in the world we inhabit (as opposed to the world of the model) changes in the money market actually *do* have real effects; in particular, changes in the money supply can affect both output and employment. If that majority is correct and if the model predicts otherwise, then the model must be incomplete. In Chapter 12, we will say more about the evidence on this issue.

Market Clearing and Unemployment

Voluntary unemployment:

Unemployment that occurs because individuals choose not to accept available jobs.

In the neoclassical model, the labor market is always cleared: the amount of labor that employers want to hire is exactly equal to the amount of labor that workers want to provide. Every worker who wants to work is able to do so.

This does *not* mean that there is no such thing as unemployment. What it *does* mean is that all unemployment is **voluntary unemployment**—it occurs because workers *choose* to remain unemployed.

The fact that a person's unemployment is voluntary does not mean that it is not painful. Such a person would rather have the alternative of working at a higher wage, in which case he might well choose to work; but that alternative is simply not available. Saying that someone is voluntarily unemployed does not mean that the person is happy about the situation. It only means that being unemployed is the best of the available options.

Involuntary unemployment:

Unemployment that occurs because the quantity of labor supplied exceeds the quantity demanded for labor at the going wage rate.

Figure 11-2 illustrates the sort of **involuntary unemployment** that the neoclassical model denies. At the wage rate w_1, workers want to supply L_1 hours of labor, while employers are willing to hire only L_2 hours. Those workers who would supply the additional $L_1 - L_2$ hours are involuntarily unemployed.

According to the neoclassical model, this cannot happen. Instead, some involuntarily unemployed workers will offer to work for a wage slightly lower than w_1, with the result that wages fall for everyone. At the new, lower wage, workers want to supply fewer hours, but employers want to hire more. Such downward adjustment

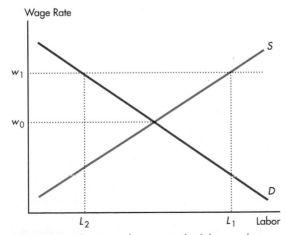

FIGURE 11-2 Unemployment in the labor market.
If the wage rate were above equilibrium (say at w_1), then workers who would supply $L_1 - L_2$ labor hours would be involuntarily unemployed. The neoclassical model denies that this can happen, as market forces would quickly depress the wage to its equilibrium level.

will continue until the equilibrium wage w_0 is reached, at which workers *choose* to supply the same number of hours that is demanded.

The neoclassical model does not rule out the possibility of high unemployment. Figure 11-3 shows a labor market equilibrium at which the wage rate is very low and the number of hours that workers choose to provide is also very low. In such a situation many workers will be voluntarily—though quite unhappily—unemployed. For them, the going wage is just so low that being at leisure is more desirable than earning income.

In reality, however, it is difficult to blame very high levels of unemployment on a picture like that depicted in Figure 11-3. During the Great Depression, unemployment reached 25 percent of the workforce. It is doubtful that the labor demand curve could have shifted far enough leftward to account for such a large decline in employment. Remember that the demand for labor depends on the marginal product of labor, which is determined by technology—and technology did not suddenly deteriorate in the 1930s.[1] More likely, some feature is lacking from the neoclassical model—something that would magnify the effects of an initial, smaller shock.

Is most of the unemployment we observe in the real world more like voluntary unemployment or more like involuntary unemployment? That turns out to be a hard question to answer, because it is difficult for an economist to be sure about exactly why people are unemployed. A question we *are* able to answer, at least in principle, is this: Which is more consistent with observed facts—a model that includes involuntary unemployment or a model in which all unemployment is voluntary?

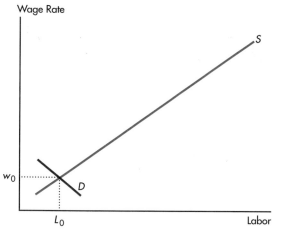

FIGURE 11-3   High unemployment in the neoclassical model.
If the marginal product of labor is very low, then the demand for labor and hence the equilibrium real wage rate are also quite low. Many workers choose to remain unemployed.

---

[1]However, the Smoot-Hawley tariff (proposed in 1929 and enacted in 1930) did substantial damage to trade opportunities and hence to productivity; some economists believe that this was equivalent to a technological shock sufficient to have triggered the Depression.

To help address this question, economists have considered two major modifications to the neoclassical model: the hypothesis that some markets do not clear immediately and the hypothesis that people do not always have enough information to foretell the future accurately. In Chapters 12 to 14 we will examine models that incorporate these two hypotheses.

Market Clearing and Recessions

The neoclassical model is inadequate in other ways. In a market-clearing model, there is no reason for output declines to affect many industries simultaneously. If demand for one good decreases, people have more income left over to spend on other goods. Hence, while the output of one good might fall, the output of another good will rise, so aggregate output is essentially unaffected. On a larger scale, a decline in one industry is likely to be offset by improvement in another, so again aggregate output is largely unchanged. Yet recessions do occur, in which output declines are economy-wide or even international.

Recessions are a part of a more general phenomenon called *business cycles,* which the neoclassical model is unable to fully explain. (The expanded models in Chapters 12 through 14 have varying degrees of success in addressing different aspects of the business cycle.) In Section 11-3, we describe real-world business cycles in greater detail, and in Section 11-4 we return to the question of how well (or poorly) the neoclassical model describes them.

Market Clearing and the Government

We have already noted that the neoclassical model does a less-than-adequate job of accounting for recessions. That model also contradicts many widespread beliefs about what the government can do if a recession does get under way. Journalists and politicians frequently assert that if the government were to increase the money supply, or increase spending, it could lower interest rates, lower unemployment, and raise output; they claim that by increasing its spending, the government can put people "back to work" and make them better off. Yet such successes are impossible according to market-clearing models, such as the neoclassical model.

Let us review what the market-clearing neoclassical model says about the tools available to governments to see why (according to the model) those tools are ineffective.

An Increase in the Money Supply

When the authorities increase the money supply, the effects are felt in the money market—Figure 11-1(*c*). But the real–nominal dichotomy in our model predicts that the effects are confined to that market. The real interest rate, the level of output, and the level of employment are still determined by the (unchanged) curves in panels (*a*) and (*b*) of Figure 11-1.

An Increase in the Growth Rate of the Money Supply

In the model, if the authorities increase the *growth rate* of the money supply, the inflation rate rises while the real interest rate remains unchanged. Once again in Figure 11-1 there is no change in either panel (*a*) or panel (*b*), and hence no change in output, employment, consumption, or investment.

Although changes in the money market have no effect on the *real* interest rate, higher inflation does mean a higher *nominal* interest rate. This is exactly the opposite of the expectation, widespread among noneconomists, that a "loose money" policy should *reduce* the nominal interest rate.

A Temporary Increase in Government Spending

All models agree that when the government spends resources to produce public goods that are undersupplied by competitive markets, there is at least a potential increase in economic welfare. But journalists and politicians frequently argue that government spending can be beneficial even without producing public goods; they say that such spending "stimulates the economy" by creating jobs, raising incomes, and thereby making people better off.

To analyze that claim, let us focus on government spending that does *not* provide public goods that are worth more than their cost; in the language of Chapter 5, let us focus on "wasteful" government spending.

Figure 11-4 traces the effects of temporary wasteful government spending in terms of the neoclassical model. For concreteness, suppose that the government undertakes a program to build a bridge to nowhere, at a cost of G. An alternative supposition could be that the government undertakes a program to build a bridge that has some value but whose cost exceeds its value by the amount G. Within the model, this is equivalent to destroying G units of output.

The first effect is therefore that the supply of current goods shifts leftward by exactly G units, as shown in Figure 11-4(*a*).

Because wasteful spending makes people poorer, the demand curve in Figure 11-4(*a*) also shifts leftward. Because the program is temporary, consumption smoothing dictates that demand shifts less than supply does. At the new equilibrium, the interest rate has risen from r_0 to r_1 and the quantity of goods available for consumption and investment has fallen from Y_0 to Y_1.

The quantity G which the government destroys is counted as output under the standard accounting systems that we studied in Chapter 2. However, our graph of the goods market does not account for wasted goods. The equilibrium quantity Y_1 does not include the government's wasteful spending.

What quantity of goods is actually produced in the economy? Prior to the government spending program, it is Y_0. After the government spending, the amount Y_1 is produced for consumption and investment, and an additional amount G is produced

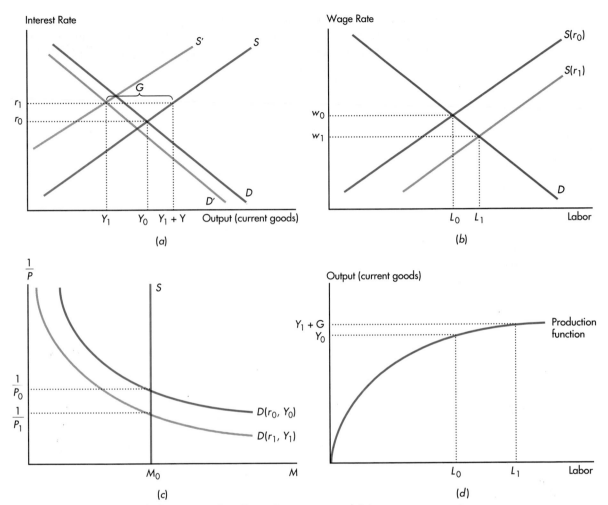

FIGURE 11-4 The effects of temporary wasteful government spending.
Assume the government wastes G units of goods. (a) The supply of goods shifts leftward the horizontal distance G. The demand for goods shifts leftward by less, because of consumption smoothing. The quantity of goods available for consumption and investment falls to Y_1. The total quantity of goods produced is $Y_1 + G$. The equilibrium interest rate rises from r_0 to r_1. (b) This interest-rate rise causes the supply of labor to shift right. Consequently, the wage rate falls from w_0 to w_1 and the amount of labor employed increases from L_0 to L_1, causing output to increase from Y_0 to $Y_1 + G$ according to the production function in (d). (c) The higher interest rate causes a drop in money demand, which in turn causes the price level to increase from P_0 to P_1. The fall in income (net of government waste) can also depress money demand.

so that the government can waste it. Total output rises from Y_0 to $Y_1 + G$ (though G units of these goods are immediately destroyed, so that only Y_1 units are available for consumption and investment).

In Figure 11-4(b), we see the effects of wasteful spending on the labor market. The labor demand curve, which is determined by the marginal product of labor, does not move. The labor supply curve shifts rightward for two reasons: The interest rate is now higher, and workers are now poorer (the income effect). Of these, the first reason is the more significant; because a temporary program makes workers only slightly poorer, the income effect is small. The new supply curve is labeled $S(r_1)$ to emphasize that its new location is primarily a result of the change in the interest rate. The quantity of labor hired rises from L_0 to L_1.

The new quantity of labor L_1 is related to the new quantity of output $Y_1 + G$ by the production function in Figure 11-4(d).

We have said that the labor supply curve in Figure 11-4(b) shifts rightward for two reasons—the interest-rate effect and the (small) income effect.

Any shift in the labor supply curve changes the equilibrium level of employment and hence the equilibrium level of output. Thus these shifts must be visible in the goods market [Figure 11-4(a)]. But the interest-rate effect and the income effect make their presence known in quite different ways.

The interest-rate effect causes a movement *along* the new supply curve S' in 11-4(a), from the point where $r = r_0$ to the new equilibrium point where $r = r_1$. No curve is shifted, so we don't even need to think about this process—the graph does all our work for us.

By contrast, the income effect causes a shift *of* the supply curve to a new curve slightly to the right of S' in 11-4(a). But because the income effect is small in this example, we can ignore that shift without substantially affecting our conclusions. We have done just that, and we shall do it again in future examples where the income effect is small.

Finally, the effects on the money market are shown in Figure 11-4(c). The money demand curve responds to both the change in the interest rate and the change in income. The increase in the interest rate causes money demand to fall. Income—or at least the component of income that is not thrown away—is down from Y_0 to Y_1; this tends to depress the demand for money still further. The two effects combine to shift the money demand curve left and hence raise the price level from P_0 to P_1.

The sum of consumption and investment is down from Y_0 to Y_1, but the sum of *all* output, including not just consumption and investment but also the output that is wasted by the government, is not down but *up*, from Y_0 to $Y_1 + G$. Which of these measures of output (or, equivalently, income) affects the money demand curve? We have assumed here that wasted output does not count, so the relevant part of income is down. This is a somewhat unconventional assumption. Some economists (and some textbooks) prefer to argue that total income is up (to $Y_1 + G$). In that case, the income effect acts to raise the demand for money, although the interest-rate effect still acts to lower the demand for money. Then either effect could dominate, and the money demand curve—and hence the price level—could move in either direction.

To summarize the conclusions of Figure 11-4, we can state the following predictions of the neoclassical model:

The effects of a temporary increase in wasteful government spending are as follows: Total output rises, consumption and investment fall, the real interest rate rises, the real wage rate falls, and the price level rises.

Concentrating in particular on the labor market, we find that real wages fall and employment rises. Workers could be earning either more or less than they earned before, depending on whether the increase in employment is larger or smaller than the decrease in wages. But *even in the case where labor earnings increase,* the spending program *still* makes people worse off. How do we know this? Recall that consumption and investment are both down. Investment affects the quantity of future consumption. So people will certainly consume less both in the present and in the future. This must mean that the taxes raised to finance the bridge-building project more than offset any gains to workers through increased employment.

The neoclassical model assumes that people care only about current consumption, future consumption, and leisure. According to that model, a bridge-building program designed solely to stimulate the economy leads to less current consumption, less future consumption, and less leisure (people work more hours in order to consume less). This makes the project a disimprovement by every possible measure.

Of course, *productive* government spending *does* have positive effects—but it would have those positive effects even if the economy weren't in a recession. The model does *not* allow for any additional mechanism whereby government spending can "stimulate the economy" out of the doldrums.

How Inadequate Is the Neoclassical Model?

We have just seen that the neoclassical model fails to support the common belief that temporary wasteful spending can stimulate the economy and make people better off. Is this an inadequacy of the model, or is it just a proof that the common belief is wrong? There is no consensus among economists on this issue, as the evidence is scanty and hard to interpret.

A far more important issue is the broader one we mentioned earlier: The neoclassical model does not appear to deal adequately with business cycles. To appreciate the extent of the problem, we must learn what happens during business cycles.

11-3   WHAT IS A BUSINESS CYCLE?

Most of the time, most economies grow from year to year. The growth rate of the U.S. economy is far from constant, but it is usually between 1 and 3 percent per year. Sometimes the growth rate slows suddenly; occasionally output during one period is

Contraction:

A period in which
there is a decline in
the growth rate of
the economy; also
called a *recession.*

Depression:

A recession that is
extremely severe.

Recovery:

The period following
a contraction in
which the economy
experiences in-
creased growth,
sometimes at a
faster-than-normal
rate.

Expansion:

A term used synony-
mously with "recov-
ery."

Business cycle:

The pattern of
changes in eco-
nomic growth that
seems to be cyclic
over time.

Trend line:

A line depicting the
average behavior of
real GDP. Contrac-
tions and expan-
sions cause actual
real GDP growth to
fluctuate above and
below the trend line.

less than it was in the preceding period. A period in which growth slows or declines is called a *recession* or a **contraction.** An extremely severe recession is called a **depression.**

Happily, after every recession the nation's economy has resumed growing at a more familiar pace, sometimes even faster, in a period called a **recovery** or an **expansion.** All five of these loosely defined terms describe the economy's behavior during a **business cycle.**

Figure 11-5 illustrates an idealized business cycle. The straight line—called a **trend line**—represents the average behavior of real GDP. The rising and falling curve represents the behavior of GDP if business cycles occurred smoothly and regularly. During an expansion, GDP grows faster than average; during a contraction, it grows more slowly or even falls. The very top of an expansion is called the *peak* and the lowest part of the contraction is called the *trough.*

Business cycles, or business *fluctuations,* have been noted for many centuries. There are many controversial questions about business cycles: What causes them? How much do they affect our economic welfare? Can they be cured or prevented? And if they *can* be cured, is it worth the effort?

In 1946, Arthur Burns and Wesley C. Mitchell's *Measuring Business Cycles* was published,[2] the first of a series of books attempting to measure exactly what happens during business cycles. Burns and Mitchell found that business cycles pervasively affect all activities in the economy. So many industries are affected and so many economic variables decline together in recessions and rise together in expansions that we cannot consider business cycles to be limited to just a few large industries. Because real GDP summarizes the average for all industries in the economy, economists use it to define the duration of recessions:

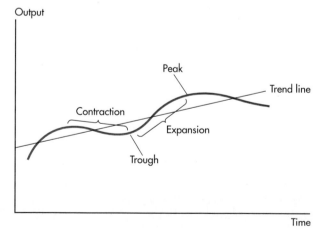

FIGURE 11-5 An idealized business cycle.

[2]New York: National Bureau of Economic Research, 1946.

Recessions are usually declared to begin when the rate of growth of real GDP declines for two successive quarters. The associated recovery is declared to begin when the rate of growth of real GDP next rises for two successive quarters.

Figure 11-6 depicts real GDP since 1960. The shaded bars indicate periods of recession, as defined by the National Bureau of Economic Research. As you can see, the pattern is anything but smooth and regular. There were sharp recessions in 1974, 1980, 1982, and 1990 and less severe recessions in 1960 and 1970. The recessions were not regularly spaced; they varied in severity and length. The recession of 1980 was followed quickly by the recession of 1982, which in turn was followed by a sharp recovery and then a sustained period of economic growth which lasted throughout the remainder of the 1980s.

Permanent Effects of Recessions

In 1982, Charles Nelson and Charles Plosser pointed out that there may be permanent effects of recessions similar to the permanent effects of a bit of bad luck in a game of chance.[3] If you lose $30 on one spin of the roulette wheel, then you are permanently $30 poorer than you would have been without that spin. If you play roulette for a long time, you will have strings of losses and strings of gains, but every loss and every gain continues to affect your wealth forever.

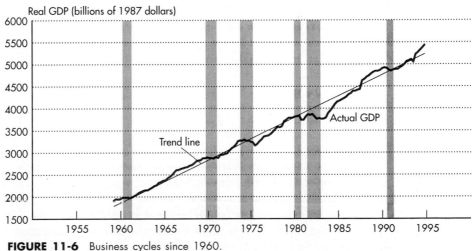

FIGURE 11-6 Business cycles since 1960.
The shaded bars represent recessions as determined by the National Bureau of Economic Research. The trend line connects the midpoints of the 1960 and 1990 recessions.

[3]C. Nelson and C. Plosser, "Trends and Random Walks in Economic Time Series: Some Evidence and Implications," *Journal of Monetary Economics* (1982).

Inspired by this analogy, Nelson and Plosser suggested that there may be no such thing as a business cycle at all. Instead, the growth rate of the economy might be determined randomly and independently each period—as if an invisible hand were flipping a coin each period to determine how much faster or slower than some base rate the economy will grow. According to this interpretation, the appearance of something like a regular "cycle" is just a statistical illusion.

Using sophisticated statistical techniques, Nelson and Plosser showed that their random-growth model was just as consistent with GDP data as the interpretation in terms of business cycles. Nevertheless, most economists continue to believe that business cycles are more than random statistical fluctuations. They base that belief on the evidence of Burns and Mitchell, who found that the outputs of different industries—ranging from ice cream to pig iron—tend to move together over the course of the (real or apparent) cycle. Moreover, interest rates, wages, prices, and other financial variables tend to behave in the same way over the course of one cycle as they do over the course of another. The fact that cycles are all so similar—economist Robert E. Lucas says that "business cycles are all alike"—suggests that they must be more than just an illusion.

If, in fact, business cycles are all alike, we are led to expect a single explanation for all business cycles: It will not do to have one explanation (say, a decrease in the money supply) for the 1982 recession and another (say, a sudden rise in the price of oil) for the 1974 recession. On the other hand, many economists believe (contrary to Lucas) that there are substantial differences from one business cycle to another. Those economists are more comfortable with the prospect of different explanations for different recessions.

What Happens during Business Cycles?

In this subsection, we examine separately the behavior of quantities and of prices over the typical business cycle.

Quantities

Procyclical variable:

An economic variable that tends to increase during expansions and decrease during contractions.

Countercyclical variable:

An economic variable that tends to decrease during expansions and increase during contractions.

From the evidence of Burns and Mitchell, as well as many subsequent studies, we know that most aggregate-quantity variables decline during recessions and rise during expansions. These variables include consumption, industrial production, business investment of all kinds, employment, government purchases, and money growth. Such variables are called **procyclical variables**—they move with the cycle. Sometimes individual industries are **countercyclical variables**—they move in the opposite direction from the cycle. For example, the output of bill collection agencies is countercyclical. So is most household production. But the output of most industries moves procyclically.

The behavior of some aggregate quantities is more *volatile* than that of others. Investment is more volatile than consumption—that is, though investment and consumption both decline during recessions, investment declines more. Similarly, investment rises more than consumption does during recoveries. If we divide consumption

goods into durable and nondurable goods, we see the same effect: durable goods, which are really a kind of capital, are more volatile than nondurable goods over the course of most cycles.

 Many quantity measurements are subject to systematic errors. For example, during recessions, many people are laid off—and hence have time to paint their own bathrooms or tackle other home improvement projects. The output from those projects is not counted in national income statistics. Thus, during recessions, *actual* output may decline less than *measured* output does.

Two aggregate quantities—business inventories and the money supply—appear to *lead* the cycle: the rates at which they increase decline rapidly before the onset of similar declines in other aggregate quantities and rise before the rises in other aggregate quantities. Do sudden declines in the money supply or in business inventories *cause* recessions? These two possibilities have surfaced time and again in economic models of business cycles. But two cautions are in order. First, the fact that one event precedes another does not prove causation; there could be a deeper cause underlying both phenomena, and it might merely be the nature of things that one event tends to occur more quickly than the other. Second, events that appear to lead the cycle might really be lagging the preceding cycle; some quantities might start falling well after other quantities have started rising. Nevertheless, a successful model of a business cycle should be able to account for the fact that business inventories and the money supply are procyclical and exhibit timing that is not perfectly in line with other aggregates.

The output declines of some particular industries, like residential construction, also appear to lead the cycle. That is, new-home construction often slows down a calendar quarter or two before the output of other industries does at the start of a recession. Thus, residential construction is often watched closely by the news media. Economists do not put much faith in attempts to predict business cycles by watching for such particular **leading indicators,** for a variety of reasons. First, the length of the lead time has been highly variable. Thus, it might be coincidence that such variables lead recessions. It is even possible that what appears to be a leading industry is actually one that is lagging the previous cycle. Moreover, economists have no well-tested models to explain why particular industries might decline first. Without such models, they are skeptical about relying on historical patterns to predict the future.

Leading indicator:
A variable that is monitored by the media as a means of predicting the business cycle.

Prices

The cyclical behavior of price variables—prices, interest rates, and wages—is far less pronounced and far more controversial than the behavior of quantity variables. While stock prices—the values of firms—are highly procyclical, goods prices and inflation are only mildly procyclical: they go up and down only slightly during expansions and recessions. To complicate matters, inflation appears to lag the cycle slightly. That i

there is some evidence showing that prices continue to rise after a peak and continue their slow growth rate following a trough. Nominal interest rates are procyclical; but the behavior of real interest rates is difficult to measure, and it appears to bear little relationship to the cycle at all.

The behavior of real wages is particularly interesting. Real wages appear to vary procyclically, rising during expansions and falling during contractions. Because the real wage is the nominal wage divided by the price level and because prices are pro-cyclical, nominal wages must be more highly procyclical—that is, they must be more volatile than prices, rising more than prices at the start of a recovery.

But it is not easy to measure the real wage. Studies of the aggregate or average real wage level in the economy might be biased over the course of a cycle because of changes in the composition of the labor force. The average worker who is employed during a recession may have very different skills than the average worker who is employed during a recovery. This suggests that a direct comparison of their wages, without correcting for skill levels, could be quite misleading.

It would be better to study changes in the wages of individual workers who remain employed throughout the cycle. However, such data are difficult to come by and difficult to interpret. Economists studying such data have reached mutually contradictory conclusions; some find that wages are completely unrelated to the cycle, while others find that they are highly procyclical.

Business Cycles Are Worldwide

Business cycles are not just nationwide—they are worldwide. Most cycles, and especially severe ones, simultaneously affect countries that trade with each other. This widely recognized fact led many nineteenth-century scientists and economists to speculate on global causes for cycles. Lowered productivity due to influenza epidemics was one candidate, but the appearance of cycles in the absence of such epidemics led to the demise of that theory. The nineteenth-century astronomer Simon Newcomb, noticing the international aspect of cycles and noticing that declines appeared to occur about 10 years apart during the early nineteenth century, suggested that sunspot activity might be the cause—perhaps affecting agriculture at regular intervals. But better measurement techniques—both astronomical and economic—demonstrated that sunspots do not correlate well with business cycles, causing that theory, too, to be rejected.

Figure 11-7 shows real GDP as a percentage of its 1980 value in the United States, France, the United Kingdom, and Japan since 1980. The period covered includes two U.S. recessions, the first in the early 1980s and the second in the early 1990s.

From the graph, it appears that the U.S. recession of 1982 was not felt in Japan. In France growth slowed slightly, but there was no marked decline in real GDP. However, in the United Kingdom real GDP declined in 1981, just prior to its decline in the United States. Were those two events—the U.S. and U.K. recessions of the early 1980s—related? Did the downturn in the United Kingdom cause U.S. output to decline? Did events in the United States signal reduced opportunities in the United Kingdom, causing British citizens to react even more quickly than U.S. citizens? Did

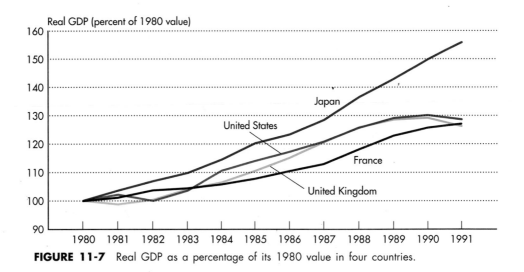

FIGURE 11-7 Real GDP as a percentage of its 1980 value in four countries.

both recessions have the same underlying cause, or were they the consequences of entirely separate economic shocks? And why were other trading partners like Japan and France so unaffected by those recessions? Much work remains to be done in analyzing how (if at all) business cycles are transmitted from one country to another.

As you can see, the recession of the early 1990s seems to have been experienced simultaneously in the United Kingdom and in the United States. France also experienced a slowdown in growth during that period, though it was less severe than the declines in the United States or the United Kingdom. And Japan's real GDP continued to grow unabated.

Over the period in the graph, Japan's only slowdown of growth was the downturn in 1986, an event that appears not to coincide with any similar events in the other three countries. Even so, it is possible that the slowdown of growth in Japan was a result of the 1982 recession or a harbinger of the recession of the early 1990s.

Have Business Cycles Changed?

You may be surprised to learn that the evidence we have on business cycles is based on very few actual cycles. We have partial information on about 12 business recessions between 1854 and 1902 and somewhat better information on 7 more through 1928. Starting with the Great Depression in 1929 (which actually consisted of two major recessions and lasted almost 10 years), the data become more reliable, reflecting more modern collection techniques. Counting the Great Depression as 2, we have solid reliable data on 13 recessions since 1929. Of those, 10 came after World War II. For most statisticians, 13 recessions do not constitute a sample large enough to justify strong conclusions.

The Great Depression seems to have begun a few months before the dramatic stock market crash of October 1929. By the spring of 1933, the lowest point of the Depression, output had fallen by almost 30 percent. Unemployment had reached 25 percent of the labor force. One factor contributing to the Depression may have been the Smoot-Hawley tariff, a 50 percent tax on most goods imported into the United States, which was proposed during the summer of 1929 and enacted in March 1930. The tariff precipitated a disastrous worldwide trade war that did not end until the close of World War II. Another contributing factor might have been severely counterproductive management of the U.S. money supply. Frantic to revive the nation's economy, the U.S. government tried all manner of policies, from establishing make-work programs to exhorting businesses to raise their prices (apparently on the theory that when times are good, prices are rising, so perhaps the reverse is also true). Much about the Great Depression is still unexplained, and economists are still not sure which policies helped and which hindered recovery.

But the Great Depression has not recurred. The blue bars in Figure 11-8 represent U.S. recessions, and the white spaces represent expansions. You can easily see that since the early 1930s, recessions have become shorter and less frequent. They have also become less severe.

What has happened? Have we learned enough about recessions so that we can control their severity? Have the world and national economic structures changed in a way that makes our economies more robust? Or have we just been lucky, so that another Great Depression could commence at any time? With so few recessions to study, it is difficult for us to know the answer.

In the postwar period between 1945 and 1974, recessions were so tame that some economists declared that the business cycle was a thing of the past. But then, in 1974, a sharp recession occurred, following soon after a large increase in the price of oil. As you can see in Figure 11-8, recessions since that time have been neither tame nor infrequent.

Nonetheless, raw data suggest that postwar recessions have been less severe than earlier recessions, even if we omit the extreme case of the Great Depression. But this may be an illusion, due to the fact that prewar statistics were not collected with modern techniques. For example, no good GDP data were available before the 1930s; modern economists had to reconstruct estimates of what the GDP might have been, based on scattered and fragmentary data on crop yields and the output of large indus-

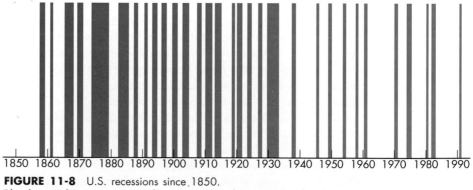

FIGURE 11-8 U.S. recessions since 1850.
Blue bars indicate recessions; the intervening white spaces indicate expansions.

tries. It is possible that the apparent reduction in the severity of recessions arises only because economists are comparing different and inconsistent types of data.

In 1986, Christina Romer presented an ingenious correction to the data.[4] Instead of trying to get better estimates of pre-1930s data, she applied reconstruction techniques to fragments of *modern* data, producing a set of data that is consistent for the entire period from the mid-1800s to the present. Her conclusion, based on that technique, is that the severity of business cycles has not abated! Romer argues that the data that were historically available were largely from relatively volatile industries and thus did not reflect many service industries like transportation that are far less volatile. But the jury is not yet in. Other studies, based on improved historical data, suggest that the original estimates were not that far off after all. So it remains controversial whether the recessions of our own day are more moderate than those of our ancestors' times.

Are Business Cycles a Problem?

When we use words like "severe" and "drastic" to describe business cycles that have high peaks and low troughs, our vocabulary betrays a value judgment. We seem to be saying that swings around the trend line of Figure 11-5 are a bad thing. But why?

To put the question another way, imagine one world where output is described by the trend line and another world where output is described by the idealized business cycle of Figure 11-5. Is there any reason to assume that people would be much happier in the first world than in the second?

Wealth—the present value of income, or of output—would be about the same in both worlds. In trough years, the world of the business cycle offers less income than the world of the trend line, but in peak years the opposite is true.

Nonetheless, the world of the business cycle is less attractive because it makes consumption smoothing impossible. People *set out* to smooth their consumption, but in bad times interest rates are driven up until people are willing to consume only what is available. Attempts at consumption smoothing must fail because there are substantially fewer goods available in some years than in others.[5]

Now the question becomes this: Just how great a misfortune is a failure at consumption smoothing? Economist Robert E. Lucas has offered some crude estimates suggesting that it is a very minor misfortune,[6] at least in comparison to the misfortune of, say, a decline in the level or the slope of the trend line.

Suppose you could replay the history of the United States since World War II, making either of two improvements along the way. Option 1 is to eliminate business cycles entirely, allowing the economy to grow along its trend line. Option 2 is to leave all postwar business cycles intact but to increase income by just one-tenth of 1 per-

----

[4]C. Romer, "Is the Stabilization of the Postwar Economy a Figment of the Data?" *American Economic Review* 76 (1986), 313–334.

[5]Consumption smoothing fails also in the world of the trend line (because consumption does increase over time), but not quite so spectacularly.

[6]R. E. Lucas, Jr., *Models of Business Cycles* (Boston: Basil Blackwell, 1990).

cent over its actual historical value each year. Lucas argues that you would make people happier by choosing option 2 than by choosing option 1.

If Lucas's estimates are correct, it is almost surely a mistake for policy makers to devote much effort to fighting small or even moderate-size fluctuations in output. Larger fluctuations—of the magnitude, for example, of the Great Depression—remain worthy of considerable attention.

11-4 BUSINESS CYCLES AND THE NEOCLASSICAL MODEL

To determine how well the neoclassical model describes recessions, we will apply to it four different kinds of shocks that could conceivably cause a recession. They are a simple supply shock, a shock to productivity, a demand shock, and a monetary shock. Our goal is to see whether any of these shocks leads to implications that are consistent with what we know about real-world recessions.

A Supply Shock

One theory of recessions is that they are produced by periods of low output caused by factors outside the economy like changes in the weather. We call these *supply shocks* because their initial effect is on the aggregate supply curve in the goods market, shifting it to the left.

Suppose, for example, that a bout of bad weather destroys some of the economy's agricultural output after it has been harvested and stored. The aggregate supply curve in Figure 11-9(a) shifts to the left by the amount of output that is destroyed, from S to S'. The resulting decline in income is temporary, so consumption demand—and hence aggregate demand—falls slightly, as is also shown in panel (a). (Here is our old friend "consumption smoothing" again.) The net effect is that the interest rate rises (from r_0 to r_1) and output falls (from Y_0 to Y_1).

In the labor market [Figure 11-9(b)], the supply curve shifts to the right because of the higher interest rate r_1 and to some extent because of the income effect of the recession (people are slightly poorer and so work more). Labor demand is unaffected, as there has been no change in the marginal productivity of labor. The net effect here is that employment increases from L_0 to L_1 and the wage rate falls to w_1.

As for the money market, the interest rate is up and income is down; the money demand curve in Figure 11-9(c) shifts to the left on both accounts. Therefore, the price level rises from P_0 to P_1.

[Notice that all of this is identical to what we found when the government spent wastefully (Figure 11-4). Government waste is just like a tornado destroying output.]

This story does capture at least two important features of recessions: Output falls, and so do wages. On the other hand, employment *increases,* a fact that does not seem to fit with our historical experience of recessions.

There are other problems with this supply-shock scenario. Specifically, it implies

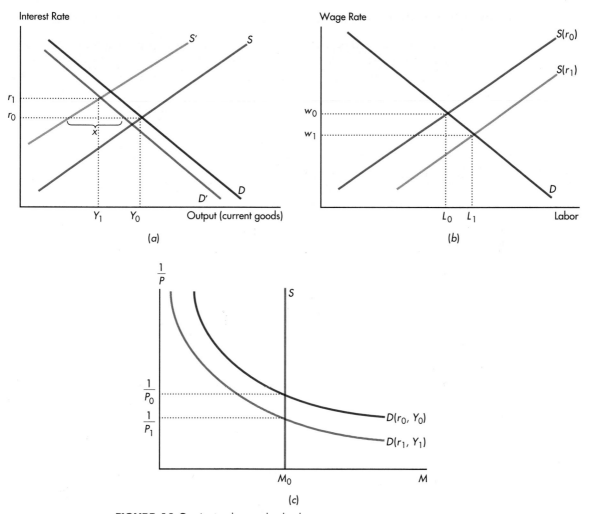

FIGURE 11-9 A simple supply shock.
Assume a tornado destroys some consumption goods. (*a*) The supply of goods shifts left by the amount of the shock, *x*, and the demand for goods shifts left only slightly because of consumption smoothing. The interest rate rises to r_1 and output falls to Y_1. (*b*) A higher interest rate causes a rightward shift in the supply of labor. (*c*) A higher interest rate and lower ouput both cause a leftward shift in the demand for money.

that the price level and the interest rate should rise during a recession, whereas most economists' reading of the evidence indicates that interest rates and prices tend to *fall* during recessions.

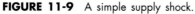

➡ *Exercise 11-2*

Trace, with diagrams, the effects of a temporary *positive* supply shock, such as a one-time unexpected gift from abroad.

A Shock to Productivity

The simple supply shock of Figure 11-9 assumes that output decreases but labor's productivity is unaffected. Next we consider a supply shock that comes about because of a drop in the marginal product of labor. The decrease could be the result of a bad harvest season, in which workers are able to gather fewer crops per hour because the crops are sparser. Alternatively, it could be the effect of a cutback in oil supplies, such as we experienced during the war with Iraq in 1991. Oil is used in production, and when less oil is available, it is reasonable to expect that the marginal product of labor will be lower. (For example, some workers who mow lawns may be forced to switch from power mowers to hand mowers.)

Figure 11-10 traces the consequences. In the goods market [panel (*a*)], the supply curve shifts leftward because of the drop in productivity, and the demand curve shifts slightly leftward in response to the temporary drop in income. Thus Figure 11-10(*a*) looks just like Figure 11-9(*a*).

In the labor market [panel (*b*)], the demand curve shifts leftward because the labor demand curve is the MPL curve and we have assumed a decline in the MPL. The supply of labor tends to increase because of the higher interest rate r_1 determined in the goods market, but it also tends to decrease because of intertemporal substitution. (People try to time their vacations to coincide with the brief period of low productivity.) The labor supply curve could thus move in either direction, to S' or S'' in Figure 11-10(*b*). In either case, at the new equilibrium point (E' or E'') the wage rate is lower than it was at the original equilibrium point (E).

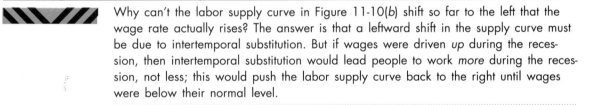

Why can't the labor supply curve in Figure 11-10(*b*) shift so far to the left that the wage rate actually rises? The answer is that a leftward shift in the supply curve must be due to intertemporal substitution. But if wages were driven *up* during the recession, then intertemporal substitution would lead people to work *more* during the recession, not less; this would push the labor supply curve back to the right until wages were below their normal level.

The money market story is exactly the same as that in Figure 11-9. The increase in the interest rate and the drop in output both lead to a leftward shift in the demand for money and hence to a rise in the price level to P_1.

Unlike the scenario of Figure 11-9, the story of Figure 11-10 allows the possibility of a decrease in employment during a recession. On the other hand, the decrease in employment is caused primarily by a shift in the demand curve for labor, and most economists are skeptical that the labor demand curve could shift far enough to explain the big swings in employment that are observed over the course of some business cycles. Furthermore, Figure 11-10 predicts that both the interest rate and the price level *rise* during the recession, but such increases, again, are at variance with much of the evidence. So this scenario is not entirely satisfactory either.

➡ *Exercise 11-3*
Trace, with diagrams, the effects of a temporary *increase* in the marginal product of labor.

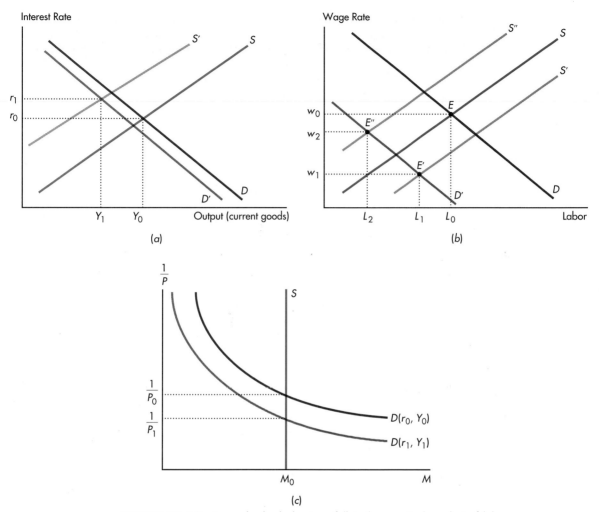

FIGURE 11-10 A supply shock due to a fall in the marginal product of labor.
(a) In the goods market, the supply curve shifts leftward, and the demand curve shifts leftward by less because of consumption smoothing. Therefore, the interest rate rises. (b) In the labor market, the demand curve shifts leftward because labor is now less productive. The supply curve shifts rightward because of the higher interest rate and leftward because of intertemporal substitution; the net effect could be a shift in either direction. (c) In the money market, the demand curve shifts leftward because the interest rate is up and output is down.

A Demand Shock

If supply shocks do not provide a satisfactory explanation of recessions, perhaps demand shocks will work better. Suppose that for some (unexplained) reason, people decide to start consuming less in the present and more in the future. Alternatively, suppose that investors decide to undertake fewer investment projects in the present. Either way, the demand for current goods falls. Figure 11-11(a) shows the demand curve shifting to the left, leading to lower output and a lower interest rate. At the lower interest rate, workers supply less labor; as shown in Figure 11-11(b), the labor supply curve shifts left, employment falls, and the wage rate rises.

In the money market, the demand curve is pushed in both directions: the interest rate has dropped, so the demand for money is up; but output has also dropped, so the demand for money is down. The new demand curve is either D' or D'' in Figure 11-11(c), and the price level could either fall to P_1 or rise to P_2.

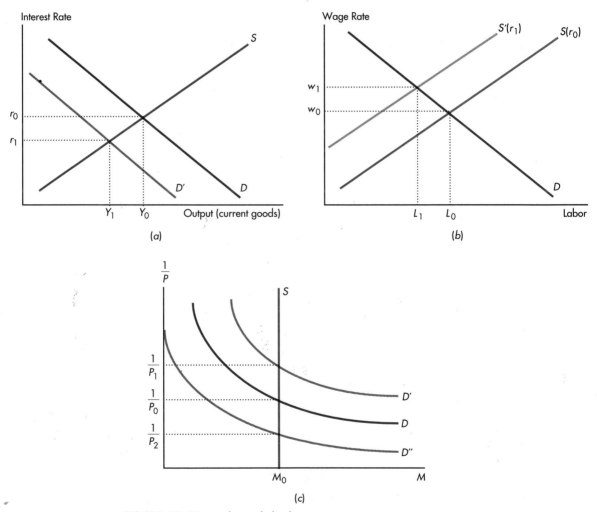

FIGURE 11-11 A demand shock.
When consumers or investors lower their demand for current goods, as in (a), the interest rate falls and so the supply of labor falls, as in (b). The wage rate rises and employment falls. The demand for money, in (c), could rise (to D') because of the lower interest rate or fall (to D'') because of the decline in income.

This story allows for the possibility of output and prices falling simultaneously, which seems to fit what we know of reality. On the other hand, it has real wages rising at the same time, contrary to our experience of real-world recessions. So the demand-shock scenario is as unsatisfactory as the supply-shock scenarios, although for a different reason.

➡ *Exercise 11-4*
Trace, with diagrams, the effects of a temporary *increase* in consumption or investment demand.

A Monetary Shock

It is sometimes argued that governments cause recessions by unwisely lowering the money supply. In particular, the recession of 1981–1982 followed close on the heels of a sharp reduction in the growth rate of the money supply, and many observers suspect a cause-and-effect relationship. Figure 11-12 shows the effect of such a *monetary shock*. Because of the real-nominal dichotomy in the neoclassical model, the effects are confined to the money market, where the leftward shift of supply to S' leads to a drop in the price level to P_1. There is no change in output, wages, or employment. This hardly seems an adequate description of a recession.

International Shocks

In an open economy, shocks abroad can lead to changes in output and employment at home. Figure 11-13 shows an open economy facing a world interest rate of r. At that interest rate, we see in panel (*a*) that domestic citizens produce Y_1 goods while demanding Y_2 goods for consumption and investment. The excess, $Y_2 - Y_1$, is imported from abroad and hence is equal to the domestic trade deficit.

We have assumed, completely arbitrarily, that Y_2 exceeds Y_1. It is equally likely that Y_1 could exceed Y_2. [This would be the case if the world interest rate were higher than the rate at which the supply and demand curves cross in Figure 11-13(a).] In that case, the economy in question would run a trade surplus.

In Figure 11-13(*b*), the labor market is initially in equilibrium at quantity L, which is the quantity necessary to produce Y_1 goods. Now suppose that events abroad cause the world interest rate to fall from r to r'. Then in Figure 11-13(*a*), domestic output falls to Y_1'. In Figure 11-13(*b*), the labor supply curve shifts leftward from S to S' and employment falls from L to L', which is the quantity necessary to produce Y_1' goods.
Thus:

A drop in the world interest rate can cause a drop in domestic output and domestic employment.

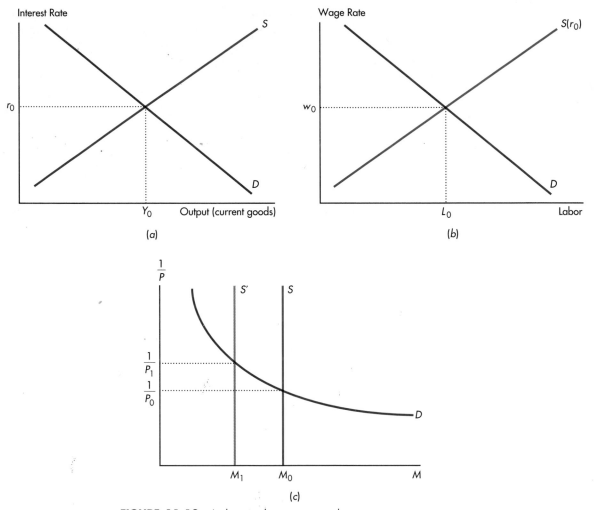

FIGURE 11-12 A drop in the money supply.
There is no change in the goods market (a) or the labor market (b). Only the money market (c) is affected, and there the price level drops.

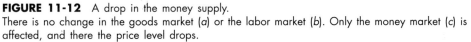

Exercise 11-5

When the world interest rate falls to r', what happens to the size of the domestic trade deficit?

Our discussion suggests an explanation of why business cycles tend to occur in many countries simultaneously. Suppose, for example, that there is a negative demand shock in Europe, causing a European recession of the sort illustrated by Figure 11-11. The world interest rate falls, leading to a simultaneous U.S. recession of the sort illustrated in Figure 11-13. Thus a European recession can cause a U.S. recession, and vice versa.

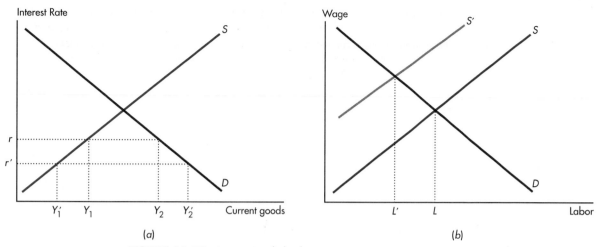

FIGURE 11-13 International shocks.
(a) A decline in the interest rate increases the quantity of goods imported from $Y_2 - Y_1$ to $Y_2' - Y_1'$. (b) The decline in output to Y_1' causes labor supply to shift leftward, causing employment to decline from L to L'.

Where Do We Go from Here?

The neoclassical model as we have presented it appears insufficient to describe what we know of business cycles. If recessions are caused by supply shocks, then the model implies (incorrectly) that prices should rise during recessions. If recessions are caused by demand shocks, then the model says (incorrectly) that wages rise during recessions. If business cycles are caused by monetary shocks, then the model implies (incorrectly) that nothing other than the price level changes during recessions.[7]

It is possible that some more complicated kind of shock, or some collection of shocks happening together, could lead to a realistic description of the business cycle within the neoclassical model. Indeed, many economists are optimistic about such a possibility. However, no economist has yet succeeded in giving a fully satisfactory account of how this could happen.

Another possibility—and one with which many economists are comfortable—is that different recessions have different causes, and we should not be surprised to learn that no single explanation fits all of them. For example, the recession of 1973–1974, unlike many others, was accompanied by a substantial increase in the inflation rate, suggesting that this particular recession can be explained by a supply shock. And indeed it is easy to identify the supply shock that is likely to have been responsible—a major interruption in oil supplies from the Middle East.

Thus it may be that we can explain the 1973–1974 recession via a supply shock and other recessions via demand shocks. If we allow ourselves this flexibility, we can

[7]Some economists might dispute the "incorrectness" of these implications; our characterizations reflect the opinions of a substantial majority of economists, though not perhaps an overwhelming one.

go a long way toward explaining a lot of history with the neoclassical model. And if we account for the fact that multiple shocks can occur simultaneously, we have even more flexibility to account for a wide variety of recessions within the model.

Still, the model's inability to give a unified explanation for all business cycles, along with the other problems that we discussed in Section 11-2, have led some economists to suggest that it could be useful to include some additional features in the neoclassical model. In Chapters 12 to 14, we explore three different modifications that economists have studied.

The models discussed in Chapters 12 to 14 are essentially variations on the neoclassical model analyzed in this chapter, as are all models that are within the mainstream of modern macroeconomics. Although we sometimes refer to them as "different models," at a fundamental level they are all really the same model, but with different bells and whistles attached.

SUMMARY

The neoclassical model is summarized by three graphs, representing the market for goods (with the interest rate on the vertical axis and the quantity of goods on the horizontal), the market for labor (with the real wage rate on the vertical axis and the quantity of labor on the horizontal), and the market for money (with the reciprocal of the price level on the vertical axis and the quantity of money on the horizontal). Underlying these graphs is the production function, which relates employment and output.

The key assumption of the model is that all markets clear (in other words, they are at their equilibrium points) at all times.

The neoclassical model appears to have several shortcomings as a model of the real-world economy:

- The model implies a real–nominal dichotomy (also called the neutrality of money), which means that changes in the money market have no effect on real economic variables such as output, employment, real interest rates, and real wages.
- The model implies that all unemployment is voluntary and that changes in the level of employment must be attributable to changes in either the demand for or the supply of labor.
- The model predicts that the government can do very little to improve economic conditions when a recession gets under way. First, the real–nominal dichotomy implies that nothing in the money market can have any real effects. Second, a temporary increase in wasteful government spending has exclusively negative effects. More specifically, it causes people to work more hours and have fewer goods to consume.

A business cycle is characterized by simultaneous declines in the output of many industries (that is, a recession) accompanied by reduced employment in the economy, followed by an eventual recovery. The price level, too, appears to behave procyclically, rising during periods of rapid output growth and falling when output falls. Real wages also appear to be procyclical, though relevant data are not definitive, leading to some disagreement among economists about the behavior of real wages over the course of business cycles.

Business cycles seem to be worldwide events. They also appear to have decreased in duration and frequency over time. But it is possible that this appearance is due at least partly to improved data collection as opposed to real changes in the economy's behavior.

The neoclassical model is apparently inadequate to explain the causes of recessions. When certain shocks are "fed into" the model, the results are contrary to experience. Because of this failure and for other reasons, we are led to modify the neoclassical model in various ways. This undertaking will span the next three chapters.

PROBLEM SET

1. Suppose the government undertakes a new *permanent* spending program that will waste $50 billion every year. The spending is financed by a head tax. What happens in the goods market? In the labor market? In the money market?

2. How would your answer to problem 1 be modified if the spending program is financed by a tax on wages instead of a head tax?

3. Look again at problem 1. What do you expect will happen to output and employment in the long run? (*Hint:* What happens to the level of investment in the present? How does this affect the supply of goods and the demand for labor in the future?)

4. Suppose the government undertakes a new *temporary* program of productive spending on public goods which effectively creates $50 billion worth of new goods this year only. What happens in the goods market? In the labor market? In the money market?

5. Suppose the economy experiences an increase in productivity, and the change is expected to be permanent. Trace graphically the effects in the markets for goods, labor, and money.

6. Suppose the government has been running a wasteful program that costs $50 billion a year but announces *today* that it will cancel the program beginning *next year*. Trace the effects in the markets for goods, labor, and money.

7. Suppose people come to believe that their labor will be far more productive in the near future than it is today. Trace the effects in the markets for goods, labor, and money.

8. Suppose the government announces a temporary program to subsidize investment. Trace the effects in the markets for goods, labor, and money. What happens to current consumption?

9. *True or false:* A productivity shock does a better job of accounting for recessions if the intertemporal substitution effect is large than if the intertemporal substitution effect is small.

10. The discussions in the text about government spending make no explicit assumption about whether that spending is financed by current taxation or by borrowing. And indeed, if Ricardian equivalence holds, it makes no difference which option the government chooses. Suppose, however, that Ricardian equivalence breaks down. *True or false:* In that case, the government can effectively combat a recession by cutting current taxes without changing its current or future spending.

11. Suppose that business cycles are caused by shocks to the labor supply. People periodically become temporarily lazy, supplying less labor and causing a recession. What does this model imply about the behavior over the business cycle of output, employment, the interest rate, real wages, and the price level? Do these results seem plausible?

12. Suppose that the interest rate and intertemporal substitution effects on labor supply are quite small. How would this affect the model's ability to explain recessions?
    a. Answer for recessions that are triggered by supply shocks.
    b. Answer for recessions that are triggered by demand shocks.
13. Add the production function to Figures 11-9 through 11-12. In which cases does the curve shift? In which direction? In which cases does the economy move along the curve? In which direction?

Chapter 12

The Sticky Wage Model

I n 1936, the developed world was in the middle of the Great Depression. In the United States, output, employment, and wages had fallen dramatically throughout the 1930s. Despite an ongoing recovery that began in 1933, the unemployment rate was still in the high teens. Great Britain had suffered even longer, enduring unemployment of over 20 percent for almost 20 years.

In the context of the classical economic model (an early version of our neoclassical model), the only way to account for such a precipitous decline was by postulating a dramatic decline in the productivity of capital and labor. But no such decline in productivity was evident.

British economist John Maynard Keynes argued that because the classical model could not plausibly explain such profound and lasting unemployment, the model's basic hypotheses should be adjusted. In particular, he questioned the assumption that all prices adjust instantly and so all markets are in equilibrium at all times. He singled out the labor market as the primary market where this assumption should be dropped. Later, Keynes's followers applied similar skepticism to the goods market.

Keynesian models:

Models in which one or more markets can be out of equilibrium.

Models in which one or more markets can remain out of equilibrium for any length of time are frequently called **Keynesian models,** in Keynes's honor.

In this chapter, we determine what happens if the labor market does not clear—that is, if the market does not move to its point of equilibrium. In Chapter 13, we will examine what happens if the goods market does not clear.

In both cases, one implication is that the government can wield powerful policy tools to improve economic conditions. By adjusting the money supply, government spending, and tax rates, the government may be able to raise output, employment, and economic welfare.

12-1   THE STICKY WAGE MODEL: AN OVERVIEW

Our first task is to produce a complete macroeconomic model incorporating the assumption that the labor market fails to clear. To do so, we will assume that the price of labor—the wage rate—does *not* automatically move to equilibrium. Instead, it is "stuck" at some nonequilibrium level.

In all other respects, our model's foundations will be identical to those of the neoclassical model in Chapter 11.

The sticky wage model can be a complement to the neoclassical model rather than a rival. Suppose that, following a shock to the labor market, wages adjust slowly to the new equilibrium. Then in the short run—before wages have moved appreciably—the economy is best described by the sticky wage model. In the long run—after the new equilibrium is reached—the neoclassical model takes over as the better description.

Real versus Nominal Wages

Whenever we discuss the wage rate, we must specify whether we mean the *real* wage rate *w*, measured in units like apples per hour or, more generally, output goods per hour, or the *nominal* wage rate *W*, measured in monetary units like dollars per hour. These two rates are related by the equation

$$w = \frac{W}{P}$$

where *P* is the price level.

In diagrams depicting the supply of and demand for labor, it is the *real* wage rate w that appears on the vertical axis. In Figure 12-1 (which we shall discuss shortly) that axis is labeled with both w and W/P as a reminder of the relation between the two wage rates.

As long as the price level P remains fixed, the *real* wage rate changes if and only if the *nominal* wage rate changes. For the time being, we assume a fixed price level, so the phrase "a change in the wage rate" will imply a change in both the real and the nominal wage rates, and we need not specify which we mean. In Section 12-2, where we will allow the price level to vary, we will be more scrupulous about distinguishing between real and nominal wages.

The Labor Market with Sticky Wages

The key assumption of the sticky wage model is that the wage rate can become *stuck* at a level above equilibrium, such as w_0 in Figure 12-1. At this wage, workers want to supply L_1 hours of labor, whereas employers are willing to hire only L_0. This leaves the difference, $L_1 - L_0$ hours of labor, as *involuntarily unemployed.*

According to standard *micro*economics, we should now proceed to tell the following story: Some workers find themselves unemployed and offer to work for less than the going wage rate w_0. Employers happily accept this offer, and the prevailing market wage is driven downward. This continues to happen until the market wage falls to its equilibrium level w_E.

The Keynesian sticky wage scenario explicitly assumes that this does *not* happen. Workers remain involuntarily unemployed because wages do *not* fall.

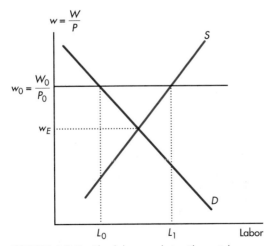

FIGURE 12-1 The labor market with a sticky wage rate.
If the real wage cannot fall below w_0, then firms will hire only L_0 hours of labor, even though workers offer L_1 hours.

Why Sticky Wages?

Sticky wage rate:

A wage rate that fails to adjust immediately to changes in the supply of or demand for labor.

What could cause a **sticky wage rate** like that in Figure 12-1? There might be a number of causative factors. Perhaps union contracts prohibit wages from falling below a prespecified level. In some industries, union contracts set nominal wages for a year or more in advance. Although unionized industries constitute only a small percentage of production in the United States, informal or *implicit* contracts may limit nominal wage changes in other industries.

But if wages are sticky because of labor contracts, then there should be sudden adjustments in the labor market at the time those contracts expire. To test this hypothesis, Professor Mark Bils of the University of Rochester asked two questions: First, what should those sudden adjustments look like if contracts keep wages sticky? Second, do actual employment figures exhibit the expected patterns?[1]

To answer the first question, Bils began with a situation like that depicted in Figure 12-1 and added a hypothesis about how the wage came to be stuck at w_0 in the first place. That hypothesis is illustrated in Figure 12-2. Initially, the labor supply curve is S, the labor demand curve is D, and the market reaches equilibrium at point A. The equilibrium wage rate w_0 is written into a union contract. Now for some reason the labor demand curve shifts leftward to D' and, because the wage rate is stuck at w_0, the market moves to point B where only L_0 units of labor are employed. Eventually, however, the contract expires, and the market can achieve its new equilibrium at C.

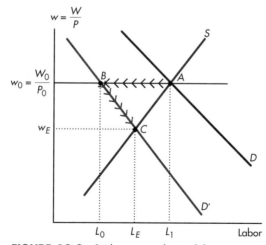

FIGURE 12-2 Sticky wages due to labor contracts.
The market is initially in equilibrium at A, and the equilibrium wage rate w_0 is written into a labor contract. Next the demand for labor shifts from D to D'; because the contract causes wages to stick at w_0, the market moves from A to B, so employment falls from L_1 to L_0. When the contract eventually expires, the market moves to its new equilibrium point C, so employment partially "rebounds" to L_E.

[1]Bils's results are reported in "Testing for Contracting Effects in Employment," *Quarterly Journal of Economics* 106 (1991).

Thus, according to Bils's hypothesis, employment should fall from L_1 to L_0 during the life of the contract and then partially "rebound" to L_E at the time the contract expires. This rebound, or adjustment, should "undo" some, but not all, of the original drop in employment.

To see whether this hypothesis fits the facts, Bils looked for evidence of the rebound in 12 manufacturing industries, and he found it in 8 of them. Figure 12-3 shows the size of the rebound in each industry. In the glass container industry, for example, 1.3 percent of all changes in employment during the life of the contract were "undone" when the contract was renewed. In the motor vehicle industry, the figure was 78.7 percent.

Because these results are generally consistent with the theory's predictions, they suggest that labor contracts can be an important source of sticky wages over significant time periods.

Labor contracts are not the only possible source of sticky wages. An alternative source is proposed in what is called the *efficiency wage* model. Note first that at the equilibrium wage w_E, workers have no fear of losing their jobs. There is no involuntary unemployment, so a worker who is fired by one firm can easily find work with another. As a result, workers might try to get away with a variety of misconduct, from shirking on the job to stealing from their employers. In such a climate, employers might choose to pay wages above w_E so that workers value their jobs and moderate their behavior.

(You should note, however, that the efficiency wage model predicts a sticky *real*

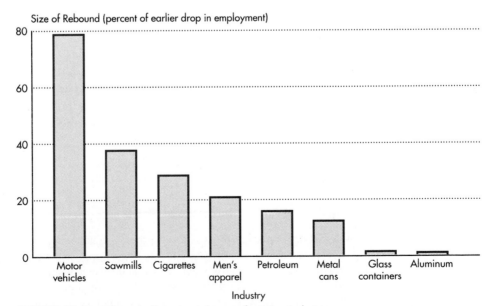

FIGURE 12-3 Rebound effects in eight manufacturing industries.
In each of these industries, a drop in employment during the life of a labor contract was offset by a partial rebound when the contract expired. The vertical axis measures the size of the rebound as a percentage of the *drop* in employment during the contract's lifetime.

wage as opposed to the sticky *nominal* wage that we will assume throughout the remainder of this chapter. When the price level is fixed, sticky real wages and sticky nominal wages are equivalent, but when the price level varies, they are not.)

Yet another possibility is that employers are simply irrational, choosing to hire workers at w_0 even when others are clamoring to work for less.

We shall not commit ourselves to any one of these explanations. We simply assume in this chapter that for some unspecified reason or reasons, possibly including some of those just listed, the wage rate in Figure 12-1 can remain stuck at w_0.

Although we do not commit ourselves to any particular explanation, it is worth noting that the choice of one over another can have significant consequences. If sticky wages result from union contracts, then we expect them to last only as long as the contracts do. If they result from efficiency wage considerations, then they may persist forever.

The Goods Market

Review of Aggregate Supply in the Neoclassical Model

Figure 12-4 is a reproduction of Figure 9-16; we shall use it here to review the relationship between the labor market and the goods market in the neoclassical model. In Figure 12-4, the labor demand curve in panel (*a*) and the production function in panel (*b*) represent the state of technology. Panel (*c*) shows the aggregate supply of goods. Points on the aggregate supply curve are derived from the information in (*a*) and (*b*) as follows:

1. Choose an interest rate, say, 10 percent. Draw the corresponding labor supply curve as in Figure 12-4(*a*) (the location of this curve depends on the interest rate).
2. Read off the equilibrium quantity of labor L_0. Use the production function to find the corresponding level of output Y_0. Then, as in Figure 12-4(*c*), plot a point to show that the interest rate 10 percent corresponds to the output level Y_0.

To find additional points on the aggregate supply curve, repeat the above procedure with different interest rates, say, 15 or 20 percent.

Aggregate Supply in a Sticky Wage Model

Now let us use the same process to find the aggregate supply curve in a sticky wage model. The details are shown in Figure 12-5. Suppose first that the interest rate is 10 percent. The wage rate is stuck at w_0, and at that wage rate employers hire only L hours of labor—despite the fact that workers would prefer to supply more than that [see Figure 12-5(*a*), where the amount of involuntary unemployment is $L_s - L$]. The level of output corresponding to L, read off the production function in Figure 12-5(*b*), is Y. So an interest rate of 10 percent corresponds to an output of Y, as graphed in Figure 12-5(*c*).

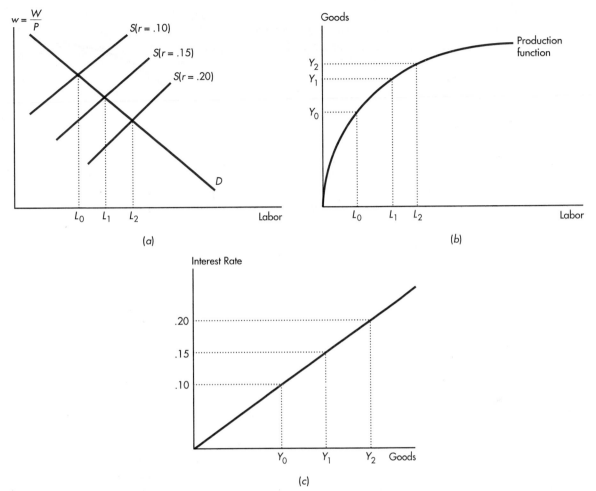

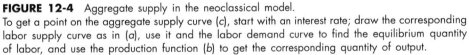

FIGURE 12-4 Aggregate supply in the neoclassical model.
To get a point on the aggregate supply curve (c), start with an interest rate; draw the corresponding labor supply curve as in (a), use it and the labor demand curve to find the equilibrium quantity of labor, and use the production function (b) to get the corresponding quantity of output.

If we repeat the process with an interest rate of 15 percent, the labor supply curve is now the middle one in panel (*a*). Workers want to supply more labor than they did at a 10 percent interest rate, but with the wage still stuck at w_0, employers are still willing to hire only L. The corresponding quantity of output from panel (*b*) is still Y, so the interest rate 15 percent *also* corresponds to the quantity Y, as graphed in panel (*c*).

And for the same reasons, the interest rate 20 percent also corresponds to the same quantity Y. The point (20%, Y) is therefore on the aggregate supply curve.

Because all of these interest rates correspond to the same quantity of output, the aggregate supply curve in Figure 12-5(*c*) is a vertical line.

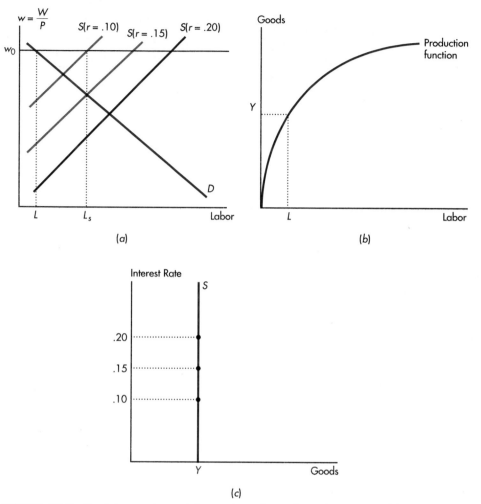

FIGURE 12-5 The labor market and the goods market in the sticky wage model.
To get a point on the aggregate supply curve (c), choose an interest rate; draw the corresponding labor supply curve as in (a) but realize that firms want to hire only the quantity of labor L; use the production function (b) to get the corresponding quantity of output (which is always Y). Plot the point (interest rate, Y) in (c).

Aggregate Supply at Low Interest Rates

We have argued that many different interest rates lead to the same quantity of output. That argument fails if the interest rate is *very* low. In Figure 12-6 you can see what happens at an interest rate of 1 percent. In panel (*a*) the labor supply curve is now so far to the left that the equilibrium wage is *above* w_0 rather than below it. In this case, only L' units of labor are hired and, consequently, panel (*b*) shows that only Y' units of output are produced. Therefore, the aggregate supply curve in panel (*c*) is vertical over most of its range but not where interest rates are very low. However, we will always assume for simplicity that the economy is operating on the vertical por-

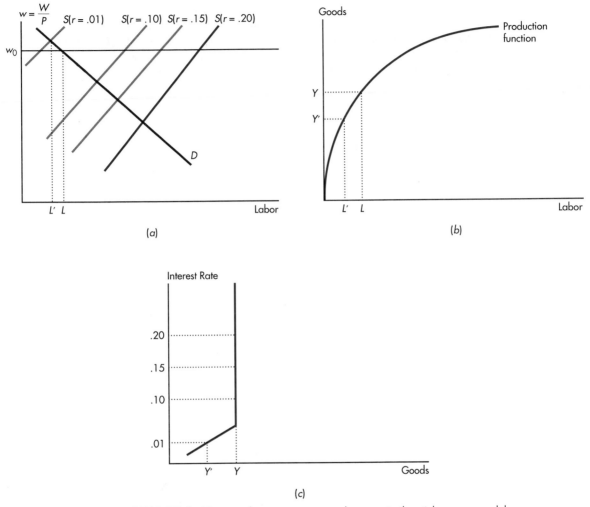

FIGURE 12-6 The complete aggregate supply curve in the sticky wage model. Most of the curve is vertical. But at very low interest rates, the model behaves like the neoclassical model, with the aggregate supply curve sloping upward.

tion of the aggregate supply curve; thus there is no harm in drawing the entire curve as if it were vertical, as we will sometimes do.

Comparing Two Supply Curves

In the early chapters of this book, we took the aggregate supply curve to be vertical, reflecting our assumption that all goods simply appeared in the economy without being produced. When we introduced the labor market in Chapter 8, we found that different interest rates call forth different levels of work effort and hence different levels of output; this led us to redraw the aggregate supply curve to slope upward, as in Figure 12-4(c).

Now that we have introduced a sticky wage, we are back in a situation where changes in the interest rate do not affect output. Because the wage rate is stuck, employers hire only L units of labor, as in Figure 12-5(a), no matter how much labor workers want to supply. Because there is no longer any mechanism by which the interest rate can affect output, the aggregate supply curve is once again vertical.

Notice in Figure 12-5(a) that as long as the wage rate is stuck above equilibrium, the quantity of labor hired (and hence the quantity of output produced) is always *less* than it would be at the neoclassical equilibrium. Thus, when wages are sticky, the aggregate supply curve lies to the *left* of where it would be if wage rates were perfectly flexible. Figure 12-7 illustrates this relationship. Wherever the sticky wage aggregate supply curve is vertical, it lies to the left of the neoclassical curve. At low interest rates, the two curves coincide.

The Complete Sticky Wage Model

Figure 12-8 illustrates the complete sticky wage model, which you should compare to the neoclassical model in Figure 11-1.

Figure 12-8(a) shows the goods market, including the vertical aggregate supply curve that we derived in Figures 12-5 and 12-6. The aggregate demand curve in panel (a) is exactly the same as in the neoclassical model.

Figure 12-8(b) shows the labor market, with its stuck wage rate, just as in Figure 12-5(a).

To complete the sticky wage model, we need the market for money, which is exactly the same as in the neoclassical model. It is depicted in Figure 12-8(c).

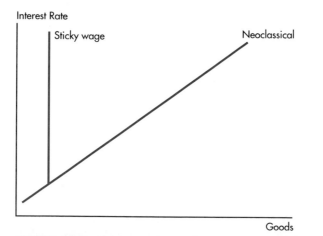

FIGURE 12-7 The aggregate supply curves in two different models.
At low interest rates, the neoclassical and sticky wage models behave identically. Once the sticky wage aggregate supply curve becomes vertical, it lies entirely to the left of the neoclassical aggregate supply curve.

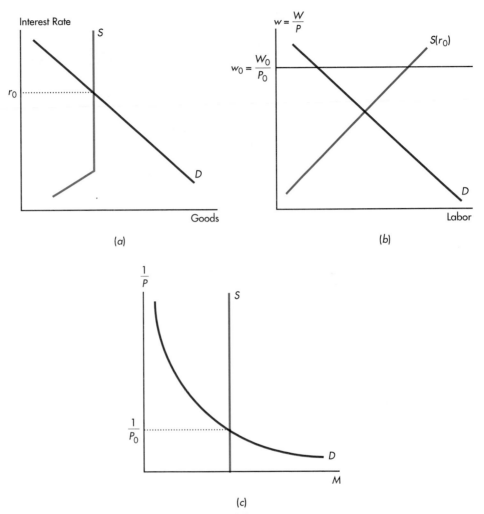

FIGURE 12-8 The complete sticky wage model.
In the goods market (a), the aggregate supply curve is as derived in Figures 12-5 and 12-6. The aggregate demand curve is that of the neoclassical model. The labor market curves in (b) are those of the neoclassical model, but this model also incorporates a stuck nominal wage of W_0, which translates to a stuck real wage of $w_0 = W_0/P_0$. The money market (c) is that of the neoclassical model.

Effect of a Change in the Price Level

In our discussion so far, we have held the price level fixed. As a result, we have not had to distinguish between a sticky real wage rate and a sticky nominal (money) wage rate.

But when the price level changes, the real and nominal wage rates cannot both remain stuck. In that case, the sticky wage model assumes that the nominal wage rate W is fixed. Therefore, an increase in the price level P causes a drop in the real wage rate W/P. In this section, we will determine the additional consequences that must follow.

The Labor Market

Suppose that the nominal wage rate is stuck at W_0. Figure 12-9 shows the labor market in a sticky wage equilibrium with the real wage rate equal to $w_0 = W_0/P_0$. Now suppose also that for some reason the price level rises from P_0 to P_1. The nominal wage rate is stuck at W_0, so the new real wage rate must be $w_1 = W_0/P_1$.

Because P_1 is greater than P_0, it follows that w_1 is less than w_0. That is, when the price level rises, the real wage rate must fall. The new, lower real wage rate w_1 is also shown in Figure 12-9. At this new, lower real wage rate, employers are willing to hire L_1 hours of labor. Therefore:

> In the sticky wage model, a rise in the price level leads to a lower real wage rate, higher employment, and less involuntary unemployment.

There is, however, a limit to the power of an increasing price level. If the price level rises so high as to drive the real wage below the neoclassical equilibrium w_E in Figure 12-9, then employers will demand more labor than workers are willing to supply. Competition among employers for a limited number of workers will put upward pressure on the wage rate. We assume that wages *can* respond to this pressure; that is, although the nominal wage is "sticky downward" (it cannot fall), it is not "sticky upward" (it is perfectly able to rise). This means that at very high price levels, the sticky wage model becomes equivalent to the neoclassical model. We will always assume, however, that the price level is in a range where the real wage is *above* w_E.

Exercise 12-1

Explain why a *drop* in the price level would *increase* the level of involuntary unemployment in the sticky wage model.

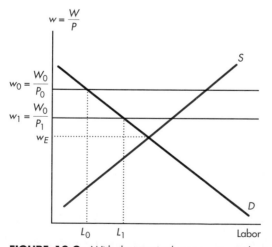

FIGURE 12-9   With the nominal wage rate stuck at W_0, a rise in the price level from P_0 to P_1 means a drop in the real wage from W_0/P_0 to W_0/P_1. This causes a rise in employment from L_0 to L_1.

The Goods Market

Figure 12-10 shows the effect of a price-level increase on both the labor market and the goods market, with the production function as the intermediary that ties the two together.

When the price level rises from P_0 to P_1 in Figure 12-10(a), the real wage falls from w_0 to w_1. The quantity of labor hired rises from L_0 to L_1. Figure 12-10(b) shows

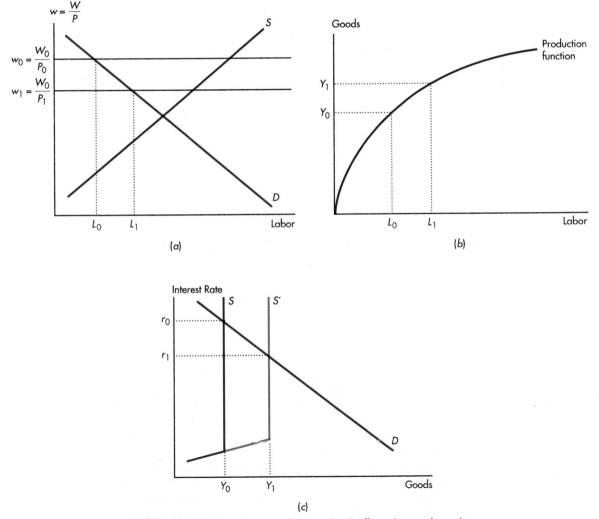

FIGURE 12-10 How a rise in the price level affects the goods market.
The nominal wage is stuck at W_0. A rise in the price level from P_0 to P_1 yields an increase in employment from L_0 to L_1 in the labor market (a). The production function (b) shows that output increases from Y_0 to Y_1. Therefore, the aggregate supply curve in the goods market (c) shifts rightward, becoming vertical at Y_1 instead of at Y_0. As a result, the interest rate drops to r_1.

that output then rises from Y_0 to Y_1. The aggregate supply curve in Figure 12-10(c), formerly vertical at Y_0, shifts right and is now vertical at Y_1. Because of the shift in supply, the equilibrium interest rate falls from r_0 to r_1.

> In the sticky wage model, a rise in the price level leads to higher output and a lower interest rate.

➡ *Exercise 12-2*
Trace the effects of a *drop* in the price level in the sticky wage model.

12-2 COMPARING THE MODELS

In Chapter 11, we criticized the neoclassical model on a variety of grounds. Let us see how the sticky wage model fares by the same standards.

The Real–Nominal Dichotomy

In the neoclassical model, the real and monetary sides of the economy are largely separate. The only link is that the real side of the economy determines the level of output (or, equivalently, income) and the interest rate, which in turn affect the demand for money. But there is no feedback from the monetary side of the economy to the real side. Changes in the price level have no real effects.

As we have seen in Figure 12-10, this is not the case in the sticky wage model. There, a rise in the price level causes the real wage to fall, employment to increase, output to increase, and the interest rate to fall. The sticky wage model offers a mechanism that links changes in the price level to real phenomena.

Which model is more accurate? In the real world, do price-level changes have real consequences or don't they?

To make the question more concrete, let us consider the specific consequences of an increase in the money supply. Figure 12-11 reminds us that (in either model), when the money supply rises, $1/P$ falls, which is to say that P increases. In the neoclassical model, that is the end of the story. The equilibria in the goods and labor markets remain unchanged.

But in the sticky wage model, the rising price level causes the real wage to fall, as in Figure 12-9. More labor is hired, and output increases.

So one way to compare the accuracy of the models is to ask this question: In the real world, does an increase in the money supply lead to an increase in output?

The question is difficult to answer, as many aspects of the economic environment are constantly changing, and when output increases, it is typically difficult to pinpoint the cause. However, in 1963, economists Milton Friedman and Anna Schwartz produced a massive detailed study of 100 years of American monetary history.[2] That study was instrumental in convincing the majority of economists that shocks to the money supply do have substantial real effects, at least over short periods of time.

The work of Friedman and Schwartz was extended by Christina Romer and David Romer.[3] The Romers investigated a series of incidents in U.S. history in which monetary authorities had deliberately cut the growth rate of the money supply. They found that these incidents were indeed followed by declines in output, contrary to the predictions of the neoclassical model. However, they also found that the declines were temporary, dying out within 33 months of the monetary shock.

A widespread view, consistent with the Romers' evidence, is that while the real-nominal dichotomy holds in the long run, there is also a short run, lasting anywhere from a few months to a couple of years, over which monetary changes have substantial real effects. That view would be justified if wages are flexible in the long run but sticky in the short run. This seems quite plausible if sticky wages are the result of union contracts or other temporary constraints.

The assertion that money supply changes can affect real variables such as output is sometimes summarized with the slogan "Money matters." The widespread view of the previous paragraph can then be summarized as "Money matters, but only in the short run."

Recently, however, a growing number of economists have begun to question

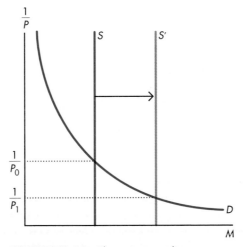

FIGURE 12-11 The money market.
An increase in the money supply from S to S' leads to a drop in $1/P$ or, equivalently, a rise in the price level P.

[2]M. Friedman and A. Schwartz, *A Monetary History of the United States, 1867–1960* (Princeton, N.J.: Princeton University Press, 1963).

[3]C. Romer and D. Romer, "Does Monetary Policy Matter? A New Test in the Spirit of Friedman and Schwartz," in *NBER Macroeconomics Annual* (Cambridge: National Bureau of Economic Research, 1989).

whether money matters at all. In 1986, economists Martin Eichenbaum and Kenneth Singleton, after carefully examining 40 years of data, concluded that the growth of the money supply is *not* a useful predictor of growth in either current or future output.[4] Commenting on their work, N. Gregory Mankiw succinctly restated Eichenbaum and Singleton's conclusion: "Money has not mattered, at least over the past forty years."[5] Mankiw went on to argue that this conclusion is both "not obviously wrong" and "not obviously right." Clearly, economists will be arguing this issue for a long time to come.

Involuntary Unemployment

The neoclassical model predicts that all unemployment is voluntary. The sticky wage model predicts, by contrast, that some unemployment is involuntary. In Figure 12-1 (which shows the labor market with sticky wages), $L_1 - L_0$ units of labor are involuntarily unemployed.

Which model is more accurate? Is all real-world unemployment voluntary?

Before we attempt to answer this question, we must stress again (as we did in Chapter 11) that a *voluntarily* unemployed worker is not the same as a *happily* unemployed worker. Workers may be voluntarily unemployed because the equilibrium wage rate is so low that working is simply not worth the trouble—perhaps the wage is even so low that it fails to cover bus fare to the workplace! Such unemployment is voluntary, but it is still extremely unpleasant.

We must also be careful about how we define involuntary unemployment in the real world. The models treat "labor hours" as a single commodity, as if every worker's hours are interchangeable with those of any other worker. For many purposes, this may be an acceptable simplification. But when we discuss real-world unemployment, it becomes necessary to recognize that different workers have different skills and that different skills command different wages.

The usual criterion for involuntary unemployment is that workers cannot sell as many labor hours as they would like to sell. Does this then mean that Woody Allen is involuntarily unemployed as a center for the New York Knicks? At the current wage for that position, Woody is undoubtedly unable to sell as many hours to the Knicks as he would like to—so perhaps by definition he is. However, we really don't want to view the fact that Patrick Ewing plays basketball and Woody Allen doesn't as an example of an economic problem. It makes far more sense to say that the going wage for the services of *people like Woody Allen* in professional basketball is extremely low (in fact, it is almost surely negative) and at that wage Woody *voluntarily* chooses not to play.

The correct real-world equivalent of our model's involuntarily unemployed worker is then a worker who would like to work at *the wage that is currently being offered to other workers with exactly the same skills* but is unable to do so. To build

[4]M. Eichenbaum and K. Singleton, "Real Business Cycles," in *NBER Macroeconomics Annual* (Cambridge: National Bureau of Economic Research, 1986).

[5]N. Gregory Mankiw, "Comment on Eichenbaum and Singleton," in ibid.

this idea rigorously into the model, we might want to consider different labor markets for different types of labor, each with its own demand, supply, and equilibrium wage.

From this viewpoint, it is not immediately evident how much real-world unemployment is of the involuntary variety. Are a significant number of workers really willing to perform existing jobs at less-than-current wages but unable to find work? (If so, then there is significant involuntary unemployment.) Or are workers unemployed primarily because their skills simply do not command a wage sufficient to draw them into the marketplace? (In that case, most real-world unemployment is voluntary.)

The Great Depression of the 1930s is a vast source of anecdotes supporting both sides of this question. In many stories, thousands of workers would show up when a plant announced a single job. Only one would be hired, and the rest would leave, involuntarily unemployed. These stories support the sticky wage model. According to the neoclassical model, the wage rate would have fallen until only one willing worker remained.

On the other hand, there are counteranecdotes that support precisely that neoclassical conclusion. The Budd Company is a major manufacturing firm in Philadelphia. When it had a job to offer in the 1930s, a manager would appear before a crowd of applicants and ask, "Who will work for a dollar an hour?" then "Who will work for 75 cents?" and so on, until only one applicant remained. The others had left unhappily but voluntarily.

Anecdotes, then, particularly when they are filtered through 60 years of memory, seem unlikely to settle the question. A more rigorous approach was offered by Robert Lucas and Leonard Rapping in 1972.[6] Lucas and Rapping evaluated the proposition that unemployment in the Great Depression was largely a voluntary response to unusually low wage rates. According to this hypothesis, workers, used to the much higher wage rates of the 1920s, did not expect the low wages of the 1930s to last for a long time; they therefore (voluntarily) turned down low-wage jobs while waiting for their salary offers to return to "normal" levels. Lucas and Rapping's examination of the historical evidence showed that a scenario along these lines seems to fit the facts pretty well at least until 1934 but less well after that. Of course, the observation that a particular hypothesis fits the facts does not make that interpretation correct; there may be alternative theories that fit the facts equally well.

The question of how much unemployment is involuntary remains an important unsolved problem in macroeconomics.

Unemployment rate:

The percentage of the labor force that is unemployed.

Labor force:

People who are employed or who have actively sought employment in the recent past.

Interpreting Unemployment Statistics

Figure 12-12(*a*) is a graph of the U.S. unemployment rate since the end of World War II. It is important to recognize that the **unemployment rate** is *not* the percentage of the population that is unemployed. Rather, it is the percentage of the *labor force* that is unemployed, where the **labor force** consists of people who are employed plus those

[6]R. Lucas and L. Rapping, "Unemployment in the Great Depression: Is There a Full Explanation?" *Journal of Political Economy* 80 (1972), 186–191.

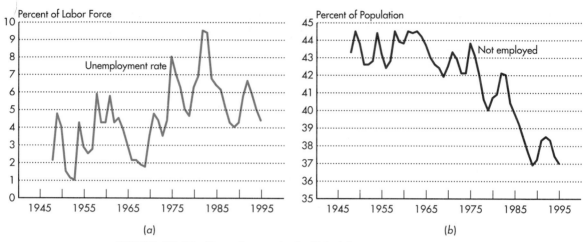

FIGURE 12-12   Unemployment in the United States.
(*a*) The unemployment rate, reported as a percentage of the labor force; (*b*) the percentage of the population that was not employed.

who have actively sought employment in the past 4 weeks. In the past 50 years, the unemployment rate has ranged from just under 3 percent to just under 10 percent. It fluctuates considerably but displays a slight upward trend.

By contrast, Figure 12-12(*b*) shows the percentage of the *total population* that was not employed during the same period. Note the steady downward trend since the early 1960s. It indicates that since 1960, a steadily increasing fraction of the population has joined the labor force. Women seeking employment outside the home account for most of the change. As a result, a given *unemployment* rate now corresponds to a very different *employment* rate than it did 30 years ago. For example, the unemployment rate in 1990 was the same as it was in 1962: 5.5 percent of the labor force. But in 1962 only 55.5 percent of the population was employed, while in 1990 the fraction had risen to 62.7 percent.

Business Cycles

As we saw in Section 11-4, the neoclassical model has some difficulty explaining short-run phenomena like business cycles; however, it does much better at explaining long-run phenomena like economic growth. Thus, when we set out to adjust the model, it makes sense to maintain our treatment of those factors that are most important in the long run and to alter our treatment of those factors that are most important in the short run.

This leads us to ask: Which factors *are* most important in the long run and in the short run, say, for explaining variations in output? To answer, let us examine the two factors that are inputs to the production process: capital and labor.

Figure 12-13(*a*) shows the values of U.S. output and U.S. capital stock (both on a per capita basis) since 1870. (The curve shows output, for which good data are readily available, and the squares show capital in those years for which estimates are avail-

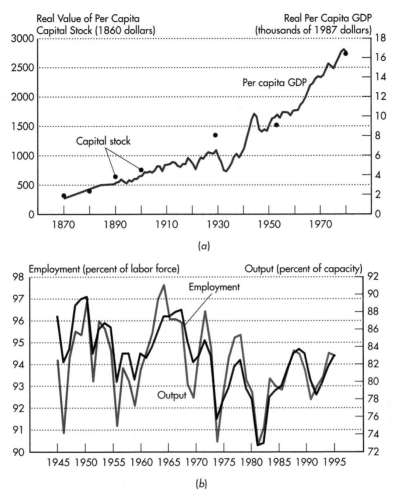

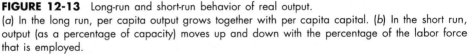

FIGURE 12-13 Long-run and short-run behavior of real output.
(a) In the long run, per capita output grows together with per capita capital. (b) In the short run, output (as a percentage of capacity) moves up and down with the percentage of the labor force that is employed.

able.)[7] As the neoclassical growth model in Chapter 8 would predict, capital and output grow together in the long run.

In Figure 12-13(b) the black curve shows the percentage of the labor force that was employed, and the blue curve shows output as a fraction of capacity (that is, as a fraction of its estimated potential) since 1948. You can see that over short periods of time, the curves move very closely together. In the short run, then, variations in labor are very closely tied to variations in output.

[7]The estimates come from R. Gallman, "American Economic Growth before the Civil War," in R. Gallman and J. Wallis, *American Economic Growth and Standards of Living before the Civil War* (Cambridge: National Bureau of Economic Research, 1992).

This suggests that if we want to modify the neoclassical model to deal more accurately with the short run, we might begin by reconsidering its treatment of the labor market. The sticky wage model does that. And indeed, sticky wages are themselves clearly a short-run phenomenon; given sufficient time, even the stickiest wage ought to be able to adjust to market conditions.

Thus it is natural to turn to the sticky wage model for a better description of real-world business cycles. We can test it by analyzing some shocks that might be responsible for a recession.

A Supply Shock

Figure 12-14 shows the effect of a negative supply shock in the sticky wage model. A loss of output (due, say, to a tornado) causes the aggregate supply curve in Figure 12-14(a) to shift leftward from S to S'. Because of consumption smoothing, the aggregate demand curve shifts slightly leftward, from D to D'. As a result, the interest rate increases from r_0 to r_1.

The new, higher interest rate causes the supply of labor in Figure 12-14(b) to shift rightward from $S(r_0)$ to $S(r_1)$. However, there is no change in the labor demand curve, because the marginal product of labor is unaffected.

The demand for money in Figure 12-14(c) falls both because the interest rate is up and because income is down [these are the effects that we discovered in panel (a)]. Thus the equilibrium price level rises from P_0 to P_1. The higher price level now leads to a lower real wage $w_1 = W_0/P_1$, indicated in panel (b). At this wage rate, employers hire L_1 units of labor instead of L_0. That is, employment increases.

We could go further: The increase in employment to L_1 in Figure 12-14(b) leads to an increase in output, pushing the supply curve in Figure 12-14(a) back toward its original position. That in turn has further effects. But we have already shifted each curve once, and we expect the second round of effects to be smaller than the first. Therefore, we can ignore that second round and still feel reasonably certain that we know the directions in which all of the variables will have moved.

We will use the same strategy repeatedly: We will shift each curve *once* and stop after we come full circle and are about to shift the same curve a second time. At this point we can be confident that every variable has changed in the proper direction.

Our analysis of Figure 12-14 leads us to the following conclusions:

In the sticky wage model, a temporary supply shock causes increases in the interest rate and the price level, a decrease in the real wage rate, and an increase in employment.

➡ *Exercise 12-3*
In what ways do these conclusions differ from those of the neoclassical model?

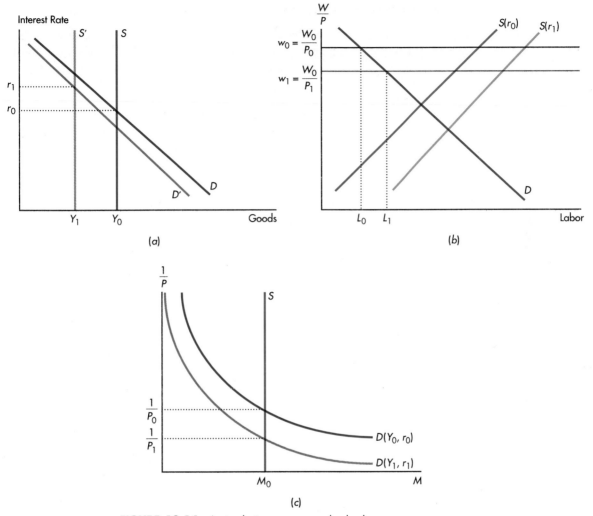

(a)

(b)

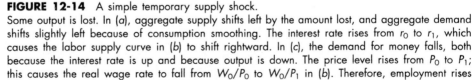

(c)

FIGURE 12-14 A simple temporary supply shock.
Some output is lost. In (a), aggregate supply shifts left by the amount lost, and aggregate demand shifts slightly left because of consumption smoothing. The interest rate rises from r_0 to r_1, which causes the labor supply curve in (b) to shift rightward. In (c), the demand for money falls, both because the interest rate is up and because output is down. The price level rises from P_0 to P_1; this causes the real wage rate to fall from W_0/P_0 to W_0/P_1 in (b). Therefore, employment rises from L_0 to L_1.

Now let's evaluate our conclusions. Our goal was to generate recessions within the sticky wage model. The central feature of recessions is a drop in output, and we modeled that by simply assuming that output is destroyed by some external source. But this assumption led us to conclude that during a recession the interest rate rises and so does employment. Both conclusions—particularly the one about employment—seem inconsistent with the facts.

A More Complicated Supply Shock

Suppose that the marginal productivity of labor falls, perhaps because of a bad harvest season or an interruption in the supply of oil. Figure 12-15 shows the consequences. Figure 12-15(a) is identical to Figure 12-14(a). The supply of goods shifts leftward, and demand shifts leftward by a smaller amount because of consumption smoothing.

In Figure 12-15(b), the demand for labor shifts leftward from D to D' because marginal productivity is down. The supply of labor S could shift either to the right

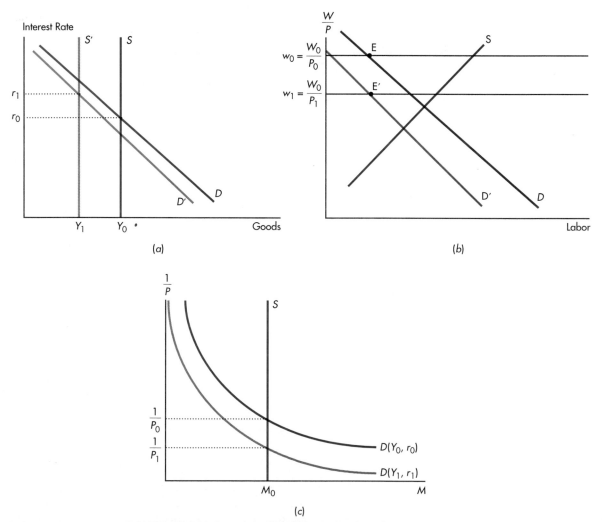

(a)

(b)

(c)

FIGURE 12-15   A temporary drop in marginal productivity.
The consequences in the goods market (a), the labor market (b), and the money market (c) are the same as those of the simple supply shock in Figure 12-14, except that the demand for labor also falls in (b). Consequently, employment could fall.

(because the interest rate rises) or to the left (because of intertemporal substitution). Fortunately, however, we don't need to know which way it shifts, because its location has no effect on the amount of labor hired. Therefore, we need not depict a shift of S in either direction.

Figure 12-15(c) is identical to Figure 12-14(c). The demand for money shifts down because of the increase in the interest rate and the decline in output. The price level thus rises from P_0 to P_1.

This change in the price level feeds back into Figure 12-15(b), where the real wage falls from W_0/P_0 to W_0/P_1. The equilibrium in the labor market shifts from point E to point E'.

Depending on the shape of the labor demand curve and depending on how far the price level (and hence the real wage) moves, E' could lie either to the right or to the left of E. Thus employment could either increase or decrease.

> In the sticky wage model, a shock to marginal productivity has consequences similar to those of a simple supply shock, except that it is possible for employment to fall.

As a means for generating recessions within the sticky wage model, a drop in the MPL does a bit better than the simple supply shock of Figure 12-14; at least it allows the possibility that employment could fall. However, to get a significant decline in employment out of Figure 12-15, the labor demand curve must shift quite far to the left. Most economists find such a large shift implausible.

In addition, Figure 12-15, like Figure 12-14, predicts rising interest rates during recessions, but that outcome contradicts most economists' interpretation of the facts.

A Demand Shock

Let's try an alternative shock. Suppose that for some reason people decide to cut back on either their current consumption, their current investment, or both. This action might be caused by a wave of pessimism about the future, which leads people to reassess either their wealth (so that consumption falls) or the productivity of capital (so that investment falls). Either way, there is a drop in the demand for current goods.

In Figure 12-16 we trace the consequences. We begin when the demand curve shifts leftward from D to D' in the goods market [panel (a)]. At this point, the supply curve is unaffected, so the equilibrium interest rate falls from r_0 to r_1.

Because the interest rate falls, the supply of labor shifts leftward from S to S' in the labor market [panel (b)]. This, however, has no effect on the quantity of labor hired, because the wage rate remains unchanged at this point.

In the money market [panel (c)], the drop in the interest rate pushes the demand for money upward from D to D' in panel (c). The equilibrium price level falls from P_0 to P_1.

Now we return to Figure 12-16(b). The nominal wage is still stuck at W_0, but the price level has changed to P_1, so the new real wage is $w_1 = W_0/P_1$. At this higher real wage, employment falls from L_0 to L_1.

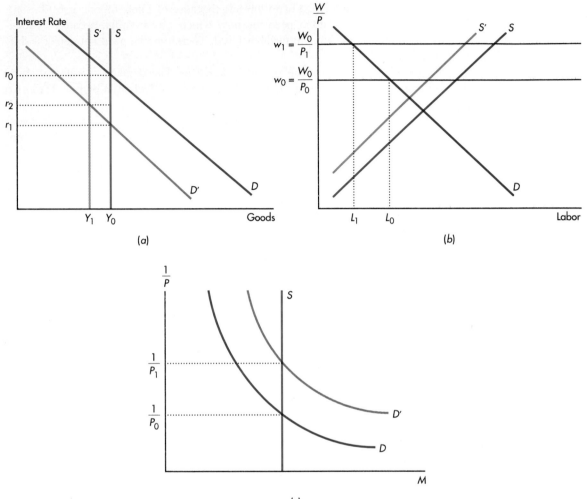

(a)   (b)

(c)

FIGURE 12-16 A negative demand shock.
In (a), the aggregate demand curve shifts leftward, causing the interest rate to fall initially to r_1.
In (b), the lower interest rate causes the labor supply curve to fall, and in (c), the lower interest
rate causes the demand for money to increase. The price level falls to P_1 in (c), causing the real
wage to rise to W_1 in the labor market (b). Now employment falls from L_0 to L_1, and consequently
output falls, as illustrated by the leftward shift in aggregate supply in (a).

Finally, the drop in employment means that fewer goods are produced, so the
aggregate supply curve in Figure 12-16(a) shifts leftward to Y_1. The equilibrium interest rate settles at r_2.

In the sticky wage model, a negative demand shock leads to reductions in
output, employment, the interest rate, and the price level and to a rise in the
real wage.

Can negative demand shocks explain recessions? To argue that the answer is yes, we must maintain that a recession is triggered by a drop in aggregate demand, which ultimately leads (through a complicated sequence of events) to a drop in aggregate supply. Along the way, the interest rate falls, employment falls, the price level falls, and the real wage rate rises. Most of this fits the facts pretty well. But not all of it: Unfortunately for the theory, the best evidence seems to indicate that real wages *fall* during recessions.[8]

For many years, economics textbooks presented this theory (or one very like it) as *the* theory of the business cycle: Wages are sticky at least in the short run, and recessions are caused by demand shocks. One prominent macroeconomist has recalled his discomfort with the theory:

> *Armed with these powerful tools of analysis, I reached the conclusion (completely on my own) that recessions must be quite popular. Sure, a few people get laid off. But most people get to enjoy the higher real wages that result when prices fall and their nominal wages do not.*

> *So I went to one of my professors . . . to ask him about this. I had the vague recollection that recessions were, in fact, politically unpopular, but this just did not make any sense to me. If high real wages accompanied low employment . . . then most households should welcome economic downturns.*

> *Well, Professor Blinder admitted to me that real wages do not move countercyclically. My conclusion did follow logically from the theory I had been taught as God's truth, but it just did not fit the facts. It was at that point that I decided to abandon macroeconomics. After all, how could I trust my macro textbook again? If (as a mere undergraduate) I had managed to uncover this big lie, how many more big lies remained undetected? I decided to stick to microeconomics.*

> *As one can see, my resolve weakened over time. Yet I have never stopped being disturbed by the cyclical behavior of the real wage.[9]*

A Monetary Shock

Let's make one more attempt to generate a realistic recession within the model. This time, suppose that the monetary authorities decrease the money supply. The initial effect is shown in Figure 12-17(c). The authorities shift the money supply from M_0 to M_1, and consequently the price level falls from P_0 to P_1.

In the labor market [Figure 12-17(b)], this causes the real wage rate to rise to $w_1 = W_0/P_1$. Therefore, employment falls from L_0 to L_1.

When employment falls, so does output; therefore, the aggregate supply curve shifts leftward from S to S' in Figure 12-17(a). In response to the decreased income,

---

[8]See, for example, the article by Rotemberg and Woodford in *NBER Macroeconomics Annual* (Cambridge: National Bureau of Economic Research, 1991).

[9]N. Gregory Mankiw, "Comment on Rotemberg and Woodford," in *NBER Macroeconomics Annual* (Cambridge: National Bureau of Economic Research, 1991).

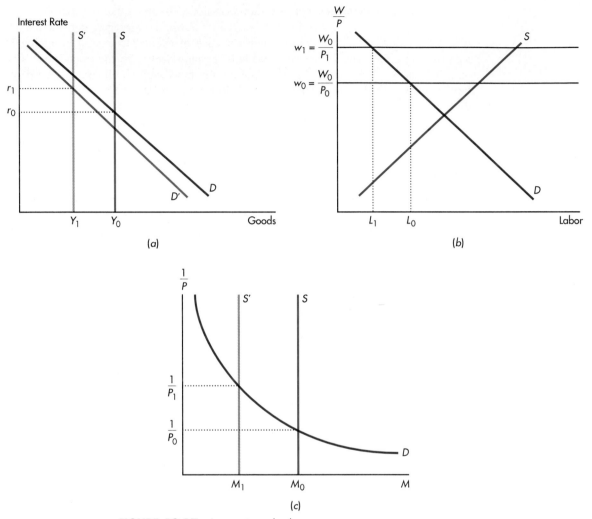

FIGURE 12-17 A monetary shock.
The authorities decrease the money supply from M_0 to M_1 in (c). The price level falls from P_0 to P_1. In (b), the real wage increases to W_0/P_1, and employment falls from L_0 to L_1. Because employment falls, output is reduced; that is, the aggregate supply curve shifts to the left in (a). Also in (a), the aggregate demand curve shifts slightly to the left because of consumption smoothing. The interest rate rises from r_0 to r_1.

the aggregate demand curve shifts left, but only slightly because of consumption smoothing. The interest rate rises from r_0 to r_1.

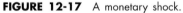

> In the sticky wage model, a monetary shock causes employment and output to fall, the real wage to rise, and the interest rate to rise.

As a theory about recessions, this one is deficient regarding both the real wage rate and the interest rate, which seem to be going in the wrong direction.

Conclusion: Business Cycles in the Sticky Wage Model

If we had an adequate model of recessions, we would almost surely have an adequate model of the entire business cycle. If, for example, negative supply shocks (or negative demand shocks or negative monetary shocks) trigger recessions, then presumably positive supply shocks (or positive demand shocks or positive monetary shocks) trigger expansions.

Unfortunately, none of these negative shocks seems able to generate a completely realistic recession within the sticky wage model. Supply shocks produce the wrong predictions for interest rates; demand shocks produce the wrong predictions for real wages; and monetary shocks produce the wrong predictions for both. On the other hand, as is true for the neoclassical model as well, these shocks do not exhaust the possibilities. Recessions may result from more complicated shocks or from several kinds of shocks happening in tandem.

Still, no economist has yet written down a completely satisfactory account of how a realistic business cycle could take place within the context of the sticky wage model.

12-3 GOVERNMENT ACTIONS

Now let us see what the sticky wage model says about the role of government. If a recession is under way, can the government take steps to improve matters? We will consider a variety of policy options.

Fiscal Policy

In Figure 12-16, we learned that a spontaneous decrease in aggregate demand causes employment and output to fall. By the same token, a spontaneous *increase* in aggregate demand can cause employment and output to rise. It is not immediately obvious that such a change represents an improvement in economic welfare: people are better off for having higher incomes but worse off for working more hours. However, if wages are sticky, then the additional hours are supplied by people whose initial unemployment was involuntary, so the net effect on welfare does turn out to be positive.

Therefore, when wages are sticky, it can be a good thing for the government to trigger an increase in aggregate demand. The question is this: How can the government possibly cause aggregate demand to shift?

Providing Public Goods

One way to increase aggregate demand is by making people wealthier. Sometimes the government can do this by undertaking programs that provide public goods whose value exceeds their cost. Virtually any economic model will recommend that projects of this sort be undertaken—independent of whether the economy is in a recession. (Of course, there is still room for considerable controversy about whether any *par-*

ticular project actually fits into this category.) Unfortunately, only a limited number of such projects can be devised.

Government Debt

Once the government has exhausted its opportunities to make people wealthier by providing valuable public goods, is there anything *else* that it can do to stimulate aggregate demand? The answer is "perhaps."

Suppose the government borrows money so that it can either increase current transfer payments or reduce current taxes. We know from Chapter 6 that the resulting increase in government debt guarantees higher taxes in the future. The present value of those taxes is exactly equal to what the government borrows. (This is the basis for the Ricardian equivalence principle.) Therefore, the average taxpayer is made neither more nor less wealthy by government borrowing.

The Ricardian equivalence principle reminds us that when wealth is unchanged, consumption demand is also unchanged. This suggests that any plan for using transfers or tax cuts to stimulate aggregate demand is doomed to failure. Such a plan will not change wealth, and so will not (according to Ricardian equivalence) change demand.

But in Chapter 6 we also discussed a variety of reasons why Ricardian equivalence might fail. Perhaps people's spending is artificially constrained by poor credit ratings; perhaps people don't care about future taxes because they don't care about their descendants; perhaps people are simply ignorant and do not perceive that today's deficits translate into tomorrow's taxes. If Ricardian equivalence does fail for these reasons or for others, then programs that increase the government's debt can have the side effect of increasing aggregate demand.

Fiscal policies:

Decisions about government spending and taxation.

Decisions about spending and taxation are called **fiscal policies.** Figure 12-18 shows the effects of a change in fiscal policy in the sticky wage model. The figure assumes that Ricardian equivalence does *not* hold, and it traces the effects of a deficit-financed increase in transfer payments or a deficit-financed cut in taxes.

In panel (a), aggregate demand shifts rightward from D to D' in response to people's sense of being wealthier. This causes the interest rate to rise initially from r_0 to r_1.

In panel (c), the new, higher interest rate causes the demand for money to shift leftward from D to D', so the price level rises from P_0 to P_1.

In panel (b), the new, higher price level causes the real wage to fall from $w_0 = W_0/P_0$ to $w_1 = W_0/P_1$. This causes employment to increase from L_0 to L_1.

In panel (a), the increase in employment means that more goods are produced, so aggregate supply shifts rightward, from S to S'. The interest rate settles at r_2.

In summary:

If wages are sticky and Ricardian equivalence fails, then an increase in the government's debt leads to increases in the interest rate, the price level, employment, and output.

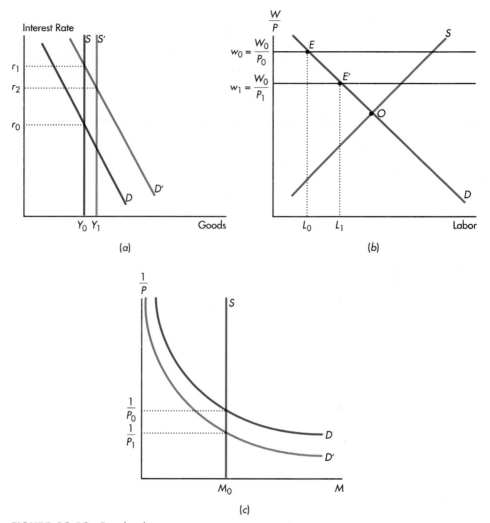

FIGURE 12-18 Fiscal policy.
The government runs a deficit to finance either transfer payments or tax cuts. If Ricardian equivalence holds, there are no effects. The diagrams here assume that Ricardian equivalence fails. Aggregate demand shifts rightward from D to D' in the goods market (a). The interest rate rises from r_0 to r_1, causing the demand for money to fall from D to D' in the money market (c). The price level rises from P_0 to P_1, causing the real wage rate to fall from w_0 to w_1 in the labor market (b). Employment rises from L_0 to L_1, causing output to rise, say, from Y_0 to Y_1, shifting the aggregate supply curve to the right in (a) and causing the interest rate to settle at r_2.

Is fiscal stimulation a good thing? To answer this question, look again at Figure 12-18(b). A perfectly functioning market with flexible prices would settle at the neoclassical equilibrium point O. By shifting the actual equilibrium from E to E', the government has moved the market closer to that ideal outcome. In that sense, the policy change has certainly improved the economy's performance.

Wasteful Government Spending without Ricardian Equivalence

Figure 12-18 tells us that if wages are sticky and Ricardian equivalence fails, then an increase in transfer payments can stimulate output and employment. It turns out that if the government is willing to spend *wastefully* instead of just giving money away, its spending can have an even bigger impact on the labor market.

First note that in Figure 12-18, the entire sequence of events is triggered by a rightward shift in the aggregate demand for goods, which raises the interest rate. The more the interest rate increases, the greater all of the subsequent effects will be. These include the shift in money demand, the rise in the price level, the drop in the real wage rate, and the increase in employment.

Now suppose that instead of making transfer payments, the government institutes a spending program whose cost exceeds its benefits. If the program is financed by future taxes that people fail to account for (that is, if Ricardian equivalence continues to fail), then the aggregate demand curve still shifts rightward, as in Figure 12-18. But now this shift is accompanied by a simultaneous *leftward* shift in aggregate *supply,* reflecting the fact that goods have essentially been destroyed by the government.

That leftward shift in aggregate supply means that the interest rate initially moves higher than r_1 in Figure 12-18(a).

The remainder of the scenario is the same as that in Figure 12-18, but all the effects are greater than before.

Exercise 12-4
Draw three graphs representing the goods, labor, and money markets, illustrating the effects of wasteful government spending in the absence of Ricardian equivalence.

Our analysis indicates that wasteful spending can do more to stimulate the labor market than mere transfers can. A bigger impact on employment means a bigger impact on the total output produced. But the production of more output does not mean that more goods are available for consumption and investment, because the quantity wasted by the government typically exceeds the additional production.

Therefore, comparing wasteful spending to transfer payments, we find the following:

> According to the sticky wage model, if Ricardian equivalence fails, then either transfer payments or wasteful government spending can stimulate employment. Of the two options, wasteful spending increases employment more, but it leaves fewer goods available for consumption and investment.

The representative agent, who prefers to work less and eat more, is better off in a world of transfer payments. But certain individuals—those hoping to find employment as a result of the government's fiscal policy—might actually prefer to see the government spend wastefully.

Wasteful Government Spending with Ricardian Equivalence

We have already observed that if Ricardian equivalence holds, then an increase in transfer payments has no effect on output, employment, the interest rate, the wage rate, or the price level.

By contrast, wasteful spending can increase employment even if Ricardian equivalence holds. Indeed, the effects of wasteful spending are exactly the same as those of a tornado that destroys output. These effects have already been illustrated in Figure 12-14. We see from Figure 12-14(b) that employment rises (from the initial L_0 to L_1). The sum of consumption and investment [determined by equilibrium in Figure 12-14(a)] decreases from Y_0 to Y_1.

Are people made better off in this scenario? The same points apply as those discussed in the preceding subsection. Because of the wasteful spending, people work more and have fewer goods to consume and to invest. Therefore, wasteful spending must make the representative agent worse off. Nevertheless, certain individuals benefit, namely, those from the ranks of the involuntarily unemployed who find jobs when employment increases.

According to the sticky wage model, if Ricardian equivalence holds, then wasteful government spending can stimulate employment even though transfer payments cannot. Although wasteful spending leads to higher employment, it reduces the quantity of goods available for consumption and investment.

An Increase in the Money Supply

An increase in the supply of money causes the reverse of what we saw in Figure 12-17: employment and output both increase. The mechanism is simple: By increasing the money supply (and hence the price level), the government allows real wages to fall, whereupon employers hire more labor to produce more goods. Thus, according to the sticky wage model, the government can use changes in the money supply to put people back to work and increase their incomes.

According to the sticky wage model, an increase in the money supply can increase both employment and output.

➡ *Exercise 12-5*
Illustrate the effects of an increase in the money supply, drawing graphs of the markets for goods, labor, and money.

Conclusion: The Role of Government

Governments can attempt to increase employment either by changing fiscal policy (increasing spending or cutting taxes) or by increasing the money supply.

According to the sticky wage model, the effectiveness of fiscal policy depends on whether Ricardian equivalence holds. In the presence of Ricardian equivalence, transfer payments and tax cuts (that is, increases in government debt) have no effects, whereas deliberately wasteful spending can increase employment while reducing the quantity of goods available for consumption and investment. In the absence of Ricardian equivalence, transfer payments and tax cuts can increase both employment and the quantity of goods available for consumption and investment; compared with transfers and tax cuts, deliberately wasteful spending has a greater effect on employment but a lesser (possibly even negative) effect on consumption and investment.

If wages are sticky, then increases in the money supply always increase employment and output.

Thus the sticky wage model implies that the government can take a number of actions that will provide clear benefits to the unemployed and perhaps to others.

By contrast, recall that in the neoclassical model, changes in the money supply have no real effects, while a temporary increase in wasteful government spending can have only negative effects. (Although employment does rise, nobody benefits from this because nobody was involuntarily unemployed in the first place. However, the real wage rate falls, and workers are all worse off.)

Thus the sticky wage model supports a much more active role for the government than the neoclassical model does. From the time it was first proposed to the late 1970s, it was the primary justification for the use of public works programs and rapid money supply increases in U.S. government attempts to combat recessions.

SUMMARY

In the sticky wage model we assume that the nominal wage rate is "stuck" above its equilibrium level and is unable to fall. As a result, the quantity of labor demanded is less than the quantity supplied. Since the quantity demanded is the amount of labor that actually gets hired, the difference between the two quantities is the amount of labor that is involuntarily unemployed.

One consequence of the sticky wage is that the labor supply curve can shift without having any effect on how much labor is actually hired. Consequently, the supply curve in the goods market is vertical (except at very low interest rates): higher interest rates fail to result in more output being produced.

If the price level rises, the real wage rate falls, so employment rises and, consequently, so does output. This breaks the real-nominal dichotomy that holds in the neoclassical model. Changes in the money market affect the price level and, consequently, now have real effects (that is, effects in the goods and labor markets).

We can examine various negative shocks to see whether they generate realistic-looking recessions (and hence business cycles) within the sticky wage model.

A simple supply shock, such as the loss of some quantity of output following a natural disaster, causes the interest rate and the price level to rise while the real wage rate falls and employment increases.

A decrease in the marginal productivity of labor has essentially the same results, though the model allows the possibility of a decrease rather than an increase in employment.

A decrease in aggregate demand causes the interest rate, the price level, and the level of employment to fall, while the real wage rate rises. Except for the increase in real wages, the demand shock seems to plausibly generate a real-world recession.

A monetary shock causes decreases in the price level and employment but increases in the real wage rate and the interest rate.

According to the sticky wage model, there are a variety of actions that the government can take to combat the effects of a recession. If Ricardian equivalence fails, then fiscal policy in the form of increased government spending or tax cuts can increase both employment and output. Wasteful spending has a bigger effect on employment at the cost of reducing the quantity of output available for consumption and investment.

If Ricardian equivalence holds, then transfer payments and tax cuts are ineffective, but wasteful spending can still increase employment, though once again at the expense of reducing the quantity of output available for consumption and investment.

An increase in the money supply can increase both employment and output, regardless of whether Ricardian equivalence holds.

PROBLEM SET

Unless directed otherwise, answer all questions in the context of the sticky wage model.

1. Suppose that, as a gesture of good will, Canada gives $100 billion worth of goods to the United States. What happens to the level of involuntary unemployment in the United States? (*Hint:* What happens to the demand and supply curves for labor?)

2. In the preceding problem, how far does the U.S. aggregate supply curve shift?

3. Suppose that a change in the climate causes the production function to become steeper. What happens to the level of involuntary unemployment?

4. Suppose that initially L_0 units of labor are employed to produce Y_0 units of output. Then the production function becomes steeper, and L_0 units of labor can produce Y_1 units of output. In the goods market, how far does the aggregate supply curve shift?

5. *True or false:* In the neoclassical model, an increase in aggregate demand can cause the price level to either rise or fall; but in the sticky wage model, an increase in aggregate demand must cause the price level to rise.

6. *True or false:* An increase in the availability of credit cards will lead to an increase in output if wages are sticky, but not otherwise.

7. Within a sticky wage model, show how to construct points on a graph that plots the price level (on the vertical axis) and the amount of involuntary unemployment (on the horizontal). Which way does the curve slope?

8. Trace through all the economic effects of a positive supply shock, assuming that the shock does not affect the marginal productivity of labor.

9. Trace through all the economic effects of a temporary increase in the marginal product of labor.

10. Trace through all the economic effects of a spontaneous decrease in the demand for money.

11. Figure 12-14 shows the impact of a temporary supply shock. In a similar figure, illustrate the impact of a *permanent* supply shock.

12. Figure 12-15 shows the impact of a temporary decrease in the marginal productivity of labor. In a similar figure, illustrate the impact of a *permanent* decrease in the marginal productivity of labor.

13. Suppose that the sticky wage model is accurate and that the government wants to increase employment. Assuming that Ricardian equivalence holds, rank the relative effectiveness of the following four plans:
   a. A temporary wasteful spending program
   b. A permanent wasteful spending program

    c. A temporary increase in transfer payments

    d. A permanent increase in transfer payments

14. Repeat problem 13, assuming this time that Ricardian equivalence does *not* hold.

15. Suppose the government wants to increase the sum of consumption and investment. It is sure that wages are sticky and that Ricardian equivalence holds. Rank the relative effectiveness of the following three plans:

    a. A temporary wasteful spending program

    b. A temporary increase in transfer payments

    c. An increase in the money supply

16. Repeat problem 15, assuming this time that wages are sticky but Ricardian equivalence does *not* hold.

17. In a sticky wage economy with an ongoing wasteful government program, what are the effects of an announcement that the program will be canceled beginning next year?

18. Suppose the government takes advantage of a temporary opportunity to provide a useful public good whose value exceeds its cost. What are the effects on employment and output in a sticky wage model? How do they differ from the effects in a neoclassical model? (In answering this question, you may assume that the program is financed out of current taxes.)

19. Suppose the government takes advantage of a temporary opportunity to provide a useful public good whose value exceeds its cost. Suppose also that Ricardian equivalence does *not* hold and that the government has not decided whether to finance the program out of current taxes or by borrowing. Contrast the effects that the two options would have on current output and employment.

20. Suppose in the *neoclassical* model that the government legislates a wage control that prevents nominal wages from rising *above* a certain fixed (below-equilibrium) level.

    a. What are the effects of a rise in the price level?

    b. What are the effects of a fall in the price level?

    c. What are the effects of a simple negative supply shock?

    d. What are the effects of a simple positive supply shock?

    e. What are the effects of a temporary fall in the marginal productivity of labor?

    f. What are the effects of a temporary rise in the marginal productivity of labor?

    g. What are the effects of a fall in aggregate demand?

    h. What are the effects of a rise in aggregate demand?

21. Make a chart, labeling the rows with potential shocks (a simple supply shock, a change in marginal productivity, a demand shock, a monetary shock) and labeling the columns with economic variables (output, employment, the interest rate, the real wage, the price level). Make entries in your chart to indicate how each variable moves in response to each shock. In doing so, assume that the sticky wage model and Ricardian equivalence both hold.

22. Repeat problem 21, continuing to assume that the sticky wage model holds but now assuming that Ricardian equivalence fails.

Chapter 13

The Sticky Price Model

The sticky wage model of Chapter 12, like the pure neoclassical model that precedes it, leaves some important macroeconomic phenomena unexplained. Additionally, many economists find the fundamental premise of the sticky wage model—an uncleared labor market—unappealing.

Nevertheless, introducing nominal stickiness into the model led to some suggestive conclusions about business cycles and government policy that were not explainable based on the pure neoclassical model. This leads us to experiment with an alternative kind of stickiness: sticky prices. In sticky price models, the labor and money markets both clear but the goods market does not. As you will see, sticky price and sticky wage models produce a number of similar predictions, and both suggest an active role in the economy for government policy.

13-1 STICKY PRICES

Sticky prices:
Sticky prices:
Prices that fail to adjust immediately to changes in the supply of or demand for goods.

If the nominal prices of goods fail to move immediately to their equilibrium values, we say that they are **sticky prices.** The **sticky price model** is a variant of the neoclassical model in which it is assumed that prices are sticky.

We begin our discussion of the sticky price model by examining some possible causes for sticky prices and the effects they would have on the markets for goods, labor, and money.

Why Sticky Prices?

Sticky price model:
A model that incorporates the possibility of sticky prices.

Do all prices adjust immediately, as is assumed in market-clearing models? The money supply changes daily; do firms really keep track of it and raise or lower prices accordingly every day? Or every week? Evidence suggests otherwise: Firms do not appear to change their prices as frequently as they would have to if the market-clearing model held exactly. As many as 40 percent of firms report that they change their prices only once a year.[1]

Price stickiness:
A tendency to leave prices unchanged in the face of changing economic conditions.

The tendency of businesses to leave prices unchanged is called **price stickiness.** The opposite of price stickiness is **price flexibility.** Price stickiness is difficult to explain in the context of microeconomic models and is an area of ongoing research. There are, however, some possible explanations.

Price flexibility:
A tendency to adjust prices immediately in the face of changing economic conditions.

Menu Costs

One reason prices might be sticky is that it is costly for firms to change their prices. Think of restaurants, where each price change requires that new menus be printed (and paid for). Despite continuous changes in the costs of raw meat and vegetables, restaurant owners might hesitate before adjusting the price of a meal—especially when the cost changes are small.

On the other hand, the printing of new menus is not so costly that it can account for a great deal of price stickiness. Surely if the price of meat doubled, restaurant owners would not hesitate to have new menus printed immediately.

But frequent menu changes can be undesirable for reasons that go beyond printing costs. Patrons like to know what a meal is going to cost before they decide which restaurant to go to, and they might be annoyed by a string of surprises.

Menu cost:
Anything that makes it costly for firms to change their prices, such as the printing of new menus in the case of a restaurant.

By analogy, anything that makes it costly for firms to change their prices is called a **menu cost.** One market where there appear to be *no* menu costs is the market for magazines on newsstands. The price of an issue has to be printed on the cover whether or not it has changed since the previous month; this suggests that there is no barrier to adjusting each issue's price according to market conditions. But the facts contra-

---

[1]A. S. Blinder, "Why Are Prices Sticky?" *American Economic Review* 81 (1991), 89–96.

dict that expectation. Stephen G. Cecchetti found that the average magazine's cover price is changed only after the general price level rises by about 25 percent.[2] No economist has explained why the publishers wait so long.

Advertised Prices

When the L.L. Bean company has its mail-order catalogs printed, it commits itself to selling overcoats at the published prices. To choose those prices, L.L. Bean must guess what the going price of overcoats will be at the time that the catalogs are delivered.

To make that guess, the company must first guess both the future price level and the future demand for overcoats. One way to guess at the demand for overcoats is to suppose that it will be equal to its historical average level. If L.L. Bean uses that method, it will make pretty much the same guess every year. In some years the resulting prices will be too low, and the company will be swamped with orders; in other years the prices will be too high, and there will later be a lot of idle time at the factory or a lot of overcoats on markdown in L.L. Bean outlet stores. But the key point is that the prices will be similar from one year to the next, and that situation is a form of price stickiness.

L.L. Bean's problem is similar to, but not identical with, that of the restaurant which is reluctant to adjust its prices. The restaurant hesitates to have new menus printed because it is costly to do so; L.L. Bean cannot have new catalogs printed because the old ones (its "menus") are already in customers' hands.

Unfortunately, there are problems with the catalog example. Firms take losses when they make mistakes, and purely competitive firms cannot afford to take such losses. Only a firm with some degree of monopoly power can survive the short-term losses that it must sometimes bear in this kind of a model. Therefore, if we want to claim that economywide prices are sticky because firms honor the prices that they've advertised, we must be willing to believe that monopoly power is fairly common. Many economists—though not all—find that belief implausible.

Adjustments to Service

Over the past few years, economist Alan Blinder has been conducting surveys in which he asks business owners why they don't adjust their prices more often.[3] Their most common response is that they frequently respond to changing market conditions not by adjusting prices but by adjusting the level of service that they offer. If the demand for IBM computers suddenly increases, neoclassical theory predicts that IBM will raise its prices. The survey data suggest that instead of raising prices, IBM might just make its customers wait longer for delivery or for technical support.

---

[2]S. G. Cecchetti, "The Frequency of Price Adjustment: A Study of the Newsstand Prices of Magazines," *Journal of Econometrics* 31 (1986), 255–274.

[3]A. S. Blinder, "Why Are Prices Sticky?" *American Economic Review* 81 (1991), 89–96.

Coordination Failure

The second most frequent response to Professor Blinder's surveys is that firms hesitate to adjust their prices before their rivals do (a situation called **coordination failure**). Even when the time is clearly ripe for an industrywide price adjustment, no firm wants to be the first to make such an announcement. Prices therefore remain sticky until demand for the product becomes high enough to encourage some firm to take the plunge.

Explicit and Implicit Contracts

Firms often have contracts with their customers which specify the price at which goods will be delivered. Over the period in which these contracts apply, prices might well be sticky. Many economists, however, object to the theory that contracts cause price stickiness; they point out that contracts can be renegotiated when the general price level changes and can even include explicit clauses allowing for periodic price adjustments. Professor Blinder's surveys provide some support for this objection; he found that renegotiation of contractual prices is quite common.

However, a lot of "contracts" are neither written down nor even precisely stated; they are understandings between suppliers and their customers that evolve over the course of a relationship and are sealed with an "invisible handshake." Economists call these understandings **implicit contracts,** as opposed to the usual **explicit contracts,** which are spelled out in writing.

Because implicit contracts are imprecise, they often cannot include provisions for price adjustments; firms that feel bound by such contracts might prefer to adjust their prices only infrequently. According to the business owners who responded to Professor Blinder's surveys, implicit contracts are far more important than explicit contracts as a source of price stickiness.

Limited Price Stickiness

No matter how many sources of price stickiness one may list, the fact remains that many prices are demonstrably flexible. Agricultural products, automobiles, computer components, bank loans—all have prices that adjust every day and even, in some cases, every minute.

However, recent and very surprising work by economists Alan Stockman and Lee Ohanian has demonstrated that even if only a small minority of goods prices are sticky, economywide variables (such as employment, output, and the price level) may behave as if *all* prices are sticky.[4] Stockman and Ohanian discovered this not by theorizing but by running computer simulations. Their finding means that the sticky price model might be applicable even in situations where its assumptions are only a poor approximation of the truth.

[4]*Bulletin of the St. Louis Federal Reserve Bank* (1995).

Invisible Price Stickiness

Economist Dennis Carlton has argued that real-world prices may be stickier than economists realize.[5] The following is an example of his reasoning.

Suppose that Robin Goodfellow supplies hockey pucks to the two major American hockey leagues. He charges the National Hockey League (NHL) $30 per puck, but he charges the American Hockey League (AHL) only $20 per puck—perhaps because somebody at the AHL was a shrewd bargainer. These prices are perfectly sticky.

Now suppose that in 1996 each league buys 100 pucks. The average price of those pucks is $25. Suppose also that in 1997 the NHL buys 150 pucks at $30 apiece while the AHL buys only 50 at $20 apiece. The average price of those pucks is $[(150 \times \$30) + (50 \times \$20)]/200 = \$27.50$.

An economist looking only at average prices will see a 1-year increase from $25 to $27.50—a 10 percent annual increase. From that observation, the economist might draw the incorrect inference that the price of hockey pucks is quite flexible. But the truth is that the price *to each customer* is perfectly sticky.

Carlton wondered whether such errors are commonplace. To test that possibility, he gathered data on prices to individual customers in various industries, and he found that the prices did indeed change less often than the *average* prices of those same goods. Thus there may be quite a bit of stickiness that is invisible to economists who deal only with average prices.

In many industries, prices to individual customers remained fixed for nearly a year or longer, as Figure 13-1 indicates.

The Money Market with Sticky Prices

Consider Figure 13-2, with our familiar money demand and money supply curves. Remember that the money supply curve is fixed by decisions of the monetary authorities, while the location of the demand curve is affected by both income and the interest rate.

Suppose the price level is sticky at level P_0, determined by the intersection of current money demand and supply—point A in Figure 13-2. Now suppose the money supply increases, from S to S'. If prices were not sticky, there would be a new equilibrium at point B, requiring that the price level rise to P_1. But by assumption this is impossible—the price level cannot move.

The money market can stay in equilibrium only if the demand curve shifts rightward to D'. This would allow the market to achieve a new equilibrium at point C without any change from the original price level.

But what could make the demand curve shift to the right? The answer is either a fall in the interest rate or a rise in income (or both). Many different combinations of interest rates and income can combine to yield the money demand curve D'. To

[5]D. Carlton, "Rigidity of Prices," *American Economic Review* 76 (1986), 637–658.

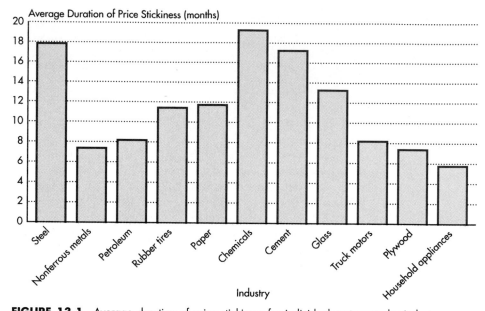

FIGURE 13-1 Average duration of price stickiness for individual customers, by industry. [*Source:* D. Carlton, "Rigidity of Prices," *American Economic Review* 76 (1986), 637–658.]

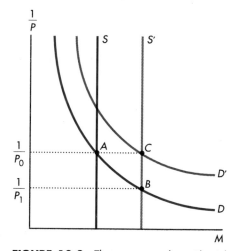

FIGURE 13-2 The money market with sticky prices.
The money market is initially in equilibrium at point *A*. Then the money supply increases from *S* to *S'*. If prices were flexible, the new equilibrium would be at point *B*, with a price level of P_1. But because prices are sticky, the price level must remain fixed at P_0. If the money market is to remain in equilibrium with supply curve *S'* and price level P_0, then the economy must end up at point *C*. And this can happen only if the demand curve shifts rightward to *D'*. This shift, in turn, requires a rise in income, a drop in the interest rate, or both.

maintain equilibrium in the money market, the economy must move to one of those combinations.

For the time being, we will not be so ambitious as to ask exactly *which* combination the economy moves to. (We will return to this question in Section 13-2.) Instead, our goal in this section is to examine the possibilities.

Our next task, then, is to determine the various combinations of interest rate and income that can yield a particular money demand curve, such as *D* or *D′*. We will represent those combinations by the points of a curve called the **LM curve.**

The *LM* Curve

Every point in Figure 13-3 represents a particular combination of interest rate and aggregate income (here measured in apples).

For example, point *X* represents an interest rate of 5 percent and an aggregate income of 10,000 apples. These interest-rate and income values determine the level of money demand; any movement away from point *X* can affect that demand. If we move upward in the graph (say, toward point *Z*), the interest rate rises, so money demand falls. If we move rightward (say, toward point *Y*), income rises, so money demand rises.

Suppose we move upward and rightward from point *X*. Then the simultaneous drop in money demand (due to the interest-rate rise) and rise in money demand (due to the income rise) might just happen to cancel each other out, leaving money demand unchanged. In other words, there may be other combinations of interest rate and income that yield the same money demand as point *X* docs.

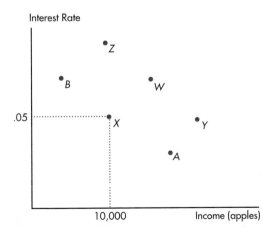

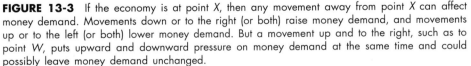

FIGURE 13-3 If the economy is at point *X*, then any movement away from point *X* can affect money demand. Movements down or to the right (or both) raise money demand, and movements up or to the left (or both) lower money demand. But a movement up and to the right, such as to point *W*, puts upward and downward pressure on money demand at the same time and could possibly leave money demand unchanged.

Point *W* could represent such a combination. There the interest rate is above 5 percent (which leads us to expect a *lower* money demand than at point *X*), and income is above 10,000 apples (which leads us to expect a *higher* money demand than at point *X*). It is *possible* that the two effects could cancel and thus yield the same money demand at *W* as that at *X*.

In general, to find points yielding the same money demand as point *X*, we need to look for points to the northeast or southwest of *X*, not to the southeast (like point *A*) or the northwest (like point *B*).

Point *X* is shown again in Figure 13-4(*a*), and the associated money demand curve D_1 is shown in Figure 13-4(*b*). (That is, an interest rate of 5 percent and an income of 10,000 apples yield the money demand curve D_1.) The curve through *X*, labeled LM_1, connects all the other points that yield exactly the same money demand curve D_1. It is the *LM* curve we have been seeking. Because every point on the *LM* curve must lie to either the northwest or the southeast of every other point on the curve, the *LM* curve slopes upward to the right.

For every money demand curve there is an associated *LM* curve, and vice versa. In Figure 13-4(*a*), we can look for all the combinations of interest rate and income that yield the money demand curve D_2. Then we can plot these points and connect them to obtain the curve LM_2. Note that LM_2 lies below and to the right of LM_1: to get the higher money demand curve D_2, we must have a lower interest rate, a higher income, or both.

 The letters "LM" stand for "liquidity preference" (which is another term for "money demand") and for "money supply." You might wonder what the "M" is doing there,

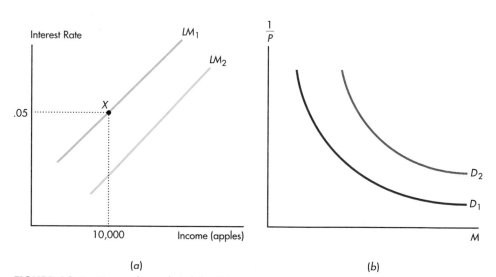

(a)   (b)

FIGURE 13-4 Money demand and the *LM* curve.
Each money demand curve has an associated *LM* curve. The *LM* curve in (a) shows all the combinations of interest rate and income that yield the associated money demand curve in (b). The points on LM_1 yield D_1, and the points on LM_2 yield D_2.

as our derivation of the *LM* curve is based entirely on money demand and has nothing whatever to do with the money supply. The answer is tied to the fact that there are alternative ways to think about the *LM* curve, which we have not made use of here.

Money Supply Shocks and the *LM* Curve

In this subsection we want to see what happens to the *LM* curve when the money supply is changed.

Figure 13-5(*b*) shows the money demand and supply curves of Figure 13-2. The economy is initially in equilibrium at point *A*, at the intersection of the money supply curve S_1 and the money demand curve D_1. The *LM* curve associated with D_1 is labeled LM_1 in Figure 13-5(*a*).

Now suppose the money supply is increased to S_2. Because the price level is stuck at P_1, something must happen to shift the money demand curve rightward to D_2. What happens? Does the interest rate fall? Does income rise?

At this point we can't say for sure how much either one of these variables changes. But we *can* say for sure that the new combination of interest rate and income must lie somewhere on the curve LM_2 associated with the demand curve D_2. By definition, LM_2 shows all the combinations of interest rate and income that could possibly yield D_2.

In the sticky price model, then, any increase in money *supply* must trigger an increase in money *demand*. The new money demand curve is associated with a new *LM* curve, below and to the right of the original. The economy must be located on that new *LM* curve.

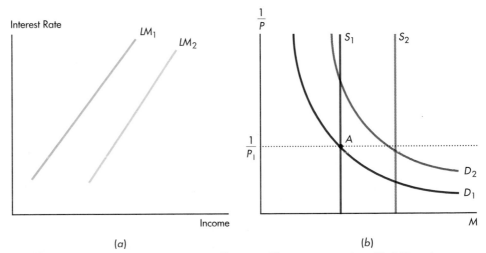

FIGURE 13-5 The money market is initially in equilibrium at point *A* in (*b*). When the money supply increases from S_1 to S_2, money demand must shift from D_1 to D_2 in order to maintain the (stuck) equilibrium price level P_1. This means that the *LM* curve must shift from LM_1 to LM_2 in (*a*).

When prices are sticky, a rise in the money supply causes a rightward shift of money demand. This in turn causes the *LM* curve to shift down and to the right. Similarly, a drop in the money supply requires a leftward shift of money demand. This in turn requires that the *LM* curve shift up and to the left.

 We've left *two* important questions unanswered. First, where on the new LM curve does the economy end up? Second, what forces cause the economy to move to that point? For example, if the economy moves to a point with a lower interest rate, what induces people to bid the interest rate down to that new level? If the economy moves to a point with higher output, what induces people to produce that extra output? We will continue to keep these questions on hold for now, but we will return to them in Section 13-2.

Price Level Shocks and the *LM* Curve

Now we want to see what happens to the *LM* curve when the price level changes.

It might sound like a contradiction in terms to talk about a change in the price level when prices are sticky. But we can imagine the economy jumping from one "stuck" price to another and then being unable to move from the new sticking point.

Figure 13-6 illustrates what happens when the price level jumps upward from P_1 to P_3 and then sticks at P_3. Because the money supply is unchanged, the equilibrium point must move from A to B in Figure 13-6(*b*). This requires that the demand for money shift downward from D_1 to D_3. The lower money demand curve D_3 requires higher interest rates or lower incomes or both; therefore, the *LM* curve shifts up and to the left, from LM_1 to LM_3 in Figure 13-6(*a*).

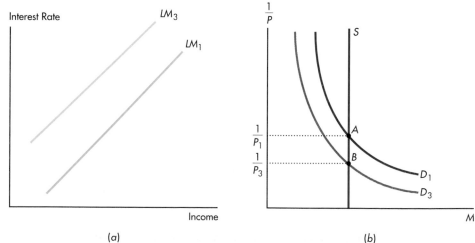

FIGURE 13-6 Suppose that the price level jumps from P_1 to P_3 in (*b*). For the money market to stay in equilibrium, money demand must jump from D_1 to D_3. Therefore, the *LM* curve must jump up and to the left, to LM_3 in (*a*).

When prices are sticky, a rise in the price level causes the *LM* curve to shift up and to the left. Similarly, a drop in the price level causes the *LM* curve to shift down and to the right.

Money Demand Shocks and the *LM* Curve

Let's see how a change in money demand affects the *LM* curve.

Suppose that the demand for money falls for reasons unrelated to income or the interest rate. For example, the demand for money would fall if credit cards became easier to obtain or if automatic teller machines became more common.

In Figure 13-7(*b*), the demand for money initially drops from *D* to *D'*. *This shift does not require that the* LM *curve move* because the same combinations of income and interest rate that used to yield the demand curve *D* now yield the demand curve *D'*.

However, because the price level is stuck at P_0 and because the money supply is unchanged, the money demand curve must return to its original level *D* to produce an equilibrium. In order for money demand to rise from *D'* to *D*, the interest rate must fall or income must increase or both. That is, the *LM* curve must shift down and to the right, to *LM'* in Figure 13-7(*a*).

When prices are sticky, if money demand shifts down for reasons unrelated to the interest rate or income, it must return to its original level. This return requires that the *LM* curve shift down and to the right. Similarly, if money demand increases for reasons unrelated to the interest rate or income, it must return to its original level, requiring that the *LM* curve shift up and to the left.

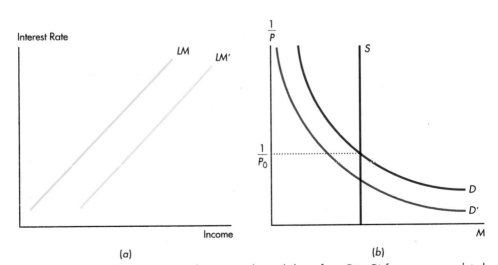

(a)   (b)

FIGURE 13-7   In (*b*), we suppose that money demand drops from *D* to *D'* for reasons unrelated to income or the interest rate. To maintain the stuck price level of P_0, money demand must shift back to its original level *D*. This shift requires that the *LM* curve shift down and to the right, to *LM'* in (*a*).

A Digression: The Sticky Inflation-Rate Model

Sticky inflation-rate model:

A model in which the inflation rate cannot adjust immediately to changing economic conditions.

A variation of the simple sticky price model is the **sticky inflation-rate model,** in which the price level is not fixed but, instead, rises at some fixed rate and is unable to deviate from this rate.

When the inflation rate rather than the price level is sticky, the *LM* curve behaves somewhat differently.

Suppose, first, that the money supply and the price level are both rising at the same rate, say, 4 percent per year. As indicated in Figure 13-8(*b*), this produces movement along a fixed money demand curve. Because the money demand curve *D* never shifts, the associated *LM* curve in Figure 13-8(*a*) never moves.

> In the sticky inflation-rate model (as opposed to the sticky price model), when the money supply and the price level both change at the same rate, there is no change in the *LM* curve.

Suppose now that the annual growth rate of both the money supply and the price level jumps upward, say, from 4 to 6 percent. In Chapter 10 we learned to expect *overshooting*: At the onset of the new inflation rate there is a downward jump in the demand for money, say, from *D* to *D'* in Figure 13-9(*b*). This would ordinarily cause an upward jump in the price level. But because the inflation rate is stuck at 6 percent, the expected price-level jump cannot occur. To prevent the price level from jumping upward, the money demand curve must return to its original level *D*.

When the money demand curve first shifts from *D* to *D'*, the *LM* curve does not shift: the combinations of interest rate and income that yield the demand curve *D* in a world of 4 percent inflation are the same combinations that yield the lower demand

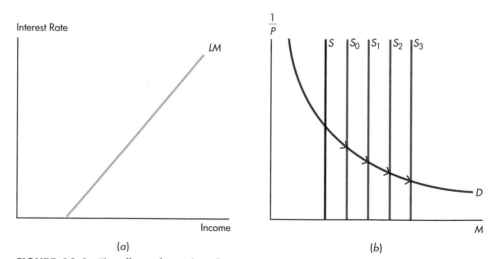

FIGURE 13-8 The effects of a sticky inflation rate.
If the money supply and the price level grow at the same rate, as in (*b*), the demand curve never shifts and therefore neither does the *LM* curve, in (*a*).

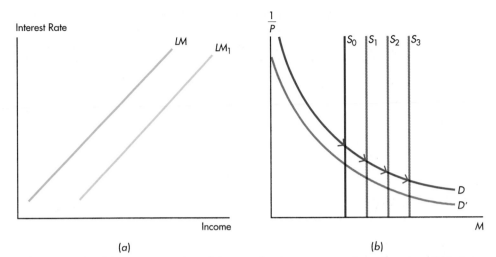

FIGURE 13-9 If the money supply and the price level start growing faster than they did before, the demand for money jumps downward from D to D' in (b). Ordinarily this would cause the price level to jump upward. But if the sticky inflation rate prevents such a jump, then the demand curve must return to its original level D, necessitating a shift in the LM curve to LM_1 in (a).

curve D' in a world of 6 percent inflation. But when the demand curve returns to its original level D, the LM curve must shift rightward to LM_1 in Figure 13-9(a).

> In the sticky inflation-rate model, a rise in the inflation rate causes the LM curve to shift down and to the right.

Another way to say this is that when the money demand curve shifts down to D' in Figure 13-9(b), it does so for reasons unrelated to income or the interest rate. Therefore, the logic of Figure 13-7 applies: When the money demand curve shifts back up to D, the LM curve must shift down and to the right in Figure 13-9(a).

13-2 STICKY PRICE EQUILIBRIUM

Our detailed discussion of the LM curve has still not answered the question of which point on that curve the economy will settle on. In this section we introduce the goods market and the labor market so that we can answer that question and several others.

The Goods Market in the Sticky Price Model

For the moment, let us pretend there is no government. Then aggregate income is equal to the sum of all the goods available for consumption and investment. (With government, we would also have to add in any goods that the government "wastes.")

This very nice coincidence allows us to draw the *LM* curve on the same graph as the demand and supply curves for current goods. The *LM* curve has income on the horizontal axis; the goods market curves have the total of consumption and investment goods on the horizontal axis. So when income equals consumption plus investment, we can display all the curves on the same graph.

Goods market equilibrium occurs at the intersection of the demand and supply curves, point *A* in Figure 13-10(*a*). Point *A* corresponds to a particular interest rate and income, which determine the location of the money demand curve D_1 in Figure 13-10(*b*). The demand curve *D* has an associated *LM* curve, LM_1 in panel (*a*). Because point *A* is one of the points that yield the demand curve D_1, it must lie on the curve LM_1. Thus the demand, supply, and *LM* curves all pass through the point *A* in Figure 13-10(*a*).

Shocks and the Short Run

In Figure 13-10, both the goods market and the money market are in equilibrium. But with sticky prices, it is not possible for both markets to remain in equilibrium following a shock. Suppose, for example, that there is a drop in the money supply, say, from S_1 to S_2 in Figure 13-11(*b*). Just as in the neoclassical model, this has no effect on the supply of or demand for goods. However, in order for the money market to remain in equilibrium with the sticky price level P_1, the money demand curve in Figure 13-11(*b*) must shift leftward to D_2. The associated *LM* curve, LM_2 in Figure 13-11(*a*), lies above and to the left of the original *LM* curve, LM_1.

If the goods market stays in equilibrium at *A*, the economy is off its new *LM* curve, LM_2, so the money market must be out of equilibrium. But the sticky price

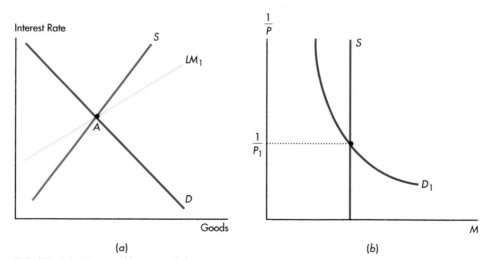

(*a*)   (*b*)

FIGURE 13-10 Equilibrium and the *LM* curve.
The goods market (*a*) is in equilibrium at point *A*. Point *A* determines the interest rate and income, which determine the location of the money demand curve D_1 in (*b*). Associated to D_1 is the curve LM_1 in (*a*).

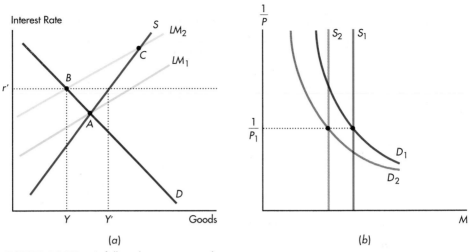

FIGURE 13-11 A fall in the money supply.
Initially the goods market (a) is in equilibrium at A. The money supply and demand curves are S_1 and D_1 in (b), and the equilibrium price level is P_1. Now suppose that the money supply falls to S_2. To maintain money market equilibrium at the sticky price P_1, the money demand curve must shift to D_2. This causes the LM curve to shift left to LM_2 in (a), where it no longer passes through the goods market equilibrium point A. To stay on the LM curve, we must sacrifice equilibrium in the goods market, moving to point B or point C. The sticky price model posits that the economy moves to the intersection of LM and demand (point B).

model assumes that the money market is *always* in equilibrium. In other words, the economy must move to a point on the curve LM_2, sacrificing goods market equilibrium in the process.

That means that the goods market can be on the demand curve [at point B in Figure 13-11(a)] or on the supply curve (at point C), but not on both at once. To complete the sticky price model, we make that choice by assuming that output is *demand-driven;* that is, we place the economy at point B on the demand curve rather than at point C on the supply curve.

The new interest rate is then r'. At this interest rate, suppliers want to supply more goods (Y') than demanders are willing to buy (Y). Under such circumstances, you might expect suppliers to offer lower prices to encourage buying. But the sticky price assumption states precisely that suppliers cannot do this. Therefore, the economy remains stuck at point B.

Long-Run Adjustment

Figure 13-11 shows that as long as the price level remains stuck at P_1, the goods market remains out of equilibrium, at point B. However, we do not expect prices to remain sticky forever. When the price level eventually adjusts to the new economic conditions, the demand curve D_2 in Figure 13-11(a) can return to its original level D_1. The money supply remains at its new level S_2 and the money market achieves equilibrium at the intersection of D_1 and S_2. With the restoration of the original money demand curve in Figure 13-11(b), we also have the restoration of the original LM curve, LM_1, in Figure 13-11(a). At this point, the goods market can return to equilibrium at point A.

Adding the Government

Now let us add to the model a government that, at least sometimes, spends wastefully. This requires that we make an explicit assumption about the nature of money demand. When we say that money demand depends on income, should we include *all* income—even that which is essentially discarded—or just that portion of income which is actually used for consumption and investment?

We could, of course, develop two versions of the sticky price model—Sticky Prices Mark I (where all income enters money demand) and Sticky Prices Mark II (where only "useful" income—that is, income that is ultimately used for either consumption or investment, either in private markets or by the government—enters money demand). But we will restrain our enthusiasm and stick with one choice. Most macroeconomics textbooks, for no compelling reason, choose Mark I. We shall choose Mark II, mostly because Mark II is easier to present with the particular graphs that we happen to have already developed.

So we assume that money demand depends only on the consumption-plus-investment part of income. This means that we can continue to plot the LM curve as well as the supply of and demand for goods on the same graph, the graph with consumption plus investment on the horizontal axis.

The bottom line is that our sticky price model *with* government looks exactly like our sticky price model *without* government, given our auxiliary assumption about the nature of money demand.

The Complete Sticky Price Model

Now we can add the labor market, complete the sticky price model, and do some comparative-statics exercises.

Figure 13-12 shows the complete sticky price model.

Figure 13-12(a) shows the demand curve for goods together with the LM curve. The economy is assumed to be at the intersection of these two curves (rather than at the intersection of demand and supply, as in the neoclassical model). Just as in the neoclassical model, the demand curve is derived from consumers' preferences; it shifts in response to changes in wealth. The key facts about the LM curve are that it shifts right when the money supply increases and left when the price level jumps upward (to a new sticky price). (We do not draw the supply curve for goods because it plays no important role in the sticky price model.)

Figure 13-12(b) shows the labor market, which we include here for the first time in this chapter. The labor supply curve is exactly as in the neoclassical model; in particular it shifts to the left when wealth increases and to the right when the interest rate increases. The demand curve for labor is taken to be vertical at whatever quantity L_0 is necessary to produce Y_0 units of output, as indicated by the production function in Figure 13-12(d).

Figure 13-12(c) shows the money market. Because the price level is stuck at P_0, any change in the money supply must be accompanied by a corresponding change in money demand, which requires that the *LM* curve shift.

Comparative Statics

Now that we have a complete model, we can trace through the consequences of various shocks. Specifically, we will consider the effects of an increase in the money supply and an increase in wealth.

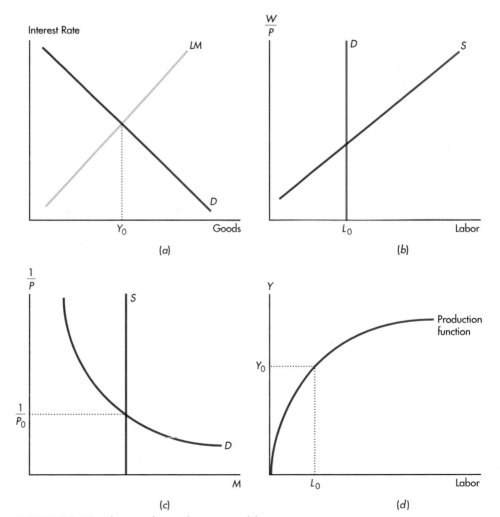

FIGURE 13-12 The complete sticky price model.
The output of goods (Y_0) is determined by the intersection of demand and *LM* in the goods market (a). The quantity of labor (L_0) needed to produce that output can be read off the production function (d). In the labor market (b), labor demand is vertical at the quantity L_0. Labor supply in (b) and the money demand and supply curves in the money market (c) are exactly as in the neoclassical model.

An Increase in the Money Supply

Suppose the government increases the money supply from S to S' in Figure 13-13(c). Money demand must shift rightward to D' to maintain the sticky price level P_0.

Because of the shift in money demand, the LM curve in Figure 13-13(a) (the goods market) shifts rightward, so output increases from Y_0 to Y_1 and the interest rate falls from r_0 to r_1.

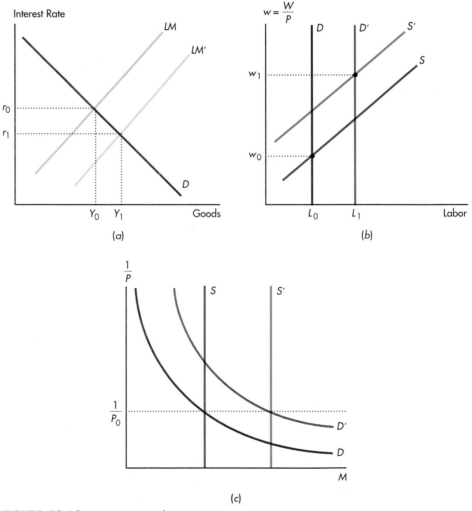

FIGURE 13-13 A money supply increase.
The money supply is increased from S to S' in the money market (c). To maintain the sticky price level P_0, money demand must increase from D to D'. This requires that the LM curve shift to LM' in the goods market (a), so output rises from Y_0 to Y_1 and the interest rate falls from r_0 to r_1. To produce more output, firms must hire more labor—L_1 instead of L_0 in the labor market (b). The supply of labor falls (shifts left to S') because the interest rate has dropped. The real wage rate increases from w_0 to w_1.

In Figure 13-13(*b*), the labor market, the lower interest rate causes a leftward shift in labor supply. At the same time, the increase in output (which requires more labor) causes a rightward shift in labor demand, from *D* to *D'*. The net effect is that the real wage rate rises from w_0 to w_1.

> According to the sticky price model, an increase in the money supply causes an increase in output, a drop in the interest rate, an increase in employment, and a rise in the real wage rate.

That much is evident from the graphs. It is also instructive to consider the scenario that underlies all of the curve shifts. It is as follows.

When the money supply increases, prices would ordinarily be bid up by people who find themselves holding more money than they want. But because prices are stuck, people are forced to hold the extra money. In an effort to rid themselves of the money, they buy bonds (that is, they lend), thereby driving interest rates down. At lower interest rates, consumers and investors demand more goods [that is, they move along the demand curve in Figure 13-13(*a*), from the old to the new equilibrium point]. Because output is demand-driven, output rises, and because more output is produced, more labor is hired.

In the end, people are willing to hold the extra money after all [that is, the demand for money in Figure 13-13(*c*) shifts rightward], both because their incomes have risen [from Y_0 to Y_1 in Figure 13-13(*a*)] and because the interest rate has fallen (from r_0 to r_1).

Notice that *all* these effects flow from the inability of prices to move upward. If prices were flexible, a monetary shock would have no effect on the real (goods and labor) markets.

A Permanent Increase in Nonlabor Income

Suppose now that a new invention allows people to produce an additional *x* units of output per year with no additional labor. Figure 13-14 uses the sticky price model to predict the consequences.

In Figure 13-14(*a*), the goods market, the demand for goods shifts exactly *x* units rightward to *D'*: a person who *receives* an additional *x* goods per period can smooth consumption only by *consuming* an additional *x* goods per period. The *LM* curve does not move because neither the (sticky) price level nor the money supply has changed. The equilibrium point shifts from *A* to *B*. The interest rate rises from r_0 to r_1, and output increases from Y_0 to Y_1.

In Figure 13-14(*d*), the production function rises to reflect the fact that L_0 units of labor can now produce $Y_0 + x$ goods. But output is only Y_1, which is less than $Y_0 + x$, so employment must fall from L_0 to L_1. (In other words, people enjoy part of their windfall by increasing their consumption and part by increasing their leisure.) This is reflected also by the leftward shift of the labor demand curve in Figure 13-14(*b*).

The labor supply curve could shift either to the left (because of the rise in income) or to the right (because of the rise in the interest rate). In Figure 13-14(*b*), the labor market, we have assumed that these two effects cancel out and the supply curve remains fixed. But it could actually shift in either direction, producing either a rise or a drop in the wage rate.

Nothing changes in the money market, shown in Figure 13-14(c).

 How do we know that there is no shift in the money demand curve of Figure 13-14(c)? Income has increased from Y_0 to Y_1, a change which should shift the

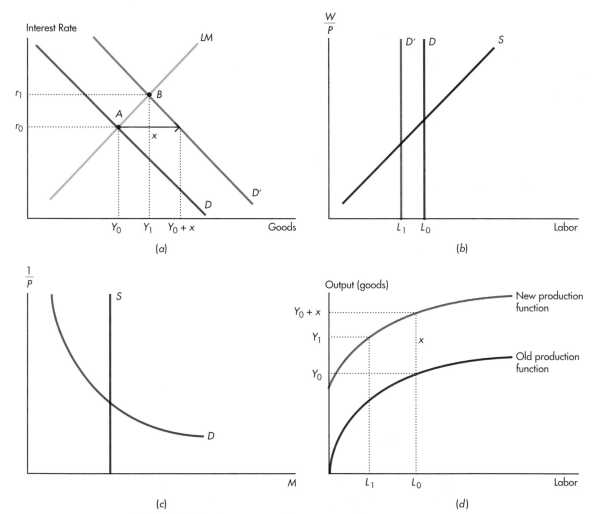

FIGURE 13-14 A permanent increase in nonlabor income.

Initially L_0 units of labor are employed to produce Y_0 goods. Now people begin to receive an additional x goods per period (for a given amount of labor). They want to consume their new wealth, so the demand for goods in (a) shifts x units to the right. The quantity of output rises from Y_0 to Y_1, which is less than $Y_0 + x$, so employment must fall from L_0 to L_1 in (d). This is illustrated also by the leftward shift of the labor demand curve in (b). The labor supply curve could shift either left (because income is up) or right (because the interest rate is up). Nothing changes in the money market (c).

money demand curve rightward, while the interest rate has increased from r_0 to r_1, a change which should shift the money demand curve leftward. Thus you might be tempted to think that the money demand curve might shift in either direction, depending on which effect is stronger. But in fact the two effects must exactly cancel each other, and here is why: The new combination (Y_1, r_1) [point B in Figure 13-14(a)] and the old combination (Y_0, r_0) (point A) both lie on the same LM curve and thus must yield exactly the same money demand curve.

According to the sticky price model, a permanent increase in nonlabor income leads to a rise in output, a rise in the interest rate, and a drop in employment. The wage rate could move in either direction.

Exercise 13-1
Draw graphs like those in Figure 13-14 to illustrate the effects of a permanent *decrease* in nonlabor income in the sticky price model.

Again it is instructive to consider the scenario that underlies all the curve shifts: When their incomes increase, people demand more money, which they at first attempt to acquire by selling goods. Ordinarily we would expect these attempts to bid down the price level until people are satisfied with the money they have. But when prices are stuck, this cannot happen. Therefore, people attempt to acquire more money by selling bonds (that is, by borrowing), and this drives up the interest rate. At the higher interest rate, consumers are unwilling to increase their consumption by the full amount of the windfall, so employment must fall to reduce output to an acceptable level.

A Temporary Increase in Income

In our earlier models, it has been important to distinguish between temporary and permanent changes in income in order to know whether the aggregate demand curve shifts as far as the aggregate supply curve does. But in the sticky price model, this distinction is unimportant because the aggregate supply curve plays no role. Therefore, the graphs in Figure 13-14 apply to both temporary and permanent changes.

The only difference is that when income increases temporarily, the demand for goods does not shift as far to the right. This reduces the magnitudes of all the effects in Figure 13-14 but leaves their directions the same as in the figure.

An Increase in Productivity

In our earlier models, it has been important to distinguish two potential sources of increased prosperity: a pure windfall in the form of nonlabor income, and an increase in the productivity of labor. The distinction has been important because in our earlier models a pure windfall has no effect on the labor demand curve, whereas an increase in the productivity of labor causes the labor demand curve to shift.

But in the sticky price model, the theory of labor demand is much simpler than in the other models: The labor demand curve is vertical at whatever quantity is required to produce the output that is determined in the goods market; its shifts are independent of labor productivity changes.

Therefore, the graphs in Figure 13-14 apply equally well to the case of a productivity increase.

The Short Run versus the Long Run

Many economists believe that the sticky price model is more accurate than the neoclassical model over the short run and that the neoclassical model is more accurate than the sticky price model over the long run. These economists do not agree among themselves about how short and long the short run and long run are.

John Maynard Keynes famously dismissed concerns about the long run by noting that "in the long run, we are all dead." Economists who believe that the long run is on the order of 18 months—or in some cases 18 minutes—have been unimpressed with that argument.[6]

One thing on which economists largely *do* agree, however, is this: It is important to distinguish between a sticky price equilibrium S that is to the *left* of the neoclassical equilibrium N, as in Figure 13-15(a), and a sticky price equilibrium that is to the *right* of the neoclassical equilibrium, as in Figure 13-15(b).

In the first case, the sticky price equilibrium might be able to survive for a con-

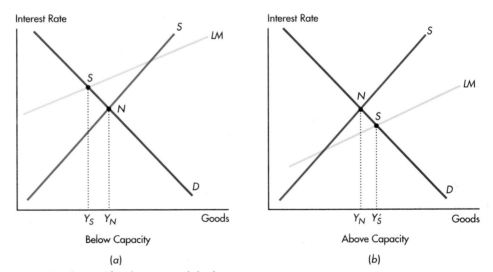

FIGURE 13-15 The short run and the long run.
In the long run, the economy tends toward the neoclassical equilibrium N. In the short run, can it spend a while at the sticky price equilibrium S before moving? When S is to the left of N, as in (a), the answer is "possibly." When S is to the right of N, as in (b), the answer is almost surely no.

[6]It is worth quoting Keynes at greater length: "In the long run we are all dead. Economists set themselves too easy, too useless a task, if in tempestuous seasons they can only tell us that when the storm is long past, the ocean is flat again."

siderable time before prices move to restore the neoclassical equilibrium. But in the second case, the sticky price equilibrium certainly cannot last very long.

The idea here is that the neoclassical equilibrium is a sort of measure of the economy's natural "capacity"; it shows the quantity of output that would be produced if all markets functioned smoothly. It seems reasonable to believe that the economy can operate *below* its natural capacity [at Y_S in Figure 13-15(a)] for many months or even years. But it is far more difficult to believe that the economy can operate *above* its natural capacity [at Y_S' in Figure 13-15(b)] for long periods of time. Economists disagree about the plausibility of the former, but are close to unanimous in dismissing the plausibility of the latter.

Therefore, when the sticky price equilibrium S is to the right of the neoclassical equilibrium, we expect prices to "unstick" themselves quite quickly and begin rising. To determine the new equilibrium in that situation, we would use the neoclassical model, not the sticky price model.

13-3 COMPARING THE MODELS

Let us now see how the sticky price model compares with the neoclassical and sticky wage models according to the same yardsticks we used in Chapter 12.

The Real–Nominal Dichotomy

In the neoclassical model in Chapter 11, the real and monetary sides of the economy are essentially separated. In the sticky wage model in Chapter 12, this real–nominal dichotomy is overthrown, and a change in the price level can influence real wages, output, and employment. The sticky price model shares this feature.

To see the effects of an increase in the money supply, you can look back to Figure 13-13. According to the sticky price model, the interest rate falls (from r_0 to r_1), output rises (from Y_0 to Y_1), employment rises (from L_0 to L_1), and the real wage rate rises (from w_0 to w_1). Clearly, a purely monetary shock has substantial real effects in this model.

Why do sticky prices cause monetary shocks to have real effects? When the authorities supply more money than is demanded, people are unable to bid up prices in response. Consequently, they attempt to rid themselves of excess money by buying bonds, thereby driving the real interest rate down. Once the real interest rate moves, a chain of other real effects is set in motion; most notably, people demand more goods for current consumption and investment, and in order to produce these goods, employers demand more labor.

Involuntary Unemployment

The sticky price model shares with the neoclassical model the assumption that the labor market clears. Unemployment certainly exists according to the models, but it is not involuntary because the real wage adjusts freely downward, discouraging work-ers from sitting outside the doors of firms waiting endlessly for jobs that are not going to materialize.

Business Cycles

Let us, as we did in Chapter 12, apply several shocks to the sticky price model to see whether any of them might generate a recession.

A Shock to Productivity

Let us see how well a temporary decrease in productivity can explain a recession in the sticky price model.

The effects of a temporary *increase* in productivity are shown in Figure 13-14.[7] A temporary *decrease* in productivity has the exact opposite effects, as shown in Fig-ure 13-16. In Figure 13-16(a), the goods market, the demand curve shifts leftward because people are made poorer by the decrease in productivity. There is no change in the LM curve. Therefore, output falls from Y_0 to Y_1, and the interest rate falls from r_0 to r_1.

Because the decrease in productivity is temporary, people are made only slightly less wealthy, so the shift in the demand curve is not very large and Y_1 is only slightly smaller than Y_0. To produce almost as many goods with labor that has become less productive, firms must hire *more* workers. The demand curve for labor in Figure 13-16(b) shifts to the right.

The supply curve for labor could shift right because people are poorer or left because of the drop in the interest rate. Here we assume that these effects cancel out, and so the curve in panel (b) does not shift. But no matter how the supply curve shifts, employment rises from L_0 to L_1.

Thus, according to the sticky price model, if recessions are caused by produc-tivity shocks, then employment must *rise* in a recession. Few economists would con-sider this to be an accurate description of reality.

A Demand Shock

Consider a temporary reduction in the demand for, say, investment goods. (Our con-clusions will hold also for reductions in the demand for consumption goods.)

Figure 13-17 shows the consequences in the sticky price model. In Figure 13-17(a), the demand for goods falls from D to D', leading output to fall from Y_0 to Y_1 and the interest rate to fall from r_0 to r_1. A drop in output combined with a drop in the interest rate seems consistent with what we observe in real-world recessions.

Figure 13-17(b) shows the labor market. Because firms now produce less output, they demand less labor; the labor demand curve shifts to the left. Because the inter-

---

[7]The caption to Figure 13-14 describes the effects of a permanent increase in nonlabor income. However, as the text fol-lowing the discussion of the figure explains, a temporary increase has the same effects as a permanent increase, and an increase in productivity has the same effects as an increase in nonlabor income.

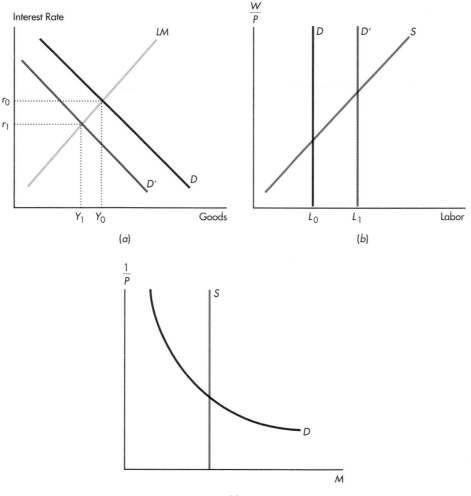

(a)

(b)

(c)

FIGURE 13-16 A temporary decrease in productivity.
In the goods market (a), demand falls because people are slightly poorer. This causes output to fall (slightly) from Y_0 to Y_1. In order to produce almost as much output with labor that has become less productive, firms must hire more workers, increasing employment from L_0 to L_1 in the labor market (b). As in Figure 13-14, the money market (c) is unaffected.

est rate is down, the labor supply curve moves to the left as well. The wage rate could move in either direction, depending on which curve shifts farther.

Recall that in the sticky wage model, a drop in the demand for goods leads unambiguously to a rise in the real wage (see Figure 12-16); we considered this a deficiency of the model. The sticky price model is thus an improvement in the sense that it allows the possibility that real wages can fall during demand-induced recessions.

In fact, as long as the interest-rate effect on the labor supply is small, and hence the labor supply curve does not move very far to the left, the sticky price model predicts that real wages *will* fall during demand-induced recessions.

➡ *Exercise 13-2*
Explain why the preceding sentence is true.

A Monetary Shock

Suppose the money supply is decreased. The effects are exactly the opposite of those of a money supply *increase,* which is depicted in Figure 13-13. Now the interest rate rises, output falls, employment falls, and wages fall.

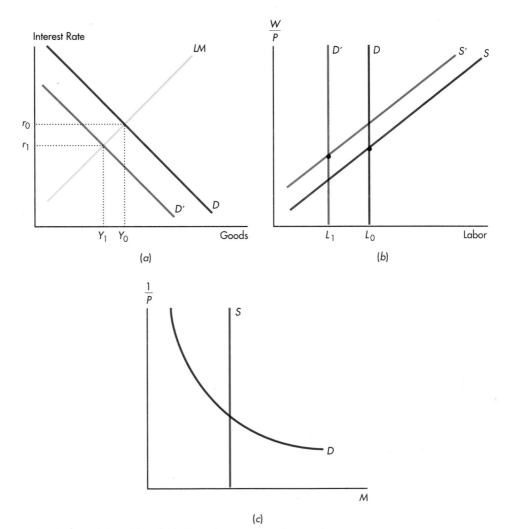

FIGURE 13-17   A demand shock.
A drop in the demand for goods leads to lower output and a lower interest rate in (a) and hence to decreases in both the demand for and supply of labor in (b). There is no change in the money market (c).

These interest-rate and output effects are the same as those predicted by the sticky wage model. The predicted rise in the interest rate does not appear to be in accord with our experience of recessions.

➡ *Exercise 13-3*
Draw graphs illustrating the effects of a decrease in the money supply. Your graphs should be similar to those in Figure 13-13 but should show all of the effects going in the opposite directions.

13-4 GOVERNMENT ACTIONS

In a sticky price equilibrium like that of Figure 13-15(*a*), output (and therefore employment) is below its neoclassical equilibrium level. If government policies can stimulate output, they can bring the economy closer to the neoclassical equilibrium.

What can the government do to stimulate output and employment? We will consider some of the same policy options that we considered in Chapter 12 and will determine what the sticky price model has to say about their effectiveness.

Fiscal Policy

In Figure 13-17, we examined the effects of a decrease in aggregate demand: output and employment both fall. An *increase* in aggregate demand has exactly the opposite effects: output and employment both rise. Therefore, the government can improve economic conditions if it can find a way to increase aggregate demand.

➡ *Exercise 13-4*
Draw graphs similar to those in Figure 13-17 to demonstrate that an increase in demand causes output and employment to rise.

How can the government cause aggregate demand to increase? One possibility is to alter tax laws or regulatory policies to encourage investment. Another possibility is to encourage consumption by making people wealthier.

As in the discussion of fiscal policy in Chapter 12, we note that the most efficient way for the government to make people wealthier is to provide public goods that are worth more than their cost. Assuming that such opportunities have been exhausted, we turn next to tax cuts and transfer payments, financed by an increase in the government's deficit.

Government Debt

Again, the lessons of Chapter 12 continue to apply. If Ricardian equivalence holds, then tax cuts and transfer payments have no effect on consumption demand. But in the absence of Ricardian equivalence, a cut in taxes or a deficit-financed transfer payment causes consumption demand to increase. This could be the case if people fail to fully perceive future tax burdens or if their current spending is limited by their credit ratings.

> If prices are sticky and Ricardian equivalence fails, then an increase in the government's debt leads to higher consumption demand and hence to higher output and employment.

Wasteful Spending

Suppose that instead of making transfer payments, the government spends wastefully. As we shall soon see, the sticky price model predicts that when the government is wasteful, its spending can have an even bigger positive impact on output and employment.

More precisely, for cases in which Ricardian equivalence holds, we have already seen that transfer payments have no effect on output and employment—whereas we shall see here that wasteful spending has a positive effect. And for cases in which Ricardian equivalence fails, we have already seen that transfer payments have a positive effect on output and employment—whereas we shall see here that wasteful spending has an even bigger positive effect.

Figure 13-18 shows the effects of wasteful government spending in the sticky price model. Wasteful spending makes people poorer and therefore generates a drop in the demand for goods from D to D' in Figure 13-18(a). (If the wasteful spending is temporary, this drop in demand is small.) The interest rate falls from r_0 to r_1.

The sum of all goods used for consumption and investment falls from Y_0 to Y_1. However, the total amount of goods produced is equal to Y_1 *plus* the quantity of goods (call it G) that the government purchases and throws away. That amount, $Y_1 + G$, is greater than Y_0.

You might wonder how we know that $Y_1 + G$ exceeds Y_0. The answer is that when the government wastes G, consumption smoothing dictates that the demand curve move left by less than G (if the waste is temporary) or by approximately G (if the waste is expected to be repeated every year). Either way, the geometry of Figure 13-18(a) dictates that the difference between Y_0 and Y_1 be less than G. (The amount $Y_0 - Y_1$ would just equal G if the demand curves D and D' were vertical.)

On the production function in Figure 13-18(d), you can see that the amount of labor employed must *increase* to produce $Y_1 + G$ goods. It changes from L_0 to L_1.

Figure 13-18(b) shows this increase in labor demand (from D to D'). At the same time, the drop in the interest rate leads to a leftward shift in labor supply (from S to S'). The two effects combine to yield a higher real wage along with the increase in employment.

This means that during a recession, the government can take action to increase output, employment, and wages by spending wastefully. Like the sticky wage model, the sticky price model supports an active role for the government during recessions.

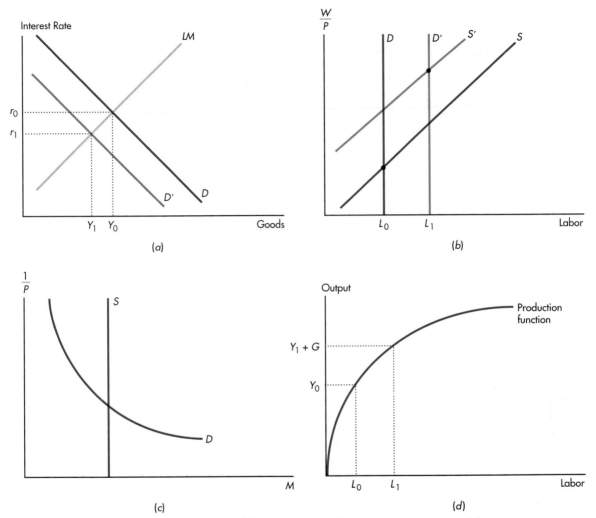

FIGURE 13-18 Wasteful government spending in the sticky price model.
When the government spends wastefully, people are made poorer, so the demand for goods shifts slightly to the left in (a). Consumption plus investment falls from Y_0 to Y_1. But the amount of goods that must be produced is not just Y_1; it is $Y_1 + G$, where G is the amount the government wastes. Producing $Y_1 + G$ goods requires that employment rise from L_0 to L_1 according to the production function in (d); this rise translates into a rightward shift in labor demand in (b). Labor supply shifts leftward because the interest rate drops. The wage rate increases. Nothing changes in the money market (c).

The implication that wasteful spending lowers the interest rate depends crucially on our earlier assumption (in Section 13-2) that money demand is a function of only consumption plus investment. (That assumption was the difference between the models we temporarily called "Sticky Prices Mark I" and "Sticky Prices Mark II.") We have not developed a model in which money demand depends on *all* income, including that which is wasted. If we did work out such a model, we would find that wasteful spending drives interest rates up, not down.

Transfers versus Waste

We have seen that transfer payments have no effect on output or employment unless Ricardian equivalence fails. By contrast, wasteful spending has the effects shown in Figure 13-18 even if Ricardian equivalence holds.

If Ricardian equivalence fails and the government's wasteful spending is financed by deficits, then the demand curve in Figure 13-18(*a*) might shift to the right rather than the left. In that case, the government's spending policy would be even *more* effective at stimulating output and employment.

> In the sticky price model, wasteful spending stimulates output and employment. It does so even if Ricardian equivalence holds, but it does so more effectively when Ricardian equivalence fails.

Does the U.S. Government Believe the Sticky Price Model?

When government officials want to build a new highway or buy a new aircraft carrier, they frequently justify the expenditure by arguing that it will help to revive a sluggish economy. Embedded in such justifications is an implicit appeal to the stickiness of prices or of wages. Unlike the neoclassical model with market clearing, the sticky price and sticky wage models imply that the government can effectively fight recessions by temporarily increasing its purchases.

Do government officials really accept the premises of price and wage stickiness, or are they just making a convenient argument for spending that they really support on other grounds? (Those other grounds could range from a conviction that the aircraft carrier is critical for national defense to a desire to funnel business to a large campaign contributor.)

One way to attack this question is to see whether increases in government purchases really do tend to coincide with recessions—as the sticky price model says they ought to. If government officials are sincerely motivated by the sticky price model, then purchases during recessions should be higher than those immediately before and immediately after.[8]

The evidence is mixed. Figure 13-19 shows real government purchases (measured in 1987 dollars) in the United States since 1970. The five recessions in that period are indicated by rectangles.

The recessions of the early 1970s and early 1990s were indeed times of unusually high government purchases (compared with the years immediately preceding and

---

[8]Spending might not increase until the recession is well under way, because it can take time for the government to recognize and react to a change in economic conditions.

FIGURE 13-19 Real government purchases in the United States since 1970. The rectangles indicate recessions. Data are at quarterly intervals.

following those recessions). The recession of the mid-1970s shows an increase in government purchases that continued for a short time after the recession but was then followed by a small dip in purchases. The recession of the early 1980s does show a small peak in purchases. The recession of the mid-1980s was a time of increasing purchases, which continued pretty much unabated after the recession was over.

We can gather some additional evidence by looking at what happens when the economy is *not* in a recession. Government purchases grew quite steadily and dramatically throughout the late 1980s with no recession in sight. This at least shows that recessions are not the *only* reason why government purchasing expands. In fact, given the growth of government purchases in the 1980s, it is clear that factors other than recessions must play a major role in that growth.

Try looking carefully at Figure 13-19 and deciding for yourself whether the government has used its purchasing power specifically to fight recessions. One question you might ask yourself is this: "If the recessions were not marked on the graph, could I have guessed where they were on the basis of the government's purchasing patterns?" Could you have made some reasonable tentative guesses?

Government purchases frequently increase rapidly even in times of economic prosperity. Figure 13-19 tells us that they might increase a bit more when there is a recession to fight. But it does appear that, compared with other factors, recessions have relatively little impact on government purchases.

Do the U.S. Monetary Authorities Believe the Sticky Price Model?

The sticky price model suggests that an increase in money supply growth can be an effective tool for fighting recessions. Do the monetary authorities in the United States make systematic use of that tool?

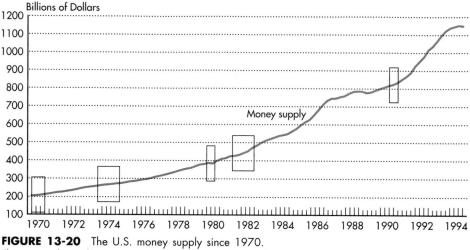

FIGURE 13-20   The U.S. money supply since 1970.
The rectangles indicate recessions. Data are at quarterly intervals.

Figure 13-20 shows the U.S. money supply since 1970, with recessions indicated by rectangles.[9] The graph contains no readily apparent evidence showing that the money supply increases more rapidly during recessions than at other times. It appears that the monetary authorities are far more concerned with other matters (such as controlling the inflation rate) than they are with using the sticky price model as a guide to fighting recessions.

SUMMARY

In the sticky price model, we assume that the price level is stuck at some historical level but the money market always clears. This means that any change in the money supply must be accompanied by a change in money demand to maintain equilibrium.

The mechanism that moves the money demand curve is a combination of changes in both the interest rate and income. When the money supply increases, people attempt to rid themselves of excess money. They attempt to buy bonds, driving down the interest rate, and the drop in the interest rate encourages more spending for consumption and investment.

The *LM* curve shows all the combinations of interest rate and income that can produce a given money demand curve. For each money demand curve, there is an associated *LM* curve.

The sticky price equilibrium in the goods market occurs at the intersection of the *LM* curve and the demand curve for goods.

The demand for labor in the sticky price model is taken to be vertical at the quantity of labor necessary to produce the equilibrium output.

In the sticky price model, the real–nominal dichotomy is overturned, because an increase

[9]In Chapter 15 you will see that there are a variety of ways to define and measure the money supply. Figure 13-20 uses the measure that is usually denoted M1. (See Chapter 15 for the precise definition of M1.)

in the money supply causes a drop in the interest rate together with increases in output, employment, and wages.

There is no involuntary unemployment in the sticky price model.

The sticky price model predicts a drop in wages during demand-induced recessions. This seems to be closer to reality than the predictions of the sticky wage model.

According to the sticky price model, governments can combat recessions through increases in the money supply and through fiscal policy. Pure transfers and tax cuts have no effect unless Ricardian equivalence fails, in which case they stimulate output and employment. Wasteful spending stimulates output and employment with or without Ricardian equivalence, though it is more effective if Ricardian equivalence fails.

PROBLEM SET

Answer all questions in the context of the sticky price model.

1. Suppose the demand for money is quite insensitive to changes in the interest rate. What does this imply about the shape of the *LM* curve?

2. Suppose the demand for money is quite insensitive to changes in income. What does this imply about the shape of the *LM* curve?

3. Suppose there is an increase in street crime, which makes people reluctant to carry money. What happens to the demand for money initially? Explain why, in the sticky price model, the demand for money must return to its original level. What happens to the *LM* curve?

4. In the sticky price (*not* sticky inflation-rate) model, depict the behavior of the *LM* curve during an ongoing inflation. How does the *LM* curve behave at the onset of the inflation?

5. Suppose there is a permanent increase in the productivity of labor, and suppose the *LM* curve is perfectly horizontal. What happens to the level of employment? What happens to the supply of labor? What happens to the equilibrium wage rate?

6. Suppose there is a permanent increase in the productivity of labor, and suppose the *LM* curve is perfectly vertical. What happens to the level of employment? What happens to the supply of labor? What happens to the equilibrium wage rate?

7. Draw graphs that illustrate all of the effects of an increase in expected future productivity.

8. Suppose the announcement of a forthcoming technological change leads people to believe that current investments will be more productive than previously expected.
   a. What happens to the demand for current goods?
   b. What happens to output, the interest rate, employment, and the wage rate?

9. Suppose business cycles are caused by shocks to the demand for money that are generated not by changes in income or the interest rate but by changes in transactions technology (the availability of credit cards, ATMs, etc.). In a recession, what would happen to the interest rate, employment, and the wage rate? (*Hint:* Make use of your answer to the preceding problem.)

10. Suppose the economy is in a recession and two economists disagree about the causes. One says the recession was caused by a demand shock, and the other says it was caused by a monetary shock. What variable could they examine to settle their dispute?

11. Suppose the economy is in a recession, and suppose also that the *LM* curve is nearly *horizontal*. Which will be more effective at stimulating employment: an increase in the money

supply or an increase in government spending? (Assume that Ricardian equivalence does not hold.)

12. Suppose the economy is in a recession, and suppose also that the *LM* curve is nearly *vertical*. Which will be more effective at stimulating employment: an increase in the money supply or an increase in government spending? (Assume that Ricardian equivalence does not hold.)

13. Draw graphs that illustrate the effects of a deficit-financed transfer payment in the absence of Ricardian equivalence.

14. Draw graphs that illustrate the effects of wasteful government spending in the absence of Ricardian equivalence.

15. Assuming that Ricardian equivalence does not hold, use your answers to the preceding two problems to explain why wasteful spending can have a bigger effect on employment than transfer payments can.

16. Use your solution to problem 14, together with the graphs in Figure 13-18, to explain why wasteful government spending can have a bigger effect on employment when Ricardian equivalence fails than when it holds.

17. Suppose that business cycles are caused by demand shocks, and that the government pursues a policy of fighting business cycles by adjusting the money supply to keep output constant. *True or false:* A side effect of this policy will be that interest rates become less volatile.

18. Suppose the demands for consumption and investment are quite insensitive to changes in the interest rate.
    a. What does this imply about the shape of the demand curve in the goods market?
    b. If the government were trying to cure a recession, would you recommend a change in the money supply or in government purchases? Why?

19. Make a chart, labeling the rows with potential shocks (a simple supply shock, a change in marginal productivity, a demand shock, a monetary shock) and labeling the columns with economic variables (output, employment, the interest rate, the real wage). Make entries in your chart to indicate how each variable moves in response to each shock. In doing so, assume that the sticky price model and Ricardian equivalence both hold.

20. Repeat problem 19, continuing to assume that the sticky price model holds but now assuming that Ricardian equivalence fails.

Chapter 14

Monetary Misperceptions and the Role of Expectations

The models presented in the preceding two chapters depart from the neo-classical model by allowing that markets might not always clear. In this chapter, we consider a quite different kind of departure: we assume that people have imperfect information about their economic environment. More specifically, we assume that people have imperfect information about the price level.

Monetary misperceptions:
Inaccurate beliefs about the money supply and/or the price level.

The resulting **monetary misperceptions** model is an alternative to the Keynesian models of Chapters 12 and 13. Although it produces many of the same implications regarding the short-term relationship between government policies and employment, it yields very different implications about the government's ability to exploit that relationship in the long run.

We begin in Section 14-1 with a summary of the recent historical relationship between inflation and unemployment, which the neoclassical and Keynesian models do not explain adequately. In Section 14-2 we develop a little extra machinery that makes it easy to compare the predictions of the various models. In Section 14-3 we introduce the monetary misperceptions model, and in Section 14-4 we work out its implications and compare them with those of the other models.

14-1 INFLATION AND UNEMPLOYMENT

The monetary misperceptions model is motivated in part by an attempt to explain the historical relationship between inflation—an ongoing rise in the price level—and unemployment. The *Phillips curve* describes that relationship.

The Phillips Curve

Trade-off:
A balance between a cost and a benefit that both result from the same action.

In 1958, economist A. W. Phillips found a statistical relationship between inflation and unemployment. According to Phillips's observations, periods of high inflation correspond to periods of low unemployment, and periods of low inflation correspond to periods of high unemployment.[1] The **trade-off** he and other economists found suggested that the benefits of inflation can be substantial: even a small inflation appeared to yield a quite considerable decrease in unemployment.

Phillips Curves during the 1960s and 1970s

Phillips curve:
A curve showing pairs of inflation and unemployment rates that have actually occurred.

Figure 14-1 shows plots of U.S. inflation versus U.S. unemployment, first for the 1960s and then for the 1970s. By connecting the data points for the 1960s in Figure 14-1(*a*), we get the **Phillips curve** for those data. As you can see, the curve slopes downward to the right. Periods of high inflation, like 1969, are associated with low unemployment, while periods of low inflation, like 1961, are associated with high unemployment. Does this mean that the government can reduce unemployment by increasing the inflation rate? The Phillips curve, at least for the 1960s, certainly suggests that such a trade-off might be possible.

Stagflation:
The condition in which high inflation and high unemployment occur at the same time.

But as the 1970s unfolded, the downward-sloping Phillips curve relationship appeared to collapse. As you can see in Figure 14-1(*b*), there is simply no obvious way to connect the data points from the 1970s and form a reasonably smooth curve. During some periods, like between 1973 and 1974, increases in inflation are associated not with decreases in unemployment but with increases. By the end of the decade, the United States had experienced several years of **stagflation**—simultaneous high

[1]Actually, Phillips measured not inflation (the rate of increase in the *price level*) but the rate of increase in *nominal wages*. If we assume that the real wage is constant, measuring the rate of increase in nominal wages amounts to the same thing as measuring inflation. Later on, Phillips's relationship was found to hold even when increases in the price level are measured directly.

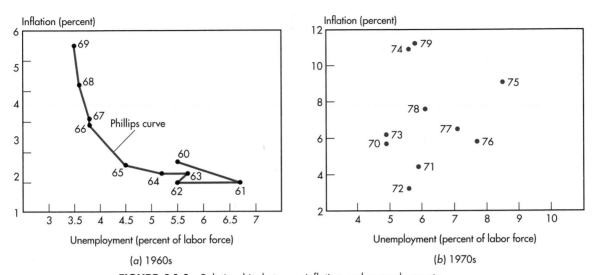

FIGURE 14-1 Relationship between inflation and unemployment.
The actual values of U.S. inflation and unemployment are plotted for each year. For the 1960s, in (a), it is easy to draw a reasonably smooth, generally downward-sloping Phillips curve through the data points. But for the 1970s, in (b), no such pattern is evident.

Monetary policy:
Collective term that refers to the deliberate actions taken by the monetary authorities to affect the economic environment.

inflation and high unemployment. Instead of suggesting a statistically reliable trade-off—say, a 3 percent drop in unemployment for each 5 percent rise in inflation—the relationship between inflation and unemployment changed from period to period. If there was a Phillips curve in the 1970s, it must have been unstable, shifting around in a manner that prevented governments from making use of **monetary policy** as a cure for unemployment.

The Phillips Curve and Economic Theory

The neoclassical model of Chapter 11, with its real–nominal dichotomy, cannot possibly account for the existence of a downward-sloping Phillips curve—or for any relationship between price-level changes and unemployment. The simple Keynesian models of Chapters 12 and 13 have the opposite problem: As you will see below, they account for the downward slope of the Phillips curve *too well,* predicting a stable relationship between prices and employment that is at odds with the erratic relationship we have observed since about 1970.

Sticky Wages and the Phillips Curve

Let us see what the sticky wage model discussed in Chapter 12 tells us about the nature of the Phillips curve.

Imagine that the nominal wage rate is stuck at some level W_0. When the price level is P_0, the real wage is W_0/P_0 and, as Figure 14-2(a) shows, $L_0 - L_0'$ labor hours are unemployed. That is, workers offer L_0 hours of labor at real wage w_0, but firms

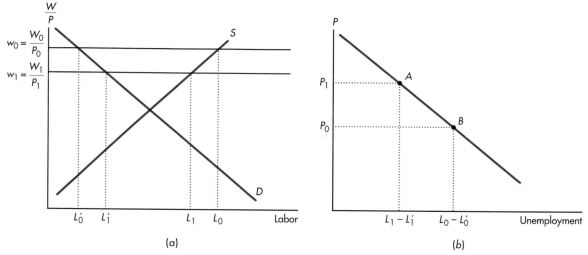

FIGURE 14-2 The price level and unemployment in a sticky wage model. (a) The labor market and (b) the price level versus unemployment in a sticky wage economy. When the price level is P_0, the real wage is W_0/P_0 and $L_0 - L_0'$ labor hours are unemployed. As the price level rises from P_0 to P_1, unemployment falls from $L_0 - L_0'$ to $L_1 - L_1'$.

hire only L_0'. This combination of price level and unemployment level is graphed as point A in Figure 14-2(b). When the price level rises to P_1, the real wage falls to W_0/P_1; at that wage, workers offer L_1 hours of labor but firms hire L_1', so unemployment falls to $L_1 - L_1'$. This combination is graphed as point B in Figure 14-2(b). [Make sure you see, in Figure 14-2(a), why $L_1 - L_1'$ is less than $L_0 - L_0'$.] Similar combinations involving other price levels reveal that the sticky wage model predicts an inverse relationship between the price level and the rate of unemployment, as drawn in Figure 14-2(b).

Figure 14-2(b) is not exactly a Phillips curve, because the vertical axis in that figure measures the price level, whereas the vertical axis in the Phillips curve measures the inflation rate. But the inflation rate for any period is the *rate of change* in the price level over that period. If we start with a given initial price level, its rate of change really amounts to the inflation rate—at least over a single period. Suppose, for example, that the initial price level is 10. Then, after a year of 10 percent annual inflation, the price level is 11, whereas after a year of 20 percent annual inflation the price level is 12. The two (identical) curves in Figure 14-3 thus illustrate exactly the same phenomenon, even though the curve in part (a) has the final price level on the vertical axis and the one in (b) has the inflation rate on its vertical axis.

At least in the short run, then, the curve in Figure 14-2(b) is equivalent to a Phillips curve. In the long run, over additional periods, the equivalence breaks down, because price levels and inflation rates are then no longer strictly proportional, as they are in Figure 14-3; in the presence of ongoing inflation, the notion of "starting from a given initial price level" ceases to be applicable.

However, inflation can be brought into the picture via a slight modification. Suppose that nominal wages are not completely stuck but, rather, are able to adjust upward

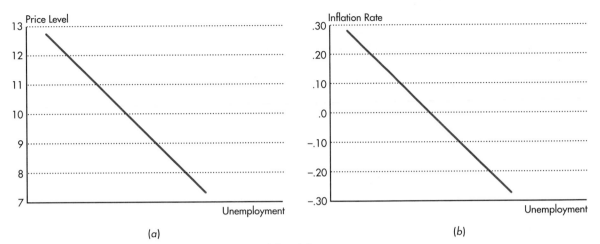

FIGURE 14-3 Two views of the Phillips curve.
(a) A plot of the price level versus unemployment; (b) a plot of the inflation rate versus unemployment. In the short run, starting from a fixed price level, the two graphs are equivalent.

only at a given rate, say, 3 percent per year. Then if price inflation proceeds at, say, 4 percent per year, real wages fall and employment rises as in Figure 14-2; if inflation proceeds at 5 percent per year, real wages fall faster and employment rises faster.

Sticky Prices and the Phillips Curve

In a strict sticky price model, there is no Phillips curve; if prices are stuck, then inflation is impossible.

Suppose however that the sticky price model holds only partially, perhaps because prices in some industries are flexible while prices in other industries are sticky. In that case, growth in the money supply could lead to price increases in flexible-price industries (which are governed by the neoclassical model) and to employment increases in sticky price industries (which are governed by the sticky price model). Then high inflation and low unemployment would tend to occur together, because they have a common cause. This observation predicts a downward-sloping Phillips curve.

(For a reminder of how a money supply increase leads to higher employment in the sticky price model, review Figure 13-13.)

There is also another way in which the sticky price model could hold partially: Suppose that all prices are partially sticky, in the sense that they move partway, but not all the way, toward their new equilibrium values following a change in economic conditions. Then we might expect the economy to respond to shocks in some way that is a sort of "average" of the predictions of the neoclassical and sticky price models. Once again, growth in the money supply will simultaneously trigger higher inflation (because the economy is partly neoclassical) and lower unemployment (because the economy is partly sticky price). Therefore, once again, high inflation and low employment will tend to occur together, and the Phillips curve will slope downward.

We can also discuss the Phillips curve in relation to the sticky inflation-rate model that we discussed briefly (as a variant of the sticky price model) in Section 13-1. With that model, we can talk about the effect of jumping from one inflation rate to another. Recall that when the inflation rate jumps up, the demand for money jumps down. Because overshooting (the condition in which a temporary increase in the inflation rate is greater than the increase in the rate of growth of the money supply and which occurs when the demand for money changes) is prohibited by the sticky inflation-rate assumption (which holds that the inflation rate cannot change at all), something must happen to push the demand for money back up to its original level. Therefore, the *LM* curve shifts right and output rises, as does employment. The sticky inflation-rate model thus predicts a downward-sloping Phillips curve—decreasing unemployment with increasing inflation.

Equilibrium and the Phillips Curve

The neoclassical model in its simplest form predicts no relationship at all between prices and employment, contrary to the experience during the 1960s and earlier decades. The Keynesian modifications of the model, in their simplest forms, predict stable inverse relationships between prices and employment, contrary to the variability or *instability* of the relationship during the 1970s (and the 1980s as well).

Much of modern macroeconomics is concerned with modifying either the neoclassical model or the Keynesian models so that they account for both types of historical experience—both inverse and variable relationships between inflation and unemployment. In Section 14-3 and 14-4, we discuss one of these modifications, called the *monetary misperceptions model*. This particular model begins with the neoclassical assumption that all markets always clear, but it adds the proviso that supply and demand curves can be affected by imperfect information about the economic environment. You will see that such a model may be able to explain both periods of stability and periods of instability in the relationship between the inflation rate and unemployment.

Before we construct the new model, we must review the old models in a new light to facilitate cross-model comparisons.

14-2 PRICES VERSUS OUTPUT: COMPARING THE MODELS

In this section we develop two graphs that relate prices to output. These graphs will allow us to conveniently compare the models we have already developed with the monetary misperceptions model to be constructed in Sections 14-3 and 14-4.

Money Market Equilibrium and the *ME* Curve

Figure 14-4(*a*) shows the money market, which behaves identically in all our economic models. The various demand curves correspond to different levels of income

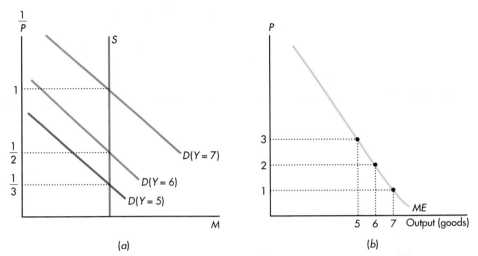

FIGURE 14-4 The derivation of the *ME* curve.
For a given income (such as 5, 6, or 7 units), draw the corresponding money demand curve in the money market (*a*). Read off the equilibrium price level (in this case, 3, 2, or 1 units) and plot it against *Y* in (*b*). Then draw the *ME* curve in (*b*) as a smooth curve through the plotted points.

Y; at higher incomes, people demand more money, and the equilibrium price level *P* changes accordingly. The graph in Figure 14-4(*b*) shows, for each level of income, the corresponding equilibrium price level *P* from part (*a*).

ME curve:

A curve that shows, for each possible level of income, the price level that would be determined in the money market.

To get a point on the graph in Figure 14-4(*b*), proceed as follows: Choose an income level (say, *Y* = 5, in whatever units are employed). Find the corresponding money demand curve in Figure 14-4(*a*), and read off the equilibrium price level *P* at which that demand curve intersects the money supply curve *S*. (In this example, the equilibrium price level is 3.) Then plot the point (*Y*, *P*), which here is (5, 3). To get another point, start with another income level (say, *Y* = 6) and follow the same procedure. Plot several points similarly, and then join them with a smooth curve.

 Remember that income (equivalently, output) is measured in terms of goods. Thus in Figure 14-4(*b*), the units on the horizontal axis are goods.

The downward-sloping curve in part (*b*) is called the **ME curve** (the letters "ME" stand for "monetary equilibrium"). It makes equal sense in all the models we have examined.

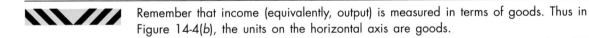 *Exercise 14-1*
Carefully explain why the points (6, 2) and (7, 1) are both on the *ME* curve in Figure 14-4(*b*), using the information in Figure 14-4(*a*).

 The *ME* curve is sometimes referred to as an "aggregate demand curve." This can be highly misleading, because it is *not* a demand curve. It is a curve that illustrates

those combinations of income and price levels that are consistent with equilibrium in the money market.

The *ME* Curve and the Money Supply

Figure 14-5 illustrates how an increase in the money supply affects the *ME* curve. When the money supply shifts right from *S* to *S'* in Figure 14-5(*a*), the equilibrium points (where supply curves intersect demand curves) all move lower on the graph. (For example, equilibrium point *A* moves to *A'*, *B* to *B'*, and *C* to *C'*.) In Figure 14-5(*a*), a lower point corresponds to a higher price level *P*. Therefore, in Figure 14-5(*b*), each income level *Y* on the horizontal axis now corresponds to a higher price level than it did before. As a result, the *ME* curve shifts vertically upward, from *ME* to *ME'*.

> An increase in the money supply causes the ME curve to shift upward. Likewise, a drop in the money supply causes the ME curve to shift downward.

The *ME* Curve and the Interest Rate

Figure 14-6 illustrates how an increase in the interest rate affects the *ME* curve. When the interest rate increases, the money demand curves in Figure 14-6(*a*) all shift down

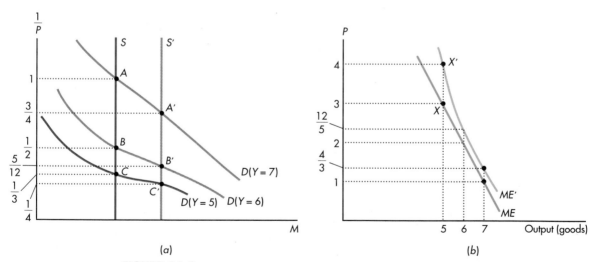

(*a*)   (*b*)

FIGURE 14-5
When the money supply increases from *S* to *S'* in the money market (*a*), the equilibrium price levels all increase (for example, the price level corresponding to *Y* = 7 rises from 1 to ⁴⁄₃), so the corresponding points on the *ME* curve in (*b*) shift upward (from *X* to *X'*, for example). That is, the *ME* curve shifts upward from *ME* to *ME'*.

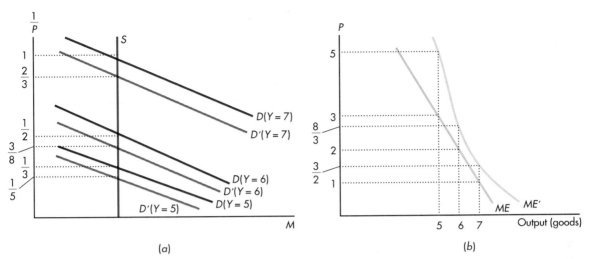

(a)   (b)

FIGURE 14-6
When the interest rate r increases, the money demand curves in (a) all shift downward from $D(Y)$ to $D'(Y)$ and the equilibrium price level corresponding to each income Y increases. (For example, the price level corresponding to $Y = 6$ rises from 2 to $8/3$.) Therefore, the corresponding points on the ME curve in (b) all shift upward. That is, the ME curve shifts upward from ME to ME'.

GE curve:
A curve that shows, for each possible price level, the level of output that would be determined in the goods market.

from D to D'. As a consequence, each income level Y now corresponds to a lower point on the graph, and hence a *higher* price level, than before. For example, the price level associated with $Y = 7$ changes from 1 to $3/2$ (because the equilibrium value of $1/P$ changes from 1 to $2/3$). In other words, the ME curve shifts vertically upward, as shown in Figure 14-6(b).

An increase in the interest rate causes the ME curve to shift upward. Likewise, a drop in the interest rate causes the ME curve to shift downward.

➞ *Exercise 14-2*
Explain carefully how to derive the price levels associated with $Y = 6$ and $Y = 5$ on the ME curve in Figure 14-6(b). Do the same for the ME' curve.

Goods Market Equilibrium and the *GE* Curve

The curve that we shall construct here shows, for each possible price level, the equilibrium quantity of output (or, equivalently, income). This equilibrium is determined in the goods market, so we shall call the resulting curve the **GE curve** (the letters "GE" stand for "goods market equilibrium").

 The *GE* curve is sometimes called the "aggregate supply curve." However, it is *not* a supply curve, just as the *ME* curve is not an aggregate demand curve.

Figure 14-7 shows the derivation of the *GE* curve for the neoclassical model. Figure 14-7(*a*) shows goods market equilibrium in that model (see also Figure 11-1, where the entire neoclassical model is shown). The equilibrium quantity of output is Y_0, and *this quantity does not change in response to price-level changes* because of the real–nominal dichotomy in the model. Therefore, the graph of price level P versus equilibrium output Y in Figure 14-7(*b*)—that is, the *GE* curve—is perfectly vertical at Y_0. At any price level, Y_0 goods are produced.

Factors Influencing the *GE* Curve

The *GE* curve reflects equilibrium in the goods market and shifts whenever that equilibrium shifts. Suppose, for example, that the economy enters a period of low productivity. In Figure 14-8(*a*), the goods market, the supply of goods shifts leftward, and the demand for goods shifts slightly leftward (because of consumption smoothing). The equilibrium output decreases from Y_0 to Y_1, and the *GE* curve in Figure 14-8(*b*) shifts accordingly.

The Sticky Wage *GE* Curve

The *GE* curve for the sticky wage model looks a bit different from that for the neoclassical model. Figure 14-9 shows how points on the curve are obtained.

Assume that the nominal wage is fixed at W_0. Now choose a price level P_0. At

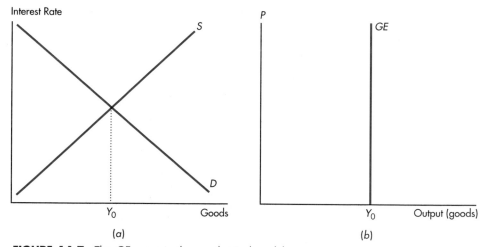

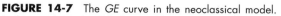

FIGURE 14-7 The *GE* curve in the neoclassical model.
In the goods market (*a*), the equilibrium quantity of output is Y_0, and this quantity does not change in response to price-level changes because of the real–nominal dichotomy in the model. In (*b*), the graph of price level P versus equilibrium output Y is the *GE* curve. The *GE* curve is vertical at whatever level of output is determined in the goods market.

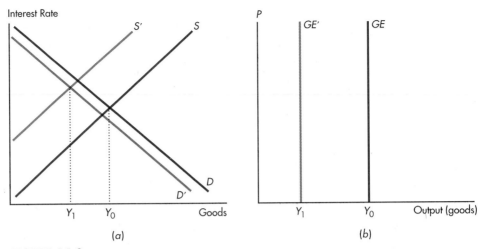

FIGURE 14-8

In the neoclassical model, if the goods market equilibrium changes, then the *GE* curve shifts accordingly. In (*a*), a temporary drop in productivity causes the supply of goods to shift to the left and the demand for goods to shift slightly to the left (because of consumption smoothing). The equilibrium output drops from Y_0 to Y_1, and the *GE* curve in (*b*) shifts left from *GE* to *GE'*.

this price level, the real wage is W_0/P_0, and we see from the labor market in Figure 14-9(*a*) that L_0 hours of labor are hired. We see from the production function in Figure 14-9(*b*) that Y_0 units of output are produced with those L_0 hours of labor. Finally, in Figure 14-9(*c*), we plot the pair (Y_0, P_0) as point *A* of the *GE* curve. If we now choose another price level P_1 and repeat the process, we obtain labor input L_1 in panel (*a*), output Y_1 in panel (*b*), and the point *B* corresponding to (Y_1, P_1) in panel (*c*). Continuing in this way, we find the *GE* curve for the sticky wage model; it slopes upward to the right, as shown in Figure 14-9(*c*): higher price levels mean lower real wages, higher employment, and increased output.

The Sticky Price *GE* Curve

When prices are sticky, only one price level is possible. The *GE* curve in the sticky price model must then be as drawn in Figure 14-10, with the price level stuck at P_0 while the quantity of output can be anything at all. The horizontal *GE* curve reflects both the fact that the price level is stuck and the fact that the goods market, which is out of equilibrium in this model, does not by itself determine the level of output.

Using the *ME* and *GE* Curves to Compare the Models

The *ME* and *GE* curves are new ways to summarize some of the things that we already knew about our models. By overlaying the *ME* and *GE* curves on the same set of

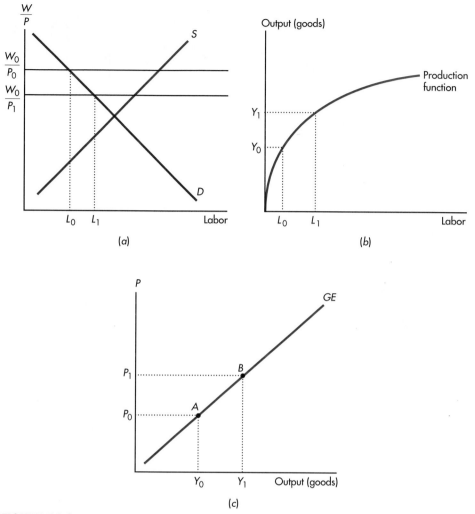

FIGURE 14-9

In the sticky wage model, the GE curve slopes upward. In (a), as the price level rises from P_0 to P_1, employment rises from L_0 to L_1. Consequently, in (b), output rises from Y_0 to Y_1. In (c), the points A (Y_0, P_0), B (Y_1, P_1), and others give us the GE curve.

axes, we can quickly contrast the predictions of the models. All three models use the same ME curve, but the GE curve changes from model to model.

Figure 14-11(a) shows the ME curve and the GE curves for the neoclassical, sticky wage, and sticky price models. Regardless of which model we are considering, the economy starts off in equilibrium—that is, at point E, the intersection of the ME curve and the GE curve. In the neoclassical and sticky wage models, point E represents equilibrium in the money market (because it is on the ME curve) *and* equilib-

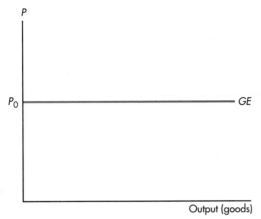

FIGURE 14-10
In the sticky price model, the *GE* curve is horizontal because the price level does not change, no matter how output changes.

rium in the goods market (because it is on the *GE* curve). In the sticky price model, point *E* represents equilibrium in the money market (because it is on the *ME* curve) and the sticky price condition in the goods market (because it is on the horizontal *GE* curve).

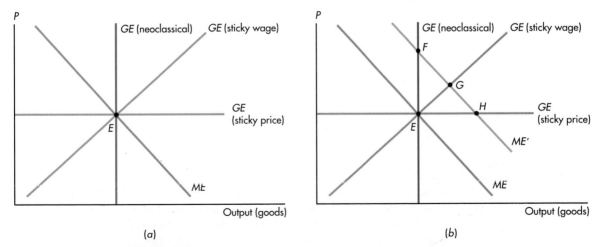

FIGURE 14-11
(a) Equilibrium in the neoclassical, sticky wage, and sticky price models as indicated by the *ME* and *GE* curves. (b) An increase in the money supply causes the *ME* curve to shift out to *ME'*. The equilibrium point moves from *E* to *F* in the neoclassical model, to *G* in the sticky wage model, and to *H* in the sticky price model.

The Effects of an Increase in the Money Supply

To see how we can use the *ME* and *GE* curves to compare the models, let us now suppose the authorities increase the money supply. This causes the *ME* curve to shift upward to *ME′*, as shown in Figure 14-11(*b*). It has no effect on the *GE* curves.

If the neoclassical assumptions are correct, then the only effect is an increase in the price level as the economy moves along the vertical neoclassical *GE* curve to point *F*. If wages are sticky, the economy moves along the sticky wage *GE* curve to point *G*, experiencing both a rise in the price level and an increase in output. If prices are sticky, the economy moves along the horizontal sticky price *GE* curve to point *H*, experiencing only an increase in output.

None of these conclusions is new. They cannot be new, because the *ME* and *GE* curves contain no new information. These curves are only new ways to record old information, in the sense that they are built from the same ingredients as all of our earlier graphs. The neoclassical conclusion that a monetary shock affects prices but not output was already available to us from Figure 11-12. The sticky wage conclusion that a monetary shock affects both prices and output was already available to us from Figure 12-17. And the sticky price conclusion that a monetary shock affects only output was already available to us from Figure 13-13. Figure 14-11 is simply a convenient way to store all this old information in the same place.

Our next step along the path toward explaining the instability of the 1970s Phillips curve is to develop a fourth model, one that will be easiest to understand if we construct it with the *ME* and *GE* curves.

14-3   MONETARY MISPERCEPTIONS: THE ROLE OF EXPECTATIONS

Monetary misperceptions model:

A model in which people's monetary misperceptions have important consequences.

The **monetary misperceptions model** is a means of explaining how people make decisions in a world where the price level sometimes changes unexpectedly. In such a world, people make guesses about the future price level and base their current actions on those guesses. However, the guesses do not always turn out to be accurate. We can explore the main ideas of the model by means of two fables about decision making in such a world.

Fable 1: The Tale of the Unemployed Worker

Stella is unemployed. She is unemployed voluntarily but unhappily. The highest wage she has been offered is $10,000 a year, and at that wage Stella can barely cover the expenses of getting to work. She prefers to remain unemployed and to use her time searching for a better opportunity. If somebody offered her a job paying $15,000, she'd jump at the chance.

Stella has just read in the newspaper that the government plans to double the country's money supply today. She recalls just enough from her college economics courses to realize that all prices are bound to double. Sure enough, when she goes out for her afternoon walk, she notices that prices in store windows and on rental advertisements are all twice what they were in the morning. When she gets home, there is a message on her answering machine from an employer, who says he is raising his offer to $20,000 a year.

Will Stella accept the job? Surely not. A wage of $20,000 this evening is worth no more than $10,000 was worth this morning; the *real* wage offer remains unchanged. In Stella's world, wages and prices can move in either direction; we know from the neoclassical model that in such a world, changes in the price level have no real effects. The real–nominal dichotomy dictates that if Stella was unemployed this morning and only the price level has changed, then she will still be unemployed tonight.

Now vary the scenario a bit: The government has doubled the money supply, but somehow Stella has missed the news. Maybe she forgot to buy a paper this morning, or maybe she was sleeping when the announcement came over the radio. Prices have already doubled, but Stella hasn't noticed yet. The only news she's gotten today is a call from an employer offering her $20,000 a year to come to work. She happily accepts.

Stella's failure to accurately perceive a change in the price level causes a breakdown in the real–nominal dichotomy. When prices change, Stella believes incorrectly that something *real* has changed (namely, her real wage rate) and she alters her *real* behavior accordingly (by accepting the job).

She doesn't keep the job for long, though. On the way home from her first day at work, Stella stops at a grocery store. Shocked by the prices, Stella figures out what has happened and immediately heads home to compose her letter of resignation.

➡ *Exercise 14-3*
Suppose that Stella is now employed at $30,000 per year but in fact would be willing to work even for $25,000. If Stella goes to bed expecting prices to triple overnight, and they only double, what will Stella's new salary be? Will she keep her job?

Fable 2: The Little Grocery Store

Roy and Lothie own a corner grocery and have three employees. Their business is small but successful, and they have no plans to expand. They do about $1000 worth of business every day. If they thought they could do $1500 worth of business a day, they might expand into the vacant lot next door and hire a few additional workers, but they don't foresee this as likely. Roy and Lothie live in the same country that Stella lives in, and they read the same newspapers that Stella reads. When the government announces it is doubling the money supply, Roy and Lothie take note and expect all prices to double. They quickly mark up everything in their store, at the same time that everything else in the economy is being marked up. Sales continue as before; customers buy just as many corn flakes, plums, and paper towels as ever, and Roy and Lothie take in $2000 a day. Nothing real has changed, and Roy and Lothie still see no reason to expand.

Now change the story a bit. Roy and Lothie, like the sleepy Stella, have somehow missed the news about the doubled money supply. They do, however, notice that food prices have doubled at all the other stores in the area, and they realize that they can command higher prices at their own store as well. Flushed with excitement and optimism, they immediately hire a builder to double the size of their store, and they place a help-wanted ad in the paper. Like Stella, Roy and Lothie soon come to recognize that they have made an error. Unlike Stella, who simply quits her new job, Roy and Lothie cannot completely undo the damage. They now have a bigger store than they would have chosen if they hadn't been fooled by rising prices, and the extra space is not going to go away. Given that they have already incurred the expense of building, they may find it in their interest to continue using the new space, or at least some of it. This means that they need a bigger workforce, not just for the short time in which they are fooled, but for a year or two thereafter.

In the long run, though, Roy and Lothie's mistake is unlikely to have much effect on grocery store employment in their area. The area can only support a given number of grocery stores, and once Roy and Lothie have expanded, some of the others will have a more difficult time surviving. Roy and Lothie's extra hiring will be balanced out by job losses elsewhere as other stores close down.

➡ *Exercise 14-4*

Suppose that Roy and Lothie expect prices to double overnight but they are wrong: in fact, there is no inflation. Explain how Roy and Lothie might get fooled into shutting down their grocery store.

The Morals

Obviously these fables are highly stylized, but many economists believe that their fundamental ideas are important in the real-world macroeconomy. When prices rise, people are not always sure whether they are seeing a rise in the general price level or a rise in the price of a particular good (the particular good being Stella's wage or Roy and Lothie's groceries). They take their best guesses, and sometimes they are wrong. Their mistakes can lead them either to supply more labor (as did Stella) or to demand more labor (as did Roy and Lothie) than they would otherwise. Most of the effects are relatively short-lived; however, some effects can persist well after mistaken ideas are corrected, such as those that arise when people undertake investment projects (like Roy and Lothie's expansion) that cannot be stopped once they are begun. In the long run, however, the supply and demand for labor do return to normal.

If these fables present an accurate picture of the world, then we can draw at least three explicit morals:

Only unexpected inflation matters; even when inflation is unexpected, it matters only in the short run; and even when inflation matters, it is undesirable.

We now expand on each of these morals.

Only Unexpected Inflation Matters

We saw in our fables that inflation affects employment only by fooling people. If inflation is expected, then nobody is fooled and there is no reason for the level of employment to change.

Unexpected component of inflation:

Actual inflation minus expected inflation.

Motivated by fables like ours, economists Milton Friedman and Edmund Phelps were led to suggest that the traditional Phillips curve (as in Figure 14-1) has the wrong variable on the vertical axis. Friedman and Phelps argued that, instead of measuring the inflation rate itself, the vertical axis ought to measure just the **unexpected component of inflation,** or the amount by which the inflation rate exceeds its expected value. If inflation is expected to be 5 percent and its actual value is 8 percent, then the unexpected component is 3 percent. If inflation is expected to be 5 percent and its actual value is 2 percent, then the unexpected component is *minus* 3 percent. Sometimes we use the phrase "unexpected inflation" as an abbreviation for "the unexpected component of inflation."

The Friedman-Phelps hypothesis can help explain both why there appeared to be a stable Phillips curve relationship in the 1960s and why that relationship broke down in the 1970s. Suppose that in the 1960s inflationary expectations were relatively constant. For a concrete example, suppose that everyone expected inflation to be 3 percent per year throughout the decade. As actual inflation ranged from around 1 percent near the beginning of the decade to almost 6 percent near the end, its unexpected component would have ranged from around minus 2 percent near the beginning to almost 3 percent near the end. The years with the highest *inflation* would have also been the years with the highest *unexpected inflation*. So, even if it is only *unexpected inflation* that has an inverse relationship with unemployment, the 1960s data could easily have fooled economists into thinking that the relationship was between *inflation* (expected or not) and unemployment.

But by the 1970s people had become more sophisticated in forming their inflationary expectations. An actual inflation rate of 6 percent no longer meant an unexpected inflation rate of 3 percent; instead, the 6 percent inflation rate might have been fully anticipated and so would have corresponded to a zero percent rate of unanticipated inflation. Under the Friedman-Phelps hypothesis, a 6 percent inflation rate yields low unemployment when it is largely unanticipated (for example, during the 1960s) but much higher unemployment when it is fully foreseen (for example, during the 1970s). That is, both a downward-sloping Phillips curve and a vertical Phillips curve are within the scope of this theory's predictions. In summary:

The slope of the Phillips curve depends on people's expectations.

Inflation Matters Only in the Short Run

Insofar as inflation works by fooling people and insofar as people are not entirely foolish, the effects of inflation should be relatively transitory. If a change in the monetary policy is not noticed by households and firms in the economy, workers are fooled into accepting jobs and employers are fooled into offering jobs; but before long they learn the true price level and revert to their old arrangements.

On the other hand, as the story of Roy and Lothie suggests, the effects of being fooled need not wear off immediately, even after the truth is revealed. Industries that have expanded do take time to return to normal.

Inflation Is Undesirable

Perhaps the most striking moral of our fables is that while inflation puts people to work, it does so for undesirable reasons. Workers do not benefit from being fooled into taking jobs that they would not accept if they understand the true (low) value of their wages. Employers do not benefit from making expansion plans that are inspired by false optimism. If these fables describe reality to any extent, then a policy maker who is genuinely concerned with economic welfare should never use inflation as a tool for stimulating employment: inflation stimulates employment, but it does so without improving welfare.

It should come as no surprise that the government can stimulate employment without improving welfare. You can stimulate employment in an ant farm by inserting a stick in the anthill and stirring it around a bit. The resulting turmoil will put a lot of ants to work, but it does not follow that you've made the ants any better off. According to our fables, inflation is like stirring an anthill: it causes a lot of scurrying around, but the end result is that people would have been far happier to have been left alone.

14-4   THE MONETARY MISPERCEPTIONS MODEL

The monetary misperceptions model formalizes the fables of the preceding section. The model is like the neoclassical model in the sense that it assumes all markets clear and all unemployment is voluntary. However, it is also like the Keynesian models in the sense that it allows that changes in the money supply can have real effects; that is, the real-nominal dichotomy breaks down. And it includes the hypothesis that only misperceptions concerning inflation have real effects.

In this section, we construct the monetary misperceptions model using *ME* and *GE* curves, and we make explicit the way in which the model relies on the expectations of the individuals in the economy. We then use the *ME* and *GE* curves to contrast the predictions of the monetary misperceptions model with those of our earlier models.

Prices and Output

The monetary misperceptions model begins with the complete neoclassical equilibrium of Figure 11-1. The level of output Y_0 is determined by equilibrium in the goods market. The general price level P_0 is determined in the money market.

According to the neoclassical model, changes in the price level have no effect on the goods market equilibrium and hence cannot change the level of output; the *GE* curve for the neoclassical model [Figure 14-7(*b*)] is vertical. According to the monetary misperceptions model, the same is true *provided the changes in the price level are fully perceived*. We will write *P* for the actual price level and P^e for the **expected price level,** by which we mean the price level that people *perceive*. Then, as long as $P^e = P$ (that is, as long as perceptions are accurate), the goods market does not devi-

Expected price level:

The price level that people perceive.

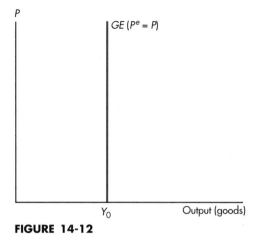

FIGURE 14-12
As long as the expected price level P^e is equal to the actual price level P, the monetary misperceptions model behaves exactly like the neoclassical model, with a vertical GE curve.

ate from its equilibrium quantity Y_0. The vertical line at Y_0 in Figure 14-12, which is the GE curve for the monetary misperceptions model given that $P^e = P$, is labeled $P^e = P$ to stress that it is applicable only in the presence of that condition.

Figure 14-13 shows the relationship between the price level and output under a different assumption about expectations. Suppose that people in the economy believe the price level to be exactly 3 (that is, $P^e = 3$) and that they retain this belief even when the actual price level is something else. In that case, higher actual price levels lead to higher output through either or both of the phenomena described by the fables: Workers are fooled into taking jobs that they would not otherwise accept, and/or

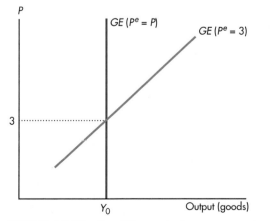

FIGURE 14-13 The GE curve in the monetary misperceptions model when $P^e = 3$.
The light blue GE curve slopes upward because higher price levels fool more firms and more workers into changing their behavior. When $P = 3$, we have $P = P^e$, so nobody is fooled and output must be Y_0, just as it is in Figure 14-12.

employers are fooled into expanding their operations. The higher the price level P, the greater the difference between it and P^e, and so the greater the number of workers or employers who are fooled (more precisely, the greater the number of workers or employers who are fooled *by enough* to cause them to accept previously unwanted jobs or take on previously undesirable expansion projects). Thus the level of output increases with the actual price level, as indicated by the light blue *GE* curve in Figure 14-13. That curve is labeled $P^e = 3$ to stress that it applies only in the presence of that condition.

Aside from the fact that the light blue curve in Figure 14-13 is upward-sloping, there is very little we can say about the location of specific points on that curve. There is, however, *one* point that we can locate precisely. Suppose that the expected price level *and* the actual price level both happen to be exactly 3. Then we have $P^e = P$, so the quantity of output must be the equilibrium quantity Y_0. Thus the point $(Y_0, 3)$ must be one point on the curve.

Figure 14-14 shows the curves from Figures 14-12 and 14-13, as well as additional curves corresponding to other expected price levels. If the expected price level is, for example, 4, then once again the level of employment (and hence output) increases with the *actual* price level; once again, the corresponding *GE* curve slopes upward. Now, however, an actual price level of 4 must correspond to the equilibrium quantity Y_0, because an actual price level of 4 means that perceptions are accurate, and accurate perceptions always yield the equilibrium outcome. Similar considerations govern the locations of the other curves in the figure.

The curves in Figure 14-14 may be compared with the *GE* curves in Figure 14-11(a). In Figure 14-11(a), the different *GE* curves come from different models—that is, models with many implications that differ from each other. By contrast, the various *GE* curves in Figure 14-14 all come from the *same* model but are applicable under different circumstances concerning expectations about inflation.

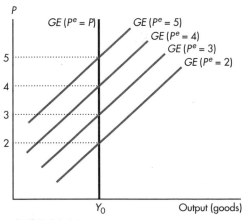

FIGURE 14-14
The monetary misperceptions model incorporates several *GE* curves. The vertical curve holds when perceptions are accurate. The curve $GE(P^e = 3)$ holds when the price level is perceived to be 3; similarly, the curve $GE(P^e = 4)$ holds when the price level is perceived to be 4; and so on.

Effects of a Monetary Shock

Let us begin our analysis of the monetary misperceptions model with an economy in equilibrium, with the price level equal to 3, and with a populace that perceives that price level accurately. In Figure 14-15, the economy is at point E. Recall that Y_0 is the equilibrium output (and income) as determined in the goods market. The curve ME represents equilibrium in the money market.

Now suppose that there is an increase in the money supply, which causes the ME curve to shift upward to a new position ME' as shown. What happens?

The answer depends on how accurately the resulting change in the price level is perceived. If people know exactly what is happening to the price level, then the equilibrium moves along the vertical line labeled $GE(P^e = P)$ and ends up at point E', with no increase in output. At the other extreme, if people go on believing that the price level is exactly 3, then the equilibrium moves along the upward-sloping curve labeled $GE(P^e = 3)$ to point E'' and output increases.

Either of these possibilities requires a rather extreme assumption about the way people form expectations. In the first case, people's expectations are always exactly accurate; in the second case, their expectations are frozen in the past, with no adjustments when circumstances change. Economists are not comfortable with either of these extremes. They often suggest, instead, a more moderate alternative called the hypothesis of *rational expectations*.

Rational Expectations

Rational expectations hypothesis:

The hypothesis that people make full use of the information available to them and, in particular, that they know and make use of the statistical behavior of economic variables.

The **rational expectations hypothesis** asserts that, on the one hand, people are not always fully informed about their economic environment but, on the other hand, they do make full use of whatever information *is* available. That is, people often do not

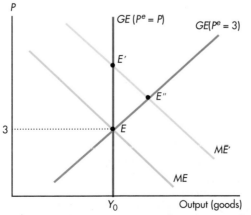

FIGURE 14-15 An increase in the money supply in the monetary misperceptions model. When the money supply increases, the ME curve shifts from its original position ME to ME'. If the change in the price level is fully perceived, the economy moves along the vertical GE curve to point E' and there is no change in output. If people expect the price level to remain fixed at 3, the economy moves along the upward-sloping GE curve to point E'' and output increases.

know the precise value of a variable such as the price level, but they do know something about its statistical behavior, and they fully exploit that knowledge when they form their expectations.

To make this concrete, consider the situation depicted in Figure 14-16. The various ME curves in the diagram correspond to various money supplies. If the money supply is 10, the ME curve has the position labeled $ME(M = 10)$; if the money supply rises to 20, the ME curve rises to the position labeled $ME(M = 20)$; and so on. We assume that the money supply fluctuates randomly between 10 and 30 but that it is 20 on the average day. On any given day, then, the money supply is as likely to be above 20 as it is to be below 20.

Citizens in this economy can never be certain of the money supply or of the price level. But they *are* sufficiently well informed to know that the money supply fluctuates around 20 and that they can minimize their errors by *assuming* that it is 20 at all times. They don't fool themselves into believing that they will never make mistakes, but they are smart enough to know that this assumption keeps their mistakes to a minimum.

On those days that are genuinely average—those days when the money supply is exactly 20—people's expectations are exactly correct. Therefore, on the average day, the economy is at point E on the $GE(P = P^e)$ curve, where the price level is 2.

Because each day's best guess is that "today is average," people behave as if they expect a price level of 2 *every* day. This keeps the economy on the curve $GE(P^e = 2)$. When the money supply falls to 10, the economy moves to point E' and the price level falls to 1.5; when the money supply rises to 30, the economy moves

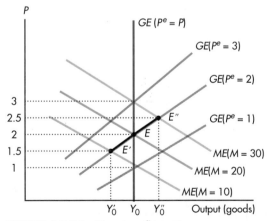

FIGURE 14-16 Monetary fluctuations.
The money supply fluctuates between 10 and 30, and the ME curve fluctuates between the positions $ME(M = 10)$ and $ME(M = 30)$. On the average day, the money supply is 20. People with rational expectations can do no better than to assume that the money supply is 20 *every* day. This leads them to expect that the price level is 2 every day, so the economy moves back and forth along the curve $GE(P^e = 2)$. Equilibrium moves back and forth along the darkened part of that curve.

to point E'' and the price level rises to 2.5. At the same time, output varies back and forth between Y_0' and Y_0'', achieving a value of Y_0 on the average day.

Changes in Monetary Policy under the Rational Expectations Hypothesis

Suppose that a government economist observes the fluctuations depicted in Figure 14-16. She is intrigued to discover that on days when the money supply is as high as 30, output rises all the way to Y_0'', whereas when the money supply falls to 10, output falls as far as Y_0'. Suppose also that this government economist views increases in output as a good thing. What will she advise her superiors?

All the economist's observations point to one conclusion: A high money supply is the road to prosperity. Armed with this conclusion, she makes a policy recommendation: Henceforth, the government should arrange for the money supply to fluctuate around an average value of 30, rather than 20.

Now what happens? According to the rational expectations hypothesis, citizens are still unable to discern the exact money supply on any *given* day, but they retain their ability to understand what is happening to them on average. As soon as the government announces its new policy, everyone's expectations are revised. People now expect the money supply to fluctuate between 20 and 40, with a value of 30 on the average day.

Figure 14-17 shows the before and after pictures. Under the old policy the money supply fluctuates between 10 and 30, around an average of 20. On the average day, as we saw, the money supply is exactly 20, so the economy is on the $ME(M = 20)$ curve. People foresee this correctly, so the economy is also on the $GE(P^e = P)$ line.

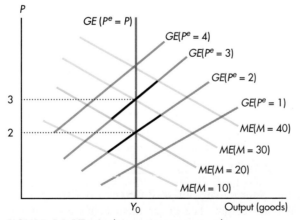

FIGURE 14-17 A change in monetary policy.
Initially, as in Figure 14-16, the money supply fluctuates between 10 and 30, and the economy moves back and forth along the black part of the $GE(P^e = 2)$ curve. Then the government decides to change policy so that henceforth the money supply fluctuates between 20 and 40. Now the economy moves back and forth along the black part of the $GE(P^e = 3)$ curve. The change in policy has no effect on average output, which remains at Y_0.

The price level on an average day is then 2, and people guess 2 to be the price level *every* day because, with the information available to them, they can do no better. Therefore, as the money supply moves back and forth between 10 and 30, the equilibrium moves back and forth along the black region of the $GE(P^e = 2)$ curve. (This is exactly the situation indicated in Figure 14-16.)

Under the new policy the money supply fluctuates between 20 and 40, around an average of 30. On the average day, the money supply is exactly 30, so the economy is on the $ME(M = 30)$ curve. People foresee this correctly because they now assume that the money supply is 30 every day, so the economy is also on the $GE(P^e = P)$ line. The price level on an average day is 3, at the intersection of the $ME(M = 30)$ and $GE(P^e = P)$ curves; people guess 3 to be the price level *every* day because, with the information available to them, they can do no better. Therefore, as the money supply moves back and forth between 20 and 40, the equilibrium moves back and forth along the black region of the $GE(P^e = 3)$ curve.

How successful is the economist's new policy? Remember that it was designed to stimulate output. But both before and after the new policy, output fluctuates around an average of Y_0. The policy is completely ineffective in changing output.

The Lucas Critique

What led the government economist astray? She was absolutely correct in her initial observation that price levels near 30 call forth more output than price levels near 20. But she was wrong to expect that this relationship would continue to hold after a change in economic policy.

Changes in the economic environment—including changes in economic policy—can cause established relationships to break down. Those relationships are actually the result of people's attempts to cope with their environment. In general:

If the economic environment changes, people's coping strategies change.

Economists like to tell the parable of the National Football League commissioner, trained in economics, who wanted to eliminate punting. He observed that punting always occurred on fourth down, and therefore he felt sure that he could eliminate it by limiting teams to three downs. But when the environment—in this case, the rules of the game—changed, so did the teams' behavior: they switched to punting on third down.

The commissioner was not so different from the government economist who wanted to increase output. The government economist observed that output always increased when the price level was high, and therefore she felt sure she could keep output high by keeping the price level high. But when the environment—in this case, the government's economic policy—changed, so did people's behavior: they switched to *expecting* high price levels, adjusted their behavior accordingly, and produced no more output than before.

Lucas critique:
The observation that
when government
policy is designed to
take advantage of a
statistical regularity,
the policy itself may
undermine the con-
ditions that created
that regularity.

Statistical regularities, even well-established ones, are liable to vanish when policy changes. Economists call this observation the **Lucas critique,** after economist Robert E. Lucas, Jr., who first called it forcefully to their attention.

Toward the end of Section 14-3 we offered a possible explanation for the breakdown of the Phillips curve relationship after 1970: Inflationary expectations had been relatively constant before 1970; but afterward, when the government became far more actively involved in manipulating the money supply in an effort to increase output, people caught on to the change in policy and made the appropriate adjustments. This is nothing but an application of the Lucas critique.

A Numerical Example of the Lucas Critique

Suppose that, in reality, the daily level of output Y is related to the unexpected component of the price level $P - P^e$ via the equation

$$Y = 20 + 5(P - P^e) \tag{1}$$

That is, when the price level exceeds its expected value by 1 unit, output is 25 units per day; when the price level exceeds its expected value by 2 units, output is 30; and so on. Suppose also that people have rational expectations, which lead them to forecast the price level accurately on the average day. Then, on the average day, $P - P^e = 0$, so output is 20 units.

Suppose also that the price level fluctuates around a value of 2, and that people therefore always expect the price level to be 2. (More precisely, 2 is always their best guess, even though they realize that they might be wrong.) Then equation (1) can be rewritten as

$$Y = 20 + 5(P - 2) \tag{2}$$

or

$$Y = 10 + 5P$$

That is, when the price level is 3 (which is the same as saying that it exceeds its expected value by 1), output is 25 units; when the price level is 4, output is 30; and so on. On the average day, the price level is 2 and output is 20 units, which coincides with what we learn from equation (1).

As long as the expected price level P^e remains fixed at 2, equations (1) and (2) make all of the same predictions. Nevertheless, it is equation (1) that expresses the *true* relationship, in the sense that changes in output are actually *caused* by changes in $P - P^e$, not by changes in P alone.

Now suppose that an econometrician gathers some data from past years. He notices that whenever the price level was 3, output was 25 units, and that whenever the price level was 4, output was 30. He notices that these data fit equation (2), and he concludes that it is the true equation guiding the economy.

Nothing in this economist's experience will ever convince him that he is wrong. Even though he has the "wrong" equation, the data fit it perfectly.

Now suppose that the government asks the economist for advice about how to raise output. Based on his belief in equation (2), the economist proposes policies designed to increase the price level (for example, he might suggest an increase in the average daily money supply). Equation (2) predicts that if the average daily price level can be driven up from 2 to 3, then average daily output will rise from 20 to 25.

Unfortunately, the recommended policy has the side effect of raising the *expected* price level to 3. The true equation

$$Y = 20 + 5(P - P^e)$$

becomes

$$Y = 20 + 5(P - 3)$$

or

$$Y = 5 + 5P$$

which is *not* the same as equation (2). In fact, with the average daily price level now at 3, average daily output is now at 20—exactly the same as it was before. Contrary to the economist's expectations, the change in policy leaves average output completely unchanged.

Because the economist made the mistake of believing equation (2) rather than equation (1) to be the "true" equation, he made incorrect predictions about what would happen after the new policy was instituted.

The Government

What can the government do to influence macroeconomic events? How should the government exercise the powers that it has? The monetary misperceptions model suggests new ways of thinking about such questions. In this subsection, we survey the most important of the insights that the model has to offer.

Policy Is a Process, Not an Event

In a model where expectations play an important role, it can be important to think of economic policy as an ongoing process, not as a one-time affair. Questions like "What happens if the government increases the money supply?" or "What happens if the government spends money on a wasteful program?" or "What happens if the income tax rate is increased?" are often meaningless in isolation. We can answer them only in context.

An increase in the money supply means one thing if it is one of a series of random fluctuations around a given average but means something quite different if it is part of a deliberate policy of increasing the money supply periodically. Suppose the government increases the money supply during a recession. Will output increase? To answer, we need to know whether the government *always* increases the money supply in response to a recession. If so, the increase will be expected and may have no real effects. If not, the increase may fool people and stimulate output.

A tax increase in 1999 will affect labor supply in one way if it is perceived as temporary, in another way if it is perceived as permanent, and in still another way if it is perceived as part of a series of further tax increases.

And similarly with any policy. One of the great lessons that economists have learned in the last couple of decades is that policies must often be interpreted as *processes,* not as *events.* Economists have learned to ask: What is the effect of a policy of doubling the money supply every year? What is the effect of allowing the money supply to fluctuate around a fixed value? What is the effect of increasing the money supply during recessions and holding it stable at other times? In contexts where the formation of expectations is important, we should *not* ask: What is the effect of raising the money supply *today?* Today's increase is an event, not a process, and its effect could be anything at all, depending on the process to which it belongs.

You Can't Fool All of the People All of the Time

If the government wants to use monetary policy to keep employment unnaturally high, then it must have a policy of always increasing the money supply by more than people expect. But it is very hard to imagine how it could be successful with such a policy. Once people figure out that the government is always trying to fool them, they will be very difficult to fool.

If the monetary authorities believe that people expect prices to double, they may try to fool them by *tripling* the money supply. But if people expect the authorities to try fooling them, then they will *expect* this tripling, so the authorities may have to resort to *quadrupling.* Once again, though, this would be perfectly foreseeable. There is no end to the game of "they think that we think that they think that we think that they think . . . ." Economists are very skeptical about the authorities' ability to win this game sufficiently often to raise average output.

Time Inconsistency

Suppose you borrow money to buy a car. But when the time comes to repay the loan, you decide you'd rather keep the money. If you are sufficiently clever (and sufficiently unethical), you may be able to avoid the bill collector and come out ahead.

Unfortunately, the bank where you get your loans may foresee this possibility and refuse to give you the loan in the first place. As a result, you never get the car.

Here then are the possible scenarios, in the order of your preference:

1. You get the loan and never repay.
2. You get the loan and do repay.
3. You don't get the loan.

If you could have gotten the loan, you could have had your first choice. Because you might have gotten your first choice, you end up with your third choice.

Interestingly, though, you would do better if your first choice were unavailable. If you could guarantee repayment, so you had no way to weasel out, then you'd get your loan and you'd have your second choice.

In this example, your desires at different times are inconsistent with each other. At the time that payment comes due, you want to renege on your commitment. At the time that you first apply for the loan, you want reneging to be impossible.

In the presence of such **time inconsistency,** you can often improve the outcome by finding a way to prevent yourself from following your true desires. If you rule out your first choice, you might convince others to allow you your second choice instead of your third.

Governments face the same problem. Suppose that people expect an annual inflation rate of 10 percent and behave accordingly. In years when the inflation rate is above 10 percent, people are fooled into working more (because they notice the rise in their nominal wages before they notice the rise in the general price level) and output goes up; in years when the inflation rate is below 10 percent, people are fooled in the opposite direction and output goes down.

Now imagine that the government would like to adjust its monetary policy to bring the inflation rate down to 2 percent. If it does so and if people continue to expect 10 percent inflation, then there will be a severe recession, which the government wishes to avoid. On the other hand, if people *believe* in the new policy, the government can take advantage of that belief by continuing to run a 10 percent inflation, fooling people into a time of extremely high productivity.

Here are the possible scenarios, in the order of the government's preference:

1. Convince people that the inflation rate is 2 percent but really keep it at 10 percent.
2. Convince people that inflation is 2 percent and really lower it to 2 percent.
3. Convince people that inflation is still 10 percent and really keep it at 10 percent.

Given these preferences, the government's claim that it is lowering inflation is no more credible than your claim that you really intend to pay your car loan. Just as your bank officer knows that as soon as you get the loan you are likely to skip town, so ordinary citizens know that as soon as their government convinces them that inflation is 2 percent it will jack the inflation rate back up to 10 percent to get them to work. As a result, citizens won't believe the 2 percent claim in the first place, and the government will get its third choice.

But if there is a way to eliminate the first choice—to convince people that the government is truly committed to a 2 percent inflation rate and cannot change its mind—then the government may be able to get its second choice instead of its third.

Unfortunately, it is difficult for governments to make credible commitments about their future behavior. In practice, they can at best attempt to send promising signals.

A government that is deeply in debt at a fixed nominal interest rate has a lot to gain from unexpected inflation, just like any other borrower. The existence of such government debt may lead people to expect that the government will attempt to engineer an unexpected inflation; if the inflation fails to materialize, then output could fall. One way for the government to send a positive signal is to borrow only for short periods of time, continually reborrowing to pay off old debt. Because any new inflation would raise nominal interest rates, a government that was continually reborrowing would have very little to gain from that inflation. So short-term borrowing can be a good strategy to convince people that the government is seriously committed to keeping inflation low.

In 1993, the U.S. Treasury significantly adjusted its borrowing policies in favor of issuing short-term bonds. At the same time, inflation dropped practically to zero despite significant increases in planned government spending. Nominal interest rates fell, suggesting that citizens trusted the sincerity of the government and its commitment to avoiding renewed inflation over the next several years. By the time you are reading this book, you will know whether that trust was justified.

Rational Expectations More Generally

In this chapter, we've added the rational expectations hypothesis to the monetary misperceptions model. But the rational expectations hypothesis can be added to *any* model in which expectations play a role. For example, let us see how the rational expectations hypothesis can be added to a version of the sticky wage model.

Suppose that firms and workers negotiate wage contracts once a year, and these contracts cannot be renegotiated until the year is up. Thus wages are perfectly flexible over the long run (in this case 1 year) and perfectly sticky over the short run.

Changes in the price level that are anticipated at contracting time will be incorporated in the negotiated wage rate. Thus, as long as the price level changes in the way that people expect it to, the real wage will be set at its equilibrium level. But changes in the price level that are entirely unexpected, of course, cannot be incorporated. Thus, when the actual price level deviates from expectations, the real wage will deviate from its equilibrium, and the level of employment can be affected.

In this model, expected changes in the price level have no real effects, while unexpected changes in the price level can affect employment (and therefore output) just as in the sticky wage model of Chapter 12. These conclusions agree with those of the monetary misperceptions model, though the reasoning that leads to those conclusions in one model is quite different from the reasoning in the other model.

In order to make predictions with this version of the sticky wage model, we need some assumption about how people form their expectations of the price level. One attractive choice is to assume that people have rational expectations. Then when the price level fluctuates randomly, it will be unanticipated and therefore have real effects. But when the price level changes because of a policy decision, it is likely to be anticipated and therefore have no real effects. Again, this model and the monetary misperceptions model reach similar conclusions through different reasoning.

Neo-Keynesian models:

Models which combine sticky wages or sticky prices with explicit models of individual behavior, frequently including rational expectations.

Models which combine Keynesian assumptions (like sticky wages or sticky prices) with explicit models of individual behavior (particularly with regard to negotiating contracts) are frequently called **neo-Keynesian models.** Rational expectations is a standard assumption in many neo-Keynesian models.

In this section we compare the model's predictions with observations of the real world.

When Does Money Matter?

Let us begin by focusing on a very specific question: Does an increase in money supply growth cause increases in output and employment?

According to the monetary misperceptions model, we must distinguish carefully between expected and unexpected monetary growth. Unexpected money supply growth surely increases output; the sticky wage, sticky price, and monetary misperceptions models all agree on this prediction (though not on the reason for it). The pure neoclassical model predicts otherwise, but most economists believe there is sufficient evidence to reject that dissenting view.

Let us then confine our attention to *expected* money supply growth, and let us review what the various models have to say on this subject.

According to the neoclassical model (with or without monetary misperceptions), expected money supply growth should have no real economic effects beyond the "convenience" costs that are imposed on people who choose to carry less cash in inflationary times.

According to the model with sticky wages, money supply growth, even when expected, raises employment, output, and prices—at least for the period during which wages are stuck.

According to the model with sticky prices, money supply growth, even when expected, raises employment and output. If we take the sticky price assumption quite literally, then of course there can be no change in prices, so we get increased output with no side effects. But no economist believes that prices are stuck *permanently*. If prices are sticky in the short run and flexible in the long run, then an expansionary monetary policy—that is, a policy of rapid money supply growth—yields real output gains in the short run at the expense of inflation in the long run.

It is more realistic, however, to expect that some prices are sticky and others are flexible; in that case, the truth lies somewhere between the pure neoclassical model and the sticky price model. Then we should expect an expansion of the money supply to increase both output and (some) prices in the short run and to increase all prices in the long run.

Finally, the monetary misperceptions model agrees with the pure neoclassical model in this case: As long as monetary growth is expected, it fools nobody and hence has no effect on output.

Which prediction is most accurate? You might think answering is just a matter of looking at the historical evidence. But the evidence is hard to interpret, because raw data will not tell you whether a given episode of monetary growth was expected or not. An influential paper by Robert Barro of Harvard University addressed this problem.[2] Barro looked at data from 1946 to 1971. For each year in this period, he first estimated the money growth rates that people ought to have expected on the basis of their historical experience up to that time. He subtracted those estimates from actual money supply growth rates and defined the difference to be the "unexpected" component of money supply growth.

Barro found—as nearly all economists would have predicted—that unexpected money supply growth is correlated with real output. That is, real output increased when there was an unexpected increase in money supply growth, and vice versa. He also found—far more controversially—that *expected* money supply growth is *not* correlated with real output. According to Barro, the evidence is consistent with the predictions of the monetary misperceptions model but not with our other models: The pure neoclassical model predicts that money *never* matters, while the sticky wage and sticky price models predict that money *always* matters (at least in the short run, until wages or prices become unstuck). Only the monetary misperceptions model distinguishes between expected and unexpected money supply growth in a way that is supported by Barro's reading of the evidence.

But Barro's paper did not settle the issue. Subsequent researchers questioned Barro's method for estimating the money growth rates that people "ought" to have expected. Using their own alternative methods and resulting estimates, those researchers have found that, contrary to Barro's findings, expected money supply growth *is* correlated with real output.

There is still much uncertainty about who is right on this issue. But even if we settle the question "Does expected money supply growth tend to be followed by changes in real output?" there will *still* be room for argument about the more important question "Does expected money supply growth *cause* changes in real output?" After all, the appearance of mistletoe in doorways tends to be followed by Christmas, but it does not follow that hanging mistletoe *causes* Christmas to arrive.

Suppose, for example, that after much statistical analysis, economists come to the conclusion that Barro was wrong and that expected money supply growth does tend to be followed by periods of growth in output. *One* possible explanation is that the money supply growth causes the output growth. A possible alternative explanation is that the Federal Reserve (the institution that controls the U.S. money supply) foresees coming output growth and increases the money supply in advance—perhaps to help keep the price level stable in the face of anticipated increases in money demand. Because much of the Federal Reserve's policy making is done in secret, it might be hard to determine which of these explanations is closer to the truth.[3]

International Evidence

Robert E. Lucas, Jr., a founder of the monetary misperceptions school, has suggested another way to test the monetary misperceptions model. Lucas points out that if the

[2]"Unanticipated Money, Output, and the Price Level in the United States," *Journal of Political Economy* 86 (1978), 548–580.

[3]In Chapter 15, we will examine the workings of the Federal Reserve in some detail.

model is right, then price-level shocks should have more impact in some countries than in others.

Here is the essence of Lucas's reasoning: Suppose that Stella, who is currently (voluntarily) unemployed, wakes up one morning to learn that her best wage offer has doubled overnight, from $10,000 to $20,000. Will she accept the job? It depends on whether she believes that the new offer represents a real wage increase or just a change in the price level. The monetary misperceptions model suggests that she could (perhaps mistakenly) believe the former and accept the job.

But what if Stella happens to live in a country where the price level fluctuates wildly all the time? Then, when she gets the message offering her a $20,000-a-year job, her most likely reaction is to think "Oh, the price level probably jumped again—just as it always does" and reject the offer as being nothing new.

In other words, changes in the price level might have big effects on employment (and thus on output) in countries where changes in the price level are unusual events capable of fooling people. But in countries where the price level is highly erratic, workers and employers learn to recognize price-level fluctuations for what they are—and hence are much harder to fool into taking new jobs or expanding their operations.

Thus, if the monetary misperceptions model is correct, we should find that price level affects output by a lot in countries where the price level has low *variance* but that it affects output much less in countries where the price level has high variance. (Variance is a statistical concept which measures the tendency of a variable to fluctuate around its average.)

Figure 14-18 tests this prediction of the model. In both parts, the horizontal axis

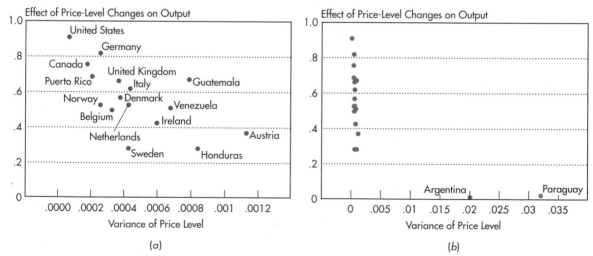

(a)   (b)

FIGURE 14-18

High variance in the price level makes it hard for changes in the price level to fool people; thus such changes have little effect on output. In (*a*), the evidence from 16 countries broadly supports this prediction. The vertical axis shows the percent change in output associated with a 1 percent change in the price level. In (*b*), 2 more countries are added to the sample. The 16 unlabeled points near the vertical axis correspond to the 16 points in (*a*).

measures the variance of the price level, and the vertical axis measures the extent to which price-level changes affect output. [For example, the value for Austria in part (*a*) is a little more than .3; this means that in Austria, a 1 percent change in the price level tends to be associated with about a .3 percent change in output.] The plotted points in Figure 14-18(*a*) clearly display a general downward-sloping trend that is consistent with the model's prediction.

Figure 14-18(*b*) expands the test by including two new countries, Argentina and Paraguay, where the price level has a much higher variance than elsewhere. To fit Argentina and Paraguay on the graph, the scale of the horizontal axis has been changed substantially, so the points from Figure 14-18(*a*) are now all bunched up near the vertical axis. Note that in Argentina and Paraguay, the price level has very little effect on output, providing two additional confirmations of the model's prediction.

SUMMARY

In the 1950s and 1960s there appeared to be a close correlation between inflation and unemployment, in that rises in inflation consistently led to drops in unemployment. This relationship is depicted by the Phillips curve. In more recent decades, the relationship between inflation and unemployment appears to have become far more complicated.

The neoclassical model predicts no relationship at all between the price level and the levels of employment and output. This seems incorrect for the 1950s and 1960s. The simple Keynesian models discussed in Chapters 12 and 13 predict a stable relationship between the price level and the levels of employment and output. This seems incorrect for more recent history.

An *ME* curve is a graph with the price level on the vertical axis and output (which is the same as income) on the horizontal axis. For each level of income, the *ME* curve shows the price level that clears the money market.

A *GE* curve, which is drawn on the same axes, shows the level of output that clears the goods market. In the neoclassical model, changes in the price level do not affect the goods market, so the *GE* curve is vertical. In the sticky wage model, higher prices correspond to higher employment and higher output, so the *GE* curve slopes upward. In the sticky price model, only one price level is possible, so the *GE* curve is horizontal.

When a model's *GE* curve and *ME* curve are superimposed, they intersect at the model's predictions for prices and output. Changes in the money supply affect the location of the *ME* curve. The economy then moves along a *GE* curve to a new equilibrium. Whether this results in more output depends on the shape of the *GE* curve.

The monetary misperceptions model gives a new explanation for the observed unstable relationship between employment and output. That explanation is based on two ideas: When the price level is higher than expected, workers are fooled about the real value of their wage offers and therefore accept jobs that they would otherwise reject. At the same time, producers are fooled about the level of demand for their products and therefore hire more workers than they would otherwise want.

This model suggests that it is not the price level but just the unexpected component of the price level that affects employment and output. When the expected price level remains fixed, every change in the price level is unexpected; then there appears to be a relationship between the price level itself and the level of employment. But this relationship is an illusion, in the sense that when expectations change, the relationship will break down.

In the monetary misperceptions model, the *GE* curve is vertical (as in the neoclassical model) when perceptions are accurate and upward-sloping when the price level is perceived as fixed. There is a different *GE* curve for each expected price level. The effects of a monetary shock depend entirely on whether the shock is accurately perceived by the individuals and firms in the economy.

Rather than assume that people perceive all shocks perfectly or, at the other extreme, that they never revise their expectations, economists often assume that people have rational expectations. That is, people have imperfect information but make the best possible guesses based on whatever information is available. Thus, when the price level fluctuates back and forth around an average, expectations are roughly correct on the average day but can be quite wrong on other days. As a result, the money supply can affect output.

However, if the government tries to take advantage of this relationship by raising the *average* price level, people revise their expectations and it is possible for the policy to have no effect.

One implication of the monetary misperceptions model is that policies should be thought of as processes, not events. The model suggests that rather than asking about the effect of a given monetary shock, we should ask about the effects of a given *pattern* of shocks.

PROBLEM SET

1. Suppose that nominal wages are "semisticky" in the sense that they can adjust immediately to foreseen changes in the price level but not to unforeseen changes. Explain how such a model could account for the shape of the Phillips curve in Figure 14-1.

2. *True or false:* According to the neoclassical model, a temporary increase in productivity causes the *ME* curve to shift upward.

3. *True or false:* According to the neoclassical model, a temporary increase in wasteful government spending causes the *ME* curve to shift upward.

4. *True or false:* According to the sticky wage model, a temporary increase in productivity causes the *ME* curve to shift upward.

5. *True or false:* According to the sticky wage model, a temporary increase in wasteful government spending causes the *ME* curve to shift upward.

6. *True or false:* According to the sticky price model, a temporary increase in productivity causes the *ME* curve to shift upward.

7. *True or false:* According to the sticky price model, a temporary increase in wasteful government spending causes the *ME* curve to shift upward.

8. *True or false:* According to the neoclassical model, a temporary increase in productivity causes the *GE* curve to shift rightward.

9. *True or false:* According to the neoclassical model, a temporary increase in wasteful government spending causes the *GE* curve to shift rightward.

10. *True or false:* According to the sticky wage model, a temporary increase in productivity causes the *GE* curve to shift rightward.

11. *True or false:* According to the sticky wage model, a temporary increase in wasteful government spending causes the *GE* curve to shift rightward.

12. Consider a model in which some but not all prices are sticky. Explain why you would expect such a model to imply the existence of an upward-sloping *GE* curve. What would happen to that *GE* curve if there were a temporary increase in productivity? What if there were a temporary increase in wasteful government spending? What if there were an increase in the money supply?

13. Suppose the government wants to use wasteful spending to stimulate employment. Will the spending program be more effective if people know about it or if they don't know about it? Why?

14. In terms of the monetary misperceptions model, describe the possible effects of a fall in the supply of money.

15. Suppose that the money supply has historically fluctuated around a given level. Suppose too that the government announces that henceforth it will continue to maintain this same average *level* but that the average size of the *fluctuations* will become bigger in both directions.

    a. Assuming that people have rational expectations, what would you expect to happen to the *slopes* of the upward-sloping *GE* curves in the monetary misperceptions model? (*Hint:* When you observe a large rise in your nominal wage rate, are you more or less likely than before to mistake it for an increase in your real wage rate?)

    b. What would you expect to happen in the long run to the aggregate supply of goods? (*Hint:* Is it now easier or more difficult to engage in productive activities?)

    c. What would you expect to happen to the magnitude of business cycles and to the average level of output over the course of one business cycle?

16. Suppose you empirically estimate Phillips curves for many different countries. That is, you plot price level and unemployment data for each country and fit a curve to the data points. Why might the curves be very different for different countries? Why, for some countries, might there be collections of data points that do not seem to fit any curve at all? What would you expect the Phillips curve to look like in a country that has had very high inflation for a very long time?

17. Do you agree with the conclusion the author comes to in the following quotation? Why or why not?

    Evaluating the effects of different economic policies with econometric models appears to be a rather straightforward procedure. An econometric model is simply a system of equations, estimated from past experience, which is thought to represent people's behavior. As input, the system requires values for certain economic variables thought to be determined outside the system, things like international developments and government policies. As output, the system predicts values of certain quantities such as employment and prices under the assumed external (input) conditions.

    Such a model can simulate the effects of different government policies on the economy. Then by comparing the outcomes of several simulations of different policy options, government policy makers should be able to choose the best one to accomplish the government's objectives.

18. Suppose that, in reality, employment *L* depends on the real interest rate *r* via the equation

    $$L = 10r + 20$$

An econometrician mistakenly believes that employment is determined by the *nominal* interest rate i via an equation of the form

$$L = Ai + B$$

where A and B are constants. Suppose also that the inflation rate has been 10 percent for a very long time.

a. If the econometrician uses historical economic data to try to discover the values of A and B, what values will he come up with?

b. Explain why the econometrician's equation will make good predictions as long as the inflation rate stays constant.

c. Suppose that it is considered desirable to increase L and that the government can affect i by controlling the inflation rate. What will the econometrician advise?

d. When the new policy is announced, what happens to A and B?

e. Explain why the recommended policy won't work.

19. Suppose that the economy is in a rational expectations equilibrium with a price level of 2. One day a tornado destroys half the country's capital stock. Suppose also that at first nobody realizes the extent of the disaster and therefore nobody expects any change in the price level.

a. What happens to the actual price level and the level of output?

b. What happens when people realize what has occurred?

c. Draw a graph showing the equilibria before the tornado, just after the tornado, and after people figure out what has happened.

Chapter 15

Monetary Institutions

So far in this book, we have taken the fundamental economic building blocks—intertemporal choice, production, consumption, investment, and the government—and used various assumptions about them to construct several complete macroeconomic models. In Chapters 15 and 16, we will enhance these models by adding some underlying details to the original building blocks. These enhancements do not change the conclusions of our models. Instead, they enrich our ability to use the models to make predictions about the world.

In our discussions about monetary policy, we have used phrases like "suppose there is an increase in the money supply" without describing exactly how the money supply grows in the real world. At times, we have imagined that the government distributes new money by dropping it from helicopters. Only rarely have we referred to the Federal Reserve. In this chapter we fill in some of the missing details.

15-1 A BRIEF HISTORY OF MONEY

Money is as old as civilization. We don't know who first invented it, but we do know something of how it has evolved in modern times.

Coins

Before the advent of modern banking, "money" usually meant coins made of gold or other precious metals. The value of those coins was determined entirely by weight: a gold coin was worth its weight in gold.

An advantage of coins over, say, gold nuggets is that they do not have to be weighed every time a transaction takes place. If 1-ounce gold coins are easily recognizable, then they are easily accepted in trade.

Traditionally, governments provided the service of converting the metal into acceptable coins. You could bring a pound of gold to the appropriate authorities, and they would mint you a pound of gold coins. For this you paid a fee—also in gold. That fee was called the *seigneurage,* or "right of the ruler," and was an explicit tax levied against people who wanted to hold money. This seigneurage was the ancestor of the modern seigniorage that we met in Chapter 10.

The system was plagued by fraud and abuse. It was very easy for the operator of the mint to make "1-ounce" coins that weighed imperceptibly less than a full ounce and then to pocket the difference. More significantly, once coins were in circulation, they were subject to further degradation: ordinary citizens would clip (shave) small pieces of gold off the edges, hoping that the damage would go unnoticed. The problem periodically reached epidemic proportions. As an example, in late-seventeenth-century England, coins became so thoroughly degraded that every commercial transaction was placed in jeopardy. According to historian Thomas Babington Macaulay,

> *The evil was felt daily and hourly in almost every place and by almost every class, in the dairy and on the threshing floor, by the anvil and by the loom, on the billows of the ocean and in the depths of the mine. Nothing could be purchased without a dispute. Over every counter there was wrangling from morning to night. The workman and his employer had a quarrel as regularly as the Saturday came round. On a fair day or a market day, the clamours, the reproaches, the taunts, the curses, were incessant: and it was well if no booth was overturned and no head broken.*[1]

➡ *Exercise 15-1*
What physical aspects of modern coins make it hard to get away with clipping them?

[1]T. Macaulay, *A History of England* (London: Longman, Brown, Green and Longmans), 1850–1861.

Paper Money and the Gold Standard

The American colonies (beginning with Massachusetts in 1690) issued the modern world's first paper money. By the 1800s, paper money was commonplace. Instead of carrying actual gold, you could store your gold with a bank (or with a goldsmith), which would then print and give you paper certificates of ownership. These certificates could be traded for goods easily and were not subject to clipping, so they were circulated as currency.

The gold held by the bank was said to be held *in reserve,* and the lightweight paper money amounted to claims on that gold. The paper money was said to be *100 percent backed* by gold.

When paper money is 100 percent backed by gold, we say that the economy is on the **gold standard.**

Gold standard:
A system under which all money is 100 percent backed by gold.

Other Standards

Although **currency** (for example, paper or coins made of inexpensive metal) is traditionally backed by gold, it can in principle be backed by any other commodity. Silver is the most frequent alternative.

Currency:
Paper money and coins.

On the Isle of Yap in Micronesia, large boulders have traditionally been used for money. At one time, each transaction required transporting a boulder from the buyer's backyard to the seller's. Over time, though, the residents of Yap developed a system whereby the largest boulders are kept together in one place and records are kept of their ownership. Now, instead of moving boulders, islanders simply keep track of who owns them. The records of ownership serve as a form of money on Yap; those records are 100 percent backed by boulders, so the Yap economy can be said to be on the boulder standard.

Fiat Currency

Banks and other issuers of currency soon noticed that on any given day, relatively few people actually tried to redeem their paper currency for gold. This meant that it was safe to issue certificates worth more than the gold being held in reserve, and issuing extra certificates meant the issuer could spend this extra money. For example, if no more than 20 percent of the certificates ever came in for redemption at the same time, a bank that held $20,000 worth of gold reserves could print $100,000 worth of certificates. Such certificates are said to be 20 percent backed by gold. Paper certificates with less than 100 percent backing of any valued asset are sometimes called **fiat currency,** or *fiat money.*

Fiat currency:
Paper money that is not 100 percent backed by any asset.

There is another form of fiat money: coins which are worth more than the value of the metal they contain. It takes about 2 cents' worth of copper and zinc to make a U.S. quarter. Because 2 cents is 8 percent of the quarter's value, the quarter is 8 percent backed by the metal it contains.

Although systems of fiat currency have proved themselves entirely workable, they have often seemed baffling to noneconomists. The great novelist Leo Tolstoy

Fiat coins:
Coins whose face value exceeds the intrinsic value of the metal they are made of.

wrote, "Paper money may deceive the ignorant, but nobody is deceived by coins of base metal that have little intrinsic value."[2] Tolstoy might have been shocked to learn that in the twentieth century, **fiat coins** would become commonplace throughout the world. They coexist with paper money, and neither coins nor paper are exchanged exclusively by the ignorant.

Government Money

Pure fiat currency:
Paper money that is not backed at all.

How much backing does a fiat currency need? Some economists believe that when *governments* issue fiat currency, it need not have any backing at all. Such **pure fiat currency** would not be redeemable for anything but would still circulate and be used as money. People would be willing to accept it at face value because of their faith in the government itself. As long as the government is willing to accept currency in payment of taxes, people can be confident that the currency has some value.

From the American Revolution to the Civil War, all the paper money that circulated in the United States was issued by private banks and other private enterprises. All this currency was at least partially backed by gold or silver. But during the Civil War, both the Union and the Confederate governments started printing their own money to finance military expenses. These currencies were initially unbacked, and the Confederate currency lost its value completely when the Confederacy was dissolved at the end of the war. However, the Union currency—popularly called "greenbacks"—continued to circulate. Eventually, in 1873, the government began backing greenbacks with gold.

In the late 1800s, the question of how to back U.S. government currency was passionately debated, and the debate played a major role in national politics. The issue was whether to use gold or silver as a backing. Advocates of silver, which was relatively plentiful, hoped that a silver standard would allow rapid money supply growth and inflation—a boon to the debtors whom they represented. Silver miners formed another powerful lobby that argued for a silver standard. William Jennings Bryan, one of the great orators in American political history and the Democratic candidate for president in 1896, went to battle in favor of silver and against the gold standard with the rallying cry, "You shall not crucify mankind upon a cross of gold." But Bryan lost the election to William McKinley, and the gold standard remained firmly in place for the next 37 years.

Vehement debates about how to back paper money have not been confined to the United States. In the 1800s, Great Britain relied increasingly on paper money that was not completely backed by gold; this reliance led to inflationary and deflationary crises throughout the 1800s. During the same period, France, Germany, Italy, Russia, Japan, Argentina, Austria-Hungary, and many other nations also experimented intermittently with issuing money backed with or without precious metals like gold or silver.

During the 1870s, Walter Bagehot, editor of the British magazine *The Economist,* highlighted a fundamental trade-off in the responsibilities of a central bank. On

---

[2]L. Tolstoy, *War and Peace,* Epilogue 2.

the one hand, he argued, the Bank of England (the British central bank) was responsible to the public for creating confidence in the currency; this suggested that the central bank should hold a high ratio of gold in its coffers to serve as backing. On the other hand, the central bank was also responsible to the public for earning interest on its assets, and gold holdings earned no interest at all. Because of this fundamental conflict in their responsibilities, the central banks of most nations have compromised by backing their currencies partially with precious metals and partially with financial assets such as parliament or treasury bills.

Until the early 1970s, most countries continued using gold—or at least a mixture of assets in which gold was an important component—to back their currencies. Many countries stored their gold in a stronghold called Fort Knox, which is located in Kentucky. During the 1970s, most countries—including the United States—shifted the backing of their currencies from gold to the bonds of stable governments. The remaining gold in Fort Knox was then transferred to vaults in the basement of the New York City Federal Reserve Bank. It can be viewed by tourists on the premises and by movie fans in their living rooms as they watch Bruce Willis take on an army of international gold thieves in *Die Hard with a Vengeance*.

Central Banks

Federal Reserve:
The central bank of the United States.

In the United States today, the money supply is controlled by the **Federal Reserve,** often called the *Fed* for short. The Fed is an example of a **central bank,** a bank designated by a country's government to control that nation's money supply. Almost all nations have them.

Central bank:
An institution designed by a country's government to control that nation's money supply.

The Federal Reserve is not technically a branch of the U.S. government, but its officers are appointed by the president and approved by Congress. It is run by a seven-member Board of Governors, each of whom serves a 14-year term. These terms overlap so that one seat on the Board becomes vacant every 2 years.

The U.S. Congress created the Federal Reserve in 1913, and continues to keep close tabs on its behavior. Congress can influence the Fed by a variety of means, including threats to pass legislation that will limit the Fed's powers.

Because it is empowered to create money, the Federal Reserve earns seigniorage of the sort discussed in Chapter 10. That is, the Fed can create money (almost costlessly) and use it to acquire valuable assets. However, the Fed pays the government a 100 percent tax on its profits, so all gains from seigniorage ultimately find their way into the U.S. Treasury.

Paper currency issued by the Federal Reserve is not backed by gold or silver. However, it is still backed. In Section 15-3 (under the heading "Open-Market Operations"), you will see that when the Fed creates dollars, it typically uses them to purchase U.S. Treasury bills. Those Treasury bills are held in storage, and you can exchange your paper money for Treasury bills at any time. The Treasury bills are valuable because the U.S. government has promised to repay the loans they represent and because the Constitution empowers the government to tax its citizens to make those payments. That is why your paper money is said to be backed by the "full faith and credit of the United States government."

European Monetary Union

Since the late 1980s, the European Union (formerly the European Economic Community) has debated the possibility of replacing the many monies of Europe with a single currency, called, say, the "euro." The move to a single money for Europe would be accompanied by unification of the various national central banks into a single monetary authority—one central bank making all the decisions about the money supply.

The proposal has the advantage of eliminating the costly currency conversions and calculations that now take place daily. (We will discuss these issues more fully in Chapter 16.) It has the disadvantage of taking away from sovereign governments the right to create their own money, including the ability to acquire seigniorage and take in revenue via an inflation tax (discussed in Chapter 10). During times of economic and political strife, and especially during wars, governments have often fallen back on these means of raising revenue, which bring in immediate funds, entail few collection costs (since no one has to send in a tax payment when inflation is the source of the tax), and do not require parliamentary debates before they can be implemented.

The idea of a single central bank and currency—that is, a monetary union—also poses an operational problem: The various governments' representatives to the combined central bank must *agree* on a monetary policy, but reaching such an agreement is likely to be difficult and time-consuming. First, representatives of various nations may disagree about the effects of monetary policy: If wages or prices are sticky, monetary expansions can influence output and unemployment during recessions, but if these variables are *not* sticky, then such expansions only result in unwanted inflation. Second, even if everyone agreed on the model to use, different economic conditions in different countries would lead to different policy goals. How should the united central bank respond in the event of a recession in Great Britain while business is booming in Spain? And third, the different nations of Europe have traditionally chosen different policies regarding inflation, with Germany's central bank carefully avoiding pressures to allow inflation during the 1970s, 1980s, and 1990s, while the central banks of nations like Italy and France have allowed more rapid inflations at times in response to economic and political pressures.

On the other hand, some politicians have argued that the very difficulty of agreeing on a coordinated monetary policy may have a substantial side benefit: it could force the leaders of various nations to become more familiar with each other's problems and to communicate with each other more effectively.

15-2   MONETARY ASSETS: AN OVERVIEW

Exactly how does a central bank go about creating money? What factors influence its decisions about how much money to create? The remainder of this chapter is devoted to answering the questions.

Before we can talk about how a central bank controls the money supply, we must decide what we mean by "money." Figure 15-1 shows a variety of assets that are

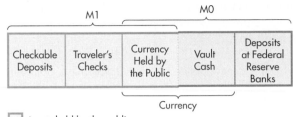

Assets held by the public

Assets held by banks (bank reserves)

FIGURE 15-1 The composition of the money supply.
The monetary base, M0, consists of currency held by the public, currency held by banks (vault cash), and the balances held by banks in their accounts at the central bank—the Federal Reserve Banks in the United States. The M1 money supply consists of currency held by the public, traveler's checks, and balances in checkable accounts held by the public.

"moneylike." In this section we briefly discuss what those assets are and how they are created. In Sections 15-3 and 15-4, we will add details to the discussion.

Currency

When you think of "money," you probably think first of currency—pieces of colored paper (green, if you live in the United States) with pictures of historical figures and slogans declaring them to be "legal tender."

You might think also of metal coins, which in the United States are issued by the Treasury Department. But in the modern world, coins are a very small part of the money supply, so we shall ignore them.

Currency can be divided into two categories: currency sitting in bank vaults **(vault cash),** and currency held by the public. Vault cash occupies the fourth box in Figure 15-1, and currency held by the public occupies the third box.

There is one other form of money that is very similar to currency, namely, traveler's checks, which are readily accepted by most merchants. In Figure 15-1, traveler's checks occupy the second box.

Vault cash:

Cash kept in bank vaults and in drawers at banks.

Where Currency Comes From

The Federal Reserve is authorized to print U.S. currency. Once it has done so, it gets that currency into circulation by using it to buy things. In principle, what those things are doesn't matter; the Fed could use newly printed money to buy toys for the children of its employees or breadcrumbs for the pigeons that nest on the roof of its main branch in Washington, D.C. In practice, however, the Federal Reserve is required by its charter to limit its purchases to several specific assets, including bonds issued by the U.S. government (such as Treasury bills), bonds issued by foreign governments or private banks, gold, and foreign currency.

If the Fed uses new currency to buy something from a bank, that currency enters the bank's vault and becomes part of its vault cash, represented by the fourth box in

Figure 15-1. If the Fed uses new currency to buy something from any source other than a bank, that currency becomes part of the currency held by the public, represented by the third box.

When the Fed prints a new dollar bill, that dollar bill is *not* counted as currency until it enters either the third or fourth box in Figure 15-1. A dollar bill sitting in a drawer at the Fed is not currency.

In 1995, the amount of U.S. currency in circulation totaled more than $350 billion, well over $1400 per American. This means that the average family of four has a total of more than $5600 cash in its pockets. Your author's family is holding less than its share, and there is an excellent chance that your own family is doing the same. Therefore, some other families must be holding far more than $5600 in currency; presumably those families transact a lot of their business in cash.[3]

Bank Deposits

One way to define money is to say that it includes whatever can be exchanged for goods and services. By that definition, the money supply must include more than just currency. Deposits in checking accounts, for example, would surely qualify as part of the (expanded) money supply.

Demand deposit:
A bank deposit that can be withdrawn on demand.

The balance in a standard checking account is sometimes called a **demand deposit** because it is available to you on demand—that is, whenever you show up at the bank and ask to make a withdrawal.

Checkable deposit:
A bank deposit that can be accessed by writing checks.

There are other accounts which are not demand deposits but can still be accessed by writing checks. These other **checkable deposits** include NOW accounts and similar accounts at credit unions and savings and loan institutions. Checkable deposits held by the public are represented by the first box in Figure 15-1.

Federal Reserve Bank:
A bank for banks, operated by the Federal Reserve.

Not all bank deposits are held by the public. The Federal Reserve operates 12 **Federal Reserve Banks** in major U.S. cities, but you cannot open an account at any of them. Only institutions—primarily other banks—can open accounts at Federal Reserve Banks. The balances in those accounts are represented by the fifth box in Figure 15-1.

Where Checkable Deposits Come From

Suppose you go to the bank and ask for a $10,000 loan to help you buy a car. When your loan is approved, the bank hands you a checkbook for a new checking account with an initial balance of $10,000. Where did the $10,000 come from? It came, in a sense, from thin air—somebody at the bank typed a few keystrokes at a computer, and suddenly your checks were as good as money.

[3]$5600 may be an overestimate if a substantial amount of U.S. currency circulates in countries other than the United States.

Some checkable deposits—such as your car loan—are created at the moment that the bank approves a loan. Others—such as, quite possibly, your personal checking account—are purchased with cash or with checks drawn on other banks. But all checkable deposits are created in the same way—by the bank's simple declaration that they exist.

If banks can create money at will, what restrains them from creating it in unlimited quantities? Banks recognize that any depositor is liable to withdraw cash at any given time. They can't create too many deposits, or they risk running out of cash.

When a customer wants cash, the bank has only two ways to get it: by removing money from its vault or by withdrawing funds from its own account at a Federal Reserve Bank. (There is actually one other possibility—borrowing the cash in a hurry. The bank can borrow either from the Fed or from another bank. We will discuss these possibilities later in the chapter.) Its **bank reserves** consist of its vault cash plus the balance in its Federal Reserve account—the darkly shaded area in Figure 15-1. So the bank needs enough reserves to meet depositors' demands for cash.

Bank reserves:
Vault cash plus bank deposits at Federal Reserve Banks.

It is safe for a bank to create checkable deposits that exceed its reserves, because banks can be quite confident that not all customers will attempt to withdraw cash at the same moment. However, a bank's reserves do put a limit on its creation of checkable deposits. A prudent bank might decide that its checkable deposits should not exceed, say, five times its reserves. Thus the bank might have $1 million in reserves and issue $5 million in checkable deposits. That bank's checkable deposits are 20 percent backed by its reserves.

Reserve requirement:
A limit on how many checkable deposits a bank can issue; expressed as a function of that bank's reserves.

A very reckless bank might want to issue checkable deposits that are, say, 100 times its reserves—and just hope that no more than 1 percent of the customers ever ask for cash at the same time. However, such recklessness is prohibited by law. The Federal Reserve is empowered to set a **reserve requirement** mandating the minimum fraction of checkable deposits that must be held in reserve. If the reserve requirement is 10 percent, then banks may issue checkable deposits equal to no more than 10 times their reserves. If the reserve requirement is 20 percent, checkable deposits must equal no more than 5 times reserves.

Where Deposits at Federal Reserve Banks Come From

Just as a private bank can create deposits for the public, so a Federal Reserve Bank can create deposits for banks. When the Fed wants to lend money to a bank, it can do so by simply increasing that bank's account balance. We will see shortly that the Fed often purchases government bonds and other assets from banks; it can pay for these assets "with a keystroke," by declaring that the bank's Federal Reserve account has grown.

We have just seen that private banks do not want to issue too many checkable deposits, for fear that too many customers will want cash at the same time. But for the Fed, coming up with cash is never a problem. If too many of the Fed's customers—the banks that hold accounts at Federal Reserve Banks—demand cash simultaneously, the Fed can just print some more cash. Unlike private banks, the Federal Reserve has an unlimited source of funds available.

Monetary base:

Currency held by the public plus vault cash plus deposits at Federal Reserve Banks.

The **monetary base,** often abbreviated M0, consists of the last three boxes in Figure 15-1: currency held by the public, vault cash (that is, currency in bank vaults), and deposits (by banks) in the central bank. (Note that currency stockpiled at the central bank itself is *not* considered part of the monetary base.) These are the kinds of "money" that are directly controlled by the central bank.

In this section we will learn more about how the central bank controls the size of the monetary base, using the U.S. Federal Reserve as our main example.

Open-Market Operations

Every Monday the U.S. Treasury (which, unlike the Federal Reserve, *is* an official agent of the U.S. government) auctions bonds to raise cash for government expenditures. These bonds—called Treasury bills or Treasury bonds, depending on their lifetimes—are available to anyone who wants to bid on them, including you.

When *you* buy a Treasury bill for, say, $9500, you pay for it with existing money. But when the Fed buys a Treasury bill for $9500, it can pay for it by printing new money. That money is then in circulation, and M0 has increased by $9500. The Treasury can use the money for some government expenditure (such as buying office equipment, paying civil servants, or distributing welfare checks).

If the Fed wants to increase the monetary base on a day other than Monday, it can do so by buying a Treasury bill from anybody who acquired one at an earlier auction. This too puts money directly into circulation.

When the Fed buys bonds, it increases the monetary base.

When the Fed wants to *decrease* the monetary base, it can do so by selling bonds and destroying the proceeds. If the Fed sells you a bond for, say, $9800, then $9800 has been taken out of circulation—stockpiled at the Fed—and is no longer part of the monetary base. We often say that the Fed has "burnt" that money, even when it has really just stuffed the money in a drawer. The real point is simply that the money—the $9800—is *not available* for anyone—private citizen or government purchaser—to use.

Open-market operation:

A purchase or sale by the Federal Reserve; results in a change in the monetary base.

When the Fed sells bonds, it decreases the monetary base.

Whenever the Federal Reserve buys or sells government bonds, we say it is engaged in an **open-market operation.** The result of an open-market operation is an increase or a decrease in the monetary base.

Avoiding the Printing Press

Earlier we noted that when the Fed purchases a Treasury bill, it pays for the bill by "printing money." In many cases, that is true only metaphorically. Let's look at what really happens.

Suppose the Fed buys a Treasury bill from Chemical Bank for $9500. It pays for that Treasury bill by adding $9500 to Chemical Bank's account balance at the New York Federal Reserve Bank. Nothing has to be "printed" except a deposit slip verifying that Chemical Bank now has additional funds in its account. This transaction adds $9500 to the fifth box in Figure 15-1, where it becomes a part of the monetary base.

When Chemical Bank wants cash, it can withdraw the $9500 from its account. The cash is taken from a drawer at the Federal Reserve Bank (where it does not count as part of the monetary base) and placed in a drawer at Chemical Bank, where it *does* count as part of the monetary base and from which it is free to circulate. If the Fed doesn't have $9500 when Chemical Bank wants to make its withdrawal, then it can order $9500 in newly printed bills. Either way, this transaction removes $9500 from the fifth box in Figure 15-1 and adds it to the fourth box; there is thus no further change in the monetary base.

This roundabout method of getting $9500 cash into the vault at Chemical Bank is essentially equivalent to the Fed's printing 9500 dollar bills and exchanging them for a Treasury bill. There is one small difference, however: Chemical Bank might decide not to withdraw the entire $9500. It might withdraw only, say, $8000 and leave $1500 in its bank account. Even so, the monetary base has still risen by the full $9500.

We usually say that the Fed is *printing money* at the moment that it increases a bank's reserves, regardless of whether the physical printing press has been fired up. "Printing money" can mean actually printing bills and spending them, or it can mean increasing the balance in a bank's Federal Reserve account.

The Fed does not actually do its own printing; it orders money from a printshop called the Bureau of Engraving and Printing, which happens to be owned by the U.S. Treasury. But only the Fed, not the Treasury, can order that money be printed.

The Discount Window

Instead of buying bonds issued by the government, the Federal Reserve could, in principle, buy bonds issued by private citizens, private corporations, or private banks. But most personal and corporate bonds carry a substantial default risk, so the Fed is prohibited from buying them. The Fed is, however, permitted to purchase bonds issued by banks; that is, the Fed is allowed to lend money to banks.

Discount window:

The mythical "window" at which banks borrow from the Fed.

When a bank borrows from the Fed, we say that it borrows at the **discount window.** The Fed prints money to lend to the bank, thereby increasing the monetary base. When the Fed gets paid back, the money supply decreases accordingly.

The discount window was originally created so that banks could borrow enough to get them through short-term cash-flow crises. We have seen that every bank keeps a certain amount of reserves to meet the normal daily demand for cash from its customers. Banks occasionally underestimate the demand for cash on a particular day, and when reserves run low, they can turn to the discount window at a moment's notice.

But the discount window is also used as a tool for controlling the monetary base. When the Fed wants to increase the monetary base, it lowers the interest rate that it charges on discount-window loans—called the **discount rate**—thereby encouraging banks to do more borrowing at the discount window. Conversely, when the Fed wants to slow the growth rate of the monetary base, it raises the interest rate at the discount window to discourage banks from asking it to print more money.

Discount rate:

The interest rate at which banks borrow at the discount window.

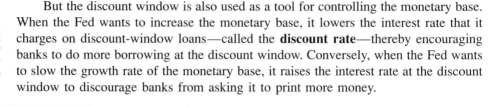

In Chapter 3, we used the phrase "discount rate" to mean the quantity $1/(1 + r)$, where r is the interest rate. We are now using the same phrase to mean something entirely different. (Historically, however, the two uses of the term are related, as the Fed used to lend to banks by purchasing discounted bonds.)

Since the inflation of the 1970s, the Fed has substantially decreased its reliance on the discount window as a tool for controlling the monetary base, relying more on open-market operations instead. However, in other countries, and particularly in Japan, central banks control the monetary base almost exclusively through the discount window.

Moral Suasion

The discount rate is consistently lower than the market interest rate. Figure 15-2 compares the U.S. discount rate to the prime rate (the rate that banks charge their most

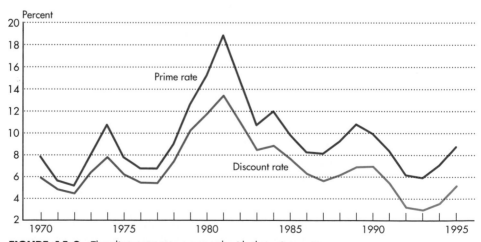

FIGURE 15-2 The discount rate compared with the prime rate.
The discount rate, at which banks borrow from the Fed, is consistently lower than the prime rate, at which banks lend to corporate customers.

creditworthy corporate customers) over a recent 20-year period. The difference between these rates creates a profit opportunity for banks, which seemingly could borrow enormous sums at the discount window and then immediately relend them at higher market rates.

The Fed controls the banks' impulse to borrow at the discount window by reminding them that the window is intended for use in cash-flow emergencies only. If a bank makes too many trips to the discount window, the Fed may even hint that the bank must not be managing its affairs very well and that perhaps those affairs should be investigated. (Besides controlling the money supply, the Federal Reserve regulates the banking industry.) The Fed applies more or less of this **moral suasion** depending on whether it wants to slow down or speed up the growth rate of the money supply.

15-4 THE MONEY SUPPLY

We noted earlier that a reasonable way to define money is to include whatever assets people use to carry out transactions. Those assets are checkable bank deposits, traveler's checks, and currency held by the public—the first three boxes in Figure 15-1. The sum of those three assets is called M1 or the M1 money supply.

Currency is part of the monetary base, and it is created by the Fed. Currency enters the hands of the public when they withdraw it from their banks; banks in turn get it from the Fed. So the Fed's policies have a strong influence on how much currency the public can carry.

Traveler's checks are issued by a variety of institutions and are nearly interchangeable with currency. But traveler's checks represent a very small proportion of the money supply—less than 1 percent—so we will not discuss them further.

In the United States, checkable deposits form the largest component of the M1 money supply. As of 1995, M1 was roughly $1200 billion, of which $800 billion—about two-thirds—was in the form of checkable deposits. We have seen that the Fed sets bank requirements and that those requirements limit the quantity of deposits that banks can issue. Thus the Fed has a strong (though indirect) influence on the supply of checkable deposits, just as it has a strong influence on the supply of currency in public hands.

Changes in the Monetary Base

When the monetary base increases, so does the M1 money supply. We examine the details of that process below.

The Money Multiplier

Suppose, to be concrete, that the Fed prints a dollar bill and uses that dollar to buy a bond from Chemical Bank. The Fed has increased M0 by $1. Chemical Bank now has that dollar in its vault and therefore feels free to create some new checkable deposits by making new loans.

But the bank knows that once the loans are made, borrowers might not want to leave the loans entirely in the form of checkable deposits: they might prefer to take them partly in cash. So Chemical Bank can foresee that, say, 20 cents of its newly printed dollar will leave the bank through withdrawals. Then only 80 cents remains in the vault.

Figure 15-3 shows that the Federal Reserve prints a dollar and that 20 cents of that dollar ends up in the hands of the public (in particular, those members of the public who withdraw it from Chemical Bank), while the remaining 80 cents ends up in Chemical Bank's vault.

Now suppose that Chemical Bank has a policy of maintaining 10 percent reserves—that is, its checkable deposits are permitted to equal 10 times the bank's reserves. (This policy might come about either because the Fed has set a reserve requirement of 10 percent or because the Fed has set a lower reserve requirement and Chemical Bank is being more cautious than the law requires.) Because its reserves have increased by 80 cents, Chemical Bank is now willing to issue $8 in new checkable deposits. In Figure 15-3, the arrow from "Vault Cash" to "Checkable Deposits" represents this $8.

Money multiplier:
The ratio of a change in the money supply to the change in the monetary base that caused it.

So when the Fed added $1 to the monetary base, M1 increased by $8.20, the sum of a $0.20 increase in currency held by the public and an $8.00 increase in checkable deposits. We say that the **money multiplier** is 8.2 in this case, because the increase in the M1 money supply is 8.2 times the increase in the monetary base.

We have ignored one complication: Some of Chemical Bank's customers might withdraw funds from Chemical Bank and deposit them elsewhere—say at Wells Fargo. But such transactions only shift reserves and checkable deposits from one bank to another; they do not affect the economywide quantities of reserves or checkable

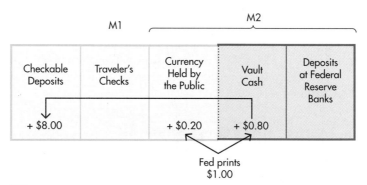

FIGURE 15-3 Effects of an increase in the monetary base.
The figure shows what happens when the Fed adds $1 to the monetary base, say, by printing a dollar bill and using it to buy a bond from a bank. Of that $1, some amount, say, $0.20, is withdrawn by the bank's customers and becomes currency held by the public. The remaining $0.80 is vault cash, which allows the bank to create additional checkable deposits—in this example, $8 worth. Thus a $1 increase in the monetary base leads to an $8.20 increase in M1.

deposits. It may very well be that in the end, Chemical Bank has 50 cents in new vault cash and $5 in new checkable deposits, while Wells Fargo has 30 cents in new vault cash and $3 in new checkable deposits. The total of all checkable deposits has still increased by $8.

Because of the money multiplier, M1 tends to be much larger than M0. Also because of the money multiplier, increases in M0 tend to be accompanied by (much larger) increases in M1. Figure 15-4 illustrates these effects by comparing the sizes of M1 and M0 in recent years.

Changing the Reserve Ratio

Reserve ratio:

The minimum allowable ratio of bank reserves to checkable deposits.

In our example we assumed that banks (in particular, Chemical Bank) keep 10 percent of deposits on hand as reserves. That 10 percent figure is called the **reserve ratio.** What if banks decided to lower their reserve ratio to 5 percent (assuming the Fed permitted that)? Then in Figure 15-3, an 80-cent increase in vault cash would lead not to an $8 increase in checkable deposits but to a $16 increase. The money multiplier would be larger than before.

A drop in the reserve ratio causes a rise in the money multiplier.

We have left one thing out of this calculation: A lower reserve ratio means more checkable deposits, and more checkable deposits probably mean more cash withdrawals—so the public now lays claim to more than 20 cents out of the original dollar. Bank reserves therefore rise by something less than 80 cents, so checkable deposits rise by something less than $16. Nevertheless, our bottom line is still correct: When the reserve ratio falls, the money multiplier rises. To get the exact relationship between the reserve ratio and the money multiplier, we need to do some algebra.

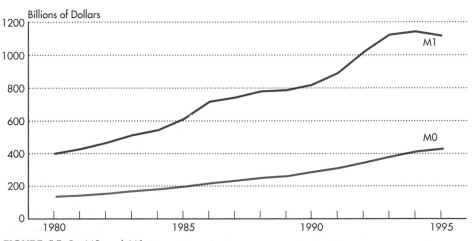

FIGURE 15-4 M0 and M1 in recent years.
The differences result not only from the money multiplier but also from the differing definitions of M0 and M1.

The Algebra of the Money Multiplier

In Figure 15-3, the Fed increases the monetary base by $1, and the money supply increases by $8.20; the money multiplier is therefore 8.2. Why does the multiplier have that value rather than some other? An inspection of Figure 15-3 reveals that the multiplier is determined by two bits of information: First, the public chooses to hold exactly $0.20 of the new money in the form of cash. Second, banks hold reserves equal to exactly 10 percent of deposits.

Here we derive a general formula for the money multiplier. We assume that the Fed increases the monetary base by an amount $\Delta M0$. Of that, the public desires to hold the amount x in currency. The rest, call it y, ends up in bank vaults. Then

$$x + y = \Delta M0 \tag{1}$$

In terms of Figure 15-3, x is $0.20, y is $0.80, and $\Delta M0$ is $1.

The banks then increase checkable deposits by an amount z. If the banks' desired (or legally mandated) reserve ratio is R, then we know that z is determined by the equation $R = y/z$. In Figure 15-3, y is $0.80 and R is .10, so z must be $8.

We next define the public's desired ratio of currency to checkable deposits as $C = x/z$. In Figure 15-3, $C = \$0.20/\$8 = .025$.

Now, by our definition, the money multiplier is the ratio of the change in M1 (call it $\Delta M1$) to the corresponding change in the monetary base (we called that $\Delta M0$). That is,

$$\text{Multiplier} = \frac{\Delta M1}{\Delta M0}$$

As we see in Figure 15-3, the change in M1 is comprised of the change x in currency and the change z in checkable deposits. So

$$\text{Multiplier} = \frac{\Delta M1}{\Delta M0} = \frac{x + z}{x + y} \tag{2}$$

The denominator here comes from equation (1).

Now look back at the equations $R = y/z$ and $C = x/z$. We can use them to rewrite x and y as

$$x = Cz \quad \text{and} \quad y = Rz$$

Substituting these terms for x and y in equation (2) yields

$$\text{Multiplier} = \frac{x + z}{x + y}$$

$$= \frac{Cz + z}{Cz + Rz}$$

$$= \frac{C + 1}{C + R}$$

➡ *Exercise 15-2*
Check that for Figure 15-3 the correct multiplier is given by the formula $(C + 1)/(C + R)$.

This formula shows that when the reserve ratio R falls, the multiplier increases (as we have already noted). It shows also that when the ratio of currency to checkable deposits C falls, the multiplier increases. Here's why: If the public decides to hold a smaller fraction of its money in the form of cash (a drop in C), then banks have more reserves and can create more deposits, so the multiplier becomes greater.

➡ *Exercise 15-3*
Suppose that the public does not want to hold any cash at all. In that case, give a simplified version of the formula for the money multiplier.

How a Central Bank Controls M1

A central bank can control the country's M1 money supply in either of two ways. First, it can control the monetary base M0 through open-market operations and the discount window. We have just seen that a single dollar in the monetary base can multiply into several dollars' worth of M1. So small adjustments to M0 yield much bigger adjustments to M1.

Second, the central bank is usually empowered by law to set the reserve requirement. If banks create as many deposits as the law allows, then a decrease in the reserve requirement will lead to more deposit creation—and hence to a rise in M1. So the central bank can adjust the reserve requirement downward to make M1 go up or adjust it upward to make M1 go down.

Changing the reserve requirement need not affect the supply of M1. Suppose, for example, that the reserve requirement is 10 percent but banks choose to hold reserves equal to 15 percent of deposits—more than the law requires. Then, if the reserve requirement is raised to, say, 12 percent, it will have no effect on deposit creation and hence no effect on the quantity of M1.

Using reserve requirements to control the supply of M1 has certain disadvantages. Banks are in the business of lending, and a higher reserve requirement means they can lend less. Thus, higher reserve requirements decrease bank income. To compensate for that, in the United States banks are allowed to lend their reserves to the Fed, which pays interest at the going market rate for government bonds. But this is still constraining to the banks, which might prefer to lend that money to private individuals at higher rates.

More importantly, the reserve requirement is a blunt instrument in the sense that even a small change in the reserve requirement can have a very large effect on the money supply. Thus, for fine tuning the money supply, the Fed relies on open-market operations rather than the reserve requirement.

Broader Definitions of Money

Time deposit:
A bank account that cannot be withdrawn until some prespecified time.

The Federal Reserve, as well as many other central banks, keeps track of several definitions of money that are more general than M1. The M2 money supply consists of M1 together with deposits in savings accounts, deposits in money market accounts, and small time deposits. (A **time deposit** is a bank deposit that cannot be withdrawn until some prespecified time after the money is deposited—usually 3 months, 6 months, or a year. Early withdrawals are often permitted but can be subject to a penalty fee. A time deposit is considered small if it is under $100,000.)

An even more general definition of money is M3, which includes all of M2 together with large time deposits. After M3 comes L, which includes M3, U.S. savings bonds, and short-term Treasury bonds.

The governors of the Federal Reserve believe that all these monetary aggregates are important determinants of the price level and other economic conditions. However, it is usually M1 and M2 that receive the most attention. When economists talk about *the* money supply, they are most often talking about M1 or M2.

Which definition of money corresponds to the abstract "money" in our economic models? If M2 increases at a time when M1 remains unchanged, should we say that the money supply has increased?

Part of the answer must be that "money" means whatever fits best with a given model's predictions about how money affects the economy. The neoclassical model says that when the money supply increases by 10 percent, so does the price level. The "right" definition of money is the one that makes such predictions most accurate. There is not yet any consensus among economists about which definition that is.

15-5   WHAT THE FED DOES

The Federal Reserve functions both as a policy maker and as a bank for banks. In this section we examine these roles in a bit more detail.

Making Monetary Policy

The chairman of the Federal Reserve is appointed for a 4-year term by the president of the United States; that term is normally scheduled to begin and end in the middle of a presidential administration, so an incoming president must wait 2 years before he can consider replacing the chairman.

The chairman administers the Federal Reserve in conjunction with the Board of Governors, who (as we saw earlier) are appointed by the president for 14-year terms. The governors meet once or twice a month with other members of the **Federal Open Market Committee (FOMC),** which consists of the governors themselves and the presidents of some of the 12 regional Federal Reserve Banks.

The FOMC meets to decide on the course of upcoming monetary policy. It sets target ranges for the various monetary aggregates (M0, M1, etc.), decides what kinds of assets the Fed should purchase, and so on.

In most countries other than the United States, the central bank's policy is set in close cooperation with the country's legislature (that is, its parliament or congress). In some countries, when the treasury—the government agency that collects taxes and pays for government purchases—wants to borrow, it sells its bonds not in the open market but directly to the central bank at an interest rate determined by the legislature. This guarantees that the government can borrow at a low interest rate. The drawback of such a policy is that whenever the treasury wants to borrow, it can force the

Federal Open Market Committee (FOMC):

A Federal Reserve committee, consisting of the Board of Governors and some of the presidents of the Federal Reserve Banks, that decides on the course of upcoming monetary policy.

central bank to purchase its bonds with newly created money; thus the money supply increases and the country experiences an inflation every time the government increases its borrowing.

An important feature of the U.S. Federal Reserve is its independence from Congress and the Treasury. (Only in Germany and Switzerland do central banks have more independence than in the United States.) The Fed is *not* required by its congressional charter to purchase any bond that the Treasury wants to sell. If the Treasury wants to borrow at an interest rate that is too low to attract a legitimate lender, the Treasury cannot force the Fed to print money for the Treasury to borrow; the Treasury has to either forgo borrowing or offer terms sufficient to attract private buyers. Thus, a government budget deficit in the United States does not necessarily force an increase in the money supply and therefore does not necessarily cause an inflation.

How important is the central bank's independence from political authorities? To answer this question, one pair of economists looked at evidence from 14 countries.[4] Their results are shown in Figure 15-5. In both panels, the horizontal axis measures the independence of each country's central bank. This subjective measure is based on the relationship between the central bank and the executive, the procedure to nominate and dismiss the head of the central bank, the role of government officials on the central bank board, the frequency of contacts between the executive and the bank, and the ability of the central bank to make monetary policy without regard to considerations such as the size of the government deficit.[5] Figure 15-5(*a*) shows quite

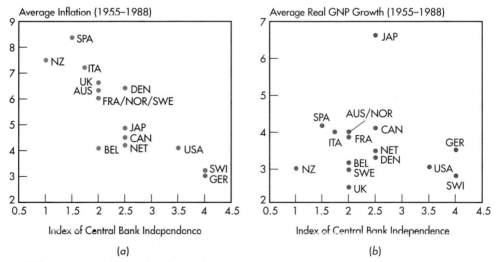

FIGURE 15-5 Central bank independence, inflation, and economic growth.
(*a*) The general downward trend shows that central bank independence is associated with low inflation. (*b*) The lack of any clear trend suggests that central bank independence is not directly tied to economic growth.

[4]A. Alesina and L. Summers, "Central Bank Independence and Macroeconomic Performance," *Journal of Money, Credit and Banking* 25 (1993), 151–162.

[5]The measures used are based on earlier work by economists Robert Bade, Michael Parkin, Vittorio Grilli, Donato Masciandro, and Guido Tabellini.

clearly that countries with more independent central banks tend to experience less inflation. On the other hand, Figure 15-5(*b*) shows that there is no clear relationship between central bank independence and economic growth. This is in accord with the neoclassical model, which predicts that monetary policy should not affect real variables such as growth.

The chairman of the Fed has the final say on how much money the Fed will create. In practice, the chairman takes into account advice and suggestions from the Board of Governors, the Treasury, and the president. Ultimately, though, the chairman has a lot of discretionary power; in setting monetary policy, he is not bound by any of this advice.

Usually, the Federal Reserve prefers to avoid influencing public opinion with its actions and goals, and hence tries to keep its purchases and sales very quiet. A large purchase of Treasury bills on a single day might be interpreted as a signal that the Fed intends to increase the growth rate of the money supply. Such an inference would in turn influence other economic variables. For example, according to the market-clearing model, an expected increase in the growth rate of the money supply would cause nominal interest rates to increase. To help keep its intentions secret, the Fed might spread its purchases of Treasury bills among different purchasing agents and brokers and across several days.

Because the Federal Reserve is a public institution, the question arises as to whether and when its policies should be revealed to the public. In particular, the meetings of the FOMC, at which monetary targets are debated, have been an object of concern. Currently, the minutes of those meetings may be legally kept secret for up to 6 months. In most other countries, there is no time limit after which the central bank must reveal to the public its minutes, its goals, or, in some cases, even the aggregate size of its previous open-market or discount-window purchases. Central banks, including the Federal Reserve, argue that secrecy about their immediate operations gives them the time they need to accomplish their objectives.

Announcement effect:

A desired change that occurs spontaneously as a result of an official announcement that alters expectations.

In part because of this 6-month gap between decisions and their disclosure, the media carefully watch for and analyze the actions and statements of the chairman of the Fed and the Board of Governors, noticing even small shifts that might indicate upcoming changes in the rate of money supply growth. The chairman of the Fed can exploit this careful observation to create a desired **announcement effect.** For example, a recent sharp rise in the nominal interest rate might convince the chairman that markets must be expecting an inflation; he could then announce the intention to slow down money growth, hoping that the announcement alone would settle the markets. Of course, the chairman's credibility would deteriorate if he announced too many things that did not subsequently occur.

The Fed as a Bank for Banks

The Federal Reserve System was created in 1913 (and began operation in 1914) with the hope that it would serve to reduce financial panics of the sort that had occurred periodically over the preceding 100 years. There had been incidents in which banks that were in perfect financial health had run out of cash on a single day—a situation that created rumors of insolvency sufficient to drive away all their depositors. The

Run on the bank (bank run):

A rush by depositors to withdraw their savings from a bank.

Lender of last resort:

The role of the Federal Reserve when it lends money to banks to help them overcome crises.

rush by depositors to withdraw their savings in such times of panic is called a **run on the bank,** or a **bank run,** a phenomenon you've seen Jimmy Stewart confront if you have ever watched the classic movie *It's a Wonderful Life*.

The original purpose of the Federal Reserve was to overcome such a crisis by printing money and lending it to the bank or banks in order to avert the panic. When the Federal Reserve acts in this capacity, it is said to be the **lender of last resort.**

Because the Fed was not always willing to create money in the necessary quantities, bank panics and other financial crises continued to occur after the founding of the Federal Reserve System. In particular, 1931 was a year of worldwide financial crises. Some economists have been very critical of the Fed for failing to do more to prevent such crises in the United States and have blamed that failure for the severity of the Great Depression.[6]

➡ *Exercise 15-4*
In what movie does Julie Andrews encounter a bank run?

The Fed scored a great success as lender of last resort in 1974, when Franklin National Bank—the twentieth largest bank in the United States—suffered a series of large losses from bad investments. Depositors, beginning to fear that Franklin would go bankrupt, rushed to close their accounts. This, of course, increased the likelihood that Franklin *would* go bankrupt and increased the number of depositors who were fearful. It began to seem likely that Franklin would collapse, taking with it a number of other institutions to which it was tied in various ways and perhaps setting off a nationwide banking panic. To avert catastrophe, the Fed opened its discount window wide to Franklin National, allowing it to borrow sufficient funds to meet all depositors' demands and restore public confidence.

A problem with having the Fed available as a lender of last resort is that its loans might prolong the life of a bank that really *is* financially unsound, allowing the bank time to do even more damage to its depositors.

Federal Deposit Insurance Corporation (FDIC):

An insurance system for banks that is run by the U.S. government.

Federal Savings and Loan Insurance Corporation (FSLIC):

A defunct insurance system for savings and loan institutions that was run by the U.S. government.

Deposit Insurance

In 1934, the U.S. government started an insurance system called the **Federal Deposit Insurance Corporation (FDIC).** The FDIC administers a fund to which banks pay premiums. In return, their customers are insured against bank failures, regardless of whether those failures are due to bad luck or poor business practices. A similar fund, the **Federal Savings and Loan Insurance Corporation (FSLIC),** was started for savings and loan institutions (sometimes called savings banks). The FDIC and the FSLIC were created to avert panics so that the Fed would not have to play such a large role as the lender of last resort.

In 1984, the FDIC was instrumental in arranging the rescue of Continental Illinois National Bank, which faced problems similar to those that Franklin National Bank had faced 10 years earlier. Since FDIC insurance applies only to small accounts

---

[6]The most effective criticism along these lines was delivered by Milton Friedman and Anna Schwartz in their book *A Monetary History of the United States* (Princeton, N.J.: Princeton University Press), 1963.

(up to $100,000), Continental's large depositors worried that if the bank went under, their funds would be lost. To reassure those depositors and avert a bank panic, the FDIC announced that it would cover the losses of all Continental depositors, without regard to the $100,000 limit. Together with other dramatic actions—arranging enormous loans for Continental from the Fed and from private banks, and ultimately taking complete control of Continental—the FDIC's quick response averted disaster.

A problem with insurance programs like the FDIC and the FSLIC is that if many banks fail simultaneously, as can happen in a recession, there may be insufficient funds to rescue all of them. That is exactly what happened in the early 1980s. Savings banks were suffering from market interest rates that had been rising for years and that were, at the time, very high. The savings banks had to pay these rates to attract depositors, even though they were collecting much lower interest rates on outstanding loans (like home mortgage loans) they had made years or decades earlier. Liberal accounting procedures had allowed many of these institutions to continue appearing solvent long after there was any realistic prospect of their survival. And the FSLIC was bound to make up for the losses of depositors in banks that failed. However, as the savings banks began to topple, it became clear that the FSLIC did not have enough funds to rescue all the banks that were certain to fail.

After several banks did fail, the Federal Reserve stepped in as a lender of last resort, providing temporary cash to protect depositors' savings. Eventually, the U.S. government took charge of the FSLIC fund. Insurance premiums have been increased, and savings banks are now subject to more rigorous accounting procedures.

The bank insurance program still faces at least one fundamental problem: The premiums paid by banks that lend to risky customers are no greater than the premiums paid by banks that lend only to very safe customers. Therefore, banks have little incentive to choose their customers with care. Depositors, who know they are insured no matter how recklessly their banks treat their deposits, have little incentive to question such recklessness or to favor more conservative institutions. In fact, because banks earn higher interest rates on riskier loans and can therefore pay higher interest rates to their depositors, depositors may even seek out banks that make riskier loans.

15-6   ISSUES IN MONETARY POLICY

We have seen that a central bank has the power to control the money supply. Now we shall turn to the questions of what a central bank like the Fed can and does attempt to accomplish with that power.

What Can Central Banks Do?

A central bank has no direct influence on income, employment, consumption, or any of the other variables that are of primary importance in our lives. It has direct influence only over the money supply. (We will soon see that it may also have something close to direct influence over nominal interest rates, at least in the short run, just by virtue of being such a large player in the market for borrowing and lending.)

Thus a central bank's power to control real variables is limited by the importance of the money supply and by the extent of the bank's ability to affect interest rates. Let us explore those limitations.

Does the Money Supply Matter?

Does money matter? To make this question more concrete, let us suppose that the central bank decides to increase the growth rate of the country's money supply. Will the nation's output of goods and services rise?

According to the pure neoclassical model—the model that most economists agree is accurate in the long run—the answer is no. But in the short run, if wages are sticky, if prices are sticky, or if monetary misperceptions play a significant role, then changes in the money supply can have significant effects on output.

Can the Central Bank Affect the Interest Rate?

Newspapers in the United States frequently report that the Federal Reserve has decided to raise or lower the interest rate. But interest rates are determined by free negotiations among individuals. So what do the newspapers have in mind?

First, the Fed does unilaterally set the discount rate—the rate at which it lends to banks. But this rate affects only very short-term (on the order of 1-day) loans in a market that is largely insulated from the rest of the economy.

Much more important is that the Fed sometimes can, and sometimes does, enter bond markets and attempt to manipulate bond prices (or, equivalently, interest rates) by offering to buy or sell large quantities.

Federal funds market:
The market in which banks lend to one another.

Federal funds rate:
The prevailing interest rate in the federal funds market.

The Fed frequently focuses its attention on the **federal funds market,** where private banks borrow and lend among themselves. Despite its possibly misleading name, the federal funds market is not run by the government or the Federal Reserve; there is not even a "market" in the sense of a physical location. Anytime one bank borrows from another, that transaction is, by definition, part of the federal funds market. The going nominal interest rate in the federal funds market is called the **federal funds rate.**

Although the Fed does not trade in the federal funds market, it trades in closely related markets where any change in the interest rate must be matched by a corresponding change in the federal funds rate. Suppose, for example, that the going federal funds rate is 5 percent and the Fed offers to borrow money in another market at 10 percent. Banks will quickly refuse to lend to each other at any rate lower than the 10 percent they can get from the Fed; in other words, 10 percent becomes the new federal funds rate.

Note, however, that when the Fed raises interest rates in this way, it simultaneously decreases the money supply. The Fed's above-market interest rate lures banks into lending money to the Fed; and once currency is in the Fed's hands, it is no longer part of the money supply.

Similarly, if the Fed wants to lower interest rates, it must be willing to expand the money supply. Suppose the prevailing federal funds rate is 5 percent and the Fed offers to lend at 3 percent. Banks will happily accept the offer, and no bank will borrow from any other at a rate higher than 3 percent. Then 3 percent becomes the new federal funds rate. But to meet the demand for loans, the Fed must supply a lot of new money.

The lesson here is this:

If the Federal Reserve wants to affect the interest rate in the federal funds market, it must sacrifice control of the money supply.

The Central Bank, the Interest Rate, and Economic Theory

In the last subsection, we asked: Can the Federal Reserve affect the market interest rate? Our answer—and this is uncontroversial among economists—was "not without sacrificing control of the money supply." But what if the Fed is willing to sacrifice that control? *Then* can it affect the market interest rate? In this subsection we will see that different economic models give different answers to that question.

Suppose the federal funds rate is 5 percent, and the Fed attempts to lower that rate by announcing its willingness to lend unlimited amounts of money at 3 percent. (The Fed's willingness to lend *unlimited* amounts is critical; if it lent only limited amounts, then some lucky borrowers would get 3 percent loans, but the market interest rate would be unaffected.) What happens when the Fed announces its offer?

To meet borrowers' demands, the Fed must create money. According to the neoclassical model, newly created money causes the price level to increase. But when the price level increases, people move along the money demand curve and demand even more money. As the Fed has pledged to make unlimited quantities of money available, it must meet that demand, thereby creating still more new money, pushing the price level up further, and causing people to demand even *more* money. We have entered a vicious circle that does not end until the money supply and the price level become infinite!

Notice that throughout this entire process, there is no effect on anything real, including the real interest rate. The lack of real effects is unsurprising, because the neoclassical model predicts a real-nominal dichotomy, so that any shock to the money market must have all of its effects confined to the money market. In our example, the Fed is committed to shocking the money market continuously until there is a change in something real. But because there is *never* a change in anything real, the shocks never end and the price level shoots off to infinity.

Conversely, suppose that the Fed tries to *raise* the interest rate, say, by offering to borrow unlimited amounts of money at 10 percent. The Fed's borrowing reduces the money supply, thereby lowering the price level; then people demand less money, so they lend even more to the Fed, and so on. In this case, the vicious circle drives the money supply and the price level to zero.

Thus:

According to the neoclassical model, when the Fed tries to maintain an interest rate other than the market equilibrium, the price level becomes either zero or infinite, but the real interest rate is unaffected.

Nevertheless, the Fed frequently appears to do exactly what the preceding paragraph says is impossible! That is, the Fed announces its intention to adjust the market interest rate either by borrowing or by lending, and the market interest rate adjusts accordingly—without the dire consequences we've just predicted.

This suggests that something very important is missing from our discussion. However, economists disagree about what that "something" is. Here are some possibilities:

- Prices may be sticky (or partly sticky) in the short run. If so, then the Fed can lend (or borrow) large amounts of money without having much immediate effect on the price level. This delays the onset of the vicious circle and allows the Fed to affect the interest rate for some period of time. However, prices do adjust in the long run, so if this explanation is correct, then the Fed must eventually retreat from its position in order to avoid disastrous consequences.

- The Fed may be following the market when it claims to be leading—creating an illusion of influence by systematically announcing plans to lower the interest rate at times when the interest rate is falling anyway. The Fed's decisions are made in secret, so noninsiders cannot be sure what triggers its interventions in bond markets. But to illustrate the kind of thing that *could* be happening, consider the following (greatly oversimplified) example: Suppose the Fed's rule is to "lower the interest rate" whenever there is a temporary increase in output. Then the Fed is simply "dictating" that markets must follow the laws of supply and demand. This can look pretty impressive—just as it would look impressive to an unsophisticated audience if an astronomer, having calculated the date and time of the next solar eclipse, were to "dictate," just moments before the event, that the moon should swallow the sun.

- It may be that for reasons economists do not entirely understand, borrowers (or lenders) are unable to respond to the Fed's offers immediately. Thus when the Fed offers to lend money, there may be some delay before an infinite amount of money is demanded. If the Fed retreats from its position before the end of that delay, it may be able to affect interest rates in the interim.

- Economists have constructed a variety of other models to explain how the Fed could affect the interest rate even when prices are flexible. One model posits that people believe there is a limit to the Fed's willingness to create new money. When the Fed offers to lend at a low interest rate, forcing itself to exceed that limit, people expect that the Fed will soon begin gradually reducing the money supply back to an acceptable level. This leads to anticipated deflation, which reduces the nominal interest rate. In this scenario, unsophisticated observers might believe that the real interest rate has fallen, even though it is only the nominal rate that has really changed.

Nobody knows for certain whether any of these scenarios is the correct one. However, it is safe to say that a substantial majority of economists would place their bets on some form of short-term price stickiness.

There is no doubt that the Fed, or any central bank, can affect *nominal* interest rates. The nominal interest rate changes when the inflation rate changes, the inflation rate changes when the growth rate of the money supply changes, and the growth rate of the money supply changes when the Fed wants it to. However, if prices are sticky in the short run, then there may be some lag between a change in the money supply and the corresponding change in the price level. Thus, all we can say for certain is that a change in the growth rate of the money supply will affect the nominal interest rate *in the long run*. Note, however, that to lower the nominal interest rate, the Fed must *lower*, not raise, the rate of money supply growth—the opposite of what many financial journalists seem to believe.

What Should the Federal Reserve Do?

We have just seen that the Federal Reserve can attempt to control the money supply or the interest rate, but not both. We have still not asked why the Fed would *want* to control *either*. In the discussion below, we address some of the goals of the Fed.

Stabilization of the Economy

Many economists believe that the Fed should use its powers to smooth business cycles by stimulating the growth of output during recessions and slowing growth during expansions. They argue that this policy will help people to achieve their goal of smoothing consumption.

Other economists believe that it is a mistake for the Fed to try to stabilize the economy, though they believe so for a variety of reasons.

Some economists object to stabilization attempts on the ground that such attempts can't work. These include economists of the monetary misperceptions school, who argue that any systematic monetary policy will be foreseen and hence will be ineffective. But as we have seen in earlier chapters, not all economists agree that foreseeable monetary policy will automatically be ineffective. Even fewer agree that interventions in the federal funds market will always be ineffective. It seems clear that if the Fed is willing to allow large changes in the money supply, it can have a major influence on the federal funds rate and hence perhaps on interest rates generally.

Other economists object to stabilization attempts on the ground that they work too well! These economists accept the Keynesian conclusion that monetary policy has important real effects in the short run, but they worry that the Fed has a history of mistiming its interventions and thus, for example, that an attempt to slow down the economy during an expansion may end up not taking effect until the middle of the next recession—when it is exactly the opposite of what is called for. An underlying problem is that it is difficult to predict how long it will take for a new policy to have noticeable effects.

Still other economists worry that by taking actions that nobody can foresee, the Fed creates an atmosphere of uncertainty that makes it difficult for people to plan their consumption and investment strategies. These economists argue that even if the Fed succeeds in smoothing the business cycle, it may do so at the cost of retarding long-term economic growth. Many of these economists would prefer to see the Fed pursue the goal of maintaining a stable price level.

Finally, there are economists who believe that business cycles might actually be a good thing. These economists point out that we don't really know what causes business cycles and that they might very well be optimal responses to changing conditions. For example, if business cycles are caused by changes in the weather, then it is certainly a good thing that people choose to eat less in a year with a bad harvest.

It is even possible that business cycles reflect a positive desire not to do too much consumption smoothing; maybe people *enjoy* alternating a few years of high income with a few years of low effort!

Some Recent Interventions

In late 1994, the Federal Reserve began a series of interventions in the federal funds market, raising interest rates each time. Its stated concern was that output (or, equivalently, income) was growing too rapidly and needed to be slowed down.

The idea that income growth can be "too rapid" strikes many economists as absurd. If you ask any wage earner to list his or her top 10 economic concerns, it is a safe bet that "income growing too rapidly" will not be among those concerns.

But many other economists reject that view. They point out that rapid growth in one period may indicate an overuse of resources that can lead to a future recession unless it is brought under control.

In the 1990s, the Fed itself has repeatedly cited the fear that rapid output growth could lead to a renewal of the inflation that was brought under control in the 1980s after many years of being both high and variable. But how can output growth lead to inflation? The neoclassical model suggests just the opposite: as output (or, equivalently, income) increases, the demand for money rises and prices should fall.

In raising the specter of inflation, the Fed seems to have been considering a much subtler scenario. Unemployment was falling rapidly in the early 1990s and the Fed apparently worried that as full employment approached, output would not be able to expand fast enough to keep pace with the demand for goods. This would then— according to some models—put upward pressure on prices.

Rules versus Discretion

We have seen that economists do not agree about what battles the Fed should be fighting. Should it try to maintain stable prices? Should it try to smooth the business cycle? Should it try to slow "excessive" growth?

Economists also disagree about what weapons the Fed should use in the battles that it fights. One of the key disagreements concerns the use of *rules* versus the use of *discretion*.

Rules:
Principles that dictate policy.

Advocates of **rules** say that the Fed should declare up front how it is going to respond to various economic situations and then stick to its declarations. Thus, for example, the Fed might announce that it will attempt to increase the money supply by 3 percent per year except that in times of recession it will aim for 5 percent per year. A more realistic policy might allow that figure of 5 percent to vary with the severity of the recession—but to vary in a preannounced way.

Discretion:
Free choice on the part of authorities in establishing policy.

Advocates of **discretion** say that the Fed should continually update its policies in response to new information and new ideas. The argument for discretion is very simple and straightforward: Knowledge is valuable, and valuable things should not be discarded. Ignoring knowledge is the same thing as discarding it. Hence the Fed should continuously modify its policies in the face of continuously updated information.

Advocates of rules say that it is important for people to be able to forecast the money supply and the price level when they make their business decisions and that having rules in place facilitates this process. They also say that rules prevent unwise or politically motivated Fed chairmen from making drastically imprudent policy choices.

Another argument for rules is that, paradoxically, a person who lives by rigid rules may accomplish his or her goals more effectively than a person who adapts well to new situations. Consider the game of "chicken," in which two cretins drive cars directly at each other until one of them loses by swerving. A self-preserving player who uses discretion will always swerve and always lose. But a player who is committed to the rule "I will never swerve" will always win (at least as long as his or her opponent uses discretion). This strategy works only if your opponent *knows* that you are truly committed: you must disable your brakes and your steering column and make sure your opponent is aware that you've done so.

The same principles apply in financial markets. Suppose, for example, that the Federal Reserve wants banks to lower nominal interest rates. It might proceed by promising to limit money growth (and hence inflation), as limited growth would keep nominal interest rates low. If the Fed is permitted to use discretion, banks will fear that after they lend at new, lower rates, the Fed may renege on its promise and engineer an inflation to accomplish some other purpose. (This difficulty with the use of discretion is an example of the time-inconsistency problem that we discussed in Chapter 14.) If, on the other hand, the Fed is bound by rules—if it disables its own ability to set monetary growth rates at will—its promise will have greater credibility and a greater chance of being effective.

SUMMARY

Historically, money has taken many forms, from coins to boulders. Paper currency is often backed by valuable assets held by the issuer of the currency. Those assets are said to be held in reserve. If the value of the assets in reserve is equal to the value of the currency, we say that the currency is 100 percent backed. If no assets are held in reserve, we say that the currency is a pure fiat currency.

Most nations in the world today, including the United States, have central banks to issue currency. The central bank of the United States is called the Federal Reserve. The Federal Reserve can create money and use it to buy valuable assets; the profits that it earns by doing so are taxed by the U.S. government at a rate of 100 percent.

Money includes both currency and bank deposits. Currency consists of paper money held by the public and paper money in bank vaults; it is printed by the Federal Reserve. Bank deposits include checkable deposits held by individuals at banks and deposits by banks at Federal Reserve Banks. Checkable deposits are created via a keystroke by the issuing bank, and deposits at Federal Reserve Banks are created via a keystroke by the Federal Reserve.

The monetary base M0 consists of currency held by the public, currency in bank vaults, and bank deposits at the Federal Reserve. The monetary base is increased through open-market operations, in which the Fed buys assets (typically Treasury bills). The Fed can pay for its purchases either by printing cash (paper money) or by increasing the Federal Reserve Bank balance of the seller. Either way, it increases the monetary base.

Another way for the Fed to increase the monetary base is by lending to banks at the discount window. Each time the Fed makes a loan, it either prints money or increases a Federal Reserve Bank balance; just as with an open-market operation, the monetary base increases.

The M1 money supply consists of currency held by the public, traveler's checks (a very small component), and checkable deposits.

When M0 increases, part of the increase finds its way into the hands of the public as cash and thus enters M1 directly. The remainder becomes part of bank reserves, thus increasing the amount that banks are permitted and/or willing to lend; this leads to the creation of new checkable deposits and so increases M1. The money multiplier is the ratio of the increase in M1 to the increase in M0. Its value depends both on what fraction of their money people choose to hold in the form of currency and on what fraction of their deposits banks hold in reserve (the reserve ratio).

The Fed can control M1 either by controlling the monetary base or by changing the required reserve ratio.

The Fed is able to influence the economy through its ability to control the money supply and its ability to affect certain interest rates by acting as a major player in the market for loans. However, the Fed can affect interest rates only by sacrificing its ability to control the money supply. To keep interest rates low, the Fed must print money, thereby creating inflation; the inflation makes low interest rates increasingly attractive to borrowers, who enter the market and bid interest rates *up*—unless the Fed continues to print more and more money.

Economists disagree about what role the Fed ought to play in attempting to stabilize the economy and in fostering conditions that are conducive to economic growth. They disagree also about whether the Fed should be bound by rules or free to exercise discretion in its policies.

PROBLEM SET

1. *True or false:* Fiat coins are less likely to be shaved than coins whose value is determined by their weight.

2. If the Fed buys $10,000 worth of Treasury bills and simultaneously sells $3000 worth of gold, what happens to the monetary base?

3. *True or false:* If the law required that all currency be 100 percent backed by gold, then the Fed would have no power to determine the monetary base.

4. Suppose the Fed purchases a $1 bond from Chemical Bank and pays for it by increasing Chemical Bank's balance at the Federal Reserve Bank. This induces Chemical Bank to make new loans, and the public takes $0.20 worth of those loans in the form of cash, which Chemical Bank supplies from previously existing currency in its vault.

   a. In Figure 15-3, what happens to the quantity of currency held by the public? What happens to the quantity of vault cash? What happens to the quantity of deposits at Federal Reserve Banks? What happens to M0?

   b. Assuming a 10 percent reserve ratio, what happens to the quantity of checkable deposits? What happens to M1?

   c. Now suppose that Chemical Bank decides to replace the $0.20 withdrawn from its vault by withdrawing $0.20 in cash from its Federal Reserve Bank account. What happens to the quantities of currency held by the public, vault cash, deposits at Federal Reserve Banks, and checkable deposits? Does this cause any changes in M0 or M1?

5. Suppose that grocery stores become more reluctant to accept checks and that shoppers therefore start carrying more cash with them.

   a. Where do shoppers get the cash?

   b. What happens to the quantity of bank reserves?

   c. What happens to the money supply?

6. Suppose that two banks with one branch apiece merge to form a single bank with two branches.

   a. What do you think happens to the amount of vault cash kept at each branch, and why?

   b. What happens to the money supply?

7. Suppose that both you and the chairman of the Federal Reserve need new cars. You finance your purchase by borrowing from a bank that has excess reserves (that is, more reserves than are necessary to meet its reserve requirement). The Fed chairman finances his purchase by printing money. Which transaction causes a bigger increase in the money supply?

8. Suppose that the public becomes very suspicious of banks and wants to hold all its money in the form of cash.

   a. What is the value of the money multiplier? Explain why it has that value.

   b. What are the implications for the Fed's ability to increase M1?

9. Explain why the money multiplier is always greater than or equal to 1. Under what circumstances is it exactly equal to 1?

10. Suppose that when the reserve requirement is 100 percent, public confidence in the banking system is so high that people hold all their money in the form of checkable deposits, whereas when the reserve requirement is 0 percent, public confidence in the banking system is so low that people hold all of their money in the form of cash. (Thus in the formula for the money multiplier, C is no longer a constant; it now depends on R.) Is the money multiplier still a decreasing function of the reserve ratio? (That is, does the multiplier still decrease when the reserve ratio increases?) If not, how does the money multiplier change as the reserve ratio grows from 0 to 100 percent?

11. *True or false:* The Fed cannot simultaneously choose arbitrary values for M0, M1, and the reserve ratio.

12. Suppose you withdraw $100 in cash from your checking account.

   a. What is the *immediate* effect on the M1 money supply?

   b. Once the bank adjusts its loan portfolio in response to your withdrawal, what happens to the money supply?

   c. Is the overall effect of your withdrawal an increase or decrease in the money supply?

13. Suppose that banks typically choose to hold more reserves than the Fed requires. Now suppose that an increase in expected future income leads to a rise in the interest rate.

   a. What happens to the reserve ratio chosen by banks? (*Hint:* When the interest rate rises, what happens to the number of loans banks want to issue?)

   b. What happens to the money supply?

   c. Suppose that the Fed does not want the money supply to change. What can it do to accomplish this goal?

Chapter 16

Exchange Rates

 U.S. citizen vacationing in rural France usually needs French francs to pay for hotel rooms and food. A Mexican citizen buying a Japanese bond typically has to acquire Japanese yen before the transaction can be consummated. An Indian clothier who wants to import British-made suits usually has to pay for them in British pounds rather than Indian rupees; if the British suitmaker does agree to accept rupees, he will soon want to exchange those rupees for British pounds.

Foreign exchange:
Currency issued by a foreign government.

Foreign exchange markets:
Markets in which the currencies of various governments are exchanged.

Domestic citizens acquire foreign money, also called *foreign currency* or **foreign exchange,** and foreign citizens acquire domestic money by trading the two in **foreign exchange markets.**

497

By making it easy to exchange one currency for another, international banking and foreign exchange markets have made it easier to travel abroad, purchase goods directly from foreign citizens, buy stock in foreign companies, and borrow from or lend to foreigners. It is almost as easy for a U.S. citizen to buy German or Mexican bonds as it is to buy U.S. bonds. At the same time, foreign citizens have easy access to U.S. financial markets without ever leaving their own countries.

Foreign money, like domestic money, is demanded and supplied according to the economic principles discussed in Chapters 10 and 15. In this chapter we see how the price of foreign money is determined.

In Chapter 15 we elaborated on the institutional differences between currency and money. Here, to simplify the discussion, we will follow customary usage and use the terms "foreign currency" and "foreign money" interchangeably to mean "foreign money."

We begin by examining some of the reasons for acquiring foreign money.

16-1 ARBITRAGE

Arbitrage opportunity:
A chance to buy low and sell high.

Arbitrage:
The act of buying low and selling high.

If you can buy candy bars downtown for 50 cents apiece and sell them to your friends at 75 cents, you have an **arbitrage opportunity**—an opportunity to buy low and immediately sell higher. The act of buying low and selling high is called **arbitrage.**

If you boast about that arbitrage opportunity to an economist, his first question will be this: Why doesn't your supplier sell directly to your friends, cutting you out of your share of the profits? There are several possible answers. Maybe it would be expensive for your supplier to deliver to your friends. Maybe the supplier faces tax disincentives that don't apply to you. Maybe selling in your neighborhood requires a license that you have and your supplier doesn't.

Having gotten an answer to the first question, the economist will come right back with a second: Well, then, why doesn't your next-door neighbor compete with you? She could buy the candy bars for 50 cents and resell them for 70 cents, undercutting you and stealing your entire market. Of course, then *you* would undercut her by selling for 65 cents. And then she would undercut you by selling for 60 cents. You could try negotiating with her to end her cutthroat competition, but it wouldn't do much good because another neighbor would stand ready to undercut both of you. Why doesn't the competitive process wash away the arbitrage opportunity?

It should, except for two possible reasons. One is that it really costs you about 25 cents (your apparent "profit") to deliver a candy bar, so your arbitrage opportunity is not as attractive as you made it sound. The other is that although *you* can make a profit delivering candy bars for 75 cents, your neighbor can't, because her delivery costs are higher than yours. Maybe you are in the habit of traveling from downtown to your friends' houses anyway, and it costs you nothing to drag some candy bars along. Your neighbor would have to make a special trip that uses 25 cents' worth of gas per candy bar.

In other words, the reason why a candy bar can sell for 50 cents in one location and 75 cents in another is that trading can be costly. Anything that makes trading costly—such as transportation costs or taxes—is called a **transactions cost.** Economists believe the following:

Transactions cost:
Anything that interferes with buying and selling.

> In the absence of transactions costs, a good must sell for the same price in all locations.

When there are no transactions costs, competition quickly whittles price differentials away. That is, competition results in the disappearance of any arbitrage opportunities. Conversely:

> In the presence of transactions costs, price differentials can exist that are equal in value to the transactions costs.

Arbitrage, Exchange Rates, and International Trade

What is true in the market for candy bars in one country alone is true in the world of international trade. If Famous Amos cookies sell for $4 a tin in the United States, then (unless there are significant transactions costs) they must sell for the equivalent of $4 a tin in England. If those cookies sell for more than $4 a tin in England, entrepreneurs will start buying cookies in the United States and selling them in England, undercutting each other until the price differential disappears. And if Famous Amos cookies sell for less than $4 a tin in England, entrepreneurs will just turn around and ship them from England to the United States until the price differential disappears again.

The process we have just described is, of course, limited by transactions costs. If it costs 10 cents to ship a tin of cookies abroad, then the price of cookies in the United States can remain 10 cents below the price in England. But in many cases transactions costs are small relative to the other magnitudes under consideration. Therefore, in this chapter we will usually assume that there are no transactions costs. Thus, a tin of cookies that sells for $4 in one country must sell for the equivalent of $4 everywhere. We call this requirement the **arbitrage condition** (more specifically, the **goods arbitrage condition**), even though it might make more sense to think of it as a *no*-arbitrage condition.

Arbitrage condition:
The nonexistence of arbitrage opportunities.

Goods arbitrage condition:
The nonexistence of arbitrage opportunities.

Among the "goods" that can be purchased in international markets is the currency of foreign nations. Suppose, for example, that British money, the "pound," sells for a price of $2 per pound. Then, according to the arbitrage condition, a tin of Amos's cookies that sells for $4 in the United States must sell in England for 2 pounds (written

"£2"), which is the British equivalent of $4. If instead pounds sell for $4 per pound, then a tin of cookies must sell for £1, again the British equivalent of $4.

Exchange Rates

Domestic exchange rate:

The price of foreign money in terms of domestic money.

Foreign exchange rate:

The price of domestic money in terms of foreign money.

The price of foreign money in terms of domestic money is called the **domestic exchange rate**, or more simply the *exchange rate*. The domestic exchange rate gives the number of units of domestic currency required to purchase a single unit of foreign currency. The price of domestic money in terms of foreign money is called the **foreign exchange rate**. The foreign exchange rate gives the number of units of foreign currency required to purchase a single unit of domestic currency. There is a domestic (and hence foreign) exchange rate for each pair of countries.

When the domestic exchange rate is e, the foreign exchange rate is $1/e$. For example, if the domestic exchange rate is $e = \$2/£1$, then the foreign exchange rate is $1/e = £0.5/\$1$.

We can express the arbitrage condition in an equation. Let p be the price of any good in the domestic country, expressed in domestic currency. Let p' be the price of that good in a foreign country, expressed in the currency of that country. If e is the domestic exchange rate, then the arbitrage condition requires that

$$p = ep'$$

In the cookie example, p is $4 per tin. If $e = \$2/£1$, then

$$p' = \frac{p}{e} = \frac{\$4/\text{tin}}{\$2/£1} = £2/\text{tin}$$

Exercise 16-1

If coffee costs $5 per pound in the United States and 25 pesos per pound in Mexico, what is the exchange rate (the price of a peso in terms of dollars)? What is the price of a dollar in terms of pesos?

Bond Arbitrage

Just as the prices of goods are brought into alignment by arbitrage, so too are the rates of return on bonds equalized. In the absence of transactions costs, two equivalent bonds (that is, bonds representing identical risks and terms of repayment) must have the same return in all locations. Let's see how this works.

A bond that promises to pay foreign currency in the future in exchange for foreign currency today is said to be *denominated* in foreign currency. We will call a bond denominated in foreign currency a *foreign bond* for short, though in principle the sellers and buyers of such "foreign bonds" could in fact both be domestic citizens who simply choose to write their bond contract in terms of foreign currency.

Thus, a foreign bond for which a buyer pays 1 unit of foreign currency today is a promise to pay $1 + i'$ units of *foreign* currency a year from today, where i' is the *foreign* nominal rate of interest.

By contrast, a bond denominated in domestic currency promises to pay $1 + i$ units of *domestic* currency a year from today in exchange for 1 unit of domestic currency today. We will call such bonds *domestic bonds.*

Suppose you have \$1 to spend on a bond and, prior to making your purchase, want to compare the returns from spending that dollar on a U.S. bond or a foreign bond. Suppose the U.S. bond pays interest at the nominal interest rate of 10 percent. Then if you use your dollar to buy a dollar-denominated bond, you will receive \$1.10 a year from today.

How many dollars would you end up with if you bought the foreign bond instead of the U.S. bond? To answer, we note that the transaction requires three steps. First, you use the dollar to buy foreign exchange. Then, you use the foreign exchange to buy the foreign bond. And finally, a year from today, you use the foreign currency you receive from the bond to buy dollars. If you end up with more dollars from that three-step process of buying the foreign bond, then the foreign bond is a better deal and you should use your \$1 to buy the foreign bond. If you end up with more dollars by buying the domestic (U.S.) bond with your \$1, then you should buy the domestic bond.

Let us work through this three-step process with an example. If the U.S. exchange rate today is e, then you receive $1/e$ units of foreign currency for your dollar in the first step. If $e = \$2/£1$, then you receive £0.5.

Next, using the foreign currency you received in the first step, you buy foreign bonds promising to pay $(1/e) \times (1 + i')$ units of foreign currency a year from today. If the foreign bonds pay a nominal interest rate of $i' = 8$ percent, then you will receive £0.5 × 1.08 = £0.54 a year from today. That completes the second step.

In the last step, we need to determine how many *dollars* that future foreign currency will be worth. If you expect the future exchange rate to be e^*, then you will be able to exchange the foreign currency for $e^* \times [(1/e) \times (1 + i')]$ dollars. For example, if you expect the future exchange rate to be $e^* = \$2.10/£1$, then you will end up with ($\$2.10/£1$) × £0.54, or about \$1.13 a year from today.

Since the foreign bond is a better deal in this example, you would buy the foreign bond.

The trouble is that entrepreneurs all over the world comb the bond markets for arbitrage opportunities of this sort. As a result, bond prices are bid up or down quickly until no such deals are left. If foreign bonds are a better deal, purchasers forgo U.S. bonds and buy foreign bonds. So the sellers of foreign bonds start to ask higher prices (in other words, they offer lower interest rates), and the sellers of U.S. bonds start to accept lower prices (they offer higher interest rates). The interest rates adjust until foreign and domestic bonds offer *the same* returns. Similarly, if U.S. bonds offer the better deal, then their prices are bid up and the prices of foreign bonds are bid down until the returns are the same.

In summary, the return on a domestic bond and the return on a foreign bond have to be equal. We can show this result mathematically by equating the domestic return $1 + i$ and the foreign return $e^* \times [(1/e) \times (1 + i')]$ to get

$$1 + i = e* \times \left[\frac{1}{e}(1 + i') \right]$$

or

$$1 + i = \frac{e*}{e}(1 + i')$$

Interest arbitrage (interest parity, bond arbitrage) condition:

....

The nonexistence of arbitrage opportunities in bond markets.

This equation is called the **interest arbitrage, interest parity,** or **bond arbitrage condition.**

Bond Arbitrage versus Goods Arbitrage

The bond arbitrage condition might look like a new condition, but it is actually just a special case of the goods arbitrage condition, $p = ep'$, where the "goods" are bonds. To show this, let us return to our example and compute the current prices of the domestic and foreign bonds in terms of domestic currency. As before, we use pounds as the foreign currency.

We know from Chapter 3 that the domestic bond, with interest rate i, has a current price p of $1/(1 + i)$ current dollars per future dollar.

You might think that by analogy the current price of the foreign bond is $1/(1 + i')$. But that's not quite right; $1/(1 + i')$ measures the price of the foreign bond in units of current pounds per future *pound*. But we want its price p' in units of current pounds per future *dollar*. To get that price, we must multiply by $1/e*$, because $e*$ is the expected exchange rate at the future date when the bond matures. Thus the correct expression is $p' = 1/[e* \times (1 + i')]$.

Now the arbitrage condition $p = ep'$ becomes

$$\frac{1}{1 + i} = e \times \frac{1}{e*(1 + i')}$$

Inverting both sides of this equation, we see that it is equivalent to the bond arbitrage condition.

The Evidence on Arbitrage

Studies of arbitrage opportunities across national boundaries almost always find that the arbitrage condition holds very closely. Apparent arbitrage opportunities are almost always revealed to be undermined by transactions costs—transportation costs, tariffs, taxes, legal barriers to trade, paperwork costs, or changes in the nature or quality of the goods during the process of transportation.

In the late 1980s, the U.S. news media reported that a Mercedes-Benz automobile could be bought so cheaply in Germany that it was a bargain for U.S. customers even after adding on the cost of shipping it home. Those reports enticed a lot of American Mercedes buyers to fly to Germany. They soon discovered that when they added up *all* their costs—including airfare, currency purchases, shipping, import duties, and the installation of catalytic converters to meet U.S. emissions standards—they weren't saving any money. And in exchange for the enjoyment of visiting Germany to purchase a car, they had to wait several months until the car was actually ready to drive. Some considered this a good deal, and others didn't; but nobody who traveled to Germany paid significantly less for a car.

Purchasing-Power Parity

Tradeable good:

A good that is traded across national boundaries.

Recall that the U.S. price level P is the average of the prices of all goods available in the United States (expressed in dollars per unit of goods). The British price level P' is the average of the prices of all goods available in Great Britain (expressed in pounds per unit of goods).

Let us assume that the same goods are available in both countries and that there are no transactions costs or barriers to trade, so these goods are all **tradeable goods.** If the arbitrage condition holds for each good individually, then the arbitrage condition must also hold for a basket containing all goods in representative quantities. That is, we must have

$$P = eP'$$

where e is once again the exchange rate.

Purchasing-power parity:

The condition that the price of a tradeable good in terms of a given currency should be the same no matter where the good is purchased.

The equation $P = eP'$ is called the **purchasing-power parity** equation. It says that a dollar has exactly the same purchasing power in Great Britain as it has in the United States. This follows from our assumption that all goods are tradeable and our assumption that the arbitrage condition holds (there are no transactions costs), guaranteeing that each individual good sells for the same price everywhere.

The Real Exchange Rate

Real exchange rate:

The quantity of domestic goods necessary to buy one foreign good. If all goods are tradeable and purchasing-power parity holds, then the real exchange rate must be 1.

A country's **real exchange rate** is the quantity of domestic goods required to buy 1 unit of the same foreign good. We can express the real exchange rate in terms of the price levels as

$$\text{Real exchange rate} = \frac{eP'}{P}$$

If the real exchange rate is greater than 1, then more than one unit of a domestic good is required to buy 1 unit of that foreign good. If the real exchange rate is less than 1, then more than 1 unit of a foreign good is required to buy 1 unit of that domestic good.

The higher the real exchange rate, the more expensive are foreign goods in terms of domestic goods.

If all goods are tradeable in both countries and there are no transactions costs, as we are assuming, the real exchange rate is always equal to 1.

➠ *Exercise 16-2*
If $P/P' > e$, is the real exchange rate greater than or less than 1?

 We defined the domestic country's real exchange rate above. The foreign country's real exchange rate is the quantity of foreign goods required to buy 1 unit of the same domestic good. That is, the foreign country's real exchange rate is P/eP'.

Nontraded Goods

We made two assumptions to arrive at the purchasing-power parity equation: that all goods are tradeable and that there are no transactions costs. We've already noted that our assumption about transactions costs is an approximation of the truth—but a reasonable one; now let's discuss the assumption that the same goods are available everywhere. To a large extent this is true; you can buy Coca-Cola anywhere in the world. But there are also important exceptions. Real estate on the Thames River is available in England and in no other country. A fresh, tree-ripened exotic fruit might be available only in the specific regions where it is grown because it might not retain its flavor well enough to be transported. When such *nontraded goods* play an important role, the purchasing-power parity equation may not be entirely meaningful.

Nontraded good:
A good that is not traded across national boundaries.

A **nontraded good** is a good for which transactions costs are essentially insurmountable, to the point that the good is not traded internationally. There is no acceptable cost at which a pizza can be made to survive an ocean voyage; that is why there is no intercontinental trade in pizzas. Most services are prohibitively expensive to export and hence are nontraded goods. The quality of service that is routine in a fine British clothing store might have no counterpart in the United States. The college education you are currently receiving is usually available only to those who can physically travel to the college where it is offered.

➠ *Exercise 16-3*
Explain why the instinct of American teenagers to smile when waiting on a customer and the instinct of Russian teenagers not to do so might have made dinner at McDonald's a nontradeable good even after the McDonald's Corporation opened its first restaurant in Russia.

But many goods *are* traded, and in discussing broad macroeconomic issues, we can usually get away with approximations of the truth. Hence it seems reasonable to assume that all goods are available in all nations, and we shall do so in this chapter.

The Evidence on Purchasing-Power Parity

The two conditions for purchasing-power parity *seem* to be reasonable. But what does real-world evidence tell us?

Figure 16-1 depicts the U.S. exchange rate and the ratio of price levels between the United States and an average of its 10 major trading partners since the mid-1970s. In terms of our notation, the exchange rate is e and the ratio of price levels is P/P'.

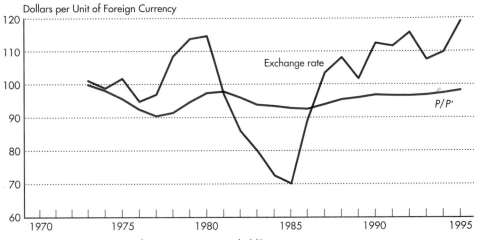

FIGURE 16-1 Does purchasing-power parity hold?
The U.S. exchange rate *e* and the ratio of price levels *P/P'*. Both are trade-weighted averages for the United States versus 10 major trading partners. There are wide deviations from purchasing-power parity that last for extended periods.

According to the purchasing-power parity equation, the two curves should be identical.

They aren't. The exchange rate *e* is more volatile than the price-level ratio *P/P'*. Though it looks like the exchange rate is perhaps on average equal to the price ratio, the value of *e* seems to keep aiming for *P/P'*, overshooting its "target," and then gradually returning to it only to overshoot in the opposite direction. Given that our equation tells us that the two curves should lie *exactly* on top of each other, the fact that they deviate from each other for extended periods is disturbing.

 Notice that the word "overshooting" is used differently in this chapter than it was in Chapter 10, where we spoke of the relationship between the price level and the growth rate of the money supply. In this chapter, "overshooting" is used in a different sense: the sense that a variable (here, the exchange rate) crosses through the level we expect it to attain, remains above or below that level for a while, and then crosses back in the other direction.

The fact that *e* and *P/P'* behave this differently suggests that there must be a lot of nontraded goods and/or high transactions costs undermining purchasing-power parity.

On the other hand, while the evidence shows large short-run differences between *e* and *P/P'*, it does indicate that over longer periods of time *e* tends to fluctuate around *P/P'*. That is, the exchange rate does not wander very far away from *P/P'* for long periods of time. Eventually it heads back toward the ratio of the price levels. This behavior suggests that many goods which are nontradeable in the short run become tradeable in the long run.

One way to make nontraded goods tradeable is to allow people to travel to them. It may be true, as we noted, that the service at a fine London tailor shop cannot be transported to the United States. But in the long run many U.S. customers can still purchase that service by shopping for clothes when they happen to be in London. And if, for example, hotel rooms and restaurant meals are unusually inexpensive in France this year and thus many people desire them, then we can expect to see more tourists traveling to France and bidding up the prices of those goods. This will help to restore purchasing-power parity, and until purchasing-power parity is restored, it is a substitute for the goods' being traded directly. Instead of the goods traveling across the borders to the people, the people travel across the borders to the goods.

Even when the goods can't travel to the customer and the customer can't travel to the goods, ingenious producers are always on the lookout for a way to bring them together. Suppose that an American pharmaceutical company invents a new drug that is too delicate to be shipped abroad. The company might still take advantage of foreign markets by opening manufacturing plants in other countries. Alternatively, a foreign firm observing the success of the drug in the U.S. market might decide to produce a similar product in its own country.

Barriers to trade do remain. International patent and licensing laws may prohibit the foreign drug producer from mimicking U.S. methods too closely. Nevertheless, in the long run we can expect that many nontraded goods will become tradeable and many transactions costs will be overcome and hence that purchasing-power parity will become a good approximation of the truth.

➡ *Exercise 16-4*
Based on Figure 16-1, during which periods was the U.S. real exchange rate greater than 1 and during which periods was it less than 1?

Real Exchange Rates and the Trade Balance

In the short run, real exchange rates do vary. At times when foreign goods are expensive in terms of U.S. goods, U.S. citizens import fewer foreign goods and curtail their foreign travel. Simultaneously, foreigners import more U.S. goods and are more likely to travel to the United States. Thus in the short run a rise in the real exchange rate should correspond to an increase in the trade balance: exports rise and imports fall when the relative price of foreign goods rises.

Figure 16-2 shows the real exchange rate and the trade balance since the early 1970s. As we expect, increases in the real exchange rate tend to be accompanied by increases in the trade balance. Similarly, decreases in the real exchange rate tend to be accompanied by decreases in the trade balance.

16-2   AN OVERVIEW OF EXCHANGE-RATE REGIMES

Foreign currency can be used to purchase foreign goods or foreign financial assets like stocks or bonds. If you want to travel from the United States to England on vaca-

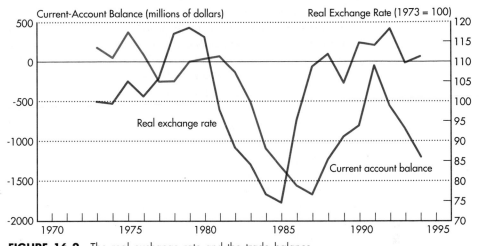

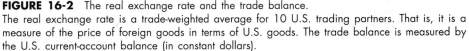

FIGURE 16-2 The real exchange rate and the trade balance.
The real exchange rate is a trade-weighted average for 10 U.S. trading partners. That is, it is a measure of the price of foreign goods in terms of U.S. goods. The trade balance is measured by the U.S. current-account balance (in constant dollars).

tion, you will probably want to purchase foreign currency—British pounds—with your domestic currency, U.S. dollars, at the going exchange rate.

If each pound costs $2, the U.S. exchange rate, e, is $2/£1. We can express the same thing by saying that the price of dollars in terms of pounds is £0.5/$1. The higher the price of the pound (in terms of dollars), the lower the price of the dollar (in terms of pounds).

In Chapter 15 we discussed the creation of currency and money by the monetary authority, focusing in depth on the U.S. central bank, the Federal Reserve. Each country's monetary authority or central bank creates reserves and prints money that is legal tender in that country. Examples include the Bank of Japan, which supplies Japanese yen; the Bank of England, which supplies British pounds; and the Bundesbank, which supplies German deutschemarks.

The one thing that you must know about central banks is this:

The only institution that can legally change the supply of a country's currency is that country's central bank.

In this chapter we often assume that there is only one foreign country and hence only one foreign currency. All our conclusions are still valid in a world of many countries.

Central banks often purchase foreign exchange. Each central bank chooses between two different policies for purchasing foreign exchange. One system is called a **fixed-exchange-rate regime;** under this policy, the central bank announces a price at which it is willing to buy and sell each foreign currency in any quantity. For example, prior to 1972, the U.S. Federal Reserve was willing to buy and sell any number of Swiss francs at a price of $0.83 per Swiss franc.

Fixed-exchange-rate regime:

A system under which central banks commit themselves to buy and sell foreign exchange at preannounced prices.

Under a fixed-exchange-rate regime, the central bank is often forced to print more of its own currency than it really wants to. Suppose that in 1970 a Swiss citizen arrived at a Federal Reserve Bank with 1 billion Swiss francs, demanding to buy dollars. The Fed's policy would have required that the Federal Reserve print $0.83 billion and make the trade. (Then the Federal Reserve would have had to figure out what to do with all those Swiss francs. Storing them in a vault is not an attractive option, because currency sitting in a vault does not earn interest.) We will discuss this and other consequences of fixed-exchange regimes in Section 16-5.

Sometimes a central bank changes from one fixed exchange rate to another. Suppose that at the beginning of the year the Canadian central bank was exchanging U.S. dollars for Canadian dollars (CD) at the Canadian exchange rate of CD1/$1; at the end of the year, however, it changed the rate to CD1.11/$1. We call such a change a **revaluation** of the U.S. dollar (because the relative price of U.S. dollars went up) and a **devaluation** of the Canadian dollar (because the relative price of Canadian dollars went down).

The alternative to a fixed-exchange-rate regime is a **flexible-exchange-rate regime** (also called a *floating-exchange-rate regime*), which is what the United States and its largest trading partners have been using since 1972. Under this regime, citizens freely buy and sell foreign exchange in private markets at whatever price they can negotiate. When the Federal Reserve wants to buy or sell foreign currencies, it does so at the going market price. Similarly, any foreign citizen or foreign central bank wishing to buy or sell U.S. dollars does so at the going market rate.

Under flexible exchange rates the relative prices of domestic and foreign currencies fluctuate constantly. A rise in the value of a currency is called an **appreciation,** and a drop in the value of a currency is called a **depreciation.** (The words "appreciation" and "depreciation" are comparable to "revaluation" and "devaluation," respectively, but the former two are used under flexible-exchange-rate systems and the latter two under fixed-exchange-rate systems.) Notice that if the dollar appreciates (say, from 100 yen per dollar to 200 yen per dollar), then the yen must depreciate (in this case, from 1 cent per yen to .5 cents per yen), and vice versa.

If we think of the United States as the domestic country, then when the U.S. exchange rate e falls, the U.S. dollar appreciates in value. And when e rises, the dollar depreciates.

To avoid confusion, remember that e is the dollar price of a unit of *foreign* currency. When the price e falls, the value of *foreign* currency falls, or depreciates. The *dollar's* price is the inverse of e; thus when e falls, the value of the *dollar* appreciates. The value of the dollar always moves in the opposite direction of e.

Many variations of the pure fixed- and flexible-exchange-rate regimes have been tried in the past, and several variations are in effect in different countries today. But all incorporate, to varying degrees, these two basic regimes, which we discuss below in some detail, starting with flexible-exchange-rate regimes.

Revaluation:
Under a fixed-exchange-rate regime, a rise in the price of domestic currency relative to foreign currency.

Devaluation:
Under a fixed-exchange-rate regime, a fall in the price of domestic currency relative to foreign currency.

Flexible-exchange-rate regime:
A system under which exchange rates can adjust freely to market conditions.

Appreciation:
Under a flexible-exchange-rate regime, a rise in the price of domestic currency relative to foreign currency.

Depreciation:
Under a flexible-exchange-rate regime, a fall in the price of domestic currency relative to foreign currency.

Nowadays most countries use flexible-exchange-rate regimes in their foreign exchange dealings. In this section we add a foreign currency to our economic models, assuming a flexible-exchange-rate regime.

The Supply of Foreign Money

When the Federal Reserve wants to increase the supply of dollars, it prints them and purchases something (usually a government bond) with them. When it wants to decrease the supply of dollars, it sells something (again, usually a government bond) and destroys the dollars it collects.

Foreign central banks control the supplies of their own national currencies in essentially the same way. When a central bank buys or sells its own national currency, it affects the *supply* of that currency. The country's money supply increases or decreases accordingly. A central bank can also buy and sell another country's currency. When a central bank buys or sells foreign currency, it affects the *demand* for that currency.

When the Bank of Japan buys U.S. dollars, it does *not* affect the *supply* of dollars; the dollars that it purchases continue to exist. Hence, a foreign central bank can affect the *demand* for dollars but not the supply. However, when the U.S. Federal Reserve buys U.S. dollars, it *does* affect the supply of dollars, because it effectively destroys the dollars that it collects.

The Determination of Price Levels and Exchange Rates in a Two-Nation Economy

In Chapter 10, we saw that the U.S. price level P is determined by the supply of and demand for U.S. dollars. [In Chapter 10 we called this the supply of and demand for *money;* here we are calling it the supply of and demand for *dollars* so as not to confuse it with the (separate) supply of and demand for foreign currency.] Further, the supply of dollars is set by the U.S. Federal Reserve, and the demand for dollars depends on, among other things, the income of U.S. citizens. People with higher incomes demand more money.

The foreign price level P' is determined analogously. The foreign monetary authority sets the supply of the foreign currency, and the demand for that currency depends on, among other things, the income of foreign citizens.

Determining the Exchange Rate

Once P is determined by supply and demand conditions in the United States and P' is determined by supply and demand conditions in the foreign country, the domestic exchange rate e between their two currencies is determined by the purchasing-power parity equation $P = eP'$. If the U.S. price level is $P = \$6$ per apple and the foreign price level is $P' = £3$ per apple, then the exchange rate must be

$$e = \frac{P}{P'} = \frac{\$6/\text{apple}}{£3/\text{apple}} = \$2/£1$$

That much is forced by the mathematics. Our goal now is to understand the market forces that bring the exchange rate to its "correct" level of $2 per pound.

Suppose the U.S. exchange rate starts out (incorrectly) at $1 per pound instead of $2. Then Americans quickly realize that they can trade a dollar for a pound, use that pound to buy one-third of an apple, and then resell that third of an apple in the United States for $2. Each time they do this, they earn a clear profit of $1.

People rushing to take advantage of this arbitrage opportunity all attempt to trade dollars for pounds at the same time. In doing so, they bid up the price of pounds in terms of dollars; that is, they bid up the U.S. exchange rate. And that exchange rate must continue to rise until the arbitrage opportunity vanishes completely, which is to say until $e = \$2$ per pound.

Suppose, on the other hand, that the U.S. exchange rate starts out at $4 per pound. Then citizens of the foreign country can trade a pound for $4, use those dollars to buy two-thirds of an apple (at the going price of $6 per apple), and then sell that two-thirds of an apple for £2 (at the going price of £3 per apple). They earn £1 each time they do so. However, that arbitrage opportunity leads to a great demand for exchanging pounds for dollars, which bids down the price of pounds in terms of dollars (that is, bids down the U.S. exchange rate) until the arbitrage opportunity vanishes with the exchange rate equal to $2 per pound.

The price levels P and P' are determined via the supply of and demand for money, each in its own country. Then the bidding away of arbitrage opportunities forces the exchange rate e to the level that makes the purchasing-power parity equation $P = eP'$ hold true.

Futures contract:

An agreement to deliver something (such as a foreign currency) at a specified future date at a price agreed upon today.

Spot price:

The current price of a good or a currency to be delivered today.

Futures price:

The current price of a good or a currency to be delivered in the future.

Expected Future Currency Prices

In the foreign exchange market, you can trade (for example) U.S. dollars for Japanese yen. You receive your yen just as soon as you deliver your dollars.

There is another market, called the *futures market* for foreign exchange, that also allows you to exchange U.S. dollars for Japanese yen. But in this market, you deliver your dollars today and receive your yen at some time in the future, say, 3 months from today. In that case, we say that you have purchased a **futures contract** for yen.

The current-dollar price of yen to be delivered immediately is what we have called the exchange rate for Japanese yen. Sometimes that exchange rate is called a **spot price,** to distinguish it from the **futures price** that you would pay for yen to be delivered in the future.

Market forces cause the futures price of the foreign exchange to be the best possible estimate of the future spot price—that is, the futures price is based on what the market *expects* the future exchange rate to be. Let us see how these market forces work.

Suppose that on January 1, the futures price for German deutschemarks to be delivered on April 1 is $0.70 per deutschemark. (That is, you pay $0.70 today to receive 1 deutschemark in 3 months.) Suppose you pay that $0.70. Suppose also that when April 1 arrives, you read in the newspaper that the spot price for deutschemarks is $0.50. Then you will regret your purchase: Instead of paying $0.70 for your futures contract, you could have waited 3 months and bought your deutschemark for $0.50. If you had correctly *expected* that spot price, you would never have bought the futures contract in the first place.

Thus, to attract buyers, a futures contract must be priced no higher than the expected future spot price. Similarly, to attract sellers, the futures contract must be priced no *lower* than the expected future spot price. For contracts to be traded at all, they must sell for exactly the market's best expectation of the future spot price.

[More precisely, the futures contract must sell for the *present value* of the expected future spot price. But for a short-term (for example, 3-month) contract, there is very little difference between the expected future spot price and its present value.]

Figure 16-3 shows the futures prices for several currencies on October 24, 1995, expressed as percentages of their spot prices on that date. Note that the futures price of yen increases slightly as a function of the delivery date. That is, market participants expected the yen to appreciate slowly relative to the U.S. dollar. On the other hand, the Canadian dollar was expected to depreciate slowly relative to the U.S. dollar, and the Mexican peso was expected to depreciate rapidly. In fact, the Mexican

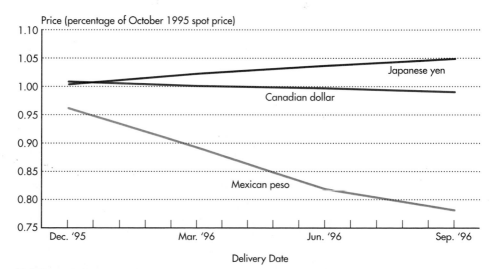

FIGURE 16-3

Futures prices on October 24, 1995, for the Japanese yen, Canadian dollar, and Mexican peso, expressed as percentages of their October 1995 spot prices. (*Source: Wall Street Journal*, Oct. 25, 1995.)

peso was expected to lose almost 20 percent of its value over the 9-month period between December 1995 and September 1996.

Using the models of the preceding chapters, we now are in a position to see how various changes in economic conditions affect the exchange rate under a flexible-exchange-rate regime.

Since the exchange rate is the ratio of the domestic and foreign price levels, in each model what happens to the exchange rate is determined by what happens to the price levels. For example, in the case of the sticky price model, the exchange rate is also sticky. A change in a country's money supply can have no effect on the exchange rate in the sticky price model, even though the exchange rate is not fixed by the government as it would be in a fixed-exchange-rate regime. (Exchange rates could change if there are nontradeable goods; in which direction they change depends on the direction in which people wish to travel across national borders, as discussed in the preceding section.) To better understand the factors influencing the exchange rate in our other models, we start by discussing the neoclassical model.

Exchange Rates and the Neoclassical Model

In the neoclassical model, a country's price level can change because of changes in a country's money supply or because of any factors leading to a change in a country's output, such as a change in fiscal policy, technology, war, weather, and so on. We consider these effects in turn.

An Increase in the Domestic Money Supply

Suppose that the U.S. money supply is increased. Then, as we saw in Chapter 10, the U.S. price level P rises. According to the purchasing-power parity equation $P = eP'$, the exchange rate e must rise also. (We assume here that the foreign price level P' remains constant.) The exchange rate *can* rise because it is a flexible, or floating, rate that is set by transactions taking place in the foreign exchange market. The exchange rate is free to move in response to market forces.

Consider the process that causes e to rise. Initially, a dollar and a dollar's worth of foreign currency, say, pounds, both buy the same number of apples. But when the U.S. price level rises, a dollar buys fewer apples than it did before. For anybody who wants to buy apples, this makes a dollar less attractive than a dollar's worth of pounds. Everyone rushes to trade dollars for pounds (that is, to buy pounds), and the price of pounds in terms of dollars—the U.S. exchange rate e—is bid up.

Equivalently, we say that the price of dollars in terms of pounds ($1/e$) goes down. That is:

An increase in the U.S. money supply causes the dollar to depreciate.

We can say a bit more about e. We know that, say, a 1 percent increase in the supply of dollars causes the U.S. price level to increase by exactly 1 percent. The purchasing-power parity equation tells us that the exchange rate e must rise by 1 percent as well. Thus, an increase in the U.S. money supply causes the dollar to depreciate *proportionately.*

An Increase in the Foreign Money Supply

An increase in the foreign money supply causes the foreign price level P^* to rise. To satisfy the equation $P = eP'$, the U.S. exchange rate e must fall. Here's why: When P' rises, each unit of foreign currency buys less. So what was a dollar's worth of foreign currency is now worth less than a dollar. People try to trade foreign currency for dollars, bidding up the price of dollars in terms of the foreign currency ($1/e$). That is:

An increase in the foreign money supply causes the dollar to appreciate.

Equivalently, we can say that the increase in the foreign money supply bids down the U.S. exchange rate e and causes the foreign currency to depreciate. Moreover, according to the parity equation $P = eP'$, a 1 percent increase in the foreign price level P' requires a 1 percent decrease in e (assuming P remains constant), and thus a 1 percent increase in the value of the dollar.

Changes in the Rate of Growth of the Money Supply: Overshooting

Exchange-rate overshooting:

The response of an exchange rate to a change in a country's inflation rate; the country's price level overshoots and hence so does the exchange rate.

Now let us shift gears from a one-time increase in the money supply to a change in the rate of growth of the money supply. Recall from Chapter 10 that if the growth rate of the money supply increases, so does the growth rate of the price level (that is, the inflation rate). Recall also that at the onset of the new growth rate, the price level jumps upward because of a drop in the *demand* for money. In Chapter 10, we called this upward jump *overshooting.*

The purchasing-power parity equation requires that changes in the price level cause changes in the exchange rate. Thus, when the U.S. money supply growth rate increases and the price level jumps upward, the exchange rate also jumps upward, just before it begins to grow at a rate proportional to the money supply. This effect is called **exchange-rate overshooting.**

We have used the word "overshooting" in two very different ways in this chapter. In the discussion of Figure 16-1, we noted that the exchange rate e sometimes "overshoots" the expected value P'/P. In other words, the data do not exactly match the predictions of our model. By contrast, when we talk about "overshooting" due to a change in the money supply growth rate, we are talking about an effect which *is* predicted by the model.

➡ *Exercise 16-5*
What is the effect on the exchange rate if the foreign country increases the growth rate of its money supply?

An Increase in Domestic Output

Suppose that U.S. output (and hence U.S. income) rises. U.S. citizens demand more dollars to carry in their wallets, and the U.S. price level P falls. According to the purchasing-power parity equation, the domestic exchange rate e must decrease as well, so the dollar appreciates.

An increase in U.S. output causes the dollar to appreciate.

➡ *Exercise 16-6*
When the U.S. price level P falls, does a dollar become more or less valuable than a dollar's worth of foreign currency? Do people try to trade dollars for foreign exchange, or vice versa?

An Increase in Foreign Output

Suppose that foreign output rises. Foreigners demand more of their own currency and bid the foreign price level P' down. The purchasing-power parity equation tells us that the U.S. exchange rate e must rise, and so the dollar depreciates.

An increase in foreign output causes the dollar to depreciate.

➡ *Exercise 16-7*
When P' falls, do people want to trade dollars for foreign exchange, or vice versa? What effect does this have on the relative price of foreign exchange and of dollars?

Exchange Rates and Other Models

The logic of the preceding discussion works for other models, such as the sticky wage model. If a change in economic conditions or government policy gives rise to an increase in a country's real income, the country's currency appreciates in value. If a change in economic conditions or government policy gives rise to a decrease in a country's real income, or to an increase in the *foreign* country's income, the country's currency depreciates in value. No matter what model is in effect, changes to the exchange rate are determined by the changes to the price levels.

Advice to Tourists

Suppose you are planning a trip to France and you hear on a news program that there's been a change in the U.S. exchange rate, from 25 cents per franc to 20 cents per franc. "Great!" you think. "Now I'll be able to buy a lot more in France with my dollars!"

Not so fast! If purchasing-power parity holds, there are only two things that could have caused the exchange rate to fall. Either the U.S. price level fell, or the French price level rose.

If the U.S. price level fell, then you don't have to go to France to reap the benefits. Your dollars will go further even if you stay at home. The economic news is good all right, but it's no better for you than it is for your neighbor who never travels.

If the French price level rose, then your dollars are not going to go any further than they did before. You'll get more francs for your dollar, but you'll pay more francs for goods in France. In this case, the economic news has no real effect on you.

Either way, the change in the exchange rate does you no good. In the first case, the drop in the price level is of benefit to you, but the new exchange rate is of no *additional* benefit. In the second case, all the advantages of the new exchange rate are undone by the disadvantages of the new French price level.

On the other hand, you may benefit if you are planning to buy a lot of nontraded goods like meals and hotel rooms while you are in France, because purchasing-power parity may not apply to such goods in the short run. But, as we saw, international trade will tend to eliminate that benefit over time.

Can a Currency Be Overvalued or Undervalued?

Occasionally someone (usually not an economist) will describe the dollar as being either *undervalued* or *overvalued*. Whoever claims that the dollar is overvalued must think that it "ought" to be worth less or, in other words, that foreign currency "ought" to be worth more. Anyone making such a claim needs to tell us what the dollar ought to be worth.

According to the reasoning behind the parity equation, the exchange rate adjusts until the value of the dollar in terms of domestic goods is identical to the value of the dollar in terms of foreign goods. Further, the dollar cannot be overvalued or undervalued unless somebody has an arbitrage opportunity. But evidence suggests that arbitrage opportunities do not exist, so the dollar is never overvalued or undervalued.

Overshooting and the Value of the Currency

One reason why people sometimes think that currencies are overvalued is that they do not understand overshooting.

If the United States increases the money supply growth rate, the U.S. price level P takes an initial jump upward before it begins to grow at the new inflation rate. This causes the exchange rate e to take an initial jump upward.

People see a gradual increase in the money supply accompanied by a sudden change in the exchange rate, and they think that the exchange rate has grown "out of proportion" to what seems reasonable. But the truth is that the exchange rate keeps pace not with the money supply but with the price level. When the price level jumps, it is quite reasonable for the exchange rate to jump with it.

The Trade Balance and Exchange Rates

Some people think currencies are incorrectly valued when a country imports more than it exports, or vice versa. Such people argue, for example, that if the United States imports more than it exports, then the dollar should depreciate, and if it fails to depreciate, then it must be overvalued. Their argument is that an excess of imports over exports suggests that traders see arbitrage opportunities in buying foreign goods and shipping them to the United States. These opportunities should cause an increase in the demand for foreign currency (with which to buy the foreign goods), a corresponding drop in the demand for dollars, and therefore a drop in the value of the dollar. If the dollar fails to lose enough value to eliminate the trade deficit, say these people, then something is wrong.

But that argument is incorrect. We saw in Chapter 5 that a trade deficit arises whenever a country's citizens want to borrow from abroad—either to increase their current consumption or to increase their current investment. Thus a trade deficit (or, similarly, a trade surplus) need not imply that there are arbitrage opportunities available.

A second flaw in the argument is that it usually relies on the official *measures* of imports and exports, which frequently fail to reflect economic reality. The most commonly cited measure, the merchandise trade balance (discussed in Chapter 2), includes many manufactured goods but ignores trade in services (such as education and banking). The merchandise trade balance can report that imports exceed exports even when broader measures like the current account (which includes services) show exactly the opposite. *Both* measures omit trade in stocks and bonds. And all these measures of international trade omit some very large sources of trade that involve travel and temporary relocation, such as education received by citizens of one country at the schools of another. The moral here is that any argument that begins by taking one of these trade measures too seriously can be very misleading.

On the other hand, our theory *does* predict a relationship between the exchange rate and the trade balance. To see this, imagine a temporary drop in the domestic country's income. We know from Chapter 5 that domestic citizens will borrow to smooth consumption and this leads to an increase in the trade deficit. At the same time, we know from Chapter 10 that a fall in income leads to a fall in the demand for money and hence a rise in the domestic price level; combining this with the comparative-statics analysis of the preceding section, we see that the exchange rate rises. Thus decreases in the trade balance tend to accompany increases in the nominal exchange rate, and vice versa. But neither causes the other; both are caused simultaneously by the underlying decline in the country's income.

Application: A Newspaper Analysis of Exchange Rates

As of October 24, 1995, the day for which Figure 16-3 depicts future exchange rates, the dollar had in fact been depreciating against several major currencies (including the yen and the German mark) for the preceding few months. One *Wall Street Journal* staff reporter wrote: "The dollar, caught in a European currency crossfire and undermined by the huge U.S. budget deficit, tumbled to an almost three-month low against the mark. And traders are betting it has further to fall."

The prediction that the dollar has further to fall is equivalent to a claim that it is overvalued. On what basis does the article claim that the dollar is overvalued? Let us first examine some of the reporter's terms. The article explains the European currency "crossfire" as follows:

> *During the past few days, the dollar has suffered at the hands of speculators and investors who have been dumping [selling] Europe's so-called peripheral currencies—specifically the Italian lira and pound—as well as the French franc, in order to seek safety in the German mark.*

An economist examining this remark would quickly point out that the explanation does not address any market forces that would tend to lower the value of the U.S. dollar. The "dumping" as described would tend to cause the lira, pound, and French franc to depreciate relative to the German mark, but the article says nothing at all about the dollar. If anything, a decline in the relative demand for those other currencies would increase the value of the dollar.

Let us turn to the next proposed explanation, the U.S. government budget deficit. While it is true that the United States had a large budget deficit at the time of the article, it is also true that the United States has had a large budget deficit every year since the late 1970s. Data from many years and many countries show little relationship between government budget deficits and exchange-rate movements.

An analyst from Citibank tried another explanation: "The dollar still suffers from its same old problem: a big trade deficit." But like the government budget deficit, the U.S. trade deficit has persisted since the late 1970s, and the dollar has had periods of both appreciation and depreciation during this time.

In summary, the article provides no grounds for believing that the dollar is overvalued or destined to fall further. The arguments in the article do not refer to predictions about changes in the exchange rate based on changes in underlying economic variables such as the money supply or real income but refer instead to less reliable predictors of exchange rates.

Central Bank Intervention

When a central bank (such as the U.S. Federal Reserve) buys or sells foreign currency, we say that it *intervenes* in the currency market.

Intervention (in currency markets): The purchase or sale of foreign currency by a central bank.

Through such **intervention,** the central bank changes the demand for foreign currency. For example, if the Fed decides to purchase Japanese yen, it adds to the demand for Japanese yen. If the intervention is large enough, it can cause a measurable drop in the Japanese price level and hence a rise in the exchange rate at which yen trade for dollars (the dollar price of yen). In practice, only the central bank of a very large country (such as the United States) can affect the demand for foreign currency by enough to have a noticeable effect on the exchange rate.

Sterilized and Unsterilized Interventions

If the Federal Reserve decides to purchase yen with dollars, it has two choices regarding where to get those dollars. It can print them, or it can acquire them by selling some other asset, such as Treasury bills.

If the Federal Reserve gets the dollars by printing them, we call the intervention *unsterilized;* if it gets the dollars by selling other assets, we call the intervention *sterilized.* Conversely, if the Federal Reserve decides to sell yen for dollars, it has two choices regarding what to do with the dollars it collects. It can either destroy them or use them to buy some other asset—again, Treasury bills are the most likely candidate. If it destroys the dollars, we call the intervention *unsterilized;* if it buys other assets, we call the intervention *sterilized.*

Sterilizing a foreign exchange transaction neutralizes the effect of the transaction on the domestic money supply. In general, an **unsterilized intervention** is one that affects the domestic money supply, and a **sterilized intervention** is one that does not affect the domestic money supply.

Unsterilized interventions affect the exchange rate in two ways. First, they change the *demand* for *foreign* currency, thereby changing the foreign price level P'. Second, they change the *supply* of *domestic* currency, thereby changing the domestic price level P in the opposite direction. Because P and P' change in opposite directions, the parity equation $P = eP'$ requires that the exchange rate e change.

Suppose, for example, that the Federal Reserve purchases Japanese yen with newly printed U.S. dollars (an unsterilized intervention). This increases the demand for yen (causing the Japanese price level P' to fall) and increases the supply of dollars (causing the U.S. price level P to rise). On both accounts, the U.S. exchange rate e must rise, and so the dollar depreciates.

Sterilized interventions affect the exchange rate in only one way. They change the demand for foreign currency, thereby changing the foreign price level P'. But they have no effect on the supply of domestic currency, so they do not affect the domestic price level P. However, because P' changes, the equation $P = eP'$ requires that the exchange rate e change.

As an example, a sterilized Federal Reserve purchase of Japanese yen increases the demand for yen and thus causes the Japanese price level P' to fall. This in turn causes e to rise, so the dollar depreciates.

Unsterilized intervention:

An intervention that is not accompanied by offsetting actions designed to prevent an overall change in the domestic money supply.

Sterilized intervention:

An intervention that is accompanied by offsetting actions designed to prevent an overall change in the domestic money supply.

⟹ *Exercise 16-8*

Describe the effects on the Japanese price level and on the exchange rate e of a sterilized Federal Reserve sale of Japanese yen. Why does the sterilized sale of yen have no effect on the supply of dollars?

Why Intervene?

When the dollar depreciates unexpectedly, the Federal Reserve is frequently urged to "shore it up" by selling foreign currencies in either sterilized or unsterilized interventions. Such urging comes from a number of sources. People who plan to purchase nontraded goods while traveling abroad do not like to see the dollar suddenly weaken.

Neither do people who have already contracted to pay debts in foreign currencies, which they must purchase with dollars.

People who are in debt to foreigners are *not* hurt by *expected* decreases in the value of the dollar, because the effects of these decreases are accounted for when the size of the debt is initially negotiated. But an *unexpected* drop in the dollar's value is bad for Americans who are in debt to foreigners.

In 1994, the value of the dollar fell dramatically. The Federal Reserve felt political pressure to intervene (by selling foreign currencies) but declined, arguing that it wanted to concentrate on its primary task of controlling the growth rate of the U.S. money supply.

By choosing not to intervene, the Federal Reserve also managed to steer clear of a secondary argument about whether the intervention should be sterilized or unsterilized. Large debtors would have been rather displeased by a large unsterilized intervention, because it would have lowered the U.S. price level and raised the real value of their debts. Not surprisingly, the U.S. Treasury Department, a notoriously large debtor, usually raises its voice in favor of sterilizing any sale of foreign currency.

Sometimes the pressure to intervene comes not from the citizens of the home country but from abroad. Governments occasionally encourage other governments to take action, particularly during times of rapid appreciations and depreciations. Of course, they do this because they feel pressure from some of their *own* citizens.

Imagine, for example, that there has recently been a substantial appreciation in the value of the French franc relative to the dollar. This discourages Americans from vacationing in France. If the French tourist industry is politically powerful, it may be able to convince the French government to ask the U.S. government to intervene and restore the original value of the franc by purchasing francs.

16-5   FIXED-EXCHANGE-RATE REGIMES

In this section we discuss fixed-exchange-rate regimes in general, as well as specific types, including the gold standard. Because fixed exchange rates were the norm from the beginnings of international trade, our discussion includes quite a bit of history.

One goal of studying history is to better understand the choices we face in the present. Which system is better—a fixed-exchange-rate regime or a flexible one? You will see that each has its advantages and disadvantages. Flexible exchange rates often change rapidly, making it hard for governments and businesses to make long-term plans. A business that depends on foreign customers can find its fortunes buffeted by exchange-rate fluctuations that are entirely beyond its control. Citizens who buy and sell foreign stocks and bonds face the same risk and uncertainty. On the other hand, fixed exchange rates also entail a loss of control—irresponsible monetary policy in one country can have undesirable repercussions all over the world.

Early Trading: A Brief History

Before the advent of modern banking, international traders usually had to pay in coin. If you lived in a country that issued 1-ounce gold coins called crowns and you wanted to purchase wheat from a country that issued 2-ounce gold coins called reales, you had to exchange 2 crowns for each reale and then use the reales to buy your wheat.

Institutions called *exchange authorities* (the precursors of modern central banks) were set up to make these exchanges. The exchange rates were based exclusively on weight. A 2-ounce gold coin, regardless of which country had issued it, was worth exactly two 1-ounce gold coins, regardless of which country had issued them. Because the exchange rate between any two currencies was fixed by their weights, market conditions (supply and demand) could not change that rate.

This exchange-rate system is an example of the gold standard, and it was the basis for the modern-day gold standard described briefly in Chapter 15. (If the coins were made of silver, the system was called a silver standard.) A gold standard is an example of a fixed-exchange-rate regime because the exchange rate between the two currencies is determined by the weights of the coins.

Bullion:
Gold bars.

In the early days of the gold standard, gold of monetary quality was frequently shipped as **bullion,** or gold bars. You could go to your country's exchange authority with, say, crowns, purchase an equivalent quantity of bullion, and carry that bullion with you to the foreign country. Once you arrived, you arranged to have your bullion melted down and minted into reales (or whatever the local currency happened to be) by the local exchange authority.

Gold Certificates

During the 1800s, integrated international banking and paper currency led to various changes in the gold and silver standards. Rather than paying for its purchases with actual gold, a country could store gold bullion and print certificates of equal value, using those certificates as payment for purchases. The country would also issue certificates to its citizens in return for gold and would convert these certificates back to gold on demand. This meant that if you traveled abroad, you no longer had to carry actual gold. You could carry paper money in the form of gold certificates, which you used to make purchases. Your foreign trading partners knew that they could exchange those certificates for gold whenever they wanted to. The gold held by the central bank was said to be held *in reserve,* and the lightweight paper money amounted to claims

Gold reserves:
Gold held by a central bank.

on the bank's **gold reserves.** That paper money was 100 percent backed by gold.

As we noted in Chapter 15, central banks soon realized that the currency they issued did not have to be 100 percent backed by gold. They began issuing *fiat currency,* which is only partially backed by valuable assets.

Modern Fixed-Exchange-Rate Systems

To implement a fixed-exchange-rate regime, a central bank simply announces an exchange rate for its currency (relative to some other country's currency). Simultaneously, it agrees to buy or sell the foreign currency at that rate from or to anyone.

To live up to its promise, the central bank must be willing to create any quantity of domestic money that is demanded at the announced price. It must also have in its coffers—or be able to acquire instantly from the foreign central bank—any quantity of foreign money that might be demanded in exchange for previously issued domestic currency.

Under a fixed-exchange-rate regime, just as under a flexible-exchange-rate regime, the purchasing-power parity equation $P = eP'$ must hold (subject to our approximations involving transactions costs and nontraded goods). However, the market forces that produce this equality are different under a fixed-exchange-rate regime.

If the U.S. price level is $P = \$6$ per apple and the foreign price level is $P' = £3$ per apple, then the U.S. exchange rate must be $e = \$2/£1$. But suppose the exchange rate starts out incorrectly at $e = \$1/£1$ instead. Americans quickly realize that they can trade a dollar for a pound, use that pound to buy one-third of an apple, and then resell that third of an apple in the United States for $2. Each time they do this, they earn a clear profit of $1. (Does this sound familiar? So far, it is the same story that we told in the world of flexible exchange rates.)

People rushing to take advantage of this arbitrage opportunity all attempt to trade dollars for pounds at the same time. With flexible exchange rates, this would bid up the exchange rate e. In a fixed-exchange-rate regime, where, say, the Bank of England has agreed to sell pounds for a dollar apiece, nobody will ever pay more than a dollar per pound. So e cannot change.

What happens instead is that everybody wants to trade dollars for pounds, and nobody but the Bank of England is willing to trade pounds for dollars. To meet demand—as it has promised to do—the Bank of England must create a large number of British pounds. This rise in the British money supply causes the British price level P' to rise. The British money supply and P' continue to rise until the profit opportunity is entirely whittled away, that is, until P' satisfies the purchasing-power parity equation. That equation is

$$P' = \frac{P}{e} = \frac{\$6/\text{apple}}{\$1/£1} = £6/\text{apple}$$

which requires that $P' = £6$ per apple.

The moral of this story is this:

Under fixed exchange rates, a central bank can control either the exchange rate or the money supply, but not both.

If the central bank fixes the exchange rate, it must agree to supply whatever quantity of money private traders demand. In losing control of the money supply, the bank also loses control of the price level. If it wants to control the domestic price level, the central bank must allow exchange rates to float freely.

Exercise 16-9

Suppose that in our example above the exchange rate starts out at $4 per pound. Explain the profit opportunity available to people who trade pounds for dollars. If the U.S. Federal Reserve maintains a fixed exchange rate, what must happen to the U.S.

money supply? What must happen to the U.S. price level? How does this restore the equation $P = eP'$?

International-Reserve Crises

Suppose that under a fixed-exchange-rate regime the U.S. Federal Reserve, acting on its own, sets an exchange rate of $1/£1. Suppose also that at this price there is a large excess demand for pounds. Traders can attempt to buy pounds from each other, but they will find none for sale at $1 each.

The traders can attempt to buy pounds from the Bank of England, but the Bank of England may not be willing to increase its money supply to help out the U.S. Federal Reserve. The only place to which traders can turn to buy pounds is the Fed, which has agreed to buy and sell pounds at a dollar apiece.

But what happens if the Federal Reserve runs out of pounds and traders want still more? It can't print them; the Federal Reserve can print only dollars, but traders want pounds, not dollars. The result is an **international-reserve crisis** in which the Fed simply cannot keep its promise to maintain an exchange rate of $1 per pound. (The term "international reserves" means the supply of gold, foreign exchange, and a few other internationally accepted assets held by central banks.)

When the Federal Reserve realizes it will soon run out of pounds at the price of $1 per pound, it has to raise the price of pounds (that is, the U.S. exchange rate) to the point where demand no longer exceeds the Fed's ability to supply pounds. We say that the Federal Reserve has been forced to *devalue the dollar* or, equivalently, to *revalue the pound*.

International-reserve crisis:

The inability of a central bank to maintain a given fixed exchange rate.

Fixed Exchange Rates and Economic Events

A fixed-exchange-rate regime creates a link between currencies such that economic conditions in one country can create crises in another. Moreover, attempts to respond to economic events at home by controlling the exchange rate can have repercussions for inflation rates; similarly, attempts to control inflation as a response to such events can result in exchange-rate crises. In this subsection we discuss a few of the possibilities.

Changes in Productivity

Suppose, for example, that the world is operating on a system of fixed exchange rates. Suppose also that there is a sudden increase in American productivity, while productivity abroad remains stagnant. As American output rises, the U.S. price level falls. Foreign entrepreneurs who want to purchase cheap American goods demand dollars, which the Federal Reserve must supply under its fixed-exchange-rate system. The rising U.S. money supply eventually restores the original price level in the United States.

But suppose now that while the rest of the world is committed to fixed exchange rates, the United States is not. In that case foreign entrepreneurs cannot get their dollars from the Federal Reserve, which refuses to supply them. Instead, they demand dollars from foreign central banks, which may not have enough to go around. The U.S. prosperity thus could trigger reserve crises in any number of foreign countries and, perhaps, the devaluation of currencies throughout the world.

Fixed Exchange Rates and Inflation

Because fixed exchange rates deprive the central bank of control over the money supply, they are sometimes hailed as the antidote to inflation.

Here is the argument: Suppose the Fed is considering increasing the U.S. money supply. Its chairman knows this will force the U.S. price level to rise. American goods will become relatively expensive, and people will want to exchange their dollars (including many newly printed ones) for gold and foreign currencies so that they can buy foreign goods instead. But the Fed has only limited amounts of gold and foreign currencies and therefore will not be able to continue to meet the demand. This imposes a discipline which prevents the Fed from raising the money supply (and inflation) in the first place.

Historically, fixed exchange rates have indeed been associated with longer periods of price stability than have flexible exchange rates. However, they have not completely prevented inflation. After the discovery of gold in the New World, inflation ran rampant in Europe. (Gold was money, and new gold meant an increase in the money supply.) The inflation began in countries like Spain, whose citizens discovered the gold, but was exported abroad as Spanish citizens tried to spend their gold in other countries. In this case, the gold standard (a fixed-exchange-rate regime) not only failed to prevent inflation but also was the mechanism by which inflation spread.

With fiat currency, governments face an enormous temptation to print more money than they can back—especially in times of financial stress. Typically, when temptation leads to actuality, they precipitate an international-reserve crisis. They then find that they must devalue their currencies.

Black Markets

In some countries that still use a fixed-exchange-rate system, citizens do not have easy access to foreign currency markets. The governments of those countries can charge their citizens a price for foreign currency that is different from the going price in world markets. They can even set different prices for different citizens, conditioned, for example, on how the citizen intends to spend the foreign currency. Thus the Romanian government might sell French francs at one price to Romanians who plan to buy foreign consumer goods and at a different price to Romanians who plan to buy foreign capital goods; both these prices might be higher than the price at which the French government sells francs.

This provides arbitrage opportunities to the Romanian who can buy francs at one of the lower prices and sell them at a higher one. To prevent its official prices from being undercut, the government must outlaw such trades. But in the face of profit opportunities, laws are broken. **Black markets in currencies**—that is, illegal private

Black markets in currencies:

Markets in which currencies trade at prices other than those officially established under a fixed-exchange-rate regime.

markets where citizens make their own currency exchanges—are common in such circumstances.

How do black marketeers acquire foreign currency? They get it from relatives living abroad (by smuggling it into the country or paying off customs agents) and from foreign tourists. In the old Soviet Union, black markets in western currencies were common, and westerners traveling to the Soviet Union were frequently approached with offers to buy their currency. After the Soviet Union broke up, it became easier for Russians to travel abroad and acquire even larger amounts of foreign currency; this forced the Russian government to bring the official prices for foreign currencies more into line with their free market prices.

The Evolution from Fixed Exchange Rates to Flexible Rates and Beyond

The International Monetary Fund

During World War II, the world went from a gold standard to a system of flexible exchange rates. This gave nations at war the freedom to control their own money supplies, and hence to raise revenue via inflation taxes. Starting immediately after the war, countries negotiated a return to fixed exchange rates. To make the fixed-exchange-rate system they envisioned work more smoothly, they created an organization called the International Monetary Fund, or IMF. Its member countries each contributed a certain amount of currency to be held in reserve by the IMF. Members were permitted to borrow from these reserves in times of international-reserve crises. The loans were temporary and carried a very low rate of interest—below the market rate, in fact. The sole purpose of the loans was to enable member countries to survive reserve crises without having to devalue their currencies. It was expected that loans would be paid back very quickly.

Structural problems:
Economic problems brought on by unwise economic policies.

It was agreed that IMF loans were not to be made available in the event of **structural problems,** such as those that a country brings on itself via unwise monetary or tax policies. A country whose growth rate temporarily lags that of the rest of the world can experience international-reserve crises (see "Changes in Productivity," page 522); but if the sluggish growth rate is determined to be a result of foolish economic policies like high taxes and tariffs, the problem is deemed structural and outside the realm of what IMF funds were intended for.

So when a country requested a big loan, the IMF had to decide whether that country's problems were structural; in other words, it had to decide whether that country's domestic economic policies were unwise. The IMF hired a lot of economists to help make those decisions. And because large amounts of money were involved, the decisions were heavily influenced by politics.

In the late 1970s and the 1980s, several countries took large loans from the IMF and were unable to pay them back on time. The reasons varied from country to country. Chile was devastated by a drop in the price of copper, which provides a substantial portion of the country's income. Brazil faced the same problem, except that it was coffee rather than copper that fell in price. Chile's problems persisted far longer than expected, and the IMF eventually decided that the problems were structural. It recommended dramatic changes in Chilean economic policy, especially in regulations that made it difficult for Chileans to produce exportable goods other than copper.

Today the world is on a system of flexible exchange rates, but the IMF's role has evolved. The IMF continues to make loans to developing nations, on condition that those nations adopt policies that the IMF approves.

The Demise of Fixed Exchange Rates

In the late 1960s and early 1970s, the United States precipitated the collapse, first, of the gold standard that had been in effect since World War II and then, ultimately, of the entire worldwide fixed-exchange-rate system. Let us take a brief look at what happened.

In the late 1960s, the United States was entangled in the increasingly costly Vietnam War. To finance the war, the government turned to an inflation tax (that is, the government created money and spent it). The Federal Reserve increased the growth rate of the money supply, and U.S. prices soon began to rise.

As American goods became more expensive, foreigners wanted fewer of them, and hence fewer dollars. They began turning dollars in to their central banks, demanding more and more of their own currencies in return. To accommodate those demands, the foreign central banks were forced to print more of their own currencies, precipitating inflations in their own countries. In essence, the trading partners of the United States paid inflation taxes that helped to finance the U.S. involvement in Vietnam.

The governments of foreign countries did not appreciate having their inflation rates dictated by the United States. The United States faced worldwide diplomatic pressure to stop using inflation as a policy tool. Foreign governments demanded a devaluation of the dollar to stem the tide.

And those foreign governments had a mighty powerful weapon to wield. Thanks to the American government's own policies, they were holding huge stockpiles of dollars that had been traded in for their own currencies. They threatened to take these dollars, all at once, to the Federal Reserve and demand gold in exchange. Because the Fed did not have enough gold to give 100 percent backing to all the dollars it had printed, it would not be able to fulfill its obligations.

By 1972, international reserves in the United States had been so lowered by ongoing demands for gold in exchange for dollars that a major international crisis loomed, and President Nixon responded by devaluing the dollar. He did so by lowering the quantity of gold for which a dollar could be exchanged at the Federal Reserve. This allowed the United States to escape an international-reserve crisis. But the credibility of the fixed-exchange-rate system, as well as that of the U.S. ability to uphold even the newly announced exchange rate, had been challenged.

Shortly thereafter, most of the developed world switched to a system of flexible exchange rates. The dollar depreciated further, and for a year or two exchange rates were highly volatile, apparently overshooting and undershooting by more than many people had expected. Some economists theorize that the volatility was part of the process of learning how to adjust to the new system of flexible exchange rates.

Today, a variety of exchange-rate regimes can be found around the world. Some countries, like the United States and Japan, have flexible-exchange-rate regimes. Other countries, particularly smaller countries with a limited number of trading partners, choose to fix their exchange rates relative to the currency of one of their large trading partners.

Still other countries, like Germany and France, choose to let their exchange rates float freely unless exchange rates rise or fall to levels outside predetermined target regions, or *bands*. If an exchange rate floats outside the band, the central banks intervene. This system, mixing fixed and flexible exchange rates, is called a **managed float.** The limits for the bands are themselves revalued or devalued when stresses on central bank reserves become too great or the problem is deemed to be structural. An example of this system in effect in Europe, called the European Monetary System, is an interlocking system of managed floats by the participating countries of western Europe.

Managed float:

A system under which exchange rates are permitted to fluctuate within a given band.

SUMMARY

The domestic exchange rate, e, is the price of a foreign money in terms of domestic money. The foreign exchange rate, $1/e$, is the price of domestic money in terms of the foreign money. It is the relative price of one currency in terms of another.

Anything that makes trading costly—such as transportation costs or taxes—is called a transactions cost. Economists believe that in the absence of transactions costs, a good must sell for the same price in all locations. Thus, a tin of cookies that sells for \$4 in one country must sell for the equivalent of \$4 everywhere. We call this requirement the arbitrage condition for goods, and it is summarized by the equation $p = ep'$, where p is the domestic price of the good and p' is the foreign price of the good.

There is an analogous arbitrage condition for bonds. The condition says that purchasing a domestic bond must yield the same return as converting domestic currency to foreign currency, buying a foreign bond, and then converting the bond's payment back to domestic currency.

If all goods are traded and there are no transactions costs, then the goods arbitrage condition holds for each individual good. In that case, the purchasing-power parity equation $P = eP'$ holds for each pair of countries, where P and P' are the domestic and foreign price levels. The domestic exchange rate is determined by purchasing-power parity according to $e = P/P'$.

A nontraded good is a good for which transactions costs are essentially insurmountable. If some goods are nontraded, purchasing-power parity will not hold in the short run and the exchange rate will not equal the ratio of the price levels. However, in the long run, travelers and creative entrepreneurs will bid exchange rates up or down until purchasing-power parity holds.

Exchange rates can be either determined in free markets, under a flexible-exchange-rate regime, or set by each central bank in a fixed-exchange-rate regime.

In a flexible-exchange-rate system, as traders demand more or less foreign currency to purchase foreign goods so as to take advantage of potential arbitrage opportunities, the value of the foreign currency appreciates (increases) or depreciates (decreases), respectively.

If a country's income increases, the resulting decline in the country's goods prices entices foreign traders to demand more of that country's currency in order to purchase goods at the lower prices; this drives the value of its currency up. In other words, the arbitrage condition requires that the currency appreciate. If a country's money supply increases, its price level increases, so the arbitrage condition requires that its currency depreciate.

Under a fixed-exchange-rate system, the central bank sets the exchange rate and offers to buy or sell foreign exchange at that price. However, a central bank can control either the money supply or the exchange rate, but not both. If it chooses to control or fix the exchange rate, then the country's money supply will be determined by the private sector. If the exchange rate is set at a level far from what the market rate would be, the central bank will either accumulate or run down its stock of foreign currency. In an extreme case, the central bank can run out of foreign currency, and hence be required to devalue (lower the value of) its own currency.

PROBLEM SET

1. If coffee costs 20 francs per pound in France and 25 pesos per pound in Mexico, what is the French exchange rate (the price of a peso in terms of French francs)? What is the Mexican exchange rate (the price of a franc in terms of pesos)? (You may assume that purchasing-power parity holds.)

2. Suppose a citizen of Zenda has 1 unit of Zendish currency (denoted "Z") with which he wants to buy a bond. A Zendish bond pays a nominal interest rate of i' per year. The citizen also considers buying a U.S. bond paying a nominal interest rate of i. The citizen can exchange currency in the foreign exchange market at the exchange rate of $e = Z6/\$1$, and he does not expect that exchange rate to change next year. Work out the interest arbitrage condition faced by this citizen.

3. Explain why a tariff (a tax on imported goods) requires that the goods arbitrage condition $p = ep'$ include a term for the tariff rate. Then answer these questions:
   a. Would the introduction of a tariff of 10 percent raise or lower the exchange rate?
   b. Write down a more general goods arbitrage condition that includes an allowance for a tariff of t percent of the price on all imported goods.

4. *True or false:* An unexpected decline in the growth rate of the money supply of the domestic country causes the domestic exchange rate to depreciate disproportionately.

5. *True or false:* If the world consists of two countries and the currency of one country appreciates, the currency of the other country depreciates.

6. Explain why the real exchange rate might not always equal 1.

7. If a country's income increases more slowly than its money supply, will its exchange rate appreciate or depreciate? Assume the country has a flexible-exchange-rate regime.

8. *True or false:* The dollar is usually overvalued because it is such a useful currency.

9. Suppose the Bundesbank decreases the growth rate of the German money supply. What effect will that have on exchange rates between German marks and foreign currencies?

10. As a country's income fluctuates, do the nation's trade balance and exchange rate move in the same direction or in opposite directions?

11. As a country's level of productive government spending fluctuates, do the nation's trade balance and exchange rate move in the same direction or in opposite directions?

12. **a.** Answer the following question assuming that purchasing-power parity holds: As a country's level of wasteful government spending fluctuates, do the nation's trade balance and exchange rate move in the same direction or in opposite directions?

    b. Now answer the question in part **a** assuming that because of the existence of non-tradeable goods, purchasing-power parity fails.

13. In a two-nation world, suppose one country on a fixed-exchange-rate regime experiences a growth spurt. What happens to its money supply? What happens to the other country's money supply?

14. Suppose a country's marginal product of capital declines. What happens to the exchange rate?

15. Contrast the effects on the value of the dollar of a sterilized and an unsterilized intervention by the Japanese monetary authority, assuming it purchases U.S. dollars.

16. *True or false:* Under a fixed-exchange-rate regime, a country can successfully reduce its inflation rate even if its trading partners are increasing their inflation rates.

17. Suppose the U.S. Federal Reserve fixes an exchange rate of $2/£1 and the British central bank fixes an exchange rate of £0.6/$1. What do you expect will happen?

18. *True or false:* Under a gold standard, inflation is impossible.

Chapter 17

Economic Policy

The U.S. government, like most national governments, touches almost every aspect of its citizens' lives. Agencies of the federal government regulate hiring practices and working conditions, maintain highways and railroads, control the flow of goods across national boundaries, subsidize higher education, and dictate environmental standards that affect the design of everything from your car to your showerhead. One agency determines which new drugs you can purchase; another monitors the content of the television shows you watch; yet another decides how fast you are allowed to drive your car.

Every decision that these agencies make has costs and benefits and can therefore be profitably subjected to economic analysis. When the consequences of a policy are concentrated in just a few markets, the tools of *micro*economics are usually most appropriate. But many government policies affect economywide variables such as the interest rate, output, employment, international trade, and the price level. Those are the policies of interest to macroeconomists—together they constitute what is called macroeconomic policy.

Fiscal policy:
The body of policies concerning government spending or taxation.

Macroeconomic policy is traditionally divided into two parts. **Fiscal policy** concerns the amount that the government spends and the amount that it taxes. **Monetary policy** concerns the money supply and its growth rate.

Monetary policy:
The body of policies concerning the level or growth rate of the money supply.

In Chapter 15, we saw that the Federal Reserve formulates and implements monetary policy in the United States. In Section 17-1, we briefly examine the institutions that formulate and implement U.S. fiscal policy. Then, in Section 17-2, we survey the most important reasons why economists sometimes give different answers when they are asked for advice on matters of policy. In that discussion, you will see how all of the models in this book are central to ongoing debates about economic policy in the real world.

17-1 HOW FISCAL POLICY IS MADE

In the United States, all federal taxes must be authorized by legislation that originates in the House of Representatives. Once that legislation has been passed by a majority of the House, it must also be approved by the Senate and then sent to the president for his signature. The president has the option of *vetoing* legislation; in that case it is returned to the House and Senate, where it must be approved by a two-thirds majority to become law.

Federal spending is authorized in exactly the same way, except that either the House or the Senate can initiate spending legislation.

Members of Congress receive economic advice from the Congressional Budget Office (CBO) and from economists on their staffs. The CBO has a difficult role to fill because it must serve representatives from both parties, who have very different agendas. Any analysis that comes from the CBO is liable to be harshly criticized by legislators from one party or the other.

Although the president plays no official role until near the end of the legislative process, he plays an important unofficial role from the beginning. Each year, the president sends to the House his recommendations for the annual budget. Those recommendations may bear little resemblance to what is ultimately approved, but they do substantially affect the direction of the debate.

In deciding what to propose, what to sign, and what to veto, the president solicits advice from a number of sources, including economists. The president's Council of Economic Advisers traditionally consists of three academic economists assisted by a staff of about a dozen more, all on 1- or 2-year leaves from universities. Their job is to give advice which is relatively untainted by political considerations.

Other departments in the administration, such as the Departments of State and of the Treasury, also hire economists. These economists traditionally offer advice that takes political considerations into account.

In 1993, President Clinton founded a new organization, the National Economic Council, to serve as a high-level clearinghouse for advice coming from various bureaus and agencies throughout the administration.

The issues that fiscal policy makers must address are these: How much should the government spend? What should it spend *on*? How much government spending should be financed by current taxes and how much by deficits? Exactly what should be taxed? What are the potential domestic and international consequences of various proposals to spend, tax, or borrow?

17-2 ISSUES IN ECONOMIC POLICY

Shortly after taking office in 1993, President Clinton, a Democrat, proposed a package of about $20 billion in new government spending designed to "stimulate the economy"—that is, to increase output, employment, or both. Republicans in Congress were quick to denounce the package as an expensive political ploy with little economic merit. Prominent economists could be found on both sides of the issue.

How can economists differ so dramatically? Why can't they just run various policy changes through standard models and pass unambiguous judgment on the consequences and desirability of those changes?

In this section we provide several answers to those questions.

Positive Issues versus Normative Issues

Positive issues:
Issues regarding the probable outcome of a given policy.

Normative issues:
Issues regarding the desirability of a given outcome.

Controversies regarding economic policy can be grouped into two broad categories. First, there are **positive issues**—questions that concern the probable *consequences* of particular policies. Second, there are **normative issues**—questions that concern the *desirability* of particular consequences.

In 1993, the Clinton economic stimulus package triggered debate over a large number of positive issues. Some economists expected that the package (if passed) would significantly increase employment, while others thought it might trigger a recession. Some economists believed that the stimulus package would raise interest rates, some thought it would raise the inflation rate, some thought it would do both, and some thought it would do neither. Some economists believed that the average American would become wealthier if the stimulus package were approved; others thought just the opposite.

But even if all those positive disputes had been resolved, economists would have continued to disagree over normative issues—questions about whether the effects of the stimulus package were desirable. Two economists might both expect a given program to employ, say, 25,000 new workers while costing the average taxpayer, say, $300, but they might still disagree about whether the benefits would be *worth* the costs.

Notice that the word "positive" here does not tell us in which direction an economic variable moves. A rise in unemployment and a drop in unemployment are *both* examples of possible positive consequences of a change in government policy. Nor does the word "positive" tell us if those consequences—and hence the underlying change—are good or bad for the citizens in the economy. A person asking if a drop in unemployment is good or bad—desirable or undesirable—is asking a normative rather than a positive question.

Sources of Positive Disagreements

Disagreements about positive issues often result from disagreement about modeling strategy. An economist who builds a model around price stickiness will reach different conclusions than one who treats all prices as perfectly flexible. An economist who believes in Ricardian equivalence will reach different conclusions than one who does not.

Even economists who use exactly the same models may reach different conclusions because of different beliefs about the slopes of various curves and the sensitivity of various responses to change. Is the consumption demand curve very steep or very flat or somewhere in between? When the interest rate rises, does the supply of labor shift by a lot or by a little? Does the demand for money shift frequently and unpredictably in response to minor changes in banking practices, or is it quite stable?

Economists try to settle positive disputes by examining data from the real world. Unfortunately, it is difficult to draw definitive conclusions because economic conditions are constantly changing. If a rise in the interest rate happens to be followed by a big leftward shift in the labor supply curve, we cannot know for certain whether that shift was caused by the interest-rate shock or by one of the dozens of other economic variables that rose or fell simultaneously.

Statisticians have developed techniques for isolating the effects of individual shocks, but those techniques often require a lot of data, which is a luxury that economists do not always have. Most macroeconomic variables were not measured accurately until about 50 years ago. There have been fewer than a dozen business cycles since then, far fewer than economists or statisticians would need to establish clear patterns of cause and effect.

Sources of Normative Disagreements

Almost every change in economic conditions creates winners and losers. To decide whether a change is desirable, we have to decide whether the winners' gains outweigh the losers' losses. Normative disputes arise when economists disagree about what kind of scale to use for weighing those gains and losses.

Many economists endorse the use of dollar values to compare gains and losses. They argue that a program which costs taxpayers $10 billion and creates $7 billion in benefits for workers (or for farmers or for poor people or for corporate stockholders) is a bad thing; if another program costs $10 billion and creates $12 billion worth of benefits, then that program is a good one.

The program with $10 billion in costs and $7 billion in benefits creates a $3 billion *welfare loss*. The program with $10 billion in costs and $12 billion in benefits creates a $2 billion *welfare gain*. Those economists who judge desirability on the basis of welfare losses and welfare gains are employing the **welfare criterion** to make their normative judgments.

There is nothing sacred about the welfare criterion. If you can design a health insurance program that imposes $10 billion worth of costs on healthy Americans in order to deliver $7 billion worth of benefits to Americans with catastrophic illnesses, a lot of economists will endorse your plan—despite the fact that it creates a welfare loss. These economists are obviously applying some normative criterion other than the welfare criterion.

In deciding what normative criteria to apply, economists are guided by considerations that come from far outside economics, including their religious and moral convictions, their attitudes toward freedom and authority, and their gut instincts about which members of society are most deserving of protection or assistance. Frequently these are the issues about which people feel most strongly and are least likely to be swayed by argument. Consequently, normative disagreements are usually the most difficult disagreements to resolve.

Positive Issues, Normative Issues, and Economic Policy

When economists are called upon to offer advice to policy makers, they must confront both positive and normative issues. In some cases, the positive issues can be resolved on the basis of logic and evidence. In other cases, the positive questions remain unresolved; but then economists may be asked to *guess* the answers, using their past experience with similar questions as a guide.

A recent example of such a situation was the debate in the early 1990s about whether the United States should lower trade barriers with its North American neighbors. This debate culminated in the ratification of the North American Free Trade Agreement, or NAFTA. While all economists tended to agree that NAFTA would improve the welfare of Americans in the long run, they also agreed that it would cause temporary disruptions, including relocations of workers and temporary decreases in U.S. employment. What economists could *not* agree on was how long those disruptions might last.

Economists who supported NAFTA on *normative* grounds (such as the belief that free international markets are justified by basic principles of liberty) tended to invest a lot of effort in convincing themselves and others to accept the *positive* proposition that the disruptions would be minor and short-lived. Those who opposed NAFTA on *normative* grounds (such as the belief that the U.S. government should have greater control over the goods and services sold in the United States) tended to invest a lot of effort in convincing themselves and others to accept the *positive* proposition that the disruptions would be large and long-lasting.

We see from this example that economists sometimes allow their normative views to influence their readings of positive evidence—particularly when the evidence is inconclusive. Many of the most persistent and heated debates about economic policy stem from such normative disagreements.

Some Points of Disagreement

In this subsection, we take a more detailed look at some of the issues which divide economists and which bear on economic policy.

Wage and Price Stickiness

The most fundamental source of conflict among macroeconomists is their variety of beliefs about the stickiness of wages and prices. It is relatively uncontroversial to say that prices are flexible in the long run and sticky in the short run. But there is a lot of dispute about whether the short run is closer to 18 months or to 18 seconds.

In *micro*economics courses, we learn that under ideal conditions, market outcomes are *efficient,* which means that they cannot be changed without making some people worse off. Those ideal conditions include an absence of monopoly power, a well-enforced system of property rights, and perfectly flexible prices.

Economists who believe that the real world closely approximates those ideal conditions—including wage and price flexibility—tend to believe that the government should not tamper with market outcomes. They argue that the neoclassical equilibrium is desirable and that the economy achieves that equilibrium without any help from the government.

By contrast, economists who believe that wages or prices are often sticky conclude that market outcomes are inefficient and can sometimes be improved by government actions. While many of these economists would agree that the neoclassical equilibrium is a *desirable* outcome, they argue that in the real world the sticky wage or sticky price equilibrium is the *actual* outcome. They favor government actions that will push the economy toward its neoclassical equilibrium and thus close the gap between what *is* and what *ought to be*.

These differences among economists are clearly evident in their attitudes toward monetary policy. The neoclassical model predicts that an increase in the money supply has no impact on output or employment. By contrast, the sticky wage model in Chapter 12 and the sticky price model in Chapter 13 both predict that an increase in the money supply causes output and employment to rise.[1]

Therefore, an economist who believes that prices are sticky might advise the government to fight recessions with increases in the money supply; an economist who believes that prices are flexible might argue that such a policy will have no effect other than to fuel inflation.

Few economists take the extreme position that monetary policy is completely ineffective. But economists of a neoclassical persuasion have argued that the impact of monetary shocks on the economy might be due not to stickiness but to monetary misperceptions. We saw in Chapter 14 that in a world of monetary misperceptions, money supply increases (at least when they are unexpected) have the same effects that they have in a world of sticky wages or sticky prices—though for very different reasons.

---

[1]See Figure 12-17 and Figure 13-11 for the reasons.

When it comes to policy recommendations, those reasons matter. Models with stickiness tell us that a money supply increase can stimulate employment by creating opportunities for the involuntarily unemployed or by enabling the goods market to move closer to its neoclassical equilibrium point. But models with flexible prices (such as the monetary misperceptions model) tell us that a money supply increase can stimulate employment by fooling workers into taking jobs that they would not want if they were fully informed. If you believe the first kind of model, you will tend to view monetary stimulation as good; if you believe the second kind of model, you will tend to view monetary stimulation as bad.

Regarding fiscal policy, the same general conclusions are true: Economists who favor models with stickiness tend to think that spending and taxing policies can be both effective and desirable; those who favor models with flexibility tend to think that such policies are often ineffective or undesirable.

Ricardian Equivalence

Attitudes toward fiscal policy are shaped not only by beliefs about stickiness but also by beliefs about Ricardian equivalence. If Ricardian equivalence holds, then all of our models agree that deficit-financed tax cuts and transfers have no effects. If Ricardian equivalence fails, then all of our models agree that deficit-financed tax cuts and transfers can increase both output and employment.[2]

Exercise 17-1
Draw graphs analogous to those of Figures 12-18 and 13-18 to illustrate why the same conclusions about output and employment hold in the neoclassical model.

Different beliefs about Ricardian equivalence therefore lead to different predictions about the *effects* of using deficits to finance tax cuts and transfer payments. At the same time, different beliefs about wage and price stickiness lead to different assessments of the *desirability* of those effects. According to the neoclassical model, all markets are initially in equilibrium, and any departure from that equilibrium reduces welfare. If tax cuts fool people into believing they have become wealthier (a failure of Ricardian equivalence), then they will consume more in the present, but they will also consume less in the future when taxes must be raised to cover the deficit—and they will have been made worse off over the course of their lifetimes.

 There are exceptions to the rule that the neoclassical equilibrium cannot be improved upon. For example, if Ricardian equivalence fails because market imperfections prevent people from borrowing at the going interest rate, government borrowing on those people's behalf can be a good thing.

[2]Review Figure 12-18 to see why this is so in the sticky wage model and review your answer to Exercise 13-4 to see why it is so in the sticky price model.

By contrast, the sticky wage and sticky price models allow the possibility that output and employment are below their equilibrium levels. Thus policies which cause output or employment to increase can improve economic welfare.

Now let us turn from tax cuts and transfers to a different issue in fiscal policy: the issue of wasteful spending. All models agree that with or without Ricardian equivalence, wasteful spending increases employment while reducing the total of consumption and investment.[3]

Exercise 17-2

Draw graphs that illustrate the effect of wasteful spending in the neoclassical model without Ricardian equivalence. (*Hint:* Adapt the graphs of Figure 11-4, adding the observation that without Ricardian equivalence, current waste which is paid for through future taxes does not necessarily make people feel poorer, so the consumption demand curve does not shift.)

All models agree that wasteful spending is always more effective than transfer payments at stimulating employment. Just as in the case of transfer payments and tax cuts, however, the models continue to disagree on whether policies that stimulate employment can improve economic welfare.

No economist believes that Ricardian equivalence holds perfectly (in the sense that future taxes have exactly the same effects as current taxes with the same present value), and no economist believes that Ricardian equivalence fails completely (in the sense that future taxes have no impact on current behavior). But there is a lot of room between those two extremes, and economists differ about which extreme is a closer approximation of reality.

Magnitudes of Effects

Even when economists are in perfect agreement about the model they want to apply, they may disagree about the slopes of curves and the magnitudes of various effects.

Consider two true believers in the neoclassical model: One thinks that labor supply is quite unresponsive to the interest rate, and one thinks that the interest rate is a major determinant of labor supply. Called upon to analyze a program of wasteful government spending, both will invoke Figure 11-4. However, the first will predict a small shift in labor supply and a small increase in employment, while the second will predict much larger effects.

Historically, a far more important controversy has concerned the slope of the *LM* curve in the sticky price model.[4] If the *LM* curve is nearly vertical, the effects of

---

[3]To see this in the neoclassical model with Ricardian equivalence, see Figure 11-4. To see this in the sticky wage model, see Figure 12-18 (with Ricardian equivalence) or your answer to Exercise 12-4 (without Ricardian equivalence). To see this in the sticky price model, see Figure 13-18 (with Ricardian equivalence) and the discussion accompanying that figure (without Ricardian equivalence).

[4]Refer to Figure 13-18 to see how wasteful spending affects employment in that model.

wasteful spending on output and employment are quite small. If the *LM* curve is nearly horizontal, those effects can be quite large.

Categories of Government Spending

In Chapter 6, we divided government spending into three categories: *productive spending,* which produces goods and services that are worth more than their cost; *pure transfers,* whose costs are exactly equal to their benefits; and *wasteful spending,* which produces goods and services that are worth less than their cost.

We have just seen how economists' attitudes toward transfers and wasteful spending are shaped by their views about wage and price stickiness and their views about Ricardian equivalence. By contrast, all economists can easily and happily agree that *productive* spending improves economic welfare, regardless of what model they use.

But when it comes to any particular spending program, there can be room for much heated argument about which category the program fits into. A plan to spend $10 billion on improving the interstate highway system can be interpreted as a productive investment that will more than pay off in the form of reduced transportation costs or as a boondoggle designed only to siphon taxpayers' money to politically favored unions and construction companies.

Most economists are cynics, but they aim their cynicism in different directions. Some focus on the fact that private markets are inadequate providers of public goods; others focus on the fact that governments are frequently in the grip of special interests. Economists who are preoccupied with failures of the market are quick to see how government spending might serve as a productive antidote; those who are preoccupied with failures of the government are quick to see how that same spending might be more wasteful than the disease it is advertised to cure.

So even when two economists give exactly the same advice in the *abstract* (for example, "Do not spend wastefully under current economic conditions"), they might still give very different advice in *practice* (one saying, "Build that highway because it is a productive use of resources that the private sector is likely to overlook," while the other says, "Don't build the highway, because you will probably do it wastefully").

Timing

Even when economists agree on a model and agree on its predictions, they might disagree about how long it will take for those predictions to have an effect. This can lead them to recommend different policies.

When the economy is in a recession, the sticky price model suggests that the government can stimulate employment by spending wastefully. Two economists who both believe that the model is correct can disagree about the probable lag time between the spending program and the boost in employment. An economist who expects the effects to be nearly immediate might recommend quick implementation of a spending policy. Another economist, believing that the effects of spending are unlikely to be felt until after the recession has run its natural course, would advise against wasting resources in a futile effort.

Some economists argue that there are almost always unpredictable lags between the advent of a new policy and the appearance of its economic consequences—partly because it takes people time to learn about the new policy and adjust their consumption demand, labor supply, and so forth. As a result, say these economists, policies designed to respond to a given set of conditions usually take effect only after those conditions have changed in ways that nobody could have foreseen. Those economists tend to oppose all attempts by the government to manipulate the macroeconomy through any kind of fiscal or monetary policy.

Is Policy a Process or an Event?

In Chapter 14 we developed the slogan "Policy is a process, not an event." According to the slogan, a single change in government expenditures, tax rates, or the money supply cannot be analyzed in isolation: it is imperative to think about how each event influences expectations of future government actions. Economists take this slogan with varying degrees of seriousness. Some insist on treating each policy decision as the beginning of a new process; others are comfortable isolating the effects of at least some individual policy choices, as we have done throughout much of this book. Different judgment calls lead to different variations of the models, and hence potentially to different predictions.

Elaborating the Models

All the models we have examined can be made much more elaborate. For example, our models treat labor as a homogeneous commodity—that is, they treat all workers as interchangeable. But it is often useful to incorporate subtler treatments of the labor market, recognizing that each worker has individual skills that are more valuable to some firms than to others and recognizing also that it takes some effort and expense for workers and firms to find each other. In analyzing the effects of a given policy, economists will reach different judgments about just how elaborate a model is called for. Once again, as a result, they will start down different paths and therefore may reach different destinations.

Moral Issues

Should the government be more concerned with increasing the total wealth (or welfare) of all its citizens or with ensuring that each citizen receives a fair share of society's wealth? Often these goals are at odds. Taxing the rich to employ the poor (and using up resources in the process) may reduce total wealth while spreading what remains more evenly. Is that a good thing?

Here is another dilemma: Suppose that the government finds a way to make us wealthier at the cost of restricting our personal freedoms. (For example, suppose that medical costs can be reduced by prohibiting people from buying certain types of medical insurance.) Is that an acceptable trade-off?

Economists, guided by highly personal religious, ethical, and aesthetic considerations, will disagree about moral issues such as these and will therefore be led to different preferences about economic policy—even if they completely agree about everything in their models.

The Importance of Growth

Should policy makers be more concerned with smoothing business cycles or with encouraging economic growth? This question has both a positive aspect and a normative one. On the positive side, economists attempt to determine which goal would contribute more to human happiness. They may investigate, for example, how much effort people expend to smooth their own consumption streams. The harder people try, the more economists believe that people would appreciate some help from the government.

On the normative side, once economists know people's preferences, they still have to make judgments about the extent to which those preferences should guide policy.

In deciding how much importance to attach to growth, economists may be forced to examine our obligations to future generations. This opens vast new areas for moral conflict and so for disputes on normative grounds.

Models versus Reality

Economic models generally include only those aspects of reality that economists think they understand, or at least partly understand. They generally omit those features of the economic landscape that remain intellectually uncharted. The omissions obviously limit the applicability of the models to policy analysis. Economists differ about the extent of the resulting limitations.

Robert Solow, the founder of modern neoclassical growth theory, has lamented economists' willingness to take his own model and some of its successors with too few grains of salt. He writes that, contrary to those models:

The (real world) markets for goods and for labor look to me like imperfect pieces of social machinery with important institutional peculiarities. They do not seem to behave at all like transparent and frictionless mechanisms for converting the consumption and leisure desires of households into production and employment decisions.[5]

What Economists Agree On

Disagreements among economists get a lot of attention. But frequently those very disagreements arise from the fact that economists generally *agree* about the foundations of their subject. Their shared beliefs about basic issues give economists a common language for expressing finer points and debating how they are likely to be resolved.

[5]R. Solow, *Growth Theory: An Exposition* (Oxford: Oxford University Press, 1987).

It was not always this way. Just a few decades ago, macroeconomics was dominated by various schools of thought that had so little overlap in their basic approaches that communication among their proponents was severely hampered. Economists could not even agree about what it was that they disagreed about.

Today the situation is very different and far more promising. There is now a broad mainstream of macroeconomic thought. That mainstream has many tributaries, and there is much dispute about where along their shores the ground is most likely to prove fertile. But economists pretty much agree that the most fruitful ground must be nourished—at least indirectly—by the mainstream.

And what ideas flow in that mainstream? First and foremost is the idea that economic events are driven by individual decision making: the choices people make about how much to consume, to invest, and to work. Moreover, those choices are made in a context of *intertemporal optimization*. Every decision about current behavior is influenced by expectations of the future. Most particularly, bond markets create opportunities to borrow and lend, and people exploit those opportunities to improve their lifetime consumption and labor patterns.

We agree that in the long run markets clear and money is neutral (that is, changes in the money supply have no effects on output). We agree that in the short run markets might not clear and money can matter. This creates the possibility for informed and productive discussion about how to measure the length of the long run and about the importance of market failures. While we sometimes disagree violently about the likely outcomes of such measurements, we at least agree about what needs to be measured.

The progress of a science is measured not by the number of questions it leaves open but by the number of questions it has answered and by its usefulness as a tool for organizing future thoughts. Currently, economists have a shared picture of the economic long run (including the determinants of long-run investment and growth), a few clear but incomplete ideas about the economic short run (including the causes of recessions and the effects of monetary shocks), general agreement about what needs to be measured in order to help clarify those short-run notions, and a shared language for formulating and testing new ideas. It's not an end, but it's much more than a beginning.

SUMMARY

In the United States, fiscal policy—policy concerned with taxing and spending—is made by the elected branches of government. Monetary policy—policy concerned with the control of the money supply—is made by the Federal Reserve.

Economists disagree over both the probable consequences of policies and their desirability. The former disagreements are called positive issues, and the latter are called normative issues. Some disagreements arise from the different assumptions that are incorporated in the economic models, for example, wage and price stickiness versus wage and price flexibility or the extent to which Ricardian equivalence is a good approximation of reality. Other important sources of disagreement include highly personal attitudes toward matters like equality and freedom.

Such differences lead to disagreements about the *goals* of government policy: Should government policies promote a general increase in incomes or a more equal distribution of incomes? Should government policies put more emphasis on fighting business cycles or encouraging long-term growth? There are also disagreements about how best to *accomplish* each of these goals: Can the authorities increase output by increasing the money supply? By cutting taxes? By increasing their spending?

Debates over these issues take place in a context where economists have largely come to agree about basic principles. They generally agree that policy analysis must rely on models which incorporate intertemporal optimization by individuals and that markets clear in the long run. There is also general agreement about what the open questions are and what sorts of information will help in resolving them. Thus the stage is set for continued progress.

PROBLEM SET

1. Illustrate the effects of a decrease in the money supply in the neoclassical, sticky price, and sticky wage models.

2. Suppose that the government increases taxes and uses the revenue to buy valuable goods and destroy them. Show the effects in the neoclassical, sticky price, and sticky wage models, assuming that Ricardian equivalence fails.

3. In the preceding problem, how would your answers have been different if Ricardian equivalence holds?

4. Make a chart with columns labeled "Neoclassical," "Sticky Wage," and "Sticky Price" and with rows labeled "Ricardian Equivalence Holds" and "Ricardian Equivalence Fails." In each box, indicate what its pair of assumptions predicts will happen to the real interest rate and the real wage rate following an increase in the money supply. For each box, justify your assertion either by referring to the appropriate figure in an earlier chapter of this book or by drawing an appropriate figure of your own.

5. Repeat problem 4, replacing the money supply increase with an increase in deficit-financed transfer payments.

6. Repeat problem 4, replacing the money supply increase with an increase in deficit-financed wasteful spending.

Index

Note: Page numbers followed by *n* indicate footnotes; **boldface** page numbers indicate definitions.